CANADIAN EDITION

BECOMING A TEACHER

Forrest Parkay
Washington State University

Beverly Hardcastle Stanford
Azusa Pacific University

Thomas D. Gougeon
University of Calgary

Allyn & Bacon Canada, Scarborough, Ontario

Canadian Cataloguing in Publication Data

Parkay, Forrest W.
    Becoming a teacher

Canadian ed.
Includes bibliographical references and index.
ISBN 0–205–19632–2

1. Elementary schools teaching — Vocational
guidance. 2. Education, Elementary — Study and
teaching (Higher). 3. Elementary teachers —
Canada — Attitudes. I. Stanford, Beverly
Hardcastle, 1938–   . II. Gougeon, Thomas D.
(Thomas Douglas). III. Title

LB1775.P37 1995   371.1'0023'73   C95–932299–X

© 1996 Allyn & Bacon Canada
A Division of the Simon & Schuster Publishing Higher Education Group
1870 Birchmount Road
Scarborough, Ontario, M1P 2J7

ISBN 0–205–19632–2

Executive Editor: Clifford J. Newman
Managing Editor: Marta Tomins
Production Editor: Imogen Brian
Copy Editor: Mia London
Production Coordinator: Anita Boyle-Evans
Cover Design: Monica Kompter
Cover Image: Jeremy Jones
Page Layout: Joan Morrison

Original English language edition published by Allyn & Bacon,
A Simon & Schuster Company, Needham Heights, MA
Copyright © 1995, 1992, 1990

1 2 3 4 5   C   00 99 98 97 96

Printed and bound in the United States

Contents

PART ONE: TEACHERS AND TEACHING

PART TWO: FOUNDATIONS OF EDUCATION IN CANADA

PART FOUR: THE FUTURE OF EDUCATION

Preface

Becoming a Teacher, Canadian Edition, will introduce you to the complexities and strengths of education within Canada's ten provinces and two (soon to be three) territories. Adapted from the third edition of the American *Becoming a Teacher* text, the Canadian edition focuses on exciting innovations in education across Canada. Whereas in the United States, education has a national focus, Canada's educational systems have a provincial focus. In reality, Canada has twelve independent provincial and territorial school systems. The differences among these systems are important to understand because many teachers move from one province to another during their careers.

The first four chapters of the book are on the theme of teachers and teaching. After reading these chapters you will be better able to determine if teaching is a good career choice for you. Among the topics we address are why people choose to teach, the realities of teaching, the paths you might follow to become a teacher, and the process of finding your first teaching position.

Chapters 5 through 10 take up the foundations of education, which every professional teacher needs to know. These foundational areas include the social, cultural, historical, philosophical, political, economic, and legal dimensions of Canadian education.

In Chapters 11, 12, and 13, we explore student characteristics and the real worlds of the classroom and the school. We examine characteristics of students at different stages of development, students as learners, the dynamics of classroom life, and the curricula that are taught in schools.

Finally, in the last two chapters we consider issues and trends that will have impact on your quest to become an effective teacher, especially the professionalization of teaching, promising innovations in education and in educational technology, comparative education in a changing world, and the challenge of acquiring the knowledge and skills you and your students will need to meet the future.

The Canadian edition includes several features to help you prepare to be a successful teacher.

- **Making a Difference** boxes provide insights from teachers across Canada who were recipients of provincial and national Hilroy Fellowships for teaching merit in 1993 and 1994. In these sections, teachers tell how they developed curricula to benefit students and, at the same time, to make their own work invigorating and exciting.

- **Education in the News** boxes present current educational issues reported in the Canadian news.
- **Professional Portfolio** features throughout the book will give you an opportunity to develop your own personal resource materials for use when initially applying for teaching positions, planning curriculum materials, or dealing with parents and other members of the community during your first years of teaching.
- Each chapter begins with a case study that presents a realistic, relevant teaching scenario, as well as several focus questions for class discussion. A summary concludes each chapter, along with a list of key terms, several discussion questions and activities.
- An updated and expanded **Teacher's Resource Guide** at the end of the book provides a rich and varied array of materials, sources, strategies, contacts, and data you can rely on for support as you enter the teaching profession. Students who have used the previous edition of this book report that the Teacher's Resource Guide has proven extremely valuable.

We congratulate you on your decision to become a teacher. You have chosen a profession that will likely change more in the next thirty years than it has since Confederation in 1867. Changes in education will be driven by societal forces and it is predicted that emergent cultural groupings in Canada will create considerable force for change by the year 2020. Equity issues will also continue to dominate the news and teaching practice will necessarily have to be sensitive to these issues. We hope that this text will serve you well as you begin to grapple with the complexities of becoming a teacher.

SUPPLEMENTAL TEACHING AIDS

- **Instructor's Manual and Handout Masters**

The *Instructor's Manual* contains extended chapter summaries, learning objectives, key terms and concepts with page references, focus questions, and teaching strategies for introducing each chapter. Handout and transparency masters are included at the back.

- **Test Item File/Computerized Test Item File**

The *Test Item File* contains over 1000 items including multiple-choice, true-false, completion, and essay questions, as well as case study applications. A Computerized Test Item File is also available to adopting instructors.

Acknowledgments

I would like to thank the professional staff at Allyn & Bacon Canada who worked with me in developing this text. Under extremely tight time frames, the text was completed only because of the commitment of the editorial and production staff who always remained positive and optimistic. I would like to thank Marta Tomins, Managing Editor of Allyn & Bacon Canada for her continued support during this project and for her gracious manner. Mia London, the copy editor, worked extremely hard under tight schedules and did a fantastic job of cleaning up the text. In addition, she used her considerable background to help me clarify points of substance within several chapters. I could not have produced this Canadian Edition on time without her skill and expertise. Imogen Brian, Associate Production Editor, worked with me during the final phases of completion of the text. I would like to thank her for the understanding and generous manner in which she communicated new deadlines to me. Overall, the entire staff at Allyn & Bacon Canada supported me and ensured that the final product was of the highest quality possible.

I appreciate the response of the many recipients of the Hilroy Teaching Fellowships who agreed to write autobiographies for this text. I also want to thank especially those who submitted material that I was not able to include. I hope that you find the contributions of eighteen excellent teachers across Canada inspiring, and I look forward to being able to highlight many more outstanding Canadian teachers in the future.

I would like to thank Forrest Parkay and Beverly Hardcastle Stanford who wrote the original American edition. I accept all responsibility for any decisions made to include or exclude American content. I also accept all responsibility for the Canadian material presented in this text. I believe *Becoming a Teacher* is the best foundations book in education available in the United States today. I hope that they will find that the Canadian Edition is of equal quality.

Finally, I would like to thank my family for their personal support while I worked on the adaptation. Thanks to my wife, Dr. Susan Hutton, for her spiritual and emotional support while I worked on my computer evenings, weekends, and holidays. And thanks to my stepson, Matt Fulton, who has incredible sensitivity and can read my non-verbal communication "like a book." Matt would unfailingly come upstairs to my office and challenge me to a game of chess just when I needed to clear my head and take a break.

Forrest W. Parkay with his daughters Catherine and Rebecca.

Tom Gougeon with 12-hour-old grandnephew Thomas Jordan Brandwagt of Mississauga, Ontario.

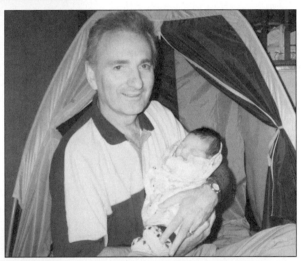

Beverly Hardcastle Stanford with her grandson Parker.

BECOMING

A TEACHER

1 Choosing To Teach

There is chalkdust on the sleeve of my soul. . . . I am as at home among blackboards, half-desks, lecterns, and seminar tables as among the furniture of my writing-room; both are the furniture of my head.

—John Barth
Teacher

Focus Questions

▼

1. What are the attractions to teaching?
2. What are the challenges of teaching?
3. How have images of teachers and teaching changed?
4. What knowledge and abilities are essential for teachers?
5. Why is self-assessment important for teachers?

Imagine that today is your first job interview. Four months ago you graduated from a teacher education program, and now you're applying for a position at a Catholic school in a multi-ethnic neighborhood of a large city.

It is 7:30 in the morning. At the suggestion of a friend who teaches at the school, you come early enough to find a parking place on the street close to the school. Arrive after 8:00, she said, and you'd probably have to park several blocks away.

While waiting for a green light to cross the busy four-lane street in front of the school, five children dash up behind you, talking loudly and breathlessly in Spanish about their plans for recess. Their restless energy momentarily held in check by the red light, the children amuse themselves by trying to stand on their toes as they wait for the walk signal.

"Yo sé que puedo correr más rápido que él," a tall thin boy exclaims.

"¡Claro, vamos a tener otra carrera y ahi les enseñaremos quien es más rápido!" another boy says, his small right fist jabbing the air for emphasis.

"Ja, José se va a llevar una sorpresa cuando pierda," a girl giggles.

With the green light, the children race across the street, their happy voices quickly growing faint as the distance between you and them increases.

You approach the brown, three-story building, the crisp air of September triggering dim recollections of your own school days. By midafternoon it will be hot and humid. On an asphalt playing field enclosed by a chain-link fence, dozens of children run about, deeply absorbed in their early morning games.

On entering the school through a set of heavy wooden doors, you see the main office straight ahead. You hold the office door open a moment for a Chinese-Canadian woman and her son who are just leaving.

"Thank you," she nods as she guides her son through the doorway.

You approach the counter on which sits a plastic laminated sign that says "Welcome" in four languages. You introduce yourself to a woman seated behind a desk covered with loose papers, file folders, and assorted three-ringed notebooks.

"Mrs. Potter said she'd meet with me at 7:45," you inform her. "I know I'm a bit early. She said today was the best day for her to interview me."

"That's fine," the woman says, smiling warmly. "She's meeting with a parent right now," she adds, nodding toward the closed door to Mrs. Potter's office. "I think she'll be finished soon; then she can see you. Why don't you have a seat over there?" She motions for you to sit on the couch beneath a bulletin board titled "Announcements—Teachers and Staff."

While waiting for Mrs. Potter, you think about questions you might be asked. Why did you choose to become a teacher? What is your philosophy of education? Are you comfortable using computers in the classroom? What is your approach to classroom management? How would you involve parents in the classroom? How would you meet the needs of students from different cultural and linguistic backgrounds? Why should the board hire you?

Reflecting on these questions, you admit they are actually quite difficult. Your answers, you realize, may determine whether or not you get the job.

Though predictable, the interview questions just posed are surprisingly challenging. Why *did* you decide to become a teacher? How *will* you meet the needs of all students? What *do* you have to offer students? The answers to these and similar questions depend on the personality and experiences of the person responding. However, they are questions that professional teachers see as important and deserve careful consideration.

The primary purpose of this book is to orient you to the world of education and to help you begin to answer such questions. In addition, this book will help you answer *your own* questions about the career you have chosen. What is teaching really like? What are the trends and issues in the profession? What problems can you expect to encounter in the classroom? What kind of rewards do teachers experience?

We begin this book by examining why people choose to teach because we believe that "good teachers select themselves."[1] They know why they want to teach and what subjects and ages they want to teach. They are active in the choosing process, aware of the options, informed about the attractions and obstacles in the field, and anxious to make their contributions to the profession.

WHAT ARE THE ATTRACTIONS TO TEACHING?

People are drawn to teaching for many reasons. For some, the desire to teach emerges early and is nurtured by positive experiences with teachers during childhood. For others, teaching is a way of making a significant contribution to the world and experiencing the joy of helping others grow and develop. And for others, life as a teacher is attractive because it is exciting, varied, and stimulating.

LOVE OF TEACHING

The foreword to *The Metropolitan Life Survey of the American Teacher 1992, The Second Year: New Teachers' Expectations and Ideals* includes the following statement: "[F]rom the outset, teachers have made it clear that most join the profession—and stick it out—for one reason above all others: *teachers love to teach*. Even though they recognize the host of problems that continue to beset schools, those who entered the profession in 1990 are, if anything, redoubling that sense of idealism."[2] The survey, based on a nationally representative sample of 1000 K–12 teachers who began teaching in fall 1990, goes on to report that 70 percent found their work with students "very satisfying" and 27 percent found it "somewhat satisfying." Similarly, a 1989 Metropolitan Life survey of 2000 teachers who taught an average of sixteen years or more found that 81 percent "strongly agree" that they love to teach and 16 percent "agree somewhat." Why do beginning and experienced teachers find teaching so satisfying? What does it mean to *love* teaching?

Love of Students   The teachers in the surveys might have meant a love of students. Though the conditions under which they work may be poor, and segments of their communities unsupportive, many teachers teach simply because they care about students. As one elementary school teacher put it: "I love kids; I love kids; I love kids. . . . I get lots from the kids. I get a reason to get up in the morning. I get— definite reasons to be able to go to sleep at night!"[3]

The day-to-day interactions between teachers and students build strong bonds. Daily contact also enables teachers to become familiar with the personal as well as the academic needs of their students, and this concern for students' welfare and growth outweighs the difficulties and frustrations of teaching. Teachers who know they are needed find it hard to leave the profession.

Others, no doubt, love students because they appreciate the unique qualities of youth. Like the following teacher, they enjoy the liveliness, curiosity, freshness, openness, and trust of young children, or the abilities, wit, spirit, independence, and idealism of adolescents:

> I have always enjoyed teaching, and I like the children. I've taught first, third, and fifth grades, and I think each grade level was the best age to teach. I stay in teaching because it keeps me connected to the spirit and vitality of childhood, a connection I don't want to lose.[4]

The opportunity to work with young people, whatever their stage of development, is a key reason people are drawn to teaching and remain in the profession.

Love of Subject   Some teachers who expressed a love of teaching may have meant that they love teaching in their discipline. The opportunity to continually learn more in one's profession and to share that knowledge with students is a clear attraction. Most of us can recall teachers who were so excited about their subjects that they were surprised when students were not equally enthusiastic. The affinity of such teachers toward their subjects was so great that we tended to see the two as inseparable—for instance, "M. Gilbert the French teacher" or "Ms. Montgomery the math teacher." Though other factors may draw teachers to their work, a love of subject is clearly one of them.

Love of the Teaching Life   For those teachers who always enjoyed school, it is often the life of a teacher that has appeal—to be in an environment that encourages a high regard for education and the life of the mind. John Barth, novelist and English professor, wrote eloquently of his love of the teaching life: "There is chalk-dust on the sleeve of my soul. In the half-century since my kindergarten days, I have never been away from classrooms for longer than a few months. I am as at home among blackboards, half-desks, lecterns, and seminar tables as among the furniture of my writing-room; both are the furniture of my head."[5] These are the teachers who are ready to return to the classroom when fall begins or when stores

Which one of the attractions to teaching might have influenced this teacher the most in choosing to teach?

display their back-to-school signs. The rhythm of their lives is synchronized with that of the school.

Others enjoy the drama and unpredictability of teaching. A new class or school year offers them an excitement similar to opening night in the theater. They view themselves—at least in part—as actors who enjoy performing for their audience of students.

Love of the Teaching-Learning Process   To love teaching can also mean to love the act of teaching and the learning that can follow. Many teachers, like the following high school special education teacher, focus on the *process* rather than on the subject or even the students: "I enjoy what I do. . . . I've been teaching long enough that when the fun stops . . . I'll get out. But it hasn't stopped yet, after thirty-four years. Every day is different. Every day is interesting."[6] Persons with this orientation are attracted by the live, spontaneous aspects of teaching and are invigorated by the need to think on their feet and to capitalize on teachable moments when they occur. They relish the "simultaneity" of teaching,[7] the times when several learning opportunities occur at once, and they constantly work to identify the full array of chesslike moves they can make in leading students to new insights. For them, the teaching-learning process is fascinating.

INFLUENCE OF TEACHERS

It seems reasonable to assume that the process of becoming a teacher begins early in life. Figure 1.1, for example, shows that most people who decide to become teachers make that decision before university. Although it is not true that some people are born teachers, their early life experiences often encourage them to move in that direction.[8] A teacher's influence during his or her formative years may have been the catalyst. In most cases, the adults who have the greatest influence on chil-

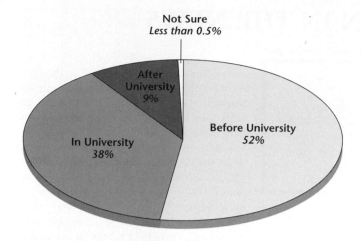

FIGURE 1.1

When Students Decide to Become Teachers

Source: *The Metropolitan Life Survey of the American Teacher, 1990, New Teachers: Expectations and Ideals.* Based on a survey of 1002 graduates who began teaching in a public school in 1990–91.

dren—beyond their parents or guardians—are their teachers. In the words of one student teacher, "When I was a child, I knew I wanted to become a teacher. Teachers were so important in my life."

Evidence also suggests that those in teacher training programs recall their teachers more positively than others. For example, educational researchers Benjamin Wright and Shirley Tuska, in a study of nearly 4500 teacher trainees, found a much higher incidence of teachers being remembered as "admired" and "influential" than in a group of almost one thousand nonteachers. The nonteachers recalled their teachers with negative associations more often than the teacher trainees.[9] Similarly, it has been suggested that teachers behave according to "internalized" models of their own teachers.[10] These internalized models are not always based on good teachers; when they are, however, students and the teaching profession benefit.

A DESIRE TO SERVE

Many teachers choose to teach because they want to serve others; they want the results of their labor to extend beyond themselves and their families. Some decide to leave teaching to earn more money elsewhere, only to return to teaching, confiding that they found the other work lacking in meaning or significance. Being involved in a service profession is their attraction to the field.

Whether motivated by a wish to do work of significance, to respond to a societal obligation, or to pursue a mission, the desire to serve is the reason many choose to teach. Of all the reasons to teach, a desire to serve is the best motivation because through it teachers selflessly empower others to have more fulfilling lives.

REWARDS OF TEACHING DIVERSE LEARNERS

Teaching is an exciting, energizing profession with many rewards. In particular, teachers derive significant rewards from meeting the needs of diverse learners. While students from our nation's more than one hundred racial and ethnic groups and students with special needs are increasing in number, effective teachers recognize that their classrooms are enriched by the varied backgrounds of students. To enable you to experience the satisfaction of helping *all* students learn, significant

EDUCATION IN THE NEWS

Report Cards

Today's report cards are quite different from the ones students used to receive. Thirty years ago children received letter grades or percentages reflecting their knowledge of core subjects and a few comments about appearance or work habits. Current report cards appear to give more information and teachers are often at pains to write individualized comments for each student but many no longer give letter grades. Instead they might write that skill in a particular subject is "not yet apparent," "beginning to develop," "developed," or "highly developed." Anyone can read between the lines and translate "highly developed" into an "A," but the question remains: Why has this shift occurred?

Many of today's parents do not want to hear negative comments about their children. Teachers tell stories about parents complaining to the school administration about negative comments on report cards, removing children

from schools, or demanding that the comment be deleted from the records. As a result, teachers have developed a jargon to say what they want, but they convey the information euphemistically.

So how can parents who want to know what the teacher is really saying interpret their children's report cards? If a teacher writes, "We are encouraging Mike to be honest and to respect the rights of others," it may mean that Mike has been lying and stealing from other children. But it may not. Perhaps it is time to get back to clear communication on report cards. Although it is unlikely that a new report card format will end obfuscation and jargon, clearer writing may better represent the wishes of parents in the 1990s. Perhaps a balance is needed between enhancing the self-esteem of a child and clearly reporting the child's progress to his or her parents. If so, how can such a balance be achieved?

Source: Based on *The Globe and Mail,* Apr. 20, 1995.

---

portions of this book are devoted to **student variability** (differences among students in regard to their developmental needs, interests, abilities, and disabilities) and **student diversity** (differences among students in regard to gender, race, ethnicity, culture, and socioeconomic status). An appreciation for such diversity, then, will help you to experience the rewards that come from enabling each student to make his or her unique contribution to classroom life.

PRACTICAL BENEFITS OF TEACHING

Not to be overlooked as attractions to teaching are its practical benefits. These include working hours and vacations, rising salaries, and the accessibility of a teaching career.

Hours and Vacations   Teachers' hours and vacations are widely recognized as benefits. Though the number of hours most teachers devote to their work goes far beyond the number of hours they actually spend at school, their schedules do afford them a measure of flexibility not found in other professions. For example, teachers with school-age children can often be at home when their children are not in school.

For most of those who make the transition to a nonteaching career, the reduced vacation time is an adjustment. The lengthy holiday breaks are replaced by a scant few weeks in their new workplaces. Only after an employee has worked for several years will vacation time be increased significantly. In contrast, all teachers, regardless of their years of experience, receive the same generous vacation time: holiday breaks and a long summer vacation.

High Salaries   The general belief that teachers in Canada are well paid is supported by Statistics Canada figures. The median annual earnings of 1990 university graduates across all fields of study and working full time in 1992 was $32 000 with a bachelor's degree, $44 000 with a master's degree, and $46 000 with a doctorate. The median annual earnings of graduates in education, in contrast, was $33 000 with a B.A., $52 000 with an M.A., and $55 000 with a Ph.D. Thus, two years after receiving their degrees, teachers with bachelor's degrees were ahead of their counterparts in other fields of study in salary by 3 percent. Two years after graduation, those with master's degrees and doctorates had outpaced their counterparts by 18 and 20 percent respectively. Salaries, of course, vary within Canada from province to province and within provinces from region to region. A teaching position advertised in 1994 for Fort Good Hope in the Northwest Territories offered a beginning teacher with a bachelor's degree a salary of $54 000, well above the median starting salary across Canada.

Teachers' salaries are geared to the importance of their work. This competitiveness may change over the short term as Canadian governments struggle to gain control of their budgets and to reduce the public debt which in 1994 exceeded $600 billion in total. Teachers, as public sector employees, will continue to be pressured to cut back their salaries until the debt is reduced. But teacher salaries will remain high compared to other employment sectors, reflecting the emphasis on education in our society today and the importance of having a highly skilled Canadian work force to ensure Canadian competition globally.[11]

Career Accessibility   Entry into teaching is relatively accessible because teaching has a "wide decision range," according to Dan Lortie, the author of *Schoolteacher: A Sociological Study*.[12] In other words, it is rarely too late or too early to decide to become a teacher. People may decide to teach when they are young or after they have completed a full career in another field.

Teaching is also perceived as easy to enter. Lortie refers to this as the "subjective warrant" and notes that "occupations with stringent warrants will lose more would-be members through self-discouragement than will those with permissive warrants."[13] Although teaching may in some respects be an easier field to enter than others, it is our thesis throughout this book that teaching is a complex, demanding profession. In short, it is not easy to become a professional teacher.

WHAT ARE THE CHALLENGES OF TEACHING?

Why should an introductory text on teaching confront undesirable or difficult aspects of the profession? Shouldn't such discussions be reserved for those who have already entered the field? Won't students learn soon enough about the hazards of being a teacher?

We do not think so. We believe that prospective teachers need to consider the problems as well as the pleasures they are likely to encounter. Students need to be informed of what to expect if they are to make the most of their professional preparation programs. With greater awareness of the realities of teaching, they can more purposefully and meaningfully go about the business of (1) reflecting on and refining their personal philosophies of education, (2) acquiring teaching strategies and management techniques, and (3) developing a knowledge base of research and theory to guide their actions. In this manner, they can become true professionals—free to savor the joys and satisfactions of teaching while being confident of their ability to deal with its frustrations and challenges.

As professionals, teachers must remain aware of public attitudes toward education, as they provide valuable information on the public's perception of the school system. A sample of 1345 Albertans, 18 and over was interviewed in spring 1991 on a variety of issues, including education. When asked about student learning, most were satisfied with how students learned skills, such as math, science, problem solving, reading, writing, and communication. But fewer were satisfied with how students learned to develop a sense of self worth, self confidence, or social values such as tolerance and cooperation. (See Table 1.1.) This survey suggests that teachers in the future will need to address students' sense of self and sense of social values as thoroughly as they now address reading, writing, and arithmetic.

Although we have noted that the work schedule and vacations for teachers are quite good, other working conditions need improvement. Though working conditions vary from school to school and from board to board, some problems are common to many schools. We briefly discuss five of them here: (1) classroom management, (2) drug abuse prevention, (3) long working hours, (4) gaining parental support, and (5) gaining professional empowerment.

Classroom Management   Discipline is a major concern among students in introductory education classes. Before teachers can teach they must manage their classrooms effectively. Even when parents and the school community are supportive and problems are relatively minor, dealing with discipline can be a disturbing, emotionally draining aspect of teaching.

In addition, many schools have high teacher-student ratios, which can make classroom management more difficult. Feeling the press of numbers and valiantly resisting the realization that they cannot meet the needs of all their students, teachers may try to work faster and longer to give their students the best possible education. All too often, however, they learn to put off, overlook, or otherwise attend inadequately to many students each day. The problem of high teacher-student ratios becomes even more acute when complicated by the high student-mobility rates

TABLE 1.1	PUBLIC SATISFACTION WITH WHAT STUDENTS ARE LEARNING, 1991
Area of Student Learning:	*Percent Satisfied:*
Math, science, and technology	62%
Thinking and problem solving skills	60%
Reading, writing, and communicating	59%
Sense of self worth and self confidence	55%
Social values (e.g., tolerance and cooperation)	48%

Source: Education in Alberta: Facts and Figures 1991. Alberta Education.

in many schools. In such situations, teachers have trouble not only in meeting their students' needs but also in recognizing them and remembering their names!

Drug Abuse Prevention The 1990 Canadian Education Association's poll of the public's attitudes toward the public schools found that drug and alcohol abuse was the top-ranking problem facing the public schools. Students' drug problems are not always easy to detect. Their low productivity rates, inability to learn, and attitude problems demand teacher attention; yet teachers may be unaware of the source of these difficulties. Even when teachers do recognize a drug problem, they may lack the resources or expertise to help. Obviously, teachers feel frustrated when faced by the wasted potential they observe in their students. In addition, when the public calls for schools to curb the drug problem, that expectation can increase the stress teachers experience.

Long Working Hours The official working hours for teachers are attractive, but the real working hours are another matter. Not built into contracts are the after-hours or extra assignments found at all levels of teaching—from recess duty and parent conferences to high school club sponsorships and coaching. Also not obvious are the hours of preparation that occur before and after school, and frequently late into the night and over the weekend. A 1992 survey by the National Education Association, for example, reported that the required school week for American teachers averages 36.2 hours, but teachers spend an average of 10.3 hours each week on additional assignments. Figures are comparable for Canadian teachers.

Copious amounts of paperwork, most related to various forms of record keeping, may be the most burdensome of the teacher's nonteaching tasks. Other non-teaching tasks include supervising students on the playground, at extracurricular events, and in halls, study halls, and lunchrooms; attending staff meetings, parent conferences, and open houses; and taking tickets or selling concessions at athletic events. Individually, such assignments and responsibilities may be enjoyable; too

Which aspect of teaching is one of the greatest concerns of beginning teachers? How do you plan to prepare to meet this challenge?

many of them at once, however, become a burden and consume the teacher's valuable time.

Gaining Parental Support   Although public opinion polls support parental involvement in schools and research indicates that parental involvement leads to increased student achievement and improved attitudes toward school, parents are not as involved in their children's education as teachers would like them to be. According to *The Metropolitan Life Survey of the American Teacher 1992,* lack of parental support is a major source of dissatisfaction among second-year teachers—even more daunting to them than drug abuse or violence. Among teachers who planned to leave teaching, "lack of support or help for students from their parents" was identified most often as the major factor in their decision.

The low rate of parental participation in their children's schooling is reflected in the National Education Association's finding in 1991 that only 32 percent of the parents of grade eight students reported belonging to their school's parent-teacher organization, and less than 29 percent said they had visited a classroom during the academic year. Nevertheless, the 1992 Gallup Poll of the Public's Attitudes Toward the Public Schools revealed that 59 percent of the public would be willing to help in their local schools without pay if needed. According to the poll, public school parents were more willing to serve as unpaid volunteers (72 percent willing) than those with no children in school (51 percent willing) or with children in private schools (49 percent willing).

Gaining Professional Empowerment   Although teachers are in the best position to recognize the needs of their students and to select teaching methods, management strategies, and materials to address those needs, they are commonly excluded from participating in the decision-making processes concerning these issues. Administrators, legislators, and even architects—all of whom are removed from the realities of classroom life and the concerns of teachers and students—can make decisions that profoundly affect teachers. In addition to the frustration caused by their lack of efficacy in matters of immediate concern to them, teachers may be demoralized if they believe that decision makers question their professional abilities.

In an interview with journalist Bill Moyers, noted Harvard educator Sara Lawrence Lightfoot eloquently describes why teachers desire **professional empowerment:**

> [Teachers are] saying, "I haven't had the opportunity to participate fully in this enterprise." Some teachers are speaking about the politics of teachers' voice. They're saying, "We want more control over our lives in this school." Some of them are making an even more subtle point—they're talking about voice as knowledge. "We know things about this enterprise that researchers and policy makers can never know. We have engaged in this intimate experience, and we have things to tell you if you'd only learn how to ask, and if you'd only learn how to listen."[14]

Although some teachers may experience frustration in their efforts to gain professional empowerment, we wish to point out that efforts to empower teachers and to "professionalize" teaching are leading to unprecedented opportunities for today's teachers to extend their leadership roles beyond the classroom. As *Teachers as Leaders: Evolving Roles,* a 1992 book published by the National Education Association, points out, "Recently, there have been calls for expanded, and qualitatively different leadership opportunities for teachers . . . the nation is coming to realize a need for more authentic forms of school reform or restructuring to meet the needs of an increasingly diverse student population and our rapidly changing society."[15]

HOW HAVE IMAGES OF TEACHERS AND TEACHING CHANGED?

At times, teachers and their profession have received scant praise from the media and from the public at large. From the scrutiny of colonial communities to the recent, occasionally negative press reports, the public has not always boosted the morale of those to whom it entrusts the minds of its young.

During the 1980s, the image of teachers in the United States was badly battered by ominous sounding commission reports, a dramatically negative press, and the resultant public outcry for better schools. Canadian media carried stories of these American reports and, because Canada does not have a National Department of Education, these reports, several of which declared that American education was shockingly inadequate, if not a failure, carried weight throughout Canada.

THE PUBLIC'S ATTITUDES TOWARD SCHOOLS

The Canadian Education Association's poll of the public's attitudes toward public schools is a useful barometer of the image of teaching, teachers, and schools. The survey asks if schools are better, worse, or the same as they were five years ago. In 1979, 1200 respondents over 18 years old from across Canada were generally evenly split in their attitudes (see Table 1.2). Responses in the four categories (the fourth choice was "no opinion") were all between 20 and 30 percent. By 1984, however, respondents were more split. Nearly half (44 percent) thought schools had improved while over a third (36.6 percent) thought that schools had deteriorated. By 1990, over 40 percent of respondents believed the quality of schools had not changed while a quarter thought that the quality had either improved or worsened. The present attitudes toward teachers and schools are particularly challenging, because the trend is toward more parental involvement. If teachers are not perceived as agents of change, parents may decide to intervene and break the stalemate they see occurring between parental forces for change and school forces for the status quo.

TEACHERS' ATTITUDES TOWARD TEACHING

A definite decrease during the early 1990s in the percentage of teachers who reported that they may leave teaching suggests that teachers' perceptions of their profession are improving. Two thousand American teachers were asked the following question for *The Metropolitan Life Survey of the American Teacher 1989*: "Within the next five years, how likely is it that you will leave the teaching profession to go into some different occupation?" Twenty-six percent responded "very likely" or "fairly likely." The *Metropolitan Life Survey* of 1000 teachers who completed their second year of teaching in 1992, however, found that only 19 percent believed it was "very likely" or "fairly likely" that they would leave teaching.

TABLE 1.2	QUALITY OF SCHOOLS		
Are schools better, worse, or the same as they were five years ago?			
	1979	*1984*	*1990*
No Change	25%	13%	42%
Improved	26%	44%	30%
Worse	25%	37%	20%
No Opinion	22%	8%	10%

Source: Canada's Schools: Report Card for the 1990s. A CEA Opinion Poll.

CANADIAN TEACHERS WHO MAKE A DIFFERENCE

Many of Canada's most talented young teachers as well as many dedicated veterans retain the desire to teach. In part, the desire endures because teachers have been positively influenced by one or more teachers of their own who enriched, redirected, or significantly changed their lives. The desire also endures because teachers recognize the many joys and rewards the profession offers.

Reflecting on dedicated teachers and their contributions to our lives, we are led to teaching because of the benefit it brings to others. In doing so, we retain the belief that education can improve the quality of children's lives. This belief is more powerful than all our images of teachers and is alive across each province in classrooms in which outstanding teachers work.

WHAT KNOWLEDGE AND ABILITIES ARE ESSENTIAL FOR TEACHERS?

Contemporary images of the teaching profession aside, we must ask what knowledge and abilities teachers need to teach well. Unfortunately, the complexities of teaching make it very difficult to answer this question without a good deal of elaboration and qualification. For one thing, there is no single, universally accepted definition of what good teaching is. For another, the **knowledge base** on which teaching as a profession rests is uncertain. Educational researchers are still learning *what* good teachers know and *how* they use that knowledge. An examination of different views of teachers' knowledge and abilities follows.

A PERSONAL-DEVELOPMENT VIEW

One view of what teachers need to know and be able to do places primary emphasis on who the teacher is as a person. According to this view, teachers should be concerned with developing themselves as persons so that they may learn to use themselves more effectively. Arthur Combs, a well-known advocate of this view, has suggested that "teacher effectiveness . . .is a function of how teachers use themselves. . . . The skillful use of self and the creation of conditions for significant learning is a truly professional achievement."[16]

One way of viewing teaching and learning is as a relationship. The rapport and connections established between teachers and their students is the link between teaching and learning. Thus, the main tool in the teaching process is the teacher herself or himself. Teachers cannot connect with students just through the newest and most effective technology. All the technologies in the world will not help students learn if their teachers have not established positive, authentic relationships with them.

What this approach requires is that teachers continually develop their powers of observation and reflection so that they can most effectively respond to the needs of students. Teaching is seen as more than a mechanical, craftlike implementation of specific procedures; it becomes an authentic, growth-oriented encounter between teacher and students.

Another important dimension of the **personal-development view** is the teacher's need for self-knowledge, particularly as a learner. As Arthur Jersild wrote in *When Teachers Face Themselves,* a 1955 book still timely today, "A teacher's understanding of others can be only as deep as the wisdom he possesses when he looks inward upon himself."[17] If teachers do not know themselves well, if they have not taken time to reflect on what they think and feel, on how they have grown and developed as human beings, they present and model a hollow self for others. In turn, they are unable to see beyond the surface of their students' behavior. Regarding yourself as separate from a role and taking time to reflect on your beliefs and values about education will help you become a more authentic teacher.

RESEARCH-BASED COMPETENCIES

Since the late 1980s, several larger school boards have developed lists of **research-based competencies** that beginning teachers must demonstrate. These competencies are derived from educational research that has identified what effective teachers do. Typically, the districts have developed *behavioral indicators* for each competency which trained observers use to determine to what extent applicants for teaching positions might actually exhibit the target behaviors in the classroom.

The Calgary Board of Education, with over 94 000 students, is one of the largest urban school districts in Canada. The CBE's Department of Human Resources has adopted a commercially available set of research-based competencies as a guide in interviewing and hiring new teachers. Selection Research Incorporated (SRI) from Nebraska created the SRI Perceiver instrument to choose and develop people in education.[18] The philosophy behind their research is that, because a teacher is a person and not a role, the research must focus on how outstanding teachers relate to and interact with peers and students. SRI summarizes its research findings as follows.

A teacher is a person—a real, authentic person who believes that students can and want to learn. A teacher is convinced that, as a teacher, he or she can make a significant contribution to the development of others. Teachers are often particularly sensitive to the feelings or states of mind of other people; they possess an ability to put themselves in another person's place because they are in tune with their own thoughts and feelings.

An outstanding teacher will push to build relationships with students because rapport between teacher and student is seen as a necessary precondition of learning. Relationships are most effectively built one on one, demonstrating concern for individual students. Good teachers learn the interests and needs of each student and make every effort to personalize each student's program. By listening carefully to each student, teachers gain insight into personalities and students are freed to think out loud and to work through thoughts and feelings in the process: to learn.

Teachers are active learners, ready to share what they have learned and eager to find materials, experiences, or ideas they can use to help other people learn. Because they are open to ideas, they have a storehouse of techniques, methods, approaches, and materials to stimulate students to think, to respond, to feel, to grow.

Good teachers are willing to try new ideas and techniques. They are able to creatively put information and experiences together into new configurations. At the same time, they want to know the facts before acting, and prefer to understand the total situation rather than reacting impulsively.

Good teachers have a unique blend of structure and flexibility. They see organization as a way to facilitate the learning process, not as an end in itself. They fit the structure to the individual students and can help students develop a sense of organization and ability to complete tasks.

Teachers receive a sense of reward and reinforcement from the response of students. As students learn, grow, and develop, the teacher is renewed and able to invest more time and energy in the lives of others.

When candidates for teaching positions are interviewed, they are asked a series of open-ended questions that require them to link together concepts from their own experiences so that interviewers are able to identify candidates' life themes. These themes are the following:

Focus: Focus is demonstrated when a person has models and goals, and when her or his life is moving in a planned direction. Teachers know what the goals are and choose activities keeping these goals in mind.

Objectivity: Objectivity is shown when a teacher responds to a situation by getting the facts and understanding the whole picture rather than reacting compulsively.

Gestalt: The gestalt theme indicates the teacher desires completion. He or she sees patterns and is uneasy until work is finished. When gestalt is high, the teacher tends toward perfectionism. Nonetheless, although form and structure are important, the individual student is considered first. The teacher fits the structure to the individual.

Innovation: Innovation is demonstrated when a teacher tries new ideas and techniques. A certain amount of determination can be seen in the teacher because she or he has to implement the idea. Creativity is a higher level of innovation in which the teacher has the capability to put information and experience together into new configurations.

Activation: Activation indicates that the teacher is capable of stimulating students to think, to respond, to feel—in short, to learn.

Input Drive: Teachers demonstrate the input drive theme when they seek out new experiences, information, ideas, and materials. They show the desire to study and learn all the time.

Investment: The investment theme is shown by the teacher's capacity to receive satisfaction from the growth of students, satisfaction that comes from the learner's response rather than from the teacher's performance.

Listening: The listening theme is evident when a person listens to others carefully and caringly. Listening is more than hearing. It should be a benefit to the person speaking.

Individualized Perception: Individualized perception means that the teacher thinks about the interests and needs of each student and makes every effort to personalize each student's program.

Rapport Drive: The rapport drive is evidenced by the teacher's ability to relate to each student. The teacher likes students and expects them to reciprocate. Rapport is seen by the teacher as a necessary condition of learning.

Empathy: Empathy is the understanding and acceptance of another person's state of mind. It gives the teacher feedback about individual students' feelings and thoughts.

Mission: Mission is what allows some individuals and groups to rise above the mainstream in order to ensure the quality of that mainstream. Mission is a deep underlying belief that students can grow and attain self-actualization. A teacher with mission has a goal to make a significant contribution to other people.

Districts that use the SRI Perceiver method of choosing teachers try to reinforce desirable behaviors in experienced, tenured teachers through staff development and professional development activities.

A JOB-ANALYSIS APPROACH

A third view of what teachers need to know and be able to do is based on the job analyses that some school boards conduct. Typically, a **job analysis** begins with a review of existing job descriptions and then proceeds to interviews with those currently assigned to the job and their supervisors regarding the activities and responsibilities associated with the job. These data are then analyzed to identify the dimensions of the job. Finally, interview questions based on the dimensions are developed and used by personnel responsible for hiring.

To illustrate the job-analysis view of the knowledge, skills, and attitudes needed by teachers, we present the twelve dimensions identified by a Florida School District as essential for the position of elementary teacher.

Oral Communication/Presentation: Effective expression in individual or group situations (includes gestures and nonverbal communication)

Written Communication: Effective expression of ideas in writing and with good grammar

Initiative: Active attempts to influence events to achieve goals; self-starting rather than passive acceptance. Taking action to achieve goals beyond what is necessarily called for; originating action

Tolerance for Stress: Stability of performance under pressure and/or opposition

Job Motivation: The extent to which activities available in the job overlap with activities and responsibilities that result in personal satisfaction

Sensitivity: Actions that indicate a consideration for the feelings and needs of others

Individual/Group Leadership: Utilization of appropriate interpersonal styles and methods in guiding individuals and groups toward task accomplishment

Technical/Professional Knowledge: Level of understanding and ability to use technical/professional information

Planning and Organizing: Establishing a course of action for self and/or others to accomplish a specific goal; planning proper assignments of personnel and appropriate allocation of resources

"Have you had any experience working with children?"

Control/Monitoring: Establishing and/or using procedures to monitor and/or regulate processes, tasks, or activities of students and personal job activities and responsibilities

Judgment/Decisiveness: Developing alternative courses of action and decisions that are based on logical assumptions and that reflect factual information. Decisiveness is the readiness to make decisions, render judgments, take action, or commit oneself

Work Standards: Setting high goals or standards of performance for self, subordinates, others, and the organization.[19]

PROFESSIONAL VIEWS

What teachers should know and be able to do varies from province to province. The Alberta Teachers' Association (ATA) released a document in 1993 entitled "Trying to Teach."[20] Although the document focused on teaching in one province, the concerns it raises are experienced by teachers throughout Canada. A committee of the ATA reviewed eight recent trends and initiatives in education: integration of students with special needs, results-based curriculum, individual educational plans, portfolio assessment, continuous progress, increased external testing, program continuity, and vision statements. The committee surveyed teachers, school superintendents, universities, specialist councils, and locals of the teachers' union. The survey asked three key questions: (1) What is the present situation? This question asked for an analysis of where teachers are, where they seem to be going, and how teachers view these developments. (2) What should be the situation? This

MAKING *a DIFFERENCE*

Judith Wyatt
Kingston, Ontario

Most high school English curriculums present students with only North American and British literature, clearly a narrow perspective of the world and human experience. I wish to foster students' appreciation of literary styles and traditions different from our own and increase their knowledge of other countries of the world through research and a study of indigenous literature.

Several years ago, when I decided to introduce an international component to the literature studied in the grade 12 advanced English class, I thought that it would be a simple matter of choosing appropriate anthologies. I wanted a selection of English translations of short stories from around the world with four or more stories per country. First I called publishers, then I called curriculum consultants for large boards of education. When nothing suitable was to be found, I began my own collection and after two years I had selected 56 appropriate stories from ten countries.

The stories cannot be properly understood out of context, however, so I prepared a series of questions to guide the students in their background research on a chosen country. The students learn about the country's environment, history, economics, politics, law, education, religion, language, architecture, art, music, fashion, and cuisine.

Since the medium of film is an excellent way to enter a culture, I've found ten videos to correspond with many of the countries in the unit. All are shot on location. Three of the six feature films are made by indigenous filmmakers and are produced in the native language with English subtitles.

While studying foreign literature extensively and intensively and creating a 70-minute group presentation on a particular country, the students develop important communication and cooperative skills. Even more significant, however, are the affective skills they acquire. For the first time, students in my high school are studying and learning to appreciate literature and culture that is not North American or British. For the first time, they are viewing and learning to appreciate foreign films, with subtitles in English. They understand ways in which Canadian values, world views, family life, and culture differ from those of other regions and, most important, they understand the similarities shared by peoples around the world.

question asked what direction was necessary and desirable for education in Alberta. (3) How do we get there? This question asked for a plan of action to achieve the desired goals.

Integration   The increasing frequency of integration caused teachers the greatest concerns. Defined as "the practice of educating children with special needs in the regular classroom in their neighborhood school with their non-handicapped same-aged peers," integration was seen by many teachers to cause educationally unsound situations. Teachers felt that students with special needs were being "dumped" into regular classrooms without the necessary resources or teacher aides. Teachers generally felt that integration was good for some students but not all, and that it was up to teachers to find ways to adjust to the changing situations in their classrooms.

Results-Based Curriculum   A results-based curriculum is "one which describes, in observable terms, what students need to know and be able and willing to do (knowledge, skills, and attitudes)." A traditional curriculum, on the other hand, describes what teachers should teach or how they should teach but does not clearly state what students should learn as a result of the teaching.

Teachers generally approved of this curriculum approach but were concerned that it emphasizes some aspects of learning at the expense of others. This approach might focus on learning that is observable and measurable and miss learning that is intuitive, creative, or inventive. Teachers using results-based curriculum must avoid being mechanical in their teaching and merely attending to input and output dynamics, and must be open to the complex relationship of teachers, students, ideas, concepts, and context.

Program Continuity   Program continuity means "assessing what students know and can do and then teaching so that every student is learning the next steps. Every facet of classroom instruction, assessment, school organization, recording and reporting student achievement needs to be connected to the fundamental idea of the maximum gain for each student, each year, across all areas of the curriculum—knowledge, skills, and attitudes." This type of programming requires a major shift from teacher-centered to child-centered practice and a conceptual shift from a behaviorist to a developmental model in which the needs of each individual student are determined and met. This is a difficult stretch for most teachers to make which they can easily lose sight of day to day in the classroom.

Continuous Progress   Continuous progress or continuous learning is often called "age-appropriate placement" or "ungraded classrooms." Continuous progress is an attempt to accommodate children who learn at different rates and in different ways. Children are not "retained" in grades but continue to move through the grades with their peers while learning at their own rate. Implications for teachers are profound. As children move from year to year, they may experience ever-widening learning deficits. They may need to be grouped with younger and younger children in reading or arithmetic and consequently suffer lower self-esteem. Teaching styles must change to accommodate the increased need to remediate rather than to teach new concepts. Teachers must balance the loss of ability to make professional judgments as to whether to retain a child with the gain of treating children more humanely.

Individual Educational Plans (IEPs) "IEPs are an established feature of special education where it has long been a common practice to develop an individualized program to meet the special needs of each child." But as special needs children are being integrated into regular classrooms, all teachers are becoming increasingly responsible for IEPs. In addition, pressure is increasing for all children to have IEPs because each child is special in some way. Teachers are challenged to find the time needed to design IEPs while at the same time developing unit plans for "regular" students. Indeed, as more regular classrooms have several students with profoundly special needs in them, teachers are challenged to adjust and prepare class activities so that all students may be involved.

Increased External Testing External testing is becoming more prevalent and more contentious. Many school systems have developed batteries of tests for Grades 3, 6, and 9 in addition to the requirement in some provinces for diploma exams. Increased testing increases school and board accountability and appears to be an appropriate response to Canada's poor showing in international student achievement comparisons. Teachers find this trend to be in conflict with the aims of continuous progress and struggle to balance the two, both intellectually and in practice.

Portfolio Assessment Portfolios are collections of each student's work over a school term. "Portfolios of student work have long been used by some teachers to enhance learning and to aid in their assessment of students' work. What is new is a trend towards authorities mandating their use in schools and school systems." Debate is ongoing over what constitutes a portfolio, how portfolios should be used, who gets to decide their content, and whether portfolios are appropriate for all curriculum areas. Teachers have expressed concern over the amount of time it takes to assess the collection of products contained in portfolios and, as the practice of portfolio assessment is mandated, teachers' resistance increases. Teachers who use portfolio assessment practices need to decide what amount the portfolio will contribute to final student grades.

Vision Statements Vision statements in education are generally imposed by the minister of education or by school system leaders. Teachers are concerned that, to be meaningful, vision statements must be developed at the school level. In the midst of "drugs, violence, broken-down family relationships, AIDS, sexual abuse, physical abuse, alcohol, hunger, gangs, weapons, technology, poverty, etc., all the esoteric vision statements in the world are not going to help deal with the realities that every teacher in Alberta faces every day in the classroom." Teachers must strike a balancing act, dealing with the immediate realities in the classroom while keeping the long-range visions in mind. The greatest struggle is acting every day in a manner congruent with the vision of the future.

In light of the four differing views of what teachers ought to know and be able to do, it seems clear that becoming a teacher is complex and demanding. We believe that effective teachers use five kinds of knowledge and skills to meet the challenges of the profession. Such teachers are guided by **reflection** and a **problem-solving orientation**. On the basis of this reflection and problem solving, they use knowledge of self and students (including cultural differences), subject matter, and educational theory and research to create optimum conditions for learning.

FIGURE 1.2
Essential Knowledge and Skills for the Professional Teacher

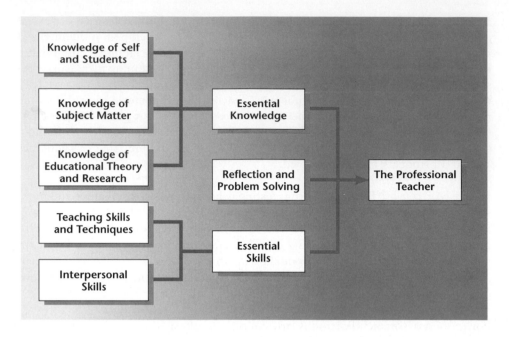

WHY IS SELF-ASSESSMENT IMPORTANT FOR TEACHERS?

Self-assessment is a necessary process in the professional development of teachers. Now that you have begun your journey toward becoming a teacher, you should acquire the habit of assessing your growth in knowledge, skills, and attitudes. As you do so, however, remember that professional development is a lifelong process; any teacher, at any stage of development, has room for improvement.

At this point, you should have a general idea of the extent to which you currently possess the knowledge, skills, and attitudes reviewed in the previous section. In which areas are you already strong? Which areas will require hard work on your part? How will you acquire the knowledge you need? How will you develop the skills you need? How can you come to know yourself more fully and deeply? To help you with the self-assessment process, the following Professional Reflection feature is designed to focus on several characteristics that may indicate your probable satisfaction with teaching as a career.

You may wish to collect the results of your reflections and self-assessments in a professional portfolio. A **professional portfolio** is a collection of work that documents an individual's accomplishments in an area of professional practice. An artist's portfolio, for example, might consist of a résumé, sketches, paintings, slides and photographs of exhibits, critiques of the artist's work, awards, and other documentation of achievement. Recently, new approaches to teacher evaluation have included the professional portfolio. Teacher education programs at several universities now use portfolios as one means of assessing the competencies of candidates for teacher certification.[21] Also, many school districts are beginning to ask applicants to submit portfolios that document their effectiveness as teachers.

PROFESSIONAL REFLECTION

For each of the following characteristics, indicate on a scale from 1 to 5 the extent to which it applies to you.

	Very applicable			Not at all applicable	
1. Love of learning	1	2	3	4	5
2. Success as a student	1	2	3	4	5
3. Good sense of humor	1	2	3	4	5
4. Positive attitudes toward students	1	2	3	4	5
5. Tolerance toward others	1	2	3	4	5
6. Patience	1	2	3	4	5
7. Good verbal and writing skills	1	2	3	4	5
8. Appreciation for the arts	1	2	3	4	5
9. Experiences working with children (camp, religious groups, tutoring, etc.)	1	2	3	4	5
10. Other teachers in family	1	2	3	4	5
11. Encouragement from family to enter teaching	1	2	3	4	5
12. Desire to serve	1	2	3	4	5

Total score _____

Now that you have completed the self-assessment, calculate your total score; the highest score = 60, the lowest = 12. Interpret the results of your self-assessment with caution. A high score does not necessarily mean that you will be dissatisfied as a teacher, nor does a low score mean that you will be highly satisfied.

PROFESSIONAL PORTFOLIO

To help you in your journey toward becoming a teacher, we have added the Professional Portfolio feature. Each chapter includes an entry for your professional portfolio. If you make these entries, at the end of this course you will be well on your way toward developing a portfolio that contains evidence of the professional knowledge and skills you have acquired. As you take additional courses in your teacher education program, your instructors may ask you to continue adding to your portfolio. On completion of your program, then, you would have a portfolio that reflects the richness and complexity of teaching and documents your growth and development over time.

Your portfolio should represent your *best work* and give you an opportunity to become an advocate of *who you are* as a teacher. Because a primary purpose of the professional portfolio is to stimulate reflection and dialogue, you may wish to discuss what entries to make in your portfolio with your instructor or other teacher education students.

What will your portfolio contain? Written materials might include the following: lesson plans and curriculum materials, reflections on your development as a teacher, journal entries, writing assignments set by your instructor, sample tests you have prepared, critiques of textbooks, evaluations of students' work at the level for which you are preparing to teach, sample letters to parents, and a résumé. Non-print materials might include video- and audiotapes featuring you in simulated teaching and role-playing activities, audiovisual materials (transparencies, charts, etc.), photographs of bulletin boards, charts depicting room arrangements for cooperative learning or other instructional strategies, sample grade book, certificates of membership in professional organizations, and awards.

For your first portfolio entry, prepare a journal entry (or videotaped version) describing what has drawn you to teaching. Describe or list your reasons for deciding to become a teacher. What will the rewards of teaching be for you? What aspects of teaching will you find satisfying?

CHAPTER SUMMARY

People are drawn to teaching for different reasons. A love of teaching, the influence of previous teachers, a desire to serve, the rewards of teaching diverse learners, and the practical benefits of teaching are among the factors commonly cited by those who decide to become teachers. Whatever draws you to teaching, you should assess your motives and aptitudes for teaching and base this self-assessment on a realistic view of the teacher's world.

Developing an awareness of the challenges of teaching is a necessary step in the journey toward becoming a teacher. Such awareness enables you to acquire the knowledge, skills, and attitudes that lead to professional effectiveness and satisfaction. Among the significant challenges of teaching are classroom management, drug abuse prevention, long working hours, gaining parental support, and gaining professional empowerment.

In addition, you should be aware of how Canada's images of teachers, teaching, and schools have changed over time. In spite of persistent negative attitudes about teaching, the public maintains respect for teachers and finds hope in the determined spirits of those who choose to teach.

Different views have been advanced regarding the knowledge and abilities that are essential for teachers. Among those considered in this chapter are personal development, research-based competencies, job analysis, and professional portfolios. In spite of these different perspectives, effective teachers are guided by reflection and problem solving, and they use three kinds of knowledge (knowledge of self and students, subject matter, and educational theory and research) and two kinds of skills (teaching skills and techniques, and interpersonal skills).

KEY TERMS AND CONCEPTS

job analysis, 17

knowledge base, 14

personal-development view, 15

problem-solving orientation, 21

professional empowerment, 12

professional portfolio, 22

reflection, 21

research-based competencies, 15

self-assessment, 22

student diversity, 8

student variability, 8

APPLICATIONS AND ACTIVITIES

Teacher's Journal

1. Consider your reasons for deciding to become a teacher. How do they compare with those described in this chapter?

2. Make a list of recent portrayals of teachers in the movies, television, and other media. Analyze the portrayals in terms of the type of teacher image they present—positive, neutral, or negative.

3. Clip all education-related articles in a major newspaper for a two-week period. Analyze the clippings in terms of the type of teacher image they present—positive, neutral, or negative.

4. Describe a former teacher who has had a positive influence on your decision to teach. In what ways would you like to become like that teacher?

5. What is your impression of the public's image of teachers in your province or community? What factors might be contributing to the kind of attention or lack of attention teachers are receiving?

6. Reflect on your suitability as a teacher. What knowledge, skills, and attitudes do you already have that suit you well for teaching? What other knowledge do you hope to acquire that you feel will make you even better suited?

Field Assignments

1. Volunteer to assist a teacher at a local school, preferably at the level and in the subject area for which you are preparing to teach. During this field experience, ask yourself these questions: Do I have the aptitude to become a good teacher? Am I willing to acquire the essential knowledge and skills teachers need? Do I really want to become a teacher?

2. Design a questionnaire and conduct a survey of students who are planning to become teachers. Why did they decide on teaching as a career, and what do they think they need to know and be able to do in order to teach?

3. Visit a local school and interview several teachers for their perceptions on the rewarding and challenging aspects of teaching. Present your findings to the rest of your class in the form of a brief oral report.

4. Interview a school administrator to find out what kind of knowledge, skills, and attitudes he or she looks for in a new teacher. Exchange your findings with others in your class. Do you note any differences according to level (i.e., elementary, intermediate, or secondary)?

2 What Is Teaching Really Like?

There are endless contradictions, conflicts, polarities, tensions, and oppositions that structure the pedagogical experience.
—Max van Manen
The Tact of Teaching: The Meaning of Pedagogical Thoughtfulness

Focus Questions

1. What are the complexities of teaching?
2. How do good teachers view their work?
3. What are six basic realities of teaching?
4. How do teachers benefit from educational research?

Shortly before lunch time, Mark Ogawa, a fourth-year university student, watched Karen Long as she worked with one of four reading groups in her grade two classroom at Diefenbaker School. Three weeks earlier, Mark had begun his student teaching experience. Now, a week remained before he would take over Karen's class.

Karen, well known throughout the district and community as a talented, caring teacher, was in her mid-thirties and had been at Diefenbaker for eight years. Last April, the local newspaper ran a feature article on how Karen's students used computers to communicate with students in other parts of the country.

As he watched, Mark wondered what it would feel like next week when he assumed responsibility for the twenty-four grade two children who now seemed so absorbed in learning. He felt anxious about how the children would respond and about whether he could focus their attention and energy as skillfully as Karen. Always smiling and soft-spoken, Karen seemed to have a gift for motivating students to do their best. Furthermore, she always seemed to be in control, even when students were working in small groups on different projects at the four learning centers located at the back of the large classroom.

"Does everyone have paper and pencil?" Karen asks the three boys and four girls seated with her at the low round table. Almost in unison, the children nod their heads slightly to indicate their readiness. Karen smiles warmly and continues.

"Jill, do you have enough room? Okay, good. Everybody sit up nice and straight. Good. Now, who remembers the four consonant combinations we looked at yesterday?" Three children excitedly wave their hands, and Karen nods to Artrise that she can respond.

"CH, SH, TH, and WH," Artrise says softly, as she beams a broad smile back at her teacher.

"All right. Very good, Artrise," Karen says, turning to glance quickly across the cheerfully decorated room to the other three groups. Satisfied that the children in each group are writing in their journals, she returns her attention to those seated at the table with her. "Now, who remembers which day of the week starts with one of the combinations we've been studying? George?"

"Thursday," says George.

"And which consonant combination does it start with?" Karen asks.

"TH," says George.

"Okay, remember a consonant combination is when we take two consonants and put them together so they make a brand new sound. It doesn't sound like either one of the consonants usually sounds."

As he watched from a student desk nearby, Mark thought about how animated and energetic Karen was when she interacted with the children. He was impressed with her approach to teaching reading—how she skillfully integrated the district's required basal readers and the latest whole-language techniques. He hoped the children responded as openly and enthusiastically to his teaching.

After ten minutes passed, Karen had her students line up at the doorway for lunch. Two girls approached Karen and asked if they could work on their puppets that afternoon. When Karen told them that they would have time to work on their projects, the girls jumped up and down and, together, shrieked, "Oh, goody!" Karen patted them on the back and motioned for them to return to their place in line.

As the children filed out of the room for lunch, Karen turned to Mark. "Well, in three more days *you'll* be the teacher. The kids are really excited. They're eager to begin the science lessons you told them about yesterday."

"I'm really looking forward to it," Mark said. Although he sounded enthusiastic, Mark felt uneasy. He thought to himself, "I hope it goes well. There's so much to keep track of. A teacher never really knows how the kids'll respond. How does Karen do it? She always seems to know just what to do."

What is it really like to be a teacher? What are the realities of teaching that Mark will soon experience? How can Mark learn to deal with the ambiguities of teaching?

———

Each of us is able to recall, at least dimly, the years during which we were taught the basics—reading, writing, mathematics, and oral communication. We also remember, no doubt, reading and writing about other subjects—geography, science, and history, for example. We acquired other knowledge and skills that school boards, teachers, curriculum committees, and an array of interest groups felt we ought to learn. Courses such as woodworking, health, music, art, physical education, typing, home economics, and a foreign language rounded out the curriculum we were taught at the elementary, intermediate, junior, and senior high schools we attended.

Although the teachers who taught us had different personalities, methods, and expectations, we would probably find that our lives as students were more alike than different. The recollections we share with one another about teachers who were good or bad, easy or hard, interesting or dull are drawn from a commonly shared set of experiences. The universality and apparent sameness of these experiences lead us to conclude that we *know* what teaching is really like and what teachers do.

But, is teaching the sum total of the overt behaviors that students observe in their teachers? Clearly not. Teaching is much more complex. Because dynamic interactions among human beings are at the heart of teaching, "the roles of a teacher are extremely complex and difficult,"[1] and teaching is an "imperfect human enterprise."[2]

WHAT ARE THE COMPLEXITIES OF TEACHING?

One of the most important steps you can take toward becoming a professional teacher is to try to appreciate the complexity of the career you have chosen. As you progress through your teacher education program, you will come to realize that it is impossible to know all of the factors that determine how much any student learns. Our hope, though, is that you will become an expert at determining just where to target your energies and resources in the classroom.

To develop this expertise, you must recognize that teachers "are problem posers and problem solvers; they are researchers; and they are intellectuals engaged in unraveling the learning process both for themselves and for the young people in their charge."[3]

THE CHALLENGE OF THE PROFESSION

To meet the challenge of the profession of teaching, however, will not be easy. At best, the task is difficult; at worst, it may be close to impossible. As Haim Ginott suggests, "Teachers are expected to reach unattainable goals with inadequate tools. The miracle is that at times they accomplish this impossible task."[4]

In spite of the difficulties that confront all teachers, we want you to keep this important distinction in mind: Though the outcomes of teaching may be unsatisfying if students do not learn all that you would like them to learn, the *experience* of teaching others is very satisfying.

Anyone who aspires to become an effective teacher should have a personal vision—a sense of what he or she values and is committed to. As Roland Barth observed in *Improving Schools from Within*, vision and a sense of purpose can help one respond to the complex realities of school life:

> [The] lives of teachers, principals, and students are characterized by brevity, fragmentation, and variety. During an average day, for instance, a teacher or principal engages in several hundred interactions. A personal vision provides a framework with which to respond and to make use of the many prescriptions and conceptions of others. Without a vision, I think our behavior becomes reflexive, inconsistent, and short-sighted as we seek the action that will most quickly put out the fire so we can get on with putting out the next one. . . . As one teacher put it in a powerful piece of writing, "Without a clear sense of purpose we get lost, and our activities in school become but empty vessels of our discontent."[5]

Commitment is also a vital component of professional effectiveness. However, as Tom Peters and Nancy Austin point out in *A Passion for Excellence*, it is not easy to make a commitment to excellence:

> Whether we're looking at a billion dollar corporation or a three-person accounting department, we see that excellence is achieved by people who muster up the nerve (and the passion) to step out—in spite of doubt, or fear, or job description. . . . They won't retreat behind office doors, committees, memos or layers of staff, knowing this is the fair bargain they make for extraordinary results. They may step out for love, because of a burning desire to be the best, to make a difference, or perhaps, as a colleague recently explained, "because the thought of being average scares the hell out of me."[6]

How committed are you to achieving excellence in your teaching? The following Professional Reflection feature is designed to give you an indication of your level of job commitment.

PROFESSIONAL REFLECTION

For an approximation of your level of commitment to teaching, respond to the Teaching Commitment Scale that follows. The scale contains sixteen items that ask how you will feel once you become a teacher. Indicate the extent to which you agree or disagree with each item by writing in the appropriate number. When you total your score, reverse-score items 6, 8, and 16. Your total score will range from a low of 16 to a high of 64, with 64 representing the highest level of commitment to teaching.

Responses: 1–Strongly Disagree, 2–Disagree, 3–Agree, 4–Strongly Agree

After I have become a teacher:	1	2	3	4
1. Most of the important things that will happen to me will involve my work.	–	–	–	–
2. I will spend a great deal of time on matters related to my job, both during and after school.	–	–	–	–
3. I will feel bad if I don't perform well as a teacher.	–	–	–	–
4. I will think about teaching even when I'm not working.	–	–	–	–
5. I would probably continue teaching even if I didn't have to work.	–	–	–	–
6. I will have a perspective on my job that will not let it interfere with other aspects of my life.	–	–	–	–
7. Performing well as a teacher will be extremely important to me.	–	–	–	–
8. Most things in my life will be more important to me than teaching.	–	–	–	–
9. I will avoid taking on extra duties and responsibilities in my work.	–	–	–	–
10. I will enjoy teaching more than anything else I do.	–	–	–	–
11. I will stay overtime to finish a job even if I don't have to.	–	–	–	–
12. Sometimes I will lie awake thinking about the next day at school.	–	–	–	–
13. I will be able to use abilities I value.	–	–	–	–
14. I will feel depressed when my teaching does not go well.	–	–	–	–
15. I will feel good when I teach well.	–	–	–	–
16. I would not teach if I didn't have to.	–	–	–	–
Total				———

Source: Adapted from Becky Heath Ladewig and Priscilla N. White, "Dual-Earner Marriages: The Family Social Environment and Dyadic Adjustment." *Journal of Family Issues, 5* (1984): 343–362.

HOW DO GOOD TEACHERS VIEW THEIR WORK?

Let's begin by examining how four junior and senior high school teachers, identified as highly successful by their principals, view their work. We asked these teachers to describe those moments when they knew they were teaching effectively. As you listen to their individual voices, notice how they try to describe something that is beyond easy observation and measurement. And note, too, how they convey the idea that teaching is not entirely a logical, sequential process.

> *Teacher 1:* Sometimes you see this little light . . . especially in math. You're explaining something, and you see all these puzzled looks on their faces. And you think, "Oh, gosh, they don't understand any of this." And then all of a sudden it hits them and I think, "Aha, they got it!" And they really do!

> *Teacher 2:* I don't really know how to determine when I'm definitely reaching kids. That's what makes this job so difficult. But it's when they respond. . . . I don't know how to measure it exactly. It's just a feeling. I just feel like I have the kids with me.

> *Teacher 3:* Well, sometimes it's lightbulb clear. Boom . . . it's there, and you can see it. The kids really responding, actually learning. I don't know how you see it, but you know it.

> *Teacher 4:* I have to grab the kids that don't want to do math at all and somehow make them want to do this work. I'm not sure how I do it, but kids just want to do well in my class. For some mysterious reason, and I don't care why, they really want to do well.

In some respects, the essence of teaching is difficult to describe. Certainly, we can describe in elaborate detail the interactions of effective teachers and their students—and these data are rightly included in quality teacher education programs—but our descriptions cannot capture, with richness and completeness, *all* that a teacher does (or doesn't do) to teach. Just as the attraction between two persons may be the result of a mysterious chemistry, the relationships between teachers and their students are charged with a difficult-to-measure emotional energy. The more effective teachers are somehow able to direct this energy toward learning the subject at hand.

The above comments confirm the difficulty of arriving at a comprehensive definition of teaching. Our quest to answer the question "What is teaching really like?" leads us to the inescapable conclusion that we can't fully define what it is. It may be in the way we describe the good teachers we have had that we find the closest approximation of what teaching really is. David Denton describes that special quality this way: "We come close to the 'It' of teaching with such terms as 'magic,' or 'the vibrations are great,' or 'he's altogether.' Student language, not scientific language, but student language emerges from that shared existential space where teaching is—whatever It is."[7]

When we recall our favorite teachers, we probably think of particular people, not idealizations of the teacher's many roles. Five **modes of teaching,** more general and significant than a discussion of the teacher's roles, can help you understand what teaching is really like. You may recognize these modes in the writings of gifted teachers when they reflect on their work, and may even acknowledge them as deeper reasons for your decision to teach.

When you recall your favorite teachers from the past, which aspects of their characters and work leap to your mind?

TEACHING AS A WAY OF BEING

Teaching is ideally more like wearing an academic robe than a stiff and binding straitjacket, and, once you put it on, you rarely take it off. When you travel, when you read, and when you learn something, the robe is there, its weight prompting you to think, "How can I use this in class?"

The robe is also with you as you move about in your life outside of school, reminding you when you encounter students, parents, and others in the community that you are no longer just yourself. For good or ill, you are also "Mr. Burke, the basketball coach," "Mr. Montgomery, the new math teacher," or "Ms. Tam, our son's grade six teacher."

In much the same way that becoming a spouse or parent changes you, so does becoming a teacher, for you must take on the role and let it become a part of you. Increasingly, the learning of facts can be achieved easily with good books, good TV, and good computer-assisted teaching; what cannot be done in these ways is to teach styles of life, to teach what it means to be, to grow, to become actualized, and to enlarge one's self. The only way a teacher can teach these qualities is to assume them.[8]

TEACHING AS A CREATIVE ENDEAVOR

Teaching is a creative endeavor in which teachers are continually shaping and reshaping the lessons, events, and experiences of their students. Ann Lieberman and Lynne Miller discuss this dimension of teaching in their book, *Teachers, Their World, and Their Work,* when they share their perceptions of teaching as a craft and teachers as craftspeople:

Teachers struggle to adjust and readjust, to make routines, and establish patterns, only to recast what has been done in a new form to meet a new need or a new vision. [Thus] the reality of teaching is of a craft learned on the job, [and] when viewed as a craft, teaching makes sense as a messy and highly personal enterprise, for it concerns itself with the making and remaking of an object until it satisfies the standards of its creator.[9]

Similarly, in *The Complex Roles of the Teacher,* Shirley Heck and C. Ray Williams address the creative dimensions of teaching by comparing the work of teachers and artists:

> [T]he complex roles of the teacher operate simultaneously and function interdependently. The complex and integrated structure might be compared to the construction of a mosaic in which the artist has an overall vision of how each part will relate and contribute to the total picture. The artist is well aware that the completed mosaic will be far greater than the sum of the individual pieces. It is this awareness that enables him or her to make the thousands of decisions for selecting specific colors, shades, and shapes. Similarly, it is the teacher's overall perspective of the teaching-learning phenomenon that helps him or her to see how the roles are related and to make decisions concerning which role may need greater emphasis at any specific moment.[10]

Thus, the creative dimension of teaching replenishes the spirit.

TEACHING AS A LIVE PERFORMANCE

Teaching is a live performance with each period and each day containing the unpredictable. Furthermore, teachers are engaged in live dialogues with their classes and individual students. The experience of teaching is thus an intense, attention-demanding endeavor—an interactive one that provides minute-to-minute challenges.

Some teachers embrace the live performance aspect of teaching more than others, believing that within it lies true learning. Sybil Marshall, who is such a teacher, writes about the process and effect of teaching dynamically in her book *An Experiment in Education*, an account of her experiences as a teacher in a one-room school in England: "To control a class in freedom, to learn with each child instead of instructing a passive class, to be a well of clear water into which the children can dip all the time, instead of a hosepipe dousing them with facts, is the most exhausting way of doing a teacher's job."[11] This mode of teaching can be best understood through actual experience.

TEACHING AS A FORM OF EMPOWERMENT

Power is the dimension of teaching most immediately evident to the new teacher. It is recognized in the grade one student's awed "Teacher, is this good?" on through the grade twelve student's "How much will this paper count?" Customarily, the respect and deference teachers receive derives, at least initially, from their power to enhance or damage their students' academic status and welfare.

Even in the most democratic classrooms, teachers have more influence than their students because they are responsible for what happens when students are with them, establishing the goals, selecting the methods, setting the pace, evaluating the progress, and deciding whether students should pass or fail. Accordingly, teachers' authority can be regarded as the heaviness of the academic robe we mentioned earlier, the part of teaching that is particularly serious.

How you use this power is crucial. The teacher and writer John Holt wrote about the psychological wars that insecure and frightened teachers conduct with their students. In his book *How Children Fail*, Holt gave a vivid example of one battle in such a war:

> A mother told me not long ago that on one of her five-year-old son's first days in kindergarten he began to talk to a friend. Having never in his short life been told that he couldn't talk to people, he didn't know this was a crime. Instead of just telling him her rule, the teacher scolded him loudly in front of the class. Then she made a long red paper "tongue," which she pinned to his shirt, after which she began to make fun of him, calling him Long Tongue and inviting the other children to do the same—an invitation they could hardly refuse. In such ways is the war waged. Not much will be learned while it goes on.[12]

The war is not confined to kindergarten, as we all know, for students at any level can be humiliated by teachers who misuse their power. For example, a high school student quoted in Patrick Welsh's *Tales Out of School* complained:

> Last year the highest grade given on a test in my advanced modern language course was my C. Most of the other grades were D's and F's. This teacher treated us like dirt. She told one boy who was struggling, "You're stupid—what are you doing here?"[13]

You can support as well as defeat with your power, turning students around and swaying them to appreciate your subjects, or school, or most important themselves through your belief in them. Sometimes your influence will surprise you when a passing comment or words of genuine praise come back to you as reasons for a student's success.

TEACHING AS AN OPPORTUNITY TO SERVE

To become a teacher is to serve others professionally—students, the school, the community, and the country, depending on how broad the perspective is. Most who come to teaching do so for altruistic reasons. As Herbert Kohl, the teacher in a high-needs school who first came to our attention twenty years ago with his book *36 Children*,[14] notes in a recent work:

> I believe the impulse to teach is fundamentally altruistic and represents a desire to share what you value and to empower others. Of course, all teachers are not altruistic. Some people teach in order to dominate others or to support work they'd rather do or simply to earn a living. But I am not talking about the job of teaching so much as the calling to teach. Most teachers I know, even the most demoralized ones who drag themselves to oppressive and mean schools where their work is not respected and their presence not welcome, have felt that calling at some time in their lives.[15]

The altruistic dimension of teaching is at the heart of the motivation to teach. The paycheque, the public regard, and the holidays have little holding power compared to the opportunity to serve. When teachers speak of this, their reason for remaining in the profession becomes obvious. Torey Hayden, a special education resource room teacher and popular author, enlivens her accounts of her teaching experiences with frequent illustrations of just such satisfaction.

> What was important was a scrawny seven-year-old kid waving a twenty-five-year-old pre-primer at me from across the room, squealing delightedly, reading out the

text to Boo and Benny and the finches. Come what might in her future, I knew I had given her the best I had. Never again could anyone say she could not read. She now could prove that false. Lori Sjokheim was not anybody to be messed with. Lori Sjokheim could read.[16]

Sara Lawrence Lightfoot describes a similar phenomenon at the secondary-school level when she writes about certain special relationships between teachers and students in her book *The Good High School*:

> In every school I visited, several students spoke of developing these bonds that were highly individualized and mutual, and very different from the generalized affection of a kind and popular teacher. A lanky, awkward senior at Carver told me how it felt when, in his sophomore year, an English teacher described his writing as "poetic." "I couldn't believe what she was saying . . . so I asked her to say it again." Every day he finds a way of stopping by her room, even if it is just for a brief greeting. She traces him through the day, knows most of the details of his life, and gets "a rare pleasure" from their relationship.[17]

Whatever form the altruistic rewards of teaching take, they ennoble the profession and remind teachers of the human significance of their work.

WHAT ARE SIX BASIC REALITIES OF TEACHING?

In this section we examine six basic **realities of teaching** that illustrate why teaching is so demanding *and* why it can be so exciting, rewarding, and uplifting. And when we say that teaching is demanding we mean more than that Mr. Smith's third-period math students just can't seem to learn how to compute the area of a triangle; or that Ms. Lavallée's grade six class can't remember whether to use *there* or *their*; or even that one out of four teachers in a large American city has said that teaching makes him or her physically ill.[18] While there are many frustrating, stressful events with which teachers must cope, the difficulty of teaching goes much further, or deeper, than these examples suggest.

Before we look at the six realities of teaching, we want to clarify our perspective. Though these six realities highlight the demanding (perhaps even impossible) dimensions of teaching, we do *not* mean to suggest that the efforts of teachers are wasted or that teachers do not make a difference. Clearly, what teachers do in the classroom matters a great deal.

REALITY 1: THE UNPREDICTABILITY OF OUTCOMES

The outcomes of teaching, even in the best of circumstances, are neither predictable nor consistent. Any teacher, beginner or veteran, can give countless examples of how the outcomes of teaching are often unpredictable and inconsistent. Life in most classrooms usually proceeds on a fairly even keel—with teachers able to predict, fairly accurately, how their students will respond to lessons. The best-laid lesson plans, however, may be accompanied by students' blank stares, yawns of boredom, hostile acting out, or expressions of befuddlement. On the other hand, lack of preparation on the teacher's part does not necessarily rule out the possibility of a thoroughly exciting discussion in class, a real breakthrough in understanding for an individual student or the entire class, or simply a good, fast-paced

EDUCATION IN THE NEWS

Year-Round Schooling

Year-round schools began in the United States in 1968 and today over 1.5 million students, mainly in California and Utah, attend school throughout the year.

The Ontario ministry of education endorsed year-round schools over 15 years ago but so far none has been launched. Year-round schools have started to take hold in British Columbia where several school districts have implemented them to address severe facility shortages and a rapid growth in student enrollment. In a pilot project in Alberta, one school in a small district north of Calgary switched about one third of its students to a year-round schedule while the other two thirds remain on a traditional ten-month school year. The project is designed to determine which school experience is better for both children and their parents.

However, most school districts consider year-round schedules to save money rather than to improve children's learning. With a year-round schedule, schools can house 25 to 50 percent more students than on a ten-month school

year. Holidays are staggered so that at any one time a group of students and teachers are out of the building. A group of students and teachers on vacation return to the space used by another group just beginning their holidays.

Parents and students do not seem to object to moving from room to room. What they mind is losing their summer holidays. Canadians have grown up in a society with ten months of school and two months of holiday from school. Parents want to pass along their experiences of freedom and relaxation to their children. Moreover, Canadians take vacations in the summer. Holidays during the year in a year-round schedule are called intercession, are shorter, and do not necessarily coincide with summer at all.

Canadians are caught up by strong cultural and economic traditions that are tied to summer holidays and that prevent us from seeing school as continuous and year-round, even though this type of schooling might better educate children. Do you see year-round schooling as an issue of quality of education or as an issue of economics?

Source: Based on *The Globe and Mail,* Jan. 2,4,5; 1995

---

review of previously learned material. In short, teachers are often surprised at students' reactions to a lesson.

In an article titled "The Way Teaching Is," Philip Jackson quotes Sir William Osler, the famous Canadian physician and professor of medicine, who had an apt metaphor for the unpredictable quality of teaching. As Osler put it: "No bubble is so iridescent or floats longer than that blown by the successful teacher." Jackson then goes on to say, "Osler's metaphor intrigues me because it calls attention to the fragile quality of the psychological condition that is created and maintained by the teacher. Class sessions, like bubbles, tend to be shortlived, and after a teaching session is finished, its residue, like that of a burst bubble, is almost invisible."[19]

Students' Responses   Contrary to the popular notion that teaching consists entirely of a specific number of competencies or observable behaviors, the reactions of students to any given lesson cannot be guaranteed. Furthermore, it is incorrect to assume that teachers, like other professionals, can control all the results of their efforts.

An example of how the outcomes of teaching are unpredictable is given in this teacher's account of his first year on the job. We see how creativity and planning do not necessarily ensure a successful lesson and how the inability to obtain positive outcomes can lower a teacher's professional self-esteem.

I brought in movies, had exercises with the newspaper, had the class write their own newspaper, did map exercises, and had them work on problems I brought in, but I felt that I was only occupying them—a sort of military holding action. I sensed no growth. I felt like Mr. Jonas, the teacher I had observed the year before. What a disappointing self-image! I began watching the clock, hoping the minutes would race by. They never did. It seemed like an eternity before the bell would ring. It would finally come, and I would drag myself to the first floor and prepare to get away from it all. Thank God it was my last class. I would be completely drained of emotional and psychic energy. Some days I would come home and fall asleep from four o'clock to ten o'clock. I am sure it was a symbolic return to the womb.

The next morning I would be reborn again and I would trudge off to school to face another day of trying to be a teacher.[20]

As the preceding example shows, students' unexpected reactions may cause teachers either to scrap their carefully executed plans or to press ahead and make the best of things. However, surprises in the classroom are not always bad. One teacher we interviewed, for example, describes how her grade sixes let her know that they enjoyed, not disliked, a particular lesson.

Yesterday, the kids seemed real lethargic when I questioned them about the paragraphs they had read. They hardly had anything to say and I thought to myself, "I am really boring these kids with this stuff. So why don't we get off this tomorrow?"

So, for today I had the greatest lesson plan in the world ready—a lesson on speed reading. Well, I couldn't even get into it. Two or three kids said, "Let's read some more paragraphs. Let's do what we did yesterday." Then the whole class started in. They wanted more paragraphs!

When you have a positive response like that from the kids, they must be getting something out of it. So I shelved the speed reading lesson and we read more paragraphs. It was absolutely the best class I've ever had with this group. Everyone was just about frantic to read aloud and answer questions. It was beautiful! It was like I could see them begin to understand what reading for comprehension is all about.

How can teachers best prepare themselves for the unpredictability of students' responses?

Philip Jackson describes this dynamic dimension of teaching in *Life in Classrooms* when he notes that "as typically conducted, teaching is an opportunistic process. . . . Neither the teacher nor his [or her] students can predict with any certainty exactly what will happen next. Plans are forever going awry and unexpected opportunities for the attainment of educational goals are constantly emerging."[21]

Results in the Future   Teachers strive to effect behavioral changes in their students for the future as well as for the here and now. In *Life in Classrooms*, Jackson labels this the preparatory aspect of teaching. Few teachers have the sole purpose of having students perform better on next Monday's unit exam or on a criterion-referenced test mandated by the province. Instead, students are expected to apply their newly-acquired skills and knowledge at some indeterminate, usually distant, point in the future. As one English teacher points out, it may take some time for students to display what they have learned from teachers:

> English particularly is so much a business of increasing [students'] ability to think for themselves, to write their thoughts, get them down on paper, that sometimes you don't know until they're seniors whether what you have taught them as sophomores has penetrated at all. . . . Sometimes it doesn't work until they're in college.[22]

Just as months or years may pass before the results of teaching become manifest, teachers may wait a long time before receiving positive feedback from students. The following comment by a kindergarten teacher illustrates the delayed satisfaction that can characterize teaching:

> About a month ago I had a 22-year-old boy knock on the door. He said, "Miss R?" I said, "Yes." He is now in England, an architect; he's married and has a little girl. I thought, "This is not happening to me. I had you in kindergarten." If you teach high school and a kid comes back and he's married in two or three years, that's expected, but 16 years or 18 years—first year in kindergarten. It's rewarding . . . be it one year, or ten years down the road. . . . There are daily satisfactions—"She got it!"—that's a reward in itself, but I think it's a little bit down the road that you get your satisfaction.[23]

REALITY 2: THE DIFFICULTY OF MEASUREMENT

It is difficult to measure what students learn as a result of being taught. The ultimate purpose of teaching is to lead the student to a greater understanding of the things of this world. But, as even the most casual appraisal of human nature will confirm, it is difficult, perhaps impossible, to determine precisely what another human being does or does not understand. Although the aims or intentions of teaching may be specified with exacting detail, one of the realities of teaching, as the following junior high school teacher points out, is that some of what students learn may be indeterminate and beyond direct measurement:

> It's most difficult to assess the work you're doing—especially this thinking business. I've looked around for a test I could give the advanced placement children to measure their thinking . . . to give a posttest later on and see if I've done them any good. . . . I'm looking for something concrete and I'm afraid that it's most difficult to achieve. . . . There is no science to this.[24]

In spite of provincial efforts to institute standardized tests of basic skills and thereby hold teachers accountable, the conventional wisdom among teachers is

Shanks

"Well, Brooks, I'm giving you a C. I believe this effort deserves an F for ability to follow instructions but an A for realization of full potential."

that they are often uncertain about just what their students learn. We have kilometres of computer printouts with test data, but very little knowledge of what lies behind a child's written response and little understanding of how the child experiences the curriculum. As one educational researcher concludes: "The inaccessibility of data is similar both in science and in learning. We cannot directly 'see' subatomic particles, nor can we 'see' the inner-workings of the mind and emotions of the child. Both are inferential: both are subject to human interpretation."[25]

Years ago, John Dewey called for teachers who would be sensitive to the inner lives of children and therefore aware of what students were learning (or failing to learn) as a result of their exposure to the curriculum. That he refers to this high degree of sensitivity as "insight into soul-action" suggests how difficult it is for teachers to develop the capacity to know what their students learn:

> As every teacher knows, children have an inner and an outer attention. The inner attention is the giving of the mind without reserve or qualification to the subject at hand. It is the first-hand and personal play of mental powers. As such, it is a fundamental condition of mental growth. To be able to keep track of this mental play, to recognize the signs of its presence or absence, to know how it is initiated and maintained, how to test it by results attained, and to test *apparent* results by it, is the supreme mark and criterion of a teacher. It means insight into soul-action, ability to discriminate the genuine from the sham and capacity to further one and discourage the other.[26]

On the one hand, then, teachers must recognize their limited ability to determine what students actually learn; on the other, they must continuously work to become more sensitive to what students learn. To reduce uncertainties about students' learning, Philip Jackson suggests four basic approaches available to teachers (see Figure 2.1). The first two are indirect: carefully observing students for signs of involvement and creating a classroom climate in which they feel comfortable enough to admit learning problems. The second two are more direct: questioning students to determine their level of understanding and testing them on material

FIGURE 2.1

Reducing the Uncertainties of Teaching: Four Strategies

Source: Reprinted by permission of the publisher from Jackson, Philip W., *The Practice of Teaching* (New York: Teachers College Press, © 1986 by Teachers College, Columbia, University. All rights reserved.)

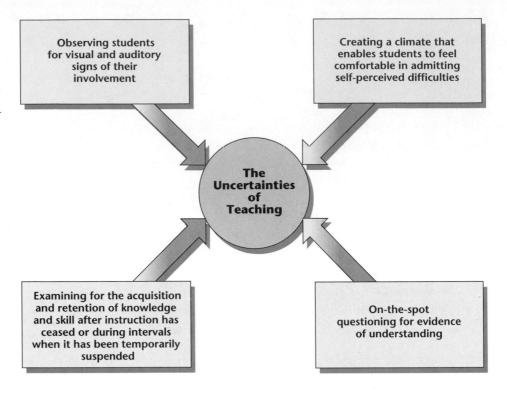

they have been taught. None of these approaches, however, will tell teachers all they might wish to know about students' learning.

REALITY 3: THE NEED FOR TEACHER-STUDENT PARTNERSHIP

The teacher's ability to influence student behavior is actually quite limited. The very fact that we refer to the *teaching-learning process* indicates the extent to which classroom events are "jointly produced"[27] and depend upon a teacher-student partnership. In regard to this partnership, Dewey suggests that the teacher sells and the student must buy:

> Teaching may be compared to selling commodities. No one can sell unless someone buys. We should ridicule a merchant who said that he had sold a great many goods although no one had bought any. But perhaps there are teachers who think that they have done a good day's teaching irrespective of what pupils have learned. There is the same exact equation between teaching and learning that there is between selling and buying.[28]

To the extent that we believe that learning *always* results in observable, measurable changes in student behavior (a currently popular, though limited, view), teaching becomes even more of a challenge. Arthur Combs rejects the notion of a direct correlation in a book aptly titled *Myths in Education: Beliefs That Hinder Progress and Their Alternatives*:

> A teacher's influence on all but the simplest, most primitive forms of student behavior, even in that teacher's own classroom, cannot be clearly established. The older children get, the less teachers can influence even those few, primitive forms

of behavior. The attempt to hold teachers responsible for what students do is, for all practical purposes, well nigh impossible.[29]

It should be obvious that a teacher cannot change a student's behavior with the ease with which a surgeon removes a patient's tonsils or a factory worker tightens a nut and bolt. At best, a teacher tries to influence a student so that he or she makes an internal decision to behave in the desired manner—whether it be reading the first chapter of *The Pearl* by Friday or solving ten addition problems during a mathematics lesson. In contrast, the patient under anesthesia is passive, and the surgeon is no more dependent on the vagaries of an interactive doctor-patient relationship than an auto assembly-line worker is dependent on a worker-chassis relationship.

Teaching, therefore, is uniquely demanding because the work of teachers is evaluated not in terms of what teachers do but in terms of what their clients (students) do. "It is the student who does the learning, and he or she is the most powerful person in the teaching/learning situation. His or her intelligence, adaptability, creativity, motivation, and general configurations of personality are much more important determiners of how much he or she will learn than anything the teacher or curricular system can do."[30]

REALITY 4: THE IMPACT OF TEACHERS' ATTITUDES

With the role of teacher also comes the power to influence others by example. Albert Bandura writes that "virtually all learning phenomena resulting from direct experience occur on a vicarious basis by observing other people's behavior and its consequences for them."[31] Clearly, students learn much by imitation, and teachers are the ones they often choose to imitate. In the primary grades, teachers are idolized by their young students. At the high school level, teachers have the potential to inspire their students' emulation, and, at the very least, to establish the classroom tone by modeling expected attitudes and behaviors.

Teachers' attitudes toward individual students, groups of students, the subjects taught, and learning itself can have powerful effects on their students' thinking and behavior. The specific attitudes teachers provide for imitation can significantly influence the quality of life in classrooms and, in some cases, the future lives of students.[32]

In *The Tact of Teaching: The Meaning of Pedagogical Thoughtfulness*, Max van Manen clearly states the importance of teachers' attitudes toward students:

> An educator needs to believe in children. Specifically he or she needs to believe in the possibilities and goodness of the particular children for whom he or she has responsibility. My belief in a child strengthens that child—provided of course that the child experiences my trust as something real and as something positive.[33]

And, an elementary teacher expresses the same idea in this manner: "I'm teaching children. I'm not teaching reading, writing, math. That's secondary. I really think that if you can't reach them, you can't teach them."[34]

Teachers model attitudes toward the subjects they teach as well as the way they treat their students. This helps to explain why many principals report first looking for enthusiasm in teacher candidates, no doubt thinking that if they feel positive about the subject matter, students also are more likely to.

Although the love of what one teaches is a crucial ingredient for good teaching, it is something that cannot be feigned, because students of all ages are too perceptive. If teachers become bored with the subjects they teach, they need to find new ways to be interested in them again—new approaches for teaching them, new dimensions of the subjects to study. If they feel inadequate in a subject area, they must master the skills and change their attitudes or they will pass on their insecurities and dislikes.

Finally, teachers' attitudes toward learning are important models for their students. The teachers who are learning to ski, sketch, play the piano, speak French, or who continually seek more information about nutrition, investments, politics, literature, or archaeology are teachers who show students through their example that learning is an ongoing, life-enriching process that does not end with diplomas and graduations. With their love of learning, they confirm the message of Sir Rabindranath Tagore that is inscribed above the doorway of a public building in India: "A teacher can never truly teach unless he is still learning himself. A lamp can never light another lamp unless it continues to burn its own flame."[35]

REALITY 5: THE DRAMA AND IMMEDIACY OF TEACHING

Interactive teaching is characterized by events that are rapid-changing, multidimensional, and irregular. We have already discussed how the outcomes of teaching are unpredictable and inconsistent. Yet the challenges of teaching go beyond this. The face-to-face interactions teachers have with students—what Jackson has termed **interactive teaching**[36]—are themselves rapid-changing, multidimensional, and irregular. One of us realized during his first year of teaching that

> from the moment I and my students encountered one another in the classroom, the flux of counter-educative events I had to contend with was often confusing, if not overwhelmingly chaotic, in its complexity. What any [teacher] found in a given classroom was not a cohesive, task-oriented group but several small, very strong, often opposing subgroups that somehow the teacher had to rally around the common goal of learning.[37]

When teachers are in the **preactive teaching** stages of their work—preparing to teach or reflecting on previous teaching—they can afford to be consistently deliberate and rational. Planning for lessons, grading papers, reflecting on the deviant behavior of a student—such activities are usually done alone and lack the immediacy and sense of urgency that characterize interactive teaching. While actually working with students, teachers must be able to think on their feet and respond appropriately to complex, ever-changing situations. They must be flexible and ready to deal with the unexpected. During a discussion, for example, the teacher must operate on at least two levels. On one level, he or she must respond appropriately to students' comments, monitor other students for signs of confusion or comprehension, formulate the next comment or question, and be alert for signs of misbehavior. On another level, the teacher must ensure that participation is evenly distributed among students, evaluate the content and quality of students' contributions, keep the discussion focused and moving ahead, and emphasize major content areas.

During interactive teaching, the awareness that one is solely responsible for the forward movement of the group never lets up. Teachers are the only professionals who practice their craft almost exclusively under the direct, continuous gaze of up to thirty or forty clients. Jackson sums up the experience: "The *immediacy* of classroom events is something that anyone who has ever been in charge of a roomful of students can never forget."[38]

MAKING a DIFFERENCE

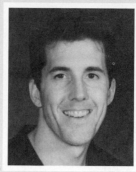

Todd Zazelenchuk
Saskatoon, Saskatchewan

It's true what they say about the progression of a teacher. In your first year, you're pretty much self-absorbed. All you can think about is how you are going to manage all the work and responsibilities of your new job. Over time, your confidence builds and your focus shifts to where the content you are teaching becomes the priority. Finally you reach the stage where your main concern is for the individual students in your classroom.

For me, it was at the start of my third year of teaching that I think I finally reached the latter stage. My goal at the start of the year was two-fold: First, I wanted to challenge my students with a large group project. I had always placed a great deal of importance on teamwork and cooperation and I knew there was life-long satisfaction to be gained by contributing to a large group effort. Combined with this goal was my desire for the group project to be technologically based. I had personally become quite familiar and enthused by multimedia technology by this time in my career and I was confident that my students would benefit greatly from the problem-solving skills and creativity that it fostered.

With these ideas in mind, my remaining goal crystallized following a European vacation one summer.

For as long as I can remember, I had always held a sentimental place for the topic of Remembrance Day and the sacrifices that Canadians made during the two world wars. The impact of their contribution never really hit me, however, until I visited a number of the actual battlefields in person. It was then that I realized how difficult it is for Canadians to truly appreciate this part of our history when we are so far removed from it. It struck me that I had just discovered the perfect topic for my large group project. Had I known at that time just how large it was going to be, I might never have continued.

During the next calendar year, *Gone But Not Forgotten* raised a budget of over $40 000 and received both provincial and national awards for education. Additional support came from the Royal Canadian Legion, the University of Saskatchewan, and an entire community of veterans and volunteers. By the time the year was over, my students had gained skills in researching, writing, interviewing, and computers that they might not have achieved without the project. The feelings of accomplishment and the experiences shared by class members throughout that year were unique.

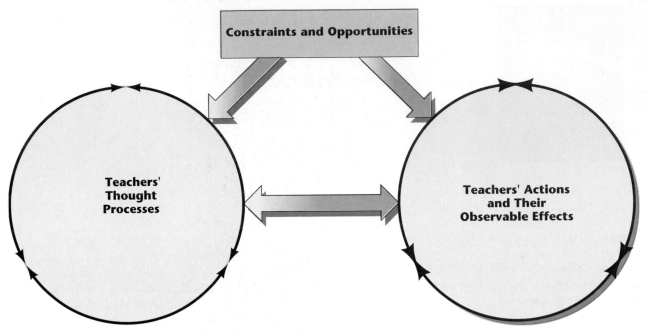

Figure 2.2   A Model of Teacher Thought and Action

Source: From "Teachers' Thought Processes" by Christopher M. Clark and Penelope L. Peterson. Reprinted by permission of Macmillan Publishing Company from *Handbook of Research on Teaching,* Third Ed. Edited by Merlin C. Wittrock. Copyright © 1986 by the American Educational Research Association.

REALITY 6: THE UNIQUENESS OF THE TEACHING EXPERIENCE

Teaching involves a unique mode of being between teacher and student—a mode of being that can be experienced but not fully defined or described. On your journey to become a teacher, you will gradually develop your capacity to listen to students and to convey an authentic sense of concern for their learning. Unfortunately, we can offer no precise, easy-to-follow formula for demonstrating this to students. You will have to take into account your personality and special gifts to discover your own best way for showing this concern.

One reason it is difficult to describe teaching is that an important domain of teaching, **teachers' thought processes,** cannot be observed directly. Figure 2.2 shows how this domain interacts with and is influenced by the observable domain of teachers' actions and their effects. The model also illustrates a further complexity of teaching—namely, that the relationships between teacher behavior, student behavior, and student achievement are reciprocal. What teachers do is influenced not only by their thought processes before, during, and after teaching but also by student behavior and student achievement. This complexity contributes to the uniqueness of the teaching experience.

HOW DO TEACHERS BENEFIT FROM EDUCATIONAL RESEARCH?

Since the 1970s, educational researchers have developed increasingly sophisticated methods for observing and analyzing the behavior of teachers and their students.

This line of research, often referred to as **teacher effectiveness research,** has shown us that, while we may not fully understand the artistic dimensions of teaching, there are particular teacher behaviors that tend to result in greater student learning. Much of what goes on in classrooms can have significant, measurable effects on student attitudes and achievement. For example, researchers have identified the following as strongly associated with how much students actually learn:

- Teacher praise and reinforcement
- Students' time-on-task
- Teachers' thought processes
- Teachers' expectations that students will (or will not) learn
- The amount of time students spend practicing what they have learned
- The amount of time teachers spend actively (or directly) teaching students
- How teachers organize and manage their classrooms
- How teachers respond to low and high achievers
- The instructional strategies teachers use

Although research can provide teachers with useful tools for analyzing their teaching, it should not be viewed as a recipe or a set of easy-to-follow steps for solving particular problems. Instead, it is most accurate to think of educational research as providing general rules of thumb for teachers to follow. After all, part of being a professional is the ability to decide *how* and *when* to use research to guide one's actions.

We believe that teachers for the 1990s and beyond need to be aware of theories and research that can be applied to teaching students from different backgrounds. Increasingly, teachers are finding students in their classrooms whose race, first language, religion, values, and social class differ from their own. Over 200 000 immigrants arrive in Canada each year.[39] Over 64 000 live in Toronto, another 30 000 in Montreal, and 49 000 in Vancouver. Eight thousand move to Edmonton and Calgary each. The populations of many Canadian schools are becoming more and more diverse, but teachers do not represent the same diversity. In the ten-year period from 1981–82 to 1991–92 Canadian teachers aged significantly; the average age rose four years to 42. By 1991–92, only 11 percent of teachers were under the age of 30, while 19 percent were over 50. The number of middle-aged teachers increased from 42 percent in the early 1970s to over 70 percent by 1991-92. This means that teachers of diverse races, ethnic groups, and cultures are not being hired at the same rate as the Canadian population is changing while all teachers are required to teach a student population that is becoming increasingly diverse.

SOURCES OF EDUCATION RESEARCH REPORTS

Employing methods that range from carefully designed experiments with intricate statistical analyses of data—often termed *quantitative* research—to studies that make use of methods borrowed from the field of anthropology—often termed *qualitative* research—educational researchers are continuing their quest to understand teaching more fully. Their findings are reported in scores of educational research journals (see "Resources in Educational Research: Publications" in the Teacher's Resource Guide). In addition, there are several excellent reviews of research with which you should become familiar during your professional preparation. The most impressive of these is the third edition of the *Handbook of Research on Teaching* (Macmillan, 1986), a project sponsored by the American Educational Research Association. Its more than one thousand pages are devoted to synthesizing research in the following five areas: (1) theories and methods of research on teaching, (2) research on teaching and teachers, (3) the social and intellectual context of teaching, (4) adapting teaching to differences among learners, and (5) research on teaching at various grade levels and in various subject areas. Other comprehensive, authoritative reviews of research that you might wish to consult include the following:

- *Handbook of Research on Science Teaching and Learning* (Macmillan, 1994), sponsored by the National Science Teachers Association
- *Handbook of Research on the Education of Young Children* (Macmillan, 1993)
- *Handbook of Research on Mathematics Teaching and Learning* (Macmillan, 1992), sponsored by the National Council of Teachers of Mathematics
- *Research Ideas for the Classroom* (Macmillan, 1993), three volumes sponsored by the National Council of Teachers of Mathematics
- *Handbook of Research on Music Teaching and Learning* (Macmillan, 1992), sponsored by the Music Educators National Conference
- *Handbook of Research on Teaching the English Language Arts* (Macmillan, 1991), sponsored by the International Reading Association and the National Council of Teachers of English
- *Handbook of Research on Social Studies Teaching and Learning* (Macmillan, 1991), sponsored by the National Council for the Social Studies

PROFESSIONAL PORTFOLIO

To learn more about the sources of information available to teachers, this professional portfolio entry will be a notebook containing brief summaries (or descriptions) of articles, books, videos, educational programs, or training materials that focus on an educational issue of interest. For example, the sources of research discussed in this chapter could be consulted to provide up-to-date information on topics such as teaching scientific concepts to elementary-age children, tutoring programs for potential dropouts, demographic changes in schools, or partnerships between schools and businesses.

CHAPTER SUMMARY

Though we have all spent hundreds of hours being taught, we tend to believe that the skills of teaching may be easily described and readily acquired. However, the complexities of teaching suggest that this is not the case.

Teaching is more than the sum total of observable teacher behaviors. Teaching also involves the teacher's inner dialogue about how to respond appropriately to the complex and constantly changing conditions of the classroom. Diligently pursued, such reflections lead the teacher toward greater understanding of the factors that both promote and hinder learning.

Not only are the realities of teaching more complex than they appear to the casual observer, it is also difficult for "good" teachers to describe what actually accounts for their effectiveness. In the end, it may be that students' descriptions of their teachers give us the most complete picture of what teaching is.

By considering the following five modes of teaching—that is, different ways of describing teaching—we can further appreciate what teaching is really like: teaching as a way of being, a creative endeavor, a live performance, a wielding of power, and an opportunity to serve.

In addition, the realities of teaching shed light on the challenging nature of teaching. The following six realities are professional challenges that, if little understood, can result in stress and frustration. If understood, however, they can lead to incomparable joy and satisfaction.

1. The outcomes of teaching, even in the best of circumstances, are neither predictable nor consistent.
2. It is difficult to measure what students learn from what they are taught.
3. The teacher's ability to influence student behavior is actually quite limited.
4. With the role of teacher also comes the power to influence others by example.
5. Interactive teaching is characterized by events that are rapidly changing, multidimensional, and irregular.
6. Teaching involves a unique mode of being between teacher and students—a mode of being that can be experienced but not fully defined or described.

Finally, the many complex dimensions of teaching are being studied by educational researchers. Although teachers can use research findings to increase their understanding of teaching, they should remember that research provides general rules to follow, not specific solutions to particular problems.

KEY TERMS AND CONCEPTS

interactive teaching, 42
modes of teaching, 31

preactive teaching, 42
realities of teaching, 35

teacher effectiveness research, 45
teachers' thought processes, 44

APPLICATIONS AND ACTIVITIES

Teacher's Journal

1. Think about a time when a teacher motivated you to learn. What are some of the things that teacher did to motivate you? Do you believe other students in the class had the same reaction to this teacher? Why or why not? Does the analysis of your experience suggest any principles about how people learn? How might you incorporate these principles into your own teaching?

2. How might you prepare yourself to deal effectively with one of the realities of teaching discussed in this chapter?

3. Review carefully the quotes from Dewey on page 39. What does Dewey mean by children's inner and outer attention? How do they differ? Why is the inner attention a "fundamental condition" of mental growth? How does a teacher differentiate between outer and inner attention? To what extent is Dewey correct in suggesting that the

teacher "sells" and the student must "buy"? Are there any limitations to this comparison?

4. ➤ Reflect on your personal vision as a teacher. What do you think you would like your students to remember most about you?

5. Recall and describe specific experiences you had with teachers in elementary school, middle school, junior high school, or high school. Were you ever made uncomfortable because of a teacher's power over you? Were you ever ridiculed or diminished by a teacher? Have you experienced the opposite—being elevated by a teacher's regard for you?

6. Describe aspects of your style of learning as a student. By what outward signs have your teachers been able to tell when you are involved in your learning?

7. Describe an activity that requires you to think on your feet and make spontaneous decisions about what to do. What is the best way for you to prepare for that activity?

Field Assignments

1. Ask your instructor to arrange a group interview session between students in your class and several school teachers. Ask the teachers to comment on the extent to which they agree or disagree with each of the six realities of teaching discussed in this chapter.

2. Arrange to observe a teacher's class. During your observation, note evidence of the five modes of teaching discussed in this chapter. Following your observation, arrange to check your perceptions with the teacher during an informal, postobservation interview.

3. Have your instructor arrange group interviews between students in your class and students at some local schools. At each interview session, ask the students what characterizes good and bad teachers. As well, ask the students what advice they would give a university student in the process of becoming a teacher. Following the interviews, compare the characterizations and advice given by students at the different levels.

4. Visit a first-year teacher (possibly a graduate from your institution) and ask him or her about their first impressions of becoming a teacher. What aspects of teaching were difficult? Which easy? What surprises did this first-year teacher encounter? How would this person have prepared himself or herself differently?

Teaching ultimately requires judgment, improvisation, and conversation about means and ends. Human qualities, expert knowledge and skill, and professional commitment together compose excellence in this craft.

—National Board for Professional Teaching Standards (United States)

Focus Questions

▼

1. What three kinds of essential knowledge must teachers have?
2. How is preservice training for teachers organized?
3. What are the four approaches to teacher education?
4. What field experiences are available to preservice teachers?

Thérèse Carmen looked out over her class of seventeen grade one students and smiled as she watched them prepare for the science lesson.

"Maybe I love grade one students so much," she thought, "because they are so defenseless, so needy." Thérèse walked up one aisle and down the next, helping one child make a place for his math book in his desk and another fit her crayons back into their box. The children, while fidgety and noisy, were responsive to Thérèse's attention, and their immature behavior and dependence did not bother her.

Once all the desks were clear, Thérèse began her introduction to the lesson. She perched at the edge of her desk and held several circles of different colors and sizes. "What are these?" she asked.

Some children responded, "Balls, dots . . ."

"Yes, these look like balls and dots. What *shape* are they?" Thérèse emphasized the word *shape* and pointed to a bulletin board that showed circles, squares, and triangles.

"Circles." Most of the children called out the answer.

"Good. These are circles. Are all the circles the same?"

The children were quiet. Some were no longer watching Thérèse. William called out, "Some are different."

"How are they different, William?"

"Some are red."

"Yes, some are red. Let's put the red ones here." Thérèse put the red circles on the flannel board and looked out at her students. Three or four had opened their desks and were looking inside. Other students were bouncing in their seats or talking to the children next to them. Fewer than half of the students were watching her.

"It's this science curriculum," Thérèse thought as she observed her students. The curriculum seemed poorly matched to the needs of her students and to their maturity levels. Regardless, she plunged ahead.

"OK, everybody. Eyes front. Look at Miss Carmen. Rosa, Anthony, Jacob." As she called the names of several students, all the children turned toward her.

"William told us that some circles are different because they are red. Kelly, how are some other circles different?"

Kelly shook her head but didn't answer.

"Tiffany, do you know?"

"Some are round."

"Yes, all circles are round. How are they *different?*"

When none of the students responded, Thérèse answered her own question. "Some of the circles are yellow," she said as she placed the yellow circles underneath the red ones on the flannel board.

"What color do I have left?"

"Blue," several students responded.

"Good," Thérèse said enthusiastically as she put the blue circles on the flannel board. "We have circles that are different *colors*. What colors are they, class?"

A few children answered, but most were no longer looking at the teacher or the flannel board. Again, Thérèse thought about what a poor idea it was to teach classification in this way to grade one children. It occurred to her that tomorrow might be better because the lesson involved animals, and she knew that the children would be more interested in animals than in circles.

But she had to get through today's lesson before she could introduce tomorrow's, so she again sought the children's attention to continue the discussion.[1]

As a second-year teacher, Thérèse is starting to learn that teaching involves more than just following a curriculum step by step. Her concern about the appropriateness of the science curriculum for her students is but one example of how teachers reflect their work. With time, Thérèse will learn how to modify the curriculum to fit the readiness levels of her students. If so, she also will have learned that, as the quotation at the beginning of this chapter from the National Board for Professional Teaching Standards in the United States points out, "Teaching ultimately requires judgment, improvisation, and conversation about means and ends."[2]

Among the factors that will contribute to Thérèse's success as a teacher are her ability to draw from what she has learned in her teacher education program and the support, guidance, and encouragement she receives during her first years of teaching. During the last decade, widespread efforts have been made to ensure that beginning teachers such as Thérèse have the knowledge and skills to be successful.

What do other teachers contribute to beginning teachers' success? In the spring of 1995, several Alberta teachers who had been recognized for teaching excellence were asked to reflect on their teaching experience and to present their thoughts to members of the Calgary chapter of Phi Delta Kappa. PDK is an educational fraternity with chapters throughout Canada and is committed to teaching, research, and service. Two of the teachers share their beliefs below.

Joanne Brown of the Calgary Catholic School District is an elementary teacher. She focused on the need for teachers to establish and maintain caring relationships with their students:

> When first asked to speak here tonight, I began to reflect on my teaching and to try to understand why I was recognized as an excellent teacher by my peers in the province. I thought of all the letters that parents and administrators had written to me. Then I remembered the quote from Rosemary and Henry Wong's book, *The First Days of School*, which still holds special meaning for me. "The mediocre teacher tells, the good one explains, the superior one shows, the great one inspires." I try to use this as a personal guide to follow.

Then I thought back to the teacher I liked best in my own schooling, and I remember her well. Her name was Miss Johnson, my grade three teacher. But why was she my favorite? She let us have chewing gum day—was that it? She was funny—was that it? She hugged me even when I wasn't hurt. That was it! She listened, she responded, she loved her students. I ask you to think back to your favorite teacher. I don't think you would say this teacher was your favorite "because she or he taught you to learn your multiplication." I think your favorite teacher cared about you, loved you, inspired you, and listened to you.

The next thing that I thought about was what did I value in my students. First of all was self-esteem. I strive to make all of my students feel great, not good, but great about themselves. If I can help them believe in themselves, then almost anything is possible. From September to December we work very hard on self-esteem. For example, I don't let my students take books home to read before January because parents might not think their children are reading very well when they phonetically stumble through words. But when they do take those books home in January, they dazzle their parents with how much they learned.

Another aspect that I feel is important is making school fun and exciting. When planning a unit I always leave room for celebrations, exploration, and experiences. I want to take a unit and make it come alive. When we did our ocean unit we got fishing nets, suspended them from the ceiling and hung our handmade ocean creatures to swim around the nets. We had an aquarium donated to our class, so we then went to the local pet store and purchased six fish and named them. We had a science corner with real sea shells, starfish, oysters, a lobster tail, and crab legs that we wrote reports on.

Who would have thought we were learning when we wore our shorts and bathing suits and lay on beach towels in our classroom watching a video on underwater life?

It's my job to make school magical, fun, and inspiring. Fortunately for me I love fun, I love kids, and they give me my inspiration to improve, to conduct action research, and become not mediocre, not good, but to be the best that I can be for my students. The day that I can't inspire children to learn, give a child a hug, let them rest their head on my shoulder, have my patent shoes polished by their wet fingers, be told I look beautiful just like their 80-year-old grandmother and see the humor and sincerity, is the time to retire from teaching and let the next excellent teachers begin their career.

Ellen Guderyan is a primary teacher with the Calgary Catholic School District. She also focused on the importance of establishing caring relationships with students but adds another dimension in her understanding of being a good teacher:

In order to prepare to speak to you this evening, I had to reflect on what was important to me to be a successful teacher. It is my opinion that an effective teacher possesses two qualities: one, to have a genuine love of children and, two, to have the ability to instill in them a quest for lifelong learning.

To demonstrate a love of children, we as teachers must build a sense of caring and community within both our classrooms and schools. We must give our students opportunities to feel safe enough to take risks and to challenge them to reach their full potential. After all, we are simply guiding them on their personal journey.

Just as we want our students to be lifelong learners, so must we as teachers. It is through constantly challenging ourselves to grow and improve, persevering and taking risks, continually evaluating and re-evaluating our own teaching practice, that we can create and maintain healthy, thriving schools and classrooms.

Teachers must be open to change and, in fact, I believe have a professional responsibility to stay current with trends in education yet, at the same time, be able to maintain sound instructional practice. I can attribute much of my success as a teacher to the countless in-services, conferences, and university courses I have attended over the past several years. Professional reading as well as dialogue among colleagues is also an invaluable tool in aiding us as teachers to become more effective. I have also had the opportunity to facilitate and lead several in-services for my colleagues. This has been an extremely valuable experience for me. I firmly believe that teachers teaching teachers is a powerful tool to enhance the professional growth in all of us.

It is also my belief that excellent teachers must demonstrate enthusiasm and commitment to their students. We must have a clear vision and set goals to meet these objectives.

Research has certainly played a major role for me in achieving these visions. I would like to share with you one specific example of how research has had a direct and positive impact on my teaching practice as well as my students' learning—the use of *student portfolios* for both instructional and assessment purposes. This example is typical of the process I follow to improve my teaching.

As a primary teacher I am always searching for better ways to communicate with my students' families not only their child's progress and academic achievement but, and maybe even more importantly, the *process* their child goes through in their own learning.

I have found an excellent tool through the use of portfolios. This has been quite a process for me starting several years ago with reading research in the area of portfolio assessment. Then I attended a conference on portfolios which in turn led to completing two university courses on this subject. During this time, I engaged my class in building their own portfolios. I had constant communication with my administrator who encouraged and supported me each step of the way. I believe it is crucial for success to have this support. Today, three years later, each of my grade one students has three personal portfolios, one for math, one for writing, and one of their own choice. They are also involved in self-assessment as well as student-led parent/teacher conferences. They are accountable and take responsibility for their learning and are able to share with their families all their successes. These are quite the accomplishments for a six-year-old.

Three weeks ago, my class had their third occasion to share their portfolios with their families. It was quite a night of excitement and celebration. As a teacher, I find there is no greater reward than seeing my students brimming with pride over their accomplishments and their parents praising their fine efforts.

As I suggested earlier, teachers must embrace change and take risks and the whole idea of portfolios was a risk that has paid endless dividends to me, my students, and their families. New ideas such as this keep me motivated and challenged, and reinforce to me that teaching children is the greatest profession there is.

These teachers speak clearly about the kinds of knowledge that are essential to teachers. Joanne Brown talked about the importance of caring, loving, inspiring, and listening to students. Ellen Guderyan also thought that teachers must be able to form a loving, caring relationship with students, and added that instilling a quest for lifelong learning was essential. To do that, she continued, teachers must be lifelong learners who take university courses, attend workshops, read journals, and think of themselves as researchers.

WHAT THREE KINDS OF ESSENTIAL KNOWLEDGE MUST TEACHERS HAVE?

In Chapter 1, we identified three kinds of knowledge that students preparing to become teachers must have before they can enter the classroom legitimately and confidently: knowledge of self and students, knowledge of subject, and knowledge of educational theory and research. It is to this essential knowledge that we now turn.

SELF-KNOWLEDGE AND KNOWLEDGE OF STUDENTS

Effective teachers are aware of themselves and sensitive to the needs of their students. Although it is evident that teachers should understand their students as fully and deeply as possible, it is less evident that this understanding depends on their level of self-knowledge. If teachers are knowledgeable about their needs (and, most important, able to take care of those needs), they are better able to help their students. As Arthur Jersild wrote in 1955, "The teacher's understanding and acceptance of himself is the most important requirement in any effort he makes to help students to know themselves and to gain healthy attitudes of self-acceptance."[3]

Two somewhat surprising emotions that teachers experience when they teach are anxiety and loneliness. Promoting the anxiety are three conditions clouding teachers' efforts: (1) the interminable nature of teaching (i.e., their work is never completed), (2) the intangible and often unpredictable characteristics of teaching results, and (3) the inability to attribute learning results to specific teachers' instruction. Unlike architects, lawyers, and doctors, teachers can never stand back and admire *their* work. If a student does well, that success rightfully belongs to the student. Furthermore, the work teachers do with certain students one year may not take effect until the next, and the sudden blooming of students this year may be due to the fine work of last year's teachers. Thus, teachers need to develop the ability to tolerate ambiguities and to reduce their anxieties about being observably effective.

The second emotion, loneliness, is hardly to be expected in a profession devoted to the service of others; yet both elementary and secondary school teachers commonly experience it, albeit for different reasons. Elementary teachers tend to feel isolated from adult companionship because of their need to remain in their classrooms, supervising their students at all times for safety, legal, and pedagogical reasons. Even to leave the classroom to go to the washroom, they must make arrangements with other teachers to cover their classes.

Secondary teachers usually have more free time in common, but they too experience loneliness and isolation because of their subject matter separations. "So strong is subject matter compartmentalization that it is common for the shop teacher and the English teacher to never interact in the course of a school day, or in fact, in the course of a school year," write Ann Lieberman and Lynne Miller.[4] The physical space of high schools, they note, is also designed to separate subject areas, with the math department sectioned off in one corridor, the foreign language in another.

In their book, *Beyond Bias: Perspectives on Classrooms,* Jean Carew and Sara Lawrence Lightfoot describe the sense of isolation that exists for teachers psychologically as well as physically: "Behind closed doors, they are asked to perform a complex and demanding job alone, without companionship and supportive criticism, often without reinforcement and reward; and their lack of adult contact and interaction gives them a distorted view of their own power and maturity.[5]

Knowledge of students is also important. The case study of Thérèse presented at the beginning of this chapter illustrates how important it is for teachers to be knowledgeable about student characteristics such as their readiness to learn new material. Without an understanding of these characteristics, teachers' efforts to help students learn and grow are likely to be inappropriate and, in some cases, counterproductive.

KNOWLEDGE OF SUBJECT

Clearly, with the title of teacher comes an assumption of knowledge. Those outside the field of education expect a teacher to be a ready reference for all sorts of information: How do you spell *esophagus*? When should *mother* be capitalized? What is the plot of *King Lear*? Which countries border the Mediterranean? Who is the prime minister of Israel? What is the significance of the Monroe Doctrine to Canada? Teachers are expected to be informed and to hold defensible positions on

PROFESSIONAL REFLECTION

You probably have had more experience as a teacher than you realize. Maybe you took charge of a group such as guides or scouts, 4-H, summer camp, or a club in high school. If you were responsible for what the group learned from the experience, you were a teacher. Maybe you tried to tutor someone. You might have been a peer tutor. Or perhaps your friend, brother, or sister needed something explained or demonstrated. Even as a babysitter you might have had to explain or demonstrate something occasionally. The subject matter might have ranged from algebra to sharing toys to tying shoes. This exercise is intended to help you inventory past experience as a teacher. Completing it should result in a greater awareness of previous teaching experience and a more informal basis for choosing future field experiences. Use a form similar to the one below to list your teaching experiences.

Inventory of Teaching Experiences

Experience	Subject matter	Learner's age or grade level	Context (e.g., school, camp, youth group)	Ways different from you (e.g., racial, cultural, socioeconomic)
0	Swimming	Age 7–9	Summer camp	City kids
1				
2				
3				
4				
5				

Source: From *Field Experience: Methods of Reflective Teaching*, 2/e, by George J. Posner, (New York: Longman, 1989), p. 9. Copyright © 1989 by Longman Publishing Group.

a full range of issues, from local politics to English literature to Canadian history to world geography. Obviously, training in methods of classroom instruction alone will not provide the knowledge, perspective, and intellectual habits that facilitate the development of an educated person, which in turn is what the public expects a teacher to be.

Teachers who have extensive knowledge of their subjects are also better equipped to help their students learn. Because these teachers "have a rich understanding of the subject(s) they teach and appreciate how knowledge in their subject is created, organized, linked to other disciplines and applied to real-world settings,"[6] they are able to present that knowledge to students in ways that increase student learning. According to the National Board for Professional Teaching Standards in the United States, such highly skilled, knowledgeable teachers

> command specialized knowledge of how to convey and reveal subject matter to students. They are aware of the preconceptions and background knowledge that students typically bring to each subject and of strategies and instructional materials that can be of assistance. They understand where difficulties are likely to arise and modify their practice accordingly. Their instructional repertoire allows them to create multiple paths to the subjects they teach, and they are adept at teaching students how to pose and solve their own problems.[7]

What should this teacher know about her students in terms of both their variability and their diversity?

KNOWLEDGE OF METHODS FOR APPLYING EDUCATIONAL THEORY AND RESEARCH

Much is known about learners and learning that can be of great value to teachers. Study of the contributions of Jean Piaget, Maria Montessori, John Dewey, Jerome Bruner, Erik Erikson, B. F. Skinner, Albert Bandura, and other cognitive and learning theorists, for example, can provide future teachers with several perspectives on the learner and the learning process. You may also wish to take courses in child or adolescent development and educational psychology to increase your understanding of how learning takes place.

Theories about learners and learning guide the decision making of professional teachers. Not only do such teachers know that a certain strategy works, but they also know *why* it works. Because they recognize the importance of theories, they have at their disposal a greater range of options for problem solving than teachers who have not developed their repertoire of theories. Your ultimate goal as a professional is to apply theoretical knowledge to the practical problems of teaching. To the extent that you realize this goal, you will have confirmed what noted social psychologist Kurt Lewin said about theories: "There is nothing so practical as a good theory."[8]

To illustrate the usefulness of research on students' learning, we present six **teaching functions** that educational researcher Barak Rosenshine found enhance students' learning of the basic skills. The effectiveness of each function is supported by carefully designed research studies in actual classrooms.

1. Daily review, homework check, and, if necessary, reteaching
2. Rapid presentation of new content and skills in small steps
3. Guided student practice with close monitoring by teachers
4. Corrective feedback and instructional reinforcement
5. Independent practice in seatwork and homework with a success rate greater than 90 percent
6. Weekly and monthly review[9]

For teaching higher-level thinking skills, Rosenshine and a colleague, Carla Meister, found that effective teachers use the following steps:

1. Present the new cognitive strategies
2. Regulate difficulty during guided practice
3. Provide varying contexts for student practice
4. Provide feedback
5. Increase student responsibility
6. Provide independent practice[10]

It may be helpful to think of educational research as providing teachers with rules of thumb to guide their practice. Rosenshine and Meister, in cautioning teachers about how to implement their research findings for teaching higher-order thinking strategies, put it this way: "The teaching of cognitive strategies is a higher-level operation itself; there is no specific, predetermined, or guaranteed path of instructional procedures to follow. Rather, there are sets of procedures [and] suggestions . . . that a teacher selects, develops, presents, attempts, modifies, and even abandons in order to help students learn the cognitive strategy.[11]

EDUCATION IN THE NEWS

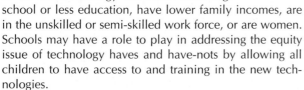

Schools and Technology

If the promise of computers and telecommunications is realized, technology may be the new stumbling block to social and class mobility. The world has become divided between the technology "haves," those who own or have access to computers and other new technologies, and the technology "have-nots." According to studies, those who tend to be the technology have-nots have high

school or less education, have lower family incomes, are in the unskilled or semi-skilled work force, or are women. Schools may have a role to play in addressing the equity issue of technology haves and have-nots by allowing all children to have access to and training in the new technologies.

However, like families, schools too are technological haves and have-nots. Schools in urban or wealthier areas may have strong parent advisory groups who can raise money to buy new computers or arrange for local businesses to donate used computers for the students to use. Perhaps have schools can twin with have-not schools to distribute resources more equitably.

Simply having computers, however, is not enough. Teachers must be able to use the potential of technology within their own classrooms and learn to integrate computer and telecommunications into their daily curriculum. The curriculum itself must devolve from its present form of segregated subjects to become more global and integrated. Teachers must reconceptualize both their and the students' role as knowledge workers and learners. Schools that have done so find their students are more sophisticated in writing compositions and have greater mastery of spelling, grammar, and syntax.

For example, it has been found that students who write by hand do not generally share their work with others. With computers, they look at each other's work more and work more cooperatively. Furthermore, with handwritten work, students must recopy the entire piece of writing several times to produce the final, "good" draft. With computers, children can write longer stories because of the convenience of the editing and spelling functions. Do you believe all schools and teachers should be technological haves?

Source: Based on *The Globe and Mail,* Jan. 3, Mar. 24, 31, Apr. 7; 1995

*H*OW IS PRESERVICE TRAINING FOR TEACHERS ORGANIZED?

Although programs in teacher education vary from province to province, they provide preservice teachers with an enduring set of resources and experiences they can draw from as teachers. Preservice training for teachers refers to the preparation of individuals for teaching, or people's experience before certification. Recall our observation that Thérèse, profiled at the beginning of this chapter, could modify her curriculum to meet the needs of her students by applying what she had learned in her teacher education program.

In a similar manner, a beginning junior high school teacher quoted in Robert Bullough's book, *First-Year Teacher: A Case Study,* describes how a course provided her with specific techniques that she could apply to meet the challenges of her first teaching assignment:

> [The professor] always said, "Take the students from where they are to where you want them to go." She was always very questioning about what your [purposes] were [but she didn't just ask,] "What's your objective?" It was more than that; "What is the student thinking? Where is he or she? What do you want [them] to

be doing?" Whenever I have to prepare a lesson, I'm thinking about how to be creative [with it]; she always [emphasized] creative things. I go back to those [things she taught]. Sometimes I even go back and thumb through lessons that [the students in her classes] did [and shared] with each other. That helps a lot.[12]

Criteria for admission to teacher education programs in this country vary. For some, admission into the university is all that is needed for acceptance into a program; for others, a student may have to pass a test in basic skills and general knowledge, pass a test of writing proficiency, submit documentation of supervised work with youth, be interviewed by an admissions committee, or achieve a certain grade point average (GPA) in university-level courses taken before admission.

Should teacher education students be thoroughly prepared with an arts or science degree and then receive professional training, or should the mixture of general and professional courses be more equal and occur simultaneously during the undergraduate years? The balance between the two types of knowledge—liberal and professional—has been a fundamental concern in teacher education over the years.

Citing M. L. Borrowman's review of teacher education programs, Judith Lanier and Judith Little outline three stances commonly taken regarding the mixture of professional and liberal education studies: (1) future teachers need to receive a thorough four-year liberal education and then study an additional year for professional training; (2) the two types of courses should be mixed and organized "around a set of professional functions of teaching or a general social problems core;" and (3) "the eclectic or ad hoc approach," which mixes the professional and liberal education courses early in students' academic study, should be used.[13]

There is still no consensus on the value of making graduate work necessary for certification, although a number of universities are experimenting with the five-year program.

WHAT ARE THE FOUR APPROACHES TO TEACHER EDUCATION?

Teacher education programs also differ in that many present students with approaches that are oriented toward a particular view of how reflective, problem-solving teachers should be prepared. Among those that have been widely documented are the post-degree approach, the reflective, inquiry-oriented approach, the theory-into-practice approach, and the collaborative approach.

POST-DEGREE PROGRAMS

Several teacher education programs across the country now require students to complete an extended course of study before becoming eligible to receive a teaching certificate. Normally, **post-degree programs** require that students acquire a bachelor's degree and extensive preparation in an academic area before taking professional education courses. In spite of recent recommendations to extend teacher preparation beyond four years, four-year programs are most common.

APPROACHES FOR REFLECTIVE TEACHING

Teacher education programs oriented around the concept of **reflective teaching** are designed to prepare teachers who are reflective decision makers. As Donald

Cruickshank, one of the primary architects of reflective teaching, observed: "Rather than behaving according to technique, impulse, tradition, and authority [reflective teachers] deliberate on their teaching."[14] Several universities in Canada have developed teacher education programs based on reflective teaching. Classroom instruction in faculties of education in many universities across Canada is being integrated with teaching practice in schools. Experiences during practicum observation days and university classes are connected, and students are expected to spend more time in the schools and less time on the university campus. The Faculty of Education at the University of Ottawa has developed a site-based program; students are in schools four days and at the university one day each week. This program helps students develop skills in critical reflective thinking as part of their education studies.

INSTRUCTIONAL THEORY INTO PRACTICE PROGRAMS

Several teacher education programs are designed to enable students to master the **Instructional Theory into Practice (ITIP)** model developed by Madeline Hunter at the University of California at Los Angeles. According to Hunter, teaching consists of a series of professional decisions that influence student learning. These decisions are in three areas: those involving content to be learned, those that focus on how students will learn, and those that involve specific teacher behaviors. In terms of this three-part framework, then, teacher education students learn how to develop lessons that contain the seven essential elements shown in Figure 3.1: anticipatory set, objective and purpose, input, modeling, check for understanding, guided practice, and independent practice. Although Madeline Hunter had a great deal of influence in Canadian schools and universities in the 1970s and 1980s, the ITIP model has begun to be replaced by both the reflective teaching approach and the collaborative approach.

COLLABORATIVE APPROACHES

Using approaches similar to those suggested by Goodlad in *Teachers for Our Nation's Schools,* several innovative teacher education programs have been collaborating with school-based teachers and administrators in the preparation of teachers. Universities in Canada have responded to the needs of remote communities by developing satellite programs in collaboration with several small and medium-sized districts. Simon Fraser University has external programs in Prince George, Fort St. John, Terrace, and Prince Rupert in northern British Columbia. The program in Prince George serves the Burns Lake, Nechako, Quesnel, Williams Lake, and Prince George school districts. Arctic College also offers several on-site programs for teacher preparation in small communities throughout the Northwest Territories. Other universities in Canada collaborate with each other to offer teacher preparation programs in remote areas. The Brandon University Northern Teacher Education Program (BUNTEP) is a joint program offered by Brandon University, the University of Winnipeg, and the University of Manitoba to provide on-site teacher education in northern Manitoba communities. Universities draw heavily upon the resources of local school districts to offer these programs and in their concept approach Goodlad's idea of collaboration.

FIGURE 3.1

Seven Elements of
Instructional Theory
into Practice

1. **Anticipatory Set:** The teacher develops in students a "mental set" that focuses them on the content to be learned. For example, "How many of you know how to find out the area of a circle?"

2. **Objective and Purpose:** The teacher tells students what they are going to learn and why it will be useful to them. For example, "Today we are going to learn how to write a business letter so that you will be able to write for information about careers that interest you."

3. **Input:** The teacher presents new information related to the knowledge, processes, or skills students are to learn. This may be accomplished through lecture, demonstration, simulation, or other appropriate activity.

4. **Modeling:** In this step, the teacher provides examples of the knowledge, processes, or skills being taught. In other words, the teacher "models" what students are expected to do.

5. **Check for Understanding:** As the lesson unfolds, the teacher conducts periodic checks to see what students have learned. The teacher may check for understanding concurrently with the next step.

6. **Guided Practice:** Students are given an opportunity to practice the new knowledge, processes, or skills under the teacher's guidance.

7. **Independent Practice:** In the final step, the teacher assigns activities that require students to practice on their own what they have learned.

WHAT FIELD EXPERIENCES ARE AVAILABLE TO PRESERVICE TEACHERS?

Field experiences are designed to give students opportunities to experience first-hand the world of the teacher. Through field activities, students are given limited (and usually carefully structured) exposure to various aspects of teaching. Observing, tutoring, instructing small groups, operating instructional media, student teaching, and completing various noninstructional tasks are among the most common field experience activities.

CLASSROOM OBSERVATIONS

A vital element in all field experiences is classroom observation. Students report that these experiences aid them greatly in making a final decision about entering the teaching field. Most become more enthusiastic about teaching and more motivated to learn the needed skills; a few decide that teaching is not for them. Recognizing the value of observations, a number of universities are trying to incorporate such fieldwork earlier in their teacher education programs.

Observations are more meaningful when they are **focused** and conducted with clear purposes. Observers may focus on the students, the teacher, the interactions between the two, the structure of the lesson, or the setting. More specifically, for example, observers may note differences between the ways boys and girls or different ethnic groups communicate and behave in the classroom. They may note student interests and ability levels, study student responses to a particular teaching strategy, or analyze the question and response patterns in a class discussion. Much of what observers will notice will be determined by the questions that have been raised before they enter the classroom. For example, Figure 3.2 presents a helpful set of questions on motivation.

When conducting observations, students need to guard against three types of observation errors—errors of omission, commission, and transmission—according to Martin O. Juel, retired professor, Southwest Texas State University. Errors of omission result from not having the necessary information or not seeing or under-

FIGURE 3.2
Guiding Questions for Observing Motivation

Directions: As you observe, note the ways that students are motivated intrinsically (from within) and extrinsically (from factors outside themselves).

Intrinsic Motivation
- What things seem to interest students at this age?
- Which activities and assignments seem to give them a sense of pride?
- When do they seem to be confused? bored? frustrated?
- What topics do they talk about with enthusiasm?
- In class discussions, when are they most alert and participating most actively?
- What seems to please, amuse, entertain, or excite them?
- What do they report as being their favorite subjects? favorite assignments?
- What do they report as being their least favorite subjects and assignments?
- How do they respond to personalized lessons (e.g., using their names in exercises)?
- How do they respond to activity-oriented lessons (e.g., fieldwork, project periods)?
- How do they respond to assignments calling for presentations to groups outside the classroom (e.g., parents, another class, the chamber of commerce)?
- How do they respond to being given a choice in assignments?

Extrinsic Motivation
- How do teachers show their approval to students?
- What phrases do teachers use in their praise?
- What types of rewards do teachers use in their praise?
- What reward programs do you notice (e.g., points accumulated toward free time)?
- What warnings do teachers give?
- What punishments are given to students?
- How do teachers arouse concern in their students?
- How do students motivate other students?
- What forms of peer pressure do you observe?
- How do teachers promote enthusiasm for an assignment?
- How do teachers promote class spirit?
- How do teachers catch their students' interest in the first few minutes of a lesson?
- Which type of question draws more answers: recall or open-ended?
- How do teachers involve quiet students in class discussions?
- How do teachers involve inactive students in their work?
- In what ways do teachers give recognition to students' accomplishments?

standing the whole story; errors of commission are caused by including more information than is actually there (i.e., projecting one's opinions into the situation); and errors of transmission occur when careless mistakes are made while keeping a written record of the observation. Because our expectations strongly influence what we see, observer bias is difficult to overcome. It can be reduced by using such tactics as writing comments in two columns—one for objective reporting of what is seen and a second for subjective reactions—or viewing a lesson from two perspectives, a student's and the teacher's, and comparing the two.

With reform efforts to improve education in Canada has come the development of instruments to facilitate the evaluation of teacher performance, a task now widely required of school administrators. Students preparing to teach can benefit by using these evaluative instruments in their observations. A sample instrument is shown in the Appendix at the end of this chapter.

CLASSROOM EXPERIENCES

Because of the need to provide opportunities to put theory into practice before student teaching, many teacher education programs enable students to participate in microteaching, teaching simulations, field-based practicum experiences, and classroom aide programs.

Microteaching   Introduced in the 1960s, **microteaching** was received enthusiastically and remains popular. The process calls for students to teach brief, single-concept lessons to a small group of students (five to ten) while concurrently practicing a specific teaching skill, such as positive reinforcement. Often the microteaching is videotaped for later study.

As originally developed, microteaching includes six steps. The student:

1. is assigned, or selects, a specific teaching skill to learn about and practice;
2. reads about the skill in one of several pamphlets;
3. observes a master teacher demonstrate the skill in a short movie or on videotape;
4. prepares a three- to five-minute lesson to demonstrate the skill;
5. teaches the lesson, which is videotaped, to a small group of peers;
6. critiques, along with the instructor and the student's peers, the videotaped lesson.

Based on the level of skill performance shown, the student may either reteach the skill or prepare a new lesson from nearly twenty skills that have been categorized into five clusters: response repertoire, creating student involvement, questioning skills, increasing student participation, and presenting skills.

Simulations   As an element of teacher training, **teaching simulations** provide opportunities for vicarious practice of a wide range of teaching skills. In simulations, students analyze teaching situations that are presented in writing, on audiotape, in short films, or on videotape. Typically, they are given background information about a hypothetical school or classroom and the pupils they must prepare to teach. After this orientation, students role-play the student teacher or the teacher who is confronted with the problem situation. Following the simulation, participants discuss the appropriateness of solutions and work to increase their problem-solving skills and their understanding of the teacher's multifaceted role.

Practica   A **practicum** is a short-term field-based experience (usually between four and seven weeks long) that allows teacher education students to spend time observing and assisting in classrooms. Though practica vary in length and purpose, students are often able to begin instructional work with individuals or small groups. For example, a cooperating teacher may allow a practicum student to tutor a small group of students, read a story to the whole class, conduct a spelling lesson, monitor recess, help students with their homework, or teach students a song or game.

Classroom Aides   Serving as a teacher's aide is another popular means of providing field experience before student teaching. Assisting teachers in classrooms familiarizes university students with class schedules, record-keeping procedures, and students' performance levels, and provides ample opportunity for observations. In exchange, the classroom teacher receives much needed assistance.

STUDENT TEACHING

The most extensive and memorable field experience in teacher preparation programs is the period of student teaching. The importance of student teaching is described in the following excerpt from *The Student Teacher's Handbook:*

> The 10, 15, or 20 weeks of your student teaching will have almost exact counterparts to the medieval apprenticeship system. One of its often unrecognized purposes is to contribute to your socialization into the teaching profession, to prepare you for your regular job by having you experience how real-life (i.e., not textbook) teachers behave in class, in school, and in relationships with students, other teachers, the principals, and parents.
>
> Also, as the apprentice, you will be working with an experienced if not yet master teacher. You will have the opportunity under his or her scrutiny to use the tools and materials of your new trade, and to gain experience first in small ways with individual students and later in larger ways with groups of students and with the class as a whole. When this time comes, you will likely recognize that although the courses and the fieldwork that preceded it helped ready you for student teaching, it is the teaching experience itself that caps and gives fullest meaning to all your previous education and training.[15]

Provinces require students to have a set number of weeks of student teaching or practicum experience in the schools before certifying them as teachers. The nature of student teaching varies considerably among teacher education programs. Typically, a student is assigned to a cooperating (or sponsor) teacher in the school, and a university supervisor makes periodic visits to observe the student teacher. Some programs pay cooperating teachers an honorarium.

Student teaching is a time of responsibility. As one student teacher put it, "I don't want to mess up [my students'] education!" It is also, as two other student teachers suggest, an opportunity for growth, a chance to master critical skills.

> I went in with some confidence and left with lots of confidence. I felt good about what was going on. I established a comfortable rapport with the kids and was more relaxed. Each week I grew more confident. When you first go in you are not sure how you'll do. When you know you are doing O.K. your confidence improves.

> I had some bad days, but overall I felt like I improved. I felt like, wow, I can deal with these kids. They're not so intimidating. They're not so smart. But the first few days it was kind of scary.

MAKING a DIFFERENCE

Linda Bennett
Whitehorse, Yukon

I am a grade seven junior secondary teacher from Porter Creek Junior Secondary School in Whitehorse, Yukon. In the spring of 1991, I was given a unique opportunity to participate in a project with a teacher from Juneau, Alaska. The fact that Juneau is our sister city enabled us to promote the goals of the sister-city agenda in a pragmatic way.

Initially, the project focused on teacher visits in which teaching ideas and strategies were shared. However, as the teacher from Juneau and I became more excited and enthusiastic about the international aspect of this project, we decided to have our students become actively involved, not only through student correspondence and student visits, but also through the development of theme boxes. Our theme boxes included a variety of activities that promoted historical, geographical, and cultural aspects of our Canadian north.

One of these activities, a game based on a trip up the Alaska Highway, gave the thrust to this project. As it was the fiftieth anniversary of the Alaska Highway and as the Alaska Highway was a joint project of both countries, we were provided with an excellent opportunity for students to learn about and become involved with an actual event occurring in our community.

From this origin, the project gained momentum. The game, which was a part of the theme box, not only heightened awareness and interest among sister-city groups, it also facilitated interaction between the students. At all times, teachers and students were enthusiastically engaged. Students in particular enjoyed the experience of becoming involved in their own learning and participating in local events as they happened.

The exchange between the sister cities continues. In 1994–95 students from my class produced a variety of projects based on the history of the RCMP in the Yukon to tie in with local events surrounding the RCMP Centennial. These projects were presented by my students to their peers in Juneau, Alaska.

As a teacher, my personal and professional life has been enriched through the life-long friendships that have been the result of this project. Taking the time and spending the energy to create this project has helped me to stay enthusiastic about and committed to teaching.

This student teacher is being observed by his teaching supervisor. What specific measures can he take to best maximize the benefits of his student teaching experience?

Actual teaching time for student teachers gradually increases over the practicum. When they are not teaching, their remaining time is devoted to observing and participating in classroom activities. The amount of time one actually spends teaching, however, is not as important as one's willingness to reflect carefully on the student teaching experience. Two excellent ways to promote reflection during student teaching are journal writing and maintaining a reflective teaching log.

Student Teacher Journal Writing   Many supervisors require student teachers to keep a journal of their classroom experiences so that they can engage in reflective teaching and begin the process of criticizing and guiding themselves. We share here two entries that give brief glimpses of the student teaching experience and illustrate the instructive benefit of journal writing. The first was written by a student teaching in a grade three classroom.

> *February 3*
> If there is one thing that *really* drives me crazy about these kids, it's how they don't listen to directions. Today in my language lesson all they had to do was rewrite a paragraph—not make corrections, just rewrite. We are working on paragraph form. I explained the directions once and had one of the students read it out loud again. Then I asked for any questions—none. Then as soon as I said "begin" the questions started flying. But what really got me was that they were all questions I had already explained or that were in the directions right there on their papers. I finally said they would have to ask their neighbors for the answer. It was *so* frustrating. Mrs. B. said for me to tell them next time that I would explain the directions once and ask for questions, then that was it. They would have to ask someone else! What a day!

Gaining skill in giving directions effectively resulted from this student's exasperation. The next entry is from a student teacher in a grade five classroom who discusses a problem less easily remedied—the recurrence of misbehavior.

He turned right around 30 minutes later and took another person's pencil. Needless to say I was very disappointed in the little boy who stole and in myself for my ineffective discipline. My cooperating teacher saw the disappointment in my face. She sat down next to me, patted me on the back and said, "You know the song 'We've only just begun . . .'? Well, you have just started in this business and even someone like me with 15 years of experience still thinks about that song every time I discipline a new child each year. Sometimes you're effective and sometimes you're not." That made me feel so much at ease with myself and with my career choice.

Relatively unstructured, open-ended journals, such as the ones from which these entries were selected, provide student teachers with a medium for subjectively exploring the practicum experience.

Reflective Teaching Logs   To promote the practice of reflecting more analytically, some supervisors ask their student teachers to use a more directed and structured form of journal keeping, the **reflective teaching log**. In this a student lists and briefly describes the daily sequence of activities, selects a single episode to expand on, analyzes the reason for selecting it and what was learned from it, and considers the possible future application of that knowledge.

To illustrate the reflective teaching approach to keeping a log, we share here a complete entry for one episode that was recounted and critiqued by a university student tutoring a high school student in life sciences. The entry is of particular interest because it provides us with a glimpse of a university student's first experience teaching an academic subject and it addresses two common problems: failure to pay attention and apparent lack of motivation.

Log for February 17, 2:30–4:15

Events

We went over her old notes, homework, quizzes and tests, looking for the relationship between them. We also talked about her lab work and how she liked that aspect of the course. We then shifted our attention to the textbook and worked about halfway through chapter one.

Episode

When I talked to Anne's teacher and his assistant, they both felt her main problem was attention and motivation. Perhaps that is why I so easily noticed the former problem today. I realize it was a Friday afternoon and few people are into schoolwork at that point, but it was still amazing how quick[ly] her attention would wander.

We were working in the school library, trying to pull the central meaning out of the text sections. For instance, we would read the section on bacteria characteristics and then try to make an outline, but she wasn't really there. I don't wish to exaggerate this because she was paying some attention though I felt it wasn't much. I felt annoyed, but I also felt anxious because I might be just boring and not teaching "right." This is really the first teaching I've done dealing with an academic subject and consequently I am in need of improvement.

Analysis

I can't truthfully say I have any solution to this problem or that I had previously thought about it. I just assumed we would work on the material and on "understanding-type problems." Understanding is not the main problem; bringing attention to the subject is. At first glance through her biology book I thought, at the risk of sounding arrogant, that it was so basic that even people who are not considered smart could work through it. But I'm beginning to see that I was really off the mark as to the problem. One reason this is so interesting to me is because it sounds somewhat like myself in high school. Attention is something both Anne and I have a problem with, but in my case I rely on my relatively good learning ability. Anne can't. I don't see how to change her attitude or even if it is my responsibility or right, but I do think her attention can be worked on.[16]

INDUCTION AND INTERNSHIP PROGRAMS

In response to widespread efforts to improve education, many provinces and local school districts, often in collaboration with universities, have begun teacher induction and/or internship programs.

Induction programs provide beginning teachers with continued assistance, at least during the first year. **Internship programs** also provide participants with support, but they are usually designed primarily to provide training for those who have not gone through a teacher education program. In some instances, however, the terms *induction* and *internship* are used interchangeably. Internship programs are offered by the University of Lethbridge. Students undergo four months of teacher training after they complete a 13-week practicum. Each student intern is placed with a school district to work in a school for the four months, and most are offered teaching contracts before they finish their internship.

Besides helping students find jobs, most induction and internship programs serve a variety of purposes:

1. To improve teaching performance
2. To increase the retention of promising beginning teachers during the induction years
3. To promote the personal and professional well-being of beginning teachers by improving teachers' attitudes toward themselves and the profession
4. To satisfy mandated requirements related to induction and certification
5. To transmit the culture of the system to beginning teachers.[17]

To accomplish these purposes, induction programs offer such resources as workshops based on teacher-identified needs, observations by and follow-up conferences with individuals not in a supervisory role, support from mentor (or buddy) teachers, and support group meetings for beginning teachers.

PROFESSIONAL PORTFOLIO

Observe a classroom in which there is likely to be some teacher-student interaction (for example, questions and answers, discussion, or oral checking and feedback). Divide the time devoted to your observation into two equal parts (for example, two fifteen-minute segments).

1. During the first part, count separately the number of teacher-to-student and student-to-teacher interchanges that occur, and record the occurrence of each with a tally in the appropriate box. A teacher question addressed to a student would count as one tally, and a student response back to the teacher as another.

Teacher Exchange Directed to Student	Student Exchange Directed to Teacher
~~||||~~ ~~||||~~ |||	~~||||~~ |||

2. During the next segment of your observation, continue observing teacher-student interaction, but this time record the number of student-to-teacher and teacher-to-student exchanges that pertain to (a) lesson content, (b) procedural matters (for example, directions and clerical tasks), and (c) discipline or classroom management (restating rules, giving warnings, assigning punishment, etc.). Use the following boxes to tally the number of teacher-student exchanges in each of these areas during this part of your observation.

Exchange	Exchanges Involving		
	Lesson Content	Procedural Matters	Discipline or Classroom Management
Student to Teacher			
Teacher to Student			

Now, for each of the preceding two observation records, state one general conclusion, supported by the data you have collected, about life in this classroom.

Source: Adapted from Gary D. Borich, *Observational Skills for Effective Teaching* (Columbus, Oh.: Merrill/Macmillan, 1990), pp. 19–21. Reprinted by permission from Macmillan College Publishing Company, Inc.

CHAPTER SUMMARY

The effectiveness of teachers depends, to a great extent, on their ability to apply the knowledge and skills they acquired in their teacher preparation programs. Outcome-based or performance-based programs, a recent trend in teacher preparation, require education students to demonstrate mastery of specific outcomes rather than simply present documentation that they have completed an approved sequence of courses. Although approaches to teacher preparation vary, three kinds of knowledge must be part of any program: knowledge of self and students, knowledge of subject, and knowledge of educational theory and research. Knowledge of self is important because teachers who understand their own needs are in a better position to understand the needs of their students. As student variability (differences in developmental needs, interests, abilities, and disabilities) and student diversity (differences in gender, race, ethnicity, culture, and socioeconomic status) increase, it becomes even more critical for teachers to have extensive knowledge of their students.

Teachers with extensive knowledge of the subjects they teach are able to present those subjects in ways that facilitate learning. Such teachers understand students' background knowledge and are able to create multiple paths to learning the subject.

Knowledge of educational theory and research also makes a significant contribution to a teacher's effectiveness in the classroom. Though educational theory and research do not specify exactly what a teacher ought to do in a given situation, they do provide rules of thumb for meeting the challenges of teaching.

Teacher education programs differ greatly. Criteria for admission and the structure of general and professional education components vary considerably. In post-degree programs, students acquire a broad, liberal education before taking professional education courses. Programs that emphasize reflection and inquiry are designed to prepare teachers who are effective problem solvers. Programs based on the Instructional Theory into Practice (ITIP) model emphasize the decisions teachers make regarding the content to be taught, how students will learn, and specific behaviors they (the teachers) will use. Last, many teacher education programs have developed a collaborative approach for involving school personnel in the preparation of teachers.

Among the field experiences that give students opportunities to experience the realities of teaching are classroom observations, microteaching, simulations, practica, classroom aide programs, and student teaching. Journal writing and reflective teaching logs are two strategies for getting the most out of student teaching, the most important experience in a teacher education program. Finally, induction and internship programs play a critical role in the ongoing professional growth of teachers.

KEY TERMS AND CONCEPTS

collaborative approach, 61
field experiences, 62
focused observations, 63
induction programs, 69

Instructional Theory into
    Practice, 61
internship programs, 69
microteaching, 64
post-degree programs, 60

practicum, 65
reflective teaching, 60
reflective teaching log, 68
teaching functions, 58
teaching simulations, 64

APPLICATIONS AND ACTIVITIES

Teacher's Journal

1. This chapter points out that teachers will encounter challenges related to student variability (differences in developmental needs, interests, abilities, and disabilities) and student diversity (differences in gender, race, ethnicity, culture, and socioeconomic status). To begin thinking about how teachers acquire knowledge about student variability and diversity, write a brief profile of yourself in regard to such differences. Show what you were like during your years in elementary, middle, or senior high school.

2. Teacher education students consistently rank classroom observations as one of the most valuable components of their teacher education programs. To help in planning your forthcoming observations, develop a list of questions you would like to ask the teachers whom you will observe.

3. Reflect on your education as a teacher. What are your primary concerns about the preparation you are receiving? What experiences do you think will be most helpful to you as you move toward becoming a teacher?

4. ➤ What does self-knowledge mean to you? Why is self-knowledge important in teaching? What steps can you take to achieve greater self-knowledge?

5. Think about areas for focused observations of teaching, such as classroom management, student involvement, questioning techniques, evaluation, or teacher-student rapport. For one or more areas, brainstorm and order in logical sequence a set of questions you could use to guide your next observations.

Field Assignments

1. Interview a student who has completed student teaching at your university. What tips does he or she have for developing a positive relationship with a cooperating teacher?

APPENDIX: Formative Observation of Effective Teaching Practices Instrument

Key Behavior	Indicators of Effectiveness	Observed* (✓)	Observed* (✓)	Indicators of Lack of Effectiveness
Clarity	1. Informs learners of skills or understandings expected at end of lesson			Fails to link lesson content to how and at what level of complexity the content will be used
	2. Provides learners with an advance organizer with which to place a lesson content in perspective			Starts presenting content without first introducing the topic in some larger context
	3. Checks for task-relevant prior learning at beginning of lesson and reteaches when necessary			Moves to new content without checking understanding of prerequisite facts or concepts
	4. Gives directives slowly and distinctly; checks for understanding along the way			Presents too many directives at once or too quickly
	5. Knows learners' ability levels and teaches at or slightly above their current level of functioning			Fails to recognize that the instruction is under or over the heads of students
	6. Uses examples, illustrations, or demonstrations to explain and to clarify content in text and workbooks			Restricts presentation to oral reproduction of text or workbook
	7. Ends lesson with review or summary			Fails to restate or review main ideas at the end of the lesson
Variety	8. Uses attention-gaining devices			Begins lesson without full attention of most learners
	9. Shows enthusiasm and animation through variation in eye contact, voice, and gestures			Speaks in monotone and/or is motionless; lacks external signs of emotion
	10. Varies activities with which the instructional stimuli are presented (e.g., lecturing, questioning, discussion, practice [daily])			Uses single instructional activity for long periods at a time and/or infrequently alters the modality through which learning is to occur (seeing, listening, doing)
	11. Uses a mix of rewards and reinforcers (weekly, monthly)			Fails to provide rewards and reinforcements that are timely and meaningful to the student
	12. Uses student ideas and participation to foster lesson objectives when appropriate (weekly)			Assumes role of sole authority and provider of information; ignores student input
	13. Varies types of questions and probes — Q convergent divergent			Repeatedly uses only one type of question or probe
	13. Varies types of questions and probes — P to clarify to solicit to redirect			
Task Orientation	14. Develops unit and lesson plans in accordance with text and curriculum guide			Teaches topics tangential to curriculum guide and adopted text; easily gets sidetracked by student or personal interests
	15. Handles administrative and clerical interruptions efficiently			Uses large amounts of instructional time to complete administrative and clerical tasks

APPENDIX: *Continued*

Key Behavior	Indicators of Effectiveness	Observed* (✓)	Observed* (✓)	Indicators of Lack of Effectiveness
Task Orientation (cont'd.)	16. Stops misbehavior with a minimum of disruption to the class			Focuses at length on individual instances of misbehavior during instructional time
	17. Generally, uses direct instruction strategies for teaching Type 1 behaviors and indirect instruction strategies for teaching Type 2 behaviors			Uses inefficient instructional methods for achieving lesson objectives (e.g., confuses drill and practice content with group discussion content)
	18. Establishes end products (e.g., reviews, tests) that are clearly visible to students			Fails to establish clearly identifiable weekly and monthly milestones (e.g., tests and reviews toward which the class works)
Engagement	19. Provides for guided practice			Fails to ask learners to attempt the desired behavior or skill after instruction has been given
	20. Provides correctives for guided practice in a nonevaluative atmosphere			Calls attention to the inadequacy of initial responses
	21. Uses individualized or attention-getting strategies to promote interest among special types of learners when appropriate			Does not attempt to match instructional methods to the learning needs of special students
	22. Uses meaningful verbal praise			Always uses the same verbal clichés (e.g., "OK") or fails to praise when opportunity occurs
	23. Monitors seatwork by circulating and frequently checking progress			Fails to monitor seatwork or monitors unevenly
Moderate-to-high success rates	24. Unit and lesson organization reflects task-relevant prior learning			Fails to sequence lessons based on task-relevant prior learning
	25. Administers correctives immediately after initial response			Delays in checking and correcting wrong responses after initial practice is completed
	26. Divides lessons into small, easily digestible pieces			Prepares lessons with more content or complexity than can be taught in the allotted time
	27. Plans transitions to new content in small, easy-to-grasp steps			Makes abrupt changes between lesson topics; no sign of "dovetailing"
	28. Establishes momentum (e.g., pacing and intensity gradually build toward major milestones)			Lessons lack changes in pacing (e.g., slower pace after a major event building to a faster pace just before a major event); intensity and tempo are static

*Checkmarks may be tallied over repeated observations to accumulate frequencies. Use the code "N/A" for not applicable where appropriate

Reprinted with the permission of Macmillan College Publishing Company from *Observation Skills for Effective Teaching*, 2/e by Gary D. Borich, pp. 522–524. Copyright © 1992 by Macmillan College Publishing Company, Inc.

4 Your First Teaching Position

At first I was worried about surviving student teaching. Would the kids relate to me? Could I control them? And, most importantly, could I teach them anything? Well, after a shaky start, student teaching turned out to be great! There's still a lot I need to learn, but I know I can do it. I can't wait to get my first teaching position.

—A student teacher

Focus Questions

1. What is involved in teacher supply and demand?
2. What salaries and benefits do teachers receive?
3. How do teachers become certified?
4. How do teachers find their first teaching job?
5. What can beginning teachers expect?
6. What on-the-job relationships contribute to teachers' success?
7. What are some other career opportunities for teachers?

Near the end of your student teaching practicum, you and another student teacher from your university happen to be in the teachers' lounge preparing for tomorrow's classes. With a few minutes remaining before the dismissal bell rings, you begin talking about finding a job next year. Your friend, you learn, has already had two interviews.

"What were the interviews like?" you ask.

"Well, they were both very different. For the first one I was interviewed by the principal and then by a committee of four people from the district. They asked me the usual questions like 'Why do you want to become a teacher? What's your approach to classroom management?' Then they described a hypothetical classroom situation and asked me what I would do in that case. That part was hard."

"What was the situation about?" you ask.

"It was about how I would deal with different ability levels. Some kids were grasping the material quickly and easily; the others needed more time. The high-achieving kids wanted to move faster, and they'd get bored if the teacher didn't do that. And the low-achieving kids would get lost and frustrated when the teacher sped up."

"That doesn't sound like an easy situation to deal with," you observe.

"Actually, I did pretty well. Fortunately, in our methods class we had to develop a set of strategies for modifying instruction for different ability levels. That was one of our portfolio assignments."

"What was the other interview like?"

"It was really different. I spent half an hour in the principal's office. It was like we were having a conversation. She and I talked about the kids at the school and how a lot of them come from families where English is not their first language. Then we talked about the problems some kids have to deal with in their home environments."

"Have you heard anything about either job?" you ask.

"By the end of next week I should find out. Right now, it's pretty competitive to get a teaching job in my area. So I might have to continue looking for a while."

At that moment, the dismissal bell rings. As you prepare to leave, you reflect on what you've heard. You wonder how well you will do when you begin interviewing. Also, you wonder what steps you can follow to increase your chances of finding the best possible teaching position.

————————

U pon completing your teacher education program, you will still have several important steps to take before securing your first teaching position. Preparing well for these steps will go a long way toward helping you begin teaching with confidence.

It is natural that you feel both excited and a bit fearful when thinking about your first job. While taking the courses required in your teacher education program you probably feel secure in your role as a student; you know what is expected of you. As a teacher, however, you will assume an entirely new role—a role that requires some time before it becomes comfortable. The aim of this chapter, then, is to help make the transition from student to professional teacher a positive, pleasant one. We first look at the steps you can take to identify current trends related to teacher supply and demand and teachers' salaries.

WHAT IS INVOLVED IN TEACHER SUPPLY AND DEMAND?

When you think ahead to a career in teaching, one question you are likely to ask yourself is, How hard will it be to find a job? From time to time, **teacher supply and demand** figures have painted a rather bleak picture for those entering the teaching profession. At other times, finding a position has been relatively easy.

During the early 1990s, concerns were raised about teacher supply and demand. Citing statistics related to the rising number of school-age children of baby boomers, increased teacher retirements, fewer university students going into teaching, and increased employment opportunities for women in other fields, some observers predicted a shortage of teachers by the turn of the century. Others, however, predicted that a teacher shortage would not develop. Their forecasts suggested that increases in teachers' salaries and the economic recession of the early 1990s would prevent a teacher shortage from occurring.

Despite the difficulty of predicting trends in teacher supply and demand, it is clear that, even during times of teacher surplus, talented, qualified teachers are able to find jobs. Public school teaching is one of the largest professions in Canada. With a national population of nearly 30 million in 1991–92, Canada had 2.9 million students in grades 1 to 6 and 2.4 million students in grades 7 and over.[1] There were 284 170 full-time public school teachers in Canada: 27 152 in the four Atlantic provinces, 58 915 in Quebec, 119 824 in Ontario, 21 994 in Manitoba and Saskatchewan, 26 044 in Alberta, 28 774 in British Columbia, and 1467 in the Territories.[2] Within such a large profession, annual openings resulting from retirements and career changes alone are sizable.

SUPPLY OF TEACHING JOBS DURING THE NEXT DECADE

Two major predictors for teacher demand are "expansion demand" and "replacement demand." Expansion demand occurs when student enrollment increases or when the student-teacher ratio is lowered and more teachers are hired. Replacement demand occurs when teachers retire or change careers and new teachers are needed to fill their places. Although the number of new teachers needed is difficult to determine, most analysts predict a favorable job market for teachers in Canada in the near future because of retirements. Most of the 200 000 teachers who began their careers in the 1960s and early 1970s will be retiring between 1990–91 and 2005–06[3] and will need to be replaced.

Teacher demand varies from province to province. The Canadian Teachers' Federation predicts that across Canada teacher shortfalls will increase from 650 teachers in 1990–91 to "nearly 8500 in 1998–99, and will taper off to about 3400 by 2005–06."[4] In British Columbia, teacher shortages began back in 1987 and continue today. Shortages will appear in the Atlantic region in 1996 and are already occurring in Ontario. Shortages are not expected to exist in Quebec for the next decade with the exception of certain specific regions. Shortages are most acute in remote, northern areas of Alberta, Manitoba, and Ontario.

DEMAND BY SPECIALTY AREA AND GEOGRAPHIC REGION

The ease with which you will find your first teaching position is also related to your area of specialization and to the part of the country in which you want to live. In Alberta, for example, teachers able to teach French immersion or core French were in demand in 1994. Other provinces are experiencing shortages in particular subject areas such as core French, French immersion, vocational studies, secondary sciences, computers, special education, music, drama, and Aboriginal education.

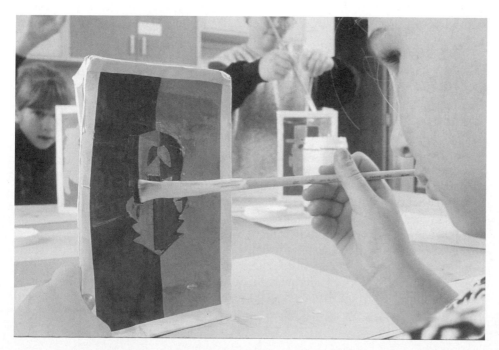

Students in this school have a full-time art teacher. How can you find out which subject areas and specialties are in the greatest demand in school districts across Canada?

Many urban school boards have a large pool of applicants from which to draw, and job seekers will find obtaining a job there quite competitive. As job seekers who live in urban areas turn to smaller surrounding towns for jobs, smaller school boards close to urban centers find they have a surplus of applicants for each position. However, school boards in smaller urban areas often have difficulty both recruiting and retaining teachers. Over the next decade job hunting will be competitive, and you may have to move to another area of the country to find a position.

WHAT SALARIES AND BENEFITS DO TEACHERS RECEIVE?

Teachers teach, in large part, because of the satisfaction of helping young people learn and grow. Although such intangible rewards represent a significant attraction of teaching, teachers are demanding that the public acknowledge the value and professional standing of teaching by supporting higher salaries.

In the 1960s a new teacher might expect to earn $6000 per year. In British Columbia in the mid-1970s, salaries leaped nearly 25 percent in one year to bring teachers' salaries in line with other professionals. Currently, when raises are minimal or non-existent, and some salaries are even being rolled back, such raises would be considered highly inflationary, even scandalous. However, teachers' salaries in Canada have continued to compare favorably with salaries in other countries. In 1984, the average salary of Canadian teachers in U.S. dollars was 35 percent higher than that of teachers from the United States, and higher than average teaching salaries in the United Kingdom, Germany, the Netherlands, Sweden, Denmark, Japan, South Korea, and New Zealand.[5]

Generally, a beginning teacher in 1995 with a four-year degree will start around $30 000 per year, and a teacher with twelve years' experience will receive around $50 000. With a graduate degree, that same teacher would receive around $55 000. Salaries vary from region to region. For example, in 1994, a teaching position in Fort Good Hope in the Northwest Territories was advertised with a beginning salary of $54 000. Higher salaries are often linked to a higher **cost of living**, for example, adjustments for travel, accommodation, and food. Salaries also vary by province. School boards in Saskatchewan, for instance, often lose teachers to Alberta or British Columbia because they have higher salary grids, and some northern B.C. boards offer more generous incentives such as paying off parts of student loans.

Teachers' salaries are typically determined by years of experience and advanced training as evidenced by graduate credit hours or graduate degrees. Many urban districts offer at least limited summer employment for teachers who wish to teach summer school or develop curriculum materials.

Teachers also receive various **fringe benefits**, such as extended medical insurance and pension plans, which are usually given in addition to base salary. These benefits vary from district to district and are determined during collective bargaining sessions. When considering a school district for your first position, carefully examine the fringe benefits package as well as the salary schedule and opportunities for extra pay.

HOW DO TEACHERS BECOME CERTIFIED?

Certification is required for teaching in public schools and in many private schools as well. A **teaching certificate** is actually a license to teach. The department of education for each province and territory sets the requirements for certification. A certificate usually indicates at what level one may teach. One might, for example, be certified for elementary or secondary education. Districts generally hire teachers and then assign them to work in particular schools. Your responsibilities in the school will largely be determined by your areas of specialty.

PROVINCIAL CERTIFICATION REQUIREMENTS

To grant a teaching certificate, provinces require different standards of academic preparation. In 1993, the Canadian Education Association surveyed all provinces and territories and provided a guide that outlines the requirements for basic teacher certificates in Canada. Six provinces—Saskatchewan, Manitoba, Nova Scotia, New Brunswick, Prince Edward Island, and Newfoundland—have an agreement that recognizes each jurisdiction's certification. Teachers can move freely between these provinces. In addition, Ontario, New Brunswick, and Quebec have bilateral agreements for teacher certification. If you are considering moving to another province, contact the appropriate office using the following list of contacts.

Northwest Territories:
Office of the Registrar
Teacher Certification, Northwest Territories Department of Education, Culture and Employment
PO Box 1320
Yellowknife, Northwest Territories X1A 2L9

Yukon Territory:
Director of Personnel
Yukon Department of Education
PO Box 2703
Whitehorse, Yukon Territory Y1A 2C6

British Columbia:
Registrar
British Columbia College of Teachers
405-1385 West 8th Avenue
Vancouver, British Columbia V6H 3V9

Alberta:
Teacher Certification and Development
Alberta Education
West Tower, Devonian Building
11160 Jasper Avenue
Edmonton, Alberta T5K 0L2

Saskatchewan:
Teacher Services
Saskatchewan Education Training and Employment
2220 College Avenue
Regina, Saskatchewan S4P 3V7

Manitoba:
Teacher Certification and Student Records
Manitoba Department of Education and Training
Box 700
Russell, Manitoba R0J 1W0

Ontario:
Registrar Services
Ontario Ministry of Education and Training
12th Floor, Mowat Block
Queen's Park
Toronto, Ontario M7A 1L2

Quebec:
Direction de la titularisation et de la classification du personnel enseignant
Direction générale de la formation et des qualifications
Ministère de l'Education
955 chemin Saint-Louis
Ville de Québec, Québec G1S 4S4

New Brunswick:
Teacher Certification
Human Resources
New Brunswick Department of Education
PO Box 6000
Fredericton, New Brunswick E3B 5H1

Nova Scotia:
Registrar, Teacher Certification
Planning and Research Division Policy Branch
Nova Scotia Department of Education
PO Box 578
Halifax, Nova Scotia B3J 2S9

Prince Edward Island:
Office of the Registrar
Administration and Finance Branch
Prince Edward Island Department of Education
Shaw Building, 95 Rochford Street
Box 2000
Charlottetown, Prince Edward Island C1A 7N8

Newfoundland and Labrador:
Registrar, Teacher Certification
Division of School Services and Professional Development
Newfoundland and Labrador Department of Education
Confederation Building, West Block
PO Box 8700
St. John's, Newfoundland A1B 4J6

Because education is a provincial responsibility, there are no national standards for teacher certification. Although education in the territories is federally funded, standards are decided locally. As Table 4.1 shows, provinces offer several types of teacher certificates that authorize teaching at different levels and of different subjects. Most require a minimum of four years of university, generally a bachelor's of education, and some recognize teacher preparation up to doctorates. Several provinces recognize the importance of Aboriginal education and provide certificates for First Nations people to teach specific Aboriginal languages and cultures.

TABLE 4.1 TEACHER CERTIFICATION BY PROVINCE

Province/Territory	Certificates Available
Yukon	Professional (K-12)
	Basic Transitional (K-12)
	Cultural (K-12)
	Letter of Permission (K-12)
Northwest Territories	Professional (K-12)
	Standard (K-12)
	Vocational (Vocational courses)
	Aboriginal Languages Specialist (K-12)
British Columbia	Professional (K-12)
	Standard (K-12)
	Basic (K-12)
	First Nations Language Teacher (K-12)
	Developmental Standard Term (K-12)
Alberta	Provisional (K-12)
	Professional (K-12)
Saskatchewan	Professional A & B (K-12)
	Vocational (K-12, limited subjects)
	Technical (K-12, limited subjects)
	Standard B (K-12, limited subjects)
	Probationary A & B (K-12)
	Letter of Eligibility (K-12)
Manitoba	Professional (K-12)
	Special Education (K-12)
	Vocational Industrial (K-12)
	Level 1 Administrator (K-12)
	Level 2 Principal (K-12)
Ontario	Ontario Teacher's Certificate (OTC) (Specified levels)
	Temporary Letter of Standing (Specified levels)
	Permanent Letter of Standing (Specified courses)
Quebec	Teaching Licence (All levels)
	Provisional Teaching Authorization (Secondary, Adult)
	Teaching Certificate (All levels)
New Brunswick	Letter of Standing 4 (Industrial)
	Certificate 4, 5, and 6 (1-12)
	Letter of Standing for persons outside New Brunswick
Nova Scotia	Class 4, 5, 6, 7, and 8 (K-12)
Prince Edward Island	Certificate 4, 5, 5A, 5B (K-12)
Newfoundland	Certificate II, III, IV, V, VI, and VII (All levels)

Source: "Requirements for teaching certificates in Canada" (May 1993), Canadian Education Association.

HOW DO TEACHERS FIND THEIR FIRST TEACHING JOB?

During your teacher education program, you will probably become increasingly concerned about finding a teaching position. In the remainder of this section we discuss five critical steps for any job search strategy: finding out about teaching vacancies, preparing a résumé, writing letters of inquiry and letters of application, being interviewed, and choosing a position.

FINDING OUT ABOUT TEACHING VACANCIES

There are many ways to find out about teaching vacancies, some worth pursuing more than others.

Newspapers   Teacher recruitment is generally the responsibility of individual school districts. How can you find out what districts are hiring in other regions of Canada? You could contact the specific provincial departments of education to obtain a list of addresses of school districts in their jurisdictions. Write or telephone those responsible for teacher recruitment to find out where they advertise teaching positions. Local libraries often carry out-of-town newspapers which you can follow.

If you want to contact the education department in a particular province, the list of addresses and phone numbers are provided:

British Columbia:
Ministry of Education
Parliament Buildings
Victoria, British Columbia V8V 2M4
(604) 387-4611, Extension 391

Alberta:
Alberta Education
West Tower, Devonian Building
11160 Jasper Avenue
Edmonton, Alberta
(403) 297-6353

Saskatchewan:
Department of Education
Parkview Place
2220 College Avenue
Regina, Saskatchewan S4P 3V7
(306) 525-6030

Manitoba:
Department of Education
Legislative Building
Winnipeg, Manitoba R3C 0V8
(204) 945-2211

Ontario:
Ministry of Education
Ministry of Colleges and Universities
Mowat Block, 900 Bay Street
Toronto, Ontario M7A 1L2
(416) 965-6407

Quebec:
Ministère de l'Education
Edifice G
1035 rue de la Chevrotière
Ville de Québec, Québec G1R 5A5
(418) 643-7095

New Brunswick:
Department of Education
PO Box 6000
Fredericton, New Brunswick E3B 5H1
(506) 453-3678

Nova Scotia:
Department of Education
PO Box 578
Halifax, Nova Scotia B3J 2S9
(902) 424-5605

Prince Edward Island:
Department of Education
PO Box 2000
Charlottetown, Prince Edward Island C1A 7N8

Newfoundland:
Department of Education
Government of Newfoundland and Labrador Confederation Building
St. John's, Newfoundland A1C 5T7
(709) 737-3027, (709) 737-2990

Northwest Territories:
Department of Education
Yellowknife, Northwest Territories X1A 2C3
(403) 873-2611

Yukon Territory:
Department of Education
Government of the Yukon Territory
PO Box 2703
Whitehorse, Yukon Y1A 2C3
(403) 667-5811

Personal Networking   There is considerable truth to the well-known maxim that it's who you know that is important in landing the right job. Personal contacts can be a very effective source of information about openings, and a contact might even be able to help you get an interview. It makes sense, then, to let people know you're looking for a job—friends, teachers at schools you've attended, faculty at the school where you student teach, and people you meet at workshops and conferences.

Letters to School Districts Though a mass mailing of your résumé to all school superintendents in your province might seem like a good idea, it usually isn't. As one director of a placement office put it: "The unsolicited shotgun approach to job hunting—mass mailing to any and all school systems—is the most popular and least effective strategy."[6] It is possible, however, that if the shortage of teachers becomes more acute during the late 1990s, mass mailings might become more effective, particularly if your specialty is in an area currently experiencing a critical shortage or if you are willing to move to a region of the country that typically has difficulty attracting teachers.

PREPARING YOUR RÉSUMÉ

A **résumé** presents a concise summary of an individual's professional experiences and education. Résumés must be typed and preferably no longer than one page, two pages at most. Although there is no right way to prepare a résumé, it should present—in a neat, systematic way—key information that will help an employer determine your suitability for a particular position. Because your résumé will most likely be your first contact with an employer, it must make a good impression. If your résumé contains errors, is poorly organized, or looks messy, an employer may conclude that your performance on the job will have the same qualities.

Ordinarily, a résumé contains the following information:

- Personal data
- Education
- Certificates held
- Experience
- Activities and interests
- Honors and offices held
- Professional memberships
- References

Figure 4.1 is a résumé prepared by Linda M. Collins. When preparing your résumé, use Collins' as a model. Hers is clear, well organized, and has an overall attractive appearance. Depending on your background, you may wish to use categories other than those Collins has used. If you have no honors or professional memberships to list, omit these categories. To prepare an effective résumé, read "Fifteen Rules for Effectively Updating Your Résumé" in the Teacher's Resource Guide.

WRITING LETTERS OF INQUIRY AND APPLICATIONS

As a job seeker, you will most likely have occasion to write two kinds of letters: letters of inquiry and letters of application. A **letter of inquiry** is used to determine if a school district has, or anticipates, any teaching vacancies. This type of letter states your general qualifications and requests procedures to be followed in making a formal application (see Figure 4.2). A letter of inquiry should include your résumé as well as a self-addressed, stamped envelope for the school district's convenience.

Be prepared not to receive a reply for each letter of inquiry you send out. Because of the volume of mail they receive requesting information on vacancies, many school districts are unable to respond to all inquiries.

A **letter of application** indicates your interest in a particular position and outlines your qualifications for that job. As most districts have several vacancies at any given time, it is important that the first sentence of your letter refer to the specific position for which you are applying. The body of the letter should then highlight why you would be an excellent choice to fill that position. Also, inform the reader that your references and transcripts will be sent on request or are enclosed. Close the letter by expressing your availability for an interview. (See Figure 4.3.)

FIGURE 4.1   Résumé

Linda Collins

Address and telephone: 948 Third Street NW
                                       Calgary, AB T2N 1N4

Education

B.Ed., Elementary Education, University of Calgary, May 1995

Certificates Held

Major Area: Elementary Education, Early Childhood Education

Experience

Student Teaching, First Round—Fall 1994
Grade 2
King Edward Elementary and Junior High School
Calgary Board of Education

Student Teaching, Second Round—Winter 1995
Grade 1
St. Rose of Lima Elementary and Junior High School
Calgary Catholic Board of Education

Volunteer Telephone Counsellor, The City of Calgary Crisis Hotline, February 1994–May 1994

Checkout Clerk, Northwest COOP Store Calgary, May 1991–September 1993

Activities and Interests

Secretary,
Education Undergraduate Society
University of Calgary

Sunday School Teacher,
St. Paul's Anglican Church
Calgary

Hobbies: Jogging, Photography, Skiing, Reading

Honors

B.Ed. with distinction, University of Calgary
Chancellor's Scholarship (4 years at $6000)

Professional Memberships

Associate Member of the Alberta Teachers' Association
Kappa Delta Pi, Calgary chapter

References

References available upon request.

FIGURE 4.2   Letter of Inquiry

Linda M. Collins
948 Third Street NW
Calgary AB T2N 1N4

April 20, 1995

Dr. Garry McKenzie
Superintendent
Golden Hills Regional School Division
PO Box 241
Strathmore, AB T4R 6V7

Dear Dr. McKenzie:

This letter is to express my interest in a teaching position in the Golden Hills Regional School Division. Specifically, I would like to know if you anticipate any vacancies at the elementary level for fall of 1995. This May I will receive my B.Ed. (with distinction) in elementary education from the University of Calgary. I specialized in Early Childhood Education.

As a student teacher this past winter semester, I taught grade one at St. Rose of Lima Elementary and Junior High School in the Calgary Catholic Board of Education. My class had 25 students, three of whom were diagnosed as having learning disabilities. I also assisted my cooperating teacher with the Spring Concert and the school yearbook.

My education at University of Calgary, I believe, has prepared me well to teach in today's classrooms and to meet the diverse needs of students. I have taken a course that focuses on meeting the needs of at-risk learners, and I completed another course in rural education. If possible, I would like a position that would allow me to work in a smaller community with students in an inclusive classroom.

Enclosed you will find my résumé which provides additional information about my experiences and activities. If there are any positions for which you think I might be suited, please send application materials in the enclosed stamped, self-addressed envelope. I appreciate the time and consideration that you have given me and my request, and I look forward to hearing from you.

Sincerely,

Linda M. Collins

FIGURE 4.3   Letter of Application

Linda M. Collins
948 Third Street NW
Calgary AB T2N 1N4

May 21, 1995

Dr. Garry McKenzie
Superintendent
Golden Hills Regional School Division
PO Box 241
Strathmore, AB T4R 6V7

Dear Dr. McKenzie:

This letter is in support of my application for the position of grade one teacher at Three Hills Elementary School in the Golden Hills Regional School Division. I have just received my B.Ed. (with distinction) in elementary education from the University of Calgary. I specialized in Early Childhood Education.

As my enclosed résumé indicates, I did my student teaching in both a public and a separate school district at the primary level. During my second round, my class had 25 students, three of whom were diagnosed as having learning disabilities. I also assisted my cooperating teacher, Mrs. Wachsmuth, with the Spring Concert and the school yearbook. In addition, I studied rural education at university and have gained an appreciation of the social complexities that exist in small remote communities.

As a result of my rewarding experiences at King Edward and St. Rose of Lima schools, and in light of the needs at Three Hills Elementary School, I believe I could make a significant contribution to the educational program at Three Hills Elementary.

I have arranged for three referees to submit confidential letters of reference directly to your address. If you require additional information of any sort, please feel free to contact me. I am available for an interview in either Strathmore or Three Hills at your convenience. I wish to thank you in advance for your consideration.

Sincerely,

Linda M. Collins

PARTICIPATING IN A JOB INTERVIEW

The interview is one of the most important steps in your search for an appropriate position. As the dialogue in the opening scenario for this chapter suggests, school districts handle interviews differently. Some ask a set of structured questions of all candidates; others hold interviews that are more informal and open-ended. In some, you might be interviewed by the principal only; in others, the superintendent, the principal, and the department chairperson might interview you; and in still others, classroom teachers might interview you. Regardless of format, the interview enables the district to obtain specific information regarding your probable success as an employee, and it gives you an opportunity to ask questions about what it is like to teach in the district.

When you are interviewed you may expect the session to begin with a short period of light conversation to put you at ease and to begin to develop rapport between you and the interviewer(s). The interviewer will then typically present a brief overview of the community, the school district, and the position to be filled. Following this, you will be asked a series of questions.

The following questions were gathered from school hiring officials and are representative of those you are likely to encounter in your job interviews. As you read, reflect on the one question in each section that you feel least prepared to answer.

Motivation/Experience/Training

1. Tell us about yourself.
2. Why did you enter the field of teaching?
3. What experiences have you had related to teaching?
4. What qualities do you have that make you an effective teacher?
5. What grade levels or subjects do you prefer to teach?
6. Have you taught or are you interested in teaching combination classes?
7. Do you have experience with special education students?
8. Why do you want to teach in our school district?
9. Do you have (multicultural, urban, rural, learning problems) teaching experience?
10. What do you remember most about your own education?

Teaching Effectiveness

11. How do you meet the range of skills and needs commonly found in a classroom?
12. When do you use an individual, group, and/or whole class teaching approach? Why?
13. Let's imagine we are going to observe a teacher teaching a lesson. I tell you in advance to expect a superb lesson. What would you expect to see in that lesson?
14. If a teacher wants to be sure pupils will learn a skill to be taught, what should he/she be sure to do when teaching?
15. How do you diagnose your students' needs?
16. How do you make sure your lessons are taught at the correct level?
17. How do you stimulate active participation in the classroom?
18. How would you use parents in the classroom?

Teacher Planning/Preparation

19. What kinds of planning do you see a teacher doing?
20. How do you plan for a year? A week? A day?
21. How do you know what you will cover?
22. What types of resource materials do you like to use?

Classroom Management/Discipline

23. What are some characteristics of a well-managed classroom?
24. Talk to us about classroom control.
25. What discipline methods work for you?
26. What is your primary goal with student discipline?
27. What are some examples of rules you would have in your classroom?
28. How would you be sure your rules are carried out?
29. How much responsibility for their learning do you feel students should have to take?
30. Are you a "let 'em go to the pencil sharpener whenever they want" type of person or a "raise your hand and ask permission" type of person?
31. What types of rewards and consequences would you use?
32. Describe your most difficult student discipline situation and how you handled it.

Staff Development/Professional Growth

33. What do you see yourself doing over the course of the next several years to improve your abilities as a professional?
34. What professional development topics most interest you?

Staff Rapport/Relationships

35. As a teacher new to a school, what would you see yourself doing to contribute to healthy staff relationships and to become part of the staff?
36. What should a principal expect from teachers?
37. What should teachers expect from the principal?

Grading Systems

38. What grading system works for you?
39. Under what conditions, if any, would most of your pupils receive D's and F's? How and why could this happen?

Closing Comments/Questions

40. What additional talents and skills do you have?
41. What extracurricular activities can you supervise?
42. Do you have questions or additional comments for us?[7]

In addition to the above questions, the Teacher's Resource Guide presents twenty-four questions *you* can ask (see "Practice Makes Perfect: Sample Interview Questions from Both Sides of the Desk"). By asking questions yourself, you demonstrate your interest in working in the district.

ACCEPTING AN OFFER

One day you are notified that a school district would like to hire you. Your job search efforts have paid off!

At first you will feel justifiably proud and excited. In the competition for positions, you have been successful. Beneath these feelings, however, may be some doubt and anxiety about whether this position is the best for you. Accepting your first teaching position is a major personal and professional step. Before signing a contract with a district, then, you should carefully consider some job-related questions, such as the following:

- In regard to my abilities and education, am I suited to this position?
- Would I like to work with this school's students, administrative staff, and teachers?
- Is the salary I am being offered sufficient?
- Will this position likely be permanent?

In addition, think about the life-style you would have if you accepted the position. Ask yourself these questions:

- Would I like to live in or near this community? Is its quality of life appealing?
- Would the cost of living in this community enable me to live comfortably?
- Are opportunities for continuing education readily available?
- What cultural and recreational activities are available in the community?

You must decide to accept or reject the offer after carefully considering the preceding questions and the possibility that you will receive another, more attractive, offer. If you accept, you will need to return a signed contract to the district along with a short letter confirming your acceptance. As a professional courtesy, you should notify other districts to which you have applied that you have accepted a position elsewhere.

WHAT CAN BEGINNING TEACHERS EXPECT?

Once you accept the professional challenge of teaching, it is important to prepare well in advance of the first day of school. During these weeks, you will want to review the texts your students will use and develop general strategies for presenting that material. This interlude before school begins is a critical time. When school is underway, you will find that your days are full and frequently hectic—with very little time available for study.

In addition to reviewing the material you will teach, you should use this time to find out all you can about the school's students and the surrounding community. Perhaps you can find another teacher or counselor who might be willing to spend some time orienting you to the culture of the school.

After making careful preparations, what can you expect when you actually begin to teach? As the following Professional Reflection feature illustrates, experienced teachers know that many realities of teaching are not as difficult as student teachers might expect. However, student teachers might be a bit more optimistic than experienced teachers are about other realities of teaching.

WHAT TO EXPECT ON THE FIRST DAY

Nearly every beginning teacher has found the first day of school both exciting and frightening. Such feelings are a natural part of beginning one's professional career.

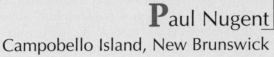

Ron Arbeau
Bath, New Brunswick

Paul Nugent
Campobello Island, New Brunswick

The area in which we teach has a very high number of welfare and single-parent families. Vandalism and crime are on the increase in the area and discipline problems were high at the school before the onset of our new program. We wanted to take a positive, proactive approach to discipline problems in the school by finding ways to enhance self-esteem in children.

We created the "Proud Monquarters" Preventative Discipline Self-Esteem Program for our classes which was later implemented schoolwide because of its success. We thought a program which helped students learn self-esteem in our classrooms would reduce the need for reactive counselling and disciplining that took up much of the time for the administration and counsellors and seemed too late for many students.

We designed several programs. Paul taught the Hole in the Fence Program for grades K-2 and Ron taught the My Quality World Program and I'm Thumbody Program for grades 3-5. We both led class discussions on self-esteem with students throughout the school.

We brought together our colleagues, students, and parents to develop a new Code of Student Behavior for the school. We then spent much time with groups of students to explain the expected behaviors and the consequences of misbehavior.

Through the Proud Monquarter, Student of the Week Program, students were recognized for their positive behavior by being awarded a special baseball cap which they got to wear all week in class. We also used the school newsletter and local media to recognize their achievement.

Students immediately responded to the programs and were excited about being involved. They designed a new school crest and created a school motto, "Bath Elementary School, Where Learning is Fun." Discipline problems were reduced and school spirit is at an all-time high. Parents responded in a very supportive way. Students have been involved in many more extracurricular programs, drama and music programs, and a new fine arts program, and intramural involvement increased.

We believe that teachers must strive to provide a caring and inviting climate as a context for their pedagogy. Learning becomes more relevant when teachers can recognize the social and emotional needs of students. And when that happens, we feel better about ourselves and the job we are prepared to do.

PROFESSIONAL REFLECTION

A study at the University of Nevada, Reno, compared the attitudes of student teachers with those of experienced teachers. A comparison of the responses of the two groups revealed that student teachers have a "greater optimism" about certain areas and "greater pessimism" about others. Read the following summary of results and then, in regard to your own attitudes, identify those items for which your expectations might be more optimistic than those of experienced teachers. What information could you gather that would enable you to develop more realistic expectations?

Category 1

Areas of Greater Student Teacher Optimism

When compared with current teachers, student teachers expressed greater optimism about:

- managing classroom behavior
- being happy with their incomes
- having input into decisions that affect their classrooms
- feeling respected by the community
- not sacrificing quality in the classroom
- paying out-of-pocket for materials
- having incomes that will reflect their educational achievements
- supporting the life-styles they desire
- being tolerant of misbehavior in the classroom.

Category 2

Areas of Greater Student Teacher Pessimism

When compared with current teachers, student teachers expressed greater pessimism about:

- being able to teach in their specialties
- having to work many after-school hours
- being liked by their students
- feeling safe at school
- having difficulty writing lesson plans, designing tests, and assigning grades

Source: Colette Dollarhide, "Student Teaching: A Chance to Test the Waters (And What to Do If You Can't Swim!)," *The Job Search Handbook for Educators: 1992 ASCUS Annual* (Evanston, Ill.: Association for School, College and University Staffing), pp. 3–4.

Creating a pleasant, work-oriented climate on the first day will contribute greatly to your success during the remainder of the year.

On the first day, students are eager to learn and are hopeful that the year will be productive. In addition, nearly all students will be naturally receptive to what you have to say. To them, you are a new, unknown quantity, and one of their initial concerns is to find out what kind of a teacher you will be. It is critical that you be well organized and ready to take charge.

ADVICE FROM EXPERIENCED TEACHERS

In our work with schools and teachers, we have gathered recommendations on preparing for the first day from experienced elementary through secondary teach-

"I thought she was a new kid, and I told her how easy it was to con the teachers here."

ers in urban, suburban, and rural schools. For example, Shirley A. Rau, an experienced teacher, offers concise, to-the-point advice for the first day:

> It's important on the first day to start building a community of learners. Rather than simply going over class rules, engage students immediately in a typical activity—talking, reading, writing about ideas. It's a great day for teachers to listen to students' ideas. Provide them with a forum so you can learn about their needs, the directions they would like the class to take during the year.

The recommendations made by other experienced teachers fall into three categories: planning, managing, and following up.

Planning   Without exception, experienced teachers stress the importance of planning. As the following teachers put it:

> An important part of preparation is having the room and all your materials ready. Ask yourself, "Where do I want students to sit?" "Do I have all the supplies I need?" You should be one-hundred percent prepared on the first day.
> —High-school mathematics teacher

> From the start, plan to get students involved. On the first day there are a lot of clerical, paperwork-type things that need to be done—distributing books, lockers, fee receipts, etc. *Before* taking care of those things, give students a short assignment or some task. With their attention focused, they're less likely to fool around. They'll know that in your class they're expected to work.
> —Elementary-school science teacher

> It really helps on the first day to have plenty of material to cover and things to do. I'd recommend taking the material you plan to cover that day and doubling it. It's better to have too much than to run out. What you don't use the first day, you use

the next. It takes a while to get a feeling for how fast the kids are going to go.
　　　　—Grade three teacher

Organizing　　Experienced teachers are unanimous in pointing out the importance of establishing effective management practices on the first day. Two of their recommendations follow.

> From the beginning, it's important to do what you're there to do—that's teach. Teach the class something, maybe review material they learned last year. That lets them know that you're in charge, you expect them to learn. They'll look to you for direction—as long as you give it to them, you're fine.
> 　　　　—Junior-high language arts teacher

> The first day is a good time to go over rules and procedures for the year. But don't overdo it. Be very clear and specific about your expectations for classroom behavior.
> 　　　　—Grade six teacher

Following Through　　Several experienced teachers stressed the importance of following through on procedures established during the first day.

> What you want to establish on the first day is a businesslike atmosphere. But you have to keep that going beyond the first day. Don't let up. Don't get lazy. Remember, there are 199 days left.
> 　　　　—High-school mathematics teacher

> What I've found very helpful is to get in touch with all my kids' parents right after the first day. I tell them a bit about how I run my class, what we're going to do that year, and how pleased I am to have their child in my room. I keep it upbeat, very positive. We're going to have a great year! It takes time to do that—everyone's so busy at the start of the year—but it's worth it. It pays off during the rest of the year.
> 　　　　—Grade one teacher

WHAT ON-THE-JOB RELATIONSHIPS CONTRIBUTE TO TEACHERS' SUCCESS?

How successful your first year of teaching is will be determined not only by the relationships you develop with your pupils but also by the contacts you have with other staff, parents, and the community. All four of these groups can contribute significantly to your effectiveness as a teacher.

RELATIONSHIPS WITH COLLEAGUES AND STAFF

Each working day, you will be in close contact with other teachers and staff members. As Shirley Rau's comments about her first year of teaching indicate, it will definitely be to your advantage to establish friendly, professional relationships with colleagues and staff.

> I was on a staff with a group of teachers who really supported me. They made it a part of their day to come into my room and see how I was doing and to share things. They made it easy to ask questions and work with them. They started me on the track of cooperating with other teachers and sharing my successes and failures with them.

They did such a good job of taking care of each other that my needs were always met. I had plenty of supplies, counseling help, administrative help. The school was a community. Anything I needed to be successful was provided.

During your first few months at the school, it would be wise to communicate to colleagues that you are willing to learn all you can about your new job and to be a team player. In most schools it is common practice to give junior teachers less desirable assignments, reserving the more desirable ones for senior teachers. By demonstrating your willingness to take on these responsibilities with good humor and to give them your best effort, you will do much to establish yourself as a valuable staff member. Taking into account your assigned duties, you might consider volunteering for a few of the numerous tasks that must be done to make any school's program a success: sponsoring a club, helping with a Parent-Teacher Association program, or helping with the library inventory.

It is important that you get along with your fellow staff members. Some you will enjoy being around; others you may wish to avoid. Some will express obvious enthusiasm for teaching; others may be bitter and pessimistic about their work. Be pleasant and friendly with both types. Accept their advice with a smile, and then act on that which is worthwhile.

Though you may find some staff members who are openly critical of certain school policies and practices, avoid expressing any criticisms of the school until you are more established as a group member. Act in a manner that will cause others to view you as a task-oriented professional.

RELATIONSHIPS WITH ADMINISTRATORS

Pay particular attention to the relationships you develop with administrators, department heads, and supervisors. Though your contacts with them will not be as frequent as with other teachers, they can do much to ensure your initial success. They are well aware of the difficulties you might encounter as a first-year teacher, and they are there to help you succeed.

The principal of your new school will, most likely, be the one to introduce you to other teachers, members of the administrative team, and staff. He or she should inform you if there are assistant principals or (at the high school level) department heads who can help you enforce school rules, keep accurate records, and obtain supplies, for example. The principal may also assign an experienced teacher to serve as a mentor during your first year. In addition, your principal will indicate his or her availability to discuss issues of concern, and you should not hesitate to do so if the need arises.

RELATIONSHIPS WITH PARENTS

Establishing friendly relationships with your pupils' parents can be an important component of your success as a teacher. A *Metropolitan Life Survey* of 1002 new American teachers who began teaching in 1990–91, for example, revealed that 91 percent "strongly agreed" and 9 percent "somewhat agreed" that teachers need to work well with their students' parents. In reality, teachers and parents are partners—both are concerned with the learning and growth of their children. It is important that you become acquainted with parents at school functions, at meetings of the Parent-Teacher Association or Organization (PTA or PTO), at various community events, and in other social situations. To develop good communication with parents, you will need to be sensitive to their needs, such as their work schedules and the language spoken in their home.

You will find that parents differ greatly in terms of how much they wish to be (or *can* be) involved with their children's school. Some parents, such as the author of the following letter, monitor their children's education quite closely:

> The time my son spends in grade five seems important as a period of transition. Grade nine seems so far away, but middle school seems right upon us. And I am concerned that he will be able to move from elementary school into middle school successfully.
>
> I like the idea of the longer school day and more requirements for graduation. Right now, in grade five, my child is a little weak in math. When he starts grade nine, he already will know that he has to take math all through high school, so it is very important to me that in the next four years his math skills improve.
>
> We want him to be involved in as many things as possible when he starts high school. In grade five, he is interested in band and hears a lot about student government from his older sister, who is in grade eleven.
>
> We expect that by the time he reaches grade nine, the schools will give a lot of attention to technology and computer training. Right now, he is very enthusiastic about school; we certainly hope that will last.
>
> We were a little surprised by how much our involvement in what he is doing could make a difference. We plan to keep in touch with the teacher and to attend all the programs the school sets up.[8]

Other parents will be known to you only by the fact that they sign their children's report cards and other routine school forms. For this reason, it is important that you consider taking the initiative and keeping parents informed of events in your classroom with a monthly newsletter. Parents greatly appreciate hearing about the

Parents might participate in evening school activities but seldom have an opportunity to observe their children learning. What are the most successful strategies for getting parents involved in their children's learning?

good things their children are doing; unfortunately, though, parents are usually contacted only when their children are in trouble. For this reason, perhaps, 14 percent of the beginning teachers in *The Metropolitan Life Survey* sample referred to above "strongly agreed" and 56 percent "somewhat agreed" that too many parents treat schools and teachers as adversaries. To improve the perceptions parents have of schools and teachers, you might consider making it a point to telephone at least one parent each day to report something positive.

By maintaining contact with parents, you can significantly enhance the achievement of your students. A study of 60 000 high school students, for example, revealed that 32 percent of the students with an A average said their parents helped them decide what courses to take; only 13 percent of the C students reported the same. In the same way, 66 percent of the A students said their parents met with or telephoned a teacher when an academic problem arose; less than 50 percent of the C students reported the same parental involvement.[9] Research has also shown, for example, that parental involvement is a key factor in children's reading achievement and reading group placement.[10] Parental involvement also increases the achievement levels of students in urban schools.[11]

Although teachers know that students learn more when parents participate, and most parents do wish to be more involved, there is a gap between the rhetoric of parental involvement and its practice. The rise in single-parent families and families in which both parents work has left parents with very little time to supervise their children's studies. For this reason, it is important that you be willing to take the extra time and energy to pursue strategies such as the following for involving parents:

- Ask parents to read aloud to the child, to listen to the child read, and to sign homework papers.
- Encourage parents to drill students on math and spelling and to help with homework lessons.
- Encourage parents to discuss school activities with their children and suggest ways parents can help teach their children at home. For example, a simple home activity might be alphabetizing books; a more complex one would be using kitchen supplies in an elementary science experiment.
- Send home suggestions for games or group activities related to the child's schoolwork that parent and child can play together.[12]
- Encourage parents to participate in school activities such as a sports booster club, career day, and music and drama events.
- Involve parents in their children's learning by having them co-sign learning contracts and serve as guest speakers.

COMMUNITY RELATIONS

Communities provide significant support for the education of their young people. They often help their schools by recruiting volunteers, providing financial support for special projects, and operating homework hotline programs. Parent Advisory Committees and School Councils are beginning to play a more critical role in the operation of schools, and there is increased understanding of the need to establish and maintain good community relations.

Most communities hold high expectations of teachers. Don't view these expectations as an imposition, however; see them as a sign that community members

EDUCATION IN THE NEWS

Accountability in Education

The accountability of schools has been a major issue across Canada. In Alberta, the government has decided to give parents and taxpayers an annual report card on all schools and school boards. Each school and school board will be rated in seven areas ranging from how many students passed math to how satisfied parents, teachers, and community members were with their role in school decision making.

British Columbia, Alberta, New Brunswick, and Newfoundland will test some of their grades three, four, seven, eight, and graduation year students to compare their education systems with 50 countries on an international mathematics and science achievement test.

The Royal Commission on Learning in Ontario has recommended that students in grades three and 11 be tested across the province. The government expanded on the recommendation by setting up testing of all students in

grades three, six, nine, and 11. An autonomous body, the Educational Quality and Accountability Office, will conduct the testing and report to the public annually.

These are examples of the accountability movement that is sweeping across Canada. The political climate has changed drastically over the past decade and education officials are under pressure to account for why Canada has one of the highest per capita education costs and yet has produced mediocre test results when compared internationally.

However, providing quality education to a particular class of students is different from guaranteeing that this same class will perform well on a standardized test. Standardized tests ignore individual needs and experiences. Although politicians argue that daily classroom teaching and global competition are linked, are teachers able to make this link during their daily interactions with their students?

Source: Based on *The Globe and Mail,* Jan. 10, 19, 25, Feb. 18; 1995.

---

view teachers as leaders—not unlike physicians, members of the clergy, or lawyers. As a professional, it is important that you take an active part in community affairs and, if the occasion arises, take a stand in regard to political and moral issues. By participating fully in the life of the community in which you live, you will also make many important contacts. Some of these individuals, for example, may have expertise related to your specialty and may be willing to visit with your students.

RELATIONSHIPS WITH STUDENTS

Needless to say, the relationships you establish with students will be among the most important (and complex) you will have as a teacher. As the range of topics addressed by this book suggests, these relationships will have many dimensions. You must see that each student learns as much as possible; this is your primary responsibility as a professional teacher. You will need to establish relationships with a great diversity of students based on mutual respect, caring, and concern. Without attention to this personal realm, your effectiveness as a teacher will be significantly limited. You will also have numerous legal responsibilities to your students, which are explained in Chapter 10. In addition, you will act in the role of disciplinarian in your classroom and you will be a role model to your students, who will be influenced by your attitudes.

WHAT ARE SOME OTHER CAREER OPPORTUNITIES FOR TEACHERS?

Our primary focus throughout this book is on becoming a professional teacher at the elementary through secondary levels. However, we wish to point out that there are a great many nonteaching jobs in education and education-related fields. Several of these were alluded to earlier: principal, vice principal, librarian, and counselor. In addition, there are many jobs that, although removed from the world of the classroom, would nevertheless enable you to use your teaching skills.

In the following outline, we list several places other than schools where individuals with teaching backgrounds are often employed. We believe that the number of education-related careers will increase dramatically during the next two decades.

ALTERNATIVE CAREERS IN EDUCATION

Industry

- Publishers
- Educational materials and equipment suppliers
- Specialized educational service firms
- Communications industries
- Research and development firms
- Management consulting firms
- Education and training consultants
- Educational divisions of large corporations—Xerox, IBM, Petro Canada, General Electric, General Motors, etc.

Government

- Federal government—Agriculture Canada, Employment and Immigration Canada, Correctional Services Canada, Environment (Parks) Canada, Health and Welfare Canada, Indian and Northern Affairs Department, Department of Multiculturalism and Citizenship, Department of National Defence, National Film Board, Public Service Commission of Canada, etc.
- Provincial governments—Department of Education, Department of Advanced Education, Rural Development, Occupational Health and Safety, Public Health, etc.
- Municipal Governments—Human Resources, Parks and Recreation, Public Information, Social Services, etc.

Other Organizations

- Research centers and foundations
- Private schools
- Community colleges
- Adult upgrading organizations
- Community action programs—private immigration services, literacy programs, etc.
- Social service agencies—United Way, Meals on Wheels, Big Brothers, etc.
- Museums
- Hospitals

OPPORTUNITIES IN NONEDUCATION FIELDS

As a former teacher who went on to become vice president of a firm that trains clients in communication skills put it, "Those who can teach also can . . . sell, compute, write, design, organize, market, advertise, run day-care centers, start meals-on-wheels programs, set up business task forces, lead community projects, and so on, ad infinitum."[13] In short, teaching requires a wide variety of aptitudes and skills that are valuable assets in many careers. Effective teachers have organizational and administrative abilities, communication skills, leadership abilities, the ability to influence and motivate, and high levels of creativity.

If you are unable to find a desirable teaching position, or if, after a few years of teaching, you realize that teaching is not for you, you may join those educators who eventually pursue careers outside of teaching.

PROFESSIONAL PORTFOLIO

Draft a preliminary professional résumé. Begin by reviewing the section in this chapter titled "Preparing Your Résumé" and "Fifteen Rules for Effectively Updating Your Résumé" in the Teacher's Resource Guide. In addition, examine the résumé prepared by Linda M. Collins (Figure 4.1).

In your résumé, under "Personal Data," provide a current address and a permanent address. Also, under "Education," specify an anticipated graduation date. Under "Experience," be sure to include work experience that indicates your ability to work with people. Begin with your most recent experiences and present information in reverse chronological order.

When you have finished your preliminary résumé, critique it against the "Fifteen Rules" presented in the Teacher's Resource Guide. After placing your résumé in the portfolio, don't forget about it. After a few months or so, reread it. Does it still make a positive impression? Could it be improved? Is there information that should be added now?

CHAPTER SUMMARY

Among the factors to consider when making the transition from being a teacher education student to being a teacher are trends in teacher supply and demand. Although some analysts believe Canada may be confronted with a teacher shortage in the late 1990s while others predict a surplus, it is clear that qualified teachers will be able to find jobs. Enrollments in elementary and secondary schools will increase slightly between now and the year 2010. At the same time many teachers who are currently teaching will retire, and these trends should result in a steady increase in the need for teachers during the same period.

An examination of teacher salaries indicates that they have exceeded the rate of inflation over the past thirty years. Salaries and benefits vary from province to province and district to district reflecting prevailing economic conditions.

Before one can begin to teach in a public school, a teaching certificate, or a license to teach, must be obtained from the Provincial Teacher Qualification Service. Certification requirements differ from province to province and you are advised to contact the TQS office in the particular province you are interested in.

To find out about teaching vacancies, job seekers may use newspaper ads, personal networking, and letters to school districts. Regardless of the steps taken to find out about teaching vacancies, the candidate should prepare a résumé, a concise summary of professional experiences and education. In addition to preparing a résumé, the job seeker may write letters of inquiry and letters of application.

The interview is perhaps the most important step in the job search sequence. Reviewing questions that an employer might ask and formulating questions in advance to ask the interviewer are two sound strategies to follow in preparing for an interview.

The weeks before the first day of school are an excellent opportunity for the beginning teacher to prepare. Although there is no single strategy to ensure success on the first day of school, experienced teachers stress the importance of planning, managing, and following up. In addition, a beginning teacher's success depends on building positive relationships not only with students but also with colleagues and staff, administrators, parents, and the community. By developing positive relationships with these groups, a beginning teacher can be assured of essential support and encouragement during the critical first years of teaching.

Because career changes are becoming increasingly common in our society, one should be aware that teachers are also qualified to pursue other careers in education and education-related fields. Among the possibilities are careers in industry, government, education-related associations, and community organizations. The knowledge and skills teachers possess also equip them for a wide variety of careers in noneducational fields.

*K*EY *TERMS AND CONCEPTS*

cost of living, 80
fringe benefits, 80
letter of application, 86

letter of inquiry, 86
résumé, 86

teacher supply and demand, 78
teaching certificate, 81

*A*PPLICATIONS *AND ACTIVITIES*

Teacher's Journal

1. Help your instructor set up a series of role-play interview sessions during which some members of your class take the part of applicants for a teaching position and others act as personnel directors. If possible, exchange résumés. The remaining class members should observe the role-plays, noting strengths and weaknesses. Review the role-plays during post-interview discussions.

2. Ask your instructor if it is possible to arrange for a member of the teachers' association

to visit your class and discuss procedures to be followed in obtaining a teaching position. Using the information presented at that session, develop a timetable for the steps you will need to follow to obtain your first teaching position.

3. ➤ What is your ideal teaching position? In your description include characteristics of the school, students, and community; resources available for effective teaching; and ideal on-the-job relationships.

4. Why does society generally regard teaching as important but often pay teachers less than workers in business and industry?

5. When you become a teacher, in what community activities will you participate? How might these activities contribute to your effectiveness as a teacher?

Field Assignments

1. If you can arrange it, observe the first day of classes at a local elementary, junior, or high school. What strategies did the teachers use to begin the year on a positive, task-oriented note? What evidence did you see that the teachers followed the advice given by the experienced teachers in this chapter? What would you have done differently? Why?

2. Review the list of education-related careers presented in this chapter and then contact or visit one of the organizations mentioned. Talk to a person who can tell you what specific jobs might be appropriate for someone with a teaching certificate. Report your findings to the class.

5 Schools and Society

As society changes, so change the dimensions of the teacher's task.
—Steven E. Tozer, Paul C. Violas, and Guy Senese
*School & Society: Educational Practice as
Social Expression*

Focus Questions

1. What are the aims of education?
2. How is cultural diversity embedded in Canadian society?
3. What are schools like as social institutions?
4. What social problems affect the schools and place students at risk?
5. What characteristics distinguish successful schools?

Carla Watkins is in her tenth year as a social studies teacher at Metropolitan High School. Metro is located in a large industrial city in Ontario. The school, in the center of a low- to middle-income area known as Uptown, has an enrollment of almost 2300 students. About 50 percent are Asian immigrants with the remaining 50 percent about evenly divided between Eastern European immigrants and Anglo European Canadians. Metro has a reputation for being a "difficult" school—a label that the school has been unable to shed.

Carla lives with her twelve-year-old son in a condominium on the edge of Uptown. She believes that teachers have an obligation to their society to address social issues. Several months ago, for example, Carla was the center of controversy when she began a two-week unit on AIDS education and the impact the disease has had on different segments of the Canadian population. She had two persons with AIDS visit her classes, and her students participated in role plays and debates that focused on how to slow down the spread of AIDS.

Many of Carla's colleagues are skeptical about her methods. On the one hand, they believe that she does her students a disservice by reducing the amount of time spent on "academics." These teachers point out that Metro parents want their children to learn the traditional basics, and they want the freedom to decide within their individual families how, if at all, they will address the issue of AIDS.

On the other hand, a small group of teachers is very supportive of Carla. They remind her detractors that students are highly involved in her classroom and that several potential dropouts have decided to remain in school because of Carla's willingness to address contemporary social issues in the classroom.

Today in the teachers' lounge Carla and two other teachers are talking about the results of a school-wide survey Carla's third-period class did on students' knowledge about AIDS. "My kids are really disturbed about the lack of students' knowledge about AIDS and the high-risk behavior of a lot of our students," Carla says. "We're thinking about starting a major school-wide AIDS awareness campaign."

"That's all well and good," says one teacher. "But I don't see where all of this is going to lead. Our responsibility as teachers is to give our kids the knowledge they need to get a better job. We need to give them the basics so they have a chance of doing well. That's what their parents want—they don't want us teaching what should be taught in the privacy of the home. Besides, a host of other agencies, like neighborhood health clinics and family planning centers, are addressing AIDS."

What is the role of the teacher as Canada prepares to enter the twenty-first century? Should teachers focus on social issues in the classroom? If you were Carla, what would you say to this teacher?

The conflict between Carla and her fellow teacher highlights the expectation of much of the public that schools (and teachers) have a responsibility to address problems that confront modern Canadian society. Those who disagree with Carla's approach to teaching social studies tend to believe that she should teach only content to students. Carla and her supporters, however, believe that teachers have an obligation to address domestic social problems. Underlying both positions are conflicting views on the aims of education.

WHAT ARE THE AIMS OF EDUCATION?

We agree that the purpose of schools is to educate. Unlike other institutions in society, schools have been developed exclusively to carry out that important purpose. That we are not always in agreement about what the aims of education should be, however, is illustrated by the fact that we disagree about what it means to *be educated*. Is a person with a university degree educated? Is the person who has overcome, with dignity and grace, extreme hardships in life educated?

Debate about the **aims of education** is not new. Aristotle, for example, expressed the dilemma this way: "The existing practice [of education] is perplexing; no one knows on what principle we should proceed—should the useful in life, or should virtue, or should the higher knowledge, be the aim of our training; all three opinions have been entertained."[1] Definitive answers to Aristotle's questions have not been achieved; instead, each generation has developed its own response to what the aims of education should be.

PROVINCIAL GOALS OF EDUCATION

Section 93 of the British North America Act, 1867, clearly states that provinces have sole responsibility for education. Since 1867, provinces have jealously guarded this right, challenging the federal government whenever it tried to influence provincial policy in education. The federal government has made inroads in education, however, under the guise of training or learning whenever they can be justified to protect the state of the nation, for example, job training to reduce unemployment. As recently as 1994, seventeen national government departments and agencies were quietly offering programs related to elementary and secondary education.[2] Moreover, the government bankrolls programs for many sectors of our population including immigrants, women, people with disabilities, and the unemployed.

Because provinces are responsible for education in their jurisdictions, each province establishes its own set of goals for education. They review them periodically and publish guidelines that link goals with proposed changes in curriculum and teacher preparation programs.

Although the goals differ from province to province and substantial differences exist, all provinces focus on the need for students to develop intellectually, emotionally, physically, and personally. For example, Prince Edward Island's goals for education state that the public education system will enable the student to develop intellectual curiosity, a sense of self worth, good mental and physical health, and a sense of pride and respect for one's community, province, and country.

Provincial goals generally also link skills taught in schools to students becoming productive citizens, for example, by developing positive work attitudes and by teaching students to use leisure time creatively and usefully. To this end, many provinces focus on developing skills such as drama and art. Many provinces also discuss how best to develop certain values in students, such as respect for the community and a sense of personal values. Some believe such values are best taught through religious education which they include as part of their mandate. All provinces refer to their obligation to provide benefits to everyone through gender equity, fundamental human rights, and equal opportunities for all.

EDUCATION FOR SOCIALIZATION

Schools are places where the young become socialized—where they learn to participate intelligently and constructively in Canadian society. Additionally, schools, more than any other institution in our society, assimilate persons from different ethnic, racial, religious, and cultural backgrounds and pass on the values and customs of the majority. It is through the schools that persons from diverse backgrounds learn English or French and learn about the importance Canadians attach to the democratic process, to bilingualism and biculturalism, and to multiculturalism; about the contributions of John A. MacDonald, Louis Riel, and Lester B. Pearson; and about the basic workings of capitalism.

EDUCATION FOR ACHIEVEMENT

Of the various aims that the schools have, achievement is the most universally agreed on. For most people, the primary purpose of schools is to impart to students the academic knowledge and skills that will prepare them either for additional schooling or for the world of work. Regardless of political ideology, religious beliefs, and cultural values, Canadians want their schools to teach academic content. However, the provincial goals for students make it clear that although academic content must be taught the goals cannot be met through content alone. Teachers cannot develop aesthetics or values through academic content by itself. Teachers know that it is not only what but how they teach that counts.

EDUCATION FOR PERSONAL GROWTH

Canadian society places great value on the dignity and worth of the individual. Accordingly, one aim of our schools is to enable the young to become all that they are capable of becoming. Unlike socialization or achievement, the emphasis on personal growth puts the individual first, society second. As Vito Perrone states in *A Letter to Teachers*, "education . . . always [begins] with children and young people and their intentions and needs."[3] According to this view, the desired outcomes of education go beyond achievement to include the development of a positive self-concept and interpersonal skills. Thus equipped, students are able to live independently and to seek out the "good" life according to their own values, needs, and wants. The knowledge and skills students acquire at schools are seen as enabling them to achieve personal growth and self-actualization.

EDUCATION FOR SOCIAL CHANGE

Schools also provide students with the knowledge and skills to improve society and the quality of life and to adapt to rapid social change. Naturally, there exists a wide range of opinion about how society might be improved. Some teachers, such as Carla, believe that one purpose of schooling is to raise the awareness of students about social problems and thereby make the world a better place. This is the principal attraction for many teachers who enter the profession.

EQUITY IN EDUCATION

Ample evidence exists that certain groups in Canadian society are denied equal economic, social, and educational opportunities. By teaching primarily to middle-class, two-parent families, schools maintain the status quo. Because most teachers are middle class, they hold middle-class values and attitudes which they, consciously or unconsciously, impart to their students. If students are unable to identify with these values and attitudes and feel excluded, they may not do well in school. Although this argument is somewhat reductionist, the evidence is clear that students who live below the poverty line are far less likely to complete high school, let alone graduate from a post-secondary institution.[4]

A remarkable correlation exists among poverty, single parent families, crime, dropping out of school, alcoholism, drug use, teenaged pregnancy, and suicide. What unites these issues is low self-esteem; children who have a low self-esteem believe they have little to look forward to and less to lose. Children with higher self-esteem tend to be more cautious about taking risks and able to think further into the future. Education seldom pays off immediately, and students with higher self-esteem are able to understand its future relevancy.

The public will to provide education equitably is strong. Eventually, schools may have to integrate their efforts with other public agencies to deal with pressing social issues such as drug use and pregnancy in an effort to lower dropout rates. Teachers will need to rethink their roles and possibly take on broader responsibilities. For example, math teachers could no longer think of the student as existing only in their classrooms but rather as a child first and a student second. The term "student" implies a certain society role different from other roles such as "gang member" or "alcoholic." Remembering that students are children or young adults first may better represent the realities of a person's life.

HOW IS CULTURAL DIVERSITY EMBEDDED IN CANADIAN SOCIETY?

Canada is officially a bilingual country and the right of Canadians to live using either English or French is guaranteed by the Constitution Act. Canada is also a **multicultural** society. How do bilingualism and multiculturalism translate from law into reality?

MAKING *a DIFFERENCE*

Ryan Lengsfeld
Calgary, Alberta

After teaching elementary students for ten years, I moved to a junior high school to teach science and became more involved with environmental science. I took students on day trips into the foothills and mountains west of Calgary. We visited four different sites regularly and were able to integrate various aspects of environmental and biological sciences with hiking, biking, and climbing. It was through these trips that I got to know Mike Mappin, the Coordinator of School Programs at the University of Calgary's Kananaskis Field Station. The Field Station offered residential environmental education programs and it was through my growing professional relationship with Michael that I was able to participate in the Kananaskis Young Scientist Program that he developed.

The program was designed to offer students an opportunity to experience the roles and expectations of scientists studying the environment in the face of human pressure. The written product encompassing student-gathered environmental data and resulting analysis and synthesis was submitted to a fictitious Land Use Committee in helping to decide the fate of a tract of land.

But as economic conditions worsened, many schools could not afford to continue the residential program and developed the Environmental Scientist Project instead. The Project carried on the same concept but was designed so that it could be conducted at various sites at a day trip level. The essential parts of the Project had to be taught before the outing and the data collected had to be analyzed and synthesized back at the school. The Project has been used at several schools and I have been encouraged to produce other creations as well, like The Canadian Endangered Species Animal Game, The Pond Game, and others.

It is clear to me that I have maintained my enthusiasm for teaching throughout my career because of the creative ventures that my students and I experience from year to year. If you are thinking of becoming a teacher, you have to ask yourself what you have to offer, how can you keep your enthusiasm for course content, and how can you make the course content come alive for students as they change from generation to generation.

For almost a decade until 1994 Canada accepted about 250 000 immigrants annually. Compared to the United States, Canada admits almost four times as many immigrants per capita and the impact on Canadian culture is correspondingly greater. According to the Alexis de Tocqueville Institute about 6 percent of the United States' population is foreign born; Britain, 8.7 percent; France, 10.5 percent; Canada, 16.2 percent; Switzerland, 17.2 percent; and Australia, 20 percent. Most immigrants settle in cities. Toronto absorbs almost 64 000 each year while Vancouver becomes home to nearly 50 000 annually. Immigrants account for 38 percent of Toronto's population, 30 percent of Vancouver's, and 21 percent of Calgary's.

Immigration has come in waves over Canada's history, beginning with the first European settlers. In the early 1900s, the majority of immigrants were from Europe; by the late 1900s, the majority are from Asian, Middle Eastern, and South East Asian countries (see Table 5.1). Early settlers were largely Christian whereas later immigrants represent the multiplicity of world religions.

The increasing **diversity** of Canadian society has enormous implications for all our social institutions, including the schools. In cities, demand is increasing for teachers who speak more than one language and for teachers who reflect a school's cultural diversity. School traditions such as Christmas and Easter concerts have been re-examined to meet the needs of all students, Christian and non-Christian. Schools in Canada today must find ways to meet the needs of all students and parents, regardless of social class, gender, or ethnic, racial, or cultural identity. Schools must provide environments in which students can learn about and appreciate the diversity that exists all around them. Familiarity will counter the increasing polarization of Canadian society and prepare students for an increasingly diverse workplace.

UNDERSTANDING THE MEANING OF CULTURE

As we pointed out in the discussion of the aims of education, one mission of the schools is to maintain Canadian culture. But what is Canadian culture? Is there a single culture to which all Canadians belong? Before we can answer that question we must define the term *culture*.

Definitions of Culture   Culture has been defined in many ways. Among the definitions suggested by sociologists and anthropologists are the following:

- The acquired knowledge that people use to interpret evidence and to generate social behavior[5]
- Whatever it is one has to know or believe in order to operate in a manner acceptable to a group's members[6]
- A shared organization of ideas that includes the intellectual, moral, and aesthetic standards prevalent in a community and the meanings of communicative actions[7]
- A world view or the way a cultural group perceives its environment, including stereotypes, role perceptions, norms, attitudes, values, ideals, and perceived relationships between events and behaviors[8]

Simply put, **culture** is *the way of life* common to a group of people. It consists of the values, attitudes, and beliefs that influence their traditions and behavior. It is also a way of interacting and looking at the world.

TABLE 5.1   COUNTRIES FROM WHICH MORE THAN 4000 IMMIGRANTS WERE ADMITTED

Country of Birth	1989–1992	Trend (positive or negative)
Hong Kong	83 126	+
China	65 946	+
Poland	60 227	−
India	51 767	+
Philippines	50 840	+
Lebanon	38 669	−
Vietnam	35 464	−
United Kingdom	26 231	−
Sri Lanka	26 051	+
Portugal	24 226	−
United States	22 033	0
Iran	21 838	+
Jamaica	20 149	+
El Salvador	20 115	+
Taiwan	17 997	+
Trinidad and Tobago	13 102	+
Guyana	12 655	0
South Korea	11 470	+
Romania	11 060	+
Pakistan	10 667	+
Somalia	10 303	+
Haiti	10 048	0
Russia and Ukraine	9 918	0
France	9 845	+
Ethiopia	9 561	0
Yugoslavia	9 032	+
Egypt	7 848	−
Malaysia	7 299	−
Germany	6 431	−
Syria	6 232	−
Peru	6 194	0
Guatemala	5 861	+
Morocco	5 382	−
Chile	5 322	−
Fiji	5 206	+
Iraq	5 083	+
Nicaragua	5 023	+
Israel	4 810	−
Afghanistan	4 635	0
Ghana	4 569	+
Mexico	4 569	0
South Africa	4 485	0
Czechoslovakia	4 212	−

Note: "0" means the number of immigrants admitted is approximately the same over the four-year period from 1989–1992.
Source: Employment and Immigration Canada, Immigration Statistics, Annual Publication, 1992.

These definitions of culture remind us that it is difficult to define Canadian culture. Although we may speak of Canadian culture in contrast to the cultures of India, Haiti, Saudi Arabia, China, or Sweden, we must remember that the primary distinguishing characteristic of Canadian culture is its diversity. It has been suggested that a "cultural mosaic" analogy captures the **cultural pluralism** of Canadian society. That is, the distinguishing characteristics of cultures are to be preserved rather than blended into a single culture.

Dimensions of Culture   Within Canada's boundaries, we find cultural groups that differ according to other distinguishing factors, such as religion, politics, economics, and geographic region. The regional culture of the Maritimes, for example, is quite different from that of British Columbia. Similarly, Ontarians are culturally different from Albertans.

Socioeconomic factors, such as income and occupation, also contribute to the culture of communities. Recall, for instance, the example at the beginning of this chapter. The culture of the Uptown community in which Carla taught included a distinct set of expectations for teachers and students at Metropolitan High School—the primary purpose of schooling is to acquire knowledge and skills that lead to a better job, social mobility, and a higher standard of living. If Carla taught at an affluent school or a rural school, different sets of expectations would undoubtedly apply.

How is cultural diversity embedded in Canadian society? Are there shared dimensions of culture? Do different cultural groups have common elements that we could call Canadian? All Canadians, regardless of their country of origin do share common perspectives such as living in the shadow of the United States. Most Canadians are aware of American culture while most Americans know little about Canada. Another common element of Canadian culture is that many Canadians identify more strongly with their region than with the nation as a whole. We tend to think of ourselves as British Columbians or Quebecers first and Canadian next. Canadians also share the sense that Canada is an urban nation. With over 77 percent of Canadians living in cities, many Canadians perceive Canada as a string of isolated cities separated by a sparsely populated, vast country. Unlike the United States or other industrialized countries which have many interstate highways, Canada has only one. Regardless of where they live, all Canadians know the Trans-Canada Highway.

Canadians may be members of their cultural groups first, residents of their cities and regions second, and Canadians third. Canadian values tend to be more clearly perceived in international settings, for example, to those travelling to Canada from abroad. Regional values are more apparent in national settings, for example, when people from different regions of Canada gather together. Cultural values will become apparent in multicultural settings such as a classroom. As a teacher, you will be challenged to understand the subtle differences in values among students, colleagues, and support staff within your school. The learning process depends on the teacher's understanding of these differences.

Language and Culture   Culture is embedded in language, a fact that has resulted in conflict among different groups in our society. Some groups, although they support the preservation of ethnic cultures, also believe that all immigrants must learn English or French if they are to function in the dominant culture.

Throughout Canada, with the exception of Quebec, primary and secondary education is provided in either English or French. Federal funds are available to school districts which choose to provide French immersion classes, classes for English-speaking children in which French is the main language of instruction. Even in towns as tiny as Masset in the Queen Charlotte Islands in British Columbia, some parents desire French immersion. French immersion can be problematic since, in many small communities, it is impossible to provide an adequate secondary school education as curriculum becomes more specialized and more teachers are required.

Many school districts have tried to recognize the growing numbers of children who speak neither English nor French at home through multicultural education. It is vital that teachers who are implementing a multicultural program understand themselves and accept who they are since it is necessary to feel comfortable with oneself in order to accept and appreciate differences in others. You will be challenged to avoid **stereotyping** other people and to find pleasure in experiencing things that are unfamiliar.

UNDERSTANDING ETHNICITY

There are many ethnic groups in Canadian society, and everyone belongs to at least one. *Ethnicity* is the quality of being a member of an **ethnic group**. Ethnic groups have been defined as

> groups whose members share a unique social and cultural heritage passed on from one generation to the next. . . . Ethnic groups are frequently identified by distinctive patterns of family life, language, recreation, religion, and other customs that cause them to be differentiated from others. Above all else, members of such groups feel a consciousness of kind and "interdependence of fate" with those who share the customs of the ethnic tradition.[9]

Some individuals mistakenly limit their view of ethnicity to people of color. As the previous definition suggests, however, all people are members of one or more ethnic groups. The 1986 Census of Canada revealed that nearly all Canadians reported that they belonged to an ethnic group. The most frequently reported groups are shown in Table 5.2.

It is also clear that racial and ethnic identities in Canada are becoming more complex. We now know that "racial and ethnic identities derive their meanings from social and historical circumstances, that they can vary over time, and that they can sometimes even be slipped on and off like a change of clothing."[10] For example, a third-generation descendent of a Japanese immigrant may choose to

---

TABLE 5.2	ETHNIC BACKGROUNDS OF CANADIANS		
British	8.5 million	Chinese	0.4 million
French	6.1 million	Dutch	0.4 million
British and French	1.2 million	South Asian	0.3 million
German	1.0 million	Jewish	0.3 million
Italian	0.8 million	Black/Caribbean	0.2 million
Ukrainian	0.5 million	Polish	0.2 million
Aboriginal	0.4 million	Portuguese	0.2 million

What dimensions of culture might distinguish these students? What dimensions of culture might they all share? How might you describe the culture of this classroom?

refer to himself or herself as a Japanese Canadian or an Asian Canadian. Furthermore, it is evident that "specific racial categories acquire and lose meaning over time."[11]

School systems across Canada have had a hundred-year tradition of integrating immigrant students from western and eastern European countries. More recently, however, schools have been under pressure to find effective ways to integrate immigrant students from the Middle East, Africa, the Caribbean, and especially parts of Asia. Asian immigrants tend to live in the more populated provinces in Canada: Ontario, Quebec, British Columbia, and Alberta. In Ontario, Asian immigrants constitute the second largest ethnic group behind Italians. In Quebec, Asian immigrants constitute the third largest group behind Italian and Jewish immigrants. In British Columbia, Asians constitute the largest immigrant group, and in Alberta, the fourth largest group behind German, Ukrainian, and Dutch immigrants.[12]

WHAT ARE SCHOOLS LIKE AS SOCIAL INSTITUTIONS?

During your career as a teacher, not only will you teach students from different cultural backgrounds but you may also teach in different kinds of schools. An **institution** has been defined as "an established organization; especially, one dedicated to public service."[13] Clearly, then, schools are the institutions our society has established for the purpose of educating the young. For the last 100 years, Canadian schools have developed complex structures, policies, and curricula to accomplish this mission.

Schools do not exist in a vacuum. They mirror the complex interaction of Canadian, regional, and religious cultures. Private, parochial, and religious schools, for example, are often maintained by groups that see the school as a means of perpetuating their preferred way of life.

THE CULTURE OF THE SCHOOL

Schools are very much alike yet each school also differs significantly. Each has a culture of its own—a network of beliefs, values and traditions, and ways of thinking and behaving that distinguishes it from other schools.

Much like a community, a school has a distinctive culture—a collective way of life. Terms that have been used to describe this way of life include *climate, ethos, atmosphere,* and *character.* Some schools are community-like places with a shared sense of purpose and commitment to providing the best education possible for all students. Other schools lack a unified sense of purpose or direction and drift, rudderless, from year to year. Still others are characterized by internal conflict and divisiveness; students, teachers, administrators, and parents may feel that the school is not sufficiently meeting their needs. Gerald Grant defines a school with a "strong positive ethos" (or culture) as follows:

> A school with a strong positive ethos is one that affirms the ideals and imparts the intellectual and moral virtues proper to the functioning of an educational community in a democracy. It attempts to commit its members to those ideals and virtues in at least a provisional way through the espousal of goals, exemplary actions and practices, ritual, celebrations and observance of norms.[14]

Formal Practices of Schools   The formal practices of schools are well known to anyone who has been educated in Canadian schools. With few exceptions, students attend school from six years of age through sixteen at least and usually to eighteen, Monday through Friday, September through June, for at least twelve years. For the most part, students are assigned to grade level based on age rather than ability or interest. Assignment to individual classes or teachers at a given grade level, however, may be made based on ability or interest.

Teachers and students are grouped in several ways in elementary school and in one dominant pattern in junior and senior high school. At the elementary school level, the **self-contained classroom** is the most traditional and common arrangement. In this type of classroom, one teacher teaches all or nearly all subjects to a group of about twenty-five children, with the teacher and students remaining in the same classroom for the entire day. Often art, music, physical education, and computer skills are taught in other parts of the school, so students may leave the classroom for scheduled periods. Individual students may also attend special classes for remedial or advanced instruction, speech therapy, or instrumental music and band lessons.

Another elementary school arrangement is **team teaching**. Teachers share the responsibility for two or more classes, dividing up the subject areas between them, with one preparing lessons in mathematics, science, and health, for instance, while the other plans instruction in reading and language arts. The division of responsibility may also be made in terms of the performance levels of the children so that, for example, one teacher may teach the lowest- and highest-ability reading groups and the middle math group, while the other teaches the middle-ability reading group and the lowest and highest mathematics groups. In many schools, team teaching arrangements are so extensive that children move from classroom to classroom for forty- to fifty-minute periods just as students do at the high school level.

In **open-space schools**, students are free to move among various activities and learning centers. Instead of self-contained classrooms, open-space schools have large instructional areas with movable walls and furniture that can be rearranged easily. Grouping for instruction is much more fluid and varied. Students do much of their work independently with a number of teachers providing individual guidance as needed.

In junior and senior high schools, students typically study four or five academic subjects taught by teachers who specialize in them. In this organizational arrangement, called **departmentalization**, students move from classroom to classroom for their lessons. High school teachers often share their classrooms with other teachers and use their rooms only during scheduled class periods.

Though not prevalent, open-space classrooms can also be found at the high school level. It is also becoming more common to find departmentalization in elementary schools.

School Traditions   School traditions are those elements of a school's culture that are handed down from year to year. The traditions of a school reflect what students, teachers, administrators, parents, and the surrounding community believe is important and valuable about the school. One school, for example, may have developed a tradition of excellence in academic programs; another school's traditions may emphasize the performing arts; and yet another may focus on athletic programs. Whatever a school's traditions, they are usually a source of pride for members of the school community.

Ideally, traditions are the glue that holds together the diverse elements of a school's culture. They combine to create a sense of community, identity, and trust among people affiliated with a school. Traditions are maintained through stories that are handed down, rituals and ceremonial activities, student productions, and trophies and artifacts that have been collected over the years.

The Hidden Curriculum   The cultures of schools also reflect the hidden, or implicit, curriculum. This refers to the behaviors, attitudes, and knowledge that schools teach students unintentionally. The **hidden curriculum** strongly influences the image students formulate of themselves and their beliefs about how they should relate to others and to society in general.

What students learn through the hidden curriculum may be either positive or negative. Some students learn positive behaviors, such as how to cooperate with others, how to postpone gratification for more significant rewards, or how to stay

These children are participating in the culture of the school. What other behaviors, formal practices, and school traditions are probably a part of their school culture?

on task in spite of temporary setbacks. Others learn negative behaviors, such as how to manipulate adults, how to get by on the effort of others, or how to cheat. Important attitudes are also acquired through the hidden curriculum: One can trust/mistrust those in authority; hard work does/does not pay off; school is/is not worthwhile; or teachers do/do not care about their students. Finally, the hidden curriculum presents students with knowledge about the ways of the world: Those in authority have more freedom than those who are not; the appropriateness of one's behavior depends on the situation and the context; or misbehavior invites certain consequences.

The School Environment   The physical environment of the school both reflects and helps to create the school's overall culture. Some schools are dreary places or, at best, aesthetically bland. The tile floors, concrete block walls, long, straight corridors, and rows of fluorescent lights often found in these schools contribute little to their inhabitants' sense of beauty, concern for others, or personal comfort. As John Goodlad observed in his landmark study of 129 elementary, 362 junior-high, and 525 senior-high classrooms in schools around the United States, "I can only conclude from our data that the schools we visited—like most of the schools I have visited over the past three decades—generally provided physical environments ranging from neutral to negative in their probable impact on the humans inhabiting them."[15]

Other schools are much more attractive. In their study of 100 "good" schools, for example, Jack Frymier and his associates found that they were "pleasant and clean places in which to be, and teachers and students [were] allowed to put things on the walls and rearrange furniture as desired."[16] Ninety-eight percent of the elementary teachers and 91 percent of the middle-level and secondary teachers reported that their school buildings were "always" or "often" pleasant.

The School Location   An additional dimension of a school's physical environment is its location. Schools in rural, urban, and suburban settings often have significantly different cultures. Rural schools are often the focal point for community life and reflect values and beliefs that tend to be more conservative than those associated with urban and suburban schools. Suburban schools are often much larger than rural schools and may lack their cohesiveness.

The cultures of urban schools vary considerably. Some are academically oriented and serve parents who are as fully involved in the education of their children as parents in the surrounding suburbs. Other urban schools, unfortunately, have the unpleasant distinction of being in the lowest percentiles of academic achievement—hardly a desirable tradition for a school to maintain.

Urban schools found in or near low-income areas often reflect the social problems of the surrounding area, such as poverty, drug abuse, and crime. The quality of such schools is a serious problem confronting Canadian education. Across the country, middle-class families who can afford to move away from low-income areas. As a result, students in low-income areas rarely mix with students from families of other social classes. As a teacher, you will find the main difference between children from various socio-economic groups is in their readiness to learn. Many students in low-income schools will be high-needs children with problems to be overcome before they are able to learn while many children from more affluent schools will exhibit greater readiness to learn.

CONCEPTUALIZATIONS OF DIFFERENCES IN THE CULTURES OF SCHOOLS

Given the wide variation in schools and their cultures, many models have been proposed for describing the distinguishing characteristics of schools. Schools can be categorized according to the focus of their curricula; for example, high schools may be academic, vocational, or general. Another way to view schools is according to their organizational structure; for example, open schools or magnet schools. A **magnet school** allows students from an entire district to attend a school's specialized program. Some magnet schools are organized around specific academic disciplines such as science, mathematics, or the basic skills; others focus on the performing and visual arts, health professions, computers, or international studies and languages.

Metaphors for Schools   Other models view schools metaphorically—what is a school like? Some schools, for example, have been compared to factories; students enter the school as raw material, move through the curriculum systematically, and exit the school as finished products. Arthur Powell has suggested that high schools are like shopping malls; there is something for everyone, and students are consumers looking for the best value.[17] Others have suggested that schools are like banks, gardens, prisons, mental hospitals, homes, religious institutions, families, and teams.

School Culture and Social Class   In her study of several elementary schools in urban and suburban New Jersey, Jean Anyon identified four categories of schools that provide a useful way for talking about their cultural dimensions.[18] Anyon maintains that schools reproduce the existing society by presenting different curricula and educational experiences to students from different socioeconomic classes. As a result of their experiences at school, students are prepared for particular roles in the wider society.

Anyon studied a small group of schools in one metropolitan area and her criteria are linked almost exclusively to socioeconomic status. Few schools actually fit the categories in all ways.

The first kind of school she calls the *working-class school*. In this school, the primary emphasis is on having students follow directions as they work at rote, mechanical activities such as completing dittoed worksheets. Students are given little opportunity to exercise their initiative or to make choices. Teachers may make negative, disparaging comments about students' abilities and, through subtle and not-so-subtle means, convey low expectations to students. Additionally, teachers at working-class schools may spend much of their time focusing on classroom management, dealing with absenteeism, and keeping extensive records.

The *middle-class school* is the second type identified by Anyon. Here, teachers emphasize to students the importance of getting right answers, usually in the form of words, sentences, numbers, or facts and dates. Students have slightly more opportunity to make decisions but not much. Most lessons are textbook based. Anyon points out that, "while the teachers spend a lot of time explaining and expanding on what the textbooks say, there is little attempt to analyze how or why things happen. . . . On the occasions when creativity or self-expression is requested, it is peripheral to the main activity or it is 'enrichment' or 'for fun.'"[19]

The *affluent professional school*, unlike the previous two types of schools, gives students the opportunity to express their individuality and to make a variety of choices. Fewer rules govern the behavior of students in affluent professional schools, and teacher and student are likely to negotiate about the work the student will do.

Anyon provides the following definition of the *executive elite school*:

> In the executive elite school, work is developing one's analytical intellectual powers. Children are continually asked to reason through a problem, to produce intellectual products that are both logically sound and of top academic quality. A primary goal of thought is to conceptualize rules by which elements may fit together in systems and then to apply these rules in solving a problem. Schoolwork helps one to achieve, to excel, to prepare for life.[20]

Teacher-student relationships are more positive than those in the working-class and middle-class schools. Teachers are polite to their students, seldom give direct orders, and almost never make sarcastic or nasty remarks.

WHAT SOCIAL PROBLEMS AFFECT THE SCHOOLS AND PLACE STUDENTS AT RISK?

A complex and varied array of social issues have an impact on schools. These problems often detract from the schools' ability to educate students according to the four aims discussed at the beginning of this chapter: socialization, achievement, personal growth, and social change. Furthermore, the schools are often charged with the difficult (if not impossible) task of providing a front-line defense against such problems. Increasingly, public schools struggle with the problem of drug abuse education in high schools and where it fits in priority with subjects like mathematics and English.

One of the most vocal advocates of the schools' role in solving social problems was George S. Counts, who said in his 1932 book *Dare the School Build a New Social Order?* that "If schools are to be really effective, they must become centers for the building, and not merely the contemplation, of our civilization."[21] Many people, however, believe that schools should not try to build a new social order. They should be concerned only with the academic and social development of students—not with solving society's problems. Nevertheless, the debate over the role of schools in regard to social problems will continue to be vigorous. For some time, schools have served in the battle against social problems by offering an array of health, education, and social service programs. Schools are beginning to provide breakfasts, nutritional counseling, diagnostic services related to health and family planning, after-school child care, job placement, and sex and drug education, to name a few. In the following sections we examine several social problems that directly influence schools, teachers, and students.

IDENTIFYING STUDENTS AT RISK

An increasing number of young people live under conditions characterized by extreme stress, chronic poverty, and lack of adult guidance. Frustrated and feeling powerless, many youths escape into music, video games, cults, movies, television, or cruising shopping malls. Others turn also to crime, gang violence, sex, or substance abuse. Not surprisingly, these activities place many young people at risk of dropping out of school.

Young people whose first language is not French or English and who need to take English as a Second Language are also at risk of dropping out of school. Dropout rates among various ethnic groups vary considerably but students with poor English language skills are particularly at risk. A 1993 study of ESL students in a Calgary high school reported that, of three cohort groups of students who enrolled in the beginner ESL classes in 1989, 1990, and 1991, the graduation rates were 6, 0, and 7 percent respectively. The average dropout rate was approximately 96 percent. Students enrolled in the intermediate ESL classes experienced a 70 percent dropout rate while advanced ESL students were at a 50 percent risk of dropping out.

It has been estimated that close to one out of every three children regardless of ethnicity will become a dropout statistic. **Students at risk** of dropping out tend to get low grades, perform below grade level academically, are older than the average student at their grade level because of previous retention, and have behavior problems in school.

The life experiences of students who are at risk of dropping out can be difficult for teachers to imagine. The following "Professional Reflection," for example, is based on the actual experiences of two students at risk of dropping out.

POVERTY AND CHILDREN

In Canada the per capita family income in 1988 for a family of four was $46 185. But despite being one of the richest countries in the world, it has not achieved an enviable record when it comes to poverty among children. The poor in Canada are not randomly distributed: They are women and children, youth, old people, and members of certain ethnic groups. Women and children make up 45 percent of all the poor in Canada, and single-parent families experience the highest levels of un-

PROFESSIONAL REFLECTION

Read the following sketches of two students at risk. Imagine that as their teacher you have learned about their personal circumstances. How comfortable would you be with such information? Would that information affect the way you react to these students in the classroom? How? What might be the consequences of your reactions?

Sketch #1

Eric has a three-year-old brother. His mother is on social assistance and stays at home. On weekends, she goes out and Eric stays with his brother. To reward Eric, she allows him to drink hard liquor.

Five years ago, Eric's mother lived with a man who was very abusive. One night he beat her severely. Eric was afraid for his mother so he grabbed a knife and stuck it in the man's neck. Eric was ten years old.

Sketch #2

Kathy's mother is in a wheelchair. She was in a car that was run over by a logging truck and has to go to the hospital several times a year for operations. During those times, Kathy becomes very worried and has difficulty concentrating on her work. She is sometimes suicidal and states that she wants to die before her mother does. Having almost lost her, eleven-year-old Kathy cannot stand the thought that her mother might die.

Kathy's parents sometimes go away for the weekend and leave her alone. At those times, she seems to get into the most trouble. After school, for example, she runs over to the high school to smoke cigarettes with the high school crowd. Kathy loves both her parents a lot and she craves attention from them.[22]

employment. Of all female-led single-parent families, 54 percent lived below the poverty line in 1988. Children account for 27 percent of all poor people in Canada; 875 000 children under 16, or 15 percent, lived in poverty. If Canada's economy slows down, the groups most severely hit will continue to be women and children and other traditionally poor groups.[23]

Poverty and education are highly correlated. Families whose heads have not graduated from high school run a high risk of living below the poverty line. In 1983, 20 percent of the heads of the household of poor families possessed primary education, 16 percent some high school, 9 percent some post-secondary, 8 percent a college diploma, and 5 percent a university degree.[24] Clearly, the more education attained, the less one is at risk of living below the poverty line.

FAMILY DISTRESS

The stress placed on families in our complex society is extensive and not easily handled. For some families, such stress can be overwhelming. The structure of fami-

lies who are experiencing the effects of financial problems, substance abuse, or violence, for example, can easily begin to crumble.

With the high rise in divorce and in women's entry into the workforce, family constellations have changed dramatically. No longer is a working father, a mother who stays at home, and two or three children the only kind of family in Canada. The number of single-parent families, stepparent families, blended families, and extended families has increased dramatically during the last decade.

Stress within the family can have a significant negative effect on students and their ability to focus on learning while at school. Such stress is often associated with health and emotional problems, failure to achieve, behavioral problems at school, and dropping out of school.

CHILD ABUSE

Recent extensive publicity has made more children and adults aware of the problem of child abuse. Clearly, the burden of having to cope with such abuse in the home environment does not prepare a child to come to school to learn.

Teachers are now required by law to report suspected child abuse. They must become well informed about physical, emotional, and sexual abuse and about the neglect and exploitation of children. These topics are discussed frequently in teachers' professional journals, but extensive, up-to-date information can also be obtained from local, provincial, and federal child welfare agencies. Such sources encourage teachers to be more observant of children's appearance and behavior in order to detect symptoms of child abuse.

SUBSTANCE ABUSE

One of the most pressing social problems confronting today's schools is the abuse of illegal drugs, tobacco, and alcohol. In one study, 1200 people based on a pro-

EDUCATION IN THE NEWS

Budget Cuts

A mood of fiscal restraint is sweeping the country; deficit and debt reduction have become the buzzwords of the 1990s and voters everywhere are asking politicians to be fiscally responsible. Alberta announced a budgetary surplus for 1994-95 and New Brunswick for 1995-96; Saskatchewan brought down a balanced budget in 1995-96.

In their moves to reduce deficits, provincial governments have had to cut deeply in the three biggest budget areas: health, education, and social services. Cuts in funds for education have been felt at all levels of the system. In Nova Scotia, school boards have had to reduce kindergarten from a full- to a half-day program, eliminate specialist teachers for physical education and music, and cut French-language instruction for the lower grades. School boards have had to defer maintenance programs and have even relied on parents to provide janitorial services. Class sizes have increased to as many as 35 students, and parents have been asked to raise money for services and equipment that governments used to supply. Teachers accepted a 3 percent rollback in their salaries; even so, 500 teaching and 49 administrative positions were eliminated.

Similar cutbacks have affected New Brunswick and Ontario. The New Brunswick government has been cutting back services since 1988. Although it announced a budget surplus in 1995-96, cuts have continued in an effort to pay down accumulated debt. To cut its education budget, the Ontario government plans to reduce the number of school boards by 30 percent. It has also imposed on school boards a formula to calculate how much they can spend on administrative services. The government has encouraged neighboring boards to cooperate to reduce duplication in transportation, computer functions, and curriculum materials.

Alberta has almost halved kindergarten time for each child per year from 400 hours to 240. The government has also imposed a 5 percent rollback on teachers' salaries, and school districts were forced to offer early retirement packages to reduce the number of teachers in their systems. School boards have been limited to spending only 4 percent of their budgets on administration. Furthermore, the government eliminated the use of property taxes for education and has instituted a basic education grant for all districts. As well as forcing some school boards to cut their budgets, a grant system may have the effect of funding education more equitably across the province.

Budget cuts and restrictions will probably be with us for some time to come. Educators must find ways to work in changing workplaces and with new expectations to ensure that students continue to have the essentials they need to learn. How can they ensure this environment continues to exist?

Source: Based on *The Globe and Mail,* Feb. 22, 24; 1995.

---

portional sample randomly drawn from the Canadian population 18 years of age and over were asked what they thought was the biggest problem facing schools today. The number one response was "drug and alcohol abuse."[25] Although substance abuse has declined since the late 1970s, the problem remains serious.

The use of drugs among young people varies from community to community and from year to year but overall it is disturbingly high. Mind-altering substances used by young people include the easily acquired glue, white correction fluid, and felt marker, as well as marijuana, amphetamines, and cocaine. The abuse of drugs not only poses the risks of addiction and overdosing but is also related to problems such as AIDS, teenage pregnancy, depression, suicide, automobile accidents, criminal activity, and dropping out of school.

For too many young people, drugs are an everyday part of life. As the following student, dangerously close to dropping out of high school, suggests, drugs are seen as a way of coping with life's problems:

I've got too many problems, too many. It's too many problems to cope with and the problem is, you know, I like to take drugs. . . . See, it's that life is crazy, you know. And everybody, you know, comes down on me, and bothers me and the only way to get away from all that is by taking my drugs cuz that's, you know, they're my friends, they talk to me. . . . It'll set me straight for the whole day. And I go outside and play some handball, go to school first period, second period, third, fourth, I'm outta there, play handball right here in the handball court. I don't like to come to school, period, so I just come and sign in and go back out. And there's nothin' that's gonna stop me from doin' what I'm doin' now unless other things in life change me.[26]

VIOLENCE AND CRIME

Crime and vandalism have increased over the past 20 years in Canada. Widespread erosion of concern for the rights and property of others has increased as a result of child abuse, television and movie violence, drug abuse, welfare and tax fraud, and corruption in business and government. Not surprisingly, violence and vandalism have also become more commonplace in our schools. Strategies for reducing violent activities in schools include the identification of violent students, implementing dress codes that ban styles of dress identified with gangs, and removing graffiti from the school.[27] Innovative intervention programs have teamed students at risk with younger low achievers to serve as tutors and have directly taught conflict mediation skills.

Although many schools have beefed up security measures, hired police or community resource officers, expelled students who commit violent acts, and taken steps to restore order, the problems, especially in large urban schools, can be hard to remedy. Clearly, students cannot learn in an atmosphere of fear and mistrust.

TEEN PREGNANCY

Since 1970, the number of teenage pregnancies has increased. Indeed, most teachers of adolescents today may expect to have at least some students who are or have been pregnant.

Because the physical development of girls in adolescence may not be complete, complications can occur during pregnancy and birth. As well, adolescents are less likely to receive prenatal care in the crucial first trimester; they tend not to eat well-balanced diets and are not free of harmful substances such as alcohol, tobacco, and drugs which are known to be detrimental to a baby's development. These young mothers "are far more likely than mature women to have premature or low-birthweight babies, who . . . account for a substantial proportion of infant deaths and suffer a host of childhood illnesses, birth injuries, and neurological defects, including mental retardation."[28]

Teen pregnancy affects the lives of young mothers and children in other lasting ways. Because many teen mothers drop out of school, forfeiting their high school diplomas and limiting their access to higher-paying job opportunities, they and their children stay at the bottom of the economic ladder.

STUDENTS AND AIDS

One of the most challenging social problems confronting schools is providing for the education of children who have AIDS (acquired immune deficiency syndrome), a condition, nearly always fatal, wherein the body is no longer able to defend itself against disease. Some school districts have been involved in litigation over the right of children with AIDS to attend school.

According to Health and Welfare Canada, by 1992, a total of 6116 cases of AIDS had been reported in Canada. Over 60 percent of these individuals had died; from 1987 to 1991 the mortality rate from the disease increased by 102 percent. Health and Welfare Canada predicted that the number of Canadians infected with HIV, the virus believed to cause AIDS, in 1992 was as high as 50 000. The provinces are increasingly requiring schools to provide information on AIDS and on how to avoid being infected with HIV. Unfortunately, the lack of national standards results in gaps in the education that some children receive. In one province, children hear about AIDS only once between grades 9 and 12.[29]

A nationwide survey of Canadians suggested that most Canadians prefer to learn about HIV/AIDS from a medical professional.[30] As a teacher you may be asked by your school administration to welcome a nurse or doctor into your classroom to provide information about HIV/AIDS. It will also be important for you to listen to your students' concerns and to answer their questions when medical professionals are not available.

SUICIDE AMONG CHILDREN AND YOUTHS

The increase in individual and multiple suicides among young people is alarming. The number of suicides in Alberta for instance has increased by nearly 25 percent in the ten-year period from 1982 to 1991.

The causes of the deep depression that drive some teens to suicide are many. Contributing factors may be conflict with parents, the end of a relationship with a boyfriend or girlfriend, rejection by peers, breakup of the family, or perceived poor performance in school. Often, as the following comments from a teenage girl who contemplated suicide indicate, no one event triggers thoughts of suicide:

> Well, lots of times I wanted to leave and sometimes just end this, end my life. . . .
> I mean actually yesterday. I was so upset. I was so depressed that I felt like my life
> was useless; I was worthless. I was so sad I didn't know what to do really.[31]

When a young person commits suicide the effect on his or her peers can be very powerful. School personnel should be understanding and supportive, ready to provide counseling to help students handle their feelings of loss and fear.

WHAT CHARACTERISTICS DISTINGUISH SUCCESSFUL SCHOOLS?

The many social problems that affect students and schools may seem daunting at this point in your professional education. However, a great many schools in all settings and with all kinds of students are highly successful, including crowded city and isolated rural schools and schools that serve pupils of all socioeconomic, racial, and ethnic backgrounds. What are the characteristics of these schools? Do they have commonalities that account for their success?

First, we must define what we mean by a *successful school*. One measure of success, naturally, is that students at these schools achieve at a high level and complete requirements for graduation. Whether reflected in scores on standardized tests or other documentation of academic learning gains, students at these schools are learning. They are achieving literacy in reading, writing, computation, and computer skills. They are learning to solve problems, think creatively and analytically, and, most important, they are learning to learn.

Another valid measure of success for a school is that it achieves results that surpass those expected from comparable schools in comparable settings. The achievement of students goes beyond what one would expect. In spite of surrounding social, economic, and political forces that impede the education process at other schools, these schools are achieving results.

Finally, successful schools are those that are improving rather than getting worse. School improvement is a slow process and schools that are improving—moving in the right direction rather than declining—are also successful.

Much research has been conducted to identify the characteristics of successful (or effective) schools.[32] The characteristics of successful schools have been described in different ways in several research projects.

- *Strong leadership*—Successful schools have strong leaders, individuals who value education and see themselves as educational leaders, not just as managers or bureaucrats. They monitor the performance of everyone at the school—teachers, staff, students, and themselves. These leaders have a vision of the school as an effective learning environment and they take decisive steps to bring that about.
- *High Expectations*—Teachers at successful schools have high expectations of students. These teachers believe that all students, rich or poor, can learn, and they communicate this to students through realistic, yet high, expectations.
- *Emphasis on Basic Skills*—Teachers at successful schools emphasize student achievement in the basic skills of reading, writing, and mathematical computation.
- *Orderly School Environment*—The environments of successful schools are orderly, safe, and conducive to learning. Discipline problems are minimal, and teachers are able to devote greater amounts of time to teaching.
- *Frequent, Systematic Evaluation of Student Learning*—The learning of students in successful schools is monitored closely. When difficulties are noticed, appropriate remediation is provided quickly.
- *Sense of Purpose*—Those who teach and those who learn at successful schools have a strong sense of purpose. From the principal to the students, everyone at the school is guided by a vision of excellence.
- *Collegiality and a Sense of Community*—Teachers, administrators, and staff at successful schools work well together. They are dedicated to creating an environment that promotes not only student learning but also their own professional growth and development.

PROFESSIONAL PORTFOLIO

Write a case study of a school's culture. Visit a school in your university community or hometown, or base the case study on a school you have attended.

The section titled "The Culture of the School" beginning on page 117 of this chapter could serve as an outline for your case study as follows:

Case Study of _____ School

1. **Formal Practices:** What grades are included at the school? How are students and teachers grouped for instruction?

2. **School Traditions:** What school-related events or activities seem to be important to students, teachers, administrators, and members of the community? What is the school known for throughout the community?

3. **The Hidden Curriculum:** Aside from explicit subject matter content, what values, attitudes, and beliefs do students acquire as a result of their experiences at the school?

4. **The School Environment:** How would you describe the school facility? Does the physical environment seem to promote or hinder effective teaching and learning?

5. **The School Location:** What is the surrounding community like? How do community members seem to view the school? With pride? Suspicion? Respect? Does the community seem to be involved in the life of the school and vice versa?

6. **Conclusions about the School's Culture:** Overall, what are some strengths and weaknesses of the school's culture? According to the "Metaphors for Schools" section (page 120), what metaphor helps to describe the school? Does the school fit one of the four categories of schools described by Jean Anyon (see "School Culture and Social Class," page 120–121)?

If possible, supplement your case study with artifacts from the school, such as the school newspaper, a yearbook, a statement of school philosophy, or other materials.

CHAPTER SUMMARY

Schools play a complex, multifaceted role in Canadian society. The public has many, often conflicting, goals that it expects schools to attain. The extent to which schools should contribute to the growth and development of students in four broad areas—socialization, achievement, personal growth, and social change—is subject to debate.

Schools are one of the leading institutions in our society for the socialization of the young. One aim of the schools is to help children learn how to become productive, concerned members of our society—to live intelligently and harmoniously with people from diverse backgrounds.

Achievement—the acquisition by students of knowledge and skills in subject matter areas—is clearly an important aim of our schools. Students must attain specific levels of achievement if they are to enter the world of work or pursue additional education.

Schools also play an important role in students' development toward self-actualization. Together with families and other institutions in society, schools can do much to help students acquire positive self-concepts and effective interpersonal skills.

Through the knowledge and skills they acquire in school, students can make significant contributions to society. School-based activities such as community volunteering enable students to experience the role that citizens can play in addressing societal problems and issues.

One of the primary challenges schools face is providing teaching that is appropriate for students from diverse cultural backgrounds. Canadian society is made up of many different ethnic groups, and students increasingly come from homes where neither French nor English is spoken.

Education in our multicultural society requires teachers who openly value diversity and recognize the unique contributions that each student makes to classroom life. Today's schools also require teachers who understand how students' values, beliefs, and life-styles affect their performance in school.

While schools are more alike than different, each has a unique culture. Various models of schools and metaphors can help us understand the culture of schools. The more teachers know about a school's traditions, its identity, and the direction in which it is moving, the more successful they will be at meeting students' needs.

Many problems and issues affect schools and, rightly or wrongly, many people look to schools to provide leadership for addressing those problems. Among the problems and issues that challenge today's teachers are equity in education, poverty, family distress, child abuse, substance abuse, violence and crime, and the education of children at risk.

In spite of social problems that affect the educational process, much is known about the characteristics of schools that successfully educate children. Successful schools are based on the assumption that *all* students—regardless of ethnic background, socioeconomic status, the culture of the surrounding community, or conditions of the home—can learn.

KEY TERMS AND CONCEPTS

aims of education, 108
cultural pluralism, 114
culture, 112
departmentalization, 118
diversity, 112
ethnic group, 115

hidden curriculum, 118
institution, 117
magnet school, 120
multicultural, 110
open-space schools, 118
school traditions, 118

self-contained classroom, 117
stereotypes, 115
students at risk, 122
team teaching, 118

APPLICATIONS AND ACTIVITIES

1. Collect and summarize several newspaper and magazine articles that contain references to the public's expectations of education and the schools. To what extent do the articles address the four aims discussed in this chapter? To what extent do they identify social problems that schools are expected to address?

Teacher's Journal

2. Defend your choice of curriculum changes that you consider most important for improving the quality of education in your province. What aims of education do your choices reflect?

3. Describe your cultural identity. What outward appearances, group memberships, beliefs, and values do you include in your cultural identity?

How might your cultural identity affect your expectations and experience as a teacher?

4. Reflect on the hidden curriculum in schools you attended and list examples of what you learned as part of the hidden curriculum.

5. Reflect on your experiences with social problems at the elementary or high school levels. Select one of the social issues or problems discussed in this chapter and describe its influence on you or your peers.

Field Assignments

1. Obtain at least one statement of philosophy or mission statement from a school with which you are familiar. Analyze the statement(s), identifying and highlighting portions that refer to the four major aims of education discussed in this chapter (socialization, achievement, personal growth, and social improvement).

2. Visit a school in your community recognized as being successful or effective. What evidence do you find of the characteristics of successful schools discussed in this chapter? Are there other characteristics you would add to the list based on your observations?

3. Collect statistics on some aspect of the student population of a school that relates to a social problem of concern in your community. You might focus on school violence, vandalism of school property, teen pregnancy, or some other issue. Share your findings with the class.

6 Equity in Education in a Diverse Society

Prejudice is a burden which confuses the past, threatens the future, and renders the present inaccessible.

—Maya Angelou

Focus Questions

1. What is the language of diversity?
2. How will diversity affect you as a teacher?
3. What does equity in education mean?
4. What is multicultural education?

Rosa is a twelve-year-old Guatemalan girl who lives with her three older brothers and two younger sisters in a half duplex in the city. Rosa and her brothers were born in Guatemala and her sisters were born in Calgary. Rosa's mother and father brought the family to Canada three years ago.

About three months ago, Rosa transferred into your class. You suspect that she's having trouble adjusting to changes. You believe her work would improve if she got more involved but she gives the impression of being afraid to risk making mistakes, especially in reading and language arts.

Because Rosa seems to trust you, you've decided to talk to her after school today—she usually waits in your classroom until her brother Domingo arrives to walk her home. As she talks, timidly at first, then more openly and naturally, you realize that Rosa is struggling to adjust to the many new challenges of living in Canada. She misses her grandmother who lived with the family in Guatemala. She believes she does not speak English well enough and is worried that the other children will tease her if she speaks out in class. You also learn that Rosa has missed school frequently because she has been having bad headaches and stomach problems. When you ask Rosa if her parents are coming to the next parent-teacher interview, Rosa tells you they probably will not come because they do not speak English.

How can you get Rosa more involved in classroom activities? What strategies could you use to help her to improve her reading, speaking, and writing skills? How might you make Rosa's parents feel welcome and comfortable at the school?

This chapter looks at educational equity for all students and takes the position that the professional teacher should see cultural diversity as an asset to be preserved and valued, not as a liability. This country has always derived strength from the diversity of its people, and all students should receive a quality education so that they are able to make their unique contributions to society.

All persons have the right to be educated "without discrimination and, in particular, without discrimination based on race, national or ethnic origin, color, religion, age, or mental or physical disability."[1] All people should be judged based on what they can do rather than who they are. Classroom teachers are confronted with the challenge of being sensitive to differences among students and at the same time treating all equally and fairly. There are no easy recipes to follow to accomplish this balancing act. It may help, though, to remember that as human beings we are more alike than different. The requirements for teaching all students, regardless of the cultural group they come from or of any special needs they might have, are basically the same. Students learn well from teachers who are knowledgeable, energetic, flexible, creative, and committed; they do not learn as well from teachers who lack these characteristics.

WHAT IS THE LANGUAGE OF DIVERSITY?

As the enrollment in our schools of students from a variety of cultural backgrounds continues to increase, it is vitally important that those entering the teaching profession understand children's different backgrounds. To prepare to teach effectively in today's classrooms, it is necessary to become familiar with key concepts related to the **diversity** you will find among your students. In particular, you should understand the concept of minority group, be able to distinguish between ethnicity and race, and learn to recognize racism.

UNDERSTANDING THE CONCEPT OF MINORITY GROUP

To understand the important concept of **minority group,** it may help to remember that, even though the term *minority* technically refers to any *group* numbering less than half of the total population, in certain parts of the country "minorities" are actually the majority. However, more important than the numbers themselves is an appreciation of how many groups of people have continuously struggled to obtain full educational, economic, political, and social opportunities in our society. Along with minority racial and ethnic groups, others who have traditionally lacked power in Canadian public life are immigrants, the poor, children and the elderly, non-English speakers, members of minority religions, and women. Groups that have been most frequently discriminated against in terms of the quality of education they have received include Aboriginal Canadians, recent non-English speaking immigrants, exceptional learners, people with disabilities, and girls and women. There is mounting evidence that many students from these groups continue to receive a substandard education that does not meet their needs or help empower them to participate fully and equally in Canadian life.

DIFFERENTIATING ETHNICITY AND RACE

Your understanding of the distinction between ethnicity and race will enable you to provide students with educational experiences that reflect ethnic and racial diversity in meaningful ways. **Ethnic group** has been defined as "an involuntary collectivity of people with a shared feeling of common identity, a sense of peoplehood, and a shared sense of interdependence of fate. These feelings derive, in part, from a common ancestral origin, a common set of values, and a common set of experiences."[2] As we pointed out in the previous chapter, everyone belongs to at least one ethnic group.

However, the concept of **race** is used to distinguish among human beings on the basis of biological traits and characteristics. Numerous racial categories have been proposed but, because of the diversity among humans and the mixing of genes that has taken place over time, no single set of racial categories is universally accepted. People can be classified into as many as 300 "races," depending on the kind and number of genetic features chosen for measurement. In his book, *Man's Most Dangerous Myth: The Fallacy of Race*, anthropologist Ashley Montagu points out that

> It is impossible to make the sort of racial classifications which some anthropologists and others have attempted. The fact is that all human beings are so . . . mixed with regard to origin that between different groups of individuals . . . "overlapping" of physical traits is the rule.[3]

RECOGNIZING RACISM

In light of the arbitrariness of the concept of race, James A. Banks points out, "In most societies, the social significance of race is much more important than the presumed physical differences among groups."[4] Unfortunately, many people attach great importance to the concept of race. If you believe "that human groups can be validly grouped on the basis of their biological traits and that these identifiable groups inherit certain mental, personality, and cultural characteristics that determine their behavior,"[5] then you hold racist beliefs. When people use such beliefs as a rationale for oppressing other groups, they are practicing **racism**.

As a teacher, you will not be able to eliminate racism in society. However, you have an obligation to all your students to see that your curriculum and instruction are free of any form of racism.

HOW WILL DIVERSITY AFFECT YOU AS A TEACHER?

As a teacher you will teach students who historically have not received full educational opportunities—students from the many racial and ethnic minority groups in Canada, Aboriginal students, students from low-income families or communities, students with exceptional abilities or disabilities, and students who are female. You will face the challenge of reaching out to all students and teaching them that they are persons of worth and can learn.

In your diverse classroom your aim is not to develop a different curriculum for each group of students—that would be impossible and would place undue emphasis on differences among students. Rather, your curriculum should help increase students' awareness and appreciation of the rich diversity in Canadian culture. As Banks suggests:

> The multicultural curriculum should enable students to derive valid generalizations and theories about the characteristics of ethnic groups and to learn how they are alike and different, in both their past and present experiences. . . . *[Each] curriculum should focus on a range of groups that differ in their racial characteristics, cultural experiences, languages, histories, values, and current problems.* (Emphasis in original.)[6]

Banks also points out that teachers who create a curriculum that is truly multicultural do more than add content about ethnic and cultural groups to their lessons. They understand that *"multicultural education is largely a way of viewing reality and a way of thinking, and not just content about various ethnic and cultural groups."*[7] Furthermore, such teachers respect students from all ethnic and cultural groups and they are alert for ways to increase their learning.

MINORITY ENROLLMENTS AND TEACHER RECRUITMENT

As this chapter's opening scenario about Rosa suggests, the need for teachers to understand students from different cultural backgrounds is critical. Minority-group students come from all social classes. Because of a history of unequal opportunities, however, some have low incomes and manifest many of the problems associated with poverty. This is particularly true of First Nations students. Unlike the French and English, whose languages, cultures, laws, and religions were protected by the Act of Union of 1840 and the BNA Act of 1867, Aboriginal Canadians were subjected to a century of assimilationist policies. Assimilation meant giving up their languages, cultures, laws, and religious beliefs. It also meant having teachers who did not honor their languages and traditions and living in poverty as a marginalized group.

Although Canada's population is rapidly becoming more diverse, the number of teachers from minority groups remains small. Look around your education classes. Is this trend about to change with the entry of your class into teaching? While some universities have specific policies to encourage First Nations peoples to enter faculties such as education, few have specific policies aimed at other disadvantaged groups. Visible minorities are not adequately represented in the teaching profession. There is a discrepancy between the classroom and the profession. As a result, effective teachers must be able to teach students from diverse backgrounds.

Why has the number of minority-group teachers remained small? Why are they greatly needed in the nation's teaching force today?

MINORITY GROUPS AND ACADEMIC ACHIEVEMENT

Minority-group students are disproportionately represented among students who have failed to master minimum competencies in reading, writing, and mathematics. In addition, many have limited abilities with English. It has been estimated that ethnic minority students are two to four times more likely than others to drop out of high school. Minority students are also expelled or suspended from school more often than nonminority students.

One of the most extensive studies comparing the academic achievement of American students was done by James S. Coleman and his associates in 1966. The Coleman report, *Equality of Educational Opportunity*, looked at the test scores of 600 000 students at 4000 schools in grades one, three, six, nine, and twelve. For each grade level, achievement for the average Mexican American, Puerto Rican, Native American, and African American was significantly lower than that for the average Asian American or Anglo-European American. Coleman also found that the achievement gap widened at higher grade levels. The reading scores of African Americans in the first grade, for example, were about six months behind; by the twelfth grade, this gap had widened to about three-and-a-half years.[8]

Coleman's findings also apply to Canada's schools. In North York schools, part of Metropolitan Toronto, students come from over 120 countries and speak over 80 languages.[9] These students can be loosely categorized into four main groups: immigrants from non-English-speaking countries, immigrants from the English-speaking Caribbean, refugees, and visa students. Students in each group have many needs in common that are important for teachers to understand.

Students from non-English-speaking countries have often had little say in the decision to immigrate to Canada; the adults in their lives usually made the decision. They often have emotional issues to deal with about leaving their friends, their extended families, their language, and their communities. If they remain angry and cannot speak the dominant language of their new country, they may express this anger through self-destructive or anti-social behaviors.

Students from the English-speaking Caribbean may have arrived in Canada after being separated from their parents for many years. Parents often come to Canada without their children and are able to sponsor them only after several years. The children must adjust to living with their parents and learn to cope emotionally with the separation from their homes. Although the children speak English, they will be living in a country that does not value their accent or their dialect.

Students from the third group arrive in Canada as refugees. They come from countries that have experienced serious conflict such as Vietnam, Afghanistan, Iran, Sri Lanka, Uganda, Hungary, or Laos. Although refugees may appreciate being in Canada, they too will feel the loss of having left their friends, family, traditions, and language behind. Some will be coping with painful memories of abuse or violence perpetrated against them or their families. In Canada, they may require substantial language and emotional help before they can participate fully in the school.

Visa students arrive to study in Canada and are often away from their family and homes for the first time. Although they usually possess a basic level of competency in English, their success will depend upon quickly becoming more proficient in English so they can participate fully in all aspects of the school's culture. These students will also need to adjust to the loneliness of being away from their family and to the unfamiliarity caused by a strange culture.

All of these students are experiencing the emotional stress of being uprooted from their culture, language, and friends. They are experiencing the mental stress of having to speak a new language and to concentrate on every word spoken. It is not surprising that some immigrants in Canada achieve poorly in school. Anyone disadvantaged by emotional and mental stress will have difficulty learning to his or her capacity.

As a teacher, you will need to learn as much as you can about your students and provide them with continuity of learning. This will involve identifying and building on the established academic and social skills of your students. Students may not understand some aspects of Canadian culture or history when you talk with them. You will need to learn when you must fill in the gaps so that they will better understand your lessons.

WHAT DOES EQUITY IN EDUCATION MEAN?

To provide equity in education to all students means that teachers promote the full development of students without regard for race, ethnicity, gender, socioeconomic status, sexual orientation, abilities, or disabilities. More specifically, teachers fulfill this important mission by continually evaluating the appropriateness of the curricular and instructional experiences they provide to each student.

In the following sections, we consider the progress that has been made to provide students from diverse groups with equal educational opportunities. As you read about each group, try to become aware of any stereotypes you might have about the group being discussed. Remember that socioeconomic status (economic wealth, parents' educational attainment, and a sense of identity with the dominant culture), not race, language, or culture, has been shown to contribute most strongly to students' achievement in school.

EDUCATION AND ABORIGINAL CANADIANS

First Nations peoples comprise Indians, both status and non-status, Inuit, and Métis. Until the 1960s, the purpose behind educating Aboriginal Canadians was assimilation into the dominant culture, thus wiping out their cultures. To this end, the government forced many Aboriginal children to attend residential schools where their birth languages were forbidden and their cultures condemned as "primitive." Education was viewed by many First Nations peoples as destructive. Today, the education system emphasizes cultural preservation and stresses the autonomy of the First Nations. The federal government funds band-controlled schools and in Saskatchewan operates an Aboriginal-run college.

Greater learning and higher levels of student self-esteem result when reserve schools are run by band councils and when Aboriginal languages are part of the curriculum. Teacher education programs in Manitoba (associated with the Brandon University Northern Teacher Education Program, BUNTEP), British Columbia (the University of Victoria), and the Northwest Territories (Aurora College and Nunavut College) focus on cultural and linguistic strategies specific to the Aboriginal Nations being taught. Because Aboriginal cultures differ significantly from the dominant Anglo-European culture, teaching strategies must also differ. Aboriginal students tend to learn through three stages: observation, hands-on practice with an adult, and private practice. Rather than singling out individuals, teachers should provide frequent opportunities for private interaction with individual children and with small groups as well as opportunities for quiet, persistent exploration.

Philip Robinson and Jason Aqqiaruq listen as Noah Piugaattuk and Aipilik Inuksuk explain the uses of artifacts.

EDUCATION FOR STUDENTS WITH LIMITED ENGLISH LANGUAGE SKILLS

Statistics Canada reported that in 1991 over 4 million Canadians had a birth tongue other than English or French. About one person in 10 in Quebec spoke a language other than French or English at home, and about one in five spoke a language other than French and English in the rest of Canada including in cities such as Calgary, Edmonton, Hamilton, Kitchener, Thunder Bay, Windsor, and Winnipeg. The ratio was even higher in Toronto (33.4 percent) and Vancouver (27.5 percent).

In the elementary grades, students not fluent in English are usually placed in regular classrooms, and teacher aides will often assist in providing the individual attention that the students need. In the secondary grades, some school systems pull these students out of regular classrooms and provide **English as a Second Language (ESL)** classes along with special electives so that students can mix with students who have stronger English-language skills. Other school systems use an early integration policy and leave all students in regular classrooms. Teachers are under no pressure to teach them the actual content of the class, for example, mathematics, but instead provide English-learning opportunities. A teacher may have a tape or video recorder in the class and non-English-speaking students may replay the lesson to learn its content while other students are working on projects or assignments.

Controversy exists over which method is better for students and research is ongoing. Proponents of early integration claim that student self-esteem and sense of belonging are enhanced when they remain in regular classes. Students will learn English less intensively and feel accepted as part of the school's student population. Proponents of more gradual integration claim that placing students in small classes with an expert teacher on language acquisition enables students to learn English more rapidly. Students are supported in their work until they have the skills to work independently.

TABLE 6.1   LANGUAGES SPOKEN IN CANADA, 1991

Language	Ability to Speak (000s)	%	Birth tongue (000s)	%
Italian	702	2.6	539	2.0
German	685	2.5	491	1.8
Chinese	557	2.1	511.9	1.9
Spanish	402	1.5	188	0.7
Portuguese	254	0.9	221	0.8
Ukrainian	250	0.9	201	0.7
Polish	240	0.9	200	0.7
Dutch	173	0.6	146	0.5
Punjabi	168	0.6	147	0.5
Arabic	164	0.6	119	0.4
Greek	161	0.6	130.5	0.5
Tagalog	137	0.5	116	0.4
Vietnamese	113	0.4	84	0.3
Hindi	112	0.4	41	0.2
Hungarian	97	0.4	84	0.3
Cree	94	0.3	82	0.3
Russian	84	0.3	38	0.1
Gujarati	54	0.2	42	0.2
Yiddish	53	0.2	28	0.1
Hebrew	52	0.2	13	0.0

Tentative evidence from an ongoing study in Calgary suggests that teachers who speak English only display different attitudes toward non-English-speaking students than teachers who speak two or more languages. Attitudes measured include willingness to accept differences in others and to understand one another. Clearly, if teachers show a lack of willingness in these areas student-teacher relationships—and learning—will be affected. Table 6.3 on page 142 presents several general strategies for improving the literacy skills of students developed by bilingual education expert Gisela Ernst and her colleagues. They point out that these strategies can be used whether or not the teacher is bilingual.

**TABLE 6.2   FASTEST GROWING, SHRINKING LANGUAGES IN CANADA
1971–1991**

	1971 (000s)	1991 (000s)
Growing		
Chinese	95	517
Spanish	12	188
Portuguese	120	221
Punjabi	52	147
Polish	135	200
Greek	145	146
Italian	538	539
Dutch	145	146
Shrinking		
German	561	491
Ukrainian	310	201

EDUCATION AND EXCEPTIONAL LEARNERS

Like many ethnic and racial groups in our society, **exceptional learners** have often not received the kind of education that most effectively meets their needs. All children require economic support, health care, security, and education, while exceptional learners are usually characterized as having needs in addition to these four. They have special educational needs. Day, Kirk, and Gallagher defined the exceptional child as one

> who deviates from the average or normal child (1) in mental characteristics, (2) in sensory abilities, (3) in neuromotor or physical characteristics, (4) in social behavior, (5) in communication abilities, or (6) in multiple handicaps. Such deviation must be of such an extent that the child requires a modification of school practices, or special services, to develop to maximum capacities.[10]

Following the enactment in the United States of Public Law 94-142, the Education of All Handicapped Children Act of 1975, educators in Canada became more sensitive to the needs of exceptional children. This awareness led to similar provincial education acts in Saskatchewan, Ontario, New Brunswick, and Alberta. By 1989 all provinces had enacted laws mandating that school systems provide for exceptional children. Furthermore, the Canadian Charter of Rights and Freedoms contains an equality clause which states,

> every individual is equal before and under the law and has the right to the equal protection of the law without discrimination and, in particular, without discrimination based on. . . mental or physical disability.

School systems began to broaden their mission to include many children who had only recently been excluded. For example, until the 1970s school districts in British Columbia distinguished between education and training and claimed that children who could not take care of their most basic needs and had to be trained could not be in the schools which were involved only in education.

Great strides have been made in obtaining equal educational opportunity for exceptional students. The learning needs of exceptional students are provided for through a variety of special education programs. **Special education** refers to "specially designed instruction that meets the unusual needs of an exceptional student."[11] Teachers who are trained in special education become familiar with special materials, techniques, and equipment and facilities for exceptional students.

> For example, children with visual impairment may require reading materials in large print or Braille; students with hearing impairment may require hearing aids and/or instruction in sign language; those with physical disabilities may need special equipment; those with emotional disturbances may need smaller and more highly structured classes; and children with special gifts or talents may require access to working professionals. Related services—special transportation, psychological assessment, physical and occupational therapy, medical treatment, and counseling—may be necessary if special education is to be effective.[12]

Just as there are no easy answers for how teachers should meet the needs of students from diverse cultural backgrounds, there is no single strategy for teachers to follow to ensure that all exceptional students receive an appropriate education. The key, however, lies in "finding and capitalizing on exceptional children's *abilities*."[13] To build on students' strengths, regular classroom teachers must work cooperatively and collaboratively with special education teachers. Furthermore, students in special education programs must not become isolated from other students.

TABLE 6.3   TEACHING IN MULTILINGUAL/MULTICULTURAL SETTINGS: STRATEGIES FOR SUPPORTING SECOND-LANGUAGE LEARNERS

Classroom Environment and Attitude

1. Relax and enjoy. Language is more caught than taught. Your relaxed, receptive, interested concern will be the magical ingredient for enhancing the teaching and learning process.
2. Provide a warm, encouraging environment in which help is readily available to ESL students.
3. Books that are sensitive to the adjustments of the new student can be shared with the class (e.g., *Crow Boy* by Yashima; *I Hate English* by Levine; *What Does the Rooster Say, Yoshio?* by Battles).
4. Fill the room with meaningful, relevant print. These are springboards for discussion and the rudiments of second-language literacy.
5. Label as many objects in the classroom as possible and invite your students to provide labels in their own language.
6. Increase possibilities for success by using a satisfactory/unsatisfactory option for grading until students are able to successfully complete classroom assignments.
7. Try to avoid anglicizing your students' names. Sometimes their names are the only connection they have with their native language, culture, and country.

Crosscultural Communication and Understanding

1. Become informed about the different cultures and languages represented in your classroom. This can be done by designing activities wherein your students become the "experts" by sharing part of their culture with the class.
2. If you find a student's behavior to be unusual or disconcerting, you might ask students or parents to clarify its meaning (e.g., Native-Canadian and Asian-Canadian students may avoid eye contact with authority figures out of respect). This could prevent misunderstandings further down the road.
3. Try to talk individually with your students as much as possible. This lets them know you are interested in them as individuals, not just as students.
4. Avoid forcing students to speak and allow a wait time for students to answer.
5. ESL students need instruction to be clear and interesting. By using exaggerated facial expressions, a slower speech rate, abundance of gestures, and enunciating clearly you can reach more students. Many times our expressions and gestures can help students understand what we are saying when our words do not.
6. Try to incorporate tutors who speak students' native languages.
7. Start by asking questions (backed by visual aids) that can be answered with yes or no. Then move, little by little, to questions requiring slightly longer answers.

Instructional Techniques and Strategies

1. Whenever possible, try to use a variety of formats that go beyond the traditional lecture format. This will enable you to target different learning styles in your classroom.
2. Organize, when possible, cooperative-learning activities. Small groups give second-language learners a chance to use their second-language skills in a non-threatening environment.
3. The use of videos, films, drama/role plays, manipulatives (great for math), pictures, artifacts, posters, music, nursery rhymes, games, filmstrips, maps, charts, and field trips can enhance teaching and learning.
4. Your school ESL specialist is a wonderful source of knowledge and information about what to do and what materials to use with your ESL students.

Encourage students to indicate when they are confused or do not understand. Students may feel more comfortable indicating understanding rather than acknowledging confusion.

When testing we need to be sensitive to students' cultural background. Culturally biased tests are a major hurdle for second-language learners. Standardized tests can be a common culprit. Misinterpreting terms, directions, or situational cues can cause your students' test performance to drop drastically.

When planning lessons or assignments, think about the following questions: What background knowledge do students have? Will the assignment use academic language or critical thinking skills unfamiliar to your students?

Restate, rephrase, summarize, and review frequently.

Literacy and Oral Language Development

1. Keep in mind specialized vocabulary that is content specific. Each content area has specific terminology that can confuse most second-language learners. Math, for example, has several terms for the function of addition (e.g., add, plus, combine, sum, increased by).
2. Whenever possible define key terms in several ways.
3. Make use of pictionaries.
4. Encourage the use of bilingual dictionaries, materials, and content-area books in students' first language. They can help students understand new concepts both in their native language and in English.
5. Consult your media specialist for books appropriate for students' reading/comprehension level.

Source: Gisela Ernst, Margaret Castle, and Lauren C. Frostad, "Teaching in Multilingual/Multicultural Settings: Strategies for Supporting Second-Language Learners," *Curriculum in Context* (Fall/Winter 1992): 14–15. Used by permission of the authors and the publisher.

In addition, teachers must understand how some people can be perceived as "different" and presumed to be "handicapped" because of their appearance or physical condition. Evidence suggests, for example, that people who are short, obese, or unattractive are often victims of discrimination, as are people with such conditions as AIDS, cancer, multiple sclerosis, or epilepsy. Significantly, many individuals with clinically diagnosable and classifiable impairments or disabilities do not perceive themselves as *handicapped*. The term itself means permanently unable to be treated equally.

Officially labeling students has become a necessity with the passage of the laws that provide education and related services for exceptional students. The classification labels help determine which students qualify for the special services, educational programs, and individualized instruction provided by the laws, and they bring to educators' attention many exceptional children and youth whose educational needs could be overlooked, neglected, or inadequately served otherwise. Detrimental aspects include the fact that classification systems are imperfect and have arbitrary cutoff points that sometimes lead to injustices. As well, labels tend to evoke negative expectations which can cause teachers to avoid and underteach these students, and their peers to isolate or reject them, thereby stigmatizing individuals, sometimes permanently. The most serious detriment, however, is that students so labeled are taught to feel inadequate, inferior, and limited in terms of their options for growth.

Students with Disabilities Imagine that it is near the end of the first week of school. Based on the comments of their teachers from last year and your experiences with them this week, you know that all of the children in your class are bright and eager to learn. However, you are concerned about two of your new students—Fred and Audrey. Fred has slight cerebral palsy and experiences mild muscle-control and speech problems. He walks with a jerky motion but he can get around on his own. He is academically talented and has always performed well in school. What steps will you take to ensure that Fred is fully included in classroom activities this year and that he continues to experience success in school?

Students like Fred or students with mental retardation and physical disabilities such as health impairments and sensory impairments have often not received the kind of education that most effectively meets their needs. Before the twentieth century, youngsters with disabilities were usually totally segregated from regular classrooms. In state-run and private schools, mentally retarded, vision-impaired, and hearing-impaired youngsters were taught by special education teachers. Around the turn of the century, however, some students were placed in special education classes in regular schools.

Meeting Audrey's needs presents you with a different set of challenges. You have found that she has an adequate vocabulary and doesn't hesitate to express herself. However, her achievement in reading and mathematics doesn't seem to add up to what you believe she can do. Audrey is restless and has a short attention span. Often, when you give the class instructions, Audrey seems to get confused about what to do. In working with her one-on-one, you've noticed that she often reverses letters and numbers—she sees a *b* for a *d* or a *6* for a *9*. What knowledge and skills must you have to help Audrey realize her full potential?

Audrey is a **learning-disabled (LD)** student. These students have problems taking in, organizing, remembering, and expressing information. Like Audrey, LD stu-

MAKING a DIFFERENCE

Susan Jay
Toronto, Ontario

Maureen Guerriero
Scarborough, Ontario

I was out of the work force for several years and when I re-entered it, I found myself spending countless hours preparing my first lessons. How fortunate I was to meet up with someone like Susan. With no hesitation Susan welcomed me into her classroom where I picked up teaching methodology that has been part of my repertoire ever since. I can speak first hand about the value of teachers sharing with others those things which have worked.

Susan knew about the demands on beginning teachers from her own experiences when she found she was too busy laying her foundation in mastery of material, classroom management, and delivery of curriculum to develop special materials or units. But we had a similar approach to teaching and we were collaborative and flexible so it seemed natural that we would create something special.

We decided to develop a unit we called the Project on the Telephone designed for new Canadians who are adult ESL high school students. We asked ourselves, "What does the student need? What are the steps that will lead to that outcome?" The answers to these questions led us to develop the unit that incorporated a range of communicative methodologies from cooperative learning through group work and role play to independent assignments.

Collaboration is a must between team-partners—bouncing ideas off each other and making use of each other's strengths. Collaboration is also needed between teachers and students to ensure that we as teachers understand the needs of our students and they in turn understand why and what we are doing.

I quickly realized that the prepared materials served only as a base from which to build learning experiences. Ongoing adjustments were necessary to meet the needs of each new set of students. As well, the materials had to be constantly updated to keep in step with the changing world. Susan and I believe it is necessary to maintain our professional growth and consequently we continue to read, provide in-service for other teachers, and participate in workshops and conferences.

dents often show a significant difference between their estimated intelligence and their actual achievement in the classroom. Estimates on the number of LD students vary; however, the public schools have identified between 4 to 5 percent of students as learning disabled, and almost half of the students identified by the public schools as needing special education are LD students.[14]

Classroom teachers play an important role in providing for the education of learning-disabled students. By being alert for students who exhibit several of the following symptoms, teachers can help in the early identification of learning-disabled students so that they can receive the special education services they need.

- Short attention span (restless, easily distracted)
- Reverse letters and numbers (sees *b* for *d*, 6 for 9)
- Reads poorly if at all (below age and grade level)
- Often confused about directions and time (right-left, up-down, yesterday-tomorrow)
- Personal disorganization (can't follow simple schedules)
- Impulsive and inappropriate behavior (poor judgment in social situations, talks and acts before thinking)
- Poor coordination (clumsy, has trouble using pencil, scissors, crayons)
- Inconsistent performance (can't remember today what was learned yesterday)
- Fails written tests but scores high on oral exams (or vice versa)
- Speech problems (immature speech development, has trouble expressing ideas)[15]

After an initial referral by a classroom teacher, a team consisting of a learning-disabilities teacher, psychologist, and social worker or nurse evaluate the student to determine if the child has a learning disability. In the event the child does, he or she may be placed in a classroom with a teacher trained in dealing with learning disabilities. In that classroom, the child is taught through techniques that involve not only the child's sense of hearing and vision but also touch and movement.

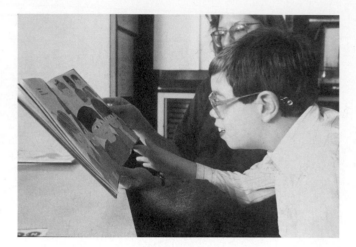

This student with disabilities is being educated in an inclusive general education classroom. How will you plan to meet the needs of your exceptional learners?

Meeting the Mainstreaming Challenge   Mainstreaming refers to the inclusion of students with different abilities in regular classes. To help teachers meet the needs encountered in diverse classrooms school districts have developed in-service programs designed to acquaint regular classroom teachers with the unique needs of disabled students. In addition, universities with preservice programs for educators have added courses on teaching students with special educational needs.

To meet the **mainstreaming** challenge, teachers must have knowledge of various disabilities and the teaching methods and materials appropriate for each. The effective teacher is also characterized by his or her positive attitudes toward special education students. In this regard, a recent study of 212 K–12 student teachers found that "developing acceptance and pupil self-confidence" was judged to be the most important competency for teaching mainstreamed students.[16]

In addition, special educators Daniel P. Hallahan and James M. Kauffman suggest that *all* teachers should be prepared to participate in the education of exceptional learners. Teachers should be willing to do the following:

1. Make maximum effort to accommodate individual students' needs
2. Evaluate academic abilities and disabilities
3. Refer [students] for evaluation [as appropriate]
4. Participate in eligibility conferences [for special education]
5. Participate in writing individualized education programs
6. Communicate with parents or guardians
7. Participate in Student Resource Committee hearings
8. Collaborate with other professionals in identifying and making maximum use of exceptional students' abilities[17]

The Debate over Full Inclusion   One interpretation of the concept of least restrictive environment holds that mainstreamed special education students must be able to keep up with general education students. A broader interpretation known as **full inclusion** calls for the inclusion of all students in regular classes and requires only that the child benefit from the opportunity to be in a regular classroom. According to the full-inclusion approach, if a child needs support services, these are brought *to the child*; the child does not have to participate in a pull-out program to receive support services. Advocates of full inclusion maintain that pull-out programs stigmatize participating students because they are separated from their general-education classmates, and pull-out programs discourage collaboration between regular and special education teachers. Those who oppose full inclusion maintain that regular classroom teachers, who may be burdened with large class sizes and be assigned to schools with inadequate support services, often lack the training and instructional materials to meet the needs of all exceptional students.

Students Who Are Gifted and Talented   You are concerned about the poor performance of Paul, a student in your eighth-period high school class. Paul is undeniably a bright young man. When he was ten, he had an IQ of 145 on the Stanford-Binet. Last year, when he was sixteen, he scored 142.

Paul's father is a physician and his mother is a professor. Both parents clearly value learning and are willing to give Paul any needed encouragement and help.

Throughout elementary school, Paul had an outstanding record. His teachers reported that he was brilliant and very meticulous in completing his assignments. He entered high school amid expectations by his parents and teachers that he would continue his outstanding performance. Throughout his first two years of high school, Paul never seemed to live up to his promise. Now, halfway through grade eleven, Paul is failing English and geometry.

Paul seems to be well adjusted to the social side of school. He has a lot of friends and says he likes school. Paul explains his steadily declining grades by saying that he doesn't like to study.

Gifted and talented students, those who have demonstrated a high level of attainment in intellectual ability, academic achievement, creativity, or visual and performing arts, are evenly distributed across all ethnic and cultural groups and socioeconomic classes. Although you might think it is easy to meet the needs of gifted and talented students, you will find that this is not always the case. "Gifted and talented students often challenge the 'system' of the school, and they can be verbally caustic. Their superior abilities and unusual or advanced interests demand teachers who themselves are highly intelligent, creative, and motivated."[18] The ability of such students to challenge the system is reflected in a 1993 U.S. Department of Education study that found that gifted and talented elementary schoolchildren have mastered 35 percent to 50 percent of the grade curriculum in five basic subject areas *before* starting the school year.[19]

Strategies for teaching students who are gifted and talented begin with effective teachers. It has been suggested that effective teachers of the gifted have the following characteristics:

- Understands, accepts, respects, trusts, and likes self
- Is sensitive to, supports, respects, and trusts others
- Has high intellectual, cultural, and literary interests
- Is flexible, open to new ideas
- Desires to learn; has high achievement needs and enthusiasm
- Is intuitive, perceptive
- Is committed to excellence
- Is democratic rather than autocratic
- Is innovative and experimental rather than conforming
- Uses problem-solving; doesn't jump to unfounded conclusions
- Seeks involvement of others in discovery
- Develops flexible, individualized programs
- Provides feedback; stimulates higher mental processes
- Respects creativity and imagination[20]

Although the preceding characteristics should apply to *all* teachers, it seems reasonable to expect that teachers of gifted students would be above the average for all teachers in regard to these attributes. In addition, a study of the differences between outstanding and average teachers of gifted and talented students showed that the outstanding teachers were characterized as having the following characteristics:

- Having enthusiasm for own work with gifted students
- Having self-confidence in ability to be effective
- Being a facilitator of other people as resources and learners
- Being able to apply knowledge of theory to practice
- Having a strong achievement orientation
- Being committed to the role of educator of gifted students
- Building program support for gifted education programs[21]

Alternatives for Gifted Education   Several innovative approaches exist for meeting the educational needs of gifted students. Some of these are briefly summarized here.

Acceleration: There seems to be increasing support for various kinds of accelerated programs for intellectually precocious students. One researcher has even advocated "extreme educational acceleration" or "radical acceleration" for gifted youth.[22] Such programs have proved successful. For example, one survey that spanned a fifty-year period and examined 200 studies of accelerated programs found that two thirds were beneficial.[23] To meet the educational needs of gifted students who have outgrown the high school curriculum, many universities now participate in accelerated programs whereby gifted youths may enroll in university courses.[24]

Self-directed or independent study: For some time, self-directed or independent study has been recognized as an appropriate way for teachers to maintain the interest of gifted students in their classes. Gifted students usually have the academic backgrounds and motivation to do well without constant supervision and the threat or reward of grades.

Individual education programs: IEPs have been promoted as an appropriate means for educating gifted students. Most IEPs for gifted students involve various enrichment experiences, self-directed study, and special, concentrated instruction given to individuals or small groups in pull-out programs.

Special or magnet schools: Several large-city school systems have developed magnet schools organized around specific disciplines, such as science, mathematics, fine arts, basic skills, and so on. The excellent programs at these schools are designed to attract superior students from all parts of the district. Many of these schools offer outstanding programs for gifted and talented youth. E. Paul Torrence, a noted researcher in gifted education and children's creative thinking skills, says of such schools: "Students in these schools [stay] for hours after school and [return] on weekends. They [are] enthusiastic, intense, and satisfied.[25]

Weekend and summer programs: Many communities have special weekend and summer programs to meet the needs of gifted and talented youth. These programs often make use of community resources—museums, theaters for the performing arts, businesses, and universities.

EDUCATION IN THE NEWS

The Marginalization of Ethnic Groups in Education

Over the last decade Toronto has absorbed more immigrants than any other city in Canada. Over 65 000 immigrants annually settle in Toronto. It is no wonder that Canadians look to the Toronto Board of Education for leadership in multicultural education.

In 1994 the Toronto Board conducted a major study, the seventh since 1970, that linked academic achievement to race and ethnicity. This study confirmed what other studies in Canada have found, that minority groups are marginalized in school systems and experience much higher dropout rates. It showed that an over-proportionate number of black, Aboriginal, and Portuguese students are in the non-academic streams and that an under-proportionate number are found in advanced, university-bound programs.

The 1995 Royal Commission on Learning in Ontario drew heavily on this study in making its recommendations

to address racism in the schools. The Commission suggested that the education of black students was in crisis in Toronto. While some black students do well, the "achievement levels of many black students left much to be desired."

Teachers and other school staff who want to avoid marginalizing minority students within their schools should work toward creating inclusive school environments. Schools should promote positive self-identity and pride in one's heritage, acceptance of people from diverse backgrounds, critical self-assessment, and action against unfairness or discrimination. To achieve this type of school, many teachers will have to reexamine who they are and what type of person they would like to be. What do you think this type of self-reflection might accomplish?

Source: Based on *The Globe and Mail,* Feb. 14, 1994, and the *Calgary Herald,* May 28, 1995.

EDUCATION AND GENDER

Females in our society have been, and still are, discriminated against in the marketplace and in the classroom, victims of **sexism**—discrimination that is based on the belief that one sex is superior to the other. Presently, slightly less than 51 percent of Canada's population is female.

It is a well-established fact that women in our society are employed at lower levels than men, and, when they are employed at the same level, they earn less. Since the 1960s, women's groups and an array of feminist publications have alerted all of us to the many forms that sex discrimination takes in our society. The old saying "Boys will be boys" is but one of many clues that powerful forces condition boys to act in one way in our society and girls to act in another.

Evidence abounds that schools have made significant contributions to the divisions between the sexes. From kindergarten on, girls have traditionally been and may still be reinforced for certain behaviors, boys for others. Girls were supposed to play with dolls, boys with trucks. Girls were supposed to be passive, boys active. On the one hand, part of the hidden curriculum girls encountered at school might make them feel that they should prepare to become homemakers by learning about home economics and family living, or secretaries by taking typing, shorthand, and bookkeeping. Girls came to believe that they might become nurses, and boys might become doctors. Girls might become teachers but boys might become superintendents. Girls might become legal secretaries but boys might become lawyers. Girls might become executive secretaries but boys might become executives.

What does equal educational opportunity for female and male students really mean? What efforts have been made to achieve gender equality in Canadian schools?

Gender-Fair Classrooms and Curricula   A clear challenge teachers face is ensuring that girls *and* boys are encouraged to develop to the full extent of their capabilities and receive an education that is free from **gender bias**—subtle favoritism or discrimination based on gender. Unfortunately, evidence such as the following suggests that boys and girls continue to experience inequities in school.

Girls

- Girls start out ahead of boys in speaking, reading, and counting. In the early grades, their academic performance is equal to that of boys in math and science. However, as they progress through school, their achievement test scores show significant decline. The scores of boys continue to rise and eventually reach and surpass those of their female counterparts, particularly in the areas of math and science. Girls are the only group in our society that begins school ahead and ends up behind.

- In spite of performance decline on standardized achievement tests, girls frequently receive better grades in school. This may be one of the rewards they get for being more quiet and docile in the classroom. However, their silence may be at the cost of achievement, independence, and self-reliance.

- Girls are more likely to be invisible members of classrooms. They receive fewer academic contacts, less praise and constructive feedback, fewer complex and abstract questions, and less instruction on how to do things for themselves.

- Girls who are gifted are less likely to be identified than are gifted boys. Those girls who *are* identified as gifted are less likely to participate in special or accelerated programs to develop their talent. Girls who suffer from learning disabilities are also less likely to be identified or to participate in special education programs than are learning-disabled boys.

Boys

- Boys are more likely to be scolded and reprimanded in classrooms, even when the observed conduct and behavior of boys and girls does not differ. Also, boys are more likely to be referred to school authorities for disciplinary action than are girls.
- Boys are far more likely to be identified as exhibiting learning disabilities, reading problems, and mental retardation.
- Not only are boys more likely to be identified as having greater learning and reading disabilities, they also receive lower grades, are more likely to be grade repeaters, and are less likely to complete high school.[26]

Following is a list of general guidelines for creating a gender-fair classroom:

1. Equalize teacher-student interactions
2. Promote girls' achievements in math and science
3. Counter young children's self-imposed sexism
4. Strengthen girls' transitions into early adolescence
5. Teach about sexism directly.[27]

Discrimination and Sexual Orientation   To help all students realize their full potential, teachers should acknowledge the special needs of students who are or believe they are gay or lesbian. Unfortunately, it may be that homosexual students are the "at-risk kids schools ignore."[28]

Based on estimates that the percentage of homosexuals in U.S. society is between 4 and 10 percent, a typical high school might have between forty and 100 homosexual students.[29] For example, a Los Angeles high school with an enrollment of 1925 students has fifty to sixty students who participate in a school counseling program for gay and lesbian youth. Canadian numbers are likely to be similar.

Homosexual students are usually invisible because they choose to hide their sexual orientation. They make the choice not to disclose for many reasons, but the majority probably hide their sexual orientation out of fear for their physical safety, of being rejected by their friends and family, and of being labeled by others as "deviant." Homophobic behavior by teachers, students, and administrators also keeps many students from disclosing. Some teenagers find ways to explore their sexual orientation discreetly, for example, by spending time or taking a part-time job in neighborhoods that are largely gay and lesbian.

WHAT IS MULTICULTURAL EDUCATION?

Multicultural education is committed to the goal of providing all students—regardless of socioeconomic status, gender, sexual orientation, or ethnic, racial, or cultural backgrounds—with equal opportunities to learn in school. Multicultural education is also based on the fact that students do not learn in a vacuum—their culture predisposes them to learn in certain ways. And finally, multicultural education recognizes that current school practices have provided, and continue to provide, some students with greater opportunities for learning than students who belong to other groups.

According to James A. Banks, "Multicultural education is at least three things: an idea or concept, an educational reform movement, and a process."[30] More specifically, Banks suggests that multicultural education may be conceptualized as consisting of five dimensions: (1) content integration, (2) the knowledge construction process, (3) prejudice reduction, (4) an equity pedagogy, and (5) an empowering school culture and social structure (see Figure 6.1). As you progress through your teacher-education program and eventually begin to prepare curriculum materials and instructional strategies for your multicultural classroom, remember that integrating content from a variety of cultural groups is just one dimension of multicultural education, and that multicultural education is an approach that enhances the education of students from *all* ethnic and racial groups.

Proponents of multicultural approaches to education assert that teachers should learn about their students' cultural backgrounds and then use this knowledge to develop appropriate educational experiences. Noted anthropologist John Ogbu suggests that teachers can learn about their students' cultures through "(a) observation of children's behavior in the classroom and on playgrounds, (b) asking children questions about their cultural practices and preferences, (c) talking with parents about their cultural practices and preferences, (d) doing research on various ethnic groups with children in school, and (e) studying published works on children's ethnic groups."[31]

In addition, teachers must carefully select the materials they use, for, as Banks points out, "[m]any of the books and other materials on each ethnic group are insensitive, inaccurate, and written from mainstream and insensitive perspectives and points of view."[32] Some guidelines for selecting multicultural instructional materials are

- Books and other materials should accurately portray the perspectives, attitudes, and feelings of ethnic groups.
- Fictional works should have strong characters from different ethnic groups.
- Books should describe settings and experiences with which all students can identify and yet accurately reflect ethnic cultures and life-styles.
- The protagonists in books with ethnic themes should have ethnic characteristics but should face conflicts and problems universal to all cultures and groups.
- The illustrations in books should be accurate, ethnically sensitive, and technically well done.
- Ethnic materials should not contain racist concepts, clichés, phrases, or words.
- Factual materials should be historically accurate.
- Multiethnic resources and basal textbooks should discuss major events and documents related to the history of many ethnic groups.[33]

In regard to instructional strategies, there is no easy way to develop the ability to be effective with students from cultures different from one's own. We are nevertheless convinced that such ability depends on being open and willing to learn about other groups.

If you participate in cultural experiences, you will begin to acquire knowledge and skills in eight areas that are essential for successful teaching in a diverse society:

1. The ability to communicate with students from other cultures
2. Skills in diagnosing the knowledge and abilities of students from other cultures

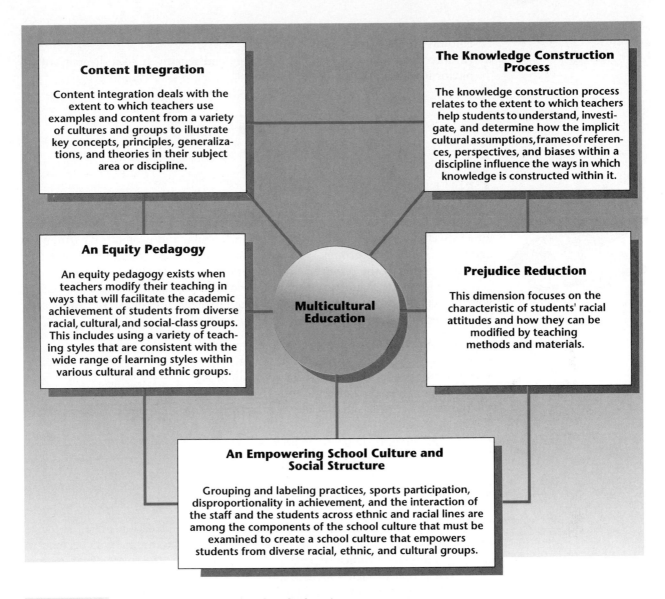

FIGURE 6.1   **The Dimensions of Multicultural Education**

(Source: From Banks, James A. *Multiethnic Education: Theory and Practice,* 3d ed, Copyright © 1992 by Allyn and Bacon. Reprinted by permission. p. 5.)

3. Knowledge about the psychology and impact of prejudice
4. The ability to discover the differences between the value systems of different ethnic and class subcultures in the school setting and to understand their effect on the teaching-learning process
5. A deeper, more sensitive knowledge of one's own and other cultures leading to the realization that human beings are more alike than they are different
6. An increased capacity for humane, sensitive, and critical inquiry into multicultural issues as they relate to multicultural education

7. An increased willingness and openness to examine and to reassess one's own cultural attitudes and values

8. An increased ability to respond positively and sensitively to a diversity of behavior involved in multicultural settings[34]

PROFESSIONAL PORTFOLIO

Consider preparing an annotated directory of local resources for teaching students about diversity, implementing multicultural curricula, and promoting harmony or equity among diverse groups. For each entry, include an annotation—that is, a brief description of the resource materials and their availability.

Resources in the directory should be available through local sources such as your university library, public library, community agencies, and so on. Among the types of resources you might include are the following:

- Films, videos, audiocassettes, books, and journal articles
- Simulation games designed to improve participants' attitudes toward diversity
- Motivational guest speakers from the community
- Ethnic museums and cultural centers
- Community groups and agencies dedicated to promoting understanding among diverse groups
- Training and workshops in the area of diversity

CHAPTER SUMMARY

Teachers face many challenges in providing equity in education for all students. Demographic projections indicate that schools and classrooms will become increasingly diverse—ethnically and culturally—well into the twenty-first century. One result is that curricula increasingly emphasize diversity and multicultural education that enables students to appreciate different points of view and the contributions that all groups have made to our society.

To develop appropriate curriculum materials and instructional strategies for diverse classrooms, teachers should understand the concept of minority group, be able to distinguish between ethnicity and race, and learn to recognize racism. In addition, teachers must understand how the lack of equal education opportunities has resulted in disproportionate numbers of ethnic minority students who have not mastered minimum competencies in reading, writing, and mathematics. Socioeconomic status—not race, language, or culture—relates most closely to academic achievement. Among the groups that have not had equal educational opportunity in our country are Aboriginal and immigrant groups.

Teachers must also meet the needs of exceptional learners—those who may have mental retardation, learning disabilities, emotional or behavioral disorders, physical disabilities, disorders of communication, autism, traumatic brain injury, impaired hearing, impaired sight, or special gifts or talents. To ensure all children with disabilities have a free, appropriate public education, the provinces passed mandatory legislation to ensure that the educational needs of exceptional children are met. One of the ways to meet the mainstreaming challenge and provide for the needs of exceptional students is to emphasize their abilities and to become careful observers of their classroom behavior.

Considerable evidence suggests that females have also been denied equal educational opportunity. Many widespread school practices contribute to sexism, the belief that one sex is superior to the other. In addition, these and other school practices reflect gender bias—discriminatory treatment of students (both female and male) that places them at an unfair advantage or disadvantage. Teachers must be alert for signs of sexism and gender bias in the classroom, and they must create gender-fair classrooms and curricula that enable all students to develop to the full extent of their capabilities. In addition, teachers should recognize that some students may experience discrimination based on sexual orientation, and they may experience problems for which their teachers can provide support.

To create classrooms that are truly multicultural, teachers must select instructional materials that are sensitive, accurately portray the contributions of all ethnic groups, and reflect diverse points of view. In addition, teachers must understand that multicultural education involves much more than integrating content from diverse cultural groups; it is based on five key elements: content integration, the knowledge construction process, prejudice reduction, an equity pedagogy, and an empowering school culture and social structure. One of the best ways for teachers to develop the aptitudes and skills necessary for teaching in a culturally diverse society is through interactions with students and members of their communities.

KEY TERMS AND CONCEPTS

diversity, 134
English as a Second Language (ESL), 139
ethnic group, 134
exceptional learners, 141
full inclusion, 146
gender bias, 150

gender-fair curricula, 150
gifted and talented, 147
individual education program (IEP), 148
learning disability (LD), 143
mainstreaming, 146
minority group, 134

multicultural education, 151
race, 135
racism, 135
sexism, 149
special education, 141

APPLICATIONS AND ACTIVITIES

Teacher's Journal

1. With which of the student groups discussed in this chapter do you feel most comfortable? Least comfortable? What reasons do you have for feeling as you do?
2. Reflecting on your experiences in schools and the five dimensions of multicultural education (see Figure 6.1), describe the steps your teachers took

to create an empowering school culture and social structure.

3. What steps can you take to examine and reassess your cultural attitudes and values?
4. In your school years, did you ever experience discrimination as a member of a "different" group? Write about one outstanding incident that you feel affected your performance as a student.
5. As a teacher, what activities and materials might you use in a specific learning context to reduce the prejudices of students toward groups different from theirs?

6. Describe an example of sex-role stereotyping or gender bias that you experienced or observed in a school setting and how you felt about it.

Field Assignments

1. If possible visit a school that has an enrollment of students whose cultural or socioeconomic backgrounds differ from your own. What feelings and questions about these students emerge as a result of your observations? How might your feelings affect your teaching and teaching effectiveness? How might you answer your questions?

2. Interview a teacher at the school identified in field assignment 1. What special satisfactions does he or she experience from teaching at the school? What significant problems does he or she encounter, and how are they dealt with?

3. Observe a classroom with exceptional students. What steps does the teacher take to meet the needs of these students? Interview the teacher to determine what he or she sees as the challenges and rewards of teaching exceptional students.

CHAPTER 7

Historical Foundations of Canadian Education

...the true business of the schoolroom connects itself, and becomes identical, with the great interests of society.

—Horace Mann
Twelfth Report, 1848

1. Why is the history of education important?
2. How did education in Canada develop prior to the twentieth century?
3. What major social factors influenced education in the twentieth century?

During your first year of teaching you are talking with five colleagues in the teachers' lounge about some of the problems schools in your province are currently facing. The discussion was sparked by a television special about how to improve schools across Canada.

"I think the program presented a realistic view of the challenges that confront today's teachers," one teacher says.

"I was really glad to see a positive, honest portrayal of teachers," another offers. "The message to viewers seemed to be, 'Let's get behind our teachers and support them more fully. The work they do is important to Canada's well-being.'" Two of the teachers listening nod their heads in agreement.

A third teacher looks up from the papers he's grading at a table near the window. "Exactly," he says. "I think the program helped people to understand that the problems in the schools are not the fault of the schools themselves. They just reflect what is happening in society." A few of the teachers murmur their approval.

Then a teacher who recently announced that she will retire at the end of the year begins to speak. Everyone listens carefully, perhaps the group's way of telling her that her opinion is especially valued.

"When I began teaching in 1958," she says, "we didn't have the problems we have today. We had a job to do and that was to teach kids. We were there to teach and the kids, believe it or not, were there to learn."

Before she continues, her attention turns to you. "Then, beginning in the late sixties, the schools became just another social service agency. We started spending our time on breakfast programs, AIDS education, and anti-racism workshops. I can't think of any good that has come out of opening up education to include everything but the kitchen sink! Can you?"

What do you say?

A country's education system is vital to how it functions and to the continuation of its culture. During times of civil unrest or war, schools are often among the first institutions to be closed. During the Cultural Revolution in China, some schools were officially closed for three years and some for as many as ten. The education of a whole generation of children and young adults was disrupted in order to permanently change how people thought and acted.

Many Europeans who emigrated to North America in the seventeenth and eighteenth centuries did so to escape the control of oppressive governments and sometimes oppressive churches. These settlers knew that to preserve their cultures and some independence they had to control the schools their children attended. During the debate that preceded Confederation, provincial leaders insisted that education remain the sole responsibility of the provincial governments. Education is a critical institution in the maintenance of culture and language. It was hoped that, by ensuring that education remained locally controlled, citizens would have some say over their schools. It was also necessary that both French and English school systems remain in place to ensure the continuation of both cultures. Thus, in forming Canada, the founders did not envision a country with only one culture or one language.

WHY IS THE HISTORY OF EDUCATION IMPORTANT?

The way Canadian schools are organized is neither "natural" nor inevitable. Rather, the fact that schools in Canada are organized and controlled by laypersons elected or appointed to boards of education is the result of several social, economic, political, and religious forces that have affected our educational system. It is impossible to understand schools today without looking at what they were yesterday. Our current system of public and private education is an ongoing reflection of the aspirations and the values of this country. It is an important part of your education as a professional to develop an appreciation for this tradition.

You may wonder, what is the value of knowing about the history of Canadian education? How will such knowledge help you to be a better teacher? First, a knowledge of this history will help you evaluate more effectively current proposals for change. It is evident that education will continue to receive great public scrutiny between now and the turn of the century. Among those groups with a keen interest in schools—parents, students, teachers, politicians, teacher educators, and others—each has an agenda for changing the schools. You will be in a better position to evaluate these changes if you understand how schools have developed and how current proposals might relate to previous change efforts.

Second, an awareness of the historical development of schools and teaching is by itself an important part of professional knowledge. The more you understand various aspects of the profession the more likely it is that you will make appropriate professional decisions. Just as an effective democracy demands enlightened, aware citizens, so too does a profession require knowledgable professionals.

Third, because of Canada's proximity to the United States, it is essential that Canadian teachers clearly distinguish for their students the Canadian knowledge base from the American knowledge base. Knowing how and why Canadian schools have developed as they have is one aspect of Canadian culture that distinguishes it from American culture, and it is important that Canadian teachers recognize both the similarities and the differences in the historical development of the two education systems.

*H*OW DID EDUCATION IN CANADA DEVELOP PRIOR TO THE TWENTIETH CENTURY?

Since the earliest days of European colonization Canada has been strongly influenced by other countries. The earliest formal teachers in Canada were four French Catholic priests who arrived with Samuel de Champlain in 1616. After the conquest of New France by the British, British methods and curricula became standard in Canada.

More recently, American influence in matters of education has been strong. Theories of progressive education developed by American philosophers heavily influenced Canadian curricula of the 1930s and 1940s. With the exception of religion in education and the importance of having two national languages, virtually every change in Canadian education in this century has followed similar changes in the United States.

Over this century, politicians and society in general have relied more and more heavily on schools as the primary institution of education, replacing the earlier assumption that the family would be the main transmitter of cultural and societal values. Schools are expected to create in their students what it means to be a Canadian. Politicians focus on the school system because it is the only institution that brings cohorts of children together regularly. To become a teacher in the 1990s requires understanding of the events that are making the roles of both student and teacher more complex. Only through this understanding can the demands on teachers be managed.

FRENCH COLONIZATION

The earliest formal teachers in Canada, or New France, were Roman Catholic priests and nuns who arrived with settlers as France struggled to establish a

In the early days of French colonization in Canada, education was closely linked to religion. The first teachers in New France were Roman Catholic priests and nuns.

foothold in North America. Although some schools existed, most learning took place within the family unit. Children were trained as farmers, homemakers, and apprentices. Some men who became priests or professionals received more formal education, but the majority of French residents in Canada could not read or write.

The missionaries focused their efforts on converting and "francisizing" the Aboriginal peoples they encountered and sought out in an effort to "civilize" those whom they misunderstood and looked down upon. In doing so, they ignored evidence of longstanding civilizations and believed themselves justified in any action to make Aboriginal peoples more like Europeans.

ENGLISH COLONIZATION AND CONFEDERATION

As in the French colonies, the home in British Canada was the primary setting for education throughout the eighteenth and early nineteenth centuries. After the British conquest of New France, politicians and officials wanted to establish Protestant or nonsectarian schools in an attempt to minimize the legacies of French language, religion, and culture that remained in Lower Canada. Their efforts were thwarted by the lack of interest among most people who saw the home as the main place for education. However, beginning as early as the 1820s a consensus began to emerge about the necessity of public education, in part in response to the already noticeable influence of the United States on the culture of British North America. People began to conceptualize governments as responsible for education rather than the church, the community, or the family.

Edgerton Ryerson in Upper Canada was a particularly determined proponent of the view that education should be publicly funded, nondenominational, and universal. He wrote a report in 1846 recommending a uniform school system for the United Province of Canada. His report reflected the belief that formal education should be associated with social purpose and that universal education could prove to be an antidote to social unrest. The ruling class of the colony, made nervous by the **Rebellion of 1837**, believed that the school system was one route by which to ensure social stability. Ryerson's report was accepted by the legislature and legislation incorporating many of its recommendations was passed in 1846 and 1850 and amended in 1871. This legislation became the model for school acts in other regions of Canada.

Edgerton Ryerson

The economy of the colony was also changing. As urbanization increased and industrialization created new demands on people, schools began to absorb children to train them for the work force. As the size of cities increased and as child labor laws became standard, many feared that gangs of disaffected working-class youth would roam the streets creating instability and danger. Generally considered to be ignorant and criminally inclined, working-class young people were sent to school to be socially trained. Compulsory education was seen as a formidable tool to inculcate the values of "natural" spheres and acceptance of the hierarchical nature of society. Rather than enabling poor children to move out of lower socioeconomic levels, schools were meant to instill acceptance and appreciation of those who had more. The benefits of compulsory universal education in accomplishing this role were seen as sufficient to overcome people's objections to paying property taxes to support them.

What does this advertisement for school desks suggest about teaching methods and attitudes about the nature of children in the late 1800s?

Teachers in these early schools, which were usually one-room schoolhouses, often lived in a room at the back of the school building and were under relatively strict ethical and moral codes of conduct. They were expected to refrain from drinking in public or courting. Teachers were generally expected to maintain the building by stoking the fire, keeping the building heated, and providing custodial services. Special training for teachers did not exist, and pay and conditions were very poor.

Throughout the eighteenth and nineteenth centuries and into the twentieth, minority language and religious education has been a volatile issue in Canada. The **British North America Act, 1867,** which gave the provinces sole responsibility for education, enshrined denominational schools that cater to specific communities. Quebec continues to have separate Protestant and Catholic school systems; Ontario has a separate Catholic school system; and all of Newfoundland's schools are denominational.

In the early twentieth century, teaching conditions continued to be poor.

WHAT MAJOR SOCIAL FACTORS INFLUENCED EDUCATION IN THE TWENTIETH CENTURY?

The twentieth century in Canada can be summed up in one word: change. The population increased 400 percent, primarily through immigration. The population, which was primarily of European descent, has become increasingly multicultural as waves of immigrants have come from Asia, Africa, and the Middle East. The provinces of Alberta, Saskatchewan, and Newfoundland joined the Confederation. The country's economic base changed radically from being primarily agricultural to being extensively industrial. Canada is no longer a rural country; over 80 percent of Canadians now live in cities.

By the early part of this century, schools were relatively well organized in eastern Canada while one-room schoolhouses continued to dominate in the west. Often, teachers were hired by a local school board which represented only two or three families. Once hired, a teacher might find himself or herself quite isolated with little access to other people or society. Some communities could be reached only by boat in the summer or on foot over ice in the winter.

Teaching conditions tended to be extremely poor. Teachers continued to live in the backs of schoolhouses, often in buildings with little insulation, or were boarded

MAKING a DIFFERENCE

Ray Brushett
Mount Pearl, Newfoundland

Having taught physical education for twelve years, I found myself growing discontented with the physical education curriculum. As well, I found myself continually quizzing other physical educators about their programs and the future direction of physical education. It became my belief that the curriculum was dated and was not fulfilling its stated intentions as outlined by the Department of Education for Newfoundland and Labrador. I felt that it was my role as a physical educator to develop a new direction for physical education, a direction that would meet the needs of the current students and challenge future students to become active participants in physical education in a changing society.

The current program, which is based on a "Play Education Model" (a sports model), was not meeting students' needs. Their discontent was displayed by low enrollments in physical education programs, especially among the female population.

My vision for physical education in the future is based on Jewett and Bain's Fitness Wellness Model. Physical education will not only concern itself with the components of physical fitness and health but also with the knowledge of how these components are affected by physical activity. This knowledge and understanding will be acquired through the integration of physical activities and will be applied by students to personalized and individualized fitness wellness programs. In this manner, physical education will meet societal and cultural changes and future trends through a personal-global approach.

My personal development through my enrollment in a Master's Degree program in Physical Education was also a contributing factor in the development of the Wellness course. My research created doubts and queries about physical education programs I was teaching. As well, it permitted me the time to become immersed in wellness concepts which helped me develop my futuristic approach to physical education.

Physical education programs must be designed to meet the needs of all individuals and assist them to become active members of society. It is my belief that "fun" must be integrated into all activities so that the process of achieving total well-being is as important as the goal itself.

ONTARIO
DEPARTMENT OF EDUCATION

Public School Second-Class Certificate

This is to Certify that *Mrs. Helen E. Jones*

having attended the Provincial Normal School at *Stratford* during the Session 1912—1913, and having passed the examinations

required by the Department of Education of the Province of Ontario, has been awarded a **Second-Class Certificate of Qualification**, as

a **Public School Teacher, valid during good behaviour.**

Dated at Toronto this 24ᵗʰ day of *August* 1913

Registered Number *266 86*

Registrar.   *Minister of Education.*

As the Canadian economy became more industrialized in the 1920s, the new model of efficiency was reflected in education. Teachers' performance began to be measured against quantifiable criteria.

with different parents in the community. Although pay was low, communities were often unable to meet their commitments, and teachers were forced to accept cash substitutes. Furthermore, although schools were small, teachers had to prepare lessons for up to ten grades with several students needing to be prepared for provincial exams.

During the 1920s, provincial governments in western Canada began to document the work of rural teachers and attempted to standardize the working and living conditions for teachers. Provincial inspectors were assigned to travel to remote schools to inspect teacher performances. Tiny school districts were amalgamated to assist the standardization. Teacher qualification became more rigorous as curricula became more standardized. Teacherages were built to provide some privacy for teachers.

As the industrial economy became dominant, school system organizations became highly influenced by the industrial model. The model assumed efficiency was the ultimate goal and an assembly-line model of operation was the best means to that goal. Learning became organized hierarchically with a provincial inspector at the top, a school board, a district superintendent, a school principal, classroom teachers, and students at the bottom. Students would take province-wide examinations to test their knowledge, and teachers would be measured against quantifiable criteria to test their performance.

PROGRESSIVE EDUCATION

A movement called **progressive education** caught the attention of educators across Canada throughout the 1930s and 1940s. Supporters of progressive education were not united by a single, overarching educational philosophy. For the most part, they were opposed to autocratic teaching methods; teaching styles that relied almost exclusively on textbooks, recitations, and rote memorization; the relative isolation of the classroom from the real world; and classroom discipline based on fear or physical punishment.

This movement recognized that students are individuals, and teachers acknowledged these differences through changes in teaching techniques, school organization, and methods of discipline. Student attitudes and motivation were considered as important as the curriculum content students were expected to learn. Progressive teachers hoped the hidden curriculum would bring balance to the classroom by emphasizing reliability, patience, ethics, and compliance. For example, for many progressive teachers, cheating in class was a more serious issue than failing a subject.

Jurisdictions across Canada were eager to implement progressive education ideas, and they endorsed sweeping changes to curricula. Standard lecture techniques were replaced with more activities in which students were active participants. Content matter was integrated and students were encouraged to do more work on their own. However, many of these changes and directives were sent to classroom teachers without being field-tested and without teachers' input. In the end, teachers did not replace the old methods completely but instead tried to integrate new progressive techniques.

Progressive education came to Canada at an unfortunate historical time. The Great Depression had created massive unemployment. Some teachers who had left the profession returned and classrooms became headed by people who did not want to be there. For many, teaching was a temporary occupation until the economy picked up; such teachers were not interested in the ideas behind progressive education. With the advent of the Second World War the economy improved but many young people who would have become teachers joined the war effort instead. There was no infusion of bright young teachers into the school system. Older teachers confronted with the pressure to change their style of teaching to a more progressive style were confused and many were reluctant to change. They were fearful of what might happen if students were encouraged to work on their own, and they lacked knowledge about child development stages and child motivation theory. When, in the mid-1940s, business people and parents were criticizing the effectiveness of schools, many school systems responded by returning to more traditional methods of teaching.

EDUCATION IN THE 1990s

As the Canadian economy continued to evolve in the 1950s, industry began to share its place with the information or high technology economy. An economy based on information requires different skills from its workers than an industrial one. Because knowledge workers were on the fringes until the 1970s, little attention was paid to their needs by the school system. In fact, teachers had little success adapting technology to the classroom. They tended to consider technology as a supplement to curriculum rather than integrated with it.

Computers have made the difference in fully integrating technology into classrooms although many teachers have resisted their use. After studying the passage of era throughout history, Don Dillman concluded that we can often determine when an old era is about to end and a new one begin when resistance to the new era is at its greatest.[2] Over the past decade, attempts have been made to make ed-

The economy of the 1990s, based on information, requires different skills from its workers. Computers are making it possible to integrate information technology into the classroom.

ucation a wholly integrated experience, a seamless environment in which the act of learning cannot be separated from the teacher, the curriculum, and the supporting technology.

In many respects, schools in the 1990s are in turmoil. They must free themselves from the more obsolete industrial mindset and seek more relevant methods to prepare students for the information age. Until it is clear what it means to be an information worker, teacher preparation programs will continue to lack an appropriate focus to prepare new teachers and schools will be forced to figure it out on their own.

School environments are also changing rapidly. Student populations are becoming increasingly multicultural, and it is important that the teaching profession become more diverse as well. The structure of the family is changing. For example, single-parent families now constitute over 17 percent of all Canadian families.[3] Teachers are responding to increasingly complex classrooms by experimenting with team teaching and multiaging.

Many of the ideas put forward by progressive educators are being reexamined and reintroduced into the classroom. Teachers are better educated and have more understanding of how learning happens while governments are investing more money in education. As a result, teachers are more comfortable with individualized learning. At the same time, teachers are concerned about how their jobs and livelihoods will be affected by the economic crunch all governments are facing. Many fear that teacher qualifications will be downgraded and that student teaching or practicum experience will be used to replace teachers.

Whatever the future brings to education in Canada, understanding the past will provide us with a clearer picture of the social forces, conflicts, and political motivations that underlie the changes of the present.

MAKING *a DIFFERENCE*

Lillian Blakey
Thornton, Ontario

For many years, I was a visual arts teacher at the secondary level. However, in the past five years I have been involved in developing strategies for equity programming in classrooms from kindergarten to grade 13 with the North York Board of Education. Although I have worked in many disciplines and with a variety of approaches, I have always come to the same conclusion: children learn best when they see themselves reflected in the learning materials and have a strong sense of belonging.

I developed a project entitled "Promoting Equity Through Bookmaking—More Than a Bilingual Project." The purposes of the project were to promote equity through bookmaking by exploring culture validation as a strategy and to involve parents in the education of their children.

Equity programming through bookmaking focuses on seeing the learning situation in the context of culture. Familiar cultural objects, cultural stories, and cultural life patterns reflected in learning materials can alleviate anxiety in an unfamiliar environment. This program differed from other bookmaking projects in that it encouraged children to explore their own cultural inheritances and depended on the joint efforts of parents and children for its success.

We are living in a time which emphasizes global communication; the boundaries between countries are being dissolved in a multitude of ways. It is crucial that the education system empower all children to understand and communicate with people from many lands. Strategies such as this bookmaking project can help to promote equity of opportunity by seeing the learning situation in the context of culture.

My belief in the importance of cultural context in the process of learning begins with the assumption that we must provide a variety of perspectives to beginning readers. We must work to help promote equity for all children so that they might become successful learners and citizens in a pluralistic society.

PROFESSIONAL REFLECTION

Read the following scenario based on a day in the life of Billy, a fifth-grade student at a school of the future. How do his school experiences differ from those you experienced as a fifth-grader? Are there any disadvantages to the education Billy is receiving? Were there advantages to your education as a fifth-grader that Billy is not experiencing?

Billy is the younger of two sons of a single, working professional woman. His mother is excited about his educational opportunities and comforted by the support services he will receive for his speech impediment.

He walks to the local bus stop. Today he is looking forward to watching a video produced by his international video pal in Uruguay. Tommy, his older friend, is on board already with his laptop computer. He is finishing his English assignment which he will send to his teacher via electronic mail.

Other students are talking, singing, and playing electronic games with friends.

Billy likes his new school. He was a fourth-grader at his last school. Here, he is part of the red team which spans an eighteen-month age group. The wider age groupings expose Billy to a broader emotional and psychological developmental experience.

His teacher starts class with a short video on a discussion topic. Students then develop discussion points to develop "a thought for the day." Yesterday, music was

(continued)

the introductory topic. The class discussed moods and emotions and emphasized listening skills, the arts, and aesthetics.

Billy's school is part of a planned community. Because of this cooperative planning, a ten-acre park site set aside for nonrecreational activities is part of the school campus and curriculum. Each of Billy's instructional activities is related to the park area.

Class continues with a review of the events over the past week. His teacher shows an instructional video of the park site explaining a plant life analysis project. The class has been measuring two species of trees planted five years ago. One grew substantially while the other was stunted. The teacher, through a projection CD ROM capability, reviews the growing process for these specific trees and illustrates how their growth is typical for this region of the country. She also presents other growth profiles that, using simple system modeling, shows how climate, air quality, and rainfall interact to affect plant life.

The withering tree interests Billy because his team has been assigned to investigate this phenomenon. His team, which includes older students, will research the greenhouse effect through the media center, CD ROM storage, and a local chemical firm. Because this topic has been in the news lately, several local experts have volunteered to discuss this topic. Also, with their teacher aide's assistance, Billy's team will conduct a conference call with a representative from an international corporation examining this issue in northern Canada.

Billy's team also checked the distance learning curriculum within the county system and found a course on this subject in several district schools. Using the in-classroom fiber optic two-way video network, they will be monitoring this course and asking the older students questions.

The team submits a weekly progress report on this project to their teacher. The report not only records the progress of the group's project, but also is electronically monitored for reading and writing skills and various achievement levels. This information is evaluated electronically and given to his teacher with a copy for his mother as needed.

Billy has recorded musical sounds to write a song expressing his feelings about the withering tree. While humming melodies about these feelings, Billy suddenly remembers his schedule for the day and realizes he may be late for his "electronic field trip."

He returns to his home classroom where he and his classmates sit in front of the large video projection screen. They can choose between several field trips including a hike in the Grand Canyon, a discussion with NASA astronauts at the Air and Space Museum in Washington D.C., or a "walk" through an African village. After a popular vote, which the teacher tabulates electronically, the African village walk wins.

Through two-way interactive communications, students see and speak with African children. Computerized synthetic voice translation creates a person-to-person exchange between French-speaking African students and Billy's class. Two of Billy's classmates fluent in French lead the discussion.

At the end of his day, Billy summarizes his day in his electronic journal and mails it to his teacher. This allows a period for reflection, stimulates creative writing, and is periodically reviewed by his teacher. She can respond with short personal comments about his thoughts and ideas.

Next, he meets with three other students and a special tutor at a satellite center for speech therapy. His services include digital voice analysis and auditory drill to be conducted with a computer simulator. Because of the time freed by technology, the tutor can focus on Billy's psychological and emotional needs.

Billy goes home after a long day and touches the scanner device at the door. A red light signals the house is safe to enter. He knows his school day is over as he sends his daily log to his teacher.

Source: Excerpted from *Images of Potential: Learning Tomorrow,* Washington, D.C.: National Foundation for the Improvement of Education (no date), pp. 13–16.

PROFESSIONAL PORTFOLIO

Prepare a video- or audiotaped oral history that focuses on the changes that have occurred over the years in local schools or an interest of local concern. You may decide to interview experienced teachers, administrators, or school board members; or you may decide to interview the older members of the community.

Before conducting your interviews, prepare several interview questions that focus on your area of interest. At the conclusion of each interview, invite the person you are interviewing to provide any other relevant information he or she might have.

CHAPTER SUMMARY

Professional teachers realize that it is difficult to understand teaching today without becoming familiar with Canada's educational past. Knowledge of our educational history is important for two reasons: First, they can use their knowledge to evaluate current proposals for change. Second, they know that an awareness of how Canada's education system has developed is an important part of professional knowledge, and those who possess this knowledge are more likely to make appropriate professional decisions.

Myriad social forces, events, and persons have influenced the character of Canadian education. The colonization of North America by France and Britain set the stage for those countries' systems of education to be transported to this land. Early education was almost exclusively in the home. Children were trained by their parents or other family members to be farmers, homemakers, and apprentices. Most early European residents of Canada could not read or write. In New France, priests and nuns were the earliest teachers, although their greatest efforts were directed toward converting Aboriginal peoples.

Formal education became common by the 1840s, in part in reaction to the Rebellion of 1837. As the economy became increasingly industrialized, child labor laws limited the employment of children, and the population grew more urban, concern increased about the potential for gangs of working-class youth wandering the streets. Compulsory education was seen as a way to reinforce social structures and to inculcate proper respect for the existing hierarchies.

Progressive education came to Canada from the United States in the 1930s with its emphasis on students' individuality. Although some progressive theories and techniques were adopted in Canadian classrooms, the movement came to Canada at a time of economic despair. Teachers were poorly trained and many had little incentive to change their approach to teaching. When complaints began to be made about the school system in the mid-1940s, many teachers went back to traditional methods with students as passive learners.

Computers and other forms of technology have continued to change the way teachers teach and the classroom looks. Many of the ideas put forward by progressive educators are being reexamined and reintroduced into the classroom. Teachers are responding to increasingly complex classrooms by experimenting with team teaching and multiaging, and by incorporating technology into their classrooms seamlessly.

Education in the 1990s will continue to be a time of great change. Although these changes will be unsettling to many, those with an understanding of Canada's history know that Canadians have been confronted with sweeping changes many times before. We must inform ourselves about the past if we are to contribute to education in the future.

KEY TERMS AND CONCEPTS

British North America Act, 1867, 163
Edgerton Ryerson, 162
Progressive education, 166
Rebellion of 1837, 162

APPLICATIONS AND ACTIVITIES

Teacher's Journal

1. Examine several textbooks currently in use at the level of education that interests you the most. Now try to locate some texts that were used at that level several decades ago. What differences do you notice? Report your findings to your classmates.
2. After forming small groups, have each group prepare a brief presentation on what it was like to teach during one of the time periods identified in this chapter. If possible, presentations should be based on written accounts by teachers from each period.
3. What is your view of the current image of teachers? How does today's image compare with those of the past? What factors in today's world might be contributing to the attention, or lack of attention, that is paid to teachers?

4. Teachers' views of children have changed greatly from those held by earlier teachers. Write a paragraph or two that presents your view of the child and begins with the following phrase: "I believe that children are..."

Field Assignments

1. Visit a museum in your area for the purpose of examining some artifacts from Canada's early educational history. Take notes on what you find and describe several of the artifacts to the rest of your class.
2. Interview a teacher or administrator at a private school in your area. Ask him or her to comment on the role of the private school in our educational history.

CHAPTER 8

Philosophical Foundations of Education

As a practical discipline, philosophy of education is an attempt to find the most rationally defensible reasons for doing education one way rather than some other.

—Foster McMurray
"Concepts of Mind and Intelligence in Educational Theory"

Focus Questions

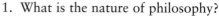

1. What is the nature of philosophy?
2. Why is philosophy important to teachers?
3. What determines your educational philosophy?
4. What are the six branches of philosophy?
5. What are six philosophical orientations to teaching?
6. How does one build an educational philosophy?

Eastside High School has ranked highest among the city's four high schools on the annual standardized test of basic skills for the last three years. Eastside is in a middle-income area of the city and has an enrollment of about 2000 students.

Roberta Chu has been teaching English at Eastside for eight years. Roberta takes what she calls a critical approach to teaching—that is, she wants her students to learn the important role they can play in improving the world. To raise her students' level of awareness, Roberta has her students consider the role that race, socioeconomic status, and gender play in political events and in societal inequities. From time to time, Roberta organizes her students to take action to address social problems. Last week, for example, as part of a unit on homeless people in the city, her students spent a weekend helping at a neighborhood soup kitchen.

In the classroom, Roberta uses creative, occasionally risk-taking strategies. Students often participate in small group projects, simulations, role-plays, and classroom debates on societal issues.

Many of Roberta's colleagues are skeptical about her methods. They believe her teaching is too political and that she does her students a disservice by making them believe they can change the world. These teachers also point out that Eastside parents want their children to learn the traditional basics rather than learn how to become social activists.

Today in the teachers' lunchroom, Roberta and two other English teachers are discussing how they teach writing. "My kids really got involved in the unit on homeless people," Roberta says. "Now they're working hard to express in writing what they experienced last week at the soup kitchen. They believe they have something to say. Two of my kids even plan to send their papers to the editorial page of the newspaper."

"Well, I think that's pretty unrealistic," says the teacher seated across the table from Roberta. "That's not what our kids need to be doing—firing off letters to the editor, getting involved in all of these causes. We should just be teaching them how to write—period. Then if they want to focus on eliminating poverty, crime, or whatever, that should be their decision."

Do you agree or disagree with Roberta's approach to teaching? What do you think the purposes of education ought to be?

As the above scenario suggests, all teachers must answer several vital questions about their work. What should the purpose(s) of education be? What is the nature of knowledge? Are students inherently good or evil—or somewhere in between? What is teaching? What knowledge is of most worth? How should learning be evaluated? To find answers to these and similar questions, teachers must make use of philosophy. "All serious discussion of educational problems, no matter how specific, soon leads to consideration of educational *aims*, and becomes a conversation about the good life, the nature of man, the varieties of experience. . . . These are the perennial themes of philosophical investigation."[1]

WHAT IS THE NATURE OF PHILOSOPHY?

Philosophy is concerned with identifying the basic truths about being, knowledge, and conduct. Although the religions of the world arrive at these truths based on supernatural revelations, philosophers use their reasoning powers to search out answers to the fundamental questions of life. Philosophers use a careful, step-by-step, question-and-answer technique to extend their understanding of the world. Through exacting use of language and techniques of linguistic and conceptual analysis, philosophers try to describe the world we live in.

The word *philosophy* may be literally translated from the original Greek as "love of wisdom." In particular, a philosophy is a set of ideas formulated to comprehend the world. Among the world's great philosophers have been Socrates, Plato, Aristotle, St. Thomas Aquinas, René Descartes, John Locke, David Hume, Jean-Jacques Rousseau, Immanuel Kant, Georg Hegel, John Stuart Mill, Karl Marx, John Dewey, Jean-Paul Sartre, and Mortimer Adler. They devoted their lives to pondering the significant questions of life: What is truth? What is reality? What life is worth living?

WHY IS PHILOSOPHY IMPORTANT TO TEACHERS?

For the teacher, philosophy can reveal principles that may be used as a guide for professional action. Every teacher, whether he or she recognizes it, has a philosophy of education—a set of beliefs about how human beings learn and grow and what one should learn in order to live the good life. Teachers differ, of course, in regard to the amount of effort they devote to the development of their personal philosophy or educational platform. Some feel that philosophical reflections have nothing to contribute to the actual act of teaching (this stance, of course, is itself a philosophy of education). Other teachers recognize that teaching, because it is concerned with *what ought to be*, is basically a philosophical enterprise. As the great educational philosopher John Dewey put it, to be concerned with education is to be concerned with philosophy: "If we are willing to conceive education as the process of forming fundamental dispositions, intellectual and emotional, toward nature and fellow men, philosophy may even be defined as *the general theory of education.*"[2]

Philosophy is also important to schools. Most schools have a statement of philosophy that serves to focus the efforts of teachers, administrators, students, and

parents in a desired direction. A school's philosophy is actually a public statement of what a school values, a description of the educational goals it seeks to attain. So important is a school's philosophy that provinces and districts evaluate schools partially on the basis of whether they achieve the goals set forth in their statements of philosophy.

WHAT DETERMINES YOUR EDUCATIONAL PHILOSOPHY?

In simplest terms, your **educational philosophy** consists of what you believe about education. It includes "the assumptions, theories, and beliefs one holds for key aspects of effective teaching, such as the purpose of schooling, perceptions of students, what knowledge is of most worth, and the value of certain teaching techniques and pedagogical principles."[3] Educational philosophy is also vitally concerned with improving all aspects of teaching. By putting into practice their educational philosophy, teachers can discover the solutions to many educational problems. Five purposes that have been identified for educational philosophy clarify how it can contribute to these solutions:

1. Educational philosophy is committed to laying down a plan for what is considered to be the best education absolutely.
2. Educational philosophy undertakes to give directions with respect to the kind of education that is best in a certain political, social, and economic context.
3. Educational philosophy is preoccupied with correcting violations of educational principle and policy.
4. Educational philosophy centers attention on those issues in educational policy and practice that require resolution either by empirical research or rational reexamination.

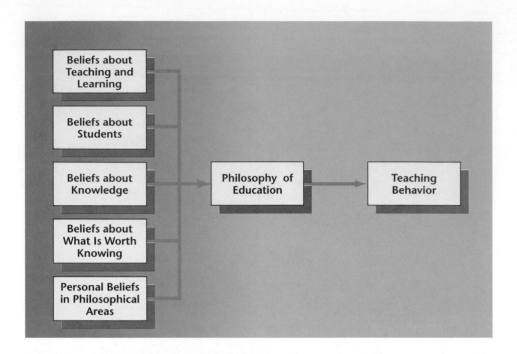

5. Educational philosophy conducts an inquiry into the whole of the educational enterprise with a view toward assessing, justifying, and reforming the body of experience essential to superior learning.[4]

There is a strong connection between your behavior as a teacher and your beliefs about teaching and learning, students, knowledge, and what is worth knowing (see Figure 8.1). Regardless of where you stand in regard to these four dimensions of teaching, you should be aware of the need to reflect continually on *what* you do believe and *why* you believe it.

BELIEFS ABOUT TEACHING AND LEARNING

One of the most important components of your educational philosophy is how you view teaching and learning. In other words, what is the teacher's primary role? Is the teacher a subject matter expert who can efficiently and effectively impart knowledge to students? Is the teacher a helpful adult who establishes caring relationships with students and nurtures their growth in needed areas? Or is the teacher a skilled technician who can manage the learning of many students at once?

How each of us views the role of the teacher says a lot about our basic conception of teaching. Some people view teaching as a science—a complex activity that is, nevertheless, reducible to a specified set of discrete, objectively determined behaviors. For others, teaching is viewed as an art—a spontaneous, unrehearsed, and creative encounter between teacher and student. And for others, still, teaching is an activity that is both science and art; it requires the artistic (or intuitive) implementation of scientifically determined procedures.

In regard to learning, some teachers emphasize the individual student's experiences and cognitions; others stress the student's behavior. Learning, according to the first viewpoint, is seen as the changes in thoughts or actions that result from personal experience; learning is largely the result of internal forces within the individual. In contrast, the second view defines learning as the associations between various stimuli and responses; here, learning results from forces that are external to the individual.

BELIEFS ABOUT STUDENTS

Your beliefs about students will have a great influence on how you teach. Every teacher formulates an image in his or her mind about what students are like—their dispositions, skills, motivation levels, and expectations. What you believe students are like is based on your unique life experiences, particularly your observations of young people and your knowledge of human growth and development.

Negative views of students may promote teacher-student relationships based on fear and coercion rather than trust and helpfulness. Opposite views may risk not providing students with sufficient structure and direction and not communicating sufficiently high expectations. In the final analysis, the truly professional teacher—the one who has a carefully thought-out educational philosophy—recognizes that children differ in regard to their predisposition to learn and grow. In regard to their beliefs about students, it is important that teachers convey positive attitudes toward their students and a belief that they *can* learn. To assess your beliefs about students, compare your expectations about teaching with those of 1002 American teachers who began teaching in the fall of 1990 (see Table 8.1). The data in Table 8.1 indicate that 99 percent of the beginning teachers who responded to this survey believed that "all children can learn."

TABLE 8.1   NEW TEACHERS' EXPECTATIONS OF THEMSELVES AND THEIR STUDENTS (PERCENTAGES)

	Strongly Agree	Somewhat Agree	Somewhat Disagree	Disagree Strongly	Not Sure	Total Agree	Total Disagree
All children can learn	93	6	*	*	*	99	1
I can really make a difference in the lives of my students	83	16	1	*	*	99	1
If I do my job well, my students will benefit regardless of how the rest of the school functions	42	47	13	1	*	89	14
Many children come to school with so many problems that it's very difficult for them to be good students	28	47	18	6	—	75	24
Even the best teachers will find it difficult to really teach more than two thirds of their students	8	38	39	15	1	44	54

*Less than 0.5%
Source: Louis Harris and Associates. *The Metropolitan Life Survey of the American Teacher 1990: New Teachers: Expectations and Ideals, Part I: Entering the Classroom* (New York: Louis Harris and Associates, 1990), p. 1. Used with permission.

BELIEFS ABOUT KNOWLEDGE

Though it may not seem immediately obvious, how a teacher views knowledge is directly related to how he or she goes about teaching. If knowledge is viewed as the sum total of small bits of subject matter or discrete facts, students will most likely spend a great deal of time learning that information in a straightforward, rote manner. As students, we have all, at one time or another, been directed to memorize certain information: the capitals of the provinces, definitions for the eight parts of speech, the exact contents of the periodic table in chemistry, and so on.

Other teachers view knowledge more conceptually, that is, as consisting of the big ideas that enable us to understand and influence our environment. Such a teacher would want students to be able to explain how decisions are made in legislatures, how an understanding of the eight parts of speech can empower the writer and vitalize one's writing, and how chemical elements are grouped according to their atomic numbers.

Finally, teachers differ in regard to whether they consider students' increased understanding of their own experiences a legitimate form of knowledge. Knowledge of self and one's experiences in the world is clearly not the same as knowledge about a particular subject, yet such knowledge is essential if one is to live a full, satisfying life. Teachers who primarily view knowledge as that which enables the individual to confront and interpret the meaning of experience will present students with opportunities to develop that ability. Thus, students would be required to reflect on how they might use the disciplines of social studies, English grammar, or chemistry to further their understanding of the world.

BELIEFS ABOUT WHAT IS WORTH KNOWING

It is obvious that teachers want students to learn as a result of their efforts, though teachers differ in regard to what they believe should be taught. Teacher A feels that it is most important that students learn the basic skills of reading, writing, computation, and oral communication. These are the skills they will need to be successful in their chosen occupations, and it is the school's responsibility to prepare students for the world of work. Teacher B believes that the most worthwhile content is to be found in the classics or the Great Books. Through mastering the great ideas from the sciences, mathematics, literature, and history, students will be well prepared to deal with the world of the future. Teacher C is most concerned with students learning how to reason, communicate effectively, and solve problems. Students who master these cognitive processes will have learned how to learn, and this is the most realistic preparation for an unknown future. Teacher D is concerned with developing the whole child, teaching students to become self-actualizing persons. Thus, the content of the curriculum should be meaningful to the student; it should contribute as much as possible to the student's efforts to become a mature, well-integrated person.

As Roberta and her colleagues illustrated in this chapter's opening scenario, there are no easy answers to the question "What knowledge is of most worth?" The following Professional Reflection feature is designed to help you begin the process of clarifying what you believe the purpose(s) of education should be.

Your beliefs about teaching and learning, students, knowledge, and what knowledge is worth knowing are the foundation of your educational philosophy. These beliefs will guide your practice as a professional teacher.

PROFESSIONAL REFLECTION

After studying the following list, cross out the ten educational purposes that you regard as least important. Then rank the remaining ten items in the order of their importance to you by numbering them from 1 to 10 from the most to the least important. To learn where you stand among the six philosophical orientations to teaching that are discussed later in this chapter, compare your results with the key at the end of the chapter on page 201.

a. Practical preparation for life and work
b. The fostering of curiosity and creativity
c. The teaching of cognitive and critical thinking skills
d. Self-actualization of the whole person
e. The teaching of basic communication skills
f. Behavior modification
g. Moral education
h. Exposure to great ideas and enduring truths
i. Preparation for whatever the future holds
j. The search for truth
k. The teaching of problem-solving skills
l. Exposure to great works in the humanities
m. The fostering of positive values and citizenship
n. The mastery of facts and scientific information
o. Transmission of a common core of knowledge
p. Cultivation of the intellect
q. The development of rational, well-rounded individuals
r. The search for personal meaning
s. Values clarification
t. The global improvement of the quality of life

WHAT ARE THE SIX BRANCHES OF PHILOSOPHY?

To provide you with further tools to use in formulating and clarifying your educational philosophy, this section presents brief overviews of six areas of philosophy of central concern to teachers: metaphysics, epistemology, axiology, ethics, aesthetics, and logic. Each area focuses on one of the questions that have concerned philosophers for centuries: What is the nature of reality? What is the nature of knowledge and is truth ever attainable? According to what values should one live life? What is good and what is evil? What is the nature of beauty? And finally, what processes of reasoning will yield consistently valid results?

METAPHYSICS

Metaphysics is concerned with explaining, as rationally and as comprehensively as possible, the nature of reality (in contrast to how reality appears). What is reality?

EDUCATION IN THE NEWS

Professional Colleges for Teachers

What is a professional college for teachers? The British Columbia College of Teachers, established in 1988, is the only one so far in Canada. It oversees all teacher training programs offered in the province. It addresses applications for teaching certificates, disciplines members, and can cancel certificates, suspend teachers, or issue letters of reprimand. Since 1988, it has cancelled 45 teaching certificates, suspended 16 teachers, and issued seven letters of reprimand.

The members of the BC College of Teachers include teachers, administrators, and other staff of both public and private schools. It reassesses the competence of teachers who have stopped teaching for a period of time and who want to return to teaching. Although it is mandated to determine competency and skill levels of practicing teachers, it has chosen not to exercise this part of its mandate.

The Royal Commission on Learning in Ontario has recommended creating an Ontario College of Teachers based on the BC model but this recommendation has faced strong opposition from the teachers' unions. The proposed college will be a self-regulating body which will provide greater control over the preparation of those entering the profession. As well, it will provide a place of recourse for parents and students who believe they have been treated unprofessionally or unethically by a teacher and will establish a greater level of confidentiality in teacher-student relationships. Unlike the BC College, the proposed Ontario college will accredit all university programs in education and teachers will be required to apply for recertification every five years. To be recertified, they will submit a portfolio of experience. Currently, other provinces, including Newfoundland and Alberta are considering requiring recertification. Do you think recertification will be a valuable process for teachers? Will it ultimately benefit students?

Source: Based on the *Globe and Mail,* Feb. 14, Mar. 6, 7, 1995.

What is the world made of? These are metaphysical questions. Metaphysics is sometimes used interchangeably with ontology, which derives from the Latin term *onto* (to be) and *ology* (the study of). Ontology is concerned with the nature of being and explores questions such as, What does it mean to exist? What is humankind's place in the scheme of things?

Because anything that is real must exist and anything that exists must be real, we will not make the fine distinctions between metaphysics and ontology that some philosophers do. What we wish to stress, however, is that such metaphysical questions are at the heart of educational philosophy. As one educational philosopher put it, "Nothing short of the fullest awareness possible of 'man's place in the cosmos' is the constant problem of the philosopher of education."[5] Or, as others have said, "Our ultimate preoccupation in educational theory is with the most primary of all philosophic problems: metaphysics, the study of ultimate reality."[6]

Metaphysics has important implications for education because the school curriculum is based on what we know about reality. And what we know about reality is driven by the kinds of questions we ask about the world. In fact, any position regarding what the schools should teach has behind it a particular view of reality, a particular set of responses to metaphysical questions.

Even though definitive answers to metaphysical questions are ultimately beyond human intelligence, teachers do convey, implicitly as well as explicitly, their views of reality to students. It is important, then, that you give serious consideration to the major metaphysical questions that confront all humankind: What is the meaning of life? Do events in the universe occur randomly or according to a purpose? Is our behavior determined or the result of our free will?

EPISTEMOLOGY

The next major set of philosophical questions that concerns teachers is called **epistemology**. These questions all focus on knowledge: What knowledge is true? How does knowing take place? How do we know that we know? How do we decide between opposing views of knowledge? Is truth constant or does it change from situation to situation? What knowledge is of most worth?

Epistemology is of central concern to teachers because a school's main task is to present knowledge of the world to students. Schools, first of all, must be confident that the knowledge presented to students is true and, second, the school must understand as much as possible how it is that students come to know.

How you answer the epistemological questions that confront all teachers will have significant implications for your approach to curriculum and instruction. First, you will need to determine what is true about the content you will teach, then you must decide on the most appropriate means of conveying this content to students. Even a casual consideration of epistemological questions reveals that there are many ways of knowing about the world. We believe that there are at least five different ways of knowing that are of interest to teachers.

1. *Knowing based on authority:* People acquire knowledge from the sage, the poet, the religious leader, or the ruler. In schools, the textbook, the teacher, the administrator are the sources of authority for students. In everyday conversations, we refer to unnamed experts as sources of authoritative knowledge: *They* say we'll have a virtual reality school by the turn of the century.
2. *Knowing based on divine revelation:* Throughout human history, supernatural revelations have been a major source of knowledge about the world. Whether it be a sun god, the many gods of the ancient Greeks, or the Judeo-Christian god, divine revelations have provided humans with knowledge about life.
3. *Knowing based on empiricism (experience):* The term *empirical* refers to knowledge acquired through the senses. When we state that experience is the best teacher, we refer to this mode of knowing. Informally gathered empirical data direct most of our daily behavior.
4. *Knowing based on reason:* We can also come to know things as a result of our ability to reason and use logical analysis. In schools, students learn to apply rational thought to such tasks as solving mathematical problems, distinguishing facts from opinions, or defending or refuting a particular argument. Many students also learn a method of reasoning and analyzing empirical data known as the scientific method. Through this method a problem is identified, relevant data are gathered, a hypothesis is formulated based on these data, and the hypothesis is empirically tested.
5. *Knowing based on intuition:* Just about everyone has at some time acquired knowledge through intuition, a nondiscursive (beyond reason) form of knowing. Intuition draws from our prior knowledge and experience and gives us an immediate understanding of the situation at hand. Our intuition convinces us that we know something, but we don't know how we know. Our intuitive sense would seem to be a mixture of instinct, emotion, and imagination.

AXIOLOGY

The next set of philosophical problems concerns values. What values should teachers encourage students to adopt? What values raise humanity to its highest levels of humanness? What values does a truly educated person hold? These are a few of the axiological questions that teachers must answer for themselves.

In essence, **axiology** highlights the fact that the teacher has an interest not only in the *quantity* of knowledge that students acquire but also in the *quality* of life that becomes possible because of that knowledge. Extensive knowledge of the basic skills, the Great Books of the Western World, or trigonometry, for example, may not benefit the individual if he or she is unable to put that knowledge to use. This idea, of course, raises additional questions: How do we define quality of life? What curricular experiences contribute most to that quality of life? All teachers must deal with the issues raised by these questions.

Ethics   The term **ethics** is sometimes used interchangeably with axiology. Although axiology addresses the question "What is valuable?" ethics focuses on "What is good and evil, right and wrong?"

A knowledge of ethics can help the teacher solve many of the dilemmas that arise in the classroom. Frequently, teachers must take action in situations in which they are unable to gather all of the relevant facts and where no single course of action is totally right or wrong. For example, a student whose previous work was above average is known—by the teacher and several classmates—to have plagiarized a term paper: Should the teacher fail the student for the course if the example of swift, decisive punishment will likely prevent other students from plagiarizing? Or should the teacher, following her hunch about what would be in the student's long-term interest, have the student redo the term paper and risk the possibility that other students might get the mistaken notion that plagiarism has no negative consequences? Another ethical dilemma: Is an elementary mathematics teacher justified in trying to increase achievement for the whole class by separating two disruptive girls and placing one in a mathematics group beneath her level?

Ethics can provide the teacher with ways of thinking about problems where it is difficult to determine the right course of action. This branch of philosophy also helps the teacher to understand that "ethical thinking and decision making are not just following the rules."[7]

Aesthetics   The branch of axiology known as **aesthetics** is concerned with values related to beauty and art. Although we expect that teachers of music, art, drama, literature, and writing regularly have students make judgments about the quality of works of art, we can easily overlook the role that aesthetics ought to play in *all* areas of the curriculum. Harry Broudy, a well-known educational philosopher, said that the arts are necessary, not "just nice."[8] Through the heightening of their aesthetic perceptions, students can find increased meaning to all aspects of life.

Aesthetics can also help the teacher increase his or her effectiveness. Teaching, because it may be viewed as a form of artistic expression, can be judged according to artistic standards of beauty and quality.[9] In this regard, the teacher is an artist and continually tries to improve the quality of his or her work.

LOGIC

If all the parties who have a genuine interest in education were to decide on a single goal that schools ought to strive for, it would most likely be to teach students how to think. Our extensive ability for various kinds of thinking is, after all, one of the major differences between us and other forms of animal life. Even a casual reflection on the great advances of civilization during the last several centuries reveals that such progress has been the result of our ability to think with ever-increasing degrees of clarity, insight, and creativity. **Logic** is the area of philosophy that deals with the process of reasoning and identifies rules that will enable the thinker to reach valid conclusions.

One hallmark of the teacher as a professional is his or her familiarity with the processes of logical thinking. Such a teacher makes regular use of logical reasoning in four important ways. First, the teacher employs logic to present ideas to students in a sequential, well-organized manner. Students are made to feel the power of the teacher's reasoning ability as he or she transforms the subject matter in such a way that students learn more effectively. Second, the teacher employs logic as a tool for the problem solving and decision making that are part of the teacher's daily life in the classroom. Third, the teacher uses logic to provide feedback to students who use fallacious reasoning and therefore arrive at erroneous conclusions. Finally, the teacher uses logic to evaluate the validity of new methods, materials, and subject-matter content. In this regard, the teacher uses hypothetical thinking to explore the probable outcomes of new approaches.

The two kinds of logical thinking processes that teachers most frequently have students master are *deductive* and *inductive* thinking. The deductive approach requires the thinker to move from a general principle or proposition to a specific conclusion that is valid. Inductive reasoning, on the other hand, moves from the particular to the general. The student begins by examining particular examples that eventually lead to the acceptance of a general proposition. Inductive teaching is often referred to as discovery teaching—where students discover, or create, their own knowledge of a topic.

Perhaps the best-known teacher to use the inductive approach to teaching was the Greek philosopher Socrates. His method of teaching, known today as the Socratic method, consisted of holding philosophical conversations (dialectics) with his pupils. Socrates questioned his pupils in a manner that led them to see errors and inconsistencies in their thinking. By using an inductive approach, Socrates believed that the truth could be discovered. The legacy of Socrates lives on in all teachers who encourage students to think for themselves.

Socrates

The six areas of philosophy that we have examined briefly in the preceding pages—metaphysics, epistemology, axiology, ethics, aesthetics, and logic—represent the mental tools that teachers can use for thinking about various aspects of teaching.

WHAT ARE SIX PHILOSOPHICAL ORIENTATIONS TO TEACHING?

As we previously mentioned, there are no absolutely correct answers to the many difficult philosophical questions raised by metaphysics, epistemology, axiology,

ethics, aesthetics, and logic. There have been, however, six major coherent philosophical orientations to teaching that have been developed in response to the questions with which all teachers must grapple. These orientations, or schools of
thought, are perennialism, progressivism, essentialism, existentialism, behaviorism,
and reconstructionism (see Figure 8.2). A brief description of each orientation is
presented in the following sections. At the end of each description, we present a
sample portrait of a teacher whose behavior illustrates that philosophical orientation in action.

PERENNIALISM

Perennialism, as the term implies, views truth as constant, or perennial. The aim
of education, according to perennialist thinking, is to ensure that students acquire
knowledge of these unchanging principles or great ideas. Perennialists also believe
that the natural world and human nature have remained basically unchanged over
the centuries; thus, the great ideas continue to have the most potential for solving
the problems of any era. Furthermore, the perennialist philosophy emphasizes the
rational thinking abilities of human beings; it is the cultivation of the intellect that
makes human beings truly human and differentiates them from other animals.

The curriculum, according to the perennialists, should stress students' intellectual growth in the arts and sciences. Students should encounter in these areas
the best, most significant works that humans have created. In regard to any area
of the curriculum, only one question needs to be asked: Are students acquiring content that represents the human race's most lofty accomplishments in that area?
Thus, a high school English teacher would require students to read Melville's *Moby
Dick* or any of Shakespeare's plays rather than a novel on the current best-seller
list. Similarly, science students would learn about the three laws of motion or the
three laws of thermodynamics rather than build a model of the CN Tower.

Perennialist Educational Philosophers   Two of the best known advocates of the
perennialist philosophy have been Robert Maynard Hutchins and, more recently,
Mortimer Adler. As president of the University of Chicago, Hutchins developed an
undergraduate curriculum based on the study of the Great Books and discussions
of these classics in small seminars. Hutchins' perennialist curriculum was based on
three assumptions about education:[10]

*Robert Maynard
Hutchins*

FIGURE 8.2
**Six Philosophical Orien-
tations to Teaching**

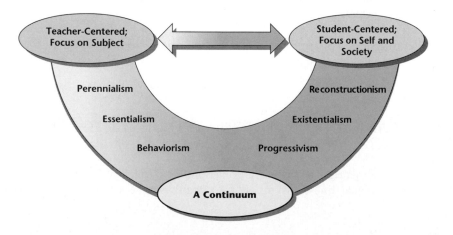

1. Education must promote humankind's continuing search for truth. Whatever is true will always, and everywhere, be true; in short, truth is universal and timeless.
2. Because the mind's work is intellectual and focuses on ideas, education must also focus on ideas. The cultivation of human rationality is the essential function of education.
3. Education should stimulate students to think thoughtfully about significant ideas. Teachers should use correct and critical thinking as their primary method, and they should require the same of students.

Noted educational philosopher Mortimer Adler, along with Hutchins, was instrumental in organizing the Great Books of the Western World curriculum. Through the study of over 100 enduring classics, from Plato to Einstein, the Great Books approach aims at the major perennialist goal of teaching students to become independent and critical thinkers. It is a demanding curriculum, and it focuses on the enduring disciplines of knowledge rather than on current events or student interests.

One of the most influential recent works in support of perennialism is Adler's *Paideia Proposal,* released in 1982. Adler's approach stresses the humanities and literature and reiterates Hutchins' idea that "the best education for the best is the best education for all."

Portrait of a Perennialist Teacher   Hannah Bernstein, a woman in her late fifties, has been teaching high school English since the mid-1960s. Among both students and teachers, she has a reputation for demanding a lot. As one student put it, "You don't waste time in Ms. Bernstein's classes."

During the 1960s, she had a difficult time dealing with students who aggressively insisted on being taught subjects that were "relevant." As a graduate of

Perennialist teachers often inspire students to seek truth, discover universalities in human experience, and celebrate human achievements. How might this lesson reflect perennialist ideas?

McGill University where she received a general arts and science education, Hannah refused to lessen the emphasis in her classes on great works of literature that she felt students needed to know, such as Beowolf, Chaucer, Dickens, and Shakespeare.

Now that the permissive, personally relevant approaches of the sixties and seventies have waned, Hannah feels less conflict related to her job. Most of her students appreciate the fact that she has high expectations of them and pushes them to think critically. She is proud of the number of her students who have gone on to university. She is especially pleased when former students return to thank her for giving them a solid foundation in English language and literature.

As far as her approach to classroom management is concerned, one student sums it up this way: "She doesn't let you get by with a thing; she never slacks off on the pressure. She lets you know that she's there to teach and you're there to learn." Hannah believes that hard work and effort are necessary if one is to get a good education. As a result, she gives students very few opportunities to misbehave, and she appears to be immune to the grumblings of students who do complain openly about the workload.

She becomes very animated when she talks about the value of the classics to students who are preparing to live as adults in the twenty-first century:

> The classics are unequaled in terms of the insights they can give students into the major problems that they will have to deal with during their lifetimes. Though our civilization has made impressive technological advances during the last two centuries, we have not really progressed that much in terms of improving the quality of our lives as human beings. The observations of a Shakespeare or a Dickens on the human condition are just as relevant today as they were when they were alive.

Hannah welcomed the public pressures to reform education in the early 1980s that called for a renewed commitment to excellence in education. In her words,

> The greatest challenge that teachers face today is to restore standards of excellence and quality to the curriculum. As educators, we need to teach students what we know they need to know—not what they want to know. Students might object today if we don't give them what they want, but tomorrow they'll thank us for giving them a good, solid education—one that is well grounded in the arts and sciences.

PROGRESSIVISM

Progressivism differs in many significant respects from perennialism. The greatest difference is that progressive education begins with the child rather than with the subject matter. John Dewey's writings in the 1920s and 1930s contributed a great deal to the spread of progressive ideas. Briefly, Deweyian progressivism is based on the following six assumptions:

1. The content of the curriculum ought to be derived from students' interests rather than from the academic disciplines.
2. Effective teaching takes into account the whole child, and his or her interests and needs in regard to cognitive, affective, and psychomotor areas.
3. Learning is essentially active rather than passive; effective teachers provide students with experiences that enable them to learn by doing.
4. The aim of education is to teach students to think rationally so that they may become intelligent, contributing members of society.
5. At school, students learn personal as well as social values.

6. Humankind is in a constant state of change, and education makes possible a future that is better than the past.

Progressive Strategies   The progressive philosophy also contends that knowledge that is true in the present may not be true in the future. Hence, the best way to prepare students for an unknown future is to equip them with problem-solving strategies that will enable them to cope with new challenges in life and to discover what truths are relevant to the present. Through continual self-analysis and reflection, the individual can identify values that are appropriate for the immediate moment.

Progressives feel that life is evolving in a positive direction and that human beings, young as well as adult, are good and may be trusted to act in their own best interests. Educators with a progressive orientation give students a considerable amount of freedom in determining their school experiences. Contrary to the perceptions of many, though, progressive education does not mean that teachers do not provide structure or that students are free to do whatever they wish. Progressive teachers begin with where students are and, through the daily give-and-take of the classroom, lead students to see that the subject they are learning can enhance their lives.

The teacher's role in a progressively oriented classroom is to serve as a guide or resource person whose primary responsibility is to facilitate student learning. The teacher is concerned with helping students learn what is important to them rather than passing on a set of so-called enduring truths. Toward this end, the progressive teacher tries to provide students with experiences that replicate everyday life as much as possible. Students are given many opportunities to work cooperatively in groups, often solving problems the group, not the teacher, has identified as important.

Portrait of a Progressive Teacher   Alan Barkan teaches high school social studies in a well-to-do part of the city. In his mid-thirties, Alan usually works in casual attire—khaki pants, soft-soled shoes, and a sports shirt. He seems to get along well with students. Alan likes to give students as much freedom of choice in the classroom as possible. His room is divided up into interest and activity centers, and much of the time students are free to choose where they want to spend their time. One corner at the back of the room has a collection of books, an easy chair, and an area rug; the other back corner is set up as a project area and has a worktable on which sit several globes, maps, large sheets of newsprint, and assorted drawing materials. At the front of the room in one corner is a small media center with three cassette tape recorders with headphones and a slide-viewing machine about the size of a small portable television.

Alan makes it a point to establish warm, supportive relationships with his students. He is proud of the fact that he is a friend to his students. "I really like the kids I teach," he says in a soft, gentle voice. "They're basically good kids and they really want to learn if we—teachers, I mean—can just keep their curiosity alive and not try to force them to learn. It's up to us as teachers to capitalize on their interests."

The visitor to Alan's class today can sense his obvious regard for students. He is genuinely concerned about the growth and nurturance of each one. As his students spend most of their time working in small groups at the various activity centers in the room, Alan divides his time among the groups. He moves from group to group and seems to immerse himself, as an equal participant, in each group's

These children are active learners as whole people in a real or relevant context, and they are constructing their own meanings through direct experience. How might this lesson be seen as combining progressive and existential ideals?

task. One group, for example, has been working this term on making a papier-mâché globe. Right now, several students are animatedly explaining to him how they plan to transfer the flat map of the world they have drawn to the surprisingly smooth sphere they have fashioned out of the papier-mâché. Alan listens carefully to what his students have to say and then congratulates the group on how cleverly they have engineered the project. When he speaks to his students he does so in a matter-of-fact, conversational tone, as though speaking to other adults.

Although Alan uses the approved social studies textbook, he makes it a point to go beyond the text and help students to identify problems that they can get excited about and involved in. During a recent unit on world hunger, for example, one group of students presented to the class its findings on local provisions to feed the hungry. Another group looked at population trends in the province during the last hundred years and then, based on its findings, wrote a skit on what life would be like in their city during the year 2020.

As much as possible he likes to bring textbook knowledge to life by providing his students with appropriate experiences—field trips, small-group projects, simulation activities, role-playing, and so on. Alan believes that his primary function as a teacher is to prepare his students for an unknown future. Learning to solve problems at an early age is the best preparation for this future, he feels.

The increase in the amount of knowledge each decade is absolutely astounding. What we teach students as true today will most likely not be true tomorrow. Students have to learn how to learn and become active problem solvers. In addition, students need to learn how to identify problems that are meaningful to them. It doesn't make much sense to learn to solve problems that belong to someone else.

To accomplish these things in the classroom, teachers have to be willing to take the lead from the students themselves—to use their lives as a point of departure for learning about the subject. What this requires of the teacher is that he or she be willing to set up the classroom along the lines of a democracy, a close community of learners whose major purpose for being there is to learn. You can't create that kind of classroom atmosphere by being a taskmaster and trying to force kids to learn. If you can trust them and let them set their own directions, they'll respond.

ESSENTIALISM

William C. Bagley

Essentialism is a conservative philosophy of education that was originally formulated as a response to progressive trends in schools. William C. Bagley (1874–1946), a professor of education at Teachers College, Columbia University, was the founder of the Essentialistic Education Society. To promote the essentialist philosophy, he founded the educational journal, *School and Society*.

Bagley and several other like-minded educators had become very critical of progressive educational practices in the United States, contending that the movement had damaged intellectual and moral standards among young people.[11] Following the Second World War, criticism of progressive education became even more widespread and seemed to point to one conclusion: Schools were failing in their task of transmitting the country's social and intellectual heritage.

Essentialism, which has some similarities to perennialism, holds that our culture has a core of common knowledge that the schools are obligated to transmit to students in a systematic, disciplined way. Unlike perennialism, which emphasizes a set of external truths, essentialism stresses what advocates believe to be the essential knowledge and skills that productive members of our society need to know. Several books have been written that lament the decline of rigorous schooling in the United States and call for an essentialist approach to schooling. Among them have been James D. Koerner's *The Case for Basic Education* (1959), H. G. Rickover's *Education and Freedom* (1959), Paul Copperman's *The Literacy Hoax: The Decline of Reading, Writing, and Learning in the Public Schools and What We Can Do about It* (1978), and John W. Friesen, *Reforming the Schools—for Teachers*.

According to essentialist philosophy, schooling should be practical and provide children with sound instruction that prepares them to live life; schools should not try to influence or set social policies. Critics of essentialism, however, charge that such a tradition-bound orientation to schooling will indoctrinate students and rule out the possibility of change. Essentialists respond that, without an essentialist approach, students will be indoctrinated in humanistic and/or behavioral curricula that run counter to society's accepted standards and need for order.

The Back-to-Basics Movement   The back-to-basics movement that began in the mid-seventies is the most recent large-scale push to install essentialist programs in the schools. Above all else, the essentialists contend, the schools must train students to communicate clearly and logically. The core skills in the curriculum should be reading, writing, and speaking, and the school has the responsibility for seeing that all students master these skills.

Essentialists are critical of many innovations in the schools, citing them as examples of pedagogy gone soft, a trend, they claim, that has led to a lowering of standards and a dramatic decline in achievement. What schools need to do, according to essentialist thinking, is get rid of fads and frills in the schools and restore sound, traditional teaching to the classroom. Schools should also provide special programs for talented youth whose needs are not met by curricula that have been reduced to a level of common mediocrity.

The essentialist curriculum emphasizes the teaching of facts; it has little patience with the indirect, introspective approaches promoted by progressivism. Some essentialists even view the arts and humanities as frills and feel that the hard sciences and technical and vocational courses are the true essentials that students need in order to contribute to society.

Though the essentialist educator does not view the child as evil, neither does he or she view the child as naturally good. Unless children are actively and vigorously taught the value of discipline, hard work, and respect for authority, they will not become valuable members of society. The teacher's role, then, is to shape children, to hold their natural, nonproductive instincts (e.g., aggression, mindless gratification of the senses, etc.) in check until their education has been completed.

Portrait of an Essentialist Teacher   Reg Samuels teaches mathematics at a junior high school in a poor section of a major city. Before coming to this school six years ago, he taught at a rural elementary school.

Middle-aged and highly energetic, Reg is known around the school as a hardworking, dedicated teacher. His commitment to children is especially evident when he talks about preparing "his" children for life in high school and beyond. "A lot of teachers nowadays have given up on kids," he says with a touch of sadness. "They don't demand much of them. If we don't push kids now to get the knowledge and skills they're going to need later in life, we've failed them. My main purpose here is to see that my kids get the basics they're going to need."

Reg has made it known that he does not approve of the methods used by some of the younger, more humanistically oriented teachers in the school. At a recent staff meeting, for example, he was openly critical of some teachers' tendency to let students do their own thing and spend time expressing their feelings. He called for all teachers to focus their energies on getting students to master subject-matter content, "the things kids will need to know," rather than on helping students adjust to the interpersonal aspects of school life. He also reminded everyone that "kids come to school to learn." All students would learn, he pointed out, if "teachers based their methods on good, sound approaches that have always worked—not on the so-called innovative approaches that are based on fads and frills."

Reg's students have accepted his no-nonsense approach to teaching. With few exceptions, his classes are orderly, business-like operations. Each class period follows a standard routine. Students enter the room quietly and take their seats with a minimum of the foolishness and horseplay that mark the start of many other classes in the school. As the first order of business, the previous day's homework is returned and reviewed. Following this, Reg presents the day's lesson, usually a fifteen- to twenty-minute explanation of how to solve a particular kind of math problem. His mini-lectures are lively, and his wide-ranging tone of voice and animated, spontaneous delivery convey his excitement about the material and his belief that students can learn. During large-group instruction, Reg also makes ample use of the blackboard, overhead transparencies, and various manipulatives such as a large abacus and colored blocks of different sizes and shapes.

Following the presentation of the day's new material, Reg has students work through several practice problems. At this time, he has four to five students work their practice problems at the board. Using the work that students have displayed on the board, Reg comments on the correct procedures to be followed. During the final fifteen minutes or so of class, students begin to work on their homework assignment, usually a set of problems in the textbook or on a dittoed worksheet. As students work at their desks, the room takes on an atmosphere of subdued yet earnest industriousness. Without exception, all students address themselves to the task at hand. Reg moves about the room, stopping here and there to check on a student's work or to answer a question.

EXISTENTIALISM

Jean-Paul Sartre

Existential philosophy is unique in that it focuses on the experiences of the individual. Other philosophies are concerned with developing systems of thought for identifying and understanding what is common to *all* reality, human existence, and values. **Existentialism**, on the other hand, offers the individual a way of thinking about *my* life, what has meaning for *me*, what is true for *me*. In general, existentialism emphasizes creative choice, the subjectivity of human experiences, and concrete acts of human existence over any rational scheme for human nature or reality.

The writings of Jean-Paul Sartre (1905–1980), well-known French philosopher, novelist, and playwright, have been most responsible for the widespread dissemination of existential ideas. According to Sartre, every individual first exists and then he or she must decide what that existence is to mean. The task of assigning meaning to that existence is the individual's alone; no preformulated belief system of philosophy can tell one who one is. It is up to each of us to decide who we are. According to Sartre, "Existence precedes essence. . . . First of all, man exists, turns up, appears on the scene, and, only afterwards, defines himself."[12]

Two Existentialist Views   There are two schools of existential thought—one *theistic*, the other *atheistic*. Most of those belonging to the first school refer to themselves as Christian Existentialists and point out that humankind has a longing for an ultimate being, for God. Though this longing does not prove the existence of God, people can freely choose to live their lives as if there is a God.[13] The Spanish philosopher Miguel de Unamuno expresses this position well: "Let life be lived in such a way, with such dedication to goodness and the highest values, that if, after all, it is annihilation which finally awaits us, that will be an injustice."[14]

Most existentialists, however, point out that it is demeaning to the human condition to say that we must entertain a fantasy in order to live a life of moral responsibility. Such a stance absolves humans of the responsibility for dealing with the complete freedom of choice that we all have. It also causes them to avoid the inescapable fact that "we are alone, with no excuses," and that "we are condemned to be free."[15]

Life, according to existential thought, has no meaning, and the universe is indifferent to the situation humankind finds itself in. With the freedom that we have, however, each of us must commit ourselves to assign meaning to *our* life. The human enterprise that can be most helpful in promoting this personal quest for meaning is the educative process. Teachers, therefore, must allow students freedom of choice and provide them with experiences that will help them find the meaning of their lives. This approach, contrary to the belief of many, does not mean that students may do whatever they please; logic indicates that freedom has rules, and respect for the freedom of others is essential.

Existentialists judge the curriculum according to whether or not it contributes to the individual's quest for meaning. The ideal curriculum is one that provides students with extensive individual freedom and requires them to ask their own questions, conduct their own inquiries, and draw their own conclusions.

Portrait of an Existentialist Teacher   Right after he first started teaching English eight years ago at a suburban high school, Fred Gianelli began to have doubts about the value of what he was teaching students. Although he could see a limited, practical use for the knowledge and skills he was teaching, he felt he was doing little to help his students answer the most pressing questions of their lives. Also, Fred had to admit to himself that he had grown somewhat bored with following the narrow, unimaginative curriculum guides.

During the next eight years Fred gradually developed a style of teaching that placed emphasis on students finding out who they are. He continued to teach the knowledge and skills he was required to teach, but he made it clear that what students learned from him they should use to answer questions that were important to them. Now, for example, he often gives writing assignments that encourage students to look within in order to develop greater self-knowledge. He often uses assigned literature as a springboard for values clarification discussions. And, whenever possible, he gives his students the freedom to pursue individual reading and writing projects. His only requirement is that students be meaningfully involved in whatever they do.

Fred is also keenly aware of how the questions his students are just beginning to grapple with are questions that he is still, even in his mid-thirties, trying to answer for himself. Thoughtfully and with obvious care for selecting the correct words, he sums up the goals that he has for his students:

> I think kids should realize that the really important questions in life are beyond definitive answers, and they should be very suspicious of anyone—teacher, philosopher, or member of organized religion—who purports to have the answers. As human beings, each of us faces the central task of finding *our own* answers to such questions. My students know that I'm wrestling with the same questions they're working on. But I think I've taught them well enough so that they know that my answers can't be their answers.

Fred's approach to teaching is perhaps summed up by the bumper sticker on his car: "Question authority." Unlike many of his fellow teachers, he wants his students to react critically and skeptically to what he teaches them. He also presses them to think thoughtfully and courageously about the meaning of life, beauty, love, and death. He judges his effectiveness by the extent to which students are able and willing to become more aware of the choices that are open to them.

BEHAVIORISM

Behaviorism is based on the principle that desirable human behavior can be the product of design, rather than accident. According to behaviorists, it is an illusion to say that humans have a free will. Although we may act as if we are free, our behavior is really *determined* by forces in the environment that shape our behavior. "We are what we are and we do what we do, not because of any mysterious power of human volition, but because outside forces over which we lack any semblance of control have us caught in an inflexible web. Whatever else we may be, we are not the captains of our fate or the masters of our soul."[16]

Although behaviorists are quick to point out that their beliefs are a psychological system based on science, not philosophy, we include behaviorism in our discussion of philosophical orientations to teaching because it is a comprehensive worldview that serves as the basis for the way many teachers approach teaching.

Founders of Behavioristic Psychology   John B. Watson (1878–1958) was the principal originator of behavioristic psychology and B. F. Skinner (1904–1990) its best-known promoter. Watson first claimed that human behavior consisted of specific stimuli that resulted in certain responses. In part, he based this new conception of learning on the classic experiment conducted by Russian psychologist Ivan Pavlov (1849–1936). Pavlov had noticed that a dog he was working with would salivate when it was about to be given food. By introducing the sound of a bell when food was offered and repeating this several times, Pavlov discovered that the sound of the bell alone (a conditioned stimulus) would make the dog salivate (a conditioned response). Watson was so confident that all learning conformed to this basic stimulus-response model (now termed classical or type S conditioning) that he once boasted, "Give me a dozen healthy infants, well-formed, and my own specified world to bring them up in, and I'll guarantee to take any one at random and train him to become any type of specialist I might select—doctor, lawyer, artist, merchant-chief and, yes, even beggar-man and thief, regardless of his talents, penchants, tendencies, abilities, vocations, and race of his ancestors."[17]

B.F. Skinner

Skinner went beyond Watson's basic stimulus-response model and developed a more comprehensive view of conditioning known as operant (or type R) conditioning. Operant conditioning is based on the idea that satisfying responses are conditioned, unsatisfying ones are not. In other words, "The things we call pleasant have an energizing or strengthening effect on our behaviour."[18] For the teacher, this means that desired student behavior should be reinforced, undesired behavior should not. Furthermore, the teacher should be concerned with changing students' behavior rather than trying to alter their mental states.

In his novel *Walden Two* (1962), Skinner portrayed how "behavioral engineering" could lead to the creation of a utopian society. The book describes how a community with a desirable social order was created by design rather than by accident. In much the same way, educators can create learners who exhibit desired behaviors by carefully and scientifically controlling the educative process. The teacher need merely recognize that all learning is conditioning and adhere to the following four steps:

1. Identify desired behaviors in concrete (observable and measurable) terms.
2. Establish a procedure for recording specific behaviors and counting their frequencies.
3. For each behavior, identify an appropriate reinforcer.
4. Ensure that students receive the reinforcer as soon as possible after displaying a desired behavior.

Portrait of a Behaviorist Teacher   Camille Leblanc teaches grade four at a school with an enrollment of about 500 in a small Saskatchewan town. Now in her fifth year at the school, Camille has spent the last three years developing and refining a systematic approach to teaching.

Her primary method is individualized instruction. Students proceed at their own pace through modules she has put together. The modules cover five major areas: reading, writing, mathematics, general science, and spelling. She is working on a sixth module, geography, but it won't be ready until next year. She has developed a complex point system to keep track of students' progress and to motivate them to higher levels of achievement. The points students accumulate entitle them to participate in various in-class activities: free reading, playing with the many games and puzzles in the room, drawing or painting in the art corner, or playing video games on one of the two personal computers in the room.

Camille has tried to convert several other teachers at the school to her behavioristic approach, and she is eager to talk to anyone who will listen about the effectiveness of her systematic approach to instruction. When addressing this topic, her exuberance is truly exceptional. She smiles a great deal and speaks rapidly, traits that reflect her excitement about her work rather than nervous energy:

> It's really quite simple. Students just do much better if you tell them exactly what you want them to know and then reward them for learning it. So, for every subject I teach I've got a set number of behavioral objectives that students have to master. Each subject has a certain number of modules with anywhere from ten to twenty objectives in each module.
>
> For completing the activities in each module and passing the module's test, a student will get a certain number of points. For each 100 points a student gets so much time to spend on a special activity in class. Right now, the video games are really popular, so the kids have to get 200 points before they can do that.

Camille can be rather critical about some of the methods employed by some of her colleagues. She knows some teachers in the school who teach by a trial-and-error method and "aren't clear about where they're going." She is also impatient with those who talk about the "art" of teaching; in contrast, everything that she does as a teacher is done with precision and a clear sense of purpose. "Through careful design and management of the learning environment," she says, "a teacher can get the results that he or she wants."

Although Camille enjoys positive relationships with her students, she does not feel that teachers should necessarily strive to be friends with students. "The teacher's main role is clear: to manage the important business of students learning what they need to know to become productive members of society. A teacher who is effective and efficient serves students better than one who is merely a friend."

As a behaviorist, Camille does not recognize a separation between knowledge and action, or knowing from doing. She is single-minded in her emphasis on changing behavior. Her success is measured only in terms of whether students achieve clearly stated learning outcomes. "Students get frustrated with teachers who want them to 'know,' to 'appreciate,' or to 'understand' the material," she says. "That's too vague, and kids don't know what you want them to do."

RECONSTRUCTIONISM

As the name implies, **reconstructionism** holds that schools should take the lead in reconstructing the current social order. Theodore Brameld (b. 1904), acknowledged as the founder of reconstructionism, bases his philosophy on two fundamental premises about the present: (1) We live in a period of great crisis, most evident in the fact that humans now have the capability of destroying civilization overnight, and (2) humankind also has the intellectual, technological, and moral potential to create a world civilization of "abundance, health, and humane capacity."[19] In this time of great need, then, the schools should become the primary agent for planning and directing social change. In short, schools should not only *transmit* knowledge about the existing social order; they should seek to *reconstruct* it as well.

MAKING *a DIFFERENCE*

Tom McGrath
St. John's, Newfoundland

As a high school teacher, I felt that capable students needed to see the applicability of their education to their futures. I thought they would benefit if they could interact with a highly professional group of people, especially if they could assimilate the qualities required for professional success.

I decided that many of these needs could be met through the development of a Co-op Law Program. Through this program, I could expose students to the relationship between law and politics in the formation, practice, and enforcement of law. Students could rotate through four different co-op placements to gain this exposure.

I developed the program to include grade twelve students who are seventeen and eighteen years of age from all socio-economic groups. The students were required to complete a series of modules which were scheduled four afternoons each week with the fifth afternoon scheduled back at the school for debriefing. The first three-week module was in pre-employment and was designed to prepare students for the work force. During this module, the students toured the Law Society library, various courts, and the House of Assembly, and would hear several guest speakers. Following the pre-employment module, students were assigned to their legal placements for six to eight weeks. During this time they worked in either a private firm or a corporate office under the supervision of a practicing attorney. Students assisted the lawyers by researching cases, taking notes in court, attending discoveries, making phone call inquiries, and participating in client interviews.

Then the students were required to take a five- to seven-week module which would bring them into close contact with cabinet ministers, executive assistants, and government members. Then they would take a two-week module at the headquarters of the Royal Newfoundland Constabulary where they would see firsthand the intricacies of police work and its relation to the formation and practice of law. They then finished off with a one-week module at the John Howard Society where students would observe rehabilitation and meet with former offenders.

When the students returned to the school, the Co-op Coordinator attempted to link the realities of practical experience with classroom instruction. The classroom activities incorporated a variety of educational strategies to foster creative and critical thinking on such topics as "Women in the Legal Profession," "Young Offenders," and "Criminal Negligence."

The exciting part of this program is that it draws directly upon the expertise of law practitioners in a variety of forums. They were exposed to four different placements during their co-op semester, each one offering a different aspect of law. As a teacher, it was exciting to see my students become actively involved in the process of learning.

Reconstructionism and Progressivism   Reconstructionism has clear ties to progressive educational philosophy. Both attach primary importance to the kind of experiences students have. The classroom should be characterized by extensive interactions between teacher and students and among students themselves. Furthermore, both philosophies place a premium on bringing the community, if not the entire world, into the classroom. Student experiences often include field trips, community-based projects of various sorts, and opportunities to interact with persons beyond the four walls of the classroom.

Through a reconstructionist approach to education, students learn appropriate methods for dealing with the significant crises that confront the world: war, economic depression, international terrorism, hunger, inflation, and ever-accelerating technological advances. The curriculum is arranged to highlight the need for various social reforms and, whenever possible, allow students to have firsthand experiences in reform activities. Teachers realize that they can play a significant role in the control and resolution of these problems, that they and their students need not be buffeted about like pawns by these crises.

According to Brameld, the educative process should be based on a continuous quest for a better society. The logical outcome of this quest would be the eventual realization of a world-wide democracy.[20] Unless we actively seek to create this kind of world through the intelligent application of present knowledge, we run the risk that the destructive forces of the world will determine the conditions under which humans will live in the future.

Portrait of a Reconstructionist Teacher   At the urban high school where she teaches social studies and history, Martha Perkins has the reputation for being a social activist. On first meeting, she presents a casual and laid-back demeanor. Her soft voice and warm smile belie the intensity of her convictions about pressing world issues, from terrorism and hunger to peaceful uses of space and the need for all humans to work toward a global community.

During the late 1960s, Martha participated as a high school student in several demonstrations in support of women's rights. This also marked the beginning of her increased awareness of social injustice in general. Like many young people of that era, Martha vigorously supported a curriculum that focused on students understanding inequities and identifying resources that might eliminate them from society. Before she graduated from high school, Martha had formulated a vision of a healthier, more just society, and she vowed to do what she could to make that vision become a reality during her lifetime.

In her teaching, Martha takes every appropriate opportunity to confront her students with social problems and then help them work toward solutions. Within the last few months, for example, her students have spearheaded an in-school drug education program, written letters to the prime minister expressing their views on the Young Offenders Act, and completed ten-hour service projects at a nearby nursing home. When she can, Martha also likes to arrange guest speakers and field trips for her classes.

Martha feels strongly about the importance of having students learn about social problems as well as discovering what they can *do* about them. "It's really almost immoral if I confront my students with a social problem and then we fail to do anything about it," she says. "Part of my responsibility as a teacher is to raise the consciousness level of my students in regard to the problems that confront all human beings. I want them to leave my class with the realization that they *can* make a difference when it comes to making the world a more humane place."

For Martha to achieve her goals as a teacher, she frequently has to tackle controversial issues—issues that many of her colleagues avoid in the classroom. She feels that students would not learn how to cope with problems or controversy if she were to avoid them.

> I'm not afraid of controversy. When confronted with controversy, some teachers do retreat to the safety of the more "neutral" academic discipline. However, I try to get my students to see how they can use the knowledge of the discipline to attack the problem. So far, I've gotten good support from the principal. She's backed me up on several controversial issues that we've looked at in class: the landfill site that was to be built here in this county, the right to die, and absentee landlords who own property in the poorer sections of the city.

*H*OW DOES ONE BUILD AN EDUCATIONAL PHILOSOPHY?

As you read the preceding brief descriptions of six philosophical orientations to teaching, perhaps you felt that no single approach fit perfectly the kind of teacher you want to become. Or there may have been some element of each approach that seemed compatible with your own emerging philosophy of education. In either case, don't feel that you need to identify a single educational philosophy around which you will build your teaching career; in reality, few teachers follow only one educational philosophy. Remember that our portraits of six teachers were drawn with purposefully bold, one-dimensional contrasts to illustrate the different orientations.

In addition, keep in mind that your educational philosophy is only one determinant of the professional decisions you will make as a teacher. As Figure 8.3 sug-

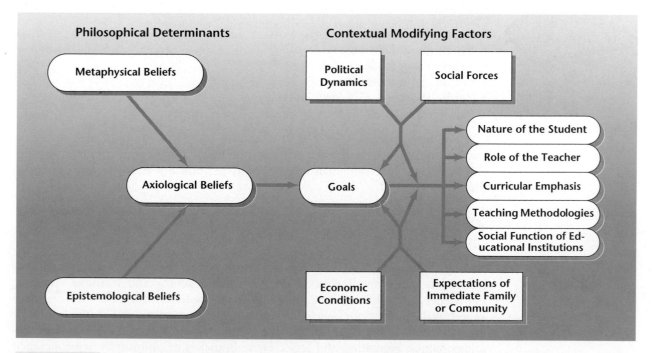

FIGURE 8.3   **The Relationship of Philosophy to Educational Practice**

Source: George R. Knight, *Issues and Alternatives in Educational Philosophy,* 2d ed. (Berrien Springs, Mich.: Andrews University Press, 1990), p. 33.

gests, the educational goals a teacher sets are influenced by factors such as political dynamics, social forces, the expectations of one's immediate family or community, and economic conditions.

It has been our observation that most teachers develop an *eclectic* philosophy of education, which means they have developed their own unique blending of two or more philosophies. Many effective combinations are possible. One might be a perennialist when it comes to selecting content and a behaviorist in regard to motivating students to learn that content. Or, one might be both a progressivist and an existentialist, one who pays particular attention to the needs of the whole child as well as the child's need to develop a personal meaning for life.

We encourage you to reflect on the philosophies we have discussed, incorporating from each the features that are most congruent with your personality and the kind of teacher you wish to become. To help you with this reflection, we have included a philosophic inventory in the Appendix to this chapter. One characteristic of the professional teacher is that he or she continually tries to arrive at a clearer, more comprehensive answer to one basic philosophical question: Why do I teach the way I do?

PROFESSIONAL PORTFOLIO

For this portfolio entry, prepare a written (or videotaped) statement describing a key element of your educational philosophy. To organize your thoughts, focus on *one* of the following dimensions of educational philosophy:

• Beliefs about teaching and learning
• Beliefs about students
• Beliefs about knowledge
• Beliefs about what is worth knowing
• Personal beliefs about the six branches of philosophy

On completion of your teacher education program, you may wish to review your portfolio entry and make any appropriate revisions. Similarly, you may decide to review your statement of philosophy periodically after you have begun to teach.

CHAPTER SUMMARY

Clearly, philosophy is vital to the work of the teacher. A teacher's educational philosophy is made up of personal beliefs about teaching and learning, students, knowledge, and what is worth knowing. For the teacher who wishes to formulate sound, well-thought-out beliefs in these four areas, familiarity with the following main currents of philosophical thought is essential: metaphysics, epistemology, axiology, ethics, aesthetics, and logic. These branches of philosophy are concerned with answering six fundamental questions that are central to teaching: What is the nature of reality? What is the nature of knowledge? What values should guide one's life? What is good and evil, right and wrong? What is beautiful? What processes of reasoning will yield optimum results for the individual?

How a teacher answers such questions determines what the teacher does in the classroom and reveals his or her philosophical orientation to teaching, each representing a unique stance toward life and the educative process:

1. *Perennialism*—Students should acquire knowledge of enduring great ideas.
2. *Progressivism*—The aims of education should be based on the needs and interests of students.
3. *Essentialism*—Schools should teach students, in a disciplined and systematic way, a core of "essential" knowledge and skills.
4. *Existentialism*—In the face of an indifferent universe, students should acquire an education that will enable them to assign meaning to their lives.
5. *Behaviorism*—By careful control of the educational environment and with appropriate reinforcement techniques, teachers can cause students to exhibit desired behaviors.
6. *Reconstructionism*—In response to the significant social problems of the day, schools should take the lead in creating a new social order.

Few teachers teach according to a single philosophical orientation. Instead, they develop an eclectic philosophy based on two or more orientations and on their response to factors such as political dynamics, social forces, the expectation of their immediate families and communities, and economic conditions.

KEY TERMS AND CONCEPTS

aesthetics, 184
axiology, 184
behaviorism, 194
educational philosophy, 177
epistemology, 183

essentialism, 191
ethics, 184
existentialism, 193
logic, 185
metaphysics, 181

perennialism, 186
philosophy, 176
progressivism, 188
reconstructionism, 196

ANSWER KEY FOR PROFESSIONAL REFLECTION

Items most closely associated with each philosophical orientation to teaching: perennialism—*c, h, j, l, p*; progressivism—*b, i, k, m, q*; essentialism—*a, e, g, n, o*; existentialism—*d, r*; behaviorism—*f*; reconstructionism: *s, t*.

APPLICATIONS AND ACTIVITIES

Teacher's Journal

1. In this chapter we referred to the work of several educational philosophers. Select one of them and prepare a written report on the contributions he or she has made to education.

2. Conduct a survey of current journals in education and try to locate articles that reflect the six philosophical orientations discussed in this chapter. Which orientations appear to have the greatest representation?

3. Conduct a comparative survey of an education journal at ten-year intervals and try to determine if there have been any significant changes over the years in regard to the philosophical orientations to teaching reflected in the journal.

4. Imagine that you are a colleague of Roberta Chu who was profiled in this chapter's opening scenario. Write a memo to her in which you react to her philosophical orientation to teaching.

5. ▷ Of the six branches of philosophy discussed in this chapter (metaphysics, epistemology, axiology, ethics, aesthetics, and logic), which one concerns you most in regard to your future as a teacher? How does this concern relate to the dimensions of educational philosophy identified in this chapter's Professional Portfolio activity?

6. Recall one of your favorite teachers in grades K–12. Which of the six educational philosophies you have just read about (perennialism, progressivism, essentialism, existentialism, behaviorism, and reconstructionism) best captures that teacher's approach to teaching?

Field Assignments

1. Interview a teacher for the purpose of clarifying his or her educational philosophy. Formulate your interview questions in light of the philosophical concepts discussed in this chapter. Report your findings to the rest of the class.

2. If possible, arrange a short interview with a professor of philosophy on your campus. Ask her or him to comment on the contributions that philosophy can make to education. Give the rest of the class a report on your visit.

3. Observe the classes of two different teachers at the level at which you plan to teach. Which *one* of the six philosophical orientations to teaching discussed in this chapter most characterizes each teacher? Share your findings with the rest of your class.

4. Visit a school and interview the principal about the school's educational philosophy. Ask him or her to comment on what is expected of teachers in regard to achieving the goals contained in the statement of philosophy.

APPENDIX: Philosophic Inventory

The following inventory is to help identify your educational philosophy. Respond to the statements on the scale from 5 "Strongly Agree" to 1 "Strongly Disagree" by circling the number that most closely fits your perspective.

Strongly Agree   *Strongly Disagree*

5   4   3   2   1   1. The curriculum should emphasize essential knowledge, *not* students' personal interests.

5   4   3   2   1   2. All learning results from rewards controlled by the external environment.

5   4   3   2   1   3. Teachers should emphasize interdisciplinary subject matter that encourages project-oriented, democratic classrooms.

5   4   3   2   1   4. Education should emphasize the search for personal meaning, *not* a set fixed body of knowledge.

5   4   3   2   1   5. The ultimate aim of education is constant, absolute, and universal: to develop the rational person and cultivate the intellect.

5   4   3   2   1   6. Schools should actively involve students in social change to reform society.

5   4   3   2   1   7. Schools should teach basic skills, *not* humanistic ideals.

5   4   3   2   1   8. Eventually, human behavior will be explained by scientific laws, proving there is no free will.

5   4   3   2   1   9. Teachers should be facilitators and resources who guide student inquiry, *not* managers of behavior.

5   4   3   2   1   10. The best teachers encourage personal responses and develop self-awareness of their students.

5   4   3   2   1   11. The curriculum should be the same for everyone: the collective wisdom of Western culture delivered through lecture and discussion.

5   4   3   2   1   12. Schools should lead society toward radical social change, *not* transmit traditional values.

5   4   3   2   1   13. The purpose of schools is to ensure practical preparation for life and work, *not* to encourage personal development.

5   4   3   2   1   14. Good teaching establishes an environment to control student behavior and to measure learning of prescribed objectives.

5   4   3   2   1   15. Curriculum should emerge from students' needs and interests; it *should not* be prescribed in advance.

5   4   3   2   1   16. Helping students develop personal values is more important than transmitting traditional values.

5   4   3   2   1   17. The best education consists primarily of exposure to great works in the humanities.

5 4 3 2 1   18. It is more important for teachers to involve students in activities to criticize and transform society than to teach the Great Books.

5 4 3 2 1   19. Schools should emphasize discipline, hard work, and respect for authority, *not* encourage free choice.

5 4 3 2 1   20. Human learning can be controlled and anyone can be taught to be a scientist or a thief; therefore, personal choice is a myth.

5 4 3 2 1   21. Education should enhance personal growth through problem solving in the present, *not* emphasize preparation for a distant future.

5 4 3 2 1   22. Because we are born with an unformed personality, personal growth should be the focus of education.

5 4 3 2 1   23. Human nature is constant—its most distinctive quality is the ability to reason; therefore, the intellect should be the focus of education.

5 4 3 2 1   24. Schools perpetuate racism and sexism camouflaged as traditional values.

5 4 3 2 1   25. Teachers should efficiently transmit a common core of knowledge, *not* experiment with curriculum.

5 4 3 2 1   26. Teaching is primarily management of student behavior to achieve the teacher's objectives.

5 4 3 2 1   27. Education should involve students in democratic activities and reflective thinking.

5 4 3 2 1   28. Students should have significant involvement in choosing what and how they learn.

5 4 3 2 1   29. Teachers should promote the permanency of the classics.

5 4 3 2 1   30. Learning should lead students to involvement in social reform.

5 4 3 2 1   31. On the whole, school should and must indoctrinate students with traditional values.

5 4 3 2 1   32. If ideas cannot be proved by science, they should be ignored as superstition and nonsense.

5 4 3 2 1   33. The major goal for teachers is to create an environment where students can learn on their own by guided reflection on their experiences.

5 4 3 2 1   34. Teachers should create opportunities for students to make personal choices, *not* shape their behavior.

5 4 3 2 1   35. The aim of education should be the same in every age and society, *not* differ from teacher to teacher.

5 4 3 2 1   36. Education should lead society toward social betterment, *not* confine itself to essential skills.

PHILOSOPHIC INVENTORY SCORE SHEET

In the space available, record the number you circled for each statement (1–36) from the inventory. Total the number horizontally and record it in the space on the far right of the score sheet. The highest total indicates your educational philosophy.

Essentialism

Essentialism was a response to progressivism and advocates a conservative philosophic perspective. The emphasis is on intellectual and moral standards that should be transmitted by the schools. The core of the curriculum should be essential knowledge and skills. Schooling should be practical and not influence social policy. It is a back-to-basics movement that emphasizes facts. Students should be taught discipline, hard work, and respect for authority. Influential essentialists include William C. Bagley, H. G. Rickover, Arthur Bestor, and William Bennett; E. D. Hirsch's *Cultural Literacy* could fit this category.

_____ + _____ + _____ + _____ + _____ + _____ = _____
1   7   13   19   25   31   Total

Behaviorism

Behaviorism denies free will and maintains that behavior is the result of external forces that cause humans to behave in predictable ways. It is linked with empiricism, which stresses scientific experiment and observation; behaviorists are skeptical about metaphysical claims. Behaviorists look for laws governing human behavior the way natural scientists look for empirical laws governing natural events. The role of the teacher is to identify behavioral goals and establish reinforcers to achieve goals. Influential behaviorists include B. F. Skinner, Ivan Pavlov, J. B. Watson, and Benjamin Bloom.

_____ + _____ + _____ + _____ + _____ + _____ = _____
2   8   14   20   26   32   Total

Progressivism

Progressivism focuses on the child rather than the subject matter. The students' interests are important; integrating thinking, feeling, and doing is important. Learners should be active and learn to solve problems by reflecting on their experience. The school should help students develop personal and social values. Because society is always changing, new ideas are important to make the future better than the past. Influential progressivists include John Dewey and Francis Parker.

_____ + _____ + _____ + _____ + _____ + _____ = _____
3   9   15   21   27   33   Total

Existentialism

Existentialism is a highly subjective philosophy that stresses the importance of the individual and emotional commitment to living authentically. It emphasizes individual choice over the importance of rational theories. Jean-Paul Sartre, the French philosopher, claimed that "existence precedes essence." People are born, and each person must define himself through choices in life. Influential existentialists include Jean-Paul Sartre, Soren Kierkegaard, Martin Heidegger, Gabriel Marcel, Albert Camus, Carl Rogers, A. S. Neill, and Maxine Greene.

_____ + _____ + _____ + _____ + _____ + _____ = _____
4   10   16   22   28   34   Total

Perennialism

The aim of education is to ensure that students acquire knowledge about the great ideas of Western culture. Human beings are rational and it is this capacity that needs to be developed. Cultivation of the intellect is the highest priority of an education worth having. The highest level of knowledge in each field should be the focus of curriculum. Influential perennialists include Robert Maynard Hutchins, Mortimer Adler, and Allan Bloom.

_____ + _____ + _____ + _____ + _____ + _____ = _____
　5　　　　11　　　　17　　　　23　　　　29　　　　35　　　　Total

Reconstructionism

Reconstructionists advocate that schools should take the lead to reconstruct society. Schools have more than a responsibility to transmit knowledge, they have the mission to transform society as well. Reconstructionists go beyond progressivists in advocating social activism. Influential reconstructionists include Theodore Brameld, Paulo Friere, and Henry Giroux.

_____ + _____ + _____ + _____ + _____ + _____ = _____
　6　　　　12　　　　18　　　　24　　　　30　　　　36　　　　Total

Source: Prepared by Robert Leahy for *Becoming a Teacher: Accepting the Challenge of a Profession,* 3d ed., 1995. Used by permission of the author.

9 Governance and Support of Education in Canada

There is currently in Canada, as in many other countries, a high level of cynicism about politicians. Many people feel that our current political processes are not serving their needs, that politicians are all self-serving, interested in their own re-election, and that somehow politics has become preoccupied with the wrong things, while the big issues facing our country are not being addressed.

—Benjamin Levin and Jon Young, *Understanding Canadian Schools*

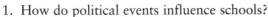

Focus Questions

1. How do political events influence schools?
2. What is the role of the local community in school governance?
3. What is the impact of restructuring on schools?
4. What is the province's role in developing education policy?
5. What assistance do regional educational service agencies provide schools?
6. How does the federal government influence education?
7. How are schools financed in Canada?

You've just entered the teachers' lounge for your planning period. It's obvious that the three teachers in the room have been having a heated discussion.

"I don't see how you can say that we make those kinds of decisions," says Kim, a language arts teacher who came to the school two years ago. "The books I can use are chosen by the province. Next April all my kids have to take a mandated test. And . . ."

"Hold it," says Betty, raising her hand to silence her. "How can you say that we don't control the schools? Unless I'm mistaken, I was the only one teaching in my classroom just before I came in here. I've been here eight years and no one's ever told me what to do." Betty takes a quick sip of her drink.

"It's the politicians; they're starting to run the schools more and more," says Lara, looking up from the mathematics book she is evaluating. "Look," she continues, "the politicians even set up a beginning teacher program to try to tell this new teacher how to teach and what to teach." She motions for you to have a seat at the table. Feeling a bit uncomfortable but anxious to fit in with your new colleagues, you take a seat.

"Lara's right," says Kim. "The other day, Robin Matthews, who teaches over at Crestview, told me that someone at his school figured out that teachers there have a total of over 100 provincial and board guidelines they have to follow. Can you imagine that!" She rolls her eyes to emphasize the point.

"Right," Lara says, "I'm surprised the number isn't higher—not only do you have provincial tests, you've got mandated standards for grading, for graduation, for placement in special programs, for suspending kids, for just about anything you can think of."

"That's an exaggeration," says Betty. "We've got the freedom to decide what we want to teach and how we want to teach it. Sure, there are guidelines but they're there to help us and the kids."

"Help us?" says Kim, rolling her eyes again. "How can you say that?"

"We've got a difficult enough job to do without the politicians making it harder," says Lara.

"I hear what you're both saying," says Betty, "but you've got to remember why we're here—for the kids. The politicians, the school board . . . they're just looking out for the kids."

"Well, who's looking out for us?" asks Kim. "If we meet all their guidelines, then we've got less time to teach the kids. Is that helping kids?"

"Well, I still think you're overreacting," says Betty. "Why don't we ask the new teacher here. What do you think?"

The three teachers look at you, awaiting your response. What do you say?

In preparing to become a teacher, your primary concern is probably how to become effective in dealing with the six realities of teaching discussed in Chapter 2. Compared to these realities, understanding how schools are governed and supported may not seem very important. Though teachers must acquire the specific knowledge and skills that will enable them to survive their first months of teaching, true professionals also recognize the need to understand the political forces that influence their work. An appreciation for the political dimensions of teaching can have positive results, as the following examples suggest:

- As members of the Local School Council (LSC) for a high-needs school in a poor area, two teachers organized a group of parent volunteers that has been very effective at reducing student truancy and improving students' attitudes toward school.
- Three high school English teachers who were awarded a provincial grant to develop a humanities program had submitted letters of endorsement for their project from the chairperson of the board of education and the superintendent.
- A group of concerned teachers was instrumental in getting special provincial money to fund a much-needed remodeling and expansion project at their school.

HOW DO POLITICAL EVENTS INFLUENCE SCHOOLS?

Before we look at how political events influence schools, we wish to point out that education is not and never will be apolitical. Our discussion of the historical foundations of education in Chapter 7, for example, showed how political forces have shaped the character of our schools since their early beginnings.

Some teachers might prefer not to dirty their hands with politics, but it is a fact of life that school policies are developed in a political setting. Whenever educators try to enlist government support for a particular approach to schooling, they are acting politically. In fact, some educators feel that it is quite appropriate to act in this way:

> Each time educators or lay leaders take action to influence educational policy, or policies in other areas of society, they are involved in politics. Thus, educational leadership to upgrade educational standards is political. And if educators and citizens desire changes in school programs, they must be good politicians. Performing as a politician to develop quality schools is a perfectly legitimate, statesmanlike activity.[1]

Many complex political forces currently shape schools in Canada. During the 1980s, for example, numerous groups pressed to have school policies reflect their special, often conflicting, interests. During the last half of the 1990s we will see a continuation of this struggle to control various aspects of the educational system. Among the groups that will continue to have a keen concern for shaping educational policies, at least nine can be identified:

1. *Parents*—Concerned with controlling local schools so that quality educational programs are available for their children
2. *Students*—Concerned with policies related to freedom of expression, dress, behavior, and curricular offerings
3. *Teachers*—Concerned with improving conditions of the workplace, terms of employment, and other professional issues
4. *Administrators*—Concerned with providing leadership so that the constructive energies of various interest groups are channeled into the development of quality educational programs
5. *Taxpayers*—Concerned with maintaining an appropriate formula for determining local and provincial financial support of schools
6. *Provincial authorities*—Concerned with the implementation of guidelines and legislation related to the operation of schools
7. *Minorities and women*—Concerned with the availability of equal educational opportunity for all and with legal issues surrounding administrative appointments, terms of employment, and evaluation
8. *Educational theorists and researchers*—Concerned with using theoretical and research-based insights as the bases for improving schools at all levels
9. *Businesses and corporations*—Concerned that graduates have the knowledge, skills, attitudes, and values to help an organization realize its goals

Out of the complex and often turbulent interactions of these groups school policies are developed. And, as strange as it may seem, no one of these groups can be said to control today's schools. In fact, some observers suggest that the period since 1960 might be characterized as the "era of nobody in charge."[2] Those who we might imagine control schools—principals, superintendents, and boards of education—are in reality responding to shifting sets of conditions created by those who have an interest in the schools. In addition, schools are influenced by several out-of-school factors—what sociologists have termed *environmental press*. Because schools reflect the society they serve, they are influenced directly and indirectly by an almost infinite number of factors. The following are some of the more obvious factors that exert pressure on the schools:

media	political climate	religion
legislation	educational research	technology
international events	economics	demographic shifts
community attitudes	social issues	

It is difficult to untangle the web of political forces that influence schools. Figure 9.1 shows graphically how school authorities are confronted with the difficult task of funneling the input from various sources into unified, coherent school programs. In the next four sections of this chapter, we examine the many political forces that have an impact on the schools by looking at how they are influenced at the local, provincial, and regional levels.

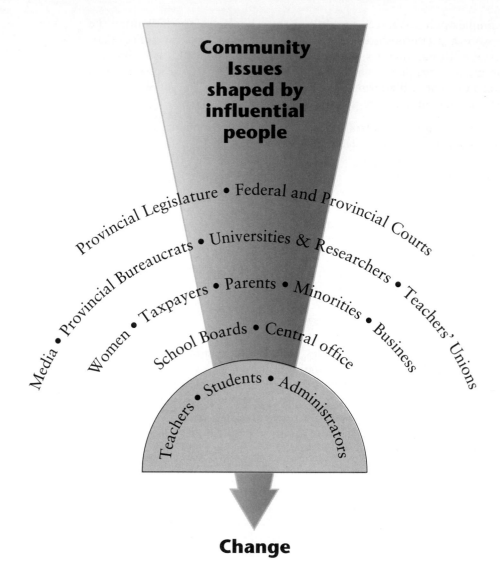

Community Issues shaped by influential people

Provincial Legislature • Federal and Provincial Courts

Media • Provincial Bureaucrats • Universities & Researchers • Teachers' Unions

Women • Taxpayers • Parents • Minorities • Business

School Boards • Central office

Teachers • Students • Administrators

Change

FIGURE 9.1

Political Forces that Influence Schools to Change

WHAT IS THE ROLE OF THE LOCAL COMMUNITY IN SCHOOL GOVERNANCE?

Section 93 of the BNA Act, now the Constitution Act, 1982, provides that provinces have exclusive rights to make laws in all matters of education. The provinces, in turn, created school districts with responsibility for the daily operation of public schools. They further provided that local community members within each school district would be elected to provide governance for the system.

LOCAL SCHOOL DISTRICT

Local school districts vary greatly in demographics such as number of school-age children; educational, occupational, and income levels of parents; operating budget;

number of teachers; economic resources; and number of school buildings. Some serve wealthy communities, others impoverished neighborhoods or rural areas. School districts in Canada range from the very small and remote to the highly ur-banized. An isolated one-teacher school district in northwestern Ontario might serve approximately 14 students while school districts in Calgary and Montreal might have hundreds of teachers and serve nearly 100 000 students each. Because the smaller, more isolated districts cannot provide the same range of services for students as the larger, more urban districts, the smaller districts must rely on the regional offices of the ministries of education to offer these supplementary services.

Large school districts tend to have more complicated structures than smaller districts. They have human resource departments to interview and hire hundreds of teachers per year. They may have curriculum departments to develop materials to supplement the provincial curriculum. Curriculum departments are also re-sponsible for providing on-going training, in-service, to help teachers deal with emerging areas of concern or new guidelines. In smaller districts, superintendents, deputy or assistant superintendents, and school principals carry out the human re-source function along with their other responsibilities. Similarly, small school dis-tricts usually delegate the responsibility for curriculum to a deputy or assistant superintendent.

Local school districts deal with a broad range of issues. To respond equitably to requests from community or special interest groups and to establish uniform standards among several hundred schools, school districts establish policies, some-times on an enormous range of issues. Larger local school districts tend to have more complex policies to guide their daily operations. For example, the Calgary Board of Education has policies on everything from AIDS to x-ray examinations. Hundreds of policies are listed in a 25-page alphabetical index of policies.[3] These topics deal with issues that range from the critical to the mundane.

School districts have varying influences on the conditions under which teach-ers work. Some of these differences are readily apparent. For example, in many dis-tricts the central office determines how funds will be spent. In others, principals and teachers have a considerable say in how money will be spent. As well, many districts are decentralizing and giving their schools greater freedom to determine policies and how resources will be allocated.

SCHOOL BOARD

The primary governing body of a district is the **school board**. The board, acting as an agent of the province, is responsible for the following important activities: approving the teachers, administrators, and other school personnel hired by the superintendent; developing organizational and educational policies; and deter-mining procedures for the evaluation of programs and personnel.

School board members are elected in general elections. Board members typ-ically serve two to three years, and their terms of office are sometimes staggered. School boards usually range in size from five to fifteen members, with five or seven frequently suggested as the optimum size. Although board members in urban areas are usually paid, board members in most other areas are not.

Nearly all school board meetings are open to the public; in fact, many com-munities even provide radio and television coverage. Open meetings give parents and interested citizens an opportunity to express their concerns and to get more information about problems in the district.

The primary governing body of a district is the school board. Most school board meetings are open to parents and interested citizens.

Each board meets its responsibility for controlling local schools in various ways. However, all school boards must follow provincial guidelines. One study of the communication and decision-making processes at board of education meetings concluded that school board meetings differ in the following six areas:[4]

1. Topics on the agenda—curriculum, finances, student services, discrimination, performance evaluation, etc.
2. Individual or group who sets the agenda—school board, superintendent, staff experts, the public
3. Participants in the discussion
4. How participation varies according to topic of discussion
5. Individual or group who proposes policy
6. The degree to which the board defers to the recommendations of the superintendent of schools

Although school boards currently have a significant influence on local schools, there is a growing belief that improvements in education will come only when teachers and principals begin to make policy decisions currently reserved for school boards. As Figure 9.2 shows, most of the American public believes that teachers and principals should have more say in how schools are run and that schools could be effectively governed by local school councils composed of teachers, principals, and parents.

Several provinces are considering mechanisms to ensure a greater role for parents in schools. For example, the Alberta government is in the process of creating Parent School Councils with some responsibility for staffing, hiring principals, curriculum, textbook selection, and teaching strategies. The Ontario government has proposed similar legislation to create Parent Advisory Councils. The councils in Ontario will have to be chaired by a parent, not an educator or administrator.

SUPERINTENDENT OF SCHOOLS

Though school boards operate very differently, the **superintendent** is usually the key figure in determining a district's educational policy. The superintendent is the chief administrator of the school district, the person charged with the responsibility of seeing that schools operate in accord with provincial guidelines as well as policies set by the local school board. Though the board of education delegates broad powers to the superintendent, his or her policies require board approval.

The specific responsibilities of the superintendent are many. Among the most important are the following:

1. To serve as professional adviser to the board of education and to make policy recommendations for improving curricular and instructional programs
2. To act as employer and supervisor of professional and nonteaching personnel (janitors, cafeteria workers, etc.)
3. To represent the schools in their relations with the community and to explain board of education policies to the community

Who Should Control the Schools?

Question #1

In most school districts the school superintendent and school board have more to say about how the local public schools are run than the principals and teachers. Would you favor or oppose giving the principals and teachers more say about how the public schools in this community are run?

Question #2

In most school districts, policy decisions and changes are made by the school board and its administrative staff. In a few districts, however, some of these decisions are made by councils composed of local public school teachers, principals, and parents. Which way would you prefer to have policy decisions made in the schools in this community: by the school board and its administrative staff or by a council of teachers, principals, and parents?

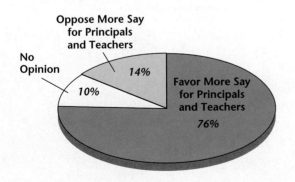

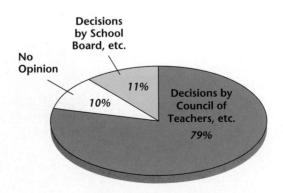

FIGURE 9.2

Who Should Control the Schools?

Source: Based on data presented in Stanley M. Elam, Lowell C. Rose, and Alec M. Gallup, "The 23rd Annual Gallup Poll of the Public's Attitudes toward the Public Schools," *Phi Delta Kappan* (September 1991): 52.

4. To develop policies for the placement and transportation of students within the district
5. To prepare an annual school budget and adhere to the budget adopted by the school board

How the superintendent and his or her board work together appears to be related to the size of the school district; superintendents and school boards in larger districts are more likely to be in conflict. Schools boards in smaller districts, however, are more effective when they do oppose the superintendent. In large districts, the board's own divisiveness makes it less likely that the board will successfully oppose the superintendent.[5] Superintendents have also observed how widely the political climate of school districts can vary. "In some schools, changing the location of a bicycle rack will cause parents to call the principal. In other schools, we can cut the school day from seven periods to six periods without neighborhood reaction."[6]

Superintendents must have a great deal of skill to respond appropriately to the many external political forces that demand their attention. As one observer has put it, "Conflict is the DNA of the superintendency," and effective superintendents demonstrate that they are able to play three roles simultaneously: politician, manager, and teacher.[7] It is a demanding position, and turnover is high. Research has shown that the average tenure in office for superintendents is between three and four years.[8] In an environment characterized by political turbulence and demands from competing interest groups, the superintendent cannot be an omnipotent, insensitive figure; he or she must be a "negotiator-statesman."[9]

THE ROLE OF PARENTS

Parents may not be involved legally in the governance of schools but they do play an important role. As we learned in Chapter 5, for example, one characteristic of

Successful schools develop close working relationships with parents and guardians. Such a relationship is of great benefit to children.

successful schools is that they have developed close working relationships with parents. Children whose parents or guardians support and encourage school activities have a definite advantage in school.

Groups such as the **Parent-Teacher Association (PTA)**, Parent-Teacher Organization (PTO), or **Parent Advisory Council (PAC)** give parents the opportunity to communicate with teachers on matters of interest and importance to them. Through these groups, parents can become involved in the life of the school in a variety of ways—from making recommendations regarding school policies to providing much-needed volunteer services, or to initiating school-improvement activities such as fund-raising drives.

Parents are beginning to acquire a greater role in the governance of schools in several provinces. In the past, most parent advisory councils were directly or indirectly controlled by school principals; council members traditionally volunteered in the schools and donated money for special projects. In the future parents will be more involved in deciding what teaching strategies ought to be used in schools and how to best use resources in the classrooms. Principals will have to communicate effectively with parent councils and to include parents in more decisions such as programming, budgets, educational standards, and management.

WHAT IS THE IMPACT OF RESTRUCTURING ON SCHOOLS?

At many schools across the country exciting changes are taking place in regard to how schools are controlled locally. To improve the performance of schools, to decentralize the system of governance, and to enhance the professional status of teachers, some districts are **restructuring** their school systems. Restructuring goes by several names: shared governance, administrative decentralization, teacher empowerment, professionalization, bottom-up policy-making, school-based planning, school-based management, and shared decision making. What all these approaches to school governance have in common is allowing those who know students best—teachers, principals, aides, custodians, librarians, secretaries, and parents—the freedom to decide how to meet students' needs.

In response to the need to reduce government debt, the Alberta government in the 1990s decided to amalgamate small school districts into larger ones. Local school boards resisted because they wanted to retain control over local schools. They feared that larger school boards would be less responsive to local needs. In response, the government tried to compensate for reduced accountability within larger school districts by restructuring school district governance systems, decentralizing the decision making to the local school level. The idea was that rural communities may have lost direct control over their school boards but they would gain control over their local schools. Whether this will work in practice remains to be seen.

SCHOOL-BASED MANAGEMENT

One of the most frequently used approaches to restructuring schools is **school-based management (SBM)**. Most SBM programs have three components in common:

MAKING *a DIFFERENCE*

Carolyn MacDonald
Igloolik, Northwest Territories

Teaching in Igloolik provides many opportunities for innovation. While volunteering as a field assistant with Dr. Susan Rowley on surveys and salvage projects at endangered archaeological sites on Igloolik Island, I was struck by the degree of interest and commitment shown by the participating young people. Accordingly, we developed a three-level summer archaeology field course for our high school students. It has received official recognition by the Department of Education of the Northwest Territories and gives students the chance to earn up to 15 credits in Archaeology.

The main purpose of this archaeology program is to provide our students with an opportunity to appreciate their area's rich cultural heritage from an archaeological point of view as well from the traditional perspective of Inuit elders. Students are taught the basic skills needed for successful field archaeology including mapping, surveying, excavating techniques, and artifact conservation. An important component involves student/elder interviews focusing on the local traditions and history of the sites.

To increase local appreciation and understanding of the Island's archaeological record, each summer's excavation concludes with a major public exhibit presented and interpreted by the students. Invariably well attended, these exhibits contribute to a strengthening of the bond between community and school.

Students experience the excitement of discovery. They come to appreciate and respect the value of preserving knowledge about the human history of their area. Team work and cooperation are essential ingredients building, in turn, self-confidence and self-respect. Importantly, students have the opportunity to apply classroom knowledge in practical situations—mathematics for surveying, Inuktituk for artifact exhibits, English for data notation, and art for illustrations. In short, the knowledge learned in school is reaffirmed.

Students master the accurate and often painstaking work required for archaeological excavation and receive a good understanding of applied science. Finally, the program has become a generational meeting point inspiring dialogue at many levels between Inuit elders and students. Most students come away expressing genuine respect for the knowledge and experiences of the elders. What better rewards can a teacher receive?

1. Power and decisions formerly made by the superintendent and school board are delegated to teachers, principals, parents, community members, and students at local schools. At SBM schools, teachers can become directly involved in making decisions about curriculum, textbooks, standards for student behavior, staff development, promotion and retention policies, teacher evaluation, school budgets, and the selection of teachers and administrators.
2. At each school, a decision-making body (known as a board, cabinet, site-based team, or council) made up of teachers, the principal, and parents implements the SBM plan.
3. SBM programs operate with the whole-hearted endorsement of the superintendent of schools.[10]

The primary aim of school-based management is to provide teachers, administrators, staff, and, indeed, the entire school community with a greater sense of ownership and efficacy in the operation of schools. Such empowerment, it is believed, will result in greater cooperation, satisfaction, and pride among those directly involved in educating children. The assumption is that, if people have a greater say in the decisions that affect them, they will become more involved and, ultimately, their schools will become more successful. Although some Canadian school districts have experimented with SBM, other countries, including New Zealand, Australia, England, and the United States, have done much more with it. In the words of the president of the local teachers' union that helped implement an SBM program in Florida:

> We are convinced that kids are going to get a better education when the decisions that affect them are made in the schools they're attending, by the people who are there in the classroom.[11]

The restructuring of programs increases communication among teachers, principals, parents, students, and other groups concerned with the operation of schools. With increased communication comes a greater awareness of what needs to be done to improve education at the local school site. As a middle school teacher involved in restructuring said: "We were convinced that what we wanted to change was possible.... The thing we learned is that communication is very, very important."[12]

The range of management decisions that can be made by teachers is broad. As Superintendent Joseph A. Fernandez said of his approach to implementing school-based management in Florida, his former district: "The instructions were very simple. We told them the sky is the limit."[13]

Among the changes implemented at some SBM schools are the following:

- Offering Saturday classes to teach students in a more informal setting
- Initiating various before- and after-school programs
- Hiring aides instead of assistant principals
- Creating new positions, such as discipline manager and enrichment coordinator
- Having teachers give up some of their planning time to reduce class size during basic-skills instruction
- Creating a developmental program for five-year-olds that includes monthly hands-on workshops for parents
- Having teachers create their own report card to give parents more detailed information about their children
- Instituting a high school teacher-as-adviser program in the middle of the day to counsel students about suicide, drug abuse, and stress-related problems[14]

EXAMPLES OF SCHOOL-BASED MANAGEMENT IN CANADA

School-based management was pioneered in Canada by the Edmonton school district in the early 1980s. Although the Edmonton school board did not delegate political or governance functions to the schools, they did transfer administrative functions, professional staffing, and budgeting. After the change it became evident that the board still retained substantial control. School staffs did not have much control over maintenance or cleaning of the school, transportation of students, capital projects, or collective bargaining.

Dan Brown, a professor at the University of British Columbia, has studied decentralization and school-based management in Canada.[15] He studied the Edmonton case as well as the Langley and Peace River North School Districts in British Columbia. Brown concluded that SBM should not be implemented to reduce education costs. Instead, it is an effective way of delegating authority to those on whom the responsibility for offering education services exists. In a more traditional centralized system, the authority to offer education services generally rests with the school board and the superintendent while the responsibility lies with school principals and teachers. Theoretically, with SBM, both the authority and responsibility rest with school principals and teachers.

In Canada, SBM usually means decentralizing only administrative functions. For example, in Edmonton, staffing and budget decisions were delegated to schools. But SBM can also mean decentralizing political and governance functions such as collective bargaining, capital development, and staffing decisions. But few districts have gone this far.

Brown found that SBM can help a staff respond to their school's unique needs. For example, school staff in Langley could decide on how best to deal with particular children's speech and language difficulties. A district-wide policy normally makes it impossible for a school to tailor its programs to the unique needs of its students. Peace River North schools found they could make decisions that made people's jobs easier. School staff in Edmonton could decide whether to buy extra equipment, such as audio-visual equipment for each floor, eliminating the need for teachers to haul equipment up and down stairs between classes. A Langley school's staff decided to hire a teacher's aide rather than buying a new photocopier as mandated by a district-wide policy. Decisions such as these demonstrate the benefits of bringing the authority to make decisions that affect education services to the level at which the responsibility to offer these services exists.

Alberta is currently experimenting with giving parent councils expanded authority. These councils may soon have the authority to participate in hiring, budgeting, curriculum, and teaching strategy decisions. Although it is still too early to tell, a policy that expands the role of parent councils may open up the possibility of administrative and political SBM province-wide.

WHAT IS THE PROVINCE'S ROLE IN DEVELOPING EDUCATION POLICY?

Above the board or district level, provinces have an enormous influence on the governance of schools. Sparked by widespread criticism of education in the early 1980s, many provinces considered ways to achieve greater accountability through:

- tougher requirements for graduating from high school
- career ladders for teachers and master teacher programs
- higher expectations for students, including testing of basic skills
- testing graduates of teacher education programs before certification

Provinces have the exclusive right to pass legislation on matters of education. Each province has its own school act that defines how education is provided and how powers are delegated. Although each province is aware of how other provinces educate their citizens and ministers of education of all the provinces meet regularly, each province has developed a unique educational system. However, many similarities exist.

To meet the responsibility of maintaining and supporting schools, provinces have several powers:

- the power to tax for the support of schools and to determine provincial aid to local school districts
- the power to set curricula and to identify approved textbooks
- the power to determine minimum standards for teacher certification
- the power to establish standards for accrediting schools
- the power to pass legislation necessary for the proper maintenance and support of schools

To carry out the tasks implied by these powers, the provinces have adopted a number of different organizational structures, all of which are hierarchical.

THE ROLES OF THE PROVINCIAL GOVERNMENT IN EDUCATION

Various persons and agencies within each provincial government play a role in operating the education system within that province. Though provincial governments differ in many respects, the legislature, the courts, and the ideology of the party in power have a direct, critical impact on education in their province.

The Legislature   In every province, the legislature is responsible for establishing and maintaining public schools and for determining basic education policies within the province. To accomplish these ends, the legislature has the power to enact laws related to education.

Among the policies that the legislature may determine are the following:

- how the ministry of education will function
- the composition of local and regional districts
- how higher education will be organized and financed
- how local school boards will be elected and what their powers will be

In addition, the legislature may determine how taxes will be used to support schools, what will or will not be taught, the length of the school day and school year, how many years of compulsory education are required, and whether the province will have community colleges and/or vocational/technical schools. Legislatures may also make policies about pupil attendance, admission, promotion, teacher certification, teacher tenure and retirement, and collective bargaining. For example, in 1992 the Newfoundland legislature considered extending the school day and adding full-time kindergarten programs, while New Brunswick considered focusing on preschool programs and programs to help children in need of special services. In

EDUCATION IN THE NEWS

School Responsibilities May Devolve to School Councils

The volume of discussion on the issue of more parental input into schooling has risen across the country over the past year. Canadian schools have traditionally had parent advisory committees that spent their time raising money for special trips or equipment. More recently, politicians have begun to consider giving parents and community members more say in the running of schools.

The 1995 OISE national survey reported that 85 percent of those polled support the creation of parent advisory councils and that 68 percent said they were willing to serve on them. The issue of greater parental involvement in schools seems to have struck a chord across Canada. With the perception growing that family, community, and religion are in decline, the idea of strong and parent-run schools seems to be resonating with Canadians. Schools may become the next institution through which local values are articulated and community authority exercised. Parent advisory councils may have a say in budgeting, curriculum, scheduling, and hiring.

In February 1995, parent advisory councils in Alberta were replaced by new, more powerful school councils. Each council was instructed to develop a charter that would define the school's mandate. In Saskatchewan, community schools are becoming involved in the discussions of how many and which responsibilities should devolve to the parent advisory councils. In Ontario, the Royal Commission on Learning has recommended that parent advisory councils be created with greater responsibilities than parent groups now hold.

School councils might one day take over disciplining students and provide mentors, volunteers, social workers, and counsellors. Might school councils simplify the roles and expectations of teachers and administrators? How can we prevent school councils from being taken over by special interest groups, cliques, or zealots, and guarantee that the community at large has a voice?

Source: Based on the *Globe and Mail*, Feb. 2, 3, 10, 11, Mar. 10, 17, 1995.

1994, Saskatchewan planned to improve collaboration between schools and various social services agencies to help children who were at risk of dropping out.[16]

Although legislatures implement policy through legislation, individual ministries write rules and regulations. By doing so, government bureaucrats translate political intentions into practice. Ministries also conduct studies to provide politicians and the public with information. For example, in 1989, the Planning and Policy Secretariat of the Alberta Department of Education reported on the population's changing demographics and on trends that affect families and youth such as the growth of single-parent families, teen pregnancy, substance abuse, and suicide.[17] Government policy makers used this information to decide how schools could move beyond their traditional roles to address these issues.

These examples demonstrate the direction that educational policy is beginning to take. Rather than regarding schools as agents which fulfil only custodial, training, and educative roles for children, provincial legislatures are increasingly considering how schools can be caregivers as well. Until recently, schools have generally assumed that families, religious bodies, and communities would ensure children were ready to learn, and it was the school's role to teach children. Schools resisted adopting social service roles. But provincial legislatures are beginning to view schools as integral to children's emotional health and are developing legislation accordingly.

Legislatures also develop policies that apply to private schools in the province—policies related to health services, building construction, safety, textbooks, and testing of pupils, for example. In general, legislatures pass laws that provide for the reasonable supervision of private educational institutions.

The Premier The premier has a great deal of influence in how a province is governed. He or she is the leader of the party with the greatest number of seats in the legislature and has also been elected by the party membership to lead the party. Thus the premier has a mandate from both the party members and from the electorate.

Premiers influence and direct the issues and legislation that come before the legislature. If a premier considers education a priority, it will probably be a priority during his or her term. Furthermore, premiers appoint the ministers of education and help to write budgets that set the amounts allocated to education. They may also choose to use any accumulated balances in the provincial treasury for education.

MINISTRY OF EDUCATION

Ministries of education have a broad set of responsibilities that affect every school, school district, and teacher education program in a province. In general, the **ministry of education** is concerned with policy making and with the day-to-day implementation of those policies.

Traditional responsibilities of ministries of education include (1) certifying teachers, (2) distributing provincial funds to school districts, (3) reporting to the public the state of education within the province, (4) ensuring that school districts follow provincial guidelines, (5) accrediting schools, (6) monitoring student transportation and safety, and (7) sponsoring research and evaluation projects to improve education within the province.

Until the 1970s, ministries of education collected evaluative data on education programs within the province. But the economy became more information driven and the number of post-secondary spaces increased substantially. Parents wanted to ensure their children had access to this education. As parents became increasingly concerned about the education their children were receiving, ministries were pressured to provide data on the performance of specific districts, schools, and programs.

During the 1980s, ministries of education also became increasingly involved with other ministries and with issues that traditionally belonged to social service agencies. In 1985 in British Columbia, for example, educators were mandated to report any suspicion or evidence of child abuse to the appropriate social service authorities. Teachers were made criminally liable if they were found to ignore clear indications of child abuse.[18] Previously, spotting child abuse was considered outside teachers' domain or skills. Now, teachers and principals were compelled to defer to other agencies. Other social issues with which ministries of education became involved include substance abuse, homelessness, poverty, and health issues such as teenage pregnancies and AIDS.

MINISTER OF EDUCATION

The minister of education is a member of the provincial legislature and is appointed by the premier to be the central educational authority in the province. He or she is a member of the cabinet and provides direction to the government on policy development. Ministers of education have tremendous influence over policy for the entire public school system. The priority education receives in any province depends to some degree on the power wielded by the individual minister.

Although the specific responsibilities of the minister of education vary from province to province, several held in common are the following:

1. Responsibility for the ministry of education
2. Making decisions on a range of educational priorities
3. Recommending policies, rules, and regulations to the provincial cabinet deemed necessary for efficient governance of the schools
4. Interpreting provincial school laws, policies, rules, and regulations
5. Ensuring compliance with applicable laws, policies, rules, and regulations
6. Arranging for studies, committees, and task forces as necessary to study educational problems and recommend plans for improvement
7. Reporting on the status of education within the province to the premier, legislature, and public[19]

As the aforementioned responsibilities indicate, the minister of education is a very influential person. He or she is frequently called on to tell the premier, the legislature, and the people of the province what steps should be taken to improve education.

WHAT ASSISTANCE DO REGIONAL EDUCATIONAL SERVICE AGENCIES PROVIDE SCHOOLS?

When we think of how schools are governed and the sources of political pressure applied to them, we typically think of influences originating at two levels: local and provincial. There is, however, an additional source of control—the **regional**, or intermediate, **unit**. Through the intermediate unit, local school districts can receive support services that, economically and logistically, they could not provide for themselves.

Regionalization can be achieved through two processes: consolidating school districts into larger regional districts and establishing a middle bureaucratic structure to operate between the school districts and the ministry of education. For example, before 1994 Alberta had several hundred public and separate school districts, many of which had only one school. To provide these small districts with the support services that larger districts normally have, the Department of Education created five regional offices. Although several regional offices were later closed, school districts were also forced to consolidate, ensuring that smaller isolated schools continued to have support services.

The primary role of the intermediate unit is to provide assistance directly to districts in the areas of staff development, curriculum development, instructional media, and program evaluation. Intermediate or regional units also help school districts with their school improvement efforts by providing help in targeted areas such as French immersion, vocational education, computer education, and the education of gifted and talented and handicapped students.[20] Although intermediate units do monitor local school districts to see that they follow provincial educational guidelines, "local districts [actually] exert more influence over the intermediate unit and often specify what services shall or shall not be rendered by the regional unit."[21] Other regional support units do not provide a monitoring function. For instance, smaller school boards often form such units voluntarily to share services that an individual district could not otherwise afford.

HOW DOES THE FEDERAL GOVERNMENT INFLUENCE EDUCATION?

Although the Constitution gives exclusive responsibility for education to the provinces, the federal government has increasingly found ways to influence education by funding special services. In 1994 the federal government funded educational initiatives through 29 departments and agencies.[22] Hundreds of millions of dollars are channeled into education and training because issues such as the school dropout rate, youth crime, unemployment, poverty, and industry/schools cooperation have national implications.

High school dropout levels will affect a country's productivity and competitiveness. Children at risk of becoming dropouts can be identified as young as seven years old. The federal government makes resources available for educators, parents, business, and community groups to encourage youth to stay in school. The federal government is also interested in reducing dependence on unemployment insurance, and there is a direct correlation between levels of education and employment.

The federal government is solely responsible for matters related to First Nations Canadians. The locus of control for education of Aboriginal Canadians living on reserves has recently shifted from the Department of Indian and Northern Affairs to individual band councils.

Employment Canada, another federal department, wants to improve relations between the private sector and the public education system. Federal funds have been made available to schools which commit to developing job training programs targeted at specific sectors of the work force. Such programs have the additional benefit of bringing previous dropouts back into the system.

HOW ARE SCHOOLS FINANCED IN CANADA?

To provide free public education to all school-age children in Canada is a costly undertaking. It costs about one dollar for every five dollars provinces have. It is second only to the cost of health care, which is about 50 percent more. In 1993, Canadians spent approximately $35 billion to educate over 5.2 million students.[23] Even though the number of students in Canada decreased from 5.8 million in 1971 to 5.2 million in 1993, the costs increased from $5.4 billion to $35 billion. Thus financing education is a major concern for provincial government politicians.

LOCAL FUNDING OF EDUCATION

With the exception of Prince Edward Island, New Brunswick, the Northwest Territories, and most recently Alberta, local school boards in Canada raise a portion of their annual budgets from property taxes. The proportion of income that boards raise varies greatly and depends upon provincial policy. For example, Manitoba, Ontario, and Saskatchewan provide roughly half of the money to local boards and the rest is raised through property taxes.[24]

Provinces that require school districts to raise money through local property taxes have to constantly adjust their contributions to achieve a level of equity among the various districts. Because some districts have greater wealth than others, they may have more funds available. Rural districts have large transportation

To develop additional sources of funding, many local school districts have established community partnerships with businesses, such as the Bank of Montreal.

costs while urban districts may have no transportation costs at all. Provincial authorities monitor these discrepancies and provide equalization payments to ensure that educational opportunities are as equitable as possible.

An additional challenge for local funding is developing guidelines to assess the value of property. The fair market value of property is difficult to determine, and the qualifications and training of assessors vary greatly. Moreover, individuals and groups in a community sometimes pressure assessors to keep taxes on their property as low as possible.

Most provinces specify by law the minimum property tax rate for local school districts to set. Voters have a say about property tax increases at the next school board election. If a tax hike is considered unwarranted, the voters may not re-elect trustees. Some provinces place no cap, or upper limit, on tax rates, and other provinces set a maximum limit.

Community-School Partnerships To develop additional sources of funding, many local school districts have established partnerships with community groups interested in improving educational opportunities in the schools. Some groups raise money for schools. Other partners are businesses that work with school systems, such as Alberta Government Telephones (AGT) which, together with the Calgary School District, created Canada's first workplace school.

Business-school partnerships take many forms. Businesses may contribute funds or materials needed by a school or may give employees release time to visit classrooms. In some dropout prevention programs, business people adopt individual students, visiting them at school, eating lunch with them once a week, meeting their

Community group funding is often used to pay for field trips and other non-core activities.

families, and taking them on personal field trips. Community groups may also provide a variety of special services, such as museum-in-the-schools programs, outdoor education, local history projects, and model government activities. Community-based fraternal, civic, and service organizations also provide valuable support. They may sponsor sports teams, recognize student achievement, or award scholarships.

PROVINCIAL FUNDING OF EDUCATION

Most provincial revenues for education come from sales taxes and income taxes. Sales taxes are added to the cost of items such as general goods, gasoline, amusements, alcohol, and insurance. Income taxes are placed on individuals, business, and industry.

The percentage of funding for education contributed by the provinces varies. Alberta, New Brunswick, Prince Edward Island, and the Northwest Territories contribute nearly 100 percent. Newfoundland, Nova Scotia, Quebec, British Columbia, and the Yukon pay between 80 and 93 percent, while Manitoba, Ontario, and Saskatchewan give about 50 percent.

School boards and districts are generally given a lump sum of money called a block grant, and the board or local school decides how to spend its allocation. Provinces may also provide categorical grants, monies that must be spent as the province dictates. This type of grant is often linked to special programs, administrative allowances, or kindergarten programs. Finally, provinces may give equalization grants to ensure that all districts are able to spend roughly the same amount per student. Such grants may be tied to certain specific expenses such as transportation or to account for low property values in some communities.

All provinces pay for new school buildings from capital funds. When a district identifies the need for new buildings, it applies for funding from the province. The

FIGURE 9.3

Public Spending on Education as a Percent of Gross Domestic Product: An International Comparison

Source: The Research Department of the American Federation of Teachers, Research Report: *Survey & Analysis of Salary Trends 1992* (Washington, D.C.: American Federation of Teachers), p. ix.

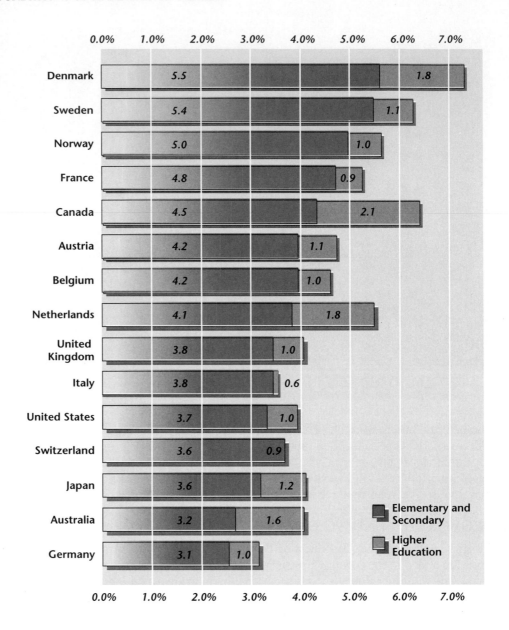

province in turn rank orders all requests and approves some. Once a district receives permission to build, virtually all costs associated with construction are covered by the province.

FEDERAL FUNDING OF EDUCATION

The federal government gives all provinces transfer payments to partially pay for social services, welfare, health, and post-secondary education. These payments account for more than 40 percent of total revenue in smaller provinces such as Newfoundland and Prince Edward Island and as little as 10 percent in larger provinces such as Ontario, British Columbia, and Alberta. In recent years, the federal government has capped the amount it will give the provinces through transfer payments and is considering further reductions. Although the federal government does not specifically earmark funds for education, any reductions in transfer payments will inevitably have an impact on overall provincial budgets and consequently on education.

Compared with most other industrialized nations, Canada spends significantly more. Figure 9.3 shows the percentage of the 1987 gross domestic product spent on education in fifteen countries including Canada. Canada was fifth behind Denmark, Sweden, Norway, and France in spending on elementary and secondary education, but second only to Denmark in total education spending. In 1991, Canada spent 7.1 percent of its gross domestic product on education.[25] In 1994, Canada spent the highest percentage of its gross domestic product on education of all industrialized countries in the world.[26] It is only a matter of time before the federal and provincial governments decrease their total spending, including spending on education.

PROFESSIONAL PORTFOLIO

For this portfolio entry, prepare a profile of a school district. The district may be in your home town, your university community, or a community in which you would like to teach. Information on the district may be obtained from your university library, public library, school district office, ministry of education, or professional teacher associations.

Keeping in mind that school district statistics are more readily available in some cases than in others, your profile might include the following types of information:

- Organizational chart showing (if possible) personnel currently assigned to each position
- Tables showing numbers of school buildings, students, teachers, administrators, support personnel, etc.
- Graduation/dropout rate
- Total annual budget
- Expenditures per pupil
- Demographic characteristics of population living in the area served by the district—age, race/ethnicity, socioeconomic status, unemployment rate, etc.
- Volunteer groups serving schools in the district
- Pupil-teacher ratio
- Percent of ethnic minority students, students with disabilities, etc.
- Percent of students going on to post-secondary education

CHAPTER SUMMARY

One of the professional challenges teachers face is learning to understand the political and economic forces that influence their work. Although some might believe that politics and teaching should remain separate, it is a fact of life that school policies are developed in a political milieu. Moreover, many groups have a keen interest in influencing education policies, among them, parents, students, teachers, administrators, taxpayers, provincial and local authorities, minorities, women, educational theorists, researchers, businesses, and corporations.

An examination of who controls today's schools reveals that those whom we might expect to be in control, principals, superintendents, and school trustees, are for the most part responding to a variety of social forces and pressures. Schools in each province reflect the society they serve, and the extent to which any individual or group controls the school is limited indeed.

Locally, the primary responsibility for the daily operation of public schools lies with the local school board and the superintendent of schools. School districts vary greatly in their organizational structures and operating procedures with many districts moving toward greater organizational complexity and ever-larger operating budgets.

To improve their schools, many school districts are implementing various restructuring programs. Some have begun to decentralize school governance and enhance the status of teachers. Examples of school-based management are found in the Edmonton, Langley, and Peace River North school districts.

Schools in Canada are supported by revenues from local and provincial sources, with more than half and sometimes all coming from the provinces. Locally, it is a continuing challenge to provide equality in educational opportunities regardless of the wealth of the surrounding community. In provinces that pay the entire cost of education, the quality of education is not tied to the wealth of the community.

KEY TERMS AND CONCEPTS

community-school partnerships, 226
funding of education, 225
minister of education 223
ministry of education, 223

parent advisory council (PAC), 217
parent-teacher association (PTA), 217
regional unit, 224
restructuring, 217

school-based management (SBM), 217
school board, 213
school districts, 212
superintendent, 215

APPLICATIONS AND ACTIVITIES

Teacher's Journal

1. Would you prefer working in a large, medium, or small school district? Discuss the reasons for your choice.

2. If you were able to arrange a fifteen-minute meeting with the minister of education in your province, what would you tell him or her about the concerns of prospective teachers?

3. Imagine that you have vouchers to send your child to any school in your province. What factors would you consider in making your choice?

4. Think of businesses and groups in your community that may make good candidates for a partnership with a school. Choose one and develop a proposal outlining the nature, activities, and benefits of the partnership you envision.

Field Assignments

1. Attend a meeting of the local school board and observe the communication and decision-making processes at that meeting. Note the following: topics on the agenda, who set the agenda, who participates in the discussion, how participation varies according to topic, who proposes policy, and the extent of agreement between superintendent and board. Note also the harmony or lack of harmony among board members. Finally, do you see evidence of single-issue interests?

2. Interview a school superintendent and ask him or her to comment on how federal, provincial, and local forces affect education in the district. To what extent do influences at these three levels help (and/or hinder) the district in accomplishing its goals?

3. Develop and administer a questionnaire to teachers on the subject of restructuring and school-based management. Design your questions to discover what teachers think about shared decision making and local governance of schools, and share your findings with classmates.

10 Legal Concerns in Canadian Education

. . . by its very nature, the law is often complex and uncertain. New issues and new perspectives on old issues arise continually; questions that once seemed settled are reexamined as notions about government and law evolve.

— Michael Imber and Tyll van Geel
Education Law

Focus Questions

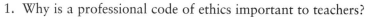

1. Why is a professional code of ethics important to teachers?
2. What are the legal rights of teachers?
3. What are the legal rights of students?
4. What are the rights and responsibilities of student teachers?

Rich, a student in your third-period class at the rural high school where you teach, follows every game of a professional basketball team. To show his support, he wears a team jacket and cap to school each day. Until recently, Rich's choice of dress has been no cause for concern—other than an occasional comment to Rich about the performance of his team during the most recent game, you and his classmates have paid little attention to what Rich wears.

Three weeks ago, however, Rich's appearance changed. Every day now he wears the same type of clothing—a starched white T-shirt, baggy khaki pants that ride ridiculously low on his hips, and high-top basketball shoes. And, last week, Rich started coming to class wearing slicked-back hair. Yesterday, you even had to interrupt your lesson for a moment to ask him to stop applying a sweet-smelling yellow gel to his hair. With a scowl and moan of disgust—a surprising departure from his usually affable, easygoing demeanor—Rich complied and reluctantly shoved the tube of gel into his pants pocket.

Since Rich began dressing like this, some students have begun to tease him. When a student recently asked Rich about the name of the gang he was starting, you began to wonder if Rich's new appearance might be gang-inspired. Rich has always been a "good kid," and his playful attitude makes it hard to believe that he really intends to start a gang in this peaceful farming community.

As your students enter class today, you notice that Eric, a good friend of Rich's, is dressed in a similar manner. His long black hair is slicked back, as though he just stepped out of a shower. Like Rich, he is wearing tan khaki pants, a T-shirt, and basketball shoes. Rich joins Eric, and they saunter nonchalantly around the perimeter of the room. Both are laughing and guffawing, delighting in the fact that everyone's eyes are on them. Several students giggle and point at them. For a moment, Rich and Eric return the stares with menacing leers, but then they, too, start laughing. After some prodding from you, the two boys finally slide into their seats. Several of their classmates continue to point at them and snicker.

"O.K., class," you begin. "Let's settle down. We've got a lot of work to do today if we're going to be ready for tomorrow's test."

Even with the reference to tomorrow's test, it's more difficult than usual to get your students' attention. Clearly, the appearance of Rich and Eric has unsettled the whole class.

As you continue with the lesson, you wonder if you have the right to speak to Rich and Eric and request that they change their appearance. Or, do they have the right to wear whatever they want to school?

_____

In this chapter we examine significant legal decisions that affect the rights and responsibilities of teachers, administrators, and students. Teachers must act in accordance with a wide range of federal and provincial legislation and court decisions. As a teacher, you may need to deal with such legal issues as the teacher's responsibility for accidents, discriminatory employment practices, freedom of speech, student rights, and circumstances related to termination or dismissal. Without a knowledge of the legal dimensions of such issues, you will be ill-equipped to protect your rights and the rights of your students.

WHY IS A PROFESSIONAL CODE OF ETHICS IMPORTANT TO TEACHERS?

The actions of professional teachers are determined not only by what is legally required of them, but also by what they know they *ought* to do. They do what is legally right, and they *do the right thing*. A specific set of values guides them. A deep and lasting commitment to professional practice characterizes their work. They have adopted a high standard of professional ethics and they model behaviors that are in accord with that code of ethics.

There is no single code of ethics to guide teachers across Canada; instead, each teachers' association has adopted a code of ethics. The Alberta Teachers' Association, for instance, has a Code of Professional Conduct that stipulates minimum standards for its membership to follow. Part of the Code is included here to give you an idea of the standards teachers are typically required to follow.[1]

IN RELATION TO PUPILS

1. The teacher teaches in a manner that respects the dignity and rights of all persons without prejudice as to race, religious beliefs, color, sex, physical characteristics, age, ancestry, or place of origin.
2. (1) The teacher is responsible for diagnosing educational needs, prescribing and implementing instructional programs and evaluating progress of students. (2) The teacher may not delegate these responsibilities to any person who is not a teacher.
3. The teacher may delegate specific and limited aspects of instructional activity to noncertified personnel, provided that the teacher supervises and directs such activities.
4. The teacher treats pupils with dignity and respect and is considerate of their circumstances.
5. The teacher may not divulge information about a pupil received in confidence or in the course of professional duties except as required by law or where, in the judgment of the teacher, to do so is in the best interest of the pupil.

6. The teacher may not accept pay for tutoring a pupil in any subjects in which the teacher is responsible for giving classroom instruction to that pupil.
7. The teacher may not take advantage of a professional position to profit from the sale of goods or services to or for pupils in the teacher's charge.

IN RELATION TO SCHOOL AUTHORITIES

8. The teacher protests the assignment of duties for which the teacher is not qualified or conditions which make it difficult to render professional services.
9. The teacher fulfils contractual obligations to the employer until released by mutual consent or according to law.
10. The teacher provides as much notice as possible of a decision to terminate employment.
11. The teacher adheres to agreements negotiated on the teacher's behalf by the Association.

IN RELATION TO COLLEAGUES

12. The teacher does not undermine the confidence of pupils in other teachers.
13. The teacher criticizes the professional competence or professional reputation of another teacher only in confidence to proper officials and after the other teacher has been informed of the criticism.
14. The teacher, when making a report on the professional performance of another teacher, does so in good faith and, prior to submitting the report, provides the teacher with a copy of the report.
15. The teacher does not take, because of animosity or personal advantage, any steps to secure dismissal of another teacher.
16. The teacher recognizes the duty to protest through proper channels administrative policies and practices which the teacher cannot in conscience accept; and further recognizes that, if administration by consent fails, the administrator must adopt a position of authority.
17. The teacher as an administrator provides opportunities for staff members to express their opinions and to bring forth suggestions regarding the administration of the school.

IN RELATION TO THE PROFESSION

18. The teacher acts in a manner which maintains the honor and dignity of the profession.
19. The teacher does not engage in activities which adversely affect the quality of the teacher's professional service.
20. The teacher submits to the Association disputes arising from professional relationships with other teachers which cannot be resolved by personal discussion.
21. The teacher makes representations on behalf of the Association or members thereof only when authorized to do so.
22. The teacher accepts that service to the Association is a professional responsibility.

RIGHTS AND RESPONSIBILITIES OF TEACHERS

The Alberta Teachers' Association Member Handbook also outlines the rights and responsibilities of ATA members. The statements of rights and responsibilities have been separated into columns to highlight more clearly the tensions that exist between these two aspects of a teacher's role.

RIGHTS	RESPONSIBILITIES
Teachers have the right	**Teachers have the responsibility**
• to base diagnosis, planning, methodology, and evaluation on professional knowledge and skills	• to review constantly their own level of competence and effectiveness and to seek necessary improvements as part of a continuing process of professional development
• to expect standards of pupil behavior necessary for maintaining an optimal learning environment	• to use reasonable methods to achieve such standards
• to a voice in all decisions of a professional nature which affect them	• to seek the most effective means of consultation and of collaboration with their professional colleagues
• to criticize educational programs	• to do so in a professional manner
• to work in surroundings that are sanitary, healthful and conducive to teaching and learning	• to assess conditions encountered and to seek improvement of unacceptable conditions
• to a reasonable allotment of resources, materials and services of support staff	• to use them in an efficient manner
• to fair and reasonable evaluation of professional performance	• to give sincere consideration to any suggestions for improvement
• to protest and in extreme cases to refuse the assignment of teaching duties when they believe their qualifications and experience will not provide adequate service and safety to pupils	• to consider any special circumstances under which the duties were assigned

- to be protected against discrimination on the basis of prejudice as to race, religion, color, sex, physical characteristics, age, ancestry, or place of origin

- to refrain from practicing these forms of discrimination in their professional duties

ETHICAL TEACHING ATTITUDES AND PRACTICES

Teaching is an ethical enterprise—that is, a teacher has an obligation to act ethically, to follow what he or she knows to be the most appropriate professional action to take. The best interests of students, not the teacher, should determine what is ethical and what is not. Behaving ethically is more than a matter of following the rules or not breaking the law—it means acting in a way that promotes the learning and growth of students and helps them realize their potential.

Unethical acts break the trust and respect on which good student-teacher relationships are based. An example of unethical conduct would be public ridicule of the appearance of Rich and Eric, the two students described in this chapter's opening vignette. Other examples would be using grades as a form of punishment, expressing rage in the classroom, or intentionally tricking students on tests. You could no doubt think of other examples from your own experience as a student. The ATA Code of Professional Conduct identifies specific behaviors a teacher should avoid. Examine this code carefully. Do you disagree with any of the items? Should any be added?

"Wilson, about your interest center on statistics and probability..."

ETHICAL DILEMMAS IN THE CLASSROOM AND SCHOOL

Teachers routinely encounter **ethical dilemmas** in the classroom and in the school. They often have to take action in situations in which all the facts are not known or in which no single course of action can be called right or wrong. At these times it can be quite difficult to decide what an ethical response might be. Dealing satisfactorily with ethical dilemmas in teaching often requires the ability to see beyond short-range consequences to consider long-range consequences.

Consider, for example, the following three questions based on actual case studies. Based on the information given, how would you respond to each situation?

1. Should the sponsor of the high school literary magazine refuse to print a well-written story by a budding writer if the piece appears to satirize a teacher and a student?
2. Is a reading teacher justified in trying to increase achievement for an entire class by separating two disruptive students and placing one in a reading group beneath his or her reading level?
3. Should a chemistry teacher punish a student (on the basis of circumstantial, inconclusive evidence) for a laboratory explosion if decisive, swift punishment will likely prevent the recurrence of a similar event and thereby ensure the safety of all students?[2]

As these cases suggest, responding ethically to a dilemma can be difficult. The first case poses a choice between censorship and disrespect, the second between class disruption and individual low achievement, and the third between inappropriate punishment and the possibility of accidents. Teachers must be prepared to go beyond their first impulse, to carefully weigh alternatives and to consider possible consequences.

WHAT ARE THE LEGAL RIGHTS OF TEACHERS?

It is frequently observed that with each freedom comes a corresponding responsibility to others and to the community in which we live. As long as more than one individual inhabits this planet, laws will be needed to clarify individual rights and responsibilities. This necessary balance between rights and responsibilities is perhaps more critical to teaching than to any other profession. As one observer put it, the "rights of teachers are simultaneously simple yet complex; straightforward yet convoluted; and, clearly established yet little understood. These apparently mutually exclusive qualities exist because there are two sources of the rights that teachers enjoy: (1) their general rights as individual citizens, and (2) adjustments in those rights required by the special nature of their occupation."[3]

While "adjustments" may apply to the legal rights of teachers, their right to **procedural fairness** cannot be violated. Teachers, like all citizens, are protected from being treated arbitrarily by those in authority. A principal who disagrees with a teacher's methods cannot suddenly fire him. A school board cannot ask a teacher to resign merely by claiming that her political activities outside of school "disrupt" the educational process. A teacher cannot be dismissed for "poor" performance without ample documentation that the performance was, in fact, poor and without sufficient time to meet clearly stated performance evaluation criteria.

In addition to the right to procedural fairness, prospective teachers should know about their legal rights in the areas of teacher certification, employment, evaluation, discipline, termination, off-duty conduct, immorality and crime, alcohol and drugs, and life-style choices.[2] These concerns are discussed below, drawing from several provinces' requirements.

TEACHER CERTIFICATION

Teacher certification is a provincial responsibility under the authority of the minister of education. Certification determines at what category and classification teachers are placed. A teacher's certification level depends on his or her post-secondary education and number of years of teaching experience. A teacher's salary depends on what certification he or she possesses although the actual dollar figure is determined by the collective agreement struck between the teachers' union and the school board.

Establishing a classification structure is usually a joint process by the Ministry of Education, the School Trustees' Association, and the Teachers' Association. School boards are obligated to pay a minimum salary depending on a teacher's classification but they may choose to recognize non-board teaching experience and pay a higher amount. Previous military service and private school experience have both been recognized by public boards as relevant experience.

TEACHER EMPLOYMENT

New teachers are often hired on probation. Several provinces have argued that they cannot reasonably be expected to assess the capabilities and skills of a job ap-

What duties will be expected of this teacher that are not spelled out in the contract? What kinds of noncontractual duties can teachers refuse?

plicant from a two-page résumé and a 30-minute interview. Instead, new teachers are assessed over a period of time without the protection of a permanent contract. The length of the probationary period varies from province to province.

Teacher contracts take many forms. Besides **probationary and permanent contracts,** temporary or casual contracts are used for teaching positions for a fixed term usually less than one school year. In Ontario, an occasional teacher is employed to substitute for another teacher for a term less than a school year, for example, to replace a teacher on maternity leave. Teachers hired as substitutes or part-time teachers may have fewer benefits than teachers hired on standard probationary or permanent contracts.

Some part-time contracts automatically terminate at the end of the school year and teachers who have such contracts have to wait until late spring or even August to find out whether their contract will be renewed.

TEACHER EVALUATION

Teachers are generally evaluated annually. Evaluations may be used as the basis of promotion, retention, or dismissal, or to determine salary increases. Evaluations are usually based on observation by the teacher's supervisor. Following the evaluation, the supervisor will produce a report outlining his or her opinions and recommendations. The teacher is asked to sign the report, indicating that he or she has read and understood it, not necessarily agreed with it. Teachers will sometimes write their own comments on the report so that the supervisor receives feedback on the report's content.

It is a basic principle of procedural fairness that employees must have the opportunity to correct substandard or unacceptable behavior. Supervisors must take into account the nature of the class the teacher has, the subject the teacher teaches, and the number of visits the supervisor has made to observe. Criteria for evaluation must be applied consistently for all teachers across the district or board.

TEACHER DISCIPLINE AND TERMINATION

Teacher discipline may mean terminating the contract, written warnings, suspension, or demotion. Because collective agreements usually include a clause about discipline for "just cause," teachers are able to challenge a discipline decision through the grievance procedure and arbitration. Just cause or procedural fairness provisions provide both the teacher and his or her employer with a process for reaching a decision about a dispute that binds both sides. Just cause provisions enable parties frequently to resolve issues without resorting to the courts.

OFF-DUTY CONDUCT OF THE TEACHER

School districts can make rules concerning the off-duty conduct of teachers, but they must prove that the conduct is legitimately connected to the specific role of the teacher. Canadian courts have generally accepted that teachers cannot escape from their responsibility to be a role model even when not working. However, the teacher's actual conduct must be directly connected to the responsibility of teaching. For example, although in the past school districts regulated how long a pregnant teacher could work, most districts today have eased such restrictions. However, Catholic school districts may still require that teachers be practicing Catholics and that they follow all tenets of Roman Catholicism.

IMMORALITY, CRIME AND THE TEACHER

Immorality committed by the teacher while on duty is considered clear grounds for dismissal. In cases of sexual misconduct the student's age is irrelevant. School districts can even request a psychiatric examination of a teacher if the board suspects the teacher's emotional or mental health is putting students at risk and makes a proper case to the courts. Boards can also dismiss teachers whose life-styles run counter to the morality of the board, particularly with Catholic boards. While teaching is a moral act in that teachers enter into special relationships with students, criminal immorality is distinguished as acts against others that run counter to the law.

ALCOHOL, DRUGS, AND THE TEACHER

The concern of school boards and supervisors over teachers who misuse alcohol or drugs is usually related more to a teacher's performance than morality. Teachers with a substance abuse problem may have high rates of absenteeism, become markedly less efficient, or have specific physical impairments. Concern is especially high if these teachers supervise students in laboratories, technical shops, or gymnasiums where students may get injured.

While the dangers of abusing some drugs are similar to the dangers associated with alcohol, many recreational drugs are illegal. Conviction for possession of marijuana has in itself been grounds for dismissal in Canada. Courts have also upheld dismissals based on the fact that teachers were encouraging students to use alcohol and illegal drugs. The courts' judgments cited the belief that teachers should be role models and the concern that teachers' effectiveness and credibility in the classroom would be diminished.[5]

THE TEACHER AND LIFE-STYLE CHOICES

Canadian courts have recognized teachers' right to privacy. The two questions a court will examine in determining whether a life-style choice should be grounds for

TABLE 10.1   **Physical and Behavioral Indicators of Child Abuse and Neglect**

Type of child abuse/neglect	Physical indicators	Behavioral indicators
Physical Abuse	Unexplained bruises and welts: • on face, lips, mouth • on torso, back, buttocks, thighs • in various stages of healing • clustered, forming regular patterns • reflecting shape of article used to inflict (electric cord, belt buckle) • on several different surface areas • regularly appear after absence, weekend, or vacation • human bite marks • bald spots Unexplained burns: • cigar, cigarette burns, especially on soles, palms, back, or buttocks • immersion burns (sock-like, glove-like, doughnut-shaped on buttocks or genitalia • patterned like electric burner, iron, etc. • rope burns on arms, legs, neck, or torso Unexplained fractures: • to skull, nose, facial structure • in various stages of healing • multiple or spiral fractures Unexplained lacerations or abrasions: • to mouth, lips, gums, eyes • to external genitalia	Wary of adult contacts Apprehensive when other children cry Behavioral extremes: • aggressiveness • withdrawal • overly compliant Afraid to go home Reports injury by parents Exhibits anxiety about normal activities, e.g., napping Complains of soreness and moves awkwardly Destructive to self and others Early to school or stays late as if afraid to go home Accident prone Wears clothing that covers body when not appropriate Chronic runaway (especially adolescents) Cannot tolerate physical contact or touch
Physical Neglect	Consistent hunger, poor hygiene, inappropriate dress Consistent lack of supervision, especially in dangerous activities or long periods Unattended physical problems or medical needs Abandonment Lice Distended stomach, emaciated	Begging, stealing food Constant fatigue, listlessness, or falling asleep States there is no caretaker at home Frequent school absence or tardiness Destructive, pugnacious School dropout (adolescents) Early emancipation from family (adolescents)
Sexual Abuse	Difficulty in walking or sitting • torn, stained, or bloody underclothing Pain or itching in genital area Bruises or bleeding in external genitalia, vaginal, or anal areas Venereal disease Frequent urinary or yeast infections Frequent unexplained sore throats	Unwilling to participate in certain physical activities Sudden drop in school performance Withdrawal, fantasy, or unusually infantile behavior Crying with no provocation Bizarre, sophisticated, or unusual sexual behavior or knowledge Anorexia (especially adolescents) Sexually provocative Poor peer relationships Reports sexual assault by caretaker Fear of or seductiveness toward males Suicide attempts (especially adolescents) Chronic runaway Early pregnancies
Emotional Maltreatment	Speech disorders Lags in physical development Failure to thrive (especially in infants) Asthma, severe allergies, or ulcers Substance abuse	Habit disorders (sucking, biting, rocking, etc.) Conduct disorders (antisocial, destructive, etc.) Neurotic traits (sleep disorders, inhibition of play) Behavioral extremes: • compliant, passive • aggressive, demanding Overly adaptive behavior: • inappropriately adult • inappropriately infantile Developmental lags (mental, emotional) Delinquent behavior (especially adolescents)

Source: C. C. Tower, *How Schools Can Help Combat Child Abuse and Neglect*, 2d ed. (Washington, D.C.: National Education Association, 1987), 162–163. Adapted from *Early Childhood Programs and the Prevention and Treatment of Child Abuse and Neglect*, by D. D. Broadhurst et al., The User Manual Series, 1979, Washington, D. C.: U.S. Department of Health, Education and Welfare.

dismissal are the following: First, does the given behavior affect students, colleagues, or the school? Second, how important is the behavior to the teacher's sense of self? Hair style, clothing, place of residence, and leisure activities have all been recognized as unreasonable grounds for punitive action. The more public a teacher's behavior is, the less likely a court is to rule that the teacher has the right to privacy and the more likely it is to rule in support of his or her dismissal.

In one case in which an unmarried woman teacher became pregnant and was dismissed, the courts upheld the dismissal because she taught for a Roman Catholic board. The court ruled that she could not be fired for being unmarried and pregnant but she could be dismissed for violating the Catholic doctrine forbidding premarital sex. The courts have also upheld the dismissal of a teacher employed by a Catholic board who converted to the Salvation Army. In public boards, however, teachers cannot be fired for breaking religious rules.[6]

REPORTING CHILD ABUSE

Teachers are now *required* by law to report any suspected child abuse because they are in positions to monitor and work against the physical, emotional, and sexual abuse and the neglect and exploitation of children. Teachers' professional journals and information from local and provincial child welfare agencies encourage teachers to be more observant of children's appearance and behavior in order to detect symptoms of child abuse. Such sources often provide lists of physical and behavioral indicators of potential child abuse, similar to those shown in Table 10.1. Many communities, through their police departments or other public and private agencies, provide programs adapted for children to educate them about their rights in child-abuse situations and to show them how to obtain help. Teachers in school systems that do not take advantage of these services may encourage their administrators to do so.

Schools usually have a specific procedure for dealing with suspected abuse cases, involving the school principal and nurse as well as the reporting teacher. Because a child's physical welfare may be further endangered when abuse is reported, caution and sensitivity are required. Before the school year begins teachers need to know the procedural expectations of their school. Teachers are in a unique position to help students who are victims of child abuse, both because they have daily contact with them and because children learn to trust them. It is imperative that they be informed about this problem and alert to signs of abuse in their children.

WHAT ARE THE LEGAL RIGHTS OF STUDENTS?

As a prospective teacher, you have an obligation to become familiar with the rights of students. Since the 1960s students have increasingly confronted teachers and school districts with what they perceive to be illegal restrictions on their behavior. In this section we discuss briefly some students' rights related to suspension and expulsion, physical punishment, privacy, and nondiscrimination.

Increasingly, the courts have moved in attitude from treating children as the property of their parents to viewing them as persons with inherent rights. Consequently, courts have increasingly intervened to guarantee specific rights for children. Children are acknowledged to hold legal rights separate from those of their parents or schools. Since the Canadian Charter of Rights and Freedoms, enacted

MAKING *a DIFFERENCE*

James Wallach
Kirkland, Quebec

I am an elementary phys. ed. instructor and several years ago I witnessed a dream come true. I wanted to train my students to compete in a triathlon and fifteen students took up the challenge and trained to swim one hundred yards [90 m], to bike three miles [5 km], and to run one mile [1.6 km]. My dream came true when they all completed the course and crossed the finish line, which was the objective. The following year, twenty hearty souls, including four veterans of the initial event, came out to train for the second annual triathlon.

The triathlon curriculum that I developed is a holistic curriculum that incorporates mental, physical, and affective domains of students' experiences. The students learn about the science of triathloning. The purpose of this program is to develop in students positive attitudes, awareness of the theory of "cross-training," increased physical fitness, improved enthusiasm for learning, improved mental capacities, and enhanced decision-making skills. The curriculum is divided into four main areas including triathlon concepts, skills, theory, and benefits. The methods used for the program involve actual skill teaching and, as skills are built and refined, many mental and affective areas of the child's world are touched.

I learned that I could not develop this program nor generate the level of interest needed to make it successful without the commitment of many students and parents. In fact, the local community pool staff were fantastic in helping to prepare for and staging the triathlon. The roles I found myself playing the most were those of guide, moderator, and coach as students struggled to achieve their different personal goals. I found that students responded more positively to me when I was a caring and helpful person and I found that I spent a tremendous amount of time with students encouraging them to complete the training.

I believe that we, as educators, must try to provide positive and meaningful experiences for our students. We must strive to influence our students in a positive way. The "TRI-TRI, AGAIN" program may involve the whole school and may be modified for handicapped students as well as for whole family participation. Its limitations are only bounded by the imagination of the person incorporating it. It is a program for all students, regardless of their skill levels, and can not only improve individual performance but can also develop a greater sense of self and of self-worth.

in 1982, is so recent, few cases relating to students' rights have gone through to the Supreme Court. However, with the Charter, certain student rights are constitutionally protected and school administrators and teachers will need to be vigilant in protecting them.

STUDENT RECORDS[7]

Who has access to student records and what type of information can be placed in them? The **confidentiality** of student records must be protected. In general, any information that will benefit teachers in their professional duties can become part of a student's records. However, information that discloses a contravention or an alleged contravention of a federal or provincial law cannot be written into the records. The one exception to this rule is that information about the student's conduct, school infractions, or disciplinary action may be included even if they disclose a contravention of the law.

School officials must preserve the secrecy of student records. Only parents and guardians are permitted to examine a student's records and only if the student is a minor. The parents of an adult student need written permission to see the records of their child. Without written consent, officials must refuse access to the records to all others, including social service agencies. They can give the police access only if ordered by the courts.

With divorced or separated parents, custody must be clearly demonstrated to school officials before the custodial parent is permitted to see the records. The onus is on the custodial parent to provide the school with a certified copy of the document establishing custody. If custody is not yet determined or is not clear, school officials should check with their legal counsel before allowing access.

CHILD ABUSE

Children have the right to be protected from abuse. All provinces and territories have created guidelines that compel teachers and administrators to report any suspected case of child abuse. All school boards are required to develop guidelines that specifically direct teachers and administrators to act quickly. Teachers are not absolved of responsibility simply by reporting their suspicions to their superiors; they must ensure that their suspicions are reported to the proper authorities.

STUDENTS UNDER CHILD CARE SERVICES

Students under the protection and care of social services, whether in a foster home, group home, or halfway house, have the right not to be discriminated against by educational authorities. They have the right to be treated equitably in the same uniform manner as all other children. Caregivers must exercise discipline as a kind, firm, and judicious parent would. Teachers should know that child care providers are specifically directed not to use corporal punishment on the child.

STUDENT DISCIPLINE

How do the rights of the student balance with the school's need to maintain an orderly learning environment? To begin, students have the right not to be disciplined in arbitrary or humiliating ways. School authorities may write rules for student behavior but they cannot prescribe punishments in advance. For example, the school may include in a rule that breaking the rule *may* result in a maximum of five days' suspension but it cannot say that breaking the rule *will* result in the suspension. Although the rule may be definite, any consequences or punishment must be applied case by case. If a disciplinary measure is appealed, the courts examine whether the rule has been applied equitably and uniformly.

Disciplinary actions can range from a private reprimand to **expulsion**. In between lie the following: public reprimand, removal from the class for a short period, denial of privileges (for example, participation in sports or field trips), extra work, detentions, **corporal punishment**, and **suspension**. Choosing the appropriate measure is a matter of judgment and is usually done in consultation with the principal or another school authority. It should be noted that, with the exception of suspension and expulsion, disciplinary measures are not meant to impair or interrupt the education of the student.

Many school districts have banned the use of all forms of corporal punishment. In the early 1970s, the government of British Columbia abolished corporal punishment for all school districts within that province. Although section 43 of the Criminal Code permits teachers to use "force by way of correction toward a pupil," public resistance to using any form of violence against children is increasing, and corporal punishment is rarely used today.

HAIR AND DRESS CODES

From the courts' point of view, schools seem to spend considerable time on hair and dress codes; certainly many cases have dealt with these matters. In general, courts require that, at least in the public system, an educational purpose be served by the enforcement of hair and dress codes. If a school or a school board cannot

Legal matters involving schools often focus on dress codes. However, if a school cannot show a connection between a hair or dress code and health, education, achievement, or discipline, courts in Canada will not order a student to follow the code.

EDUCATION IN THE NEWS

School Boards Under Scrutiny Across Canada

The 1995 Ontario Royal Commission on Learning did not see the trend toward reducing the number of school boards as all positive. When schools boards amalgamate, they combine personnel who were working under different contracts for differens salaries and benefits. When the new school board negotiates one contract for all employees who do similar work, the wages of the lowest paid workers are generally raised to the level of the highest paid ones. In the short term, amalgamation may not save money.

Alberta, Prince Edward Island, and New Brunswick have already reduced the number of boards in those provinces. British Columbia, Saskatchewan, Manitoba, Ontario, Nova Scotia, and Newfoundland are considering

similar measures. Quebec has decided to leave its boards alone but has decentralized some of their powers to the level of the local school.

The issue of reducing the number of school boards is always a political hot potato. The electorate often views the move not as one of fiscal responsibility but as one of centralizing control away from the local people.

The Alberta government moved to reduce community control over districts while simultaneously giving greater control to local school councils. How might the process of reducing numbers of school boards affect teachers and their relationships with their school communities?

Source: Based on the *Globe and Mail*, Feb. 22, 25, 1995.

---

show a connection between a hair or dress code and health, education, achievement, or discipline, a court will not order a student to follow the code. Canadian courts have rejected arguments that long hair on boys makes it difficult for teachers to determine students' gender, or that long hair on boys takes too long to dry after showering during physical education classes, or that the surrounding community objects to the clothing or hair style.

Courts across the country have not been consistent; in one case, the court agreed that a football coach could require his players to have short hair, although only during the football season, while in a similar case, another court held that the coach could not require his players to cut their hair. Similarly, one court supported the school when a student wearing jeans was ejected from a graduation ceremony while another court supported the student. In general, courts are more likely to uphold a school's code when a certain hair or clothing style actually disrupted the academic environment and to strike down a regulation that prohibits certain hair or clothing styles in all circumstances.

It is worth noting that the courts have tended to treat private schools differently from public ones. They have usually ruled that the parents' decision to send the child to the school binds both the parents and the student to conform with the school's rules and regulations.

THE YOUNG OFFENDERS ACT

In 1984 the **Young Offenders Act**[8] replaced the Juvenile Delinquents Act and has been plagued with controversy ever since. The media have painted adult criminals enlisting young people to become criminals because of the widespread belief that teens under 18 will get off without serious consequences. The media describe young offenders who laugh at both the risk of getting caught and at the consequences. Many people believe that children caught carrying drugs or crawling through basement windows will receive community service or probation while the adults who enlisted them would have received much stiffer sentences if convicted. But are the media giving a balanced perspective?

The Young Offenders Act sets out six principles that govern how young offenders should be handled:

1. While young offenders should bear responsibility for their actions, they may not always be held accountable in the same manner as adults.
2. Society must be protected from illegal activities of young persons, but society must also take responsibility for preventing illegal conduct of young persons.
3. Young persons have certain guaranteed rights and freedoms. In fact, they should have guarantees of special rights not granted to adults.
4. Young offenders require supervision, discipline, and control, but it must be recognized that they have special needs and require guidance and assistance as well.
5. Whenever it can be justified, that is, whenever it is consistent with the protection of society, authorities should consider how to help young persons avoid the court process and instead become involved with alternative processes.
6. Parents have the primary responsibility for the care and custody of their children. Young persons should be dealt with within the family setting whenever appropriate.

Several of these principles seem to be in conflict, especially the wish to balance the protection of society with the preservation of the family as an institution. Many experienced teachers know the difficulty they have in gaining the support of some parents whose children are doing poorly in school or who are at high risk of dropping out. For example, at parent-teacher conferences teachers are confronted every year with the fact that the parents who do attend are often the parents teachers do not need to see. Many parents of children in trouble with the law do not have the skills to alter their children's behavior.

The Young Offenders Act is more likely than the Juvenile Delinquents Act was to involve teachers and schools in the court process. Courts are ordering more predisposition reports that describe the child's environment and behavior, both at home and in school.

If a teacher or principal suspects a student is connected with illegal activity, the Young Offenders Act is clear on how the school should proceed in questioning the student. Because the courts assume teachers and principals are in a position of authority over students, educators must follow the same procedures as the police when questioning students. The person in authority must make it clear to the student that any statement is voluntary and freely given; that the statement can be used against the student as evidence; that the student has the right to consult a lawyer, parent, or another appropriate adult before making any statement; and that the person consulted can be present when the statement is made. Judges will rule a statement inadmissible if they believe it was made under duress; it is both advisable and preferable to safeguard the student's rights in the first place.

Teachers and principals who are asked to provide information about a student to a court or the police must request that the parent sign a release of information form or a court order. The school will normally supply grades, attendance records, any involvement with counsellors or psychologists, failure at any grade with a description of the circumstances, and a description of any difficulty in relationships with teachers and peers.

If a student commits a criminal offence at school, the principal and teachers may be asked by the court to allow the student to do community service at the school as a way of fulfilling probation. Students may also be required to attend school as part of probation. If teachers or principals are asked to write progress reports to the student's probation officer, they should do so objectively.

AVOIDING CIVIL LIABILITY IN SCHOOLS[9]

Teachers and schools have a duty of care toward their students. While at school, children should have the opportunity to acquire knowledge and skills, discipline should be fair and uniform, and the learning environment should be safe. Schools or teachers have been found civilly liable because of inadequate supervision; improper, defective, or inadequate equipment; failure to warn students properly of dangers related to a particular activity; failure to train students in the safe use of equipment; failure to take reasonable precautions; incompetent or poorly trained staff; and failure to treat an injury.

Teachers and principals are generally expected to act as a prudent parent would. However, a teacher with special skills, such as a physical education or a technical teacher, might be held to a higher standard because of his or her specialized knowledge. In one case, a sewing teacher was expected to exhibit the care of a "reasonably prudent sewing teacher" in predicting the danger to students of learning how to use a sewing machine. Similarly, principals are expected to be more cautious than the parents of a large family and to exercise care over the entire student body.

Liability before and after school hours is a source of concern for many school administrators. When is the school responsible for a young person and when are his or her parents responsible? What happens when a child arrives at school too early or hangs around after hours? During their hours of operation schools are responsible for the children. They must display their hours of operation prominently and maintain them consistently. Courts have agreed that parents have the responsibility to ensure that their children do not arrive at school too early. Schools are not liable for the injuries of a child who arrives before the school is open.

Schools are obliged to ensure that students arrive home safely if the school is closed early unexpectedly. Principals and teachers must not send children home without confirming that they will be safe and cared for when they arrive home. In some cases courts have found for the parents and in some for the schools when students have been hurt walking home from school. Teachers are advised to instruct their students on how to walk home from school safely.

Teachers are allowed to detain students at schools but they must do so carefully by telling students to show up at a certain place at a certain time. Detaining a person wrongfully or without authority is false imprisonment and is a risk teachers take if they arbitrarily or capriciously detain students against their will. If a student decides to bolt from the classroom, let him or her go and notify the

The liability of teachers before and after school hours is a source of concern for many school administrators. While teachers are responsible for the safety of children during school, can they be expected to monitor behavior after the school day has ended?

principal and the parents immediately of the circumstances. Do not try to restrain the student or lock the door.

Assault and battery are commonly used but often misunderstood terms. Assault is any intentional act that causes another person to believe that he or she is about to be harmed. No physical contact is necessary. Assault can be both verbal and non-verbal; threatening gestures such as surrounding a person or blocking his or her path can constitute assault. To avoid charges of assault, teachers should avoid using threatening gestures or body language.

Battery means an intentional act in which there is direct contact with the person or with something directly connected to the person. Courts have accepted, among other actions, spitting, striking, pushing, tripping, and burning as constituting battery. Even if a student provokes the attack, a teacher might be found liable for battery if there is direct and intentional contact.

No teacher in Canada has been sued for educational malpractice (and such suits in the United States have rarely been successful) but it may happen in the future. Evidence is mounting that incompetent teaching reduces both a child's self-esteem and employment potential. If a school system fails to provide a student with basic knowledge and literacy skills, it is possible that courts may support a student's claim that the school board has been negligent and award damages for malpractice. Similarly, if a school board or district knowingly retains an incompetent teacher, it is possible that the courts will find the school board liable for educational malpractice.

SEXUAL HARASSMENT

Teachers should recognize the need to be careful about any form of physical contact with students. A casual pat on the head, a hand placed on the shoulder, or an encouraging hug can reassure or motivate a student, but for some individuals and groups and in some contexts such behavior can be easily misinterpreted as **sexual harassment**. In light of recent increases in reported instances of child exploitation, molestation, and sexual harassment, teachers would be wise to exercise reasonable caution.

Though few victims report it, sexual harassment may affect as many as four out of every five teenagers in schools across the nation, according to a 1993 survey sponsored by the American Association of University Women. Although most teens report that they are harassed by their schoolmates, one fourth of the girls and one tenth of the boys said they had been harassed by school employees. Canadian figures, although unavailable, are probably similar. Figure 10.1 shows the percentage of students reporting various types of sexual harassment. In addition, the survey indicated that only 7 percent of the victims told the school about the sexual harassment, and more than half didn't even know if their school had a policy on sexual harassment. As a school superintendent put it, "There's no question but that the attitudes of personnel in schools are changing because of the many cases [of sexual harassment] that have come up across the country. I think all of us are being extremely cautious in how we handle students and in what we say and do with students and employees"[10] To address the problem, many school districts have suggested guidelines that teachers can follow to show concern for students, offer them encouragement, and congratulate them for their successes.

WHAT ARE THE RIGHTS AND RESPONSIBILITIES OF STUDENT TEACHERS?

Do student teachers have the same legal status as certified teachers? Read the following case study:

> Meg Grant had really looked forward to the eight weeks she would spend as a student teacher in Mrs. Walker's high school English classes. Meg knew that Mrs. Walker was one of the best supervising teachers she might have been paired with, and she was anxious to do her best.
>
> In Mrs. Walker's grade 12 class, Meg planned to teach *The Stone Angel*. Mrs. Walker pointed out to Meg that this book was controversial and some parents might object. She asked Meg to think about choosing an additional title that students could read if their parents objected to *The Stone Angel*. Meg, however, felt that Mrs. Walker was bowing to pressure from conservative parents, so she decided to go ahead and teach the book.
>
> Two weeks later Meg was called down to the principal's office where she was confronted by an angry father who said, "You have no right to be teaching my daughter this trash; you're just a student teacher." What should Meg do? Does she have the same rights as a fully certified teacher?

A student teacher such as Meg has the same rights and responsibilities as a fully certified teacher. The most prudent action for Meg to take would be to apologize to the father and to assure him that she will provide alternative titles if she assigns any controversial books in the future. In addition, Meg should learn how important it is for a student teacher to take the advice of his or her supervising teacher. Student teachers should be aware that the potential for liability exists with them just as it does with certified teachers.

One area of debate regarding student teachers is whether they can act as substitutes for their cooperating teachers or even other teachers in a school building.

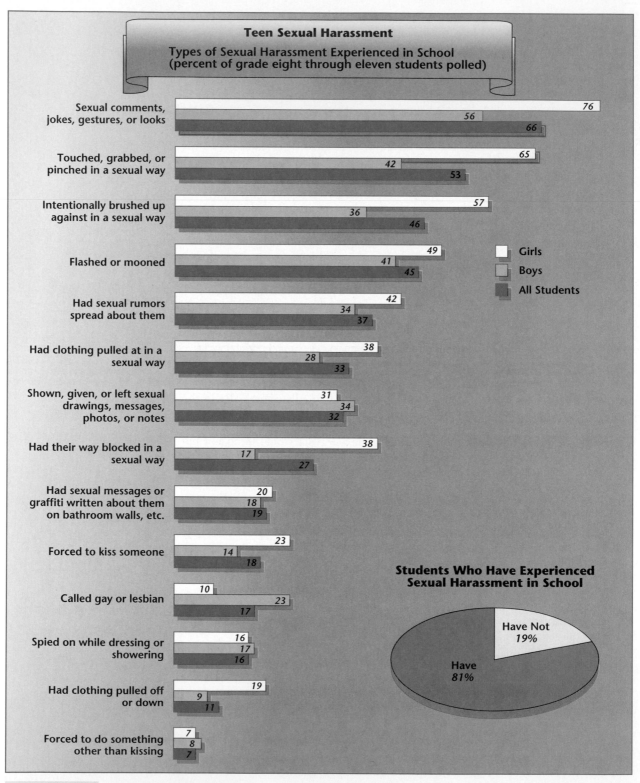

FIGURE 10.1   Teen Sexual Harassment

Source: American Association of University Women. Figure prepared by Associated Press and reported in the *Moscow-Pullman Daily News* (June 2, 1993): IA.

Unfortunately, many school districts have no policy regarding this practice. However, a student teacher may substitute under the following conditions:

- A substitute teacher is not immediately available.
- The student teacher has been in that student teaching assignment for a minimum number of school days.
- The supervising teacher, the principal of the school, and the university supervisor agree that the student teacher is capable of successfully handling the teaching responsibilities.
- A certified classroom teacher in an adjacent room or a member of the same teaching team as the student teacher is aware of the absence and agrees to assist the student teacher if needed.
- The principal of the school or the principal's representative is readily available in the building.
- The student teacher is not paid for any substitute service.[11]

The status of student teachers is ambiguous and it is important that you begin your student teaching assignment with a clear idea of your rights and responsibilities.

*P*ROFESSIONAL PORTFOLIO

For this portfolio entry, survey a group of students, teachers, and/or parents regarding a legal issue in education. Among the legal issues and questions you might address are the following:

- Under what circumstances should restrictions be placed on *what* teachers teach and *how* they teach?
- Should parents be allowed to provide home schooling for their children?
- Are parents justified in filing educational malpractice suits if their children fail to achieve in school?
- Under what circumstances should restrictions be placed on students' freedom of expression?
- Should schools have the right to implement dress codes? guidelines for students' hairstyles?
- Should corporal punishment be banned? If not, under what circumstances should it be used?
- How should schools combat the problem of sexual harassment?
- To combat drug abuse, should schools implement mandatory drug testing of students? of teachers?

- Should students have access to their educational records? Should their parents or guardians?
- As part of an AIDS prevention program, should condoms be distributed to high school students? Should parental approval be required for participation?

The report summarizing the results of your survey should include demographic information such as the following for your sample of respondents: gender, age, whether they have children in school, level of education, and so on. When you analyze the results, look for differences related to these variables. Last, because your professional preparation should include opportunities to develop cooperative learning skills and collegiality, you may wish to work with a small group of your classmates in preparing this portfolio entry.

CHAPTER SUMMARY

Scores of laws and court decisions affect the rights and responsibilities of teachers and their students. It is essential that teachers have a knowledge of education and the law. In addition, because professional teachers not only do what is legally right but also what is ethically right, it is also important for them to understand the ethical dimensions of teaching and the ethical dilemmas that teachers encounter.

Among the legal concerns that typically concern the beginning teacher are the following: the code of professional conduct required of all members of the teachers' association, teacher certification, teacher evaluation, teacher discipline and termination, off-duty conduct of the teacher, immorality or crime by the teacher, life-style choices, child abuse, student discipline, the Young Offenders Act, and avoiding civil liability.

Because students' rights are increasingly being respected, both constitutionally and by society, teachers and school systems are adapting their rules and regulations to better balance these rights with the needs of the school system. It is important for teachers to understand how freedom of expression and religion, suspension and expulsion, physical punishment, sexual harassment, assault and battery, and the right to nondiscrimination are expressed within the school setting and through their students.

Though the legal status of student teachers has been clarified, it is important for student teachers to be aware that the potential for liability exists for them just as it does with certified teachers.

It is clear that the law touches just about every aspect of the teacher's professional life. The teacher is no longer quite as free as in the past to determine what happens behind the closed classroom door. A complex array of court decisions and provincial and federal laws must be taken into account. Because school law is constantly changing and is interpreted and applied differently from province to province, the beginning teacher may wish to consult current publications on school law in his or her province.

KEY TERMS AND CONCEPTS

civil liability, 249
confidentiality, 245
corporal punishment, 246
ethical dilemmas, 238
expulsion, 246

permanent contract, 240
probationary contract, 240
procedural fairness 238
professional code of ethics, 234
sexual harassment, 250

suspension, 246
Young Offenders Act, 247

APPLICATIONS AND ACTIVITIES

Teacher's Journal

1. What limits do you believe should be placed on *what* teachers teach? on *how* they teach?
2. What is your position regarding corporal punishment? Are there circumstances under which its use is justified?
3. Review the section on the legal rights of students (pp. 243-249). Can you recall a time when you believe your rights as a student (or the rights of a classmate) were denied?

Field Assignments

1. Interview a lawyer and ask him or her to comment on the legal dimensions of teaching that should concern teachers. Present your findings to your classmates in the form of a brief oral report.

2. Interview several students at a middle school or high school to get their views regarding the legal rights of students discussed in this chapter. Present the results of these interviews to your class in the form of a brief oral report.
3. Interview a school superintendent or principal to find out how much litigation occurred in the district during the last year or so. As well, ask him or her to identify procedures the district has in place to ensure procedural fairness for teachers and students. Report your findings to the class.
4. With the assistance of your instructor, set up several role-plays based on hypothetical conflicts related to the rights of teachers. At the end of each role-play, those who did not participate should provide feedback to those who did. If time permits, do some role-plays that focus on the rights of students.

11 Students: The Focus of Your Teaching

Teaching, after all, is about knowing children well.

—Vito Perrone
A Letter to Teachers

Focus Questions

▼

1. What are the influences of family life on students?
2. What differences among students relate to gender?
3. How do students vary in intelligence?
4. How do students vary in abilities and disabilities?
5. How do students differ in their stages of development?
6. What are the concerns of students in childhood and adolescence?

Fifteen-year-old Alecia and her twin brother, Herb, live with their mother in a subsidized housing building. Their mother divorced her second husband three years ago, after she learned that he had been sexually abusing Alecia. Since then, Alecia's mother has been struggling to make ends meet with her job at a supermarket.

Alecia wishes her mother and Herb didn't fight so much. The fights usually revolve around Herb missing school and his drinking. Just last night, for example, Herb came home drunk and he and his mother got into another big fight. Herb stormed out and went down to spend the night at his cousin's apartment on the second floor.

At 6:30 that morning, Alecia awoke just as her mother left for work. The hinges on the apartment door, painted over by a careless maintenance worker, creaked loudly as she closed the door behind her. Alecia felt reassured by the sound of her mother locking the dead bolt—the apartment beneath them had been burglarized just last week. Like Herb, she wasn't getting along well with her mother lately so it would be nice to have the apartment to herself while she got ready for school.

Alecia got up slowly, stretched, and looked around the cluttered living room of the one-bedroom apartment. Her mother slept in the bedroom, and Herb, when he wasn't out all night or at his cousin's, slept on the other couch in the living room.

She had trouble sleeping last night. Now that it was winter, the radiator next to the beige couch on which she slept clanked and hissed most of the night. Also, she was worried—two weeks ago a doctor at a neighborhood clinic confirmed that she was pregnant. Yesterday, she had finally got up enough courage to tell her boyfriend. He got angry at her and said he "wasn't gonna be a father."

Alecia knew she ought to be seeing a doctor, but she dreaded going alone. Her mother took a day off from work—without pay—when she went two weeks ago. Right after that, her mother complained about missing work and said, "Don't expect me to take off from work every time you go to the doctor. You should have thought about that before you got in trouble."

Later that morning, Alecia is in your class, sitting in her usual spot in the middle of the back row. While your students work on an in-class writing assignment, you glance at Alecia and wonder why she hasn't been paying attention during the last few weeks as she usually does. At that moment Alecia, wearing the same clothes she wore yesterday, stifles a yawn.

As you continue to move about the room, checking on students' progress and answering an occasional question, you wonder if you should talk with Alecia after class. You don't want to pry into her life outside of school, but you're worried about what might be causing her to act differently.

As the preceding scenario about Alecia suggests, teachers must understand and appreciate how students differ. They must also be willing to explore the special issues and concerns of students at three broad developmental levels—childhood, early adolescence, and late adolescence. The need to learn about the intellectual and psychological growth of students at the age level you plan to teach is obvious. Understanding how their interests, quests, and problems will change throughout their school years will better equip you to serve them now.

Though you are well aware that people differ, as a teacher you will discover how extensive and challenging the variations can be. Your students may be approximately the same age, live in the same area, be exposed to similar community values, and even dress alike, but their abilities, interests, and concerns will not be the same. As we learned in Chapter 5, students are members of different ethnic groups. In addition, individual students belong to many different **microcultural groups,** that is, subgroups within the larger Canadian culture.[1] For example, your students will be members of microcultural groups that are based on gender, social class, race, religion, geographic region, and abilities and disabilities. To begin exploring how students vary as individuals, let us look at five areas of difference among students: family life, gender, intelligence, abilities and disabilities, and learning styles.

WHAT ARE THE INFLUENCES OF FAMILY LIFE ON STUDENTS?

In some schools during certain periods in our history, teachers had to make home visits at the beginning of the school year and at various other times. What they gained in those visits was a special and intimate understanding of their students and their families that many contemporary teachers miss. Today's school open houses and parent conferences are formal, somewhat awkward, and school-oriented. Teachers take advantage of school open houses to outline the school curriculum, explain testing programs, and communicate their expectations of student behavior and performance. Overlooked in these sessions, or at least considerably deemphasized, are the lives of the students in the context of their families. The focus in parent-teacher encounters has clearly shifted from a discussion of how the school is meeting the students' needs (home-visit orientation) to how the student is meeting the school's expectations (parent-conference orientation). The consequences of this shift can be significant, especially for students who are at risk of dropping out.

COMPOSITION OF FAMILIES

Teachers need to deliberately seek out information about their students' families. For instance, teachers may learn much simply by being informed about their students' family structures. With the high divorce rate and women's entry into the workforce, family constellations have changed dramatically. No longer is there a typical Canadian family with a working father, a mother who stays at home, and two or three children. In its place is a mixture of structures:

- Single-parent families with parents (who may be widowed, divorced, separated, or never married) living alone with their children or with other single parents to share expenses. According to Statistics Canada, in 1994 about 20 percent of all children under eighteen live with only one parent, and more than half of all families below the poverty level are lone parent families.
- Stepparent families with children living with their natural parent and a stepparent
- Blended families with two single-parent families blended by a remarriage that creates various combinations of step-siblings and half-siblings
- Extended families which include relatives such as aunts, uncles, and grandparents. Increasing numbers of parents are having to act as primary caretakers for their children's children. Many young parents, who are addicted to drugs, unemployed, or undereducated, for example, are unable to care for their own children.
- Nuclear families which consist of two parents living alone with their birth children, adopted children, or providing a foster home
- Families headed by unmarried couples, lesbians, gay men, older siblings, or grandparents

Each family's structure and economic arrangement places different demands and expectations on the children in them. As well, changes in family structure can bring about subtle or obvious changes in students' behaviors and attitudes at school. When their parents divorce, students may suddenly be burdened with adult responsibilities and concerns, along with their own grief over the breakup of their family, the real or imagined loss of the noncustodial parent, and the reduction in attention received from either parent. School may seem irrelevant and performances and grades may plummet. In other cases, the arrival of new siblings or step-siblings will shift students' positions in their family, changing their roles at home and their attitudes at school. As psychologist Rudolph Dreikurs has written, "It is upon this one fact—the child's subjective impression of his place within the family constellation—that much of his future attitude toward life depends."[2] Some personality theorists believe that individuals are influenced more by their siblings—especially the sibling most unlike them—than by their parents.

DIVERSITY IN FAMILY STYLES

Just as there is diversity in the composition of today's families, so, too, there is diversity in the styles with which children are raised in families. As a result of increases in the paid employment of women and the fact that almost one half of current marriages will eventually end in divorce, an alarming number of children, often referred to as **latchkey children**, are unsupervised during much of the day. To meet the needs of latchkey children, many schools offer before- and after-school programs.

Many middle-class couples are waiting longer to have children. Although children of such couples may have more material advantages, they may be "impoverished" with respect to the time they spend with their parents. In *When the Bough Breaks: The Cost of Neglecting Our Children*, for example, Sylvia Ann Hewlett points out that the "total contact time" between parents and children has declined by as much as 40 percent during the last few decades.[3]

As a result of dramatic changes that have occurred in today's families, the "natural transfer of authority from home to school"[4] is not as strong as it has been in the past, and schools and teachers are being called on to play an increased role in the socialization of young people.

LIFE SETTINGS OF STUDENTS AT RISK

Many children in Canada live in families that help them grow up healthy, confident, and skilled, but many do not. Instead, their life settings are characterized by problems of alcoholism or other substance abuse, family violence, unemployment, poverty, poor nutrition, teenage parenthood, and a history of school failure. Margret Winzer from the University of Lethbridge reports that, some time in their lives, one out of two females and one out of three males is the victim of some unwanted sexual acts. The peak years for unwanted sexual advances are between 12 and 18; during childhood one in three girls and one in ten boys is subjected to unwanted sexual advances.[5] Considering all the other possible forms of abuse, it is clear that an alarming number of elementary-age children come to school sick, disturbed, or abused. Such children live in communities and families with many problems. They are frequently unable to provide their children with the support and guidance they need. With their futures dimmed by such conditions, these young people are at risk of dropping out of school.

Children at risk are from families of all ethnic and racial groups and all socioeconomic levels. Children from wealthy backgrounds who use drugs run the same risk as children from poor backgrounds of becoming disconnected from society. They may share the same feelings of hopelessness and despair.

Many youths leave their immediate families in search of a better life, placing themselves at greater risk of becoming a dropout statistic. Canadian society bombards young people with mixed messages. Television commercials and shows suggest that being an adult means drinking, smoking, and living a glamorous life. They rarely balance these images with the school work young people must do and the education they must obtain to enjoy the glamor. Instead, for many, the choice is between these societal messages and the ones they receive from their parents which are often framed by frustration, anger, and impatience.

Furthermore, many young people leave home to escape an unstable or dangerous home. They may be the victims of physical or sexual abuse. For some, the streets may be safer than their homes. But the reality is that young people who leave home may find themselves homeless or on the streets working as prostitutes. Most jobs require a minimum level of education and one in five Canadians leaves school before completing grade nine.

Teachers can better understand their students by becoming aware of their family structures, belief systems, and sibling positions, and by paying attention to how well the family provides for the satisfaction of the various levels of needs. Clearly, the challenges of meeting the educational needs of students at risk are many. By becoming aware of their life settings, however, teachers can help students at risk learn

In what specific ways might the structure, functioning, values, and life-style of this family affect the academic success of its children?

and can give them a sense of belonging, hope, and purpose. Teachers who do that have taught their students the greatest lesson of all—that education can improve the quality of their lives.

WHAT DIFFERENCES AMONG STUDENTS RELATE TO GENDER?

Students differ not only by sex but also by society's traditional expectations of them as males and females. Families, the media, the schools, and other powerful social forces condition boys and girls to act differently. Moreover, as part of the Western heritage, males have traditionally been accorded higher status. This heritage has created many inequities, some of which are reflected in the classroom.

As we mentioned in Chapter 5, one of the aims of schools is to socialize students to participate in our society. One dimension of the **sex role socialization** process conveys to students certain expectations about the way boys and girls are "supposed" to act. Evidence suggests that schools tend to socialize girls to become dependent and passive, and they socialize boys to become competitive and to assume leadership roles.[6] You may be able to recall, for example, instances from your own schooling when teachers complimented girls on their neatness, pretty handwriting, grooming, and clothing, and they complimented boys on their competitiveness and accomplishments.

Students may also be socialized into particular gender-specific roles as a result of the curriculum materials they use at school. By portraying males in more dominant, assertive ways and portraying females in ways that suggest that they are passive and helpless, textbooks can reinforce expectations about the way girls and boys "should" behave. Within the last few decades, though, publishers of curriculum materials have become more vigilant about not reinforcing these stereotyped roles.

The feminist movement and sociological research of the past few decades have drawn attention to the problem of **sex-role stereotyping** and sex discrimination in our society. Evidence abounds that schools have significantly contributed to these problems. From kindergarten on, girls were often reinforced for "feminine" behaviors and roles (such as playing with dolls and preparing for careers as homemakers) and boys for "masculine" ones (such as playing with trucks and preparing to become executives or to run their own businesses). In the not-so-distant past, if girls were planning careers other than homemaking, they were encouraged to become nurses or secretaries rather than doctors or lawyers. Girls are still often subtly encouraged to be passive, dependent, unassertive, and unambitious.

Teachers may not be aware of how their behavior and attitudes promote sex-role stereotyping. For example, "teachers [may] say nice things about boys concerning their academic work and bad things about their behavior—throwing chalk and making noise. Girls tend to have more compliments given them about their nonacademic work—how neat and clean they are, how pretty they look."[7]

Although the Charter of Rights and Freedoms guarantees equality to both sexes, girls and boys today still experience inequities in school. Teachers face the challenge of providing an education that is free from gender bias and fair in encouraging all students to develop their capabilities to the fullest extent.

HOW DO STUDENTS VARY IN INTELLIGENCE?

Students differ in their intellectual capacity. Unfortunately, test scores, and sometimes intelligence quotient (IQ) scores, are treated as accurate measurements of students' intellectual development because of their convenience and long-time use. What is intelligence and how has it been redefined to account for the many ways in which it is expressed? Though many definitions of intelligence have been proposed, the term has yet to be completely defined. One view is that **intelligence** is the ability to learn. As David Wechsler, the developer of the most widely used intelligence scales for children and adults, said: "Intelligence, operationally defined, is the aggregate or global capacity to act purposefully, to think rationally, and to deal effectively with the environment."[8] Other proposed definitions of intelligence include the following:

- Goal-directed adaptive behavior
- Ability to solve novel problems
- Ability to acquire and think with new conceptual systems
- Problem-solving ability
- Planning and other metacognitive skills
- Memory access speed
- What people think intelligence is
- What IQ tests measure
- The ability to learn from bad teaching[9]

INTELLIGENCE TESTING

The intelligence tests that we now use can be traced to the 1905 Metrical Scale of Intelligence designed by French psychologists Alfred Binet and Theodore Simon, who were part of a Paris-based commission for "dealing with the problem of subnormal children in the public schools."[10] Their scale was a set of increasingly dif-ficult subtests that had successfully distinguished between below-average and bright children and between younger and older children in their research. Binet revised the scale in 1908 and established the use of mental ages for scores, indi-cating how children perform in terms of the performance of others in their age group. Figure 11.1 shows that approximately 67 percent of the population have an IQ between 85 and 115—the range of normal intelligence.

Individual intelligence tests are valued by psychologists and those in the field of special education because they can be helpful in diagnosing a student's strengths and weaknesses. However, group intelligence tests given for the purpose of classi-fying students into like-score groups have received increasing criticism.

The most significant and dramatic criticism of group IQ tests has been that test items and tasks are culturally biased, drawn mostly from white middle-class expe-rience. Thus, the tests are more assessments of how informed students are about features in a specific class or culture than of how intelligent they are in general. Another criticism of intelligence tests is that they are timed and rely heavily on stu-dents' abilities to work quickly, to withstand the press of time, and to be motivated to do well. Students who are not so motivated or who experience test anxiety take their time answering questions and consequently score poorly. Emotional factors may also influence how well a student performs. If self-esteem is low or if the stu-dent is upset, sick, or tired, performance on an IQ test may be lower than normal. The one-time, one-sitting score is a recognized drawback.

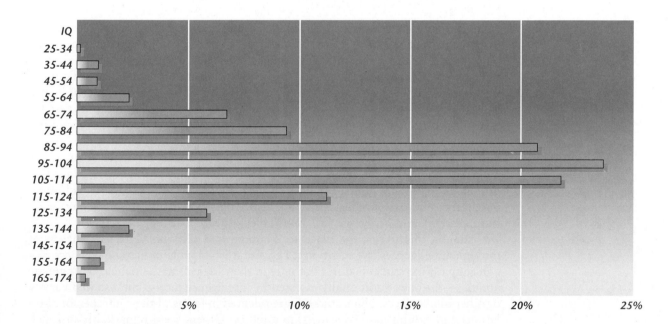

FIGURE 11.1   Distribution Curve for IQ Scores

Source: The Diagram Group, *The Brain: A User's Manual* (New York: Perigree Books, 1982), p. 112.

TABLE 11.1	The Seven Intelligences	
Intelligence	*End-States*	*Core Components*
Logical-mathematicial	Scientist Mathematician	Sensitivity to and capacity to discern logical or numerical patterns; ability to handle long chains of reasoning
Linguistic	Poet Journalist	Sensitivity to the sounds, rhythms, and meanings of words; sensitivity to the different functions of language
Musical	Composer Violinist	Abilities to produce and appreciate rhythm, pitch, and timbre; appreciation of the forms of musical expressiveness
Spatial	Navigator Sculptor	Capacities to perceive the visual-spatial world accurately and to perform transformations on one's initial perceptions
Bodily-kinesthetic	Dancer Athlete	Abilities to control one's body movements and to handle objects skillfully
Interpersonal	Therapist Salesperson	Capacities to discern and respond appropriately to the moods, temperaments, motivations, and desires of other people
Intrapersonal	Person with detailed, accurate self-knowledge	Access to one's own feelings and the ability to discriminate among them and draw on them to guide behavior; knowledge of one's own strengths, weaknesses, desires, and intelligences

Source: H. Gardner and T. Hatch, "Multiple Intelligences Go to School: Educational Implications of the Theory of Multiple Intelligences," *Educational Researcher*, *18*(8) (1989): 6. Copyright © 1989 by the American Educational Research Association. Reprinted by permission of the publisher.

MULTIPLE INTELLIGENCES

Many theorists believe that intelligence is a basic ability that enables one to perform mental operations in the following areas: logical reasoning, spatial reasoning, number ability, and verbal meaning. Others, such as Howard Gardner, believe that such a view of intelligence is limited to the logical-mathematical or scientific intelligence especially valued in Western culture. Instead, Gardner proposes that "there is persuasive evidence for the existence of several relatively autonomous human intellectual competencies, [referred to] as 'human intelligences.' . . . [The] exact nature and breadth of each has not so far been satisfactorily established, nor has the precise number of intelligences been fixed."[11] Drawing on the theories of others and research findings on *idiots savants*, stroke cases, child prodigies, and so-called normal children and adults, Gardner suggests that there are at least seven human intelligences: logical-mathematical, linguistic, musical, spatial, bodily-kinesthetic, intrapersonal, and interpersonal. (See Table 11.1.)

Though this is not the place to examine and critique Gardner's theory of **multiple intelligences**, we mention it because it is valuable in helping teachers recognize that their students differ not only in their logical-mathematical or linguistic abilities—the ones traditionally assessed by intelligence tests—but also in a variety of other intelligences. Some students are talented in terms of their interpersonal relations and exhibit natural leadership abilities. Others seem remarkably in touch with their own feelings, thinking, and development, revealing intrapersonal strengths. Differences in musical, athletic, and mechanical abilities can be recognized by even the minimally informed observer. Because these intelligences are not tested or highlighted, they may go unnoticed, with the possible consequence of their being wasted. We encourage you to guide students' intellectual growth by recognizing and promoting all forms of intelligence and adapting your teaching to their interests and intellectual abilities.

LEARNING STYLE DIFFERENCES

Students vary greatly in their learning styles, that is, the approaches to learning that work best for them. The U.S. National Task Force on Learning Style and Brain Behavior suggests the following definition of **learning style:**

> Learning style is that consistent pattern of behavior and performance by which an individual approaches educational experiences. It is the composite of characteristic cognitive, affective, and physiological behaviors that serve as relatively stable indicators of how a learner perceives, interacts with, and responds to the learning environment. It is formed in the deep structure of neural organization and personality [that] molds and is molded by human development and the cultural experiences of home, school, and society.[12]

Students' learning styles are determined by a combination of hereditary and environmental influences. Some quickly learn things they hear; others learn best when they see material in writing. Some need a lot of structure; others learn best when they can be independent and follow their desires. Some learn best in formal settings; others learn best in informal, relaxed environments. Some need almost total silence to concentrate; others learn well in noisy, active environments. Some are intuitive learners; some prefer to learn by following logical, sequential steps.

There is no one "correct" view of learning styles to guide teachers in their daily decision making. Culture-based differences in learning styles are subtle, variable, and difficult to describe. Moreover, critics have pointed out flaws in many learning-style schemes that have been proposed. You should be aware of the concept of learning styles and realize that any given classroom activity may be more effective for some students than for others. Knowledge of your own and your students' learning styles will help you to individualize instruction and motivate your students.

HOW DO STUDENTS VARY IN ABILITIES AND DISABILITIES?

Students also differ according to their special needs and talents. Some enter the world with exceptional abilities or disabilities; others encounter life experiences that change their capabilities significantly; and still others struggle with conditions that medical scientists have yet to understand. Where possible, all of these exceptional children and youth are given a public education in Canada. Between 1988 and 1992, all provinces passed legislation ensuring that all children have access to public education.

Children "who require special education and related services if they are to realize their full human potential"[13] are referred to as **exceptional learners.** They are taught by special education teachers (perhaps you or some teacher education students you know are seeking certification in special education) and by regular teachers into whose classrooms they have been integrated or *included.* Among the many exceptional children that teachers may encounter in the classroom are students who have physical, mental, or emotional disabilities and students who are gifted or talented.

EDUCATION IN THE NEWS

Kindergarten

Under the NDP government, Ontario embarked on an ambitious and controversial kindergarten/early childhood education initiative in Canada. By the year 2000, all school boards would be required to offer full-day kindergarten for all four- and five-year-olds. The overarching idea behind this plan is the seamless day and a desire to minimize the number of adult relationships a child must build. Parents would drop their children off for an early morning breakfast club, morning kindergarten, and afternoon day care before picking them up at the end of the working day.

Junior and senior kindergarten curricula would be developed provincially and all school boards would be required to develop early literacy plans and remedial programs for early identification of students with learning

problems. This change in the role of kindergarten was seen to be a response to the changing needs of families. (The current conservative government is reevaluating this initiative).

Alberta has embarked in a different direction. Alberta now invests the fewest resources into early childhood education. While all other provinces offer publicly funded half- or full-day programs for five-year-olds, Alberta has reduced its commitment to 240 hours or a quarter-year program. School boards may offer 400-hour programs if they pay for them themselves or charge parents for the extra 160 hours. Choices by various school boards have left Alberta with a patchwork of programs across the province. Is early childhood education the best place to invest resources?

Source: Based on the *Globe and Mail*, Feb. 22, Mar. 6, 17, 1995.

STUDENTS WITH DISABILITIES

Margret Winzer reports that approximately 7 percent of children under 15 years of age in Canada have disabilities.[14] This equates to over 502 000 children in 1994. About 25 percent are learning disabled, 12 percent are behaviorally disabled, 10 percent are mentally disabled, 8 percent have heart disease, and the remainder have relatively low incidence conditions such as deafness and visual impairment. About 15.5 percent of the Canadian school population will require special educational services at some point. Given that enrollment in Canadian schools has been relatively stable since 1971 at about 5.3 million students, the school system could be required to provide special services to over 830 000 students in any given year. The percentage of special services provided varies by province and territory from a low of 1 to 2 percent in Manitoba and Saskatchewan to a high of 13 to 15 percent in Quebec and the Northwest Territories.[15]

Geography may have an effect on the wide range of students with handicaps served from province to province and in the territories. Provinces with rural populations tend to have difficulty offering students with handicaps special services whereas provinces with large urban populations do not. With the advent of distant delivery formats, universities are beginning to train special education teachers in isolated and small school districts.

Various tests and other forms of assessment are used to identify individuals with disabilities. A system of classification, though imperfect, helps educators determine the special needs of exceptional learners.

Though it is beyond the scope of this book to present instructional strategies that teachers can use to address the needs of **students with disabilities,** the following general guidelines are appropriate for exceptional students who are integrated into regular classrooms. To increase your knowledge of teaching students with disabilities, you may wish to take special education courses at your university.

1. Present material on tape for students who cannot read successfully. School volunteers, older students, or parents can be asked to make recordings of assigned material.
2. Allow students to tape-record answers if writing is difficult or their handwriting is illegible.
3. Provide lots of visual reminders (pictures, maps, charts, graphs) for students who have trouble listening or attending.
4. Present handouts that are clear, legible, and uncrowded. Blurred copies [can be] very hard for [students with disabilities] to read.
5. Break directions and assignments into small steps. Completion of each step is an accomplishment—reward it.
6. Give tests orally if the child has trouble with reading, spelling, or writing. Testing which demonstrates what the student knows rather than language skills gives you a clearer picture of the student's abilities. The student demonstrates abilities, not disabilities.
7. Emphasize quality rather than quantity of writing.
8. Be consistent with directions, rules, discipline, and organization.
9. Arrange the class schedule so the exceptional student does not miss important activities when he or she goes to the resource room.
10. Dispense encouragement freely but fairly. If students make errors, help them find the correct answers and then reward them.
11. Discover the exceptional student's strengths and special interests. Capitalize on them in the regular classroom.
12. Carefully establish routines so that the student does not become further handicapped by the confusion of unclear expectations.
13. Arrange desks, tables, and chairs so every person can be easily seen and every word easily heard. Remember, students with hearing impairments need to see your face as you speak.
14. If possible, schedule difficult subjects when there are no outside noises, such as a class at recess.
15. Provide carrels or screens—an "office"—for students who are easily distracted.
16. When checking students' work, check correct answers rather than incorrect answers. The student is still informed of mistakes but sees his or her successes emphasized.
17. Allow the exceptional student to tape lectures or arrange for a classmate who writes neatly to use carbon paper. Either the carbon copy or a copy of the teacher's notes can be given to the exceptional student.
18. Correct deficient lighting, glare from windows, and light-blocking partitions. Small light problems can be big distractions for some exceptional students.
19. Fit the furniture to the child. Discomfort leads to distraction and restlessness.
20. Generally, become sensitive to the obstacles which prevent the exceptional student from exercising his or her abilities.[16]

GIFTED AND TALENTED STUDENTS

In addition to students with disabilities, you may find students with exceptional abilities in your classroom. Some may be **gifted and talented,** that is, have exceptional abilities in one or more areas. Such children are quick, eager learners, often capable of mastering a subject or skill with an ease that other students (and some teachers) may resent. Gifted and talented students are often critical of teachers who fail to stimulate and challenge them. To ignore or limit the potential of this special population, our most talented young people and children, is a grave mistake. Teachers need to become attuned to these students, recognizing their strengths and promoting their growth, talents, and productivity.

Giftedness may take many forms; the trend during the last few decades has been to broaden our view of what characterizes giftedness. In 1961, Louis Fliegler proposed that gifted persons demonstrate at least two of the following qualities: high intelligence, high creativity, high achievement, or a talent.[17] An even more comprehensive definition, proposed by Sidney Marland, a former U.S. Commissioner of Education, has since been widely used:

> Gifted and talented children are those identified by professionally qualified persons who, by virtue of outstanding abilities, are capable of high performance. These are children who require differentiated educational programs and/or services beyond those normally provided by the regular school program in order to realize their contributions to self and society.
>
> Children capable of high performance include those who demonstrated achievement and/or potential ability in one or more of the following areas:
>
> 1. General intellectual ability
> 2. Specific academic aptitude
> 3. Creative or productive thinking
> 4. Leadership ability
> 5. Visual and performing arts
> 6. Psychomotor ability
>
> It can be assumed that utilization of these criteria for identification of the gifted and talented will encompass a minimum of 3 to 5 percent of the school population.[18]

Educators disagree on the best criteria for identifying gifted and talented students. Some rely exclusively on IQ scores and set a score of 130 and above for identifying the gifted and talented. Others believe that the cutoff IQ score should be 160 or above. Broader criteria identify students with exceptional abilities in the performing arts, visual arts, and sports. Depending on the criteria used, estimates of the number of gifted and talented students range from 2 to 5 percent of the total population.

In general, Joseph Renzulli and C. H. Smith believe that gifted and talented persons exhibit the following characteristics:

> 1. High ability (including but not limited to intelligence)
> 2. High creativity
> 3. High task orientation (the motivation to initiate and complete a task)[19]

LABELING EXCEPTIONAL LEARNERS

Special-needs students are often referred to synonymously as *handicapped* or *disabled*. However, it is important for teachers to distinguish between a disability and a handicap:

> A disability is an inability to do something, a diminished capacity to perform in a specific way. A handicap, on the other hand, is a disadvantage imposed on an individual. A disability may or may not be a handicap, depending on the circum-

stances. Likewise, a handicap may or may not be caused by a disability. For example, blindness is a disability that can be anything but a handicap in the dark. In fact, in the dark the person who has sight is the one who is handicapped. . . . When working and living with exceptional individuals who have disabilities, we must constantly strive to separate the disability from the handicap. That is, our goal should be to confine their handicap to those characteristics that cannot be changed and to make sure that we impose no further handicap by our attitudes or our unwillingness to accommodate their disability.[20]

In addition, teachers should know that current language use emphasizes the concept of "people first." In other words, a disabling condition should not be used as an adjective to describe a person. Thus, one should say "a child with a visual impairment," not a "blind child" or even a "visually impaired child."

Teachers should also become aware that the definitions for disabilities are generalized, open to change, and significantly influenced by the current cultural perception of normalcy. Consider, for example, the definition of learning disabilities proposed by the Learning Disabilities Association of Canada:

Learning disabilities is a generic term that refers to a heterogeneous group of disorders due to identifiable or inferred central nervous system dysfunction. Such disorders may be manifested by delays in early development and/or difficulties in any of the following areas: attention, memory, reasoning, coordination, communicating, reading, writing, spelling, calculation, social competence, and emotional maturation. Learning disabilities are intrinsic to the individual and may affect learning and behavior in any individual, including those with potentially average, average, or above average intelligence. Learning disabilities are not primarily due to visual, hearing, or motor handicaps; to mental retardation; emotional disturbance; or environmental disadvantage although they may occur concurrently with any of these. Learning disabilities may arise from genetic variation, biochemical factors, events in the pre- to postnatal period, or from any other subsequent events resulting in neurological impairment.[21]

Cautions about labeling also apply to gifted and talented students. Unfortunately, people commonly have a negative view of gifted and talented youngsters. Like ethnic groups, gifted students are different and thus have been the target of many myths and stereotypes, as Laurence Coleman points out:

The presence of negative images about gifted persons is obvious. . . . Popular sayings or proverbs, such as "the cream always rises to the top" and "a flash in the pan," are prime examples. The frail, bespectacled, loud-mouthed child and the idealistic, misguided professor are frequently seen on our TV screens. Perhaps the simplistic notion of compensation, that bright persons are physically weak, is a form of hostility toward high ability.[22]

In addition, the gifted are often stereotyped as emotionally or mentally unstable, socially unskilled, overspecialized, strange or odd, or conceited. Gifted students can also experience negative attitudes from their peers, as the following high-achieving student's comments indicate:

Today, one of the students said I was frantic, you know, 'cause I got through with all my work. I felt funny about it, 'cause here I am trying to do all my work to try and get an "A" because we're supposed to finish eleven units for this marking period. I'm really trying and they're putting me down because I'm ahead.[23]

Even though specific descriptors for exceptionalities may change, the students who are affected by them still need special treatment and programs. Teachers can best serve such students by seeking a better understanding of their abilities and disabilities and by regarding them, and *all* of their students, as unique individuals with varying needs.

HOW DO STUDENTS DIFFER IN THEIR STAGES OF DEVELOPMENT?

After reviewing some of the ways that students differ, we now turn to an examination of students at different **stages of development**. Development refers to the predictable changes that all human beings undergo as they progress through life from conception to death. Although developmental changes "appear in orderly ways and remain for a reasonably long period of time,"[24] it is important to remember that students develop at different rates. Within a given classroom, for example, some students will be larger and physically more mature than others; some will be socially more sophisticated; and some will be able to think at a higher level of abstraction.

As humans progress through different stages of development, they mature and learn to perform the tasks that are a necessary part of daily living. There are several different types of human development. For example, as children develop physically, their bodies undergo numerous changes. As they develop cognitively, their mental capabilities expand so that they can use language and other symbol systems to solve problems. As they develop socially, they learn to interact more effectively with other people—as individuals and as groups. And, as they develop morally, their actions come to reflect a greater appreciation of principles such as equity, justice, fairness, and altruism.

MODELS OF COGNITIVE, SOCIAL, AND MORAL DEVELOPMENT

Because no two students progress through the stages of cognitive, social, and moral development in quite the same way, teachers need perspectives on these three types of development that are flexible, dynamic, and, above all, useful. By becoming familiar with models of cognitive, social, and moral development, teachers at all levels, from preschool through post-secondary, can better serve their students. Three such models are Piaget's theory of **cognitive development**, Erikson's stages of **psychosocial development**, and Kohlberg's stages of **moral reasoning**.

Piaget's Model   Jean Piaget, the noted Swiss biologist and epistemologist, made extensive observational studies of children. He concluded that children reason differently from adults and even have different perceptions of the world. Piaget surmised that children learn through actively interacting with their environments, much as scientists do, and proposed that a child's thinking progresses through a sequence of four cognitive stages. (See Figure 11.2.) According to Piaget's theory of cognitive development, the rate of progress through the four stages varies from individual to individual.

During the school years, students move through the **preoperational stage**, the **concrete operations stage**, and the **formal operations stage**; yet, because of individual interaction with the total environment, each student's perceptions and learning will be unique. According to Piaget,

FIGURE 11.2
Piaget's Stages of
Cognitive Growth

1. **Sensorimotor Intelligence (birth to 2 years):** Behavior is primarily sensory and motor. The child does not yet "think" conceptually; however, "cognitive" development can be observed.

2. **Preoperational Thought (2 – 7 years):** Development of language and rapid conceptual development are evident. Children begin to use symbols to think of objects and people outside of their immediate environment. Fantasy and imaginative play are natural modes of thinking.

3. **Concrete Operations (7 – 11 years):** Children develop ability to use logical thought to solve concrete problems. Basic concepts of objects, number, time, space, and causality are explored and mastered. Through use of concrete objects to manipulate, children are able to draw conclusions.

4. **Formal Operations (11 – 15 years):** Cognitive abilities reach their highest level of development. Children can make predictions, think about hypothetical situations, think about thinking, and appreciate the structure of language as well as use it to communicate. Sarcasm, puns, argumentation, and slang are aspects of adolescents' speech that reflect their ability to think abstractly about language.

A student who achieves a certain knowledge through free investigations and spontaneous effort will later be able to regain it; he will have acquired a methodology that can serve him for the rest of his life. . . . At the very least, instead of. . . subjugating his mind to exercise imposed from outside, he will make his reason function by himself and will build his own ideas freely.[26]

Erikson's Model   Erik Erikson's model of psychosocial development delineates eight stages, from infancy to old age (see Table 11.2). For each stage a **psychosocial crisis** is central in the individual's emotional and social growth. Erikson expresses these crises in polar terms; for instance, in the first stage, that of infancy, the psychosocial crisis is trust versus mistrust. Erikson explains that the major psychosocial task for the infant is to develop a sense of trust in the world but not to give up

TABLE 11.2   **Erikson's Eight Stages of Development**

Stage	Psychosocial Crisis	Virtue
Infancy	Trust vs. Mistrust	Hope
Early Childhood	Autonomy vs. Shame and Doubt	Will
Play Age	Initiative vs. Guilt	Purpose
School Age	Industry vs. Inferiority	Competence
Adolescence	Identity vs. Role Confusion	Fidelity
Young Adult	Intimacy vs. Isolation	Love
Adulthood	Generativity vs. Rejectivity	Care
Mature Love	Integrity vs. Despair	Wisdom

Source: Adapted from *Childhood and Society,* 2d ed. by Erik H. Erikson, by permission of W. W. Norton & Co., Inc. Copyright 1950, © 1963 by W. W. Norton & Company, Inc. Copyright renewed 1978 by Erik H. Erikson.

TABLE 11.3   Kohlberg's Theory of Moral Development

I. **Preconventional Level of Moral Reasoning**
   Child is responsive to cultural rules and labels of good and bad, right or wrong, but interprets these in terms of consequences of action (punishment, reward, exchanges of favors).
   Stage 1: Punishment-and-obedience orientation
   Physical consequences of action determine its goodness or badness. Avoidance of punishment and deference to power are valued.
   Stage 2: The instrumental-relativist orientation
   Right action consists of that which satisfies one's own needs and occasionally the needs of others. Reciprocity is a matter of "You scratch my back and I'll scratch yours."

II. **Conventional Level of Moral Reasoning**
   Maintaining the expectations of the individual's family, group, or society is perceived as valuable, regardless of consequences.
   Stage 3: The interpersonal concordance or "good boy-nice girl" orientation
   Good behavior is that which pleases or helps others and is approved by them.
   Stage 4: The "law and order" orientation
   Orientation toward fixed rules and the maintenance of the social order. Right behavior consists of doing one's duty and showing respect for authority.

III. **Postconventional, Autonomous, or Principled Level of Moral Reasoning**
   Effort to define moral principles that have validity and application apart from the authority of groups.
   Stage 5: The social-contract, legalistic orientation
   Right action defined in terms of rights and standards that have been agreed on by the whole society.
   Stage 6: The universal-ethical-principle orientation
   Right is defined by conscience in accord with self-chosen *ethical principles* appealing to logic and universality.

Source: Adapted from Lawrence Kohlberg, "The Cognitive-Developmental Approach to Moral Education," in *Curriculum Planning: A New Approach*, 6th ed., eds. Glen Hass and Forrest W. Parkay (Boston: Allyn and Bacon, 1993), p. 154. The original version appeared in *Journal of Philosophy*, 70, 18 (October 25, 1973): 631–632.

totally a sense of distrust. In the tension between the poles of trust and mistrust, a greater pull toward the more positive pole is considered healthy and is accompanied by a virtue. In this case, if trust prevails, the virtue is hope.

When we examine the issues and concerns of students in childhood and in early and late adolescence later in this chapter, we will return to Erikson's model of psychosocial development. For further information on this significant and useful theory of development, we recommend that you read Erikson's first book, *Childhood in Society.*[26]

Kohlberg's Model   According to Lawrence Kohlberg, the reasoning process people use to decide what is right and wrong evolves through three levels of development. Within each level, Kohlberg has identified two stages. Table 11.3 shows, at Level I, the preconventional level, that the individual decides what is right on the basis of personal needs and rules developed by others. At Level II, the conventional level, these decisions reflect a desire for the approval of others and a willingness to conform to the expectations of family, community, and society. At Level III, the postconventional level, the individual has developed values and principles that are based on rational, personal choice and may be separated from conventional values.

Kohlberg suggests that "over 50 percent of late adolescents and adults are capable of full formal reasoning [i.e., they can use their intelligence to reason abstractly, form hypotheses, and test these hypotheses against reality], but only 10 percent of these adults display principled (Stages 5 and 6) moral reasoning.[27] In addition, Kohlberg found that maturity of moral judgment is not highly related to IQ or verbal intelligence.

Some individuals have criticized Kohlberg's model as being too systematic and sequential, limited because it focuses on moral reasoning rather than actual behavior, or biased because it tends to look at moral development from a male perspective.[28] Carol Gilligan, for example, suggests that male moral reasoning tends to address the rights of the individual and female moral reasoning addresses the individual's responsibility to other people. Thus, when confronted with a moral dilemma, females tend to suggest solutions based more on altruism and self-sacrifice than on rights and rules.[29]

Criticisms of Kohlberg's model aside, the question remains, can moral reasoning be taught? Can teachers help students develop so that they live according to principles of equity, justice, caring, and empathy? Kohlberg suggests that the following three conditions can help children internalize moral principles:

1. Exposure to the next higher stage of reasoning
2. Exposure to situations posing problems and contradictions for the child's current moral structure, leading to dissatisfaction with his [her] current level
3. An atmosphere of interchange and dialogue combining the first two conditions, in which conflicting moral views are compared openly[30]

PROMOTING CHARACTER DEVELOPMENT

One approach to teaching that helps students grow morally and develop a sense of social responsibility is service learning. Through service learning, "students participate in systematic activities that result in real assistance to others, as well as personal growth. Service experiences . . . also impart or reinforce commonly accepted values such as a sense of justice, compassion for others, or an acceptance of the obligations of citizens."[31] Following are service-learning activities that teachers have used in various content areas:

English

- Writing letters for senior citizens or persons with disabilities
- Writing stories for a weekly neighborhood newspaper
- Performing community service and then writing stories, poems, or plays using the experience as a starting point

Mathematics

- Tutoring younger students in math skills
- Conducting surveys on community needs and analyzing the results
- Helping food banks, food co-ops, or local businesses with their monthly or quarterly inventories

Social Studies

- Helping to restore local historical sites such as farms, Aboriginal sites, or the homes of noted people
- Working with local officials to solve problems such as graffiti, shoplifting, drug abuse, and so on
- Assisting immigrants with the process of becoming citizens

Arts

- Painting public murals on community themes
- Designing public spaces such as parks and playgrounds
- Teaching art to younger children through community education programs

Although there is no single way to develop character, Table 11.4 suggests several steps that teachers can follow in working toward that goal.

WHAT ARE THE CONCERNS OF STUDENTS IN CHILDHOOD AND ADOLESCENCE?

According to Erikson, elementary school students are concerned with the psychosocial issue of industry versus inferiority and developing competence. Of special concern to those who teach at the elementary level are the challenges and consequences of **childhood** stress. Turning to the concerns of students in adolescence, we must first look at the continuum along which they develop. Thus our exploration of adolescence begins with an examination of the substages of **adolescence**.

DEVELOPMENTAL TASKS OF CHILDHOOD

During Erikson's school-age stage, children strive for a sense of industry and struggle against feelings of inferiority. If they are successful, they gain the virtue of competence, believing in their abilities to do things. The self-confidence and sense of control that come with mastering new skills and producing acceptable projects is self-generating. Successes build on success and promote a positive attitude toward learning and participating actively and enthusiastically in their worlds.

If children find evidence that they are inferior to others, if they experience failure when they try new tasks, and if they struggle without ever gaining a sense of mastery, then they feel incompetent. These negative feelings also perpetuate themselves, and the children experiencing them will protectively pull back from learning opportunities, regarding them as unpleasant and threatening.

Children gain the sense of industry needed at this age by playing seriously, mastering new skills, producing products, and being workers. When they first go to school they are oriented toward accomplishing new things (some kindergartners expect to learn to read their first day of school and are disappointed when they don't). For young schoolchildren, the idea of work is attractive; it means that they are doing something grown-up. They may hope to have homework (until they really do) and enjoy bragging about having lots of work to do in school.

TABLE 11.4	**DEVELOPING CHARACTER**

Character education calls on the individual teacher to:

- *Act as caregiver, model, and mentor,* treating students with love and respect, setting a good example, supporting positive social behavior, and correcting hurtful actions through one-on-one guidance and whole-class discussion
- *Create a moral community,* helping students know one another as persons, respect and care about one another, and feel valued membership in, and responsibility to, the group
- *Practice moral discipline,* using the creation and enforcement of rules as opportunities to foster moral reasoning, voluntary compliance with rules, and a respect for others
- *Create a democratic classroom environment,* involving students in decision making and the responsibility for making the classroom a good place to be and learn
- *Teach values through the curriculum,* using the ethically rich content of academic subjects (such as literature, history, and science) as vehicles for teaching values and examining moral questions
- *Use cooperative learning* to develop students' appreciation of others, perspective taking, and the ability to work with others toward common goals
- *Develop the "conscience of craft"* by fostering students' appreciation of learning, capacity for hard work, commitment to excellence, and sense of work as affecting the lives of others
- *Encourage moral reflection* through reading, research, essay writing, journal keeping, discussion, and debate
- *Teach conflict resolution,* so that students acquire the essential moral skills of solving conflicts fairly and without force
- *Foster caring beyond the classroom,* using positive role models to inspire altruistic behavior and providing opportunities at every grade level to perform school and community service
- *Create a positive moral culture in the school,* developing a schoolwide ethos that supports and amplifies the values taught in classrooms
- *Recruit parents and the community as partners in character education,* letting parents know that the school considers them their child's first and most important moral teacher

Source: Thomas Lickona, "The Return of Character Education," *Educational Leadership* (November 1993): 10–11. Reprinted with permission of the Association for Supervision and Curriculum Development. © 1993. All rights reserved.

Older elementary students, who have encountered some of the unpleasant realities of schoolwork, can still lose themselves in their own learning endeavors—designing and building a science project, reading a series of books by the same author, studying the biographies of famous people, writing their own books. Unless thwarted by unpleasant school experiences, boring exercises, or the pressure of anxious parents, elementary students have a natural inclination for industry and an inner desire to gain competence.

COPING WITH CHILDHOOD STRESS

What are some of the areas of concern for elementary school children? Though a wide range of concerns exists, we will confine our discussion to the general area of childhood stress. Is childhood a time of carefree play or a period of stress? Certainly the answer depends upon the life circumstances and personalities of the individual child. Many adults are surprised to learn that stress is a common feature in the lives of most children. We are prone to look back on our own childhoods nostalgically, recalling the happy times and forgetting the anxieties we felt.

MAKING *a DIFFERENCE*

Tim Varro
Vancouver, British Columbia

As a secondary teacher, I have always wanted to truly engage my students in active learning processes where the process of learning would become more important to students than the end goal, the content. I decided that my students would video a story about the life of Robert Burnaby for the 1992 Burnaby Centennial celebrations. Through this project, I was able to integrate available technology across the school curriculum and use this technology as a catalyst for learning communication and literary skills and improving analytical skills. I was able to integrate the teaching of history and the development of the Canadian community with technology of instant communication using video at its center. In doing so, I saw the change in those involved from passive viewers to active adjudicators, and I sensed that the success or failure of the project became a side issue.

Recently, educators have begun to experience and experiment with entirely new approaches to learning and teaching. Some of the discoveries point to the students as those who have the most to gain from these new approaches. At the center of these approaches are the students' perceptions of themselves as active learners: posing questions, making judgments, integrating criticisms, reconsidering problems, and investigating new possibilities. Within this framework, that of becoming accurate adjudicators of their own efforts, they must first come to recognize their roles and responsibilities. Somehow, somewhere, they should be taught and given ample opportunities to build on their strengths and correct their weaknesses.

Within this context we need to ask ourselves, what are we as teachers doing? Is it moving beyond words-alone instruction in order to enhance an interdisciplinary approach to learning? Could it be expanding and even opening new pathways to learning for many of our students by sparking disciplined inquiry in ways other than language-only, lecture-type instruction? I propose that the essential elements of preparing our students for their roles as responsible citizens in the community, the country, and throughout the world, rest in our abilities as educators to offer our students an active part in being able to understand the connections between what they are learning in school and what is happening in the world around them. Schools and the education they can offer must meet the challenges of today and the uncertainties of tomorrow.

How can we motivate students to learn? This is best accomplished in an environment where the teacher/student relationship is personal. What happens in the classroom between people is more important than any curriculum assignment, procedure, or content. If people can relate to each other in an environment of acceptance and trust, content and competence will grow. As a result of this kind of relationship students would be able to sense that what they are doing in school is important to what they will need to know as adults in the "real world." Students want the knowledge that they are learning to make sense to them, to have meaning for them today, and to have relevance to their future.

"You gave me a D- on the paper I wrote? I
suppose this means the movie deal is off."

Serious stress is experienced by latchkey children who are left on their own or
in each others' care for part or all of the day without adult supervision. These
children are placed at risk in terms of both their physical safety and their emotional
sense of well-being. Their parents, often single, may be equally stressed, feeling
guilty and anxious about their children's lack of supervision; yet they see no alternatives because of their economic situation.

Children are subject to many other forms of stress. An alarming number of
children must endure, for example, the stress of coping with physical, sexual,
and/or psychological abuse.

The pressures to handle situations beyond their abilities, whether at home or
in a classroom, can deprive children of their childhoods and darken the years when
they should be feeling cared for and secure. Parents, teachers, and the community
need to make certain that children have physically and psychologically safe settings
in which to grow.

HELPING CHILDREN DEVELOP

What can teachers do to help children develop competence? First, teachers need to
be attuned to the importance of their students' struggles to avoid feeling inferior
and incompetent. One effective way to directly promote a sense of competence in
students is to provide a climate in which children are so secure that they will risk
making mistakes. Another way is assigning work that children can perform successfully and still be challenged. Praising more than criticizing, taking students and

their work seriously, respecting their dignity, and encouraging them by expressing genuine belief in them are sound teaching practices.

Teachers can also focus directly on promoting students' sense of self-esteem by planning activities that boost morale. Games that require students to compliment each other, certificates awarded for particularly fine work, and bulletin boards and interviews devoted to "student of the week" are a few examples of exercises that teachers can use to enhance students' self-concepts.

Teachers can promote a sense of industry and competence by providing opportunities for elementary school students to do projects of their own—to compose stories and poems, create and perform dramas, build models of historical sites, prepare science experiments, videotape and edit films, design and use computer programs, and plan and produce art pieces. In addition, teachers can give students a greater sense of importance by arranging for older students to help tutor younger ones or by having their class adopt a younger class. For the children, a sense of competence is gained by helping those less competent and by assuming responsibilities.

DEVELOPMENTAL TASKS OF ADOLESCENCE

An increasing number of psychologists believe that adolescence contains two distinct stages: an early period covering the ages of ten to twelve through the ages of fourteen to sixteen and a late period from approximately fifteen to sixteen through nineteen. Although a continuity exists in each individual's life, the psychosocial issues of adolescence—coping with change and seeking identity—vary in form and importance as individuals progress through the transition from childhood to adulthood. In early adolescence changes are multiple and rapid, peers are paramount, and vulnerabilities are high; in late adolescence a quest for personal meaning supersedes the regard of peers, moving the individual toward the establishment of a feeling of efficacy and a more integrated sense of identity.

In Erik Erikson's model of the eight stages of humans, identity versus role diffusion is the psychosocial crisis for the adolescent years. Although the quest for identity is a key psychosocial issue for both early and late adolescence, many believe that Erikson's identity-vs.-role diffusion stage fits best for early adolescence. During this time, young adolescents, using their new thinking abilities, begin integrating a clearer sense of identity. Erikson's role diffusion refers to the variety of roles that adolescents have available to them.

According to Erikson's theory, when adolescents do identify themselves with a group, with a school, or with a cause, their sense of fidelity—the "virtue" of this stage—is clear and strong. At this stage adolescents are loyal and committed, sometimes to people or ideas that may dismay or alarm their parents, sometimes to high ideals and dreams.

The hazard of this stage, according to Erikson, is being overwhelmed by the options and roles open to them. Some may respond by overidentifying with other people, developing crushes, and losing a sense of themselves in their imitation of others. Still other young people may respond by doing nothing, making no decisions or commitments, or dropping out of school.

In late adolescence, the period between the ages of fifteen to sixteen and nineteen years, the quest for identity shifts from others to self. Young people continue to work on strengthening their sense of identity in late adolescence, but as they do so they draw less on the reactions of their peers and more on their own regard for

How might these teens volunteering at a food relief collection center explain their actions morally? According to Kohlberg, what three conditions help people internalize moral principles?

what matters. During this stage, the needs of the adolescent are best met by allowing them "to do things of importance—to do real work of real consequence in the real world."[32] Those who work with late adolescents should not cause them to remain in early adolescence by applying unneeded restrictions and direction that are more appropriate in the earlier stage. Instead, we need to grant older adolescents opportunities to make significant contributions, respecting their new abilities to handle responsibilities and to think and work independently. To do otherwise is to risk their experiencing school and life as meaningless and to turn instead to self-destructive escape activities.

Although young people in late adolescence possess an array of interests, talents, and goals in life, they share a desire to achieve independence. More like adults than children, late adolescents are anxious to use newly acquired strengths, skills, and knowledge to achieve their own purposes. Whether through marriage, parenthood, full-time employment, education beyond high school, or military service, late adolescents are eager to prove to others and to themselves that they are independent.

COPING WITH PROBLEMS OF ADOLESCENCE

The list of alarming concerns in adolescence includes academic failure, accidents, anorexia, assaultive behavior, criminal activity, cultism, depression, discipline problems, dropouts, drug abuse, incest, prostitution, runaways, school absenteeism, suicide, teenage pregnancy, vandalism, and contracting sexually transmitted diseases. Clearly, all of these concerns merit our attention and study, but examining them extensively is beyond the scope of this text. In addition, we must remind ourselves that these problems often occur in conjunction—and are not limited to only one stage of adolescence.

Young people in early adolescence are especially vulnerable to a full range of life stresses because they mature more quickly physically than they do cognitively or socially. This fact, coupled with the freedom given to young people in our society, places early adolescents in positions where they "are able to, and do, make many fateful decisions that affect the entire life course, even though they are immature in cognitive development, knowledge, and social experience."[33]

Young adolescents have a paramount need to cope with physical, cognitive, and emotional changes that occur concurrently and rapidly. The newness of so many features in their lives and the confusion or insecurity caused by the pace of personal change contribute to adolescents' drive to be accepted by their peers. Though a strong need for approval from others is common during this stage of development, teachers should be alert, as the following Professional Reflection suggests, to signs that a student may not be moving in the direction of developing an adequate self-concept.

HELPING ADOLESCENTS DEVELOP

Those who teach early adolescents must be prepared on occasion to intervene and take preventive action. To help prevent the problems that place young people at risk, an energetic, creative, and multifaceted approach is recommended. Practically, teachers can provide a structured classroom environment where students feel secure, and have opportunities to discuss values, morals, consequences, preferences, and so on. You can help students practice problem-solving skills and learn methods of avoiding unwanted activities without losing face or alienating others. In addition, you can gather and convey current information on subjects of special concern to students. More broadly, groups and individuals in all sectors of our society—businesses, schools, religious groups, and government agencies—need to join in the effort to seek solutions to the damaging problems that affect too many of our young people during adolescence.

Teachers of late adolescents must be aware of their strong need to become independent and must provide them with appropriate ways to express that independence. Although occasionally challenging and stressful, helping youth to make the transition between late adolescence and early adulthood can be very rewarding for teachers.

PROFESSIONAL REFLECTION

Near the beginning of the school year, a teacher has students complete an "interest inventory" to learn about their backgrounds and interests. One student turns in the following inventory. In terms of Erikson's stages of personality development, what issues seem to be of concern to this student? What steps might the teacher take to strengthen this student's self-concept? Is there any information about this student's home situation that might be helpful to the teacher?

SENTENCE COMPLETION INTEREST INVENTORY

1. My father likes me best when *I don't know. He doesn't come around the apartment very often.*

2. My mother likes me best when *I do what she tells me to do. If I don't, she gets mad.*

3. I feel most proud when *never. I am not very good at most things.*

4. My biggest fear is *making a mistake and having my mother get real angry.*

5. My friends *I don't really have any. I like to be alone most of the time.*

6. Home is *doing what your supposed to do and staying out of trouble.*

7. I wish *I could get a job and move away.*

8. I am happiest when *I am left alone and I can do what I want to.*

9. What I like most about school is *reading – but I don't like to read in front of other people.*

10. On the weekends, I like to *watch television and read.*

PROFESSIONAL PORTFOLIO

For this portfolio entry, prepare an annotated directory of local organizations and businesses that you could use as resources for developing service-learning projects. The entry will consist of ways that students and teachers can connect classroom learning in specific subject areas to community needs. (For suggested service-learning activities, review "Promoting Character Development," pp. 346–347.)

For each entry, include the name of the organization or business and the purpose of the project (e.g., to visit care centers for senior citizens or persons with disabilities, to collect household goods for an agency that cares for the homeless, etc.). In addition, you will probably want to include information such as the following:

- A brief description of the organization or business
- Address
- Phone number
- Key contact person
- Hours when each resource is available
- Directions to the resource site
- Number of students who can participate at one time
- Any special instructions that should be followed

Depending on the resource, you may also want to describe orientation activities that are available for students: films, formal presentations, tours of the site, and so on.

CHAPTER SUMMARY

The hallmark of the professional teacher is an extensive understanding of students. Familiarity with their intellectual and psychological growth and an appreciation of their concerns and problems is essential for today's teachers. Though students are typically grouped according to similarities such as age and achievement levels, students vary greatly. Among the differences that should concern teachers are differences in family life, gender, intelligence, learning styles, and abilities and disabilities.

Family life has a significant influence on students. Differences among families in their composition, childrearing practices, cultural styles, beliefs, attitudes, and values, positions of siblings within the family, and ability to satisfy basic needs powerfully affect the lives of children. In regard to gender differences among students, teachers should understand the dynamics of sex-role socialization and guard against sex-role stereotyping. In addition, teachers should appreciate the limitations of intelligence tests and adapt their teaching to the various forms of intellectual abilities and learning styles they find among their students. Finally, in regard to exceptional students—those with disabilities and the gifted and talented—teachers should be informed about their needs and guard against using labels that overlook their strengths and abilities.

Teachers must also understand their students from a developmental perspective and consider the major cognitive, psychosocial, and moral stages through which they progress. To achieve this understanding, three developmental theories are helpful: Piaget's theory of cognitive development, Erikson's theory of psychosocial development, and Kohlberg's theory of moral development.

Finally, teachers must familiarize themselves with several developmental issues and areas of concern during childhood and adolescence. During childhood, elementary school students desire to gain a sense of competence through industrious behavior. Students in early and late adolescence must learn to cope with change and begin to develop an identity that will serve as a foundation for meeting the challenges of early adulthood.

Whether they are in childhood, early adolescence, or late adolescence, students need teachers who are committed to facilitating their development. To provide students with such support, teachers must understand the developmental stages through which students grow.

KEY TERMS AND CONCEPTS

adolescence, 274
childhood, 274
cognitive development, 270
concrete operations stage, 270
exceptional learners, 265
formal operations stage, 270
gifted and talented, 267

intelligence, 262
latchkey children, 259
learning style, 265
microcultural groups, 258
moral reasoning, 270
multiple intelligences, 264
preoperational stage, 270

psychosocial crisis, 271
psychosocial development, 270
sex-role socialization, 261
sex-role stereotyping, 262
stages of development, 270
students with disabilities, 267

APPLICATIONS AND ACTIVITIES

Teacher's Journal

1. What is your sibling position and how has it affected you in your schooling? Note that if a sibling is five or more years older than you, you are more like an only child than the younger or youngest.
2. Recall an example of sexist behavior or sex-role stereotyping that you observed in a school setting. Describe the events that took place and discuss how you felt. What will you do to ensure that your classroom is gender fair?
3. Think about why group IQ tests are criticized by some. What is unfair about them? Who might not do well on such tests? How could these test scores hurt students?
4. Think back to your elementary school days. What things worried you? What things made you afraid? Which life events were stressful to you?

Field Assignments

1. Observe and interview a student in the age group you wish to teach. Conduct a brief case study that focuses on common developmental tasks for that age group and the areas of individual differences highlighted in this chapter. Then prepare a written portrait of the student.
2. Visit a school at the level you plan to teach. Interview the counselor, asking questions about the problems that bring students to the counselor most often. If possible, shadow the counselor for a day.
3. Attend an extracurricular event such as a high school basketball game or a track and field meet. Observe the students on the field as well as any students watching the players. Notice the differences between the students in terms of their physical appearance, clothing and hairstyles, athletic abilities, social skills, and evidence of personal interests and confidence. Share your observations in class.
4. Have everyone in the class write a description of a student in early adolescence and one in late adolescence, drawing on personal memories and adding specific experiences when possible. Analyze the set of descriptions in terms of the psychosocial issues and concerns present in each stage.
5. Invite several school counselors from the elementary and secondary school levels to your class. Have them discuss the most frequent student needs they encounter and suggest ways that teachers can help students with those needs.

12 Dynamics of Classroom Life

[One] characteristic of effective teachers is that they are long-term planners and thinkers. They know what the end results of their work will be. . . .

—Gary D. Borich
Clearly Outstanding: Making Each Day Count in Your Classroom

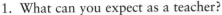

Focus Questions

▼

1. What can you expect as a teacher?
2. What determines the culture of the classroom?
3. What are the keys to effective classroom management?
4. What teaching skills are essential?
5. What are the characteristics of effective teaching?

Terry-Sue slid lower in her seat, propped her feet on the chair in front, her head on the desk behind, closed her eyes, and slipped away. Philip sat alert, hands folded on a pile of books and binders, pencils sharpened, ready for whatever I had to dish out. Steven sat muttering self-deprecating remarks to anyone who would listen; no one would, we had heard them all before.

After writing about Shakespeare's England and reading Charles and Mary Lamb's version of *Romeo and Juliet*, we were ready to begin reading the play. I had no idea how the language would be handled by students of such low ability, so I began reading aloud to them. Previously, I had told them that there were two things that they must always do when reading: have a pencil in hand for underlining key words and putting question marks in the margins beside points that they wanted to return to for clarification and use a finger or pencil for tracking while reading.

We read line by line, scene by scene, discussing as we went along, until we had finished act I. They wrote about what they had read and heard, interpreting and summarizing on their own. They shared their writing and talked some more. It was late December, time to wish each other happy holidays and go home.

Throughout the holidays I found myself trying to puzzle out ways to make the reading easier. The vocabulary seemed to be just too difficult. At one point I considered abandoning the play, but I knew that this would have been a big disappointment for all of us and we could not afford such a setback. Nothing was resolved when I returned to work in January. As it turned out, David had the answer.

David scoots by me and into the classroom, tapping my shoulder (the far one) as he goes by. Reflexively, I look the wrong way to see who has touched me. He laughs, his big, crossed, brown eyes twinkling with delight, "Gotcha!" he cries. I laugh, too. We do this every day.

David loves to be the center of things. To this end, he has entertained classes year after year with clever, clownish antics, until this year he was suspended from school and the bus for continuing to "moon" the neighborhood after repeated discussions and warnings. His seemingly harmless pranks have evolved into a pattern of disruptive behavior. David is now trying hard to break out.

"How come you never let us read aloud?" he asks. Perched on my stool at the front of the class, I feel choked as I scrounge for an answer. I think all the wrong things and I know that they are the wrong things. "Your skills are too weak, you're not capable, it's too hard. . . . " I choose to lie. "I was just about to ask for volunteers," I answer. David's hand shoots up. The others, all but Terry-Sue, follow his lead. "Act II, scene i, *Romeo and Juliet*," he falters, and then continues reading laboriously, monotone through to the end of the first speech. The group, including Terry-Sue this time, responds by clapping, pounding their desks, and shouting out the names of the parts that they want to read. David beams at me and I beam back. We are on the road to Verona.[1]

The opening scenario for this chapter, written by a special education teacher at a high school, illustrates how teachers make decisions based on the unfolding dynamics of classroom life. Sensitivity to the ebb and flow of classroom events is the hallmark of a professional, reflective teacher. Attention to classroom dynamics not only reveals when students are ready to learn, it helps teachers address students' needs more effectively. For example, the teacher who wrote the scenario comments on how her view of teaching changed as a result of preparing the narrative:

> The immediate effect of this reflection is that I feel more focused in my teaching. I had to watch individuals and the group more closely than I would have in the natural course of the daily routines. The result is that I have become more knowledgeable about the needs and strengths, goals, and shortcomings of my students. I have also found that there is a rhythm or series of cycles to my teaching of which I had previously been unaware.[2]

For teacher education students such as yourself, making the transition from the study of teaching to actual teaching can be a challenge. A unit plan or course design that is perfect in theory could fail completely in the classroom because of its inappropriateness for a particular group of students or its being presented at the wrong time in terms of the group's development or the school's schedule of vacations. The more teachers know about "the types of classroom conditions and student behaviors that provide good learning environments," the better prepared they will be to make the transition smoothly.[3]

WHAT CAN YOU EXPECT AS A TEACHER?

One study of beginning elementary teachers revealed that they commonly experience reality shock because the real world of the students violates so many of the teachers' expectations.[4] It may take time to adjust to the fact that some students can be rude, lazy, hostile, or unreceptive to adult guidance. Depending on your personality, you may experience a degree of psychological buffeting if students try to weaken your self-esteem through such behaviors as complaining that the class is boring, failing to cooperate, or being critical of the class in general.[5] Estelle Fuchs found that some teachers experience symptoms similar to those anthropologists have found in people suffering from culture shock.[6]

Of course, no two individuals experience the early days of teaching in quite the same way. The following comments of beginning teachers, however, are common:

I'm overwhelmed at the amount of work. My internship was nothing. Now, so many needs to meet and no matter what, you can't meet all their needs.

Teaching itself is what I expected; it was the other stuff, however. I'm 40 percent teacher and 60 percent social worker. I didn't expect that. So many kids, even ones from middle-class families, come with no values. They don't sit down when asked, show respect, and so on.

Although it is impossible to predict exactly what the experience of beginning to teach will be like for you, remember that anxiety is normal for anyone just entering a profession. As you acquire the knowledge and skills necessary to master the challenges of teaching, you will begin to enjoy teaching's many rewards.

I went into the classroom with some confidence and left with lots of confidence. I felt good about what was going on. I established a comfortable rapport with the kids and was more relaxed. Each week I grew more confident. When you first go in you are not sure how you'll do. When you know you are doing okay, your confidence improves.

WHAT DETERMINES THE CULTURE OF THE CLASSROOM?

As we learned in Chapter 5, one definition of *culture* is the way of life common to a group of people. In much the same way, each classroom develops its own culture. The culture of a classroom is determined by how teachers and students participate in common activities.

The activities that teachers and students engage in are influenced by several factors. "There are characteristics of the physical milieu (building, materials, resources, etc.) and social milieu (norms, rules, expectations, grouping, climate, distribution of power, accountability structure) that affect life in . . . classroom[s]."[7] Anita Woolfolk and Charles Galloway have identified the following six "interdependent and interacting sources of influence" on classroom culture:

1. The activity format, procedure, or delivery system for instruction
2. The academic content itself
3. The physical, spatial, and temporal constraints of the particular classroom
4. The accountability structure: how, when, where, against what standards, and by whom student responses (oral and written) will be evaluated
5. The players in the classroom drama
6. The dynamic interaction among participants, activities, content, materials, etc.[8]

Let us use these six influences on classroom culture to analyze a discussion of an essay that might be read in a high-school English class. What is the activity format? A discussion, directed by the teacher. And the academic content? Two or three themes in the essay and their application to students' lives. What are the physical, spatial, and temporal constraints of the classroom? An arrangement conducive to discussion is a small classroom with chairs and tables set up in a circle, square, or U-shaped pattern so that students can see each other as they talk.

What is the accountability structure that determines how students will be evaluated? Student performances in class discussions are difficult to measure but teachers can note on their rosters the students who are particularly active, engaged, or insightful in their contributions.

Who are the players in the classroom drama and what are their expectations? In our example of the discussion on an essay, the students and the teacher are the participants. Expectations are fairly clear: Students are supposed to reveal their understanding of the themes in the essay and to engage in critical thinking; the teacher is expected to motivate students to analyze, critique, and evaluate concepts presented in the essay.

What is the dynamic interaction among participants, activities, and content? This question refers to the live dimension of the discussion, which in turn raises more questions: How are the students responding to the essay's ideas? Are many students participating in the discussion? How interested is the teacher in what is happening? How lively and relevant is the discussion?

How would the lesson change if one of the six aspects of classroom culture was changed? Imagine that the activity format was a lecture instead of a discussion or substitute a test as the accountability structure and consider how the dynamics of the class would change as a result.

CLASSROOM ORGANIZATION

A factor in the culture of the classroom is **classroom organization**—the way teachers and students are grouped for instruction and the way time is scheduled in the classroom. As explained in Chapter 5, teachers and students are grouped in several ways. At the elementary-school level, the self-contained classroom is the traditional arrangement. The teacher and students remain in the same classroom for the entire day and the teacher teaches all the main subjects. Elementary teachers in self-contained classrooms sometimes organize all the day's activities around a unifying theme. In contrast, team-teaching arrangements divide responsibility for two or more classes among two or more teachers who specialize in different subject areas, skills, or ability groupings of students. In less-structured open-space classrooms, students work independently, with a number of teachers providing individual guidance.

Middle schools and junior and senior high schools typically have departmentalized classrooms. Students study four or five academic subjects taught by teachers who specialize in them and move from classroom to classroom for their lessons. Departmentalized arrangements require a more structured schedule of blocks of time, a series of separate periods lasting 45 to 75 minutes.

THE CLASSROOM ENVIRONMENT

However your classroom is organized, you will need to be concerned with the quality of its environment. When you become a teacher, the physical environment you must work in will probably be similar to that of the school where you were educated. However, we encourage you, with the help of your students, to make your surroundings as pleasant as possible. Plants, clean painted walls, displays of students' work, a comfortable reading or resource area, and a few prints or posters can enhance the quality of teacher-student relationships.

Seating arrangements and the placement of other classroom furniture can do much to shape the classroom environment. Although seating by rows may be appropriate for whole-group instruction or examinations, other arrangements may be more beneficial for other activities. For example, you can enhance small-group activities by moving desks into small clusters in different parts of the room. Figure 12.1 shows the arrangement of an elementary school classroom. The room is designed to encourage students to learn through discovery at learning centers located around the room.

However you design your classroom, take care to ensure that seating arrangements do not reduce the opportunity of some students to learn. For example, students in some classrooms receive more attention if they are seated in the "action zone," the middle front-row seats and seats on the middle aisle.[9] Teachers often stand near this area and unknowingly give students seated there more opportuni-

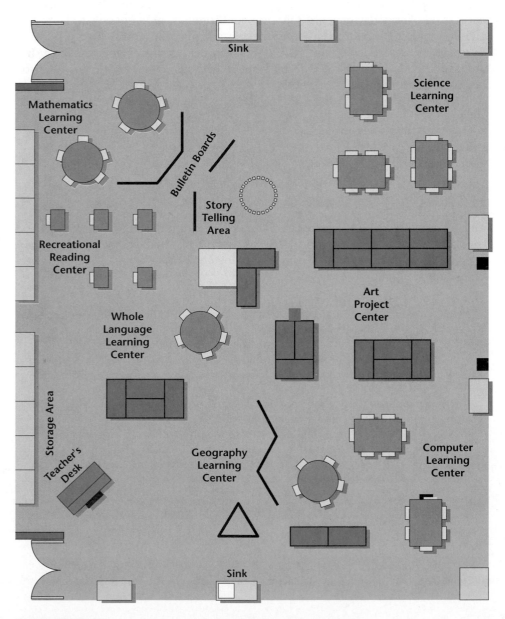

FIGURE 12.1   **Learning Centers in an Elementary Classroom**

ties to speak. Teachers also may group students by ability to instruct them more effectively. However, such arrangements often have a negative impact on relationships among students because low-ability students who are seated together, for example, may believe they have lower status than other students.

DIFFERENCES IN CLASSROOM CLIMATE

Part of the environment of the classroom is the **classroom climate**—"the ways in which the people within the classroom interact with each other."[10] Differences in classroom climates are readily apparent: Some appear to be relaxed, safe, and even homelike; others suggest businesses, efficiently productive; still others present the impression of armed camps, with teachers and students, or cliques of students, suspicious, aggressive, and defensive in their interactions. In addition to promoting learning, the classroom climate should make students feel safe and respected. It is important that your classroom foster respect for others and be a place where students can learn without fear.

The following eight dimensions have been used to describe classroom climates:

- Openness versus Defensiveness
- Confidence versus Fear
- Acceptance versus Rejection
- Belonging versus Alienation
- Trust versus Suspicion

- High Expectations versus Low Expectations
- Order versus Chaos
- Control versus Frustration[11]

The positive qualities of classroom climates are within teachers' spheres of influence and are promoted, consciously or unconsciously, by how they communicate with and treat students. Consider the following description of a classroom in terms of classroom climate:

> The front room is alive with activity. David and Maurice are building a runway with wooden blocks. Darlene, their teacher, sits in the middle of the block pile offering support and assistance. "Beautiful, David. It's going really well. Here, Maurice, use this big one, get some more of the long ones from over there."
>
> David and Maurice are intent on building the longest runway they can make. Carl comes and joins them, but they hardly notice. Their attention is on the task at hand. Shaquan and Ebony occupy a small block building in one corner where they seem to be putting dolls to bed and then waking them up. "This is my hotel," says Ebony. "And it's only for me and my friends."
>
> Maurice pushes a perilously high stack of long blocks slowly across the room toward the runway. Just as it arrives at its destination, it crashes loudly to the floor, and David laughs and rushes up to untangle the wreckage and keep the runway going.
>
> "Teacher," Pete wails. "Someone took my glue."
>
> "Doesn't everyone have a cup?" Marilyn asks.
>
> "Yeah, but she dipped in mine."
>
> "Okay, Natika. This is yours. And Pete, there's more if you run out." Changing directions, she asks, "Doesn't glue feel funny on your fingers?"
>
> Pete frowns and says, "It's yukky." Afrinique dips her whole hand in the glue and, watching the thick white drops fall back into the cup, smiles contentedly.[12]

How would you rate this classroom climate using the eight dimensions above? What changes in the teacher's behavior could transform the overall climate?

Although teachers influence the classroom climate by the way they regard and treat students, they also shape it by their instructional decisions. David Johnson and Roger Johnson, two researchers in the area of classroom communication and dynamics, describe three types of interactions promoted by instructional decisions: cooperative or positive interdependence, competitive or negative interdependence, and individualistic or no interdependence.[13] To illustrate the three types, Johnson and Johnson suggest that a group project to measure classroom furniture would promote cooperative interdependence; a race to be the first student to measure the furniture would call for competitive interdependence; and having a student measure the furniture independently would be an example of no interdependence. Johnson and Johnson believe that teachers should use strategies that foster all three forms of interactions, depending on their instructional goals, but that, ideally, the emphasis should be on furthering cooperative interdependence. As teachers increase their awareness of their influence on classroom climate, they become empowered to create the climates they prefer for themselves and their students.

For development of the classroom group, Schmuck and Schmuck describe their ideal classroom climate as

> one in which the students share high amounts of potential influence—both with one another and with the teacher; where high levels of attraction exist for the group as a whole and between classmates; where norms are supportive for getting academic work done, as well as for maximizing individual differences; where communication is open and featured by dialogue; and where the processes of working and developing together as a group are considered relevant in themselves for study.[14]

GROUPING STUDENTS FOR LEARNING

Classroom culture is also affected by student groupings. In Chapter 11, we explored the unique needs of different groups of students. A widespread method of addressing these needs is to group students on the basis of shared characteristics. Two commonly used approaches are between-class ability grouping (often called tracking) and within-class ability grouping. Between-class grouping is used at the middle and high school levels, and within-class grouping is used at the elementary level.

Students who attend schools where **between-class ability grouping** is practiced are assigned to classes on the basis of ability or achievement (usually determined by scores on standardized tests). Another form of between-class ability grouping, especially at the high school level, is based on students' goals after graduation. Many high schools, for example, have a university preparatory track, a vocational track, and a community college track.

Research on between-class ability grouping suggests that, for the most part, it does not contribute to greater achievement.[15] Its supporters nevertheless claim that teachers are better able to meet the needs of students in homogeneous groupings. Among the alternatives to between-class ability grouping are heterogeneous grouping, regrouping by subject area, the Joplin Plan (regrouping students for reading instruction across grade levels), and cooperative learning.[16]

Within-class ability grouping is often used for instruction in reading and mathematics within a class where a teacher instructs students in homogeneous, small groups. Within-class grouping is used widely at the elementary level. Perhaps you can recall learning to read in a small group with a name such as the Eagles, the Redbirds, or the Mustangs. Like tracking, within-class ability grouping can heighten preexisting differences in achievement between groups of students if teachers give high-achieving groups more attention. As well, once students are grouped, they tend not to be regrouped, even when differences in achievement are reduced.

At best, evidence to support student groupings is mixed. Whether students are grouped based on ability, curricular interests, or disabling condition, there is a danger that some group labels can evoke negative expectations, causing teachers to "underteach" certain students and their peers to isolate or reject them. The most serious consequence, of course, is that students so labeled are taught to feel inadequate, inferior, and limited in their options for growth.

Two additional approaches to grouping students for instruction are peer tutoring and cross-age tutoring. Because it is usually very difficult for teachers to provide individualized tutoring for every student, teachers can arrange for some students to be tutored by other students. In **peer-tutoring** arrangements, students are tutored by other pupils in the same class. Teachers who use peer tutoring should guard against making the tutored self-conscious about their abilities. One solution is for all students to both tutor and be tutored and for the teacher to "create the mental set that *we all learn from one another.*"[17]

Cross-age tutoring is most often used at the elementary level. For example, grade six students might tutor grade two students in reading. Research clearly shows that, with proper orientation and training, cross-age tutoring can greatly benefit both "teacher" and learner.[18] Pilot programs pairing students at risk of dropping out of school with younger children and with special needs students have proved especially successful. Some of the advantages of cross-age tutoring are evident in the following comments made by a former grade nine dropout who returned to school and became a tutor:

What form of tutoring is taking place in this picture? What are some advantages of this form of tutoring? What is required for it to be effective?

Right now I feel very good about school and would give it an eight out of ten, but [before] I would have given it a one. . . . I'm working with third-graders and some of them are passing because I worked with them. . . . I was like a teacher and I know what the teacher goes through and so I don't give them so many problems. . . . I'm so excited about graduating. . . . And I want all of my brothers to finish school also.[19]

Both peer tutoring and cross-age tutoring programs call for planning and training. Usually, a specific time of the day or week should be set aside for tutoring, and specific assignments and accompanying directions should be carefully reviewed with tutors. Young people do not know how to teach skillfully, nor can they be expected to work miracles with children whose teachers may doubt their ability to learn. For these reasons training for student tutors is essential.

THE STRUCTURE OF CLASSROOM ACTIVITIES

Of the six dimensions of classroom culture mentioned at the beginning of this section, perhaps the most significant is the "activity format, procedure, or delivery system for instruction." In short, what the teacher does and what students do have powerful influences on the quality of classroom life.

Activity Formats   Perhaps the most common **activity format** in elementary schools consists of students doing seatwork on their own or listening to their teachers and participating in whole-class recitations. In addition, however, students participate in reading groups, games, and discussions, take tests, check work, view films, give reports, and help clean up the classroom.[20]

One of the most important decisions a teacher makes is how to answer the following question: "What activity will enable me to accomplish my instructional goals?" A teacher may choose to emphasize discussion one day and lecture the next. He or she may decide to arrange a class field trip or a visit from a local business person or to use a popular television quiz show format to conduct a review rather than a teacher-led drill-and-practice format.

Use of Time   How teachers use time affects both the culture of the classroom and student learning. An important use of time is **allocated time,** the time teachers allocate for instruction in various areas of the curriculum. Teachers vary widely in their instructional use of time. Educational researchers Tom Good and Jere Brophy, for example, report that "some students may receive as much as four times more instructional time in a given subject than other students in the same grade."[21]

Perhaps even more important than the amount of allocated time is the *quality* of use, or how time is actually used. Several researchers have shown that **time on task**—the amount of time students are actively engaged in learning activities—is directly related to learning. As anyone who has ever daydreamed while appearing to pay attention to a teacher can confirm, time on task is difficult to measure. In response to this difficulty, Charles Fisher and his colleagues introduced the concept of **academic learning time**—the amount of time a student spends working on academic tasks with a high level of success (80 percent or higher).[22] Not surprisingly, learning time, like allocated time, varies greatly from classroom to classroom. For example, Fisher found that some grade two students spend between three and forty-two minutes a day successfully reading.[23]

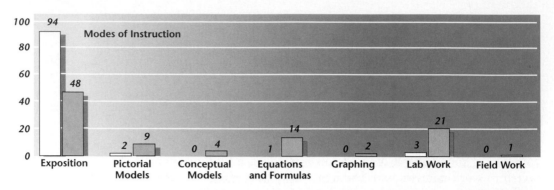

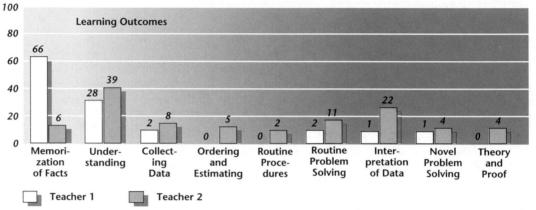

FIGURE 12.2   **Percent Instructional Time for Two Physical Science Teachers**

Source: Andrew Porter, "Opportunity to Learn," *Brief No. 7* (Madison, Wisc.: Center on Organization and Restructuring of Schools, Fall 1993), p. 3.

An additional concept that is proving useful in understanding teachers' use of time in the classroom and the kinds of educational opportunities schools provide is known as **opportunity to learn** (OTL). OTL is based on the premise that teachers must spend time to provide all students with challenging content, and they must use appropriate instructional strategies to help students learn that content.

Figure 12.2, based on the results of a study of OTL in high school science and mathematics classes, shows how two physical science teachers in different schools used time differently. Teacher 1 relied almost exclusively on lecture and student reading (exposition), and devoted two thirds of instructional time to memorization of facts. Teacher 2 spent less than 50 percent of time on exposition and 21 percent of time on lab work. As a result, students of Teacher 2 spent much less time memorizing facts and much more time learning to collect and interpret data.[24]

WHAT ARE THE KEYS TO EFFECTIVE CLASSROOM MANAGEMENT?

For most new teachers **classroom management** is a significant concern. How can you control misbehaving students so that you can teach? Unfortunately, effective classroom management cannot be reduced to a cookbook recipe. And, until recently, the best advice new teachers could find was to use whatever works.

Some teachers, however, seem to have a magic touch that gives them easy rapport with individual students, an enjoyable and productive classroom climate, and problem-free interactions with the class as a whole. Are they unusually talented or do they know some strategies for managing classrooms? In most cases, these teachers recognize "that some approaches [to classroom management] are more effective than others . . . and that *the key to successful classroom management is preventing problems before they occur.*"[25] In addition, such teachers (1) foster effective, harmonious interpersonal interactions; (2) understand how their leadership style influences students; and (3) facilitate the development of the classroom group so that it becomes more cohesive and supportive.

PROBLEM PREVENTION

How can teachers prevent discipline problems from occurring? The key to preventive discipline is excellent planning and an understanding of life in the classroom. In addition, teachers who have mastered the essential teaching skills have fewer discipline problems because students recognize that such teachers are prepared, well organized, and have a sense of purpose. They are confident of their ability to teach all students, and their task-oriented manner tends to discourage most classroom management problems.

Jacob Kounin has conducted extensive research on how teachers prevent discipline problems. In one study Kounin looked at two sets of teachers: those who managed their classrooms smoothly and productively with few disruptions and those who seemed to be plagued with discipline problems and chaotic working conditions. He found that the teachers who managed their classrooms successfully had certain teaching behaviors in common: (1) on the first day of school they established and discussed several clear comprehensive rules for behavior, (2) they displayed the proverbial eyes-in-the-back-of-their-head quality of alertness, a quality Kounin referred to as *withitness*, (3) they used individual students and incidents as models to communicate to the rest of the class their conduct expectations, Kounin's *ripple effect*, (4) they supervised several situations at once effectively, and (5) they were adept at handling transitions smoothly.[26] In addition, you will need to adjust discipline approaches to particular students and situations. For instance, older students may be embarrassed by teacher praise, and behavior modification techniques may offend the gifted student.

EFFECTIVE PROBLEM SOLVING

When management problems do emerge in the classroom, effective teachers draw from a repertoire of problem-solving skills. These skills are based on their experience, common sense, and an understanding of the teaching-learning process. Among the many structured approaches to classroom management are assertive discipline, the LEAST approach, behavior modification, the acceptance approach, reality therapy, and the no-lose method. These approaches range from those that are firm, direct, and authoritarian to those that are flexible, indirect, and democratic. None of these approaches is appropriate for all situations or for all teachers, and the usefulness of a given method depends, in part, on the teacher's individual personality and style.

Marcel Matte
Winnipeg, Manitoba

Edwin Janz
Steinbach, Manitoba

Why do teachers take on extra work to change their teaching strategies in classrooms? For some it is because of necessity. The Modern Language Department at our school saw the introduction of technology as a means of achieving better communicative/experiential learning within second language classrooms.

Fortunately, our school received special funding from the federal government through the Secretary of State for evaluation of commercial software. This provided us with computer software for proofreading, remedial grammar exercises, pronunciation drills, and vocabulary exercises. However, little of the available software actually engaged the student in meaningful communication. Since the goals of the Canadian curriculum stressed meaningful communication, we felt that another use of the technology had to be found. This led to the creation of the "Student Initiated Software" project.

Simply put, the Student Initiated Software project involves students in creating software that the school can use, and students are carefully considered for the roles they take. We begin by structuring groups of five students in the second language classroom. Each group is responsible for creating one child's story. Members of the group take on different roles depending upon their interests or skills. For example, one, who will be the liaison with computer science groups, must be concurrently enrolled in a computer science or computer applications class; another will revise the child's story written by the group, so must have achieved well in the second language; and another will create or arrange the art work, so must have skills in art or graphical illustration.

The groups create and illustrate children's stories and turn them over to the computer science classes. The computer science students scan the graphical illustrations onto disk and clean the images up. They adapt some of the illustrations into animations. Text fields are created to resemble the paper book version created by the second language groups and then the text of the stories is transferred to these fields. The final version is placed on a floppy disk and inserted into the cover of each story book.

Our students are extremely proud of their products which then go to other schools in the school district to be used by younger students. The integration of the computer into language learning has allowed students to work on a host of projects that are meaningful. The process of writing children's stories encourages students to achieve levels that before seemed impossible. We are very excited about the results our students have obtained and we will soon enter into partnerships with other disciplines in the school, such as science, and with businesses in the community.

Assertive Discipline   The assertive approach to discipline, developed by Lee Canter, calls on teachers to establish firm, clear guidelines for student behavior and to follow through with consequences for misbehavior. Canter comments on how he arrived at the ideas behind assertive discipline: "I found that, above all, the master teachers were assertive; that is, they *taught* students how to behave. They established clear rules for the classroom, they communicated those rules to the students, and they taught students how to follow them."[27] **Assertive discipline** requires teachers to do the following:

1. Make clear that they will not tolerate anyone preventing them from teaching, stopping learning, or doing anything else that is not in the best interest of the class, the individual, or the teacher.
2. Instruct students clearly and in specific terms about what behaviors are desired and what behaviors are not tolerated.
3. Plan positive and negative consequences for predetermined acceptable or unacceptable behaviors.
4. Plan positive reinforcement for compliance. Reinforcement includes verbal acknowledgment, notes, free time for talking, and, of course, tokens that can be exchanged for appropriate rewards.
5. Plan a sequence of steps to punish noncompliance. These range from writing a youngster's name on the board to sending the student to the principal's office.[28]

The LEAST Approach   Especially helpful for secondary teachers is a sequence of discipline steps outlined in the LEAST program, which can be found in *A Design for Discipline: The LEAST Approach*.[29] The acronym spells out the steps:

1. **L**eave it alone. Decide first of all if the misbehavior is worth noticing. Often it is not.
2. **E**nd the action indirectly. Have the student run an errand for you or assist a fellow student with a problem. Direct the student toward an alternative; correct behavior without a confrontation over the misbehavior.
3. **A**ttend more fully. This is the counselling component of teaching. You need to get to know the student better before you decide what to do.
4. **S**pell out directions. Specify the problem and tell them what you want them to do. Avoid using negatives. Instead say what they should start doing. At times you may need to also tell them what the consequences will be if they do not start doing what you have specified.
5. **T**rack the behavior. Keep records on how the students are doing. In this step you may have to follow through on the consequences.

Many experienced teachers recognize this sequence as the approach they have used for years. Spelled out, however, the **LEAST approach** offers the beginning teacher clear and effective procedures to follow.

Behavior Modification Strategies   Another approach to classroom management that many teachers have used with success is **behavior modification**. Based primarily on the theories of the late B.F. Skinner, a well-known psychologist, behavior modification calls for teachers to reinforce (or reward) only desired student behaviors. Teachers can reward students with effective praise, a smile, or tokens they can use to "buy" time for activities they enjoy. Behaviors that are reinforced will tend to be repeated, and those that are not reinforced will tend to be extinguished. By reinforcing only desired behaviors, the teacher can "shape" students' behavior because students soon associate the desired behavior with the pleasure of being rewarded. Those who advocate behavior modification point out that negative reinforcement makes undesired behavior disappear only temporarily.

The Acceptance Approach   Rudolph Dreikurs, a psychologist and author of several books on discipline, developed an approach to classroom management that is based on the individual's need for acceptance. According to Dreikurs, students will try to gain acceptance through socially acceptable behavior; however, if they are unsuccessful, they will try to gain recognition through misbehavior that is based on one or more "mistaken" goals: "(1) to gain attention, (2) to seek power, (3) to seek revenge, or (4) to display inadequacy (real or imagined)."[30] Teachers can recognize when a child is acting with the goal of gaining attention if they feel annoyed and/or frustrated by the child's behavior. The "treatment" for students who misbehave for this reason is to ignore the bad behavior and pay attention to the good. If the teacher feels threatened, the student is probably misbehaving with the goal of seeking power. Dreikurs suggests that teachers should avoid engaging in power confrontations and, instead, provide opportunities for students to use power productively.

When the teacher feels hurt, it is a sign that students may be misbehaving to seek revenge. Dreikurs urges teachers to cover up their hurt and show instead a caring regard for the students; those who hurt others are often deeply hurt themselves.

The most serious of the goals for misbehavior is to display real or imagined helplessness. These students have become convinced that they cannot do what is expected of them, and so they do not even try. Teachers can recognize this motivation by their own discouragement as they wonder if they can do anything that can help. For these students, Dreikurs tells teachers to give encouragement and never give up on the student.

Dreikurs' **acceptance approach** is based on three key ideas: (1) Students misbehave for different reasons, (2) teachers can use their own emotional reactions to help determine the student's motivation for misbehaving, and (3) different corrective strategies need to be used for misbehavior caused by different motivations.

Reality Therapy   The **reality-therapy** approach to classroom management was developed by William Glasser, a psychiatrist. According to Glasser, good discipline begins with teachers who create positive, caring relationships with students and encourage them to take responsibility for their behavior. Through such relationships, teachers help misbehaving students see that the choices they make may not lead to the results they want. Glasser believes that students will usually make good choices (that is, behave in an acceptable manner) if they experience success and know that teachers care about them.

In his various writings,[31] Glasser suggests the following basic steps for the reality-therapy approach to classroom discipline:

1. Establish warm, positive relationships with each student.
2. Have the misbehaving student evaluate and take responsibility for his or her behavior. Often, a good first step is for the teacher to ask, "What are you doing?"
3. Have the student make a plan for a more acceptable way of behaving. If necessary, the student and the teacher brainstorm solutions. They agree on how the student will behave in the future and the consequences for failure to follow through.

4. Require the student to make a commitment to follow the plan.
5. Don't accept excuses for failure to follow the plan.
6. Don't use punishment or react to a misbehaving student punitively. Instead, point out to the student that there are logical consequences for failure to follow the plan.
7. Don't give up on the student. If necessary, remind the student of his or her commitment to desirable behavior. Periodically ask, "How are things going?"

The No-Lose Method   In *T.E.T. Teacher Effectiveness Training,*[32] Thomas Gordon presents the **no-lose method** of resolving conflicts in the classroom. According to Gordon, there are two types of discipline problems: teacher-owned problems (that is, the teacher's needs are not being met) and shared problems (that is, the teacher and student frustrate each other's needs). The no-lose method also requires the teacher to use "I" messages—to tell the misbehaving student in a firm, nonjudgmental manner what the student is doing, how it affects the teacher, and how the teacher feels about it. Gordon's no-lose approach is based on the assumption that conflicts can be resolved by taking into account the needs of both teacher and student. The six steps of the no-lose approach are as follows:

1. Define the problem. Whose problem is it? What does each person want?
2. Generate possible solutions.
3. Evaluate solutions.
4. Identify the best solution through consensus. What are the responsibilities of each person?
5. Decide how to implement the solution.
6. Evaluate the effectiveness of the solution. Is it working? Should changes be made?

INTERPERSONAL INTERACTIONS

Interactions between teachers and students are the very core of teaching. The quality of these interactions reveals to students how the teacher feels about them. Teachers who empathize with students, respect them, and expect them to learn are more likely to develop a classroom climate free of management problems. In classrooms with positive group interactions, teachers and students work toward a common goal—learning. In classrooms with negative interactions, the energy of teachers and students may be channeled into conflict rather than into learning.

Although there is no precise formula to guarantee success in the classroom, Robert Rosenthal has developed four suggestions that teachers can follow to increase student achievement through positive interactions:

1. Establish warm social-emotional relationships with children.
2. Give students more feedback about their performance.
3. Teach students more (and more difficult) material.
4. Give students more opportunities to respond and to ask questions.[33]

Speaking and Listening   Interactions between teachers and students involve the communication skills of speaking and listening. It has been estimated that in the "typical" classroom someone is speaking about 75 percent of the time and, not surprisingly, it is the teacher who speaks about three quarters of this time. Knowl-

In classrooms with positive group interactions, teachers and students work toward a common goal – learning.

edge about the speaking and listening that occurs in classes taught by effective teachers was increased greatly by the Beginning Teacher Evaluation Study (BTES), a pioneering long-term study that in one phase focused on twenty grade two and twenty grade five classrooms. On the basis of student achievement during two-week units of instruction in reading and mathematics, the researchers identified ten "more effective" and ten "less effective" teachers at each grade level and in each subject area.

The researchers found that the behaviors of the more effective teachers created a positive climate.

> [They] enjoyed teaching and were generally polite and pleasant in their daily interactions. They were more likely to call their students by name, attend carefully to what they said, accept their statements of feeling, praise their successes, and involve them in decision making.[34]

Furthermore, the more effective teachers treated students with greater respect and were less likely to criticize students.

> The more effective teachers were less likely to ignore, belittle, harass, shame, put down, or exclude their students. Their students were less likely to defy or manipulate the teachers. Thus, the more effective classes were characterized by mutual respect, whereas the less effective classes sometimes showed evidence of conflict.[35]

Finally, the more effective teachers did not hesitate to make demands on students.

They encouraged them to work hard and take personal responsibility for academic progress, and they monitored that progress carefully and were consistent in following through on directions and demands. Thus, these teachers were pleasant but also businesslike in their interactions with students.[36]

In a comprehensive review of 8000 studies of how elementary- and secondary-level students learn best, Herbert Walberg confirmed the findings of the earlier BTES study—quality interaction between teachers and students is vital to student achievement: "Students who perceive their classroom morale as friendly, satisfying, goal-directed, and challenging and their classroom as having the required materials tend to learn more. Those who perceive student cliques, disorganization, apathy, favoritism, and friction learn less."[37]

Questioning   In addition to verbal behavior that promotes a positive classroom climate, teachers should give special attention to the questions they ask of students. Research indicates that most questions teachers ask are **lower-order questions**, those that assess a student's ability to recall specific information. Effective teachers, however, also ask **higher-order questions** that demand more critical thinking and answers to questions such as, Why? What if . . . ?

In their interactions with students, teachers should avoid treating high-achieving and low-achieving students differently. Jere Brophy and Thomas Good reviewed the research in this area and found that several teacher behaviors may indicate unequal treatment of students. The behaviors identified include waiting less time for them to answer questions, interacting with them less frequently, giving less feedback, calling on them less often, seating them farther away, failing to accept and use their ideas, smiling at them less often, making less eye contact, praising them less, demanding less, grading their tests differently, and rewarding inappropriate behaviors.[38] Effective teachers establish respectful relationships with *all* students; they listen to them, give frequent feedback and opportunities to ask questions, and demand higher-level performance.

LEADERSHIP IN THE CLASSROOM

The ability to provide leadership in the classroom may lie with the teacher, the student, or both. For good or ill, students as well as teachers exert leadership in classrooms. Wise teachers quickly identify student leaders and develop ways to focus their leadership abilities on attaining goals that benefit the entire class.

Negative student leaders, those who pull their followers away from schoolwork or destroy class spirit and cohesiveness, present challenges. If such leaders are motivated by a desire for power, teachers can grant them acceptable forms of influence, which may turn negative leadership into more positive avenues. However, if they simply seek to frustrate teachers and interfere with the progress of other students, the matter is more serious, requiring a search for the causes of the behavior and to work out ways of improving the situation. Whatever the circumstances, teachers benefit by getting to know the student leaders in their classes.

Teachers should also encourage their students to develop leadership skills. Our goal as teachers is not to train good soldiers who follow orders obediently; rather, it is to educate good citizens competent at making wise decisions and willing to be accountable for their actions. By providing leadership practice, teachers guide stu-

"Well, if you really want to know how school went today – Ms. Bradshaw relieved me of my duties overseeing the blocks-and-games cabinet, thus depriving me of my power base."

dents toward the important life goals of becoming autonomous, accepting responsibility, and influencing others to respect their opinions.

The Teacher's Leadership Style   Teachers' leadership styles vary along with the amount of authority they exert over their classes. Some, regarded as authoritarian, keep most of the power and expect students to abide by their rules; others share their power with the group and establish a democratic classroom climate; still others, usually labeled permissive, exert little power and allow their students free rein.

Which of these approaches should you use? Opinions are divided between the first two: the authoritarian, "don't smile until Christmas," camp and the democratic, "involve the learners in the process," camp. Unquestionably, the circumstances of a school and the makeup of the student population may necessitate a specific leadership style, but, optimally, the democratic approach is preferable. In an examination of the literature on leadership styles in classrooms, Jere Brophy and Thomas Good noted that "teachers with democratic styles generally were preferred to those with authoritarian style, and they generally created more positive class-room atmospheres characterized by greater student enjoyment and cooperation and less competitiveness and frustration."[39]

Teachers must be alert to the impact and consequences of the type of leader-ship they choose to exert. Autocratic and democratic teachers exhibit strikingly dif-ferent characteristics and they elicit noticeably different responses from students. According to one study, "hostility, competitiveness, and high dependency marked the autocratic group, while openness, friendly communication, and independence typified the democratically led group."[40] Teachers' leadership styles unquestion-ably affect the climate and the quality of human interactions in their classrooms.

The Democratic Classroom   In democratic classrooms and schools, students are given more power and responsibility than in autocratic systems. If they are to learn how to live in a democracy, students must be able to manage freedom responsibly.

Student councils, student judicial systems, class officers, class meetings, and school assemblies planned by students are forms of student government that offer leadership opportunities and a means of practicing democracy. Some schools pro-vide leadership conferences, enlisting the help of members of the community.

Teachers model democracy by giving their students some choices and control over some of the events that occur in their classrooms. For instance, consider the reflections of one teacher who promotes democratic decision making when a class is small enough:

> This past year my P.E. classes ranged in size from eleven to twenty-five. This size allows for relatively easy management and allowing the students to participate in the decision making increases participation and dedication. As part of the system, two different captains are selected each week, rotating alphabetically. . . . They also choose teams at the first of the week. Two or three times a week students are allowed to vote on which activities to have. An example would be voting on hav-ing a kickball game or softball game, both of which would obtain the desired ob-jectives for that day.

To create a **democratic classroom** is not easy. It takes time, patience, skill, and a willingness to share power. However, the rewards for teachers who implement democratic principles can be significant. Group spirit and school pride are often enhanced, student attitudes toward learning improve, and achievement can soar.

STAGES OF GROUP DEVELOPMENT

Richard Schmuck and Patricia Schmuck, leading theorists in the study of classroom group processes, describe four sequential **stages of group development**.

During Stage 1 of a class's group development, students are on their best be-havior. As Schmuck and Schmuck note, "The first weeks of the class's life are crit-ical times for finding out who one is in relation to the others."[41] Teachers who are aware of this "honeymoon period" use it to their advantage; they discuss and teach classroom rules and procedures, outline their goals, and deliberately set the class-room tone and standards they want. During Stage 2, teachers seeking to promote group development are advised to encourage student participation and communi-cation and to discourage the formation of cliques.

Groups that have met the requirements of the preceding stages move into Stage 3, which lasts for the majority of the expected life of the group—the semester or the school year. Stage 4, the final stage, is described by Schmuck and Schmuck as "the ideal level of maturity . . . when [the group's] norms allow for a variety of individual learning styles to be expressed and accepted, and when the group has the power to change itself toward a more effective state."[42] Classroom groups can arrive at the final cohesive stage more quickly if clear and motivating group goals are set. A class newsletter, dramatic presentations, academic or athletic competitions, fund drives, class trips, and community service work can spur on a group's development.

WHAT TEACHING SKILLS ARE ESSENTIAL?

As we pointed out in Chapter 1, along with essential knowledge teachers must possess two types of essential skills: (1) teaching skills and techniques and (2) interpersonal skills. Unfortunately, the complexities of teaching and the widely varying cultures of schools and classrooms make it difficult to identify precisely the skills teachers need in these two areas. However, one broad helpful view of essential teaching skills is the "Framework for Defining Teaching" (see Figure 12.3). According to the framework, teachers must be able to perform four teaching tasks (organize content knowledge for student learning, teach for student learning, create an environment for student learning, and develop as professionals) while taking into account differences among students and subjects. Within each teaching task, teachers should be able to perform the following:

FIGURE 12.3

Framework for Defining Teaching

Source: Carol Anne Dwyer and Ana Maria Villegas, *Foundations for Tomorrow's Teachers—No. 3, Defining Teaching* (Princeton, N.J.: Educational Testing Service, 1992), p. 6.) Reprinted by permission of Educational Testing Service.

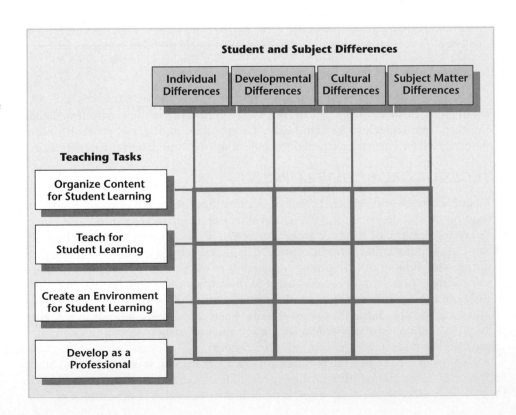

Organize content for student learning

- Articulate clear learning goals that are appropriate to the students.
- Demonstrate an understanding of the connections between past, present, and future content.
- Become familiar with relevant aspects of students' prior knowledge, skills, and cultural experiences.
- Create or select instructional materials or other resources and learning activities that are appropriate to the students and are clearly linked to the goals of the lesson.
- Create or select evaluation strategies that are appropriate for the students and clearly related to the goals of the lesson.

Teach for student learning

- Communicate high expectations for each student.
- Make specific learning expectations clear to students.
- Make content comprehensible to students.
- Encourage students to extend their thinking.
- Monitor students' understanding of content through a variety of means, providing feedback to students to assist learning and adjust lessons as needed.
- Use instructional time effectively.

Create an environment for student learning

- Create a climate that promotes equity.
- Establish and maintain rapport with students in ways that are appropriate to the students' developmental needs.
- Establish and consistently maintain clear standards of mutually respectful classroom interaction and behavior.
- Make the physical environment as safe and conducive to learning as possible.

Develop as a professional

- Reflect on the extent to which the instructional goals were met and explain how insights gained from teaching can be used in the future.
- Demonstrate a sense of efficacy and acceptance of responsibility for student learning.
- Build professional relationships with colleagues to share teaching insights and coordinate learning activities for students.
- Communicate with parents or guardians regarding student learning.[43]

As the following Professional Reflection suggests, teachers must not only master essential teaching skills such as the preceding, they must become proficient at *thinking about the complexities of teaching*.

*P*ROFESSIONAL REFLECTION

The following scenario is based on an interview with a teaching candidate participating in a pilot study in the United States for the Praxis Series: Professional Assignments for Beginning Teachers. After reading the scenario, consider the following: What evidence suggests that this teacher is able to perform the four

(continued)

tasks presented previously? How does she take into account differences among students? Their prior learning experiences? How does she create an environment for student learning? Does she accept responsibility for student learning?

A young woman in the Midwest came to teaching after earning an advanced degree in graphic arts and working for a few years as a commercial artist. She was hired by an open school to teach all subjects to a combined class of fifth- and sixth-graders. Because almost half of her students were new to the school, she knew little about them before the year started.

She quickly discovered that their reading skills were two years below level. She knew that they had worked previously with basal readers but decided not to use them because they had not helped to improve students' reading scores.

"We started out reading 'Tracker' by Gary Paulsen. I chose it because it's short and I believed it would challenge them and hold their attention. But there were neither lesson plans nor a teacher's guide, so I had to invent these and hope that what I was doing would work.

"What I did was have the students work in pairs and read to each other. This seemed to work well; the more advanced readers helped the less able ones. I also gave them a choice when it came to activities based on their reading. One set of activities I designed for the students who were struggling, and the other for the more advanced students. I never labeled them slow or fast, just gave them a choice. Given this particular group of students I feel I really should have four reading groups, but because I can't manage that many at one time, I work with two levels.

"I also used my background in graphic arts to make the classroom interesting. I wanted the students to feel excited coming into the room, so I decorated it with posters and diagrams and bright colors that would be visually stimulating. I even had more experienced teachers asking me for help with their classrooms.

"It's too early for me to tell if my approach to reading is more effective than working with basal readers. I do know that students are involved and seem to be enjoying reading. And I am more sure of my own instincts in teaching as I know the children in my class better and am discovering ways to help them learn."[44]

ORGANIZATION AND PLANNING

The ability to organize time, materials, and activities, and to plan carefully are among the most important skills of teaching. A first-year junior high school teacher explains how organization and planning helped her to have a successful first day of teaching.

All I could think about all the way home [after the first day of school] was just that it was as smooth as it could be. I was prepared. . . . I guess I just planned well enough. I knew what I was going to say.[45]

Six months later, the same teacher comments on how she came to realize that planning for control and management is also an essential teaching skill.

I thought that if you planned the *curriculum* really well, the management just falls into place. I really thought that when I was student teaching. If you are not well planned you are *going* to have problems. . . . Now [after six months], I plan a lot more things, like transition time and walking into the other room [to check on the students].[46]

Before planning a course, designing a unit, or teaching a lesson, teachers need to know what they intend to do, how they want to do it, why they want to do it, and how they will know that they have been successful. Recent studies of teachers' thinking and planning have yielded interesting findings. Christopher Clark and Penelope Peterson conclude that teachers engage in eight types of planning: lesson, daily, weekly, unit, long-range, short-range, term, and yearly, with the unit plan being considered most important.[47] Early in the school year, planning is focused on "establishing the physical environment and social system of the classroom" according to a study of elementary teachers.[48] In a study of British secondary teachers, planning was found to focus on (in order of importance) "(1) pupil needs, abilities, and interests; (2) subject matter; (3) goals; (4) teaching methods."[49]

How teachers go about making lesson plans and how education students are taught to do so may vary. A standard procedure for writing lesson plans is taught in most faculties of education, but student teachers and new teachers often discover that many experienced teachers do not use written lesson plans. Why? Some experienced teachers have internalized the process, skipping steps in the paperwork of the lesson plan but not in their thinking. Others have simply taken too many planning shortcuts and their teaching suffers in the process. On the sequence experienced teachers follow in preparing their lesson plans, *The Harvard Education Letter* reports:

> For three decades supervisors have told student teachers to plan each lesson in four steps: first specify objectives ("the students will be able to multiply improper fractions"); then select learning activities; then organize these activities; and finally, design a way to evaluate what students have learned.
>
> In fact, however, few teachers seem to proceed in this way. About a dozen studies have asked teachers to think aloud as they plan, to talk about their planning, or to keep a planning journal. For most of the teachers studied, planning was a cyclical process, which started either with what they knew about students' needs and interests or with the content to be taught. Teachers specified formal objectives only after the lesson began to take shape.[50]

Figure 12.4 illustrates the two approaches to planning.

ASSESSING STUDENTS' LEARNING

Assessing students' learning is a critical skill. **Assessment** has been defined as "the process of obtaining information that is used to make educational decisions about students, to give feedback to the student about his or her progress, strengths, and weaknesses, to judge instructional effectiveness and curricular adequacy, and to inform policy."[51] In assessing students' learning, teachers make judgments about the performance of students *and* about their own performance as teachers. Successful teachers continually evaluate the effectiveness of their teaching because they recognize that how well students learn depends on how well they teach.

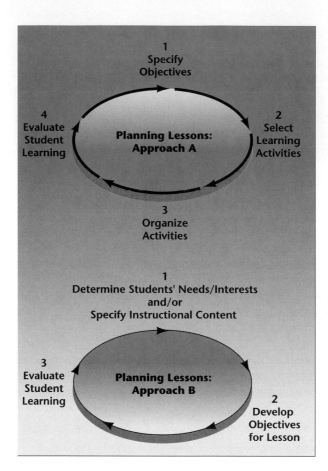

FIGURE 12.4
Two Approaches to Planning Lessons

Among the assessment techniques that teachers use are pencil-and-paper tests, oral questioning, formal and informal observations, qualitative evaluation of pupil performance and products, and the analysis of students' records. Research indicates that teachers use a variety of criteria in grading students' tests and assignments, with no single factor standing out. Among the criteria teachers consider are effort, neatness, correctness, how well students did compared with other students or their own past performance, and how long students had been studying the topic.[52]

To assess students' learning, teachers should be skilled in the following:

- Choosing assessment methods appropriate for instructional decisions
- Developing assessment methods appropriate for instructional decisions
- Administering, scoring, and interpreting the results of both externally produced and teacher-produced assessment methods
- Using assessment results when making decisions about individual students, planning teaching, developing curriculum, and school improvement
- Developing valid pupil grading procedures that use pupil assessments
- Communicating assessment results to students, parents, other non-teaching audiences, and other educators
- Recognizing unethical, illegal, and otherwise inappropriate assessment methods and uses of assessment information[53]

In the main, teachers use two approaches to evaluating student learning: formative and summative evaluation. **Formative evaluation** occurs when the teacher measures students' learning for the purpose of planning for teaching. For example, as an aid to planning for instruction, the teacher profiled in this chapter's Professional Reflection assessed her students' reading skills. **Summative evaluation** is used by teachers to determine grades at the end of a unit, semester, or year and to decide whether students are ready to proceed to the next phase of their education. At some point in your teacher education program, you will learn about **measurement**, that is, the different techniques for assessing student learning. You will also be introduced to basic statistical methods for comparing the learning of students within a group and between groups of students.

COMMUNICATION SKILLS

As we suggested in our earlier discussion of the role that interpersonal skills play in creating a well-managed classroom, successful teachers possess effective communication skills. They express themselves verbally and nonverbally (and in writing) in a manner that is clear, concise, and interesting. In addition, they are good listeners. Their students feel that, not only are they heard, they are understood. Similarly, by providing parents with regular reports of their children's progress and by conducting informative, professional parent-teacher conferences, successful teachers communicate effectively with parents.

Effective teachers relish the live, thinking-on-your-feet dimensions of classroom communication. Their communication skills enable them to respond appropriately to events that could sabotage the plans of less effective teachers: a student's clowning, announcements on the public address system, interruptions by other teachers or parents, students' private arguments or romances, or simply the mood of the class at that particular time.

One of the findings in the studies of teachers' thinking is that teachers who ignore student reactions and continue to focus on the lesson plan objectives are not as effective as those who attend to and adjust to students' responses. Closely related to this is the finding that experienced teachers were better able to read their students and thus could adjust the content of the lessons according to their students' abilities and interest levels. *The Harvard Education Letter*'s summary of this finding applies to elementary teachers, but it should be considered when observing secondary teachers as well:

> Experienced teachers, compared to beginners, know a great deal about children in general—what they do outside of school, how many are likely to need special help, and so on—and analyze classroom events in a more sophisticated way. . . .
>
> While all teachers reprimanded the unruly and aided the confused, experienced teachers were five times as likely as novices to respond to "positive cues"—a giggle of excitement, an item of news, a nod of comprehension, or an unexpected insight. . . .
>
> At all points in the processes of planning and teaching, experienced teachers keep the responses of their particular students near the center of their minds.[54]

How can new teachers use these research findings? Perhaps the best lessons to be gained are: (1) to know students well in terms of their lives outside of school as well as in; (2) to know the subject(s) thoroughly, so well that they can be adapted to the ongoing responses of students; and (3) whenever in a position to do so, to

MAKING *a DIFFERENCE*

Audrey Currie
Montague, Prince Edward Island

Excellence in teaching is portrayed in Canadian classrooms each day by caring, hardworking teachers. Most are not recognized but they quietly depict the high standards that we wish for our children. These teachers are usually motivators, set reasonable and consistent limits, are positive, and cultivate a sense of humor and fairness.

Many children who have reading problems can be easily discouraged and disillusioned about their abilities. As a special educator I have found that the most important ingredient in my students' personal success is attitude. There is truth in the old adage, "It's your attitude, not your aptitude, that determines your altitude." It may take time but once a positive attitude is instilled in a child the academics usually begin to soar.

I wanted to help cultivate a more positive attitude with a non-hearing impaired child who was a non-reader. Over three years I experimented using an FM hearing system which I approached as a lon-gitudinal study. The FM hearing system was found to have significantly affected this student's reading attitude and reading achievement levels. This student has a permanent severe figure-ground auditory processing problem and he is now reading at grade level. My study also focused on positive ways to introduce this type of technology in an effort to thwart any stigmatism.

I know that I have done my job well when former students or their parents return years later and speak about the impact I have personally made in their lives. This signifies the incredible amount of responsibility involved in teaching. I feel strongly the responsibility to create opportunities for children while at the same time it is critical to avoid unintentionally holding them back. Thus, I approach experimentation with curriculum changes or teaching strategies carefully and collect student responses before, during, and after making any changes.

310

ask teachers what they are thinking and how they are making their decisions as they plan and teach.

INSTRUCTIONAL METHODS

As we pointed out in our discussion of educational philosophy in Chapter 8, beliefs about teaching and learning, students, knowledge, and what is worth knowing influence the instructional methods a teacher uses. In addition, instruction is influenced by variables such as the teacher's personality and learning style, the learners' characteristics, the culture of the school and surrounding community, and the resources available. All of these components contribute to the "model" of teaching the teacher uses in the classroom. In *Models of Teaching*, Bruce Joyce, Marsha Weil, and Beverly Showers define a **model of teaching** as "a plan or pattern that we can use to design face-to-face teaching in classrooms or tutorial settings and to shape instructional materials—including books, films, tapes, and computer-mediated programs and curricula (long-term courses of study)."[55] Table 12.1 presents brief descriptions of five widely used models of teaching.

Each model of teaching seeks to achieve a particular set of goals that support a rationale for a particular learning style. In addition to providing a method for teaching content to students, each model also creates a particular kind of classroom environment. For example, **cooperative learning** is a model of teaching that enhances students' interpersonal skills. When students from different racial, ethnic, and cultural backgrounds and mainstreamed special needs students all contribute to a common group goal, friendships increase and group members tend to view one another as more equal in status and worth.

The contribution that cooperative learning can make to the culture of the classroom is expressed by a teacher: "The best rewards for the teacher are those signs that cooperation is becoming second nature with the children. I'm always impressed when a group finishes its work and then, without being told or even asked,

Cooperative learning, a model of teaching that enhances students' interpersonal skills, helps to create a positive classroom atmosphere.

TABLE 12.1	**Five Instructional Models**	
	Goals and Rationale	*Methods*
Mastery Learning	Virtually all students can learn material if given enough time and taught in the appropriate manner. Students learn best when they participate in a structured, systematic program of learning that enables them to progress in small, sequenced steps.	• Set objectives and standards for mastery. • Teach content directly to students. • Provide corrective feedback to students on their learning. • Provide additional time and help in correcting errors. • Follow cycle of teaching, testing, reteaching, and retesting.
Cooperative Learning	Students can be motivated to learn by working cooperatively in small groups if rewards are made available to the group as a whole and to individual members of the group.	• Small groups (four to six students) work together on learning activities. • Assignments require that students help one another while working on a group project. • In competitive arrangements, groups may compete against one another. • Group members contribute to group goals according to their talents, interests, and abilities.
Theory into Practice	Teachers make decisions in three primary areas: content to be taught, how students will learn, and the behaviors the teacher will use in the classroom. The effectiveness of teaching is related to the quality of decisions the teacher makes in these areas.	The teacher follows seven steps in the classroom: 1. Orients students to material to be learned 2. Tells students what they will learn and why it is important 3. Presents new material that consists of knowledge, skills or processes students are to learn 4. Models what students are expected to do 5. Checks for student understanding 6. Gives students opportunity for practice under the teacher's guidance 7. Makes assignments that give students opportunity to practice what they have learned on their own
Behavior Modification	Teachers can shape student learning by using various forms of enforcement. Human behavior is learned, and behaviors that are positively reinforced (rewarded) tend to increase and those that are not reinforced tend to decrease.	• Teacher begins by presenting stimulus in the form of new material. • The behavior of students is observed by the teacher. • Appropriate behaviors are reinforced by the teacher as quickly as possible.
Nondirective Teaching	Learning can be facilitated if teachers focus on personal development of students and create opportunities for students to increase their self-understanding and self-concepts. The key to effective teaching is the teacher's ability to understand students and to involve them in a teaching-learning partnership.	• Teacher acts as a facilitator of learning. • Teacher creates learning environments that support personal growth and development. • Teacher acts in the role of a counselor who helps students to understand themselves, clarify their goals, and accept responsibility for their behavior.

goes to help other groups."[56] Similarly, a grade five science teacher who uses co-operative learning describes how her students learn a variety of roles and responsibilities in addition to learning subject content:

> I have the class divided into groups of five students and each group works as a team. The job duties are as follows: principle investigator (PI), materials manager (MM), reader, recorder, and reporter. The PI is the leader of the group and helps mediate when problems occur. The PI is the only student who can come to me with questions during the actual procedure. This rule enables me to monitor the groups and also teaches the group to work independently.
>
> Students change job duties within their group each activity and every six weeks students change groups. This plan gives each student the experience of working with different classmates as well as learning the responsibility of group participation through performing the different job duties.

DEVELOPING YOUR OWN INSTRUCTIONAL MODEL

Rather than selecting and rigidly following only one instructional model, we encourage you to experiment with several. Joyce, Weil, and Shower's *Models of Teaching*, for example, provides concise, well-organized descriptions of more than two dozen models of teaching.

Effective teachers use a repertoire of teaching models, depending on their situations and the goals they wish to attain. Your teaching strategies in the classroom will most likely be eclectic, that is, a combination of several models. As you gain classroom experience and acquire new skills, your personal model of teaching will evolve, enabling you to respond appropriately to a wider range of teaching situations.

WHAT ARE THE CHARACTERISTICS OF EFFECTIVE TEACHING?

A summary of the research into teaching well-structured subjects effectively is provided by Barak Rosenshine and Robert Stevens in the *Handbook of Research on Teaching*, edited in 1986 for the American Educational Research Association. Rosenshine and Stevens note that their procedures are ideal for step-by-step knowledge and skill development but are not appropriate for less structured areas such as composition, literary criticism, discussion of social issues, and problem solving in specific subject areas. To help teachers be more successful with the structured type of instruction, Rosenshine and Stevens provide the following summary of the research findings from seven major studies conducted with students ranging in age from elementary to senior high school:

- Begin a lesson with a short review of previous, prerequisite learning.
- Begin a lesson with a short statement of goals.
- Present new material in small steps, with student practice after each step.
- Give clear and detailed instructions and explanations.
- Provide a high level of active practice for all students.
- Ask a large number of questions, check for student understanding, and obtain responses from all students.
- Guide students during initial practice.
- Provide systematic feedback and correction.

- Provide explicit instruction and practice for seatwork exercises and, where necessary, monitor students during seatwork.[57]

The above findings can help make field observations more instructive and can act as guides for preparing lessons calling for step-by-step knowledge. Similarly, descriptions of effective teachers can aid in initial observing and planning experiences. One such description, based on observations in British primary schools, is provided by researchers M. Galton and B. Simon:

> The successful teachers all engage in above-average levels of interaction with the pupils. They appear to devote considerable effort to ensuring that the routine activities proceed smoothly; they engage in high levels of task statements and questions, and provide regular feedback. At the same time, they also encourage the children to work by themselves toward solutions to problems . . . [and] make above-average use of higher-order interactions, including . . . more open-ended types of questioning.[58]

Most faculties of education offer courses in teaching strategies and on methods and materials for instruction in specific subject areas. Studying these skills will help prevent future teachers from becoming overwhelmed in their first year of teaching, thus avoiding an educationally wasteful year for students breaking in a new, unprepared teacher.

What do effective teachers do when they are teaching? How do they communicate with students? How do they manage classroom activities? What models of teaching do they use? The following sections provide answers to these questions by presenting brief portraits of three effective teachers in action. As you read each portrait, look for evidence that shows how the teachers use the essential teaching skills discussed previously in this chapter.

CASE 1: PORTRAIT OF AN EFFECTIVE ELEMENTARY SCHOOL TEACHER

Maya Dawson teaches kindergarten at a private school. As you read the following portrait, notice how effectively Maya communicates with her students.

> Maya articulates with precision. Her voice is warm and soft.... She is trim and energetic, a medium Afro forming a black halo around her open, friendly face. Her hands are in motion as she talks, softly hammering home a point, underlining a word, sweeping away an argument.
>
> "Listen to the plans now," she says. "Yesterday you painted some wonderful penguins. And the day before we painted a beautiful Antarctic background. Today I want some of you to cut out penguins and paste them on the background in the hall."
>
> "Me!"
>
> "Me!"
>
> "Me!"
>
> Maya holds up her hand. "Wait a minute. Quiet now. We'll talk first and then we'll decide who will do what. So some of you will make a mural of millions and millions of penguins. Now, who didn't make a card for Spring [a student who is moving to Italy]?"
>
> "I did!" "I made a red one."
>
> "No," Maya smiles. "No, my question is who did *not* make a card?"
>
> Not a hand goes up. "Good. Everyone made one."
>
> "I did."

"Yes!"

"Yes."

"Okay, good. Now, I wrote a message on the chalkboard, and I'd like someone to read it." About a half dozen hands shoot up, and these children go to the board one at a time to read out loud: "Dear Spring. We Will Miss You."

Maya selects five volunteers to cut out penguins.

"There's a lot of work to do there so you better get right to it. And don't forget to get scissors and paste." Off they go.

"We haven't done little books in a long time. Who wants to do little books at the table?" Ben, Vanessa, and Angola raise their hands and troop off to get supplies. "I'll be over in a minute," Maya calls after them.

"Who wants to play at the water table? Okay, Thomas and Aisha. And remember, one definite rule about the water table is you have to keep the water in the water table," she says with emphasis. "Now, you three can start working with blocks. I'll be there to see how you're doing in a short while."

The room begins to hum, and Maya moves around checking on each little group. She smiles at the block builders as they transform themselves quickly into doctors in a hospital emergency room.[59]

CASE 2: PORTRAIT OF AN EFFECTIVE MIDDLE SCHOOL TEACHER

Mr. Gebhart is a grade seven and eight art teacher at a middle school. Notice how he is able to create what he calls a "delicate balance between control and freedom" in a ceramics class.

At first no teacher is visible. Then he can be discerned in his open-necked shirt and clay-streaked pants, bending over one student's project discussing the aesthetic quality of the glaze, then over another's to suggest how to solve the problem of reattaching pieces that fell off in the first firing. Two minutes after the bell has summoned the faithful, Mr. Gebhart stands up. He has already had individual consultation with five students.

"Bo, turn off the radio please, till everyone is working."

A boy from the non-working table silences the music. Most of the students look up for a moment, then resume work. Some approach him with questions concerning evaluation of their work, further directions, or technical or aesthetic problems demanding solution. Mr. Gebhart attends briefly to them, but directs his attention to the back table where a girl is wrapping her scarf around Bo's head, talking.

"Penny, what are you working on?" She shrugs. "Don't just sit there and chat. You've had enough time to get started." Mr. Gebhart turns to somebody else. Penny pulls out a lacy clay shoe and starts smoothing out its high heel.

The radio is turned on. "Leave that off till everyone is working. I'll say when everyone is working." The radio is turned off. Students admonish one another to get to work. Fifteen minutes into the period Mr. Gebhart turns the music on. Another work-day is in progress.

Every two weeks or so Mr. Gebhart introduces a new lesson. He asks the students to gather round, which they do, some perched on the front tables, one on crutches, balanced dangerously between two tables. This lesson involves sculpting a figure, "doing something, not looking like it just died," from a small block of clay. Mr. Gebhart demonstrates the basic cuts and twists which produce a human form, telling students to attend to proportion, not detail. He shows them how to use their bodies to determine arm length. The students seem captivated by the emerging figure. Working quickly, Mr. Gebhart notes that the figure should be posed after its basic form is established, and then brings forth a seated figure, torso twisted, knee raised.

Having given basic directions, Mr. Gebhart shows the students illustrations in *Sports and Games in Art*—Bellows' boxers, Moore's abstractions, Greek wrestlers. He brings the pictures to life: "This one was probably made in clay first like you're doing." "We call this 'abstracted.' Just put in what you think is essential." "Notice how this conveys a feeling of movement." He throws his body forward to walk. "In art we create the same process by throwing the whole body off center."

Pointing to a Giacometti with slender legs, "What's the problem with this one if you were making it out of clay?" ("It wouldn't stand.") "How could you solve that problem?" With no hesitations solutions are offered, "put wire inside and clay around it"; "a platform"; "support."

Mr. Gebhart expands on the students' answers, showing further illustrations and reminding them to think about how they will present their figure. Then he recaps several tips adapting ideas from existing art pieces, planning before starting, using one's body as a guide, adding details last.

During the fourteen-minute lecture, Mr. Gebhart has the students' attention. Barb, chin on hands, has her eyes riveted to him and the book, nodding to herself. Valerie is unobtrusively observing from behind some more assertive students. Even Bo and Penny watch. "Continue with your work," concludes Mr. Gebhart. The students disperse, and the day continues in the usual manner of individual instruction. Seven or eight different types of projects are underway.[60]

CASE 3: PORTRAIT OF AN EFFECTIVE HIGH SCHOOL TEACHER

Finally, let us visit Mrs. LeFluir's high school Spanish class. Notice how Mrs. LeFluir gradually changes the demands placed on her students. She first focuses on the memorization of rules and vocabulary; then she turns to completion and fill-in exercises; and last, she has students practice their oral delivery.

MRS. LeFLUIR: Today we will study the gender of nouns. In Spanish all nouns are either masculine or feminine. Nouns ending in *o* are generally masculine, and those ending in *a* are generally feminine. Tisha, can you identify the following nouns as either masculine or feminine? (writes on board)
libro
pluma
cuaderno
gramática

TISHA: (correctly identifies each)

MRS. LeFLUIR: Now, let's see how you identified each of the words and what each word means.

TISHA: Well, I followed the rule that if it ends in an *o* it will be masculine but if it ends in an *a* it will be feminine. I think the words are book, pen, notebook, and grammar.

MRS. LeFLUIR: Good. Now for the next step, you've all used indefinite articles *a* or *an* many times in your speaking and writing. In Spanish the word *un* is used for *a* or *an* before a masculine noun, and *una* is used for *a* or *an* before a feminine noun. In Spanish the article is repeated before each noun. Now, using the vocabulary words on the board, let's place the correct form of the indefinite article in front of each word. (shifting the task demand) Why don't you take the first one, Ted?

TED: It would be *un libro.*

MRS. LeFLUIR: Mary.

MARY: *Una pluma.*

MRS. LeFLUIR: Bob and Mike, take the next two.

BOB: *Un cuaderno.*

MIKE: *Una gramática.*
MRS. LEFLUIR: OK. Now, we are ready to put our knowledge to work. I will give
                     you a sentence in English and you translate it into Spanish, being
                     sure to include the correct form of the indefinite article (shifting the
                     task demand again). For this you will need to remember your vo-
                     cabulary from last week. If you need to, look up the words you for-
                     got. Mark, let's start with you. Come up to the board and write: Do
                     you want a book?
MARK: (writes on board) *Desea usted un libro?*
MRS. LEFLUIR: Good. And how did you decide to use *un* instead of *una?*
MARK: The noun ended in *o.*
MRS. LEFLUIR: (Continues with three other examples)
                     Do you need grammar?
                     Do you want to study a language?
                     Do you need a notebook?
                     (After the students respond, she shifts the task demand again by
                     moving to the following activity.) Now, read each sentence on the
                     transparency and write down the correct form of the indefinite ar-
                     ticle that goes before the noun (shows transparency).

                     Yo necesito _____ gramática.
                     Nosotros estudiamos _____ lengua.
                     ¿Necesita Tomás _____ libro?
                     ¿Es _____ pluma?

                     (After the students respond, she moves to a final activity and yet an-
                     other task demand.) Now for the following sentences, I will speak
                     in English, and I want you to repeat the same sentence entirely in
                     Spanish. Be sure, once again, to include the correct form of the in-
                     definite article. . . .[61]

As the portraits of Dawson, Gebhardt, and LeFluir show, effective teachers are
well organized, create a positive classroom climate, establish authentic relationships with students, and promote critical thinking. Although all three use different
models of teaching, they share a commitment to working hard to promote the
learning and growth of students.

▼

PROFESSIONAL PORTFOLIO

Prepare a poster showing a classroom arrangement appropriate for the subject area
and grade level for which you are preparing to teach. The poster should indicate
the seating arrangement and location of other classroom furniture. In addition,
make a list of classroom rules that will be posted in the room. You may wish to
organize the rules using the following categories.

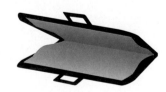

- Rules related to academic work
- Rules related to classroom conduct
- Rules that must be communicated on your first teaching day
- Rules that can be communicated later[62]

Last, prepare a flow chart depicting routine activities for a typical day. This chart could include procedures for the following:

- Handling attendance, tardy slips, and excuses
- Distributing materials
- Turning in homework
- Doing seatwork or various in-class assignments
- Forming small groups for cooperative learning activities
- Returning materials and supplies at the end of class

CHAPTER SUMMARY

An important part of becoming a professional teacher is developing an understanding of the dynamics of classroom life. Successful teachers make appropriate, moment-to-moment decisions in response to the ebb and flow of classroom events. To make the transition from the study of teaching to actual teaching one must examine the conditions and teacher behaviors that result in "good" learning environments for students.

The culture of the classroom has a significant influence on students' learning. Teachers must understand six interdependent and interacting influences on classroom culture:

1. The activity format, procedure, or delivery system of instruction
2. The academic content itself
3. The physical, spatial, and temporal constraints
4. The accountability structure
5. The players in the classroom drama
6. The dynamic interaction among participants, activities, content, and materials

In addition, teachers should understand that classroom culture is also influenced by how the classroom is organized and by the physical environment. Among the patterns for organizing classrooms are the self-contained classroom, team-teaching arrangements, open-space classrooms, and departmentalized classrooms.

Several factors influence the classroom climate or the ways in which the people within the classroom interact with each other. How the teacher groups students for instruction, structures classroom activities, and uses time greatly influences classroom climate.

Most beginning teachers are concerned about classroom management. Remember that the key to successful classroom management is preventing problems before they occur. When management-related problems do occur, however, effective teachers draw from a repertoire of systematic approaches such as the following: assertive discipline, the LEAST approach, behavior modification strategies, the acceptance approach, reality therapy, and the no-lose method. In addition, such teachers foster effective, harmonious interpersonal interactions, understand how their leadership style influences students, and facilitate the development of the classroom group so that it becomes more cohesive and supportive.

Though it is difficult to identify *all* the skills teachers need, research indicates that effective teachers have well-developed skills in four critical areas: organization and planning, assessing students' learning, communication, and instruction. How teachers employ their skills in these areas determines the instructional model they use in the classroom. Regardless of the model used, however, a look at effective teachers in action shows that they promote critical thinking in the classroom.

KEY TERMS AND CONCEPTS

academic learning time, 293
acceptance approach, 298
activity format, 293
allocated time, 293
assertive discipline, 297
assessment, 307
behavior modification, 297
between-class ability grouping, 291
classroom climate, 290
classroom management, 294

classroom organization, 288
cooperative learning, 311
cross-age tutoring, 292
democratic classroom, 303
formative evaluation, 309
higher-order questions, 301
LEAST approach, 297
lower-order questions, 301
measurement, 309
model of teaching, 311
no-lose method, 299

opportunity to learn (OTL), 294
peer tutoring, 292
reality therapy, 298
stages of group development, 303
summative evaluation, 309
time on task, 293
within-class ability grouping, 292

APPLICATIONS AND ACTIVITIES

Teacher's Journal

1. Recall the group projects that you participated in during your school career. Analyze the success or failure of one group project in terms of the stages of group development discussed in this chapter.
2. Analyze a course you are taking using the six sources of influence on classroom culture identified by Woolfolk and Galloway.
3. The LEAST approach to classroom discipline suggests that the teacher may decide *not* to respond to some instances of misbehavior in the classroom. Make a list of misbehavior that, as a teacher, you might decide to overlook.
4. Imagine that, as a teacher, you are using behavior modification strategies to manage your classroom. Develop a list of reinforcements (rewards) that you could use with your students.
5. In which area of teacher effectiveness do you feel most and least confident? What might you do or what program might you undertake to strengthen your effectiveness in areas in which you feel you lack confidence? Work your ideas into a statement of professional goals.

Field Assignments

1. Observe several teachers at the level at which you are preparing to teach. To what extent does each teacher use the behaviors Rosenshine and Stevens present in their summary of research findings on teaching (see page 385)?
2. Form a team with several other classmates and analyze three to five classrooms in terms of the eight dimensions of effective and ineffective classroom climates. Apply a ten-point scale to the continuum between the negative and positive qualities (let 10 stand for order and 0 stand for chaos) and estimate where each class fits along the continuum. Discuss your answers and report your observations to the rest of the class.
3. After observing in a classroom for several days, offer to collect data on interpersonal interactions between students and between students and the teacher. Make a seating plan of the class and whenever people interact draw a line between them on the plan. If they interact frequently, use a tallying system rather than redrawing the line. Observe the class for a 20-minute period and share your results with the teacher. Discuss with your class what you have learned from the experience. (You could also choose to code types of interactions. See Robert Rosenthal's four suggestions on page 299 to increase positive interactions.)

13 The School Curriculum

An educator is entrusted with the most serious work that confronts humankind: the development of curricula that enable new generations to contribute to the growth of human beings and society.

—William H. Schubert
*Curriculum: Perspective,
Paradigm, and Possibility*

Focus Questions

1. What is taught in the schools?
2. How is school curriculum developed?
3. What reform efforts have affected the curriculum?
4. What are the current subject-area trends?

William Mahon, a first-year teacher, is at a meeting of the school-wide curriculum development committee recently formed at his school. The committee is exploring ways to integrate the curriculum so that it treats various subject areas as a unified whole rather than as separate, disconnected parts.

The committee is discussing the pros and cons of a theme-based curriculum. The thematic approach would organize the curriculum around several themes, each of which would address a key concept (how the animal world has influenced the lives of human beings on earth, for example). As students explored such themes they would learn relevant material from areas such as language, reading, mathematics, science, social studies, art, movement and drama, and music.

At this point, Dolores Thuen, an experienced teacher who volunteered to serve as a mentor to William, is speaking in favor of curriculum integration: "It's really artificial to say that children learn best by focusing first on science, then on math, then on reading," she says. "These divisions have been created by adults and imposed on kids because . . ."

"I think that's overstating things," another teacher says, interrupting Dolores. "How are we going to be sure that our kids master the basics if we organize the curriculum around these themes? That's not what the parents of our children want. And what would students actually *do* in a curriculum that focused on how animals and humans live on earth?"

"Oh, they could do a lot of things," Dolores says, smiling. "They could study the biological characteristics of animals in science, sing about animals in music, move like different animals in physical education, and read stories about animals in reading. In math they could calculate how much animals must eat to stay alive."

William decides to get involved in the discussion. "I support the integrated approach," he says. "One of the main goals of our curriculum should be for students to go beyond the basics. We want them to know how to use the material they learn, how to solve problems. An integrated approach is the best way to accomplish that."

"I'm not sure I agree," a teacher seated across the table from William says. "The purpose of our curriculum should be to learn the basics. We want our kids to do well on tests. If they don't do well on them, they're less likely to continue their education. What we're talking about here has been tried before, and it didn't work."

What should be the purpose of the school curriculum in today's schools? How should the curriculum be organized? What learning activities should students experience? How should teachers assess students' learning?

Think back to your experiences as a student at the schools you attended. What did you learn? Certainly, the curriculum you studied included reading, computation, handwriting, spelling, geography, and history. In addition to these topics, though, did you learn something about cooperation, competition, stress, football, video games, popularity, and other people? Or, perhaps, did you learn to love chemistry and to hate English grammar?

WHAT IS TAUGHT IN THE SCHOOLS?

The countless things you learned in school make up the curriculum you experienced. Curriculum theorists and researchers have suggested several different definitions of **curriculum**, with no one definition universally accepted. Here are some definitions in current use.

1. A course of study, derived from the Latin *currere*, meaning "to run a course"
2. Course content, the information or knowledge that students are to learn
3. Planned learning experiences
4. Intended learning outcomes, the *results* of instruction as distinguished from the *means* (activities, materials, etc.) of instruction
5. All the experiences students have while at school

No one of these five is in any sense the "right" definition. The way we define curriculum depends on our purposes and the situation we find ourselves in. If, for example, we were advising a high school student on the courses he or she needs to take to prepare for university, our operational definition of curriculum would probably be "a course of study." However, if we were interviewing grade six students for their views on the K–6 elementary school they had just graduated from, we would probably define curriculum as "all the experiences that students have while at school."

For this chapter, let us posit an additional definition of curriculum: *Curriculum refers to the experiences, both planned and unplanned, that enhance (and sometimes impede) the education and growth of students.* According to this definition, the purpose of the curriculum is to educate, to promote growth. Although students have almost limitless experiences at school, not all are educative or growth-promoting. One of the challenges you will face as a teacher will be to present your students with a curriculum that contains as many experiences as possible that promote education or growth.

KINDS OF CURRICULUM

Elliot Eisner, a noted educational researcher, has said that "schools teach much more—and much less—than they intend to teach. Although much of what is taught is explicit and public, a great deal is not."[1] For this reason, we need to look at the four curricula that all students experience. The more we understand these curricula and how they influence students, the better we will be able to develop educational programs that do in fact educate.

Explicit Curriculum   The explicit, or overt, curriculum refers to what a school intends to teach students. This curriculum is made up of several components: (1) the goals and aims the school has for all students, (2) the actual courses that make up each student's course of study, and (3) the specific knowledge, skills, and attitudes that teachers want students to acquire. If we asked a principal to describe the education program at his or her school, our inquiry would refer to the explicit curriculum. Similarly, if we asked a teacher to describe what he or she wants to accomplish with a particular class, we would be given a description of the explicit curriculum.

In short, the **explicit curriculum** represents the publicly announced expectations the school has for its students. These expectations range from learning how to read, write, and compute to learning to appreciate music, art, and cultures other than one's own. The explicit curriculum usually takes the form of written plans or guides for the education of students. Examples of such written documents are course descriptions, curriculum guides that set forth the goals and objectives for a province, district, or school, texts and other commercially prepared learning materials, and teachers' lesson plans. Through the instructional program of a school, these curricular materials are brought to life.

Hidden Curriculum   As we discussed in Chapter 5, the hidden, or implicit, curriculum refers to the behaviors, attitudes, and knowledge the culture of the school unintentionally teaches students. In addition, the **hidden curriculum** addresses "aspects of schooling that are recognized only occasionally and remain largely unexamined, particularly the schools' pedagogical, organizational, and social environments, and their interrelations."[2] For example, one study of an "effective" elementary school revealed that students had "learned" that grades depended as much or more on their attitudes and behavior as on their academic ability. When asked "How do you earn grades for your report card?" the responses of grade five and six students included the following:

> If you want to earn good grades you got to hand in your work on time. You got to sit up straight and don't talk to no one.
>
> You have to be quiet, be a nice student and know how to write and read and stuff.[3]

As a result of schools' hidden curriculum, students learn more than their teachers imagine. Although teachers cannot directly control what students learn through the hidden curriculum, they can increase the likelihood that what it teaches will be positive. The following Professional Reflection, for example, reminds us of the important lessons students can learn through the hidden curriculum.

PROFESSIONAL REFLECTION

It is the first day of school, and Teacher 1 and Teacher 2 are establishing classroom rules. As a consequence of the different approaches the teachers use, what lessons might their students learn? What possible effects might the hidden curriculum of these two classrooms have on students' development beyond childhood?

(continued)

Teacher 1	"OK, class. Listen up now. One of the things I want us to make sure we understand today is our classroom rules. I've put a chart of the rules up here so everyone can see it, and you won't be able to say 'I forgot.' There aren't many rules, but they're important. To help you learn them, I want you to write them in the front of your notebooks. First, let's read them out loud, then you can write them."
Teacher 2	"Boys and girls. Today is an important day. It's our first day together and we need to spend some time getting to know one another. One thing we need to talk about is how we can make our classroom a good place for all of us. Maybe in your family you have a few really important rules. Well, we need a few important rules, too. Let's list some rules that you think are most important. Then we'll talk about them and see which ones we agree are the best rules for our classroom this year."[4]

By allowing students to help determine the content of the explicit curriculum, by inviting them to help establish classroom rules, and by providing them with challenges appropriate for their stage of development, teachers can ensure that the outcomes of the hidden curriculum are more positive than negative. The key is for teachers not to forget the hidden curriculum, to remember that one of the most important lessons students learn is what to make out of their lives at school.

Null Curriculum   Discussing a curriculum that cannot be observed directly is like talking about dark matter or black holes, unseen phenomena in the universe whose existence must be inferred because their incredible denseness and gravitational fields do not allow light to escape. In much the same way, we can consider the curriculum that we *do not* find in the schools; it may be as important as what we *do* find. Elliot Eisner has labeled the intellectual processes and content that schools do not teach "the **null curriculum** . . . the options students are not afforded, the perspectives they may never know about, much less be able to use, the concepts and skills that are not a part of their intellectual repertoire."[5]

For example, the kind of thinking that schools foster among students is largely based on manipulating words and numbers. Thinking that is imaginative, subjective, and poetic is stressed only incidentally. Furthermore, students are seldom taught anthropology, sociology, psychology, law, economics, filmmaking, or architecture.

Eisner points out that "certain subject matters have been traditionally taught in schools not because of a careful analysis of the range of other alternatives that could be offered but rather because they have traditionally been taught. We teach what we teach largely out of habit, and in the process neglect areas of study that could prove to be exceedingly useful to students."[6] Japanese schools, for example, require considerably more art, music, and literature than most Canadian schools. In addition, all Japanese students must study handicrafts and calligraphy. Japanese curricula go beyond verbal and numerical thinking to include the development of aesthetic capabilities.

You will discover that school systems grant teachers varying degrees of freedom regarding what they teach. Your goal as a professional will be to work within surrounding constraints and to offer students the subject matter your professional judgment suggests they need.

Extracurricular/Cocurricular Programs This curriculum includes school-sponsored activities—music, drama, special interest clubs, sports, student government, and honor societies, to name a few—that students may pursue in addition to their studies in academic subject areas. When such activities are perceived as additions to the academic curriculum, they are called *extracurricular*. When these activities are seen as having important educational goals—and not merely as extras added to the academic curriculum—they are called *cocurricular*. To reflect the fact that these two labels are commonly used for the same activities, we use the term *extracurricular/cocurricular activities*.

Though **extracurricular/cocurricular programs** are most extensive at the secondary level, many schools at the elementary, middle, and junior levels also provide their students with a broad assortment of extracurricular/cocurricular activities. For those students who choose to participate, such activities provide an opportunity to use social and academic skills in many different contexts.

Research shows that the larger a school is, the less likely it is that a student will take part in extracurricular/cocurricular activities. At the same time, those who do participate tend to have higher self-images than those who do not.[7] The actual effects that extracurricular/cocurricular activities have on students' development, however, are not entirely clear. In their review of research on the topic, Duane Alvin and David Morgan concluded that (1) there is little evidence to suggest that participation in sports is related to improved academic achievement, (2) participation in extracurricular/cocurricular activities does influence subsequent behavior, and (3) participation in extracurricular/cocurricular activities—particularly music, service and leadership activities, and sports—does have a positive influence on the level of education and the occupation one aspires to and eventually attains.[8]

It is clear, however, that students who might benefit the most from participating in extracurricular/cocurricular activities—those below the norm in academic achievement and students at risk—tend not to participate. In addition, students from low socioeconomic backgrounds participate less often.

As a professional, your task is to do what you can to ensure that each student has a broad range of school experiences that are worthy of being called educative. If you are able to do that, you will have gone a long way toward meeting the challenge of the profession.

CURRICULUM CONTENT

Canadian schools teach what the larger society believes young people should learn. As reported by Patty Newton and Earle Newton, when asked in which subject areas instruction should be increased and in which it should be decreased, students, teachers, and parents in Saskatchewan substantially agreed in their responses, as shown in Table 13.1.[9]

These findings are specific to Saskatchewan and are not generalizable to other regions. They indicate agreement among the different stakeholders in the school system and an emphasis on curriculum that prepares students more directly for the workplace. It is noteworthy that teachers believe that instruction should be increased or remain the same for all subjects with the exception of French. Both

TABLE 13.1	SUBJECT AREAS IN WHICH INSTRUCTION SHOULD BE INCREASED/DECREASED		
Students		**Parents**	**Teachers**
More of these courses...			
Industrial Arts		Basic Skills	Basic Skills
Counseling		Counseling	Counseling
Career Education		Life Skills	Life Skills
Computer Education		Computer Education	
Physical Education		Remedial	
Law			
Drama			
Art			
Home Economics			
Accounting			
Less of these courses...			
French		French	French
Band		French Immersion	French Immersion
Music		Other Languages	
Social Studies			

students and parents generally agree with teachers although parents also want less instruction in other languages, and students in band, music, and social studies. Although there are differences, the areas in common are substantial.

Goodlad reflects these findings when he writes that what schools teach is characterized more by uniformity than by diversity:

> Our data, whatever the source, reveal not only the curricular dominance of English/Language arts and mathematics but also the consistent and repetitive attention to basic facts and skills. Developing 'the ability to read, write, and handle basic arithmetical operations' pervades instruction from the first through the ninth grades and the lower tracks of courses beyond.[10]

HOW IS SCHOOL CURRICULUM DEVELOPED?

Although there is no easy-to-follow set of procedures for developing curriculum, Ralph Tyler has provided four fundamental questions that must be answered in developing any curriculum or plan of instruction. These four questions, known as the **Tyler rationale,** are as follows:

1. What educational purposes should the school seek to attain?
2. What educational experiences can be provided that are likely to attain these purposes?
3. How can these educational experiences be effectively organized?
4. How can we determine whether these purposes are being attained?[11]

Some educators believe that the Tyler rationale underestimates the complexities involved in curriculum development because it advocates a straightforward, step-by-step process that in reality is difficult to follow. Nevertheless, Tyler's work has been used by many school systems to bring some degree of order and focus to the curriculum development process.

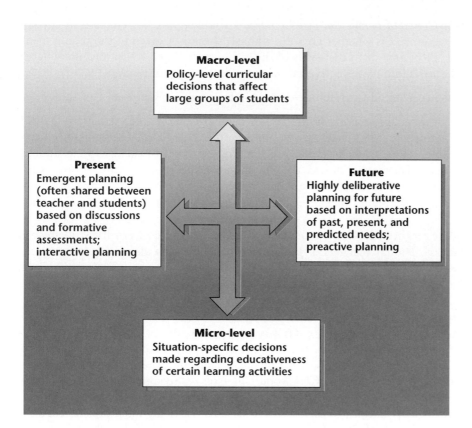

FIGURE 13.1
Two Foci of Curriculum Planning

The Focus of Curriculum Planning   In discussing curriculum development, it is helpful to clarify the focus of curriculum planning. Figure 13.1 illustrates two dimensions of this planning process: the target and the time orientation. The target of curriculum planning exists along a continuum from the macro- to the micro-level. At the macro-level, decisions about the content of the curriculum apply to large groups of students. The provincial curriculum guidelines are examples of macro-level curricular decisions. At the micro-level, curriculum decisions are made that apply to groups of students in a particular school or classroom. To some extent, all teachers are micro-level curriculum developers—that is, they make numerous decisions about the curricular experiences they provide students in their classrooms.

Another dimension of curriculum planning is the time orientation—does the planning focus on the present or the future? Curriculum planning focused on the future is a highly deliberative process, much like Philip Jackson's concept of preactive teaching that we discussed in Chapter 2. In addition to the provincial curriculum guidelines, the semester-long or monthly plans that teachers make are examples of future-oriented curriculum planning. Present-oriented curriculum planning (much like Jackson's concept of interactive teaching) usually occurs at the classroom level and is influenced by the unique needs of specific groups of students. The daily or weekly curriculum decisions teachers make are also examples of present-oriented curriculum planning.

Student-Centered versus Subject-Centered Curricula   A key concern in curriculum development is whether greater emphasis should be given to the requirements of the subject area or to the needs of the students. It is helpful to imagine where a school curriculum might be placed on the following continuum.

Student-Centered Curriculum   ◄────────►   Subject-Centered Curriculum

Although no course is entirely subject- or student-centered, curricula vary considerably in the degree to which they emphasize one or the other. The **subject-centered curriculum** places primary emphasis on the logical order of the discipline students are to study. The teacher of such a curriculum is a subject-matter expert and is primarily concerned with helping students understand the facts, laws, and principles of the discipline. Subject-centered curricula are more typical of high school education.

Some teachers develop curricula that reflect greater concern for students and their needs. Though teachers of **student-centered curricula** also teach content, they emphasize the growth and development of students. This emphasis is generally more typical of elementary school curricula.

The Integrated Curriculum   The opening scenario for this chapter is based on the integrated approach to developing the school curriculum. Used most frequently with elementary-age students, the **integrated curriculum** draws from several different subject areas and focuses on a theme or concept rather than on a single subject. In *The Integrated Early Childhood Curriculum*, Suzanne Krogh suggests that an integrated approach is more "natural" for children: "When children learn in a way that is most natural to themselves, they unconsciously integrate subject areas into a complex whole based on their current interests. Teachers who consciously adapt this method of learning to the classroom see the curriculum as a fully spun web that incorporates a number of components at one time."[12]

WHO PLANS THE CURRICULUM?

One perennial issue in Canadian education is who should plan the curriculum. Should planning be done only by the teachers who will be held accountable for implementing the curriculum? Should parents decide what they want their children to learn? Or should government officials, professional associations, or education researchers plan the curriculum? Few principals and even fewer teachers believe teachers have much influence over the curriculum.

Various agencies and persons external to the school are involved in curriculum planning. The ministries of education, for example, develop both broad aims for school curricula and specific minimum competencies for student achievement. Textbook publishers influence what is taught because many teachers use textbooks as curriculum guides. Nationally, over 70 organizations represent particular interests. These include the Canadian Educational Association, the Canadian Teachers' Federation, and the Canadian Association of Principals. Such organizations try to influence what curricula are used throughout Canada.

Within a given school, the curriculum-planning team and the classroom teacher plan the curriculum that students actually experience. As a teacher you will draw from a reservoir of curriculum plans prepared by others, thus playing a vital role in the curriculum-planning process. Whenever you make decisions about what

As a microlevel curriculum developer, what basic decisons did the teacher of this science class have to make? In what way is this class a reflection of macrolevel curriculum decisions?

material to include in your teaching, how to sequence content, and how much time to spend teaching certain material, you are planning the curriculum.

WHAT INFLUENCES CURRICULAR DECISIONS?

From the earliest schools of the settlers to schools of the 1990s, curriculum has been broadly influenced by a variety of religious, political, and utilitarian agendas. Among the factors that influence the curriculum are community pressures, students' life situations, testing results, provincial reports, teachers' professional organizations, and research results. Some factors have a more direct influence on curriculum development at the school level—students' needs and school district policies, for example. Other factors, more removed from the school setting, may have less obvious or direct effects on the school curriculum—the results of educational research or legislation, for example. (See Table 13.2.) In addition, the culture of a school itself affects how the school responds to curricular influences. Let us examine some of these influences in greater detail.

Social Issues and Changing Values   Values that affect curriculum planning include prevailing educational theories and teachers' educational philosophies. In addition, curriculum planners respond to social issues and changing values in the wider society. As a result, current social concerns find their way into textbooks, teaching aids, and lesson plans. Often curriculum changes are made in the hope that changing what students learn will help solve social problems or achieve local, provincial, or national goals. Required instructional units on water conservation or forest fire safety may reflect regional realities, for example. Locally mandated curricula addressing health, safety, and morality issues—such as AIDS, teen pregnancy, substance abuse, and drunk driving—reflect growing public concern about the behaviors and attitudes that ultimately place everyone at risk.

TABLE 13.2 FORCES INFLUENCING CURRICULUM DEVELOPMENT	
External Forces	**Internal Forces**
Textbook authors	School curriculum teams
Textbook publishers	School department heads
National education agencies	Principal
Universities	Administrative team
Teacher accrediting agencies	Classroom teachers
Other provincial agencies	Classroom volunteers
Provincial special interest groups	Parent advisory committee
Community special interest groups	Curriculum coordinators
Local school districts	Funding allocations

Because Canada is so culturally diverse, proposed curriculum changes also reflect divergent interests and values. This divergence may lead to controversies over curriculum content and conflicting calls for reform. Some groups may demand that Christian teachings and observances be included in the public school curricula, for example, or that materials regarded as objectionable on religious grounds be censored or banned. Other groups may call for the elimination of all activities or symbols that have their origins in organized religion, including secularized or commercialized ones such as Santa Claus and the Easter bunny. Curriculum changes to promote greater social integration or equity among racial or ethnic groups may draw complaints of irrelevancy or reverse discrimination. Traditionalists may object to curriculum changes that reflect feminist views. As you can imagine, consensus on many curriculum reform issues is never achieved. However, because of their public accountability, schools must consider how to respond to those issues.

Textbook Publishing   Textbooks greatly influence the curriculum. According to a survey of 12 000 K–12 teachers, 90 to 95 percent of classroom time is based on commercially published curriculum materials in the form of textbooks, workbooks, and computer software.[13] In addition, publishers influence school curricula by providing teaching objectives, learning activities, tests, audiovisual aids, and other supplements to assist their customers. This influence increases when school districts adopt a series of textbooks by one publisher—usually called a basal series. After adoption these books are used at several grade levels by all the schools in the district.

Like curriculum planners, textbook authors and publishers are influenced by trends in education and by social issues. In response to criticism, for example, publishers now try to avoid bias due to gender, religion, class, race, and culture. However, because the goal of business is profit, publishers are most responsive to market trends and customer preferences. They are often reluctant to risk losing sales by including subjects that are controversial or that may be offensive to their bigger customers. They may also modify textbooks to appeal to decision makers in larger provinces with the biggest markets, such as Ontario and British Columbia. Canadian publishers are often subsidiaries of larger American publishers, and the U.S. agenda often creeps into Canadian texts.

Educators have criticized textbooks for inoffensiveness to the point of blandness, for artificially lowered reading levels (called "dumbing down"), and for pedagogically questionable gimmicks to hold students' attention. The late child psychologist Bruno Bettelheim and his associate, Karen Zelan, for example, ask the following question about basal readers:

> Why are these primers used to teach reading, when children universally object that they find them boring, when they use an unjustifiably limited vocabulary much too repetitiously, and when they obviously fail in their purpose, since all too few of the children taught by means of these texts become literate?[14]

Although the publishing industry continually responds to such criticisms, you would be wise to follow systematic guidelines in evaluating and choosing textbooks and other curriculum materials. One survey reported that 35 percent of teachers spend less than one hour per year on the selection of materials and that 25 percent of them spend an average of only ten hours per year on the selection process.[15]

WHAT REFORM EFFORTS HAVE AFFECTED THE CURRICULUM?

The content of the curricula in Canada's schools has changed frequently since the schools of the early European settlers. These modifications came about as the goals of the schools were debated, additional needs of society became evident, and the characteristics of student populations shifted. Over time, schools have had to focus on a wide variety of goals set by society, and, through their curricula, they have tried to achieve these goals. The following list is a sampling of goals the schools have set for themselves at different times:

- Prepare students to carry out religious and family responsibilities.
- Provide employers with a source of literate workers.
- Reduce crime, poverty, and injustice.
- Help our country maintain its competitive edge in the world economy.
- Educate students for intelligent participation in a democracy.

CHURCH AND SCHOOL

Until the mid-nineteenth century the primary aim of the curriculum was to train students in religious beliefs and practices. Basic skills were taught for the purpose of learning religious catechisms and reading prayers. In addition to taking courses with religious content, students also studied such subjects as grammar, reading, writing, and arithmetic.

Early formal education was conducted primarily in the home, or in the church. Textbooks were rarely used and were usually poor in quality. Most material for instruction came from the Bible or catechisms. The quality of teachers was uneven, and nearly all were judged according to religious criteria. As you have seen, religious views still exert an influence on curriculum, especially in provinces that fund religious-based school systems, such as Ontario and Newfoundland.

FIGURE 13.2   A Chronology of Major Emphases in the U.S. School Curriculum

Religious Emphasis	1640	1636 — Latin grammar (college-prep) schools established and, like Harvard and Yale Colleges, emphasize Latin, Greek, theology, and philosophy for those preparing to enter law or religion.
	1660	1647 — Massachusetts Law of 1647 mandates a reading and writing teacher for towns of 50 or more families; a Latin teacher for towns of 100 or more. Females taught basics to enable them to carry out religious and family responsibilities.
	1680	
Political Emphasis	1700	1700s — Public schools teach reading, writing, and basic mathematics (counting, adding, and subtracting) to prepare students for jobs and apprenticeships.
	1760	Early 1750s — Academies teach secondary students a practical curriculum (drawing, surveying, navigation, merchant's accounting, etc.) to become tradespeople and workers.
	1820	1821 — First public high school teaches basic skills and history, geography, health, and physical training.
Utilitarian Emphasis	1860	1860 — First English-speaking kindergarten emphasizes growth, activity, play, songs, and physical training.
	1880	1874 — Free public schooling now includes high schools that place emphasis on vocational education and reading, writing, and mathematics.
Education for Masses		1893 — Committee of Ten asserts that high schools are for college-bound and curriculum should emphasize mental disciplines in humanities, language, and science.
	1900	1918 — Commission on Reorganization of Secondary Education focuses on individual differences. Curriculum to stress Seven Cardinal Principles.
	1920	1930s — Progressive education movement stresses curriculum based on student's needs and interests. Home economics, health, family living, citizenship, and woodshop added 1940s to the curriculum.
The Excellence Movement	1940	1957 — Russia's Sputnik sparks emphasis on science, mathematics, and languages.
		1960s — Calls for relevancy result in expanded course offerings and electives.
	1960	Mid- — Back-to-basics movement emphasizes reading, writing, mathematics, and oral 1970s communication.
	1980	1983 — Call for "five new basics"–English, mathematics, science, social studies, and computer science.
		1985 — Rigorous core curricula advocated at all levels in an effort to increase standards and to ensure quality.
		1989 — Creation of learning communities and a core academic program for middle-level students.
	1990	Mid- — National standards committees meet in the subject areas. 1990s Renewed emphasis on developing curricula for schooling in a diverse society.

INFLUENCE OF AMERICAN CURRICULUM REFORM ON CANADIAN SCHOOLS

To understand Canadian reforms in curriculum it is important to first understand American reforms because Americans dealt with educational issues nationally about one hundred years before Canadians did. Curricular concerns were a major focus in America from 1770 to 1860. The U.S. had just won its independence from England, and many policymakers believed that literacy was essential to the preservation of freedom. Accordingly, students were taught history, geography, health, and physical training, as well as the basic skills of reading, writing, and computation. In 1821, the nation's first public high school was opened in Boston, and two years later the first private normal school for teachers opened in Concord, Vermont. The first English-speaking kindergarten, taught by Elizabeth Peabody, opened in Boston in 1860.

Although Canada did not become a nation until 1867, and the Western provinces, Newfoundland and Labrador were not to join for another half century or more, political events had already occurred that would make Canadian curriculum unique. For example, the Act of Union of 1840, and the subsequent amendments of the Act in the years following clearly established that there would be two official languages, two cultures, two religions, and two legal systems. Canada would become a country based on communal rights as well as individual rights. Countries that guarantee communal rights must also ensure that education be a matter of the communal groups and not of the nation.

Canada would retain a religious emphasis in contrast to the United States which moved to a more secular orientation. Otherwise, Canada committed itself to education for the masses early on, especially in urban areas. This was in great part due to the American experience of which Canadians were very aware.

Children and School   Utilitarian goals for the curriculum were most prominent from 1860 to 1920. The turn of the century brought with it many changes that profoundly influenced the curriculum. The dawning of the machine age altered the nature of industry, transportation, and communication. The growth of cities and the influx of millions of immigrants resulted in new functions for all social institutions, and home life was forever changed. As a result, curricula came to be based on social and individual need rather than on subject matter divisions. Subjects were judged by the criterion of social utility rather than by their ability to develop the intellect. Figure 13.3, for example, shows the course of study for grades one to eight in 1902 and reflects a practical, basic skills orientation.

During this period, several national committees met for the purpose of deciding what should be taught in elementary and secondary schools. Initially, these committees espoused goals formed by educators at the college and private secondary school levels—that is, uniform curricula with standardized methods of instruction. Gradually, though, these appointed groups began to recommend curricula that were more flexible and based on the needs of children.

The Push for Mass Education   Since 1920, schools have been expected to provide educational opportunities for all citizens. During this period, curricula have been developed to meet the needs and differences of many diverse student groups: disabled, bilingual, gifted, delinquent, and learning-disabled students, for example. Moreover, these curricula have been used not only in public and private schools

Number of Lessons per Week in the Several Studies in Each Grade

	Year or Grade							
	1	2	3	4	5	6	7	8
Reading	20	10	5	5	4	4	3	3
Spelling	20	10†	5†	5†	4†	4†	2†	2†
Writing	5	5	5	4	4	4	2	2
Arithmetic	5	5	6	5	5	5	5	5
Geography			4	4	4	4	3	
Language lessons and grammar	2	2	2	2	2	2	3	4
History							3	5
Nature study	2	2	2	2	2	2	2	2
Ethical lessons	2	2	2	2	2	2	2	2
Drawing	5*	5*	4	3	3	3	3	3
Manual training and domestic science								
Music	1**	1**	1**	1**	1**	1**	1**	1**
Calisthenics	***	***	***	***	***	***	***	***
Maximum length of lessons in minutes except for spelling	20	25	25	30	30	30	30	30

* 20 min/day   ** 15 min/day   ***10 min/day   † 15 minutes/lesson

FIGURE 13.3   The Elementary-School Curriculum: 1902

Source: Presented in George Willis, William H. Schubert, Robert V. Bullough, Jr., Craig Kridel and John T. Holton, Editors. The American Curriculum: A Documentary History. Reprinted with the permission of Greenwood Publishing Group, Inc., Westport, CT. Copyright © 1993, p. 115.

but also in alternative schools: night schools, schools without walls, summer schools, vocational schools, continuation schools, schools-within-schools, magnet schools, and so on.

The Progressive Curriculum   The concern for educating all youth has drawn much of its initial energy from the progressive education movement. During the 1920s, the Progressive Education Association in the United States reacted against the earlier emphasis on the mental disciplines and called for elementary schools to develop curricula based on the needs and interests of all students. Throughout the 1930s, progressive ideas were promoted on the secondary level as well.

Though there was no single set of beliefs that united all Progressives, there was general agreement that students should be involved in activities that parallel those found in society. Furthermore, those activities should engage students' natural interests. With these guidelines in mind, the progressive education movement expanded the curriculum to include such topics as home economics, health, family living, citizenship, and wood shop.

The Eight-Year Study   One of the most ambitious projects of the progressive education movement in the United States was the Eight-Year Study, which ran from 1932 to 1940. During this period, thirty public and private high schools were given the opportunity to restructure their educational programs according to progressive tenets and without regard for college and university entrance requirements. Over 300 colleges and universities then agreed to accept the graduates of these schools. The aim of the study, according to its director, was "to develop students who regard education as an enduring quest for meanings rather than credit accumulation."[16] The curricula developed by these schools emphasized problem solving, creativity, self-directed study, and more extensive counseling and guidance for students.

Ralph Tyler evaluated the Eight-Year Study by matching nearly 1500 graduates of the experimental schools who went on to college with an equal number of college freshmen who graduated from other high schools. He found that students in the experimental group received higher grades in every subject area except foreign languages and had slightly higher overall grade point averages. Even more significant, perhaps, was the finding that the experimental group had higher performance in such areas as problem solving, inventiveness, curiosity, and motivation to achieve. Unfortunately, the Eight-Year Study failed to have any lasting impact on American education—possibly because World War II overshadowed the study's results.

Progressive education in the United States ended in the mid-1950s with the dissolution of the Progressive Education Association in 1955 and the termination of the magazine *Progressive Education* in 1957. In Canada, progressive education was initially seen as the answer to the social and economic problems that followed World War I and the Great Depression, and it was adopted by virtually every province. However, the Canadian brand of progressive education was much more moderate than that of the United States.[17]

The progressive movement could be an example of the first national reform in Canada. It became clear that to follow the ideals of Progressivism, Canada would need to have outstanding teachers, for average teachers are unable to translate the ideals into practice. It also became clear that Canada must stop adopting reforms from other countries without understanding where Canadian educational systems are developmentally and without adapting these reforms to meet Canadian needs.

The Push for Excellence   Concern with excellence in U.S. schools ran high during the decade that spanned the late 1950s to the late 1960s. More recently, excellence in the curriculum has been a hotly debated issue since the late 1970s. Though schools have always had to strive to accomplish difficult goals, the current excellence movement has attached new meanings to the terms *quality*, *standards*, and *accountability*.

The Inquiry-Based Curriculum   The prevailing view of what should be taught in the schools during the 1950s and 1960s was influenced significantly by Jerome Bruner's short book, *The Process of Education*. A report on a conference of scientists, scholars, and educators at Woods Hole, Massachusetts in 1959, Bruner's book synthesized current ideas about intelligence and about how to motivate students to learn. Bruner believed that students should learn the "methods of inquiry" common to the academic disciplines. For example, instead of learning isolated facts about chemistry, students should learn the principles of inquiry common to the discipline of chemistry. In short, students would learn to think like chemists; they would be able to use principles from chemistry to solve problems independently.

Bruner's ideas were used as a rationale for making the curriculum more rigorous at all levels. As he pointed out in an often-quoted statement in *The Process of Education*, "Any subject can be taught effectively in some intellectually honest form to any child at any stage of development."[18] Bruner advocated a spiral curriculum wherein children would encounter the disciplines at ever-increasing levels of complexity as they progressed through school. Thus, elementary students could be taught physics in a manner that would pave the way for their learning more complex principles of physics in high school.

"This is the week Mr. Conklin teaches aerodynamics."

The Relevancy-Based Curriculum   The push for a rigorous academic core curriculum was offset in the mid-1960s by a call for relevancy in the curriculum. Many educators, student groups, and political activists charged that school curricula were unresponsive to social issues. At some schools, largely high schools, students actually demonstrated against educational programs they felt were not relevant to their needs and concerns. In response to this pressure, educators began to add more courses to the curriculum, increase the number of elective and remedial courses offered, and experiment with new ways of teaching. This concern with relevancy continued until the back-to-basics movement began in the mid-1970s.

The Core Curriculum   In the early 1980s, U.S. schools were again found lacking in excellence. Several national reports claimed that curriculum standards had eroded. The 1983 report by the U.S. National Commission on Excellence in Education asserted, for example, that secondary school curricula had become "homogenized, diluted, and diffused."

The push for excellence in the high school curriculum received a boost at the end of 1987 when U.S. Secretary of Education William J. Bennett proposed an academically rigorous core curriculum for all high school students. His course of study called for four years of English consisting of four year-long literature courses; three years each of science, mathematics, and social studies; two years of foreign language; two years of physical education; and one semester each of art and music history. Twenty-five percent of his program would be available for students to use for electives.[19]

Although the push for excellence was experienced in Canada, it was experienced in a more muted form. International evidence that Canada's educational systems are more successful than U.S. systems in many areas (see Figure 13.4) helped Canadians feel more confident in the effectiveness of Canadian schools. Canadian systems continued to invest in progressive ideas and extended concerns from meeting individual needs to equity considerations, including ethical plurality, ethnicity, gender, and culture.

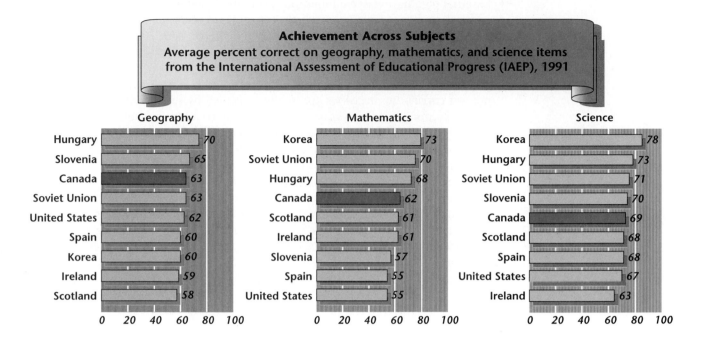

FIGURE 13.4   ACHIEVEMENT ACROSS SUBJECTS

Source: Educational Testing Service, 1992. From *The National Education Goals Report, 1992* Washington, D.C.: U.S. Government Printing Office, 1992, p. 7.

A National Curriculum?   Decisions about the operation of schools in North America are made largely at the local level. However, in some countries (Japan, Korea, and England, for example) education is centralized and teachers follow a standardized national curriculum. Since the first International Assessment of Educational Progress (IAEP) in 1991 revealed that the achievement levels of U.S. students are often below that of students from other countries (many of which have national curricula), some have proposed a national curriculum for the United States. Figure 13.4 is based on the IAEP and compares the percentages of geography, mathematics, and science questions answered correctly by thirteen-year-old students in nine countries.

Although there is widespread support for national examinations and a national curriculum, there is also widespread opposition to such a system. For example, educational researchers Thomas Kellagan and George Madaus have identified several disadvantages to a system of national examinations:

- The examinations narrow the curriculum in the sense that approaches to learning are limited and subjects and aspects of subjects not covered in the examinations are excluded or neglected.
- The cost of examining oral and practical skills is quite high, forcing most systems to rely on written tests.
- It is impossible to assess in a terminal examination such factors as student planning, perseverance, and adaptability in the execution of a project.

- External [i.e., national] examinations promote the tendency to emphasize lower-order skills in teaching, because these are more easily examined than higher-order ones.
- Examinations are unsuitable for assessing some students (particularly lower achieving ones).
- Examinations engender a diminished professional role for teachers, because important curriculum decisions are in effect decided by the examination.[20]

Canada, too, is moving toward a national curriculum and by the year 2000, the core courses will be organized on a national level. However, it is unlikely the Council of Ministers of Education will agree to a system of national examinations. Provinces have agreed to identify common knowledge among core courses but they will continue to reflect regional differences in their school systems and methods of curriculum delivery and evaluation.

As our review of curriculum reform efforts has shown, the content of the curriculum does not remain static. It is continuously refined, added to or subtracted from, based on the prevailing needs of society and our views of children and how they learn.

WHAT ARE CURRENT SUBJECT-AREA TRENDS?

The final section of this chapter examines briefly some of the current trends in what is taught in elementary, middle, junior-high, and high schools.

LITERACY

Unlike other areas of the curriculum, the public has closely monitored students' literacy skills. The importance of attaining a minimum level of literacy in our society cannot be underestimated; the language arts are the tools through which students learn in nearly all other areas of the curriculum. Most students who are deficient in reading and writing skills are at a significant disadvantage when it comes to seeking employment or additional education.

Reading   The teaching of reading at all levels should focus on acquiring basic comprehension skills and learning to appreciate literature in its various forms: novels, essays, poetry, short stories, and so on. Reading teachers, however, are currently far from united as to how these aims should be realized. Does instruction in phonics enhance reading comprehension? Is a holistic, immersion approach to the teaching of reading superior to teaching isolated decoding and comprehension skills? Should children be taught the alphabet before learning to read?

In spite of such questions, though, reading research has suggested several general guidelines for improving reading instruction, including the following:

1. Reading skills should be taught in context, not in isolation. Students cannot be taught to read outside the context of their expectations, cares, doubts, questions, loves, or hates.
2. Reading instruction should be explicitly structured and organized. Although no specific system of reading instruction works with all students, just about any system works with most if it is structured and organized.

3. Questions asked of readers should promote better understanding. Questions that ask students to predict, to relate the text to prior knowledge, and to evaluate predicted outcomes are superior to more literal and factual questions.
4. Vocabulary instruction should relate to students' present knowledge and experience. Instruction that emphasizes where a word fits in a student's present vocabulary is better than methods that emphasize word recognition vocabulary and verbatim definitions.
5. Reading teachers should give frequent, direct, and explicit instruction for comprehension skills. Current approaches to comprehension that stress only practice omit a critical element—the teacher acting as a model, demonstrating how to solve problems and showing what clues to look for in the text to find solutions.[21]

One promising approach to reading is known as the **whole-language movement**. Advocates of the whole-language approach believe that reading is part of general language development, not an isolated skill students learn apart from listening, speaking, and writing. Teachers in whole-language classrooms seldom use textbooks; instead, young students write stories and learn to read from their writing, and older students read literature that is closely related to their everyday experiences.

Writing   The Canadian public wants to ensure that all students attain at least a minimum level of literacy. Attaining this level will require that schools implement recommendations for writing instruction similar to those suggested by Stephen Tchudi, a leading researcher in the writing process:

1. Writing programs must be based on frequent, authentic writing experiences for all students—basic or advanced—with a corresponding decrease in isolated drills in so-called basic language skills.
2. Writing-across-the-curriculum projects must be developed by English and other subject matter teachers and put into place so that writing is used in all classes, not just English/language arts classes.
3. Inservice and staff development for English and content-area teachers must be expanded, preferably at the expense of testing programs.
4. Composition teachers must be given more satisfactory teaching conditions, including manageable class sizes and loads.[22]

During the last two decades, several new approaches have been incorporated into the language arts curriculum. Many English teachers have reduced the amount of time spent on grammar, electing instead to teach grammar as needed within the context of a writing program. Since the 1960s, English teachers have generally broadened their view of literature to include more varied forms of writing and the literary contributions of minority or ethnic writers. Teaching in the English classroom now frequently includes such techniques as creative writing, drama, journal writing, guided fantasy exercises, and group discussions. In addition, many teachers are using the word processing capabilities of computers to explore new ways to teach students the art of writing.

MATHEMATICS

The launching of Sputnik in 1957 by the Soviet Union spurred a wave of reform in the mathematics curriculum in the United States that spilled over the border.

MAKING *a DIFFERENCE*

Vladimir Pasek
Edmonton, Alberta

In 1972, at the age of 26, I began my teaching career in Newfoundland in Marystown. After one year, I moved to Montreal where I taught for five years. Then, I moved out west to Alberta and taught with the Edmonton Catholic School Board. I enjoy teaching because I love to help others achieve their full potential. When I teach problem solving in physics and mathematics, I guide students on how to refer to their daily experiences in order to personally relate to problems while reinforcing the academic concepts. Whenever I try to explain a concept, I try as much as possible to address both students' auditory and visual senses. I also combine concrete and abstract levels to help students gain a better understanding.

One area in which students have consistently had trouble in my classes is graphing. It seems that graphs such as distance versus time, speed versus time, and acceleration versus time have no meaning for a lot of students. Therefore, I decided that perhaps if they saw a familiar event such as a person running and then graphed the event they would have a better grasp of what the graphs convey. To achieve this goal, I decided to produce a computer-assisted interactive videodisc instruction (CAIVI) package. This is a level IIII type of interactivity whereby the

students follow the program on the computer and, with the help of a videodisc player, see different events of athletes running on the T.V. monitor. By placing a acetate sheet on the monitor, students can mark a dot at different time intervals and thereby plot a graph showing distance versus time. As well, in a different part of the program, students see an object move while the graph is being drawn. At the end, students are prompted with several questions for feedback. I am pleased that I have been able to develop this program consistent with my style of teaching.

The results showed that students enjoyed doing physics this way. They enjoyed learning at their own pace and they liked being able to go back to any section they misunderstood. They felt that they were not rushed and they commented that they could concentrate better. Another comment was that it took less time to cover the material.

It is important for teachers to use other skills to improve their teaching practice. Students may be better able to learn through interactive technology than through the interpersonal communication that normally characterizes student-teacher interaction today. It is important for teachers to try and bridge this gap whenever they can.

TABLE 13.3   **Basic Mathematical Skills for the 21st Century**

1. **Problem solving**—posing questions, analyzing situations, translating results, illustrating results, drawing diagrams, and using trial and error
2. **Communicating mathematical ideas**—receiving mathematical ideas through listening, reading, and visualizing; presenting mathematical ideas by speaking, writing, drawing pictures and graphs, and demonstrating with concrete models
3. **Mathematical reasoning**—being able to distinguish between valid and invalid arguments; using counter examples to disprove a conjecture and using models, known facts, and logical arguments to validate a conjecture
4. **Applying mathematics to everyday situations**—taking everyday situations, translating them into mathematical representations in light of the initial situation
5. **Alertness to reasonableness of results**—questioning the reasonableness of a solution or conjecture in relation to the original problem
6. **Estimation**—being able to carry out rapid approximate calculations through the use of mental arithmetic and a variety of computational estimation techniques; acquiring simple techniques for estimating measurements such as length, area, volume, and mass (weight)
7. **Appropriate computational skills**—gaining facility with addition, subtraction, multiplication, and division with whole numbers and decimals
8. **Algebraic thinking**—learning to solve practical problems that involve algebraic thinking; for example, solving ratio, proportion, percent, direct variation, and inverse variation problems
9. **Measurement**—learning to measure (in both the metric and imperial systems) distance, mass (weight), time, capacity, temperature, and angles, as well as calculate simple perimeters, areas, and volumes
10. **Geometry**—understanding concepts such as parallelism, perpendicularity, congruence, similarity, and symmetry, as well as the basic properties of simple plane and solid geometric figures
11. **Statistics**—knowing how to construct, read, and draw conclusions from simple tables, maps, charts, and graphs; being able to present information about numerical data such as measures of central tendency (mean, median, mode) and measures of dispersion (range, deviation)
12. **Probability**—understanding elementary notions of probability to determine the likelihood of future events; becoming familiar with how mathematics is used to help make predictions such as election results and business forecasts

Source: National Council of Supervisors of Mathematics, *Basic Mathematical Skills for the 21st Century* (Houston, Tex.: National Council of Supervisors of Mathematics, draft, March 7, 1988).

Students in the late 1950s and early 1960s were taught the new math. Though the new math, with its emphasis on the structure of mathematics, has since been shown to be too abstract to be easily applied to everyday problem solving, the movement did highlight the need for continuous evaluation of the mathematics curriculum.

As has been the case with nearly all areas of the curriculum in the early 1990s, the goals of mathematics have been too narrowly focused. Mathematics programs, from the elementary through the secondary level, frequently focus on the mechanical acquisition of skills identified by a select few textbooks. Using mathematics to think logically and to solve problems, though an ideal end, may be more the exception than the rule as texts and textbooks tend to measure low-level skills such as memorization—not the higher-order reasoning and problem-solving skills students need.

One promising approach to mathematics instruction is known as **problem-centered learning** in which students work in small groups on problems that have many or open-ended solutions. Rather than memorizing facts, working on sets of problems in textbooks, and competing against their real classmates, students discover concepts, solve problems similar to those they will encounter in life, and learn to cooperate in small groups.

Another approach to teaching mathematics that educational researcher Herbert Walberg describes as having "enormous" effects on students' achievement in mathematics is the use of manipulative materials such as Cuisinnaire rods, balance beams, counting sticks, and measuring scales.[23] Use of manipulatives allows students to participate directly in learning, not just follow teacher presentations. As Walberg says, "Students can handle the material, see the relation of abstract ideas and concrete embodiments, and check hypothesized answers by doing quick empirical tests—without having to wait for quiz results or teacher feedback."[24]

SCIENCE

The teaching of science in this age of technology has come under increasingly critical scrutiny. On the elementary level, the science curriculum consists of assorted science-related topics: animals, plants, seasons, light, sound, heat, weather, magnets, the stars and planets, basic electricity, nutrition, oceanography, and so on. These topics are often restudied in greater depth at the middle or junior-high level in courses variously titled Earth Science, General Science, Physical Science, or Life Science. At the high-school level, students typically may choose from only a limited number of basic science courses: Biology, Chemistry, Physical Science, Anatomy and Physiology, and Physics. Many high schools do, however, distinguish between applied science courses (for students not planning to go to university) and academic courses.

Several leading science educators have recommended changes in the science curriculum. Nearly all stress the need for students to learn more science and to acquire scientific knowledge, skills, and processes through the inquiry, or discovery, method. The teacher's primary role is to guide students in their search for knowledge rather than to act solely as a source of information and/or right answers. However, these ideals have not been easily implemented in school systems that still focus on empirically based accountability.

SOCIAL STUDIES

Goals for the social studies lack the precision that we find in other subject areas. Consider, for example, Charles Beard's comment in 1938 that the social studies aim at the "creation of rich and many-sided personalities, equipped with practical knowledge and inspired by ideals so that they can make their way and fulfil their mission in a changing society which is part of a world complex."[25] Not surprisingly, such vague and lofty goals have been translated into a patchwork quilt of social studies programs, especially at the elementary level. Here we find a wide assortment of topics addressed in no particular sequence, such as understanding the self, the family, and community; community needs and problems; provincial or Canadian history; the interdependencies of countries with respect to food, raw materials, and manufactured goods; North America's early exploration and colonization by Europeans; basic concepts of history and geography; and use of maps and

EDUCATION IN THE NEWS

Education is a Political Issue

Education has become one of the top issues in election campaigns across Canada. During times of fiscal restraint and looming cutbacks, the areas of greatest expenditure garner the most attention, and education is receiving that attention.

During Manitoba's last election, the electorate was vocal in its concerns: children who could not spell their names because their teachers did not bother with spelling; fewer teachers and larger class sizes; parents who felt excluded from the decision-making process; funding of both public and private schools; and reducing recess and lunch time for students in grades five and six to give them more instruction in core areas.

The election in Ontario showcased that province's Royal Commission on Learning and the NDP government that had commissioned it. The government was defeated

and the fate of the Commission's recommendations is unknown. Outstanding issues include eliminating grade thirteen, creating full-day kindergarten for four- and five-year-olds, creating a College of Teachers and giving it the mandate to evaluate teachers' performances, centralizing the curriculum, and capping school trustee salaries at $20 000 per year.

It is clear that education will continue to stir the passion of people from many walks of life: teachers, administrators, students, parents, taxpayers, and other members of the general public. Should education be subjected to the political winds of change or should it be protected as a resource vital to the future of the nation?

Source: Based on the *Globe and Mail*, Jan. 17, Apr. 20, 1995.

---

globes. At the high school level, the social studies curriculum becomes more uniform: Canadian history, world history, geography, and frequently a course in the history of the province or region in which the school is located.

The content of traditional social studies courses has remained comparatively unchanged during the last decade. Trends include fewer offerings in ancient history and more offerings in psychology, economics, world cultures, and the family. In addition, developing a truly multicultural curriculum is currently the subject of heated debate.

NON-CORE SUBJECT AREAS

Foreign Languages As we become increasingly aware of our interconnectedness with other countries, the small number of students who study languages other than English or French at the elementary through secondary levels is alarming. According to the American Council of the Teaching of Foreign Languages, successful foreign language programs are characterized by the following factors:

1. Extensive activities integrating language study into the fabric of school life
2. A high incidence of target language usage with special motivational techniques to promote such usage
3. An exploratory language course
4. Unusually long course sequences
5. Study and travel abroad; exchange programs
6. An especially strong, dynamic staff

7. Inservice training
8. A strong public relations effort
9. Special recruiting efforts
10. A resolve to connect language study with the practical and concrete[26]

Rarely are students introduced to foreign language study at the optimal time for learning a second language—as early as grade two. However, immersion French is available to students in all provinces from the primary grades to grade twelve. Students who do not take immersion French usually take core French beginning in grade three in some provinces and in grade eight in others. Some schools have broadened their foreign language offerings to include Spanish, Portuguese, Japanese, Chinese, and other heritage languages.

The Arts More than any other area of the curriculum, the arts hold an insecure position. When schools are faced with budget cutbacks or pressure to raise scores on basic skills tests, a cost-conscious public often considers eliminating "frills" such as music and art.

The arts, however, have much to contribute to the education of students. As Kathryn Bloom points out, "The quality of our individual lives and the quality of our society are directly related to the quality of our artistic life. We need the arts as the key to the higher order of things—our cultural heritage, our gift of expression, our creative faculty, our sense of beauty."[27]

Typically, elementary art and music are limited to one period a week, and this instruction is given either by regular teachers or by special teachers, some of whom travel from school to school. In addition, most elementary students have occasional opportunities to use crayons, watercolors, clay, and other media as they learn in other subject areas. From time to time, many children even have the opportunity to experience dance, puppetry, role-playing, pantomime, and crafts.

At the middle and junior high level, instruction in art and music becomes more structured, as well as more voluntary. Students may choose from band, chorus, arts, and crafts. At the high school level, art and music are usually offered as electives. Depending on the school's resources, however, students frequently have a wide assortment of classes to choose from: jazz band, band, orchestra, drama, girls' and boys' chorus, photography, sculpture, ceramics, and filmmaking, to name a few. In addition, middle school and high school students may receive instruction in practical arts, such as sewing, cooking, woodworking and metalworking, automotive shop, print shop, and courses teaching agricultural knowledge and skills. A noteworthy trend is for students of both sexes to take courses in all the practical arts rather than follow traditional sex-role stereotypes; that is, you increasingly find boys and girls in both the kitchen and the garage.

Physical Education The ultimate aim of physical education is to develop a desire in the individual student to maintain physical fitness throughout life. In addition, students in physical education programs may receive instruction in health and nutrition, sex education, and driver education.

Vocational Education In addition to their academic curricula, many comprehensive high schools offer programs in vocational education; some high schools may offer only a vocational education program. **Vocational education** programs vary from those that actually prepare students to take jobs in business and industry after grad-

In what grades were music classes offered when you were in elementary, junior high, or high school? Are you aware of the grades in which music is offered in your neighborhood schools today?

uation to those that merely introduce students to career possibilities. Among the areas emphasized by vocational programs are those that focus on the following:

- Consumer/homemaking skills
- Prevocational, exploratory training
- Prevocational basic skills
- Employability skills for cooperative work-study programs
- Occupation-specific programs (e.g., computer technology, hairdressing, automotive repairs, electronics, plumbing, etc.)

As Canada continues to be concerned about its productivity compared with other nations, and as employers continue to expect schools to graduate students who have mastered the basic skills and learned how to learn, it seems likely that vocational education will continue to be an important part of the school curriculum. Indeed, some vocational educators are calling for an new definition of vocational education—one based on new, rigorous standards cooperatively developed by educators and employers from various industrial sectors.[28]

PROFESSIONAL PORTFOLIO

Compare and contrast two or more textbooks or curriculum guides that are currently used by teachers in the subject area and at the grade level for which you are preparing to teach. After assessing the strengths and weaknesses of each textbook or curriculum guide, what are your conclusions? Would you use the materials in your classroom? How might they be improved?

CHAPTER SUMMARY

Although there are many different definitions of the term *curriculum*, the "correct" definition depends on our purposes and the situation in which we find ourselves. A definition that incorporates several diverse points of view follows: *Curriculum refers to the experiences, both planned and unplanned, that either enhance or impede the education and growth of students.* There are four curricula that all students experience. In addition to learning what teachers intend to teach (the explicit curriculum), students learn from the hidden curriculum, the null curriculum, and extracurricular/cocurricular programs.

From school policies to provincial politics, many factors influence what is taught in the schools. Clearly, there is no one right way to develop the curriculum. Teachers must base their curricula not only on the needs and interests of students but also on a variety of local and provincial pressures. However, the ultimate criterion for deciding what to teach is whether the planned activities will contribute to students' learning and growth.

During the course of Canada's history, several curriculum reform efforts have focused on the school curriculum. Religion, for example, has played an important role in the development of the school curriculum. The need to train students in religion was reflected in the curriculum of Canada's earliest schools, and today several groups have opposing views about whether or how religious beliefs should be included in the school curriculum. Similarly, school curricula have been viewed as a way of teaching students the knowledge, skills, and attitudes necessary to maintain our democratic way of life. The content of the curriculum largely depends on the current needs of society and the prevailing beliefs about education.

Several trends and issues are evident in the content areas addressed by today's school curricula: literacy, mathematics, science, social studies, foreign languages, the arts, physical education, and vocational education. What these trends indicate is that school curricula are not static. Because the ultimate aim of the curriculum is to prepare today's students to solve tomorrow's problems, teachers must be prepared to assume their important role in the curriculum development process.

KEY TERMS AND CONCEPTS

core curriculum, 336
curriculum, 322
explicit curriculum, 323
extracurricular/cocurricular
    program, 325
hidden curriculum, 323

inquiry-based curriculum, 335
integrated curriculum, 328
null curriculum, 324
problem-centered learning, 342
relevancy-based curriculum, 336
student-centered curriculum, 328

subject-centered curriculum, 328
Tyler rationale, 326
vocational education, 344
whole-language movement, 339

APPLICATIONS AND ACTIVITIES

Teacher's Journal

1. List in order of importance the five factors that you believe *actually* have the greatest impact on the curriculum. Then list the five factors that you believe *ideally* should have the greatest influence. What differences do you notice between your actual and ideal lists? What might be done to reduce the differences between the two lists? Compare your lists with those of other students in your class.

2. In light of calls for writing across the curriculum, develop a list of writing activities that you will involve your students in when you begin to teach.

3. Reflect on the 12 000 or so hours that you have spent in classrooms from kindergarten to the end of high school. What did the hidden curricula in these classes teach you about yourself?

4. What religious and political emphasis affected your learning as a student in elementary school or high school? Which experiences do you view as having been positive? Which do you view as having been negative for you?

5. How should teachers and schools respond to complaints about the content of instructional materials?

Field Assignments

1. Spend a half-day at a school at the level at which you plan to teach. Take note of your impressions regarding the school's hidden curriculum. If possible, chat briefly with administrators, teachers, and students. Share your observations with others in your education class.

2. Observe students outside of the classroom during a school day and record your impressions of the hidden curriculum. For each topic you list, think how it could be made a desirable and effective part of the explicit curriculum. Share your observations and ideas with others in your class.

3. Conduct an informal survey of ten people you know, asking them what they think are the four most important subjects to be taught at the elementary, middle, junior-, and senior-high levels. Compare your data with others in your class.

4. Help your instructor set up an exercise in which four to six students role-play teachers who are meeting for the purpose of revising or updating the curriculum. (The students should focus on a level and subject with which they are most familiar.) The rest of the class should observe and take notes on the educational beliefs expressed by the role-players. After the role-play (about fifteen to twenty minutes), the entire class should discuss the curriculum development process it has just observed.

14 Teaching: Your Chosen Profession

As the move to restructure schools continues, it is becoming increasingly evident that teacher participation in leadership may be the most critical component of the entire process of change.

—Ann Lieberman
Teachers as Leaders: Evolving Roles
National Education Association, 1992

Focus Questions

1. To what extent is teaching a full profession?
2. What are the characteristics of professional teachers?
3. How can teachers continue their professional development throughout their careers?
4. What professional organizations represent teachers?

It is near the end of your second year of teaching. Generally acknowledged as one of the better, more innovative schools in the district, your school was recently informed that its proposal to implement a school-based management (SBM) approach to governance next year was approved by the school board. As a member of the team that prepared the proposal, you are now meeting with six other teachers (one of whom is the school's representative to the teachers' union), the principal, the assistant principal, the school counselor, and three parents to develop plans for implementing the SBM program.

The principal has just finished pointing out that the first order of business for the group is to develop procedures for creating a School Governance Council (SGC). Eventually, the SGC will handle such matters as the school budget, hiring of new teachers, curriculum development, in-service training, scheduling and staffing of classes, and so on.

At this point, the union representative speaks. "This group needs to be aware that other teachers in the school, all of whom belong to the union, want to be certain that the membership of the SGC truly represents their interests. They want to know that under the SBM program they will be genuinely empowered. Our teachers want meaningful opportunities to function as professionals."

You reflect on the union representative's comments. What does it really mean to be a professional? What are the characteristics of a profession, and to what extent does teaching reflect those characteristics? What distinguishes the behavior of teachers who are truly professional?

In previous chapters we called teaching a profession, and you will soon be accepting the challenge of a profession. However, if we compare teaching with other professions—law and medicine, for example—we find some significant differences. As a result of these differences, current opinion is divided as to whether teaching is actually a profession. We will continue to refer to teaching as a **profession**, though others have labeled it a *semi*-profession,[1] an *emerging profession*,[2] an *uncertain* profession,[3] an *imperiled* profession,[4] and an *endangered* profession.[5]

TO WHAT EXTENT IS TEACHING A FULL PROFESSION?

Most of us use the terms *professional* and *profession* quite frequently, usually without thinking about their meanings. Professionals "possess a high degree of *specialized theoretical knowledge*, along with methods and techniques for applying this knowledge in their day-to-day work. . . . [and they] are united by a high degree of in-group solidarity, stemming from their common training and common adherence to certain doctrines and methods."[6]

From several sociologists and educators who have studied teaching come additional characteristics of occupations that are highly professionalized.[7] As you read each characteristic in Table 14.1, think about the degree to which it applies to teaching. Now let us examine the extent to which teaching satisfies each of these commonly agreed-on characteristics of full professions. As we do so, we see that teaching meets some but not all of the criteria. Also, we will understand John Goodlad's conclusion in *Teachers for Our Nation's Schools,* a comprehensive report on teacher education in the U.S. released in 1990, that "teaching remains the not-quite profession."[8]

TABLE 14.1   **Characteristics of a Profession**

---

1. Professionals are allowed to institutionalize a monopoly of essential knowledge and services. For example, only lawyers may practice law; only physicians may practice medicine.

2. Professionals are able to practice their occupation with a high degree of autonomy. They are not closely supervised and they have frequent opportunities to make their own decisions about important aspects of their work. Professional autonomy also implies an obligation to perform responsibly, to self-supervise, and to be dedicated to providing a service rather than meeting minimum requirements of the job.

3. Professionals must typically undergo a lengthy period of education and/or training before they may enter professional practice. Furthermore, professionals usually must undergo a lengthy induction period following their formal education or training.

4. Professionals perform an essential service for their clients and are devoted to continuous development of their ability to deliver this service. This service emphasizes intellectual rather than physical techniques.

5. Professionals have control over their governance, their socialization into the occupation, and research connected with their occupation.

6. Members of a profession form their own vocational associations which control admissions to the profession, educational standards, examinations and licensing, career development, ethical and performance standards, and professional discipline.

7. The knowledge and skills held by professionals are not usually available to nonprofessionals.

8. Professionals enjoy a high level of public trust and are able to deliver services that are clearly superior to those available elsewhere.

9. Professionals are granted a high level of prestige and higher-than-average financial rewards.

Institutional Monopoly of Services   Teachers have a monopoly of services. Only those who are certified members of the profession may teach in public schools. However, the varied requirements we find for certification and for teaching in private schools weaken this monopoly. (Although provincial certification and teacher education courses are not required to teach in many private schools, a university degree is usually a minimum requirement.) In addition, any claim teachers might have as exclusive providers of a service is eroded whenever there is a teacher shortage; provinces will readily reduce certification requirements to obtain more teachers.

Perhaps the most significant argument against teachers claiming to be the exclusive providers of a service, however, is that a great deal of teaching occurs in informal, nonschool settings by people who are not teachers. Every day, thousands of people teach various kinds of how-to-do-it skills: how to water-ski, how to make dogs more obedient, how to make pasta from scratch, how to tune a car's engine, and how to meditate. The teaching of others focuses on the acquisition of knowledge: knowledge about the Bible, knowledge of the stars, knowledge about cycling safety, knowledge about good health, and knowledge about investments. Finally, young people learn an enormous amount from their parents, so much so that it is no exaggeration to refer to the home as the curriculum and parents as a child's first teachers.

Teacher Autonomy   In one sense teachers have considerable autonomy. They usually work behind a closed classroom door, and only seldom is their work observed by another adult. In fact, one of the norms among teachers is that the classroom is a castle of sorts and teacher privacy a closely guarded right. Although the performance of new teachers may be observed and evaluated regularly by supervisors, veteran teachers are observed much less frequently and usually enjoy a high degree of autonomy.

Teachers also have extensive freedom regarding how they structure the classroom environment. They may emphasize discussions as opposed to lectures. They may set certain requirements for some students and not for others. They may delegate responsibilities to one class and not another. And, within the guidelines set by local and provincial authorities, teachers may determine much of the content they teach.

However, constraints are placed on teachers and their work. Teachers, unlike doctors and lawyers, must accept all the "clients" who are sent to them. Only infrequently does a teacher actually "reject" a student assigned to him or her.

Teachers must also agree to teach what provincial and local officials say they must. Their work is subject to a higher level of public scrutiny than that found in other professions. Because the public provides "clients" (students) and pays for schools, it has a significant say regarding teachers' work.

Teaching also differs from other professions in that teachers are usually evaluated by persons who are not currently teachers: principals and other supervisors appointed by the school districts. The degree of supervision that teachers actually experience varies greatly, with most teachers having considerable autonomy as long as they continue to perform at a reasonable level of effectiveness.

Years of Education and Training   As sociologist Amitai Etzioni points out in his discussion of the "semi-professions," the training of teachers is less lengthy than that required for other professionals—lawyers and doctors, for example.[9] The professional component of teacher education programs is the shortest of all the professions—only 15 percent of the average bachelor's degree program for a high school teacher is devoted to professional courses. However, as we learned in Chapter 3, several universities have begun five-year teacher education programs. If continued, this trend toward extended programs will decidedly enhance the professional status of teaching.

In most professions, new members must undergo a prescribed induction period. Physicians, for example, must serve an internship or residency before beginning to practice, and most lawyers article with law firms. Sociologists have termed this process of gradually moving from simple to more complex tasks, small to greater responsibility, as *mediated entry* into a profession. In contrast, teachers do not go through a formal induction period before assuming full responsibility for their work. Practice teaching comes closest to serving as an induction period, but it is often relatively short, informal, and lacking in uniformity. In reality, entry into teaching is abrupt, and, as the saying goes, a new teacher must either sink or swim.

In spite of the anxiety that affects just about everyone who faces a classroom full of students for the first time, teaching has been characterized as an easy-entry profession.[10] Moreover, the training teachers undergo tends not to be valued by teachers themselves, as sociologist Dan Lortie points out.

> Teachers are inclined to talk about their training as easy ('mickey mouse'); I have yet to hear a teacher complain that education courses were too difficult or demanded too much effort. Teachers do not perceive their preparation as conveying something special—as setting them apart from others. . . . Teachers do not consider training the key to their legitimation as teachers. That rests in experience.[11]

Provision of Essential Service   Throughout Canada's history, teachers have been designated by law as the primary providers of instructional services in schools. Although it is generally acknowledged that teachers provide a service that is vital to the well-being of individuals and groups, the public does need to be reminded of this fact from time to time.

The ability to function as the spark that stimulates young people to learn and grow can give teachers a sense of meaning and fulfilment they might not be able to find in other professions. A foreign language teacher summed up what many teachers feel about their choice of profession: "I feel that I get satisfaction . . . that I am a useful member of the society. I feel this is the field in which . . . I can contribute more to society than in any other field."[12]

Indeed, it is no exaggeration to say that teaching is a matter of life and death. Robert B. Howsam and his colleagues point out in their landmark study of the teaching profession that

> every moment in the lives of teachers and pupils brings critical decisions of motivation, reinforcement, reward, ego enhancement and goal direction. Proper professional decisions enhance learning and life; improper decisions send the learner towards incremental death in openness to experience and in ability to learn and contribute. Doctors and lawyers probably have neither more nor less to do with life, death, and freedom than do teachers.[13]

Degree of Self-Governance   The limited freedom of teachers to govern themselves has detracted from the profession's overall status. A quick look at the organizational chart for any school district shows that teachers are usually low in the pecking order when it comes to decision-making powers. Only students are lower. These powers, it turns out, are held by boards of education, largely made up of persons who have never taught. As a result, teachers have had little or no say over what they teach, when they teach, whom they teach, and, in extreme instances, *how* they teach.

In other, more full, professions, members of the profession, not laypersons, make decisions about practice. Nonmembers are seen as having insufficient understanding to participate in professional governance. In fact, these professions (most notably, law and medicine) have shown their ability to move swiftly and decisively to squelch any suspected movement toward lay control.

Recent efforts to empower teachers and to professionalize teaching are creating new roles for teachers and expanded opportunities to govern important aspects of their work. At schools such as the one portrayed in this chapter's opening scenario, teachers have a greater voice in decisions related to curriculum development, staffing, budget, and the school's day-to-day operation. Figure 14.1, for example,

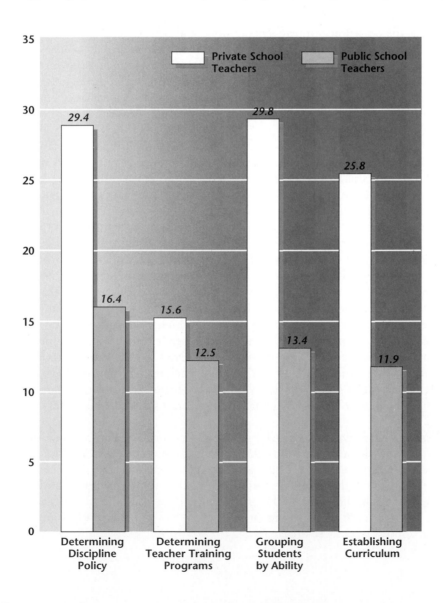

FIGURE 14.1

Percentage of Teachers Reporting "A Great Deal of Influence" over School Decision Making, 1990–91

Note: Teachers were defined as having reported "a great deal of influence" if they responded with a 6 on a 6-point scale.

Source: Based on data presented in *The Condition of Education 1993* (Washington, D.C.: U.S. Department of Education, National Center for Education Statistics), p. 367.

What characteristics distinguish teaching as a profession? What characteristics might distinguish this teacher as a professional?

compares the percentage of teachers in public and private schools who report that they have a "great deal of influence" over school-wide discipline policies, teacher training programs, grouping students by ability, and establishing the curriculum.

The paths that one follows in becoming socialized into a profession can be, if controlled by members of the profession, another form of governance. To be initiated into a profession by peers enhances professional identity and makes control by nonmembers more unlikely.

When we look at teaching we see that socialization into the profession is minimal. Due to the flat career paths of teachers (a veteran of thirty years has essentially the same status as a beginner), experienced teachers usually devote little effort to induct beginning teachers into a professional culture or way of life. Though new teachers may certainly expect veteran teachers to show them the ropes related to working at a particular school, little is done to help them identify with the profession. "Assisting occupational identity formation, encouraging collegial patterns of behavior, fostering generational trust, and enhancing self-esteem" are forms of assistance that experienced teachers tend not to provide to neophytes.[14]

The conduct of research related to practice is yet another way that professionals have of influencing their profession. When we look at research on teaching, we see that most of it is done by persons in higher education or at centers for research and development. Classroom teachers—those most intimately involved in professional practice—are only minimally involved in research efforts aimed at generating a deeper understanding of effective teaching. The development of cadres of teacher-researchers whose task it would be to focus on problems related to professional practice would greatly enhance the overall status of the profession.

Professional Associations   Teachers, like other professionals, have formed a number of vocational associations that are vitally concerned with such issues as admissions to the profession, educational standards, examinations and licensing, career development, ethical and performance standards, and professional discipline. It is clear, though, that none of the provincial and territorial teacher organizations or the national organizations has progressed as far as other professions have in gaining control over these areas.

Professional Knowledge and Skills   Professionals are granted a certain status because they possess knowledge and skills not normally held by the general public. Within the profession of teaching, however, the requirements for membership are much less precise. In spite of the ongoing efforts of educational researchers, no commonly agreed-on body of knowledge and skills exists that is considered necessary in order to teach.[15] If we ask what knowledge teachers possess that other occupational groups lack, perhaps the best answer we can come up with is knowledge about education.

Further evidence of the vaguely defined knowledge base on which teaching rests may be found in the varied programs at the 40 or so Canadian universities that train teachers. Required courses may at first glance appear similar, but closer inspection reveals almost endless differences in content.

Attempts to clarify the knowledge base for teaching are frequently hampered when members of the public routinely feel compelled to offer their usually inexpert opinions on what and how teachers should teach. As a result, discussions of the problems of education include not only observations made by members of the profession but commentaries, often uninformed and conflicting, that appear in newspapers and magazines or are offered up on television and radio talk shows.

Level of Public Trust   The level of trust that the public extends to teachers as professionals varies greatly. On the one hand, the public appears to have great confidence in the work that teachers do. Because of its faith in the teaching profession, the public invests teachers with considerable power over its children. For the most part, parents willingly allow their children to be molded and influenced by teachers, and this willingness must be based on a high degree of trust. In addition, most parents expect their children to obey and respect teachers.

On the other hand, it appears that the public's trust of teachers has eroded since the 1970s. The profession has received considerable bad press during this period. Teachers have been portrayed as incompetent, greedy, unprofessional, unintelligent, immoral, and generally unable to live up to the public's expectations.

Though all professions have some members who might be described as unprofessional, teaching is especially vulnerable to such charges. The sheer size of the teaching force makes it difficult to maintain consistently high professional standards. Moreover, teaching is subject to a level of public scrutiny and control that other, more established, professions have traditionally not tolerated. However, the era of widespread public trust may also be running out for these other professions as well. Criticism of doctors and lawyers has increased sharply over the past 20 years as public confidence has significantly eroded.

Remuneration   The status and salaries of teachers have typically not been in keeping with the professions to which teachers like to be compared. Although teachers in most provinces have made significant salary gains since the beginning of the 1970s when compared to occupations with approximately the same amount of education, they remain behind lawyers, doctors, and engineers in salary. In 1991, for example, the average elementary teacher earned $31 256 and the average secondary teacher $36 227 while librarians averaged $27 728, nurses $26 058, and social workers $26 885. In the same year, lawyers averaged $41 567, chemical engineers $45 751, dentists $52 297, and doctors $95 581.

Compared to other public service professionals such as police officers, fire-fighters, pharmacists, and veterinarians, teachers compare favorably. In 1991, police officers averaged $36 858, firefighters $35 719, pharmacists $35 106 and veterinarians $34 955. Overall, Canadian elementary teachers placed thirty-fifth in salary out of 65 occupations, and secondary teachers placed twenty-fourth.[16]

WHAT ARE THE CHARACTERISTICS OF PROFESSIONAL TEACHERS?

We believe that the current thrust among teachers, teacher educators, policy-makers, and the general public is in the direction of making teaching a full pro-fession. Be aware, too, that countless career teachers find teaching immensely satisfying. In spite of problems that confront the profession today, morale among most teachers is high. As one lifelong teacher put it:

> I hope that awareness of the problems . . . will not discourage talented young men and women from entering our profession. Some problems will be solved; the others can be lived with. All professions have their problems. If I were mak-ing a career choice in the twenty-first century, I would have no hesitation about becoming a teacher because I firmly believe that teaching, done well, is still the most personally satisfying of all the professions as well as the one offering the greatest long-range service to the human race.[17]

In the remainder of this section we look at four characteristics of teachers who are truly professional.

PROFESSIONAL BEHAVIOR

The professional teacher is guided by a specific set of values. He or she has made a deep and lasting commitment to professional practice. He or she has adopted a high standard of professional ethics and models behaviors that accord with that code of ethics. The professional teacher also engages in serious, reflective thought about how to teach more effectively. Moreover, he or she does this *while* teaching, continually examining experiences to improve practice.

Reflection-in-Action   Donald Shön has described this professional behavior as **re-flection-in-action**, and he describes how a teacher might use it to solve a problem in the classroom:

> An artful teacher sees a child's difficulty in learning to read not as a defect in the child but as a defect "of his own instruction." So he must find a way of explain-ing what is bothering the pupil. He must do a piece of experimental research, then and there, in the classroom. And because the child's difficulties may be unique, the teacher cannot assume that his repertoire of explanations will suffice, even though they are "at the tongue's end." He must be ready to invent new methods and must "endeavor to develop in himself the ability of discovering them."[18]

The professional teacher Shön describes is dedicated to making careful, sensi-tive observations of classroom events and then reflecting on the meaning of those observations. In reality, the teacher acts as a researcher—continuously experi-menting with ways to become more effective. Such a teacher has the courage and creativity to develop new ways of reaching students, ways that go beyond traditional, often limited, approaches. For example, the professional teacher has at his or her disposal not only conventional methods and materials but also a store of more effective, and sometimes unconventional, strategies. In short, teachers who use reflection-in-action are continuously alert to the differences between routine and ideal practice.

Becoming a Mentor   Because of their positions and their encounters with young people, teachers may find opportunities to become mentors for some of their students. Accepting this responsibility is another example of professionalism. Awareness of this opportunity can make it more accessible to you when you teach.

The role of **mentor** is unique in several ways. First, mentorship develops naturally and is not an automatic part of teaching, nor can it be assigned to anyone. True mentorships grow from teaching relationships and cannot be artificially promoted. Second, the role of mentor is a *comprehensive* one: Mentors express broad interest in their protégés (those whom they mentor). Third, the role of mentor is *mutually* recognized by student and teacher; both realize that their relationship has a special "depth."[19] Fourth, the role of mentor is a significant one and has the potential to change the quality and direction of protégés' lives. And fifth, the opportunity to work with a mentor is free to protégés, mentors' gifts of care.[20]

The longer teachers teach, the more they encounter opportunities for mentorships to develop, discovering that they can mentor younger teachers and student teachers as well as students. The rewards that come from the unique role of mentor may well be the most satisfying of all the teacher's roles because of the significance of the relationship to the lives of protégés.

LIFELONG LEARNING

The professional teacher is dedicated to continuous learning—both about the teaching-learning process and about the subject taught. No longer is it sufficient for career teachers to obtain only a bachelor's degree and a teaching certificate. Professional teachers see themselves as both teachers and learners.

Several provinces are considering mandating continuing education for teachers. The content of the curriculum as well as methods and materials for teaching that content are changing so rapidly that teachers must be involved in continuous learning to maintain their professional effectiveness. In addition, we feel that teachers must practice what they preach. A teacher who is not continuously learning raises serious questions for students: If it's not important for our teachers to learn, why should we? The attitude toward learning that teachers model for students may be as important as the content they teach.

Many opportunities are available for teachers to learn new knowledge and skills. Nearly every school district makes provisions for in-service training or staff development. These programs are usually offered on days when students are dismissed early or not required to attend at all. In-service training is usually given by district personnel or by faculty from a nearby university. The topics covered in in-service programs vary and are usually targeted at a particular need of the school, for example, classroom management, test-taking skills, constructing teacher-made tests, implementing research on effective teaching, and improving student achievement in the basic skills.

MAKING *a DIFFERENCE*

Sandy Wohl
Richmond, British Columbia

Ibelieve that using creativity as an important teaching and learning strategy is under-utilized. This is particularly true for secondary students where the curriculum and methods of evaluation may be content driven. I wanted to develop a series of teaching strategies and activities which encourage students to extend their thinking beyond rote memorization and copying from reference books by requiring students to use original, creative ideas to illustrate concepts taught in the classroom and compiled by students during project research.

I wanted students to benefit from using higher levels of thinking which would lead to greater achievement and involvement in their learning. I wanted them to experience self-assessment and peer-assessment which I hoped would lead to higher levels of self-esteem and satisfaction with the learning process. I wanted parents to experience greater satisfaction too.

With this is mind, when I assign students projects in junior high sciences, I ask for creativity. Students are allowed to choose from ten or more topics from a given category to research and then are encouraged to present their findings in a creative, artistic, or humorous style. Students have handed in projects that range from a late-night talk show with viruses as guests to tourist brochures for a planet. One student studying a unit about diseases wrote a mystery in which different facts about the disease were brought out as clues. Students are also responsible for self-assessment and peer-assessment, a concept I believe prepares them for later years.

Working with a team of science teachers and teachers in other disciplines such as Language Arts and English as a Second Language provides students with opportunities for curriculum integration. I have always wanted to avoid teaching classes that students would think boring, and, as long as I shift the responsibility of learning and evaluation of learning to students and I embrace their own thinking and style of humor, classes are anything but boring!

"Yo, Mrs. Wilson! Remember me, Fred Mooney — the one who looked out the window all the time?"

One of the most challenging ways to become a more effective professional is to enroll in a graduate program at a nearby university. Class schedules are usually developed with teachers in mind, with most courses offered in the evenings, on Saturdays, and during the summer. If you pursue graduate study, not only will you find the professional dialogue with instructors and fellow students stimulating, you will also acquire theories and practical approaches that you can implement in your classroom the following day. As well, you might find some other area of education—administration and supervision, guidance and counseling, special education, or curriculum development—that you want to pursue long-term.

TEACHER EMPOWERMENT

As we saw in this chapter's opening scenario, today's teacher welcomes opportunities to share decision-making power concerning education and the schools. From making decisions about the curriculum to implementing new programs designed to meet students' needs, professional teachers want to become empowered. Like other professionals, they welcome the opportunity to make decisions that directly affect their work. (See Figure 14.2 for teachers' attitudes regarding planning with their principal.)

Those who have participated in the trend toward **teacher empowerment** often report a renewed zest for teaching. Evidence indicates that the greatest opportu-

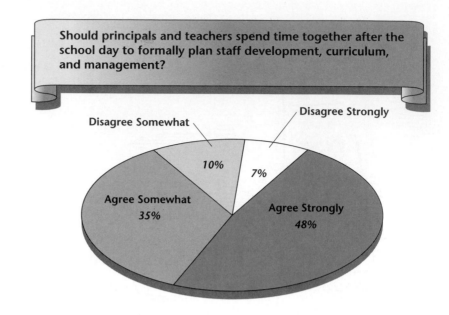

FIGURE 14.2

Principals and Teachers Should Plan Together

Note: *Survey of 2000 teachers—1048 elementary, 430 junior high/middle school, and 443 high school teachers (79 taught both junior high and high school).*

Source: Louis Harris and Associates. *The Metropolitan Life Survey of the American Teacher 1989: Preparing Schools for the 1990s* (New York: Louis Harris and Associates, 1990), p. 80. Used with permission.

nity for most teachers to participate in professional decision making is in choosing textbooks and developing the curriculum. Table 14.2, for example, shows that teachers have the least opportunity to evaluate the performance of their peers and to participate in the selection of new teachers and administrators.

INVOLVEMENT IN THE PROFESSION

The professional teacher is willing to get involved with colleagues and to press not only for increased financial rewards but for better working conditions and a greater role in professional governance. It is clear that teachers have not been given the power they need to improve the profession. This power will have to be attained in two ways. First, teachers must demonstrate by their behaviors and accomplishments that they *are* professionals. When all members of the profession—not just isolated outstanding teachers—do this, teaching will come to occupy its rightful status.

Second, teachers must more frequently demand—and in some cases even take—this power from parties who now hold it. Teachers must realize that they have the most important role in the educational enterprise. They must take a broader view of the decisions that, as professionals, they have the right to make. In some instances, power to make these decisions may have to be wrestled away from those who, because of tradition, not competence, have held it.

Although teachers may have played a limited role in school governance in the past, they currently have many opportunities to become involved in educational reform. For example, Table 14.3 on page 362 presents five streams of educational reform, each of which will offer teachers opportunities to shape policies during the next decade.

TABLE 14.2	Teacher Involvement in Professional Decision Making

Area of Decision Making	Percent of Teachers*
Choosing textbooks	79
Shaping the curriculum	63
Tracking students into special classes	45
Setting promotion and retention policies	34
Deciding school budgets	20
Evaluating teacher performance	10
Selecting new teachers	7
Selecting new administrators	7

*Based on responses from 11 827 elementary teachers and 11 651 secondary teachers.
Source: The Carnegie Foundation for the Advancement of Teaching, *Teacher Involvement in Decision Making: A State-by-State Profile, September 1988*. Data reported in National Center for Education Statistics, *Digest of Education Statistics 1990* (Washington, D.C.: National Center for Education Statistics, 1991), p. 80.

*H*OW CAN TEACHERS CONTINUE THEIR PROFESSIONAL DEVELOPMENT THROUGHOUT THEIR CAREERS?

Fortunately, changes are taking place in Canadian education during the 1990s that are designed to promote the **professionalization of teaching**. From longer and more rigorous teacher preparation programs to the creation of shared decision making/school-based management programs, today's teachers have unprecedented opportunities to enhance their professional status. Therefore, we urge you to take every opportunity to continue your professional development *throughout* your career.

SOURCES OF MOTIVATION

Once an individual becomes certified to teach, the effort to continue learning often stops, a phenomenon that seems to be due more to the prevailing image of teaching as an easy occupation than to any personal lack of initiative. A key source of motivation for professional development is the anticipation of being intellectually challenged in order to enter and then to function effectively in fields such as medicine, engineering, and finance.[21] Because teaching has yet to gain a similar reputation as an intellectually rigorous field, those who enter it must take the initiative to continue to grow professionally. New teachers may need to overcome a certain inertia. One avenue for professional development is to become a member of professional organizations and to subscribe to one or more professional journals. Continued learning can also be promoted by teachers choosing to use their free periods or professional days to observe reputedly talented and effective veteran teachers in their own and neighboring school districts. They can ask trusted colleagues to observe and critique their teaching or tap their students' perceptions through evaluative, anonymous questionnaires. Experimenting with several teaching strategies and comparing the results, reading books in the field by experts and the growing

TABLE 14.3	Five Streams of Educational Reform

1. *Reforms in subject-matter teaching (standards, curriculum, and pedagogy).* Many of the current reforms aspire to more ambitious student outcomes. Among them are the whole language and literature-based approach to language arts and the like. These reforms are incompatible with textbook-style teaching; they demand that teachers be well able to integrate various content areas into coherent lessons and to organize students' time efficiently. These demands may represent a substantial departure from teachers' prior experience, established beliefs, and present practice.

2. *Reforms centered on problems of equity and the increasing diversity of the student population.* These reforms address the persistent achievement disparities among students from differing family backgrounds and seek to improve both the demonstrated achievement and school completion rates of the lowest achieving groups. Over past decades, such reforms have focused on remedying individual student deficiencies. Recent analyses have drawn attention to the ways in which school practices define and contribute to student failure. To address the institutional failure related to low achievement, teachers must learn to identify and alter classroom practices that contribute to student failure and undermine equal opportunity to learn.

3. *Reforms in the nature, extent, and uses of student assessment.* Some reform proposals seek more widespread and rigorous use of assessment that measures what students are actually learning. Yet the technical advances in assessment are lagging behind the advances in curriculum design. Provincial and local policymakers continue to judge the success of reform efforts on the basis of standardized test scores.

4. *Reforms in the social organization of schooling.* In recent years there has been a remarkable convergence of interest, activities, and funds connected to the broad concept of school restructuring. Initiatives and special projects sponsored and supported by foundations, schools districts and the provinces have appeared across Canada. The most ambitious of these bring parents and taxpayers into the decision-making process. Restructuring poses a deep dilemma for school leadership and professional development programs because there are rarely any well-developed models of how these principles translate into specific instructional strategies and activities.

5. *Reforms in the professionalization of teaching.* Provincial professionalization reforms focus on teachers' demonstrated knowledge base (as reflected in standards for accreditation of teacher education programs and candidate assessment), on teacher licensure requirements, and on the structure of career opportunities in teaching. Reforms to professionalize teaching mean that teachers will increasingly serve as mentors to new teachers, take on new responsibilities over time, and exert more leadership through site-based decision making.

Source: Based on Judith Warren Little, "Teacher Professional Development in a Climate of Educational Reform," *Educational Evaluation and Policy Analysis* (Summer 1993): 129–151. Copyright 1993, by the American Educational Research Association; used by permission of the publisher. Excerpt taken from Consortium for Policy Research in Education, *CPRE Policy Briefs* (November 10, 1993): 2.

group of teacher-authors, and attending conferences and workshops to strengthen specific skills are still other ways that those so motivated can learn more about teaching.

OPPORTUNITIES FOR DEVELOPMENT

Many school systems and universities have in place several other sources for continuing professional education: teacher workshops, teacher centers, professional development schools, the opportunity to supervise student teachers, and graduate programs.

Throughout their careers, teachers have many opportunities for professional development. What sources might this experienced teacher use for continued development? How might his sources differ from those used by a first-year teacher?

Teacher Workshops   The quality of **in-service workshops** is uneven, varying with the size of school district budgets and the imagination and knowledge of the administrators and teachers who arrange them. For every teacher fortunate enough to participate in an in-service program, many more suffer, too frequently, through boring and irrelevant programs that offer simplistic, inapplicable solutions to complex classroom problems. It is significant that the most effective in-service programs tend to be the ones that teachers request—and often design and conduct.

Some workshops focus on topics that all teachers (regardless of subject or level) can benefit from: classroom management, writing-across-the-curriculum, or strategies of teaching, for example. Other workshops have a sharper focus and are intended for teachers of a subject at a certain level—for example, whole-language techniques for middle school students, discovery learning for high school science students, or student-centered approaches to teaching literature in the high school classroom.

Some in-service programs give teachers the opportunity to meet with other teachers at similar grade levels or with similar subject specializations for the purpose of sharing ideas, strategies, and solutions to problems. A day or part of a day may be devoted to this kind of workshop, often called an idea exchange. You may even be given released time from your regular duties to visit other schools and observe exemplary programs in action. Such visits are effective because they allow you to see how your peers address the challenges of teaching.

Teacher Centers   **Teacher centers** are quite simply "places where teachers can come together with other teachers, and perhaps with other useful persons . . . to do things that will help them teach better."[22] In contrast to in-service programs, these are more clearly initiated and directed by teachers and are usually supported by faculties of education. Some centers cooperate with a local or neighboring faculty of education and include members of the faculty on their planning committees. Their goals range from providing a setting for teachers to exchange ideas to offering information on education products and procedures to arranging instruction in new areas of responsibility, such as supervising student teachers and teaching students with special needs.

Many teachers find teacher centers stimulating because they offer opportunities for collegial interaction in a quiet, professionally-oriented setting. The busy, hectic pace of life in many schools, teachers often find, provides little time for professional dialogue with peers. Furthermore, in the teacher center, teachers are often more willing to discuss openly areas of weakness in their performance. As one teacher put it:

> At the teacher center I can ask for help. I won't be judged. The teachers who have helped me the most have had the same problems. I respect them, and I'm willing to learn from them. They have credibility with me.

Professional Development Schools Professional development schools (PDSs) have emerged recently as a way to link school restructuring and the reform of teacher education in different provinces. A **professional development school (PDS)** is an elementary, middle, or high school that has formed a partnership with a university and offers its teachers opportunities to participate in the development of the following:

- Fine learning programs for diverse students
- Practical, thought-provoking preparation for novice teachers
- New understandings and professional responsibilities for experienced educators
- Research projects that add to all educators' knowledge about how to make schools more productive[23]

Professional development schools offer teachers a wide variety of opportunities for professional growth. For example, a teacher at a PDS might team with a teacher education professor and teach a university-level course, participate in a collaborative research project, offer a professional development seminar for other teachers, arrange for the teacher educator to demonstrate instructional strategies in his or her classroom, or jointly develop relevant field experiences for prospective teachers.

Supervision of Student Teachers After several years in the classroom, teachers may be ready to stretch themselves further by supervising student teachers. Some of the less obvious values of doing so are that teachers must rethink what they are doing so that they can explain and sometimes justify their behaviors to someone else, learning themselves in the process. Furthermore, because they become a model for their student teachers, they continually strive to offer the best example. In exchange, they gain an assistant in the classroom—another pair of eyes, an aid with record keeping—and more than occasionally fresh ideas and a spirit of enthusiasm.

The benefits of supervising a student teacher are evident in the following comments of a junior-high language arts teacher:

> I find that having a student teacher keeps me intellectually alive. It's also very satisfying to pass on what I have learned. To explain to a young teacher why I do certain things in the classroom is not easy. I know what works and why it works, but it can be difficult to communicate that.

Graduate Study   A more traditional form of professional development is to do graduate study. Some teachers take only courses that are of immediate use to them; others use their graduate study to prepare for new teaching or administrative positions; still others pursue doctoral work in order to teach prospective teachers or others in their discipline at the university level. Graduate study can be a catalyst for professional growth.

WHAT PROFESSIONAL ORGANIZATIONS REPRESENT TEACHERS?

The push to make teaching more fully a profession draws much of its strength from the activities of more than 22 teacher organizations. These organizations, and the scores of hardworking teachers who run them, have been responsible for the many gains teachers have made in salaries, benefits, and working conditions during the last few decades. In addition to working for such improvements, teacher organizations also perform the important function of solidifying the professional identity of teachers.

Professional teacher organizations support a variety of activities to improve teaching and schools. Through lobbying, for example, teacher associations acquaint legislators, policymakers, and other politicians with critical issues and problems in the teaching profession. Many associations have staffs of teachers, researchers, and consultants who produce professional publications, hold conferences, prepare grant proposals, engage in school improvement activities, and promote a positive image of teaching to the public. Four major national organizations that have worked to improve the professional lives of all teachers in Canada are the Canadian Education Association, the Canadian Teachers' Federation, the Canadian Association of Principals, and the Federation of Independent Schools in Canada.

PROFESSIONAL REFLECTION

Imagine that you are near the end of your first month of teaching. The board of education has just announced that it is unable to provide job security to teachers newly hired by the district. According to the board, the school system is faced with tremendous financial problems.

Teachers at your school are very angry about the board's failure to live up to its promise. Many teachers believe that the board can find the money if it really wants to. Your school's union representative has just called a meeting of teachers to discuss the situation and to consider possible action. The day before the meeting he stops by your classroom to urge you to attend.

"This is an important meeting," he says. "As a new teacher, you need to find out how the board of education has treated teachers."

MAKING a DIFFERENCE

Ray MacLeod
Dartmouth, Nova Scotia

A native of Kentville, Nova Scotia, and a professional journalist before graduating from high school, I left Acadia University in 1965 without an undergraduate degree to pursue a career in media. Over a 12-year period this provided an eclectic life in journalism that included stints as a newspaper reporter, editor, and columnist. I was also a government information officer, publicist, and radio station news director. When I returned to university in the mid-1970s I received two degrees and began teaching in 1978 in Halifax County.

In 1989, I started using my media background to supplement high school English instruction, forming a media club which evolved into Nova Scotia's first high school credit journalism course. The Applied Broadcast Journalism (ABJ) program is built around a student-run media service with connections across Canada. Applying a strict professional media quality and rigid deadlines to all work enables me to draw the best from each student's potential, accelerating written and spoken communication skills to levels not normally expected in a high school program. My students present daily school newscasts but they go much beyond that, covering news and sports for radio stations throughout the Atlantic provinces and often across Canada. ABJ reporters have been seen on CTV, CBC, YTV, and Much Music television networks. Such youth-oriented organizations as MusicFest Canada and the Students' Commission of Canada rely on them for national media relations.

A major success has been *Teenline*, a seven-line teen news and opinion call-in service programmed by my students for the Herald Line information system run by the Halifax *Chronicle-Herald*. Up to 15 000 young people phone TeenLine monthly to plug into teen journalists covering teen matters. My students learn self-confidence in pressure communications and the reality of inflexible deadlines. Media have lavished praise on the results; one newspaper columnist referred to the hands-on, reality-based approach as "the wave of the future in communications education."

"Well," you begin, "I'm not sure. I'd like job security as much as anyone else, but if we work to rule or go on strike, what about the kids? We have a responsibility to them."

"Just a minute," he says. "This is not just about security or money. The board has a history of failing to live up to its promises. We're actually doing this for the kids. If the board gets away with this, a lot of good teachers are going to transfer out of the district. And that's going to hurt the kids."

You agree to attend the meeting, but you're still not sure how you feel about teachers' unions in general. Before the meeting, several questions keep coming to mind. If teachers are professionals, should they belong to unions? If teachers decide to go on strike, will I honor the strike? Would I cross the picket line to teach?

OTHER PROFESSIONAL ORGANIZATIONS

In addition to the organizations mentioned above, teachers' interests are represented by several other national organizations concerned with improving the quality of education at all levels and in all subject areas. Two of the most respected and influential of these groups are Phi Delta Kappa and the Association for Supervision and Curriculum Development.

Phi Delta Kappa   A professional and honorary fraternity of educators, **Phi Delta Kappa** is concerned with enhancing quality education through research and leadership activities. Founded in 1906, Phi Delta Kappa now has a membership of 168 000.[24] Members, who are graduate students, teachers, and administrators, belong to one of 677 chapters. PDK chapters exist throughout Canada. To be initiated into Phi Delta Kappa, a person must have demonstrated high academic achievement, have completed at least fifteen semester hours of graduate work in education, and have made a commitment to a career of educational service. Phi Delta Kappa members receive *Phi Delta Kappan*, an excellent journal of education published ten times a year.

The Association for Supervision and Curriculum Development   A professional organization of teachers, supervisors, curriculum coordinators, education professors, administrators, and others, the **Association for Supervision and Curriculum Development (ASCD)** is interested in school improvement at all levels of education. Founded in 1921, the association has a membership of 185 000 and has one Canadian chapter in Calgary.[25] ASCD provides professional development in curriculum and supervision, disseminates information related to educational issues, and encourages research, evaluation, and theory development. ASCD also provides a free research information service to members. Members receive *Educational Leadership*, a well-respected journal printed eight times a year. ASCD publishes a yearbook, each one devoted to a particular educational issue, and occasional books in the area of curriculum and supervision.

Subject-Area and Special-Student Associations Many teachers belong to professional organizations whose primary purpose is to identify and disseminate promising practices in specific subject areas and for special groups of students. The following are some examples.

- Association for Canadian Studies
- Association for Media Literacy
- Canadian Alliance of Home Schoolers
- Canadian Association for Curriculum Studies
- Canadian Association for Health, Physical Education, Recreation, and Dance
- Canadian Association of Immersion Teachers
- Canadian Association of School Administrators
- Canadian Association of Second Language Teachers
- Canadian Association for the Study of Educational Administration
- Canadian Association for Teacher Education
- Canadian Cable in the Classroom Association
- Canadian Council for Exceptional Children
- Canadian Council for Multicultural and Intercultural Education
- Canadian Council of Teachers of English and Language Arts
- Canadian Education Association
- Canadian Home Economics Association
- Canadian Home and School and Parent-Teacher Federation
- Canadian Music Educators' Association
- Canadian Society for Education through Art
- Canadian Teachers' Federation
- Canadian Vocational Association
- Council for Second Language Programs in Canada
- Federation of Independent Schools in Canada
- Learning Disabilities Association of Canada
- National Educational Association of Disabled Students[26]

For more information on these and other organizations, please see the Teacher's Resource Guide.

THE IMPACT OF TEACHERS' ASSOCIATIONS ON EDUCATION

Teachers' unions and other organizations can potentially have both a positive and a negative impact on education. To the extent that professional teacher organizations put the growth of students before the growth of the organizations themselves, they can have a tremendously positive influence on education. Most teacher organizations publish educational journals, fund research projects, and directly support students and teachers. And, as we have pointed out previously, teacher associations are working diligently to professionalize training and improve schools.

However, in Canada, because the responsibility for education rests with the provinces, these national organizations hold a relatively low profile with teachers. Instead, teachers are more aware of their local provincial organizations and the many curriculum-based organizations. Consult your local teachers' association and the Canadian Education Association for more information on which organizations might help you become a more professional teacher.

PROFESSIONAL PORTFOLIO

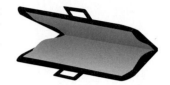

For this portfolio entry, prepare a catalogue of possible professional development opportunities for you to pursue after becoming a teacher. If appropriate, identify at what point in your career you could begin a particular activity. Among the items you might include are the following:

- In-service workshops
- Postgraduate courses and/or graduate-level study
- Professional associations

For each entry include a brief description of the activity and any other relevant information—for example, dates, address and phone number, cost, contact person(s), prerequisites (e.g., years of experience), and so on.

CHAPTER SUMMARY

For an occupation to be considered a profession, it must satisfy many criteria. Though no occupation meets all the criteria, some occupations meet more of them and therefore have a higher professional status in our society. Teaching meets some of the following nine criteria more fully than others.

1. Institutional monopoly of services
2. Teacher autonomy
3. Years of education and training
4. Provision of essential service
5. Degree of self-governance
6. Professional associations
7. Professional knowledge and skills
8. Level of public trust
9. Prestige, benefits, and pay

Though teaching does not currently satisfy all of these criteria, scores of individuals and agencies are collaborating so that teaching is rapidly becoming more professionalized.

The most potent force for improving teaching is for teachers to see that their behavior reflects professional practice, ethical conduct, a commitment to lifelong learning, a desire to become empowered, and professional involvement. Among the opportunities available for teachers who wish to grow professionally are teacher workshops, participation in teacher centers and professional development schools, supervision of student teachers, and graduate study. In addition, the following five streams of educational reform will continue to provide teachers with opportunities to grow professionally throughout their careers.

1. Reforms in subject-matter teaching (standards, curriculum, and pedagogy)
2. Reforms centered on problems of equity and the increasing diversity of the student population
3. Reforms in the nature, extent, and uses of student assessment
4. Reforms in the social organization of schooling
5. Reforms in the professionalization of teaching

Several teacher organizations work nationally, provincially, and locally to improve the teaching profession. Among the most influential are the Canadian Education Association and the Canadian Teachers' Federation.

KEY TERMS AND CONCEPTS

Association for Supervision and Curriculum Development (ASCD), 367
in-service workshops, 363
mentor, 357

Phi Delta Kappa, 367
profession, 350
professional development school (PDS), 364

professionalization of teaching, 361
reflection-in-action, 356
teacher centers, 363
teacher empowerment, 359

APPLICATIONS AND ACTIVITIES

Teacher's Journal

1. In your opinion, what accounts for the erosion of public trust in the teaching profession? What might be the best way to rebuild that trust?
2. Review several recent issues of the journal published by your provincial teachers' association. List the concerns or issues that each issue addresses.
3. In most provinces, membership in the provincial teachers' association is mandatory. List some advantages and disadvantages of mandatory versus voluntary membership.

Field Assignments

1. Visit a nearby school and talk to several teachers about what steps should be taken to improve the professional status of teachers. Take notes regarding their views. Then present a brief oral report of your findings to your class. Compare your results with those obtained by other students.
2. Interview several adults who are not involved in education to obtain their views on teaching as a profession. What image do these adults have of teaching? What are their suggestions for improving the profession?
3. Visit a school and interview a teacher who is actively involved in a professional association or teachers' union. What benefits does the teacher obtain from his or her involvement?
4. Do research to find out whether teacher strikes have occurred in your province in the recent past. What other legal mechanisms are available to resolve disputes between teachers and their employers? If strikes have taken place, find out what sequence of events led to the strike(s). What were the results of the strike(s)? Report your findings briefly to the rest of your class.

CHAPTER

15 Teaching and the Challenge of the Future

In planning for the future, we must follow the lead of innovative teachers and other change agents who today are trying new tools and breaking out of traditional constraints to improve teaching and learning.

—*Images of Potential: Learning Tomorrow*
The National Foundation for the Improvement of Education

Focus Questions

▼

1. What forces and trends are shaping the future of education?
2. What are several promising innovations in education?
3. What new technologies are being used in the classroom?
4. How can teachers and students prepare for an unknown future?

What does the future hold for education? How will teaching change? What will the classroom of the future look like? Will the following description of a student's typical school day in the twenty-first century become a reality?

8:00 A.M.

Violet grabs her textpak, which has replaced the laptop computer, as she leaves to catch the bus. She pauses momentarily as her brother's laptop on the shelf catches her eye—she wonders how he ever lugged it back and forth to school every day.

After pulling up her academic profile from her electronic locker last night, Violet was excited to see that she scored "excellent" on her math exercises. That means she could catch the late bus to school and would have time to follow her teacher's recommendation that she preview the next unit on square one videodisc in her textpak.

As Violet goes to her electronic locker and initiates a library search on robotics, she is joined by her teammates, Simon and Hue.

As in any typical middle school, they ignore the electronic announcements and review their team strategy for the day.

Day's Activities

1. Call Joan and find out why she is really out of school.
2. Math class. Large screen projection, videodisc, review. Ratios and percents.
3. Humanities. Simon leads discussion on Asian culture joined via satellite by famous Korean author.
4. Science. Continue with industrial robotics assignment. Violet has mixed emotions about this because of her dad's concern expressed at breakfast over the impact of robotic technology on his job.
5. Clubs. Bilingual track of Japanese videodisc. Violet hopes that Simon will sit with her in the cafeteria today.
6. Athletics. Simon invites Violet to come along to the Go Club meeting.
7. TLC (Teaching/Learning Corps). Hue will introduce her mother, who will discuss "Do Robots Replace People?"

After TLC, Violet returns to her electronic locker to get references on robots. She invites Simon to join her at the library, faxes Joan the materials she requested, and gets her homework assignments before boarding her bus for home.[1]

Though no one has an educational crystal ball that can give us an accurate glimpse of what the future holds for teaching, we believe the probability is high that scenarios such as the preceding will become a reality. Compare, for example, Violet's typical day at school with that of students at Lester B. Pearson Secondary School in Calgary who learn with the support of technology. The school is wired with electronic cables that run to all classrooms and seminar rooms. Video monitors are visible everywhere and work stations allow students to access information around the world, analyze data, and write reports.

Teachers work in teams and plan cross-disciplinary programs of study in a large resource room in which computer stations are arranged in groups of four. The room is alive with teachers in discussion and debate. It is a natural place for the teaching teams to maintain daily contact. Students collaborate on projects in which they study global issues and investigate and share information on their social, political, and cultural environments. They work in the open areas of the library and in seminar rooms. The student body is a diverse group, and the school's physical set-up and integrated curriculum embrace the multi-faceted experiences and attitudes of the students.

The school points the way to the future: an electronic infrastructure networked to other electronic systems, a culturally diverse student population, and teachers who view curriculum as integrated with and connected to the realities of daily experience.

WHAT FORCES AND TRENDS ARE SHAPING THE FUTURE OF EDUCATION?

What will teaching become in the twenty-first century? Of course, no one knows for certain. In spite of the impossibility of answering that question, however, it is important for us to think carefully about the kind of world we want for tomorrow. In that way, the choices we make today will increase the likelihood that tomorrow's future will be the one we prefer. In short, we should recognize the importance of planning for the future and trying to create the future we want. As Alvin Toffler pointed out in his classic book, *Future Shock*, we must choose wisely from among several courses of action:

> Every society faces not merely a succession of *probable* futures, but an array of *possible* futures, and a conflict over *preferable* futures. The management of change is the effort to convert certain possibles into probables, in pursuit of agreed-on preferables. Determining the probable calls for a science of futurism. Delineating the possible calls for an art of futurism. Defining the preferable calls for a politics of futurism.[2]

The primary aim of **futurism** is to enable a society to enter the future that it prefers. Futurists identify possible futures by analyzing current social, economic, and technological trends and then making forecasts based on those analyses.

THE FORCES OF CHANGE

Using forecasting techniques that John Naisbitt first popularized in his 1982 best-seller *Megatrends* and then updated (with Patricia Aburdene) in the 1990 *Mega-*

trends 2000: Ten New Directions for the 1990s, and drawing from the forecasts of other futurists, we have identified a number of forces and trends (see Figure 15.1) that seem to be contributing most to how we will live in the twenty-first century.

Social Forces and Trends   Although family ties will continue to remain a prominent part of our culture, evidence indicates that many marriages will end in divorce. In addition, numbers of runaway children and cases of child abuse suggest that the family is in trouble. Teachers will continue to find that more and more of their students are from families that are smaller, have mothers who work outside the home, are led by a single parent, or have unrelated adults living in the home.

There is evidence that crime and delinquency will continue to rise in the future. Much of the crime that occurs in and around schools is related to students' use of drugs. Violence and vandalism in some schools have already reached unacceptably high proportions. Certainly, the reduction of crime is one of the critical challenges of the future.

Canada will continue to grow more culturally diverse. Teachers of the future will be responsible for developing curricula and instructional methods that cultivate the potentialities of students from a wide variety of backgrounds.

With advances in health care, the life span of Canadians is steadily increasing. In addition, older Canadians in the future will be better educated and more physically, intellectually, and politically active than their predecessors. Tomorrow's elderly will recognize education as one of the keys for a satisfying, productive old age.

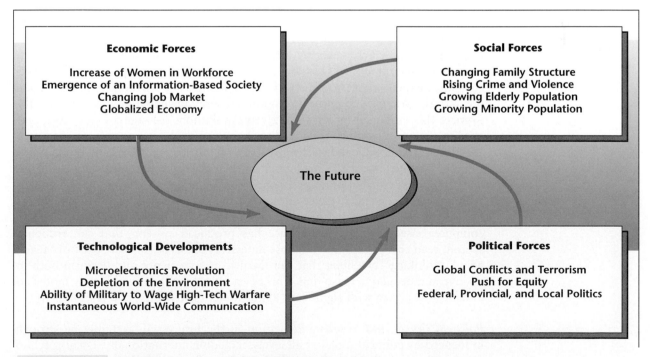

FIGURE 15.1   Significant Forces and Trends Shaping the Future

Economic Forces and Trends   The jobs we are trained for today may not exist tomorrow. During the last half decade, for example, very few occupations have been unaltered by the developments in computer technology. Today's worker must be able to learn to operate an ever-increasing array of technological devices. Workers who excel are measured not by how much they can produce but by how quickly and well they can learn new skills.

The composition of the workforce is also changing. As a result of gains made by the women's movement, for example, more and more women are not only moving out into the workforce, they are moving up. Women are obtaining increasing numbers of executive-level positions in the professions, business, and education. In fact, in *Megatrends 2000*, Naisbitt and Aburdene call the 1990s the "decade of women in leadership."[3] Slowly, the workplace is changing to accommodate the career patterns of women. Business and industry, for example, are receiving pressure from women's groups to provide childcare programs as part of their benefit packages.

Another major economic force in Canada during the last decade has been the shift from a product-oriented to an information-based, service-oriented economy. Moreover, this "new" economy is not the isolated, self-contained economy of one nation; it is a global economy. Our participation, cooperation, and competition in this global economy depends on rapid communication of information around the world. Information is steadily becoming the critical resource of our age and the ability to learn it and to use it the chief aim of education.

Technological Developments   One of the greatest influences on education is the mushrooming revolution in microelectronics. Computers, video equipment, and communication devices that use tiny silicon microchips are having profound effects on our life-styles. These technological advances are changing not only how we learn and what we learn, they are also forcing us to realize that the future will require all of us to be continuous, lifelong learners.

Technological and scientific advances have given us considerable ability to mold our environment to meet our needs for food, shelter, and safety. However, ecological experts suggest that we are so ravaging the environment that we could one day run out of vital natural resources. There are signs that we might be able to meet this challenge by harnessing more pollution-free sources of energy, conserving resources, and restoring damaged environments.

Recent technological developments such as fiber-optic cables and communication via satellite have made instantaneous, worldwide communication possible. In late 1988, the first fiber-optic telephone cable, capable of carrying 40 000 calls simultaneously, went into service and linked the United States with Europe. Today, fiber-optic cabling is being installed in countries around the world. Research in computer-based artificial intelligence has produced systems that can recognize speech, read characters, and diagnose illnesses. Prototypes already exist of "teachable," "thinking" machines that can learn from experience and perform both inductive and deductive reasoning. This research may make possible new models of human intelligence with significant applications for teaching and learning.

Political Forces and Trends   Education in the future will certainly be strongly influenced by political forces at all levels, including internationally. Locally, school districts are moving toward school-based management in which the authority to make educational decisions is held by those on whom the responsibility of teaching rests. Parent councils, administrators, and teachers will have more authority over personnel and budgets than previously. Schools will look less and less alike as school personnel decide how to address each school's unique needs.

Many provinces are amalgamating school districts and reducing the number of school boards and school trustees. This trend to centralize fiscal decision making with the province and decentralize operating decisions with the schools leaves less and less for the school districts to do. Provinces will continue to have the responsibility of developing curriculum.

The federal government will probably reduce its involvement in education and training because of the necessity of reducing the debt and deficit. As the federal government reduces transfer payments to the provinces, the trend of increasing federal involvement in education will reverse. As the global marketplace continues to set the standard for national prosperity, Canada will become increasingly sensitive to international developments in education.

THE CHANGE PROCESS IN EDUCATION

As you have seen, forces outside and within the educational system continually stimulate changes in education. And changes do occur. However, the modifications, reorganizations, and redirections are relatively slow, complex, and lackluster, especially when compared with the paths of progress in the fields of space, science, and technology, which frequently end with dazzling discoveries. The course of change in Canadian education is often more plodding, progressing undramatically on paths that at times seem circular.

Why is change so difficult to effect in education? Seymour Sarason suggests six answers to this question in his book *The Culture of School and the Problem of Change*. First, he explains, schools are complex social organizations that defy simple, single-approach innovations.[4] In the school culture, a change in one area has consequences in another. For instance, incorporating a new subject such as AIDS education into the curriculum requires all or most of the following actions: (1) obtaining approval from the school board, community, and/or administration regarding the new program; (2) reducing instructional time allotments for existing curriculum to make room for an additional subject; (3) arranging in-service training for teachers; (4) coordinating teachers' efforts in terms of common objectives and their sequence; (5) communicating with parents and the public; (6) maintaining students' skills in other areas of the curriculum; and (7) resolving conflicts that may occur in any of these areas.

A second reason why change is difficult, according to Sarason, is that it is hard to know where to start. Should the agent of change be the principal, the teachers, or the parents?[5] Obviously all will play a part but who should begin the process and provide the leadership?

Third, Sarason notes that it is also hard to know which area to target for change (e.g., the administration, the teachers, the community, the teacher-training faculties). If the change process takes the form of parent education, change could be brought about through evening programs sponsored by the parent-teacher association, administration, or school board. In this case, parents are the target for change.

Fourth, participants in the school culture are sometimes skeptical about changes because of previous negative experiences. New programs often have poor results because of the reformers' lack of knowledge of the system. For instance, teachers could be dubious about an AIDS curriculum because an earlier anti-smoking education effort had been ineffective.

Fifth, change in the school culture is difficult because "each alternative confronts one with a universe of alternatives of action."[6] The leaders initiating the change must care strongly enough about it to create a plan and then carry it through the maze of decisions and adjustments to completion.

And sixth, the time perspective of those seeking improvements often works against the success of the effort. A preference for quick solutions and an impatience with long-term processes frequently cancel innovative programs prematurely.

From Sarason comes a sampling of questions that reformers might ask. They reveal the complexity of the problem of change.

What Reformers Need to Know

- What are the different ways in which pupils can participate in preparing examinations?
- What are the different ways in which a principal can prepare for his or her position?
- What are the alternative ways of deroutinizing the school day and year?
- What are the different ways [in which] a teacher can generate and utilize question-asking behavior in children?
- What are the different ways in which a neighborhood or community can exercise "control" over schools?[7]

WHAT ARE SEVERAL PROMISING INNOVATIONS IN EDUCATION?

Recent developments in education range from applications of new scientific knowledge about the human brain to new applications of computer and telecommunications technologies. Other significant changes include new roles for teachers and students and new partnerships between communities and schools. The innovations in education described in the following sections need to be considered in terms of the complexity of the change process.

NEW KNOWLEDGE ABOUT LEARNING

Since the 1970s, educational researchers have increased our understanding of the learning process. **Learning** can be defined as "the information processing, sense making, and comprehension or mastery advances that occur while one is acquiring knowledge or skill.[8] Research into multiple intelligences and multicultural learning styles has broadened our understanding of this definition. In addition, research in the fields of neurophysiology, neuropsychology, and cognitive science promises direct relevance to education by further explaining how people think and learn.[9]

Cognitive science is concerned with the mental processes students use as they learn new material. By drawing from research in linguistics, psychology, anthropology, and computer science, cognitive scientists develop new models for how people think and learn. For the most part, cognitive scientists focus on students' thought processes while they are learning and attempt to describe how they manipulate symbols in **information processing**. Cognitive scientists have pointed out that students' learning is influenced by prior knowledge, experience, and attitudes. By studying in minute detail how students learn, cognitive scientists try to discover the "rules" that govern learning.

TRENDS IN EDUCATIONAL THEORY AND PRACTICE

Research on the thinking and learning processes has contributed to the development of innovative teaching strategies and to new methods of assessing students' learning. Two innovative forms of instruction that draw from cognitive studies are contingent teaching and the constructivist view of learning.

Contingent Teaching   Teachers who employ **contingent teaching** vary the amount of help they give children

> on the basis of their moment-to-moment understanding. If they do not understand an instruction given at one level, then more help is forthcoming. When they do understand, the teacher steps back and gives the child more room for initiative. In this way, the child is never left alone when he [or she] is in difficulty nor is he [or she] "held back" by teaching that is too directive and intrusive.[10]

The concept of contingent teaching, sometimes called *scaffolding*, is based on the word of L. S. Vygotsky, a well-known Soviet psychologist. Vygotsky coined the term **zone of proximal development** to refer to the point at which students need assistance in order to continue learning. The effective teacher is sensitive to the student's zone of development and ensures that instruction neither exceeds the student's current level of understanding nor underestimates the student's ability.

As educational psychologist David Wood points out, contingent teaching is an effective means of increasing students' abilities to process information in more complex ways:

> Contingent teaching helps children to construct local expertise—expertise connected with that particular task or group of tasks—by focusing their attention on relevant and timely aspects of the task, and by highlighting things they need to take account of. It also breaks the task down into a sequence of smaller tasks which children can manage to perform, and orchestrates this sequence so that they eventually manage to construct the completed assembly.[11]

Constructivist Views of Learning   Since the mid-1980s, several researchers have worked at identifying how students construct understanding of the material they are to learn.[12] According to the **constructivist view of learning,**

> students actively *construct* their own knowledge; the mind of the student *mediates* inputs from the outside world to determine what the student will learn. Learning is active mental work, not passive reception of teaching. In this work, other people play an important role by providing support, challenging thinking, and serving as coaches or models, but the student is the key to learning.[13]

The constructivist view of learning may be contrasted with more direct approaches to teaching in which the teacher *transmits* academic content to students in small segments. In effect, the student is seen as an empty vessel into which the teacher directly transmits knowledge.

What new knowledge about learning and new concerns about learners might have guided the teachers who developed this learning task?

New Ways to Assess Student Learning Since the mid-1970s, declining test scores, the lack of literacy among many high school graduates, and calls to hold teachers more accountable fueled a movement to evaluate the performance of students and teachers with ever-increasing numbers of tests. Recently, however, alternative forms of assessment have been developed. **Alternative assessments** require students to use higher-level thinking skills to perform, create, or solve real-life problems—not just choose one of several designated responses as on a multiple-choice test. Among the alternative assessment methods a teacher might use are individual and small-group projects, portfolios of work, videotaped demonstrations of skills, and community-based activities to assess students' learning. In science, for example, students might conduct an experiment; in mathematics, they might explain in writing how they solved a problem. Similarly, the performance of some teachers is being assessed through alternative methods such as essay exams that require the analysis of simulated teaching problems, computer simulations of classroom situations, portfolios that document the teacher's work, and videotapes of teaching.

Authentic assessments require students to solve problems or to work on tasks that approximate as much as possible those they will encounter beyond the classroom. For example, authentic assessment might allow students to select projects on which they will be evaluated or to participate in community-based projects. In addition, authentic assessment encourages students to develop their own responses to problem situations by allowing them to decide what information is relevant and how that information should be organized and presented.

NEW ROLES FOR TEACHERS AND STUDENTS

Efforts to reform education that began in the 1980s have led to new roles for teachers and students. Among the innovative strategies that are being used by many school systems are peer counseling, peer coaching, faculty teams, school houses, and charter schools.

Peer Counseling Some schools have initiated student-to-student **peer counseling** programs which are usually monitored by a school counselor or other specially trained adult. In peer counseling programs, students can address problems and issues such as low academic achievement, interpersonal problems at home and at school, substance abuse, and career planning. Evidence indicates that both peer counselors and students experience increased self-esteem and greater ability to deal with problems.

When peer counseling is combined with cross-age tutoring, younger students can learn about drugs, alcohol, premarital pregnancy, delinquency, dropping out, AIDS, suicide, and other issues. Here the groups are often post-secondary students meeting with those in high school, or high school students meeting with those in junior high school or middle school. In these preventative programs, older students sometimes perform dramatic scenes that portray students confronting problems and model strategies for handling the situations presented.

Peer Coaching Although talented, experienced teachers have always helped novice teachers, more formal peer-coaching programs are designed to extend the benefits of such exchanges to more teachers. **Peer coaching** encourages teachers to learn together in an emotionally safe environment. According to Bruce Joyce and Marsha Weil, peer coaching is an effective way to create communities of professional educators, and all teachers should be members of coaching teams:

> If we had our way, *all* school faculties would be divided into coaching teams—that is, teams who regularly observe one another's teaching and learn from watching one another and the students. In short, we recommend the development of a "coaching environment" in which all personnel see themselves as one another's coaches.[14]

Master teacher and mentor programs similarly promote teacher-to-teacher support. These approaches to staff development are expected to yield benefits in terms of improved teacher morale and teaching effectiveness.

Staff Teams The practice of team teaching is often limited by student enrollments and budget constraints. As integrated curricula and the need for special knowledge and skills increase, however, the use of staff teams will become more common.

Staff teams can be created according to subject areas, grade levels, or teacher interests and expertise. Team members make wide-ranging decisions about the instruction of students assigned to the team, such as when to use large-group instruction or small-group instruction, how teaching tasks will be divided, and how time, materials, and other resources will be allocated.

Participating on a staff team requires a willingness to devote extra time to planning and an ability to work collaboratively with others. However, the potential benefits are many: teachers spend more time teaching their areas of expertise and interests, and students are often more motivated to learn when they are taught by a team.

School Houses   Staff teams also participate in school restructuring and school-based management, especially in programs designed to create communities of teachers and learners. For example, to reduce the anonymity that students and teachers can experience in large schools and to create conditions that enhance within-school communication, some schools are restructuring into **school houses** or year-round schools—separate, autonomous groups of students and teachers within a single school. The first author of this book (U.S. edition), for example, taught at a high school that was restructured according to a 45–15 year-round plan. Teachers, students, administrators, counselors, and staff were assigned to one of four houses—A, B, C, or D. On a staggered basis, each house would attend school for forty-five days and then take a fifteen-day minivacation. A complete school year consisted of four forty-five-day sessions and four minivacations. At any given time, three houses would be in session and one house would be on holiday. As a result of this restructuring, a greater sense of community was created within each house. The first year-round school in Canada opened in July, 1995, and is based on the same 45-15 year-round plan. Terry Fox Junior High School in Calgary will provide a Canadian model for this type of restructuring, and plans are already being made to build a second school set to open within two years.

Charter schools are independent, innovative, outcome-based, public schools. "The charter school concept allows a group of teachers, parents, or others who share similar interests and views about education to organize and operate a school. Charters can be granted by a local school district or by the state [or provincial] government. In effect, charter schools offer a model for restructuring that gives greater autonomy to individual schools and promotes school choice by increasing the range of options available to parents and students within the public schools system."[15] Alberta passed the first charter school legislation in Canada in 1994. Three charter schools were approved in June 1995; one opened in Edmonton in September, 1995, and the other two are scheduled to open in September, 1996.

To open a charter school, an original charter (or agreement) is signed by the school's founders and a sponsor (usually the local school board). The charter specifies the learning outcomes that students will master before they continue their studies. Charter schools, which usually operate as autonomous school districts (a feature that distinguishes them from the alternative schools that many school districts operate), are public schools and must teach all students. If admission requests for a charter school exceed the number of available openings, students are selected by drawing lots.

Because charter schools are designed to promote the development of new teaching strategies that can be used at other public schools, they can be an effective tool for promoting educational reform and the professionalization of teaching as we enter the twenty-first century. Moreover, as Milo Cutter, one of the two teachers who founded St. Paul City Academy, the first charter school in the United States, points out, charter schools give teachers unprecedented leadership opportunities and the ability to respond quickly to students' needs:

[We had] the chance to create a school that takes into account the approaches we know will work. We listen to what the students want and need, because we ask them. And each day we ask ourselves if we are doing things the best way we can. We also have the flexibility to respond. We can change the curriculum to meet these needs as soon as we see them. Anywhere else it would take a year to change. It is much better than anything we have known in the traditional setting.[16]

NEW PARTNERSHIPS BETWEEN SCHOOLS AND COMMUNITIES

During the last decade, the concept of partnerships has been extended to include the wider community. From adopt-a-grandparent programs to adopt-a-school projects, partnerships between schools and communities take many forms and have great potential. Partnerships with parents and business, for example, help make communities valuable resources for schools. Equally important, new directions in restructuring our educational system make schools valuable resources for their communities. An example of a community-school partnership is the creation of an elementary school in a downtown building in Calgary. The school, which opened in September, 1995, is designed to accommodate parents who work downtown. They bring their children to work with them and take them home after work. This workplace school was created through the partnership of Alberta Government Telephones (AGT) and the Calgary Board of Education. AGT provided the facility and a maintenance budget while the Calgary Board of Education provided teachers and teaching materials.

Parents are encouraged to volunteer in the classrooms and to observe their children during coffee breaks and lunch hours. The curriculum is designed around the available resources, for example, substituting normal physical education curricula which depend on a gymnasium with alternative curricula in which students use available public facilities. The curriculum also makes use of nearby art galleries and theaters.

The Community as a Resource for Schools In partnerships between communities and schools, individuals, civic organizations, or businesses choose a school or are chosen by a school to work together for the good of the students. The goals of such projects are to provide students with better school experiences and to help students at risk. Rural and urban schools throughout Canada have entered into formal partnership agreements with business and service organizations. Schools enjoy benefits such as receiving used equipment and the status of being connected with a business while businesses are able to exercise their responsibilities as corporate community members.

Adopt-a-grandparent programs can be beneficial for all concerned, and relatively easy to incorporate into a school because many older citizens have the time available to serve and the desire to make meaningful contributions to their communities. Students clearly benefit from the perspective, care, and wisdom of the older generation. In many communities, senior citizens contribute to schools as paid or volunteer assistants in the library, office, or classroom, or as resources for storytelling and oral history.

Communities are resources for schools in many other ways. Community organizations may provide special services, for example. Museum in the schools programs, outdoor education, and mock government activities are some projects that may emerge from community partnerships. Businesses may contribute funds or materials needed by the school, give employees release time to participate in classroom projects, initiate prevention programs for students at risk, or offer formal career training in conjunction with the school.

This RCMP officer is participating in a partnership program between the school and the wider community.

Schools as Community Resources   A shift from the more traditional perspective that schools need support from the community is the view that schools should serve as multipurpose resources *for* the community. Proposals for year-round schools, for example, reflect not only students' educational and developmental needs but also the needs of parents and the requirements of the work world.

Proposals for making schools community resources include Bettye Caldwell's idea of an Educare system, for instance, which would provide day-long, year-round public schooling for children six months through twelve years of age.[17] Ernest Boyer of the Carnegie Foundation for the Advancement of Teaching argues that schools should adapt their schedules to those of the workplace so that parents can become more involved in their children's education, and that businesses should give parents more flexible work schedules. Drawing on the model of Japan, Boyer suggests that the beginning of the school year could be a holiday that frees parents to attend opening day ceremonies, celebrating the launching and continuance of education in the same way that we celebrate its ending.[18]

Many urban school districts have created outreach programs to provide alternatives for the students who have dropped out of school. Storefront schools or classrooms are set up in malls where many ex-students spend their time bored and without direction. Teachers make themselves available near the "store" entrance to encourage kids to come in and learn. The idea behind these outreach programs is to entice students back into the system, not to provide a complete program of studies in storefront facilities.

CORPORATE-EDUCATION PARTNERSHIPS

Business involvement in schools has taken many forms, including, for example, adopt-a-school programs, cash grants for pilot projects, educational use of corporate facilities and expertise, employee participation, and student scholarship programs. Extending beyond advocacy, private sector efforts include job initiatives for disadvantaged youths, in-service programs for teachers, and management training for school administrators.

In Canada, corporate-education partnerships have tended to focus on addressing particular local needs. The Calgary school housed in a business building is an example of a school that meets local needs. Teachers and students become more aware of parents' working environment while parents gain insights into their children's learning environment. The company benefits from their employees' greater loyalty and higher morale.

Corporate-school partnerships are mainly an urban phenomenon because rural schools or schools in medium-size and small districts have little access to corporate sponsorships. These schools tend to form partnerships with other public service agencies such as regional colleges, the public health department, and alcohol counsellors, and, in areas with a large Aboriginal population, with band councils. Schools use these agencies' resources to develop, for example, programs that deal with drug and alcohol prevention, adult education, crisis intervention, and so on.

Rural schools may also establish partnerships with community-based volunteer groups and service organizations such as the Kinsmen Club, the Lions Club, and 4-H clubs. Schools may exchange the use of school facilities for help in acquiring specialized equipment such as computers or gym equipment. These partnerships tend to be more program-specific than are partnerships between urban schools and corporations.

WHAT NEW TECHNOLOGIES ARE BEING USED IN THE CLASSROOM?

Corporate partnerships between rural schools and urban corporations do exist using technology. Increasingly, the telecommunications industry is reaching out to more isolated schools to offer distance education facilities. One such sponsorship involves a network of over 20 rural schools in Alberta which are linked by audio and video communication technology. The voices and images of students and teachers are transmitted during classes. A physics teacher can teach a full class of students who are spread out among the 20 high schools. Without the networking technology, none of the schools could afford to offer physics classes.

Other technologies include computers. For example, in a classroom hundreds of kilometres away, nine-year-old Nancy is seated in front of a computer and color monitor, about to begin a lesson on insects. On the screen is a two-story house. Nancy reaches out to the screen and touches the burnished knob on the front door and it magically opens. The next screen shows the hallway and living room. At various points on the screen are purple bugs. Nancy touches a bug near the bottom of a bookcase. The bookcase fades away and reveals dozens of ants scurrying about. A pleasant-sounding voice comes on and begins to explain how insects and humans coexist. After giving Nancy information about the ants she has discovered, the voice invites her to explore the rest of the house to see what other insects she can find.

To enhance their classroom instruction, today's teachers can draw from a dazzling array of technological devices like the ones these students were using. Little more than a decade ago, the technology available to teachers who wished to use more than the chalkboard was limited to an overhead projector, a 16-mm movie projector, a tape recorder, and, in a few forward-looking school districts, television sets.

MAKING *a DIFFERENCE*

Pia M. O'Leary
London, Ontario

Iwas born in Rome, Italy, of a French-Canadian mother and an Italian-German father. Thus, I am both a "new Canadian" and a descendant of seventeenth-century Acadians.

When I arrived in Montreal at the age of five, I spoke only Italian. By eight, when we settled in Toronto, I spoke only French. In 1979 I started the French-First language program at a high school. In 15 years I have seen it grow from one French course with 18 students and one dictionary to a full high school program involving ten French teachers.

Teaching French in a minority situation is quite a challenge. I was always looking for ways to make my classes interesting, challenging, and meaningful. The new français curriculum included media literacy with emphasis on the radio at the grade 11 level. Co-incidentally, a radio station at the University of Western Ontario offered its studios to various local community groups over the weekends. With the advice of two colleagues who had experience in professional radio I developed a unit which allows each of my grade 11 students to plan and produce a one-hour live radio program called *Paroles et Chansons*.

While becoming more discerning radio listeners my students realize the importance of clear and effective communication. French is now more than a school subject they have to pass; it is an important tool that they want to master. They are more interested in current issues and better acquainted with French popular music. They appreciate the importance of team work and deadlines. This valuable work experience develops their self-confidence and helps create an important link between the school and the French community of London, Ontario.

THE IMPACT OF THE TELEVISION REVOLUTION

Since the 1950s, television has become an omnipresent feature of life in Canada. Compared to the computer, television has had a longer and possibly a more predictable impact on education. In fact, the effects of the television revolution—both positive and negative—on all facets of Canadian life are still being studied, and for good reason. Children spend an estimated equivalent of two months of the year watching television.[19] The typical child between six and eleven years of age watches television about twenty-seven hours a week.

Critics of television point out that it encourages passivity in the young, may be linked to increases in violence and crime, often reinforces sexual and ethnic stereotypes, and retards growth and development. Some say that television robs children of the time they need to do homework, to read and reflect, and to build bonds with family members and others through interaction.

However, television can enhance students' learning. Excellent educational programs are aired by the Canadian Broadcasting Corporation and by some cable, nonprofit, and commercial networks. Television has also had a positive impact on how students are taught in schools. With the increased availability of video equipment, many schools have begun to have students produce their own television documentaries, news programs, oral histories, and dramas. Some high schools have closed-circuit television systems that teachers use to prepare instructional materials for students in the district.

Whatever the pros and cons, television is a permanent feature of modern life. It represents the explosion and globalization of knowledge and ideas. And it is clearly a primary source of students' orientations to their society and culture.

THE COMPUTER REVOLUTION

Instructional Uses of Computers   Since the early 1980s, the **microcomputer** has revolutionized classroom instruction. Instructional uses of computers include (1) record keeping through data banks and spread sheets; (2) electronic workbooks for drill and practice; (3) interactive simulations for self-directed study or problem solving; (4) word processing, involving all stages of the writing process; (5) programming, involving the development of logic and other higher cognitive functions; and (6) networking, in which teachers and students access information and communicate with others through telephone-linked computers.

Computer simulations and **networking** are particularly fascinating forms for instruction. Simulations range from the lemonade stand that elementary school students can plan and run vicariously, practicing basic arithmetic and problem-solving skills, to a mock trial in which law students can participate via videodisc and computer. Recently available are computer-based simulations that give students direct learning experiences, such as visiting the great museums of the world or the bottom of the Pacific Ocean.

Through networking, your students may create community electronic bulletin boards of their own and conduct computer conferences within the classroom or between different classes. Your students may even talk to students in other schools or different countries. Data bases and on-line experts in many fields may also change the way your students conduct research as more computerized reference works—such as directories, dictionaries, and encyclopedias—become available.

Advantages and Limitations of Computer-Assisted Instruction (CAI)   The computer revolution has clearly had an impact on education. Just how far-reaching and positive the effects have been is the subject of some debate. Early widespread excitement over the promise of the Computer Age has been tempered by practical concerns and occasional criticism. The Association for Supervision and Curriculum Development in the United States, for example, had this to say in late 1990: "Ten years after large numbers of microcomputers began appearing in U.S. classrooms, they have neither sparked a broad revolution in teaching and learning, as some advocates predicted, nor quietly faded into disuse. . . . [T]he organization and climate of most schools have yet to be changed in ways that allow teachers and students to truly take advantage of the technology's potential."[20] Table 15.1 presents several frequently voiced advantages of **computer-assisted instruction (CAI)**.

Implications of Computers for the Future   Concerns about the impact of the computer revolution on education have included images of dehumanized computer addicts—hackers—and fears of robots replacing teachers. However, computers probably have greater potential to transform education and society for the better. The following are some of the many predictions experts have offered about the likely or potential impacts of computers on teaching and learning:

- Greater individualization of instruction
- Advances in the education of children with special needs
- Diagnostic use of computers by teachers to identify learning problems
- Computer use for teacher-designed curriculum materials
- Computer use for routine tasks, giving teachers more time for students
- New teacher responsibilities as planners, coordinators, programmers, and managers
- Earlier development of students' competence as independent learners
- Stronger development of problem-solving and communication skills
- Greater development of cooperative learning modes
- Greater accumulation of, access to, and sharing of information
- Greater interest in linking together knowledge from different fields
- A democratization of the information explosion and the learning process

After all is said, we cannot underestimate the significance of the human dimension in the success of computer instruction. With any instructional media—textbooks, television, or computers—teachers have the power and opportunity to evaluate, select, and then use creatively and well the media that best suit the needs of their students and the goals of their educational programs.

CLASSROOM MEDIA MAGIC

Personal computers have so revolutionized the instructional media available to teachers that it is no exaggeration to refer to the "magic" of media. Some of the most exciting forms of media magic involve CD-ROMS, videodiscs, and interactive multimedia.

Today's book buyer can select from more than 800 000 titles. This enormous amount of information might prove overwhelming to anyone who wished to remain informed were it not for small compact discs known as **CD-ROMS**. One CD-

---

TABLE 15.1   Advantages of Computer-Assisted Instruction (CAI)

- Simply allowing students to learn at their own pace produces significant time savings over conventional classroom instruction. Computer-based instruction allows students some control over the rate and sequence of their learning (individualization).
- High-speed personalized responses to learner actions yield a high rate of reinforcement.
- The patient, personal manner that can be programmed provides a more positive affective climate, especially for slower learners. Mistakes, which are inevitable, are not exposed to peers and therefore are not as embarrassing.
- Computer-assisted instruction is effective with special learners—at-risk students, students from diverse ethnic backgrounds, and disabled students—because their special needs can be accommodated and instruction proceeds at an appropriate pace.
- Color, music, and animated graphics can add realism and appeal to drill exercises, laboratory activities, simulations, and so on.
- The record-keeping ability of the computer makes individualized instruction feasible; individual prescriptions can be prepared for all students (particularly mainstreamed special students), and their progress can be monitored.
- Computers can provide coverage of a growing knowledge base associated with the information explosion. They can manage all types of information: graphic, text, audio, and video. More information is put easily at the instructor's disposal. Computers also provide a broad diversity of learning experiences. These learning experiences can utilize a variety of instructional methods and can be at the basic instruction, remedial, or enrichment level.
- The computer provides reliable and consistent instruction from learner to learner, regardless of the teacher or trainer, the time of the day, or the location.
- Computer-based instruction can improve efficiency and effectiveness. Effectiveness refers to improved learner achievement whereas efficiency means achieving objectives in less time or at lower cost. Efficiency is very important in business and industrial applications and is becoming increasingly important in educational settings.
- One serendipitous effect of working with computers is that they force us to communicate with them in an orderly and logical way. The computer user must learn to communicate with explicit, exact instructions and responses. Any departure from precision is rejected by the computer.
- Computer users learn keyboarding or typing skills. Now very young children as well as adults are developing these skills in order to communicate with computers.
- With the advent of easy-to-use authoring systems, some instructors can develop their own customized computer-based learning programs.

Which advantages of CAI do you regard as most important? Identify some potential limitations of CAI for students, for teachers, and for schools.

Source: Robert Heinich, Michael Molenda, and James D. Russell, *Instructional Media and the New Technologies of Instruction,* 4th ed. (New York: Macmillan, 1993), pp. 223–224. Used by permission of the publisher of Macmillan College Publishing Company, Inc.

ROM can hold the equivalent of about 270 000 pages of text, or about 900 300-page books. References to any topic in the 270 000 pages can be found in less than thirty seconds. Currently, most CD-ROMs contain reference works such as encyclopedias, dictionaries, and the works of William Shakespeare, but new titles are rapidly becoming available.

Videodiscs   **Videodiscs** are discs that resemble the smaller CD-ROMs. They show still and moving pictures on a television screen and have much higher quality sound and image than videotapes. A disc can hold the equivalent of 54 000 photographic slides on each side, and the user can freeze any of the images.

What is the role of the teacher in this classroom? How can teachers capitalize on communications technology as an instructional resource?

Computer-supported **interactive multimedia** allow the user to integrate huge libraries of text, audio, and video information.

> Imagine a classroom with a window on all the world's knowledge. Imagine a teacher with the capability to bring to life any image, any sound, any event. Imagine a student with the power to visit any place on earth at any time in history. Imagine a screen that can display in vivid color the inner workings of a cell, the births and deaths of stars, the clashes of armies, and the triumphs of art. And then imagine that you have access to all of this and more by exerting little more effort than simply asking that it appear.[21]

Hypermedia   Recent advances in computer technology have made it possible for students to become much more active in shaping their learning experiences. **Hypermedia** systems consisting of computer, CD-ROM drive, videodisc player, video monitor, and speakers now allow students to control and present sound, video images, text, and graphics with an almost limitless array of possibilities. Students who use such systems can follow their curiosity, browse through enormous amounts of information, and develop creative solutions for multidimensional, real-life problems.

The term *hypermedia* refers to " 'nonsequential documents' composed of text, audio, and visual information stored in a computer, with the computer being used to link and annotate related chunks of information into larger networks or

EDUCATION IN THE NEWS

When is a School a School?

Two Alberta schools are demonstrating novel approaches to budget cutbacks. The Workplace School, the first of its kind in Canada, began in 1995. Alberta Government Telephones Ltd., Alberta's privately owned telephone company, pledged to donate 7000 square feet on the main floor of its office tower in downtown Calgary to house the school. They also pledged $200 000 to renovate the space to house the K-3 programs and another $30 000 to cover overhead expenses. The school board agreed to pay for the teachers and teaching supplies.

Parents who live in the suburbs of Calgary usually drive to work while their children are bused to school. Parents of students in the Workplace School drive to work with their children, drop them off at school on the main floor of the office tower, and take an elevator to work. They can eat lunch with their children and talk easily and frequently with their children's teachers. Teachers can use museums and theaters to augment the curriculum. The school board saves on busing, operating costs, and capital costs, while AGT saves on decreased employee absenteeism and higher worker morale.

Another school opened at the Calgary Zoo in 1995 as a result of budget cutbacks. "School Week at the Zoo" is the first of its kind in North America. With substantial private donations, two teachers were hired to guide elementary students through a one-week program at the zoo. Children spend a week in classes at the zoo and cover regular curriculum content. The zoo facility enables teachers to offer the curriculum in a different way.

Children study arithmetic and tackle problems such as determining the size of animal cages, observing orangutan behavior, determining the species of tropical butterflies, and observing slender-tailed meerkats. Children are much more spontaneous at the zoo than in regular classrooms. What better partnership could be created for the weekdays when the zoo is often mostly empty?

Source: Based on the *Globe and Mail*, Jan. 6, Mar. 15, 1995.

---

webs."[22] Hypermedia is an effective learning tool because it allows students to actively construct their own learning experiences based on their interests, preferences, and learning styles.

HOW CAN TEACHERS AND STUDENTS PREPARE FOR AN UNKNOWN FUTURE?

When you think about your future as a teacher, that future may seem at once exciting and frightening, enticing and threatening. How, you may ask, can I meet the many educational challenges identified in this book? In a very real sense, it is in the hands of persons such as yourself to shape with vision and commitment the profession of tomorrow. You must work toward the future you desire. The following "Professional Reflection" is designed to help you begin the process of planning for that future.

TOMORROW'S STUDENTS: WHAT WILL THEY NEED TO KNOW?

In light of the new patterns and trends discussed in this chapter, what knowledge and skills will prepare students to respond intelligently to an unknown future? In particular, teachers of the future will need to dedicate themselves to ensuring that all students address nine educational priorities (see Figure 15.2). Though these nine areas of learning will not be all that students will need, these areas will best enable them to meet the challenges of the future.

PROFESSIONAL REFLECTION

Following is a list of educational innovations and trends that are shaping tomorrow's classrooms. For each item, indicate with an X whether you are "highly committed," "somewhat committed," "opposed," or "neutral" toward having that innovation or trend characterize your teaching. Space is provided for you to add items not on the list.

After responding to the items, reflect on those to which you are "highly committed." What steps will you take from this point on to ensure that these items will in fact characterize your future in teaching? Next, imagine hypothetical scenarios that describe your future in teaching five, ten, and fifteen years from now. How will these items be reflected in your professional life as a teacher?

Innovation/Trend	Highly Committed	Somewhat Committed	Opposed	Neutral
1. Alternative/authentic assessment of students' learning	___	___	___	___
2. Cross-age tutoring/mentoring	___	___	___	___
3. Peer counseling/peer coaching	___	___	___	___
4. Staff teams/team teaching	___	___	___	___
5. School houses	___	___	___	___
6. Business-school partnerships	___	___	___	___
7. Community-school teaming	___	___	___	___
8. Year-round schools	___	___	___	___
9. School restructuring	___	___	___	___
10. Open enrollment/school choice	___	___	___	___
11. Telephones in the classroom	___	___	___	___
12. Student computer networking	___	___	___	___
13. Video teleconferencing	___	___	___	___
14. CD-ROMs/videodiscs	___	___	___	___
15. Interactive multimedia/hypermedia	___	___	___	___
16. Sex education	___	___	___	___
17. AIDS education	___	___	___	___
18. Moral orientation on curricula	___	___	___	___
19. Globalism/multiculturalism	___	___	___	___
20. Aesthetics orientation	___	___	___	___
21. Alcohol and drug intervention	___	___	___	___
22. Reduction of gender bias	___	___	___	___

23. Reduction of racial/ethnic prejudice   ___ ___ ___ ___
24. Teacher empowerment   ___ ___ ___ ___
25. Constructivist approaches to teaching   ___ ___ ___ ___
26. Charter schools   ___ ___ ___ ___
27. Corporate-education partnerships   ___ ___ ___ ___
28. _____   ___ ___ ___ ___
29. _____   ___ ___ ___ ___
30. _____   ___ ___ ___ ___

Literacy in Language, Mathematics, and Science   To solve the problems of the future, students will need to be able to use written and spoken language to communicate clearly and succinctly. Moreover, students will continue to need to be able to read the printed word with a high degree of comprehension. Students will also need to be able to apply mathematical and scientific concepts to solve new problems. For example, they will need to be able to pose questions, analyze situations, translate results, illustrate results, draw diagrams, and use appropriate trial-and-error methods.

New Technological Skills   Students of the future will need to understand the potentialities (as well as the limitations) of computer-based technologies. All students should acquire skills in accessing the vast stores of information that computers are routinely capable of handling today. To achieve this goal, Canada's schools will become more technologically rich, and teachers will become more sophisticated in using various technologies. In short, "the computer can and should come to be as commonplace as the pencil."[23]

Problem Solving and Critical Thinking Skills   Students of the future will need to be able to think rather than to remember. Although the information that students learn in schools may become outdated or useless, the thinking processes they acquire will not. These processes focus on the ability to find, obtain, and use information resources for solving problems or taking advantage of opportunities. Students will need to learn how to cope with change, how to anticipate alternative future developments, how to think critically and creatively, and how to analyze and synthesize large amounts of complex data.[24]

Social Awareness and Communication Skills   Tomorrow's students must be able to communicate with people from many cultures. The ability to create a better world in the future will surely depend on our willingness to celebrate our rich diversity through the kind of communication that leads to understanding and friendly social relations.

An important lesson for students will be to learn that poverty, discrimination, crime, and unequal opportunities, wherever they occur, affect us all. To solve these and other social problems, students will need to become socially aware, politically active, and skilled in conflict resolution strategies.

Global Awareness and Conservation Skills   Tomorrow's students will need to recognize the interconnectedness they share with all countries and with all people. Our

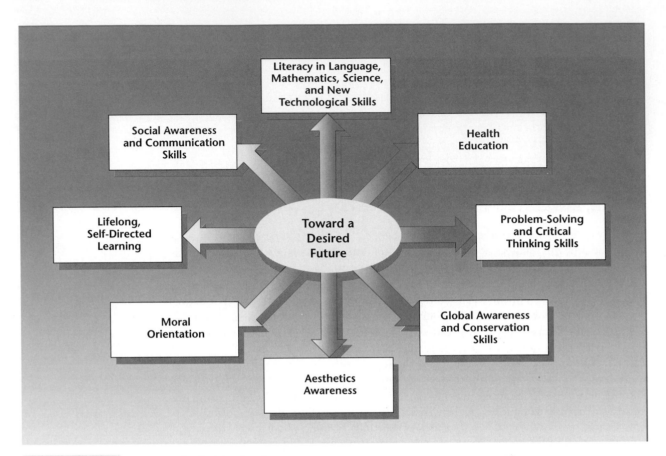

FIGURE 15.2   Educational Priorities for the Future

survival may depend on being able to participate intelligently in a global economy and to respond intelligently to global threats to security, health, environmental quality, and other factors that affect the quality of human life. The curriculum of the future must emphasize cultural diversity, interdependence, respect for the views and values held by others, an orientation toward international cooperation for resolving global issues, and practical knowledge and skills on, for example, the conservation of natural energy resources.

Health Education   With ever-increasing health care costs, the spread of diseases such as AIDS, increased risks of cancer, and longer life spans, it is imperative that students of the future acquire knowledge and skills in the area of health education. To live healthy lives, students of tomorrow will need consumer education to choose from among an increasingly complex array of health care services. In addition, they will need to be able to make informed choices among alternatives for the prevention or treatment of problems relating to substance abuse, nutrition, fitness, and mental health. Sex education, still a matter of debate in some communities, seems more critical today than at any time in the past.

Moral Orientation   School culture and the curriculum reflect both regional and community values. The traditional practice of using values-clarification activities in the classroom has been criticized by some for promoting relativism at the expense of family values or religious doctrines. Yet, as we witness the effects of family violence, sexual exploitation of children, drunk driving, false advertising, unethical business practices, and so on, many Canadians are calling for schools to pay more attention to issues of public morality.

The continuing challenge for teachers and schools will be to find ways to address these issues that are both effective with students and acceptable to their parents. At the least, teachers help students develop a moral orientation by modeling behavior, encouraging students to clarify their values, and giving students opportunities to learn respect for themselves and others, as well as for property and laws.

Aesthetics Awareness   Another challenge for teachers and schools is to encourage creativity and greater appreciation for the arts. Many observers of Canadian education point out that emotional, spiritual, aesthetic, and reflective or meditative dimensions of life receive less emphasis than analytical thinking and life skills. Although literature and drama are standard fare in curricula, most students know little, for example, about music, painting, and sculpture. Public school students are rarely taught art history or principles of design or other criteria for evaluating creative works. As a result, students may lack the concepts and experiences that lead to an appreciation of beauty and the development of aesthetic judgment.

Lifelong, Self-Directed Learning   The key educational priority that should guide teachers of the future is to create within each student the ability and the desire to continue self-directed learning throughout his or her life.

It has often been said that one of the primary purposes of schooling is for students to learn how to learn. In a world characterized by rapid social, technological, economic, and political changes, all persons must take responsibility for their own learning. Career changes will be the norm, and continuing education over a lifetime will be necessary.

A VISION OF THE FUTURE

Imagine that it is the year 2020 and we are visiting Westside Elementary School, a school in a medium-sized city in a western province. All of the teachers at Westside have been certified by the Provincial Teachers' Board, a licensing agency similar to those that certify that lawyers and medical doctors are competent to practice. The salaries of board-certified teachers are on a par with those of other professionals with comparable education and training. About half of the fifty-five teachers at Westside have also earned the advanced professional certificate offered by the Board. These teachers are known as lead teachers and may earn as much as $125 000 per year. Westside has no principal; the school is run by an executive committee of five lead teachers elected by all teachers at the school. One of these lead teachers is elected to serve as committee chair for a two-year period.

All other school personnel are in subordinate positions and have as their primary task supporting the efforts of teachers. Teacher's aides, technicians, and clerical workers, for example, are available for all teachers. In addition, the school has several paid interns and residents who are assigned to lead teachers as part of their graduate-level teacher preparation program. Each intern and resident has a bachelor's degree in the arts and sciences.

Westside's day-to-day operations are handled by several personnel who are accountable to the executive committee. These persons include a business manager, school accountant, and program administrator. Finally, teachers are assisted by such ancillary staff as a learning-style diagnostician; hypermedia specialist; computer specialist; video specialist; social worker; school psychologist; four counselors; special remediation teachers in reading, writing, mathematics, and oral communication; ESL teachers; and special needs teachers.

Westside Elementary operates many programs that illustrate the close ties the school has developed with parents, community agencies, and businesses. The school houses a daycare center that provides after-school employment for several students from the nearby high school. On weekends and on Monday, Wednesday, and Friday evenings the school is used for adult education and by various community groups. Executives from three local businesses spend one day a month at the school visiting with classes and telling students about their work. Students from a nearby university participate in a tutoring program at Westside, and the university has several on-campus summer enrichment programs for Westside students.

Westside has a school-based health clinic that offers health care services and a counseling center that provides individual and family counseling. In addition, from time to time Westside teachers and students participate in service-learning activities in the community. Currently, for example, the grade five classes are helping the city develop a new recycling program.

All the facilities at Westside—the classrooms, library, multimedia learning center, gymnasium, cafeteria, and private offices for teachers—have been designed to create a teaching/learning environment free of health and safety hazards. The cafeteria, for example, serves meals based on findings from nutrition research about the best foods and methods of cooking. The school is carpeted, and classrooms are soundproofed and well lit. Throughout, the walls are painted in soft pastels accented with potted plants, paintings, wall hangings, and large murals depicting life in different cultures.

The dress, language, and behaviors of teachers, students, and support personnel at Westside reflect a rich array of cultural backgrounds. In the cafeteria, for example, it is impossible not to hear several languages being spoken and to see at least a few students and teachers wearing non-Western clothing. From the displays of students' work on bulletin boards in hallways and in classrooms to the international menu offered in the cafeteria, there is ample evidence that Westside is truly a multicultural school and that gender, race, and class biases have been eliminated.

Each teacher at Westside is a member of a teaching team and spends at least part of his or her teaching time working with other members of the team. Furthermore, teachers determine their schedules and every effort is made to assign teachers according to their particular teaching expertise. Likewise, students are assigned to learning groups according to their preferred modes of learning. Those teachers who work well with large groups, for example, are assigned students who learn well in such situations. Other teachers, whose strengths lie in organizing and managing small groups, work with students who learn best in small groups that give them opportunities for student-teacher and student-student interactions. Students attend Westside by choice for its excellent teachers; its curricular emphasis on problem solving, human relations, creative thinking, and critical thinking; and its programs for helping at-risk students achieve academic success.

Instruction at Westside is supplemented by the latest technologies. The school subscribes to several computer data bases and cable television services, which teachers and students use regularly. The hypermedia learning center has an extensive collection of CD-ROMs and computer software, much of it written by Westside teachers. The center also has virtual-reality interactive videodisc systems, workstations equipped with the latest robotics, and an extensive lab with voice-activated computers. The computer-supported interactive multimedia in the center use the CD-ROM format and the more advanced Integrated Services Digital Network (ISDN) delivery system based on the optical fiber.

Every classroom has a video camera, fax machine, hypermedia system, and telephone that, in addition to everyday use, are used frequently during satellite video teleconferences with business executives, artists, scientists, scholars, and students at schools in other provinces and countries. Each student has a laptop computer that he or she routinely uses for drill and practice and for homework. Westside Elementary's technological capabilities permit students to move their education beyond the classroom walls; they determine much of how, when, where, and what they learn.

TOMORROW'S TEACHER

Teaching and the conditions under which teachers work may change in some fundamental and positive ways during the next two decades. Teaching will become increasingly professionalized, for example, through such changes as more lengthy and rigorous preprofessional training programs, greater teacher autonomy, and an expanded role for teachers in educational policy-making. There will be more teachers who are members of minority groups. There will be greater recognition for high-performing teachers and schools through such mechanisms as merit pay plans, master teacher programs, and career ladders. According to Forecasting International, Ltd., tomorrow's teachers will achieve new and higher levels of specialization. The traditional teaching job will be divided into parts, such as the following:

- Learning diagnostician
- Researcher for software programs
- Courseware writer
- Curriculum designer
- Mental-health diagnostician
- Evaluator of learning performances
- Evaluator of social skills
- Small-group learning facilitator
- Large-group learning facilitator
- Media-instruction producer
- Home-based instruction designer
- Home-based instruction monitor

Though we cannot claim to have handed you an educational crystal ball so that you can ready yourself for the future, we hope you have gained both knowledge and inspiration from our observations in this chapter. Certainly, visions of the future, such as the one of Westside Elementary, will not become a reality without a lot of dedication and hard work. The creation of schools like Westside will require commitment and vision on the part of professional teachers like you.

PROFESSIONAL PORTFOLIO

For this portfolio entry, prepare a catalogue of interactive multimedia resources and materials (hardware, software, etc.) that you will use as a teacher. Annotate each entry by briefly describing the resource materials, how you will use them, and where they may be obtained. As with the selection of any curriculum materials, try to find evidence of effectiveness such as the results of field tests, published reviews of multimedia programs, and testimonials from local educators.

CHAPTER SUMMARY

Though no one can predict the future, an analysis of current social, economic, technological, and political forces and trends does suggest several possible futures for teaching. In regard to these possible futures, teachers have two choices: (1) to *react* in an unfocused manner to the forces and trends that shape the teaching profession or (2) to plan in order to create a desired future for the profession. To move toward a desired future, teachers should become familiar with the complexities and requirements of implementing change in schools.

Among the recent developments that have increased our understanding of the learning process are advances in brain research (neurophysiology) and cognitive sciences. New trends in educational theory and practice such as contingent teaching, constructivist views of learning, and alternative and authentic approaches to assessing students' learning have also enabled teachers to create more effective learning environments for students. The teaching profession is also being transformed by new roles for teachers and students that are reflected in such practices as peer counseling, peer coaching, staff teams, school houses, and charter schools. In addition, new partnerships are being developed between schools and communities. Through these partnerships, the community is serving as a resource for the schools, and the schools are serving as a resource for the community.

We live in an Information Age, and, clearly, the television and computer revolutions have had a significant impact on teaching and learning. Exciting changes are taking place in classrooms as a result of computer-assisted technologies such as CD-ROMs, videodiscs, interactive multimedia, and hypermedia.

Because one of the central tasks of schools is to prepare students to solve problems in the future, teachers must ask themselves, "What will students need to know in the future?" Although such a question is not easily answered, schools and teachers should address nine educational priorities:

1. Literacy in language, mathematics, and science
2. New technological skills
3. Problem solving and critical thinking skills
4. Social awareness and communication skills
5. Global awareness and conservation skills
6. Health education
7. Moral orientation
8. Aesthetics awareness
9. Lifelong, self-directed learning

To conclude our brief survey of teaching and the challenges of the future, it is possible to imagine that teachers in the year 2020 will be well-paid, highly trained, self-governing professionals. Moreover, that vision becomes even more possible with each teacher who makes the decision to work toward attaining that future.

KEY TERMS AND CONCEPTS

alternative assessments, 380
authentic assessments, 380
CD-ROMs, 388
charter schools, 382
cognitive science, 378
computer-assisted instruction (CAI), 388
computer simulations, 387
contingent teaching, 379

constructivist view of learning, 379
futurism, 374
hypermedia, 390
information processing, 379
interactive multimedia, 390
learning, 378
microcomputer, 387
networking, 387

peer coaching, 381
peer counseling, 381
school houses, 382
staff teams, 381
videodiscs, 389
zone of proximal development, 379

APPLICATIONS AND ACTIVITIES

Teacher's Journal

1. Write a scenario forecasting how the teaching profession will change over the next two decades.
2. Choose one of the following areas and develop several forecasts for changes that will occur over the next two decades: energy, environment, food, the economy, governance, family structure, demographics, global relations, media, and technology. On what current data are your forecasts based?
3. Describe a team strategy or partnership you participated in as a student sometime in the past. What aspects of the relationship made your experience helpful or unhelpful to you?
4. In your opinion, what is the most important benefit of the computer revolution for education, and what is the most important potential drawback?
5. Think about two children you know and project them into the future, twenty years from now. What skills are they likely to need? Which talents should help them? List three of these and then consider the ways that today's schools can better promote their development.

Field Assignments

1. Interview the principal at a local or nearby school and ask him or her to describe the school in ten

years. Now interview several teachers at the school. Compare the principal's forecasts with the teachers'. What might account for any differences you find?
2. Search for examples of school-community partnership arrangements in the local school district. Find out how these partnerships are progressing and propose a specific new one based on your knowledge of the community.
3. Sample computer software in a subject area and grade level that interest you. Which programs would you prefer to use in your classroom and why?
4. Read recent professional journals to discover current areas of innovation in education. Choose one innovation that especially interests you to examine more fully and report to the class what you learn.
5. Taking turns with a partner as teacher and learner, develop role-plays illustrating the new teaching techniques and teacher-learner relationships described in this chapter. Present your role-plays to the class.
6. Working with a small group of classmates, choose specific instructional content, such as map reading or cell biology, and brainstorm ideas for alternative, authentic ways in which to assess student learning in that subject.

Notes

CHAPTER 1

1. Lucianne Bond Carmichael, *McDonogh 15: The Making of a School* (New York: Avon Books, 1981), p. 113.
2. *The Metropolitan Life Survey of the American Teacher 1992, The Second Year: New Teachers' Expectations and Ideals* (New York: Louis Harris and Associates), Foreword.
3. John Godar, *Teachers Talk* (Macomb, Ill.: Glenbridge Publishing, 1990), p. 15.
4. Cecelia Traugh, Rhoda Kanevsky, Anne Martin, Alice Seletsky, Karen Woolf, and Lynne Strieb, *Speaking Out: Teachers on Teaching* (Grand Forks: University of North Dakota, 1986), p. 53.
5. John Barth, "Teacher," in *An Apple for My Teacher*, ed. Louis Rubin (Chapel Hill, N.C.: Algonquin Books, 1987), p. 166.
6. John Godar, *Teachers Talk*, p. 244.
7. Eliot Wigginton, *Sometimes a Shining Moment* (Garden City, N.Y.: Anchor Press, 1985).
8. Benjamin Wright and Shirley Tuska, "From Dream to Life in the Psychology of Becoming a Teacher," *School Review* (September 1968): 253–293.
9. Benjamin Wright and Shirley Tuska, "How Does Childhood Make a Teacher?" *The Elementary School Journal* (February 1965): 235–246.
10. Dan C. Lortie, "Observations on Teaching as Work," in *Second Handbook of Research on Teaching*, ed. R. M. W. Travers (Chicago: Rand McNally, 1973), pp. 474–497.
11. Statistics Canada, "Survey of 1990 Graduates" (Education, Culture and Tourism Division, June, 1992).
12. Dan C. Lortie, *Schoolteacher: A Sociological Study* (Chicago: University of Chicago Press, 1975), p. 39.
13. Ibid., p. 39.
14. Bill D. Moyers, *A World of Ideas: Conversations with Thoughtful Men and Women* (New York: Doubleday, 1989), p. 161.
15. Carol Livingston, *Teachers as Leaders: Evolving Roles* (Washington, D.C.: National Education Association), p. 10.
16. Arthur W. Combs, *A Personal Approach to Teaching: Beliefs That Make a Difference* (Boston: Allyn and Bacon, 1982), p. 75.
17. Arthur Jersild, *When Teachers Face Themselves* (New York: Teachers College Press, 1955), p. 83.
18. SRI Perceivers Academies, P.O. Box 5758, Lincoln, Nebraska 68505 U.S.A.
19. "Job Relatedness Analysis Report for the Position of Elementary Teacher in Washington County" (Washington County School District, Chipley, Fla., n.d., mimeographed).
20. "Trying to Teach." (The Alberta Teachers' Association: January, 1993).
21. Teacher education programs at Washington State University, Stanford University, University of Dayton, University of West Florida, Azusa Pacific University, Washburn University, Wichita State University, and University of Houston are among those that have begun to use portfolios to assess candidates' abilities.

CHAPTER 2

1. Shirley F. Heck and C. Ray Williams, *The Complex Roles of the Teacher: An Ecological Perspective* (New York: Teachers College Press, 1984), p. xv.
2. Ann Lieberman and Lynne Miller, "Teacher Development in Professional Practice School," *Teachers College Record* (Fall 1990): 112.
3. Ibid.
4. Haim Ginott, *Teacher and Child* (New York: Avon Books, 1972), p. 15.
5. Roland Barth, *Improving Schools from Within* (San Francisco: Jossey-Bass, 1990), p. 211.
6. Tom Peters and Nancy Austin, *A Passion for Excellence* (New York: Random House, 1984), p. 414.
7. David E. Denton, *Existential Reflections on Teaching* (North Quincy, Mass.: Christopher Publishing House, 1972), p. 37.
8. Shirley F. Heck and C. Ray Williams, *The Complex Roles of the Teacher*, p. 5.
9. Ann Lieberman and Lynne Miller, *Teachers, Their World, and Their Work* (Alexandria, Va.: Association for Supervision and Curriculum Development, 1984), pp. 4–5.
10. Shirley F. Heck and C. Ray Williams, *The Complex Roles of the Teacher*, p. 189.
11. Sybil Marshall, *An Experiment in Education* (London: Cambridge University Press, 1963), p. 41.
12. John Holt, *How Children Fail* (New York: Dell, 1982), p. 281.
13. Patrick Welsh, *Tales out of School* (New York: Elisabeth Sifton Books, Penguin Books, 1987), p. 153.

14. Herbert Kohl, *36 Children* (New York: New American Library, 1967).

15. Herbert Kohl, *Growing Minds: On Becoming a Teacher* (New York: Harper and Row, 1984), p. 7.

16. Torey Hayden, *Somebody Else's Kids* (New York: Avon Books, 1981), p. 314.

17. Sara Lawrence Lightfoot, *The Good High School* (New York: Basic Books, 1983), pp. 355–356.

18. As reported in *Chicago Union Teacher* (March 1978).

19. Philip Jackson, "The Way Teaching Is," *NEA Journal* (November 1965): 62.

20. John Canfield, "White Teacher, Black School," in *Don't Smile Until Christmas: Accounts of the First Year of Teaching,* ed. Kevin Ryan (Chicago: University of Chicago Press, 1970), p. 43.

21. Philip Jackson, *Life in Classrooms* (New York: Holt, Rinehart and Winston, 1968), p. 166.

22. Dan C. Lortie, *Schoolteacher: A Sociological Study* (Chicago: The University of Chicago Press, 1975), p. 146.

23. Marilyn M. Cohn and Robert B. Kottkamp, *Teachers: The Missing Voice in Education* (Albany: State University of New York Press, 1983), pp. 42–43.

24. Dan C. Lortie, *Schoolteacher: A Sociological Study,* p. 143.

25. Arthur L. Costa, "A Reaction to Hunter's Knowing, Teaching, and Supervising," in *Using What We Know about Teaching,* ed. Philip L. Hosford (Alexandria, Va.: Association for Supervision and Curriculum Development, 1984), p. 202.

26. John Dewey, "The Relation of Theory to Practice in Education," in *The Third Yearbook of the National Society for the Scientific Study of Education,* Part I (Bloomington, Ind.: Public School Publishing Company, 1904), pp. 13–14.

27. Walter Doyle, "Classroom Organization and Management," in *Handbook of Research on Teaching,* 3d ed., ed. Merlin C. Wittrock (New York: Macmillan, 1986), p. 395.

28. John Dewey, *How We Think: A Restatement of the Relation of Reflective Thinking to the Educative Process* (Boston: D.C. Heath, 1933), pp. 35–36.

29. Arthur Combs, *Myths in Education: Beliefs That Hinder Progress and Their Alternatives* (Boston: Allyn and Bacon, 1979), pp. 234–235.

30. Bruce Joyce and Marsha Weil, *Models of Teaching,* 3d ed. (Englewood Cliffs, N. J.: Prentice Hall, 1986), p. 404.

31. Albert Bandura, *Social Learning Theory* (Englewood Cliffs, N.J.: Prentice Hall, 1977), p. 12.

32. See Chapter 13 for discussion of the hidden curriculum in classrooms.

33. Max van Manen, *The Tact of Teaching: The Meaning of Pedagogical Thoughtfulness* (Albany: State University of New York Press, 1991), p. 167.

34. Marilyn M. Cohn and Robert B. Kottkamp, *Teachers: The Missing Voice in Education,* p. 42.

35. Inscription on public building in India.

36. Philip Jackson, *Life in Classrooms,* p. 152.

37. Forrest W. Parkay, *White Teacher, Black School: The Professional Growth of a Ghetto Teacher* (New York: Praeger, 1983), p. 47.

38. Jackson, *Life in Classrooms,* p. 119.

39. Statistics Canada, *Education Statistics Bulletin.* (Ottawa: Ministry of Industry, Science and Technology, February 1994).

CHAPTER 3

1. Rita Silverman, William M. Welthy, and Sally Lyon, *Case Studies for Teacher Problem Solving* (New York, McGraw-Hill, 1992), pp. 45–46.

2. National Board for Professional Teaching Standards, *Toward High and Rigorous Standards for the Teaching Profession: Initial Policies and Perspectives of the National Board for Professional Teaching Standards,* 3d ed. (Detroit: Author, 1991), p. 13.

3. Arthur Jersild, *When Teachers Face Themselves* (New York: Teachers College Press, 1955), p. 3.

4. Anne Lieberman and Lynne Miller, *Teachers, Their World, and Their Work* (Alexandria, Va.: Association for Supervision and Curriculum Development, 1984), pp. 43–44.

5. Jean V. Carew and Sara Lawrence Lightfoot, *Beyond Bias: Perspectives on Classrooms* (Cambridge, Mass.: Harvard University Press, 1979), p. 19.

6. National Board for Professional Teaching Standards, *Toward High and Rigorous Standards for the Teaching Profession: Initial Policies and Perspectives for the National Board for Professional Teaching Standards,* 3d ed., pp. 13–14.

7. Ibid. p. 14.

8. Quoted in A. J. Marrow, *The Practical Theorist: The Life and Work of Kurt Lewin* (New York: Basic Books, 1969).

9. Barak Rosenshine, "Explicit Teaching." In *Talks to Teachers,* eds. David Berliner and Barak Rosenshine (New York, Random House, 1988), p. 75–92.

10. Barak Rosenshine, "The Use of Scaffolds for Teaching Higher-Level Cognitive Strategies," *Educational Leadership* (April 1992): p. 27.

11. Ibid p. 33.

12. Robert V. Bullough, Jr., *First-Year Teacher: A Case Study* (New York: Teachers College Press, 1989), p. 141.

13. Judith Lanier and Judith Little, "Research on Teacher Education" in *Handbook of Research on Teaching,* ed. Merlin C. Wittrock (New York: Macmillan, 1986), p. 547.

14. Donald R. Cruickshank, *Reflective Teaching: The Preparation of Students of Teaching* (Reston, Va.: Association of Teacher Educators), p. 3.

15. Andrew I. Schwebal, Bernice L. Schwebel, Carol R. Schwebel, and Milton Schwebel, *The Student Teacher's Handbook,* 2d ed. (Hillsdale, N.J.: Lawrence Erlbaum, 1992), p. 5.

16. From George J. Posner, *Field Experience: Methods of Reflective Teaching,* 2e. (New York: Longman, 1989), p. 34. Reprinted with permission by Longman Publishers USA.

17. Leslie Huling-Austin, "Teacher Induction Programs and Internships," in *Handbook of Research on Teacher Education,* ed. W. Robert Houston (New York: Macmillan, 1990), p. 539.

CHAPTER 4

1. Statistics Canada, *Elementary-Secondary School Enrolment 1991-92* (Ottawa, October 1993), Catalogue Number 81-210.

2. Statistics Canada, *The Elementary-Secondary Teaching Force* (Ottawa, February 1994), Catalogue Number 81-002 (16) 2.

3. *Teacher Recruitment and Retention: How Canadian School Boards Attract Teachers. A Report.* (Toronto: Canadian Education Association, 1992).

4. Ibid., p. 3.

5. S.M. Barro and L. Suter, *International comparisons of teachers' salaries: An exploratory study.* (Washington DC: SMB Economic Center for Education Statistics, 1988).

6. John William Zehring, "How to Get Another Teaching Job and What to Do If You Can't," *Learning* (February 1978): 49.

7. C. Bruce Johnston, Michael A. Morehead, and Carter Burns, *1992 ASCUS Annual: The Job Search Handbook for Educators* (Evanston, Ill.: Association for School, College and University Staffing), pp. 23–24. Used with permission.

8. Excerpted from *The 1985 Annual Report of the Commissioner of Education: Getting Ready for 1989* (Tallahassee, Fla.: Department of Education, 1985), p. 15.

9. *Gainesville Sun* (22 December 1985), p. 14G.

10. Claude N. Goldberg, "Parents' Effects on Academic Grouping for Reading: Three Case Studies," *American Education Research Journal* (Fall 1989): 329–352.

11. See, for example, Barbara L. Jackson and Bruce S. Cooper, "Involving Parents in Urban Schools," *NASSP Bulletin* (April 1992): 30–38; and James P. Comer, "Parent Participation in the Schools," *Phi Delta Kappan* (February 1986): 442–446.

12. *What Works: Research About Teaching and Learning* (Washington, D.C.: U.S. Department of Education, 1986), p. 19.

13. Anne Miller, "Those Who Teach Also Can Sell, Organize, Compute, Write, Market, Design, Manage . . ." *Instructor* (May 1983): 42.

CHAPTER 5

1. Aristotle, *Politics* (Book VIII), in *The Basic Works of Aristotle*, ed. Richard McKoen (New York: Random House, 1941), p. 1306.

2. H.J. Robertson. "Is There a National Role in Education? A Rationale for the Obvious." In *Is There a National Role in Education?* eds. P. Nagy and J. Lupart (Ottawa: Canadian Education Association, 1994).

3. Vito Perrone, *A Letter to Teachers: Reflections on Schooling and the Art of Teaching* (San Francisco: Jossey-Bass, 1991), p. 1.

4. R. Ghosh and D. Ray, *Social Change and Education in Canada,* 2nd ed. (Toronto: Harcourt Brace Jovanovich, 1991).

5. J. P. Spradley and D. W. McCurdy, *Anthropology: The Cultural Perspective* (New York: John Wiley and Sons, 1975), p. 5.

6. W. H. Goodenough, *Cultural Anthropology and Linguistics,* Georgetown University Monograph Series on Language and Linguistics, no. 9 (1957), p. 167.

7. R. A. LeVine, "Properties of Culture: An Ethnographic View," in *Culture Theory: Essays on Mind; Self and Emotion,* eds. R. A. Sweder and R. A. LeVine (Cambridge, England: Cambridge University Press, 1986).

8. H. C. Triandis, "Culture Training, Cognitive Complexity and Interpersonal Attitudes," in *Cross-Cultural Perspectives on Learning,* eds. R. W. Brislin, Stephen Bachner, and Walter J. Lonner (New York: John Wiley and Sons, 1975).

9. Peter I. Rose, *They and We: Racial and Ethnic Relations in the United States,* 2d ed. (New York; Random House, 1974), p. 13.

10. Ellen K. Coughlin, "Sociologists Examine the Complexities of Racial and Ethnic Identity in America," *The Chronicle of Higher Education* (March 24, 1993): A7.

11. Ibid.

12. A. Fleras and J.L. Elliott, *The challenge of diversity: Multiculturalism in Canada.* (Scarborough: Nelson, 1992).

13. *The American Heritage Dictionary of the English Language,* ed. William Morris (Boston: American Heritage Publishing Co. and Houghton Mifflin, 1970), p. 680.

14. Gerald Grant, *The World We Created at Hamilton High* (Cambridge, Mass.: Harvard University Press, 1988), pp. 188–189.

15. John I. Goodlad, *A Place Called School: Prospects for the Future* (New York: McGraw-Hill, 1984), p. 227.

16. Jack Frymier, Catherine Cornbleth, Robert Donmoyer, Bruce M. Gansneder, Jan T. Jeter, M. Frances Klein, Marian Schwab, and William M. Alexander, *One Hundred Good Schools* (West Lafayette, Ind.: Kappa Delta Pi, 1984), p. 162.

17. Arthur Powell, Eleanor Farrar, and David K. Cohen, *The Shopping Mall High School: Winners and Losers in the Educational Marketplace* (Boston: Houghton Mifflin, 1985).

18. Jean Anyon, "Social Class and the Hidden Curriculum of Work," in *Curriculum & Instruction: Alternatives in Education,* eds. Henry A. Giroux, Anthony N. Penn, and William F. Pinar (Berkeley, Calif.: McCutchan, 1981), pp. 317–341.

19. Ibid., pp. 328–329.

20. Ibid., p. 333.

21. George S. Counts, *Dare the School Build a New Social Order?* (New York: The John Day Co., 1932), p. 12.

22. The authors wish to thank Anne Remaley, a doctoral student at Washington State University, for the material on which these sketches are based.

23. P. Olson, "Poverty and education in Canada," In *Social change and education in Canada,* eds. R. Ghosh and D. Ray.

24. P. Young, "Population shifts, demands, and education," In *Social change and education in Canada,* eds. R. Ghosh and D. Ray.

25. T. William and H. Millinoff, "Canada's schools: Report card for the 1990s. A CEA opinion poll" (Toronto: Canadian Education Association, 1990).

26. John Godar, *Teachers Talk,* p. 9.

27. R. Lal, *A Study of Strategies Employed by Junior High School Administrators to Overcome Disruptive Gang-Related Activities,* Unpublished doctoral dissertation (Los Angeles: University of California, Los Angeles, 1991).

28. David A. Hamburg, "Preparing for Life: The Critical Transition of Adolescence," *1985 Annual Report* (New York: Carnegie Corporation of New York, 1985), p. 16.

29. M. Allan, "School-based HIV-AIDS Education in Canada" (Unpublished manuscript: ERIC Document ED 350 522, 1992).

30. Health and Welfare Canada, "Youth and AIDS study" (Ottawa ON: The Queen's Printer, 1988). Cited in M. Allan, "School-based HIV-AIDS Education in Canada."

31. Edwin Farrell, *Hanging In and Dropping Out: Voices of At-Risk High School Students* (New York: Teachers College Press, 1990), p. 49.

32. See, for example, Gary Davis and Margaret Thomas, *Effective Schools and Effective Teachers* (Boston: Allyn and Bacon, 1989); Sara Lawrence Lightfoot, *The Good High School: Portraits of Character and Culture* (New York: Basic Books, 1983); and Jack Frymier et al., *One Hundred Good Schools (West Lafayette, Ind.: Kappa Delta Pi, 1984).*

CHAPTER 6

1. Canadian Charter of Rights and Freedoms, 1982.
2. James A. Banks, *Multiethnic Education: Theory and Practice*, 3d ed. (Boston: Allyn and Bacon, 1994), p. 71.
3. Ashley Montagu, *Man's Most Dangerous Myth: The Fallacy of Race*, 5th ed. (New York: Oxford University Press, 1974), p. 9.
4. James A. Banks, *Teaching Strategies for Ethnic Studies*, 5th ed. (Boston: Allyn and Bacon, 1991), p. 74.
5. Ibid. pp. 74–75.
6. Ibid. p. 14.
7. James A. Banks, *Multiethnic Education*, p. 8.
8. James S. Coleman et al., *Equality of Educational Opportunity* (Washington, D.C.: U.S. Government Printing Office, 1966).
9. E. Coelho, J. Handscombe, M. Heinrich, and K. McCutcheon, *Immigrant students in North York schools: Intermediate and senior divisions.* (Toronto: North York School District. 1991).
10. C.F. Day, S.A. Kirk, and J.J. Gallagher, *Educating exceptional children*, Canadian ed. (Scarborough: Nelson Canada, 1985).
11. Daniel P. Hallahan and James M. Kauffman. *Exceptional Children: Introduction to Special Education*, 7th ed. (Boston: Allyn and Bacon, 1994), p. 14.
12. Ibid.
13. Ibid.
14. Daniel P. Hallahan and James M. Kauffman. *Exceptional Children*, p. 165.
15. S. Bever, *Building a Child's Self-Image* (St. Paul, Minn.: Association for Children and Adults with Learning Disabilities, 1980).
16. Yona Leyser, "Competencies Needed for Teaching Individuals with Special Needs," *Clearing House* (December 1985): 179–181.
17. Daniel P. Hallahan and James M. Kauffman, *Exceptional Children*, pp. 22–23.
18. Daniel P. Hallahan and James M. Kauffman. *Exceptional Children: Introduction to Special Education*, 5th ed. (Englewood Cliffs, N.J.: Prentice Hall, 1991), p. 432.
19. "Bored, Bright Students Unready to Face Competition, Report Says," *Spokesman Review* (November 5, 1993): A2.
20. Julian C. Stanley, "The Case for Extreme Educational Acceleration of Intellectually Brilliant Youths," *Gifted Child Quarterly*, 20 (1976): 66–75 and "Radical Acceleration: Recent Educational Innovation at Johns Hopkins University," *Gifted Child Quarterly* 22 (1978): 62–67.
21. Stephen P. Daurio, "Educational Enrichment Versus Acceleration: A Review of the Literature," in *Educating the Gifted: Acceleration and Enrichment*, eds. William C. George, Sanford J. Cohn, and Julian C. Stanley (Baltimore, Md.: Johns Hopkins University Press, 1979), pp. 13–63.
22. Howard H. Spiker (ed.), "University-Based Programs for Gifted Children," *Journal for the Education of the Gifted*, 5 (1982): 153–224.
23. E. Paul Torrence, "Teaching Creative and Gifted Learners," in *Handbook of Research on Teaching*, 3d ed., ed. Merlin C. Wittrock (New York: Macmillan, 1986), p. 634.
24. M. Lindsey, *Training Teachers of the Gifted and Talented* (New York: Teachers College Press, 1980), cited in Daniel P. Hallahan and James M. Kauffman, *Exceptional Children*, 5th ed., p. 432.
25. M. S. Whitlock and J. P. DuCette, "Outstanding and Average Teachers of the Gifted: A Comparative Study," *Gifted Child Quarterly*, 33 (1989): 15–21, cited in Daniel P. Hallahan and James M. Kauffman, *Exceptional Children*, 5th ed., p. 433.
26. Myra Sadker, David Sadker, and Lynette Long, "Gender and Educational Equity," in *Multicultural Education: Issues and Perspectives*, ed. James A. Banks (Boston: Allyn and Bacon, 1989), pp. 114–115.
27. Beverly Hardcastle, "Gender Equity in the Classroom" (unpublished paper), 1990, pp. 14–18.
28. Del Stover, "The at-Risk Kids Schools Ignore," *The Executive Educator* (March 1992): 28–31.
29. Ibid, p. 30.
30. James A. Banks, "Multicultural Education: Characteristics and Goals," in *Multicultural Education: Issues and Perspectives*, 2d ed., eds. James A. Banks and Cherry A. McGee Banks (Boston: Allyn and Bacon, 1993), p. 3.
31. John U. Ogbu, "Understanding Cultural Diversity and Learning," *Educational Researcher* (November 1992): 12.
32. James A. Banks, *Teaching Strategies for Ethnic Studies*, p. 118.
33. Ibid, pp. 119–120.
34. Forrest W. Parkay and Henry T. Fillmer, "Improving Teachers' Attitudes toward Minority-Group Students: An Experiential Approach to Multicultural Inservice," *New Horizons* (November 1984): 178–179.

CHAPTER 7

1. This discussion draws heavily on R.S. Patterson and N. Kach, "Education," *The Canadian Encyclopedia*, 2nd ed. (Edmonton: Hurtig Publishers, 1988).
2. Don Dillman, a rural sociologist at Washington State University, made this argument in a rural education distance program videotaped at the University of Victoria in 1987.
3. *The Calgary Herald*, February 4, 1995, p. B1.

CHAPTER 8

1. Max Black, "A Note on 'Philosophy of Education,'" *Harvard Educational Review*, 26 (1956): 154.
2. John Dewey, *Democracy and Education: An Introduction to the Philosophy of Education* (New York: Macmillan, 1916), p. 383.
3. Thomas J. Sergiovanni and Robert J. Starratt, *Supervision: Human Perspectives* (New York: McGraw-Hill, 1983), p. 304.
4. Edward J. Power, *Philosophy of Education: Studies in Philosophies, Schooling, and Educational Policies* (Englewood Cliffs, N.J.: Prentice Hall, 1982), pp. 15–16.
5. Peter A. Bertocci, "Unless Educators Be Philosophers, and Philosophers Be Educators. . . ", *Harvard Educational Review*, 26 (1956): 158.
6. Van Cleve Morris and Young Pai, *Philosophy and the American School: An Introduction to the Philosophy of Education* (Boston: Houghton Mifflin, 1976), p. 28.
7. Kenneth A. Strike and Jonas F. Soltis, *The Ethics of Teaching* (New York: Teachers College Press, 1985), p. 3.
8. Harry S. Broudy, "Arts Education: Necessary or Just Nice?" *Phi Delta Kappan*, 60 (1979): 347–350.
9. Forrest W. Parkay, "A General Theory of Aesthetics for the Conduct of Educational Research" (paper presented at the Annual Meeting of the American Educational Research Association, Montreal, 1983), p. 2.
10. Robert M. Hutchins, *A Conversation on Education* (Santa Barbara, Calif.: The Fund for the Republic, 1963).
11. William C. Bagley, *Education and Emergent Man* (New York: Ronald Press, 1934).

12. Jean-Paul Sartre, "Existentialism," in *Readings in the Philosophy of Education*, ed. John Martin Rich (Belmont, Calif.: Wadsworth, 1972), p. 98.

13. Van Cleve Morris and Young Pai, *Philosophy and the American School*, pp. 259–260.

14. Quoted in Van Cleve Morris and Young Pai, *Philosophy and the American School*, p. 260.

15. Jean-Paul Sartre, "Existentialism," p. 101.

16. Edward J. Power, *Philosophy of Education*, p. 168.

17. John B. Watson, *Behaviorism*, 2d ed. (New York: People's Institute, 1925), p. 82.

18. B. F. Skinner, "Utopia through the Control of Human Behavior," in *Readings in the Philosophy of Education*, p. 74.

19. Theodore Brameld, "Imperatives for a Reconstructed Philosophy of Education," *School and Society*, 87 (1959): 19.

20. Theodore Brameld, *Toward a Reconstructed Philosophy of Education* (New York: Holt, Rinehart and Winston, 1956).

CHAPTER 9

1. Michael Y. Nunnery and Ralph B. Kimbrough, *Politics, Power, Polls, and School Elections* (Berkeley, Calif.: McCutchan Publishing, 1971), p. 1.

2. Frederick M. Wirt and Michael W. Kirst, *Schools in Conflict: The Politics of Education* (Berkeley, Calif.: McCutchan Publishing, 1982), p. 20.

3. Calgary Board of Education, *Comprehensive Policy Manual*, June 1994.

4. Harmon Zeigler, Harvey J. Tucker, and L. A. Wilson, II, "Communication and Decision Making in American Public Education: A Longitudinal and Comparative Study," in *The Politics of Education: The Seventy-sixth Yearbook of the National Society for the Study of Education*, ed. Jay D. Scribner (Chicago: University of Chicago Press, 1977), pp. 218–254.

5. Frederick M. Wirt and Michael W. Kirst, *Schools in Conflict: The Politics of Education*, pp. 142–143.

6. Ibid., p. 145.

7. Larry Cuban, "Conflict and Leadership in the Superintendency," *Phi Delta Kappan* (September 1985): 28–30.

8. Ralph B. Kimbrough and Michael Y. Nunnery, *Educational Administration*, 2d ed. (New York: Macmillan, 1983).

9. Frederick M. Wirt and Michael W. Kirst, *Schools in Conflict: The Politics of Education*, p. 144.

10. For a comprehensive set of articles on school-based management/shared decision making, see the special theme issue of *Education and Urban Society*, August 1989.

11. Lynn Olson, "The Sky's the Limit: Dade Venture Self-Governance," *Education Week* (December 2, 1987): 18.

12. "Leading School-Based Reform: The Voices of Principals and Teachers," *Doubt & Certainties: Newsletter of the NEA Mastery In Learning Project* (June 1990): 1.

13. Lynn Olson, "The Sky's the Limit," p. 18.

14. Ibid.

15. See Daniel J. Brown, *Decentralization: The administrator's guidebook to school district change* (Newbury Park CA: Corwin Press, 1991) and Daniel J. Brown, *Decentralizaiton and school-based management* (London: Falmer Press, 1990).

16. *Globe and Mail*, February 3, 1995, p. A3.

17. "Education in Alberta: Some major social trends" (Edmonton: Alberta Education, May 1989), ERIC Document ED 314 868.

18. British Columbia Department of Education, *Inter-ministry child abuse handbook: A coordinated approach for professionals dealing with child abuse in British Columbia*, 1985, ERIC Document ED 263 706.

19. Ralph B. Kimbrough and Michael Y. Nunnery, *Educational Administration*, p. 138.

20. Carolyn Moran and Larry Hutchins, "Intermediate Service Agencies and School Improvement," in *Dissemination and School Improvement in Education Organizations*, eds. S. McKibbin and M. Malkas (Berkeley, Calif.: Far West Laboratory for Educational Research and Development, 1982), pp. 57–80.

21. Stephen J. Knezevich, *Administration of Public Education: A Sourcebook for the Leadership and Management of Educational Institutions*, 4th ed. (New York: Harper and Row, 1984), p. 190.

22. H.J. Robertson. "Is There a National Role in Education? A Rationale for the Obvious." In *Is There a National Role in Education?* eds. P. Nagy and J. Lupart (Ottawa: Canadian Education Association, 1994).

23. Statistics Canada, *Education Quarterly Review*, 1(2), 1994.

24. Statistics Canada, "A statistical portrait of elementary and secondary education in Canada," 1990. And "In Focus" (Edmonton: Alberta Education, 1995).

25. Statistics Canada, *Education Quarterly Review*, 1(2), 1994.

26. As reported in the *Calgary Herald*, March 13, 1994, p. A1.

CHAPTER 10

1. *Member Handbook* (The Alberta Teachers' Association, 1993).

2. Forrest W. Parkay, review of Kenneth A. Strike and Jonas F. Soltis, *The Ethics of Teaching* (New York, Teachers College Press, 1985), *The Educational Forum* (Fall 1985): 105.

3. Delbert Clear, "Rights of Teachers," in *Educators, Children and the Law*, eds. Lynn Sametz and Caven S. Mcloughlin (Springfield, Ill.: Charles C. Thomas, 1985), p. 60.

4. This discussion draws heavily from M.A. Zuker, *The legal context of education*. (Toronto: Ontario Institute for Studies in Education, 1988).

5. A.F. Brown and M.A. Zuker, *Education Law* (Toronto: Carswell Publishing, 1994).

6. Ibid.

7. This discussion draws heavily from M.A. Zuker, *The legal context of education*.

8. This discussion draws heavily from M.A. Zuker, *The legal context of education*.

9. This discussion draws heavily from A.F. Brown and M.A. Zuker, *Education Law*.

10. "Harassment Claims Vex Teachers," *Spokesman Review* (June 4, 1993): 1A.

11. Robert J. Shoop and Dennis R. Dunklee *School Law for the Principal: A Handbook for Practitioners* (Boston: Allyn and Bacon, 1992), p. 98.

CHAPTER 11

1. James A. Banks, *Multiethnic Education: Theory and Practice*, 2d ed. (Boston: Allyn and Bacon, 1988), p. 78.

2. Rudolf Dreikurs, Bernice Bronia Grunwald, and Floyd C. Pepper, *Maintaining Sanity in the Classroom: Classroom Man-*

agement Techniques, 2d ed. (New York: Harper and Row, 1982), p. 58.

3. Sylvia Ann Hewlett, *When the Bough Breaks: The Cost of Neglecting Our Children* (New York: Basic Books, 1991).

4. James P. Comer, "Children Can!" in *Children Can: An Address on School Improvement*, eds. Rodman B. Webb and Forrest W. Parkay (Gainesville, Fla.: Research and Development Center on School Improvement, 1989), p. 5.

5. M. Winzer, *Educational psychology in the Canadian classroom*, 2nd ed. (Toronto: Allyn & Bacon, 1994).

6. Susan F. Klein (ed.). *Handbook for Achieving Sex Equity through Education*, 2d ed. (Baltimore, Md.: Johns Hopkins University Press, 1990).

7. Carol Jacklyn quoted in Colette Dowling, *The Cinderella Complex* (New York: Summit Books, 1981), pp. 114–115.

8. David Wechsler, *The Measurement and Appraisal of Adult Intelligence*, 4th ed. (Baltimore: Williams and Wilkins, 1958), p. 7.

9. Anita E. Woolfolk, *Educational Psychology*, 5th ed. (Boston: Allyn and Bacon, 1993), p. 111.

10. George A. Miller, "The Test," *Science* (November 1984): 55.

11. Howard Gardner, *Frames of Mind*, p. 8.

12. Quoted in Christine I. Bennett, *Comprehensive Multicultural Education: Theory and Practice*, 2d ed. (Boston: Allyn and Bacon, 1990), p. 140.

13. Daniel P. Hallahan and James M. Kauffman, *Exceptional Children: Introduction to Special Education*, 5th ed. (Englewood Cliffs, N.J.: Prentice-Hall, 1991), p. 6.

14. M. Winzer, *Educational psychology in the Canadian classroom*. 2nd ed.

15. C. Crealock and D.G. Bachor, *Instructional Strategies for Students with Special Needs* (Toronto: Allyn & Bacon, 1994).

16. Pamela Maniet-Bellerman, *Mainstreaming Children with Learning Disabilities: A Guide to Accompany "L.D." Does NOT Mean Learning Dumd!* (Pittsburgh: Upward Bound Press; as presented in *Educational Psychology and Classroom Practice: A Partnership*, eds. R. R. McCown and Peter Roop (Boston: Allyn and Bacon, 1992), pp. 424–425.

17. Louis A. Fliegler, *Curriculum Planning for the Gifted* (Englewood Cliffs, N.J.: Prentice-Hall, 1961).

18. Sidney P. Marland (ed.), *Education of the Gifted and Talented: Report to the Congress of the United States* (Washington, D.C.: U.S. Government Printing Office, 1972), p. 2.

19. Joseph Renzulli and Linda H. Smith, "Two Approaches to Identification of Gifted Students," *Exceptional Children, 43*, 8 (May 1977): 512–518.

20. Daniel P. Hallahan and James M. Kauffman, *Exceptional Children: Introduction to Special Education*, p. 6.

21. C. Crealock and D.G. Bachor, *Instructional Strategies for Students with Special Needs*, p. 20.

22. Laurence J. Coleman, *Schooling for the Gifted* (Menlo Park, Calif.: Addison-Wesley, 1985), p. 5.

23. Forrest W. Parkay, *White Teacher, Black School: The Professional Growth of a Ghetto Teacher* (New York: Praeger, 1983), p. 73.

24. Anita E. Woolfolk, *Educational Psychology*, p. 26.

25. Jean Piaget, *To Understand Is to Invent* (New York: Penguin Books, 1980), p. 93.

26. Erik H. Erikson, *Childhood and Society* (New York: W. W. Norton, 1963).

27. Lawrence Kohlberg, "The Cognitive-Developmental Approach to Moral Education," in *Curriculum Planning: A New Approach*, 6th ed., eds. Glen Hass and Forrest W. Parkay (Boston:

Allyn and Bacon, 1993), p. 155. Originally published in *Phi Delta Kappan 56, 10* (June 1975): 670–677.

28. See, for example, Gerald W. Bracey, "Now then, Mr. Kohlberg, about Moral Development in Women . . ." in *Curriculum Planning: A New Approach*, eds. Glen Hass and Forrest W. Parkay, pp. 165–166. Originally published in *Phi Delta Kappan, 66*, 1 (September 1984): 69.

29. Carol Gilligan, *In a Different Voice: Sex Differences in the Expression of Moral Judgment* (Cambridge, Mass.: Harvard University Press, 1982).

30. Lawrence Kohlberg, "The Cognitive-Developmental Approach to Moral Education," p. 161.

31. Maurice B. Howard, "Service Learning: Character Education Applied," *Educational Leadership* (November 1993): 43.

32. Eliot Wigginton, *Sometimes a Shining Moment: The Foxfire Experience* (Garden City, N.Y.: Anchor Press/Doubleday, 1985), p. 236.

33. David A. Hamburg, "Reducing the Casualties of Early Life: A Preventive Orientation," *1985 Annual Report* (New York: Carnegie Corporation of New York, 1985), p. 13.

CHAPTER 12

1. Written by Judith McBride for *Becoming a Teacher: Accepting the Challenge of a Profession*, 3d ed. (Boston: Allyn and Bacon, 1994). Used by permission of the author.

2. Personal communication, Judith McBride, October 14, 1993.

3. Edmund T. Emmer, Carolyn M. Everston, Julie P. Sanford, Barbara S. Clements, and Murray E. Worsham, *Classroom Management for Secondary Teachers* (Englewood Cliffs, N.J.: Prentice Hall, 1984), p. xi.

4. M. Wagenschein, "Reality Schock: A Study of Beginning Elementary School Teachers" (Master's thesis, University of Chicago, 1950).

5. J. Gabriel, *An Analysis of the Emotional Problems of Teachers in the Classroom* (London: Angus and Robertson, 1957).

6. Estelle Fuchs, *Teachers Talk: Views from Inside City Schools* (Garden City, N.Y.: Anchor, Doubleday, 1969).

7. Anita E. Woolfolk and Charles M. Galloway, "Nonverbal Communication and the Study of Teaching," *Theory into Practice, 24*, 1 (1985): 80.

8. Ibid., pp. 80–81.

9. R. Adams and B. Biddle, *Realities of Teaching: Explorations with Video Tape* (New York: Holt, Rinehart and Winston, 1970).

10. David W. Johnson and Roger T. Johnson, *Learning Together and Alone: Cooperation, Competition, and Individualization* (Englewood Cliffs, N.J.: Prentice Hall, 1975), p. 26.

11. William J. Seiler, L. David Schuelke, and Barbara Lieb-Brilhart, *Communication for the Contemporary Classroom* (New York: Holt, Rinehart and Winston, 1984), p. 18.

12. William Ayers, *The Good Preschool Teacher: Six Teachers Reflect on Their Lives* (New York: Teachers College Press, 1989), p. 98.

13. David W. Johnson and Roger T. Johnson, *Learning Together and Alone: Cooperative, Competitive and Individualistic Learning* (Boston: Allyn and Bacon, 1991).

14. Richard A. Schmuck and Patricia A. Schmuck, *Group Processes in the Classroom* (Dubuque, Iowa: William C. Brown, 1971), p. 18.

15. See, for example, Robert E. Slavin's review of research, "Ability Grouping and Student Achievement in Elementary

Schools: A Best-Evidence Synthesis," *Review of Educational Research, 57* 3 (1987): 293–336; Adam Gamoran's "Is Ability Grouping Equitable?" *Educational Leadership, 50,* 2 (1992): 11–17 and "The Variable Effects of High School Tracking," *American Sociological Review, 57,* 12 (1992): 812–828; and M. Lee Manning and Robert Lucking's "Ability Grouping: Realities and Alternatives," in *Curriculum Planning: A New Approach,* 6th ed., eds. Glen Haas and Forrest W. Parkay (Boston: Allyn and Bacon, 1993), pp. 228–233.

16. M. Lee Manning and Robert Lucking, "Ability Grouping: Realities and Alternaties," pp. 231–232.

17. Thomas L. Good and Jere E. Brophy, *Looking in Classrooms* (Harper and Row, 1987), p. 445.

18. See, for example, A. M. Sharpley, J. W. Irvine, and C. F. Sharpley, "An Examination of the Effectiveness of a Cross-Age Tutoring Program in Mathematics for Elementary School Children," *American Educational Research Journal, 20,* 1 (Spring 1993): 103–111.

19. "Some Third Graders are Passing Because I Work with Them," *Harvard Education Letter* (March 1987): 2. Excerpted from Aurelio Montemayor, *Valued Youth Speak* (San Antonio: Intercultural Development Research Association, 1986).

20. Walter Doyle, "Classroom Organization and Mangement," in *Handbook for Research on Teaching,* 3d ed., ed. Merlin C. Wittrock (New York: Macmillan, 1986), pp. 398–402.

21. Thomas L. Good and Jere E. Brophy, *Looking in Classrooms,* 5th ed. (New York: Harper Collins, 1991), p. 31.

22. C. Fisher, N. Filby, R. Marliave, L. Cahan, M. Dishaw, J. Moore, and D. Berliner, *Teaching Behaviors, Academic Learning Time, and Student Achievement,* Final report of Phase III-B Beginning Teacher Evaluation Study (San Francisco: Far West Laboratory for Educational Research and Development, 1978).

23. Ibid.

24. Andrew Porter, "Opportunity to Learn," *Brief No. 7* (Madison, Wisc.: Center on Organization and Restructuring of Schools, Fall 1993).

25. Thomas L. Good and Jere E. Brophy, *Looking in Classrooms,* 4th ed. (New York: Harper and Row, 1987), p. 226.

26. Jacob Kounin, *Discipline and Group Management in Classrooms* (New York: Holt, Rinehart and Winston, 1970).

27. Lee Cantor, "Assertive Discipline—More Than Names on the Board and Marbles in a Jar," *Phi Delta Kappan, 71,* 1 (1989): 58.

28. R. H. MacNaughton and F. A. Johns, "Developing a Successful Schoolwide Discipline Program," *NASSP Bulletin* (September 1991): 53.

29. Robert Carkhuff, *A Design for Discipline: The LEAST Approach* (Washington, D.C.: National Education Association, 1983).

30. Rudolf Dreikurs, Bernice Bronia Grunwald, and Floy C. Pepper, *Maintaining Sanity in the Classroom: Classroom Management Techniques,* 2d ed. (New York: Harper and Row, 1982), p. 11.

31. See William R. Glasser's *Reality Therapy: A New Approach to Psychiatry* (New York: Harper and Row, 1965), *School without Failure* (New York: Harper and Row, 1969), and *Control Theory in the Classroom* (New York: Harper and Row, 1986). Also see Pauline B. Gough, "The Key to Improving Schools: An Interview with William Glasser," *Phi Delta Kappan* (May 1987): 656–662.

32. Thomas Gordon, *T.E.T. Teacher Effectiveness Training* (New York: Peter H. Wyden, 1974).

33. R. Rosenthal, *On the Social Psychology of the Self-Fulfilling Prophecy: Further Evidence for Pygmalion Effects and Their Mediating Mechanisms* (New York: MSS Modular Publications, 1974).

34. Jere Brophy and Thomas L. Good, "Teacher Behavior and Student Achievement," in *Handbook of Research on Teaching,* 3d ed., ed. Merlin C. Wittrock (New York: Macmillan, 1986), pp. 350–351.

35. Ibid., p. 351.

36. Ibid.

37. Herbert J. Walberg, "Productive Teaching and Instruction: Assessing the Knowledge Base," in *Effective Teaching: Current Research,* eds. Hersholt C. Waxman and Herbert J. Walberg (Berkeley, Calif.: McCutchan, 1991), p. 52.

38. Thomas L. Good and Jere E. Brophy, *Looking in Classrooms,* 5th ed. (New York: Harper and Row, 1991).

39. Jere Brophy and Thomas Good, *Teacher-Student Relationships* (New York: Holt, Rinehart and Winston, 1974), p. 244.

40. K. Benne and P. Sheats, "Functioning Roles of Group Members," *Journal of Social Issues,* 4 (1948): 41–49.

41. Richard A. Schmuck and Patricia A. Schmuck, *Group Processes in the Classroom,* p. 120.

42. Richard A. Schmuck and Patricia A. Schmuck, *Group Processes in the Classroom,* p. 122.

43. Carol Anne Dwyer and Ana Maria Villegas, *Foundations for Tomorrow's Teachers—No. 3, Defining Teaching* (Princeton, N.J.: Educational Testing Service, 1992), pp. 4–5. Reprinted by permission of Educational Testing Service.

44. Ibid., p. 3.

45. Robert V. Bullough, Jr., *First-Year Teacher: A Case Study* (New York: Teachers College Press, 1989), p. 23.

46. Ibid., p. 25.

47. Christopher M. Clark and Penelope L. Peterson, "Teachers' Thought Processes," in *Handbook of Research on Teaching,* ed. Merlin C. Wittrock (New York: Macmillan, 1986), pp. 255–296.

48. Ibid., p. 261.

49. Ibid., p. 264.

50. *Harvard Education Letter, II,* 4: 7.

51. American Federation of Teachers, National Council on Measurement in Education, and National Education Association, *Standards for Teacher Competence in Educational Assessment of Students,* ERIC Document No. ED323 186, 1990, p. 2.

52. *Teachers' Evaluations of Student Work,* National Center for Research on Teacher Learning (East Lansing: Michigan State University, 1993).

53. American Federation of Teachers, National Council on Measurement in Education, and National Education Association, *Standards for Teacher Competence in Educational Assessment of Students,* pp. 4–6.

54. *Harvard Education Letter, II,* 4: 7.

55. Bruce Joyce, Marsha Weil, with Beverly Showers, Models of Teaching, 4th ed. (Boston: Allyn and Bacon, 1992), p. 4.

56. Craig Pearson, "Cooperative Leaning: An Alternative to Cheating and Failure," *Learning* (March 1979): 36.

57. Barak Rosenshine and Robert Stevens, "Teaching Functions," in *Handbook on Research of Teaching* (New York: Macmillan, 1986), p. 377.

58. M. Galton, and B. Simon, *Progress and Performance in the Primary Classroom* (London: Routledge & Kegan Paul, 1980), p. 199.

59. Reprinted by permission of the publisher from William Ayer, *The Good Preschool Teacher* (New York: Teachers College Press, © 1989 by Teachers College, Columbia University. All rights reserved.), pp. 107, 122–123.

60. Lorna Catford, "Portrait of a Ceramics Class: Control and Freedom in a Delicate Balance," in *The Educational Imagination: On the Design and Evaluation of School Programs*, 2d ed., ed Elliot W. Eisner (New York: Macmillan, 1985), pp. 304–306. Reprinted with permission of Macmillan Publishing Company. Copyright © 1985 by Elliott W. Eisner.

61. Gary D. Borich, *Effective Teaching Methods*, 2d ed. (New York: Merrill/Macmillan, 1992), pp. 303–304. Reprinted with the permission of Macmillan College Publishing Company, Inc.

62. Ibid, p. 361.

CHAPTER 13

1. Elliot W. Eisner, *The Educational Imagination: On the Design and Evaluation of School Programs*, 2d ed. (New York: Macmillan, 1985), p. 87.

2. Catherine Cornbleth, *Curriculum in Context* (London: The Falmer Press, 1990), p. 48.

3. H. Felsentahl, "Factors Influence in School Effectiveness: An Ecological Analysis of an 'Effective' School," paper presented at the annual meeting of the American Educational Research Association (New York, March 1982), p. 10; as reported in Catherine Cornbleth, *Curriculum in Context,* p. 53.

4. Dorene Doerre Ross, Elizabeth Bondy, and Diane Wells Kyle, *Reflective Teaching for Student Empowerment: Elementary Curriculum and Methods* (New York: Macmillan, 1993), pp. 50–51.

5. Elliot W. Eisner, *The Educational Imagination: On the Design and Evaluation of School Programs*, p. 107.

6. Ibid., p. 103.

7. John I. Goodlad, *A Place Called School* (New York: McGraw-Hill, 1984), p. 225.

8. Duane F. Alvin and David L. Morgan, *Extracurricular Activities: Review and Discussion of the Research on Educational Practices* (Atlanta, GA: State of Georgia Department of Education, 1979).

9. E. Newton, and P. Newton, *Voices, Visions, and Vitality* (Calgary: Detselig Publishing, 1991).

10. John I. Goodlad, "What Some Schools and Classrooms Teach," *Educational Leadership* (April 1983): 14–15.

11. Ralph W. Tyler, *Basic Principles of Curriculum and Instruction* (Chicago: University of Chicago Press, 1949), p. 1.

12. Suzanne Lowell Krogh, *The Integrated Early Childhood Curriculum* (New York, McGraw-Hill, 1990), p. 77.

13. Carol B. Daniels, "Quality of Educational Materials: A Marketing Perspective," in *Quest for Quality: Improving Basic Skills Instruction in the 1980s*, ed. Forrest W. Parkay, Sharon O'Bryan, and Michael Hennessy (Lanham, Md.: University Press of America, 1984), p. 100.

14. Bruno Bettelheim and Karen Zelan, *On Learning to Read: The Child's Fascination with Meaning* (New York: Vintage Books, 1981), p. 262.

15. Carol B. Daniels, "Quality of Educational Materials: A Marketing Perspective," p. 101.

16. Wilford M. Aiken, *The Story of the Eight-Year Study* (New York: Harper and Row, 1942), p. 23.

17. R. Paterson. "The future of Progressive Education." In *Options: Reforms and Alternatives for Canadian Education,* eds. T.

Morrison and A. Burton (Toronto: Holt, Rinehart and Winston, 1973).

18. Jerome S. Bruner, *The Process of Education* (New York: Random House, 1960), p. 33.

19. William J. Bennett, *James Madison High School: A Curriculum for American Students* (Washington, D.C.: United States Department of Education, 1987).

20. Thomas Kellaghan and George F. Madaus, "National Testing: Lessons for America from Europe," *Educational Leadership* (November 1991): 91.

21. Forrest W. Parkay and Sharon O'Bryan, "Focus for Basic Skills Instruction in the 1980s," in *Quest for Quality: Improving Basic Skills Instruction in the 1980s, eds.* Forrest W. Parkay, Sharon O'Bryan, and Michael Hennessy, p. 3–4.

22. Stephen N. Tchudi, "Recent Research and New Directions in the Teaching of Writing," in *Quest for Quality: Improving Basic Skills Instruction in the 1980s,* pp. 21–22.

23. Herbert J. Walberg, "Productive Teaching and Instruction: Assessing the Knowledge Base," in *Effective Teaching, Current Research*, eds. Hersholt C. Waxman and Herbert J. Walberg (Berkeley, Calif.: McCutchan, 1991), p. 57.

24. Ibid.

25. Charles Beard, *The Nature of the Social Sciences* (New York: Charles Scribner's Sons, 1938), p. 179.

26. William D. Sims and Sandra B. Hammond, *Award-Winning Foreign Language Programs; Prescriptions for Success* (Skokie, Ill.: National Textbook Co., 1981), pp. 1–2.

27. Kathryn Bloom, "Defining the Task," in *An Arts in Education Source Book*, ed. Charles Fowler (New York: American Council for the Arts, 1980), p. 5.

28. Monika Kosmahl Aring, "What the 'V' Word is Costing America's Economy," *Phi Delta Kappan* (January 1993): 400.

CHAPTER 14

1. Amitai Etzioni, *The Semi-Professions and Their Organization: Teachers, Nurses, Social Workers* (New York: Free Press, 1969).

2. Robert B. Howsam et al., *Educating a Profession* (Washington, D.C.: American Association of Colleges for Teacher Education, 1976).

3. Arthur G. Powell, *The Uncertain Profession: Harvard and the Search for Educational Authority* (Cambridge, Mass.: Harvard University Press, 1980).

4. Daniel L. Duke, *Teaching—The Imperiled Profession* (Albany: State University of New York Press, 1984); Gary Sykes, "Contradictions, Ironies, and Promises Unfulfilled: A Contemporary Account of the Status of Teaching," *Phi Delta Kappan* (October 1983): 87–93; and S. Freedman, J. Jackson, and K. Botes, "Teaching: An Imperiled Profession," in *Handbook of Teaching and Policy*, eds. Lee Shulman and Gary Sykes (New York: Longman, 1983), pp. 261–299.

5. John Goodlad, "Teaching: An Endangered Profession," *Teachers College Record* (Spring 1983): 575–578.

6. Bengt Abrahamsson, *Military Professionalization and Political Power* (Stockholm: Allmanna Forlagret, 1971), pp. 11–12.

7. We have gleaned these characteristics from the following excellent sources: Robert B. Howsam et al., *Educating a Profession*; Gunnar Berg, "Developing the Teaching Profession: Autonomy, Professional Code, Knowledge Base," *The Australian Journal of Education, 27*, 2 (1983): 173–186; Wilbert E. Moore, *The Professions: Roles and Rules* (New York: Russell Sage Foundation,

1970); Myron Lieberman, *Education as a Profession* (Englewood Cliffs, N.J.: Prentice Hall, 1956); and Amitai Etzioni, *The Semi-Professions and Their Organization.*

8. John I. Goodlad, *Teachers for Our Nation's Schools* (San Francisco: Jossey-Bass, 1990), p. 71.

9. Amitai Etzioni, *The Semi-Professions and Their Organization: Teachers, Nurses, Social Workers,* p. v.

10. Dan Lortie, *Schoolteacher: A Sociological Study* (Chicago: Uiversity of Chicago Press, 1975).

11. Ibid., p. 160.

12. Forrest W. Parkay, *White Teacher, Black School: The Professional Growth of a Ghetto Teacher* (New York: Praeger, 1983), pp. 114–115.

13. Robert B. Howsam et al., *Educating a Profession,* p. 15.

14. Dan Lortie, *Schoolteacher: A Sociological Study,* pp. 160–161.

15. Dan Lortie, *Schoolteacher: A Sociological Study*; Henrick D. Gideonse, "The Necessary Revolution in Teacher Education," *Phi Delta Kappan* (September 1982): 15–18; and Paul Woodring, *The Persistent Problems of Education* (Bloomington, Ind.: Phi Delta Kappa, 1983).

16. Statistics Canada, *Jobs of the Future: A Guide for Youth,* Employment and Immigration Canada, 1991.

17. Paul Woodring, *The Persistent Problems of Education,* p. 121.

18. Donald A. Shön, *The Reflective Practitioner: How Professionals Think in Action* (New York: Basic Books, 1983), p. 66.

19. James G. Clawson discusses the *comprehensiveness* and *mutality* of mentoring in "Mentoring in Managerial Careers," in *Work, Family, and Career,* ed. C. Brooklyn Dorr (New York: Praeger, 1980).

20. For a fuller discussion of the gift-giving concept of mentorships, see Nathalie Gehrke, "Toward a Definition of Mentoring," *Theory into Practice* (Summer 1988): 190–194.

21. Judith Lanier and Judith Little, "Research on Teacher Education" in *Handbook of Research on Teaching,* ed. Merlin C. Wittrock (New York: Macmillan, 1986), p. 543.

22. N. L. Gage, *The Scientific Basis of the Art of Teaching* (New York: Teachers College Press, 1978), p. 57.

23. The Holmes Group, *Tomorrow's Schools: Principles for the Design of Professional Development Schools* (East Lansing, Mich.: Author), p. 1.

24. Telephone conversation with Phi Delta Kappa, February 7, 1994.

25. Telephone conversation with Association for Supervision and Curriculum Development, February 7, 1994.

26. *Ki-es-ki,* (Toronto: Canadian Education Association, 1995).

CHAPTER 15

1. The National Foundation for the Improvement of Education, *Images of Potential: Learning Tomorrow* (Washington, D.C.: The National Foundation for the Improvement of Education, n. d.), pp. 19–20.

2. Alvin Toffler, *Future Shock* (New York: Bantam, 1971), p. 460.

3. John Naisbitt and Patricia Aburdende, *Megatrends 2000: Ten New Directions for the 1990s* (New York: Avon Books, 1990), p. 228.

4. Seymour B. Sarason, *The Culture of School and the Problem of Change,* 2d ed. (Boston: Allyn and Bacon, 1981).

5. Ibid., p. 224; see also Gene E. Hall and Shirley M. Hord, *Change in Schools: Facilitating the Process* (Albany: State University of New York Press, 1987).

6. Seymour B. Sarason, *The Culture of School and the Problem of Change,* p. 224.

7. Ibid.

8. Thomas L. Good and Jere E. Brophy, *Looking in Classrooms,* 4th ed. (New York: Harper and Row, 1987), p. 328.

9. Jeanne S. Chall and Allan F. Mirsky, "The Implications for Education," in *Education and the Brain,* eds. Jeanne S. Chall and Allan F. Mirsky, The 77th Yearbook of the National Society for the Study of Education, Part II (Chicago: University of Chicago Press, 1978), p. 377.

10. David Wood, *How Children Think and Learn* (New York: Basil Blackwell, 1988), p. 81.

11. Ibid., p. 82.

12. See, for example, Graham Nuthall and Adirenne Alton-Lee, "Research on Teaching and Learning: Thirty Years of Change," *Elementary School Journal,* 90 (1990): 546–570; Nell Noddings, "Constructivism in Mathematics Education," in *Constructivist Views on the Teaching and Learning of Mathematics,* Monograph 4, eds. R. Davis, C. Maher, and N. Noddings (Reston, Va.: National Council of Teachers of Mathematics, 1990); and Linda Anderson, "Learners and Learning," in *Knowledge Base for Beginning Teachers,* ed. M. Reynolds (New York: Pergamon, 1989), pp. 85–100.

13. Anita Woolfolk, *Educational Psychology,* p. 485.

14. Bruce Joyce, Marsha Weil, with Beverly Showers, *Models of Teaching,* 4th ed. (Boston: Allyn and Bacon, 1992), p. 338.

15. Priscilla Wohlstetter and Lesley Anderson, "What Can U.S. Charter Schools Learn from England's Grant-Maintained Schools?" *Phi Delta Kappan* (February 1994): 486.

16. Quoted in *Policy Briefs, Report 1, 1993* (Elmhurst, Ill: North Central Regional Educational Laboratory), p. 3.

17. Bettye Caldwell, "Demographic Relevance—A New Challenge for Tomorrow's Schools" (address to the Kappa Delta Pi 1988 Convocation, New Orleans, April 1988).

18. Ernest Boyer, "Partners in Excellence" (address to the Kappa Delta Pi 1988 Convocation, New Orleans, April 1988).

19. John Merrow, "Children and Television: Natural Partners," *Phi Delta Kappan* (November 1985): 212.

20. Susan Mernit, "Teaching and Computers: The Guide on the Side," *Instructor* (September 1990): 77–78.

21. Sueann Ambron and Kristina Hooper (eds.), *Interactive Multimedia: Visions of Multimedia for Developers, Educators, and Information Providers* (Redmond, Wash.: Microsoft, 1988), p. vii.

22. Robert Heinich, Michael Molenda, and James D. Russell, *Instructional Media and the New Technologies of Instruction,* 4th ed. (New York: Macmillan, 1993), p. 269.

23. Seymour Papert, "Society Will Balk, but the Future May Demand a Computer for Each Child," *Electronic Education* (September 1981): 5.

24. Marvin J. Cetron, Barbara Soriano, and Margaret Gayle, "Schools of the Future: Education Approaches the Twenty-First Century," *The Futurist* (August 1985): 22.

Glossary

A

Academic learning time (p. 293): the amount of time students spend working on academic tasks with a high level of success (80 percent or higher).

Acceptance approach (p. 298): an approach to classroom management, developed by psychologist Rudolph Dreikurs, based on the individual's need for acceptance.

Activity format (p. 293): one of many types of activity classroom teachers can use to accomplish an instructional goal.

Adolescence (p. 275): the period of life (ten to nineteen years of age) between childhood and young adulthood.

Aesthetics (p. 184): a branch of philosophy concerned with making value judgments about beauty and art.

Aims of education (p. 108): what a society believes the broad, general purposes of education should be—for example, socialization, achievement, personal growth, and social improvement.

Allocated time (p. 293): the amount of time teachers allocate for instruction in various areas of the curriculum.

Alternative assessments (p. 380): an approach to assessing students' learning that requires students to use higher-order thinking skills to perform, create, or solve real-life problems—not just select one of several designated responses as on a multiple-choice test.

Assertive discipline (p. 297): an approach to classroom discipline requiring that teachers establish firm, clear guidelines for student behavior and follow through with consequences for misbehavior.

Assessment (p. 307): the process of gathering information related to how much students have learned.

Association for Supervision and Curriculum Development (ASCD) (p. 367): a professional organization for educators interested in school improvement at all levels.

Authentic assessments (p. 380): an approach to assessing students' learning that requires them to solve problems or work on tasks that approximate as much as possible those they will encounter beyond the classroom.

Axiology (p. 184): the study of values, including the identification of criteria for determining what is valuable.

B

Behavior modification (p. 297): an approach to classroom management in which the teacher reinforces (or rewards) only desired student behaviors.

Behaviorism (p. 194): based on behavioristic psychology, this philosophical orientation maintains that environmental factors shape people's behavior.

Between-class ability grouping (p. 291): the practice of grouping students at the middle and high school levels for instruction on the basis of ability or achievement, often called *tracking*.

British North America Act, 1867 (p. 163): gave the provinces sole responsibility for education.

C

CD-ROMs (p. 388): small plastic disks (usually 4.72 or 5.25 inches in diameter) that hold 600 or more megabytes of information that can be read by a computer.

Charter schools (p. 382): independent schools, often founded by teachers, that are given a charter to operate by a school district, or provincial or federal government, with the provision that students must demonstrate mastery of predetermined outcomes.

Childhood (p. 275): the period of life (two to ten years of age) between infancy and early adolescence.

Civil liability (p. 249): the responsibility a school bears towards its students beyond providing education.

Classroom climate (p. 290): the atmosphere or quality of life in a classroom, determined by how individuals interact with one another.

Classroom management (p. 294): day-to-day teacher control of student behavior and learning, including discipline.

Classroom organization (p. 288): how teachers and students in a school are grouped for instruction and how time is allocated in classrooms.

Cognitive development (p. 271): the process of acquiring the intellectual ability to learn from interaction with one's environment.

Cognitive science (p. 378): the study of the learning process that focuses on how individuals manipulate symbols and process information.

Collaborative approach (p. 61): an approach to teacher education in which school-based professionals collaborate in the on-site training of teachers.

Community-school partnership (p. 226): an association between local school districts and community groups and businesses to raise funds and otherwise improve educational opportunities.

Computer-assisted instruction (CAI) (p. 388): the use of microcomputers to provide individual instruction to students.

Computer simulations (p. 387): computer programs that present the user with multifaceted problem situations similar to those they will encounter in real life.

Concrete operations stage (p. 271): the stage of cognitive development (seven to eleven years of age) proposed by Jean Piaget in which the individual develops the ability to use logical thought to solve concrete problems.

Confidentiality (p. 245): the principle which restricts access to student records.

Constructivist view of learning (p. 379): a view of learning that maintains that students construct understanding of the material they learn—in contrast to the view that teachers transmit academic content to students in small segments.

Contingent teaching (p. 379): an approach to teaching, sometimes called *scaffolding*, in which instruction is based on (or contingent on) the student's current level of understanding and ability.

Cooperative learning (p. 311): an approach to education in which students work in small groups, or teams, sharing the work and helping one another complete assignments.

Core curriculum (p. 336): a set of fundamental courses or learning experiences that are part of the curriculum for all students at a school.

Corporal punishment (p. 246): physical punishment applied to a student by a school employee as a disciplinary measure.

Cost of living (p. 80): the amount of money needed, on average, for housing, food, transportation, utilities, and other living expenses in a given locale.

Cross-age tutoring (p. 292): a tutoring arrangement in which older students tutor younger students; evidence indicates that cross-age tutoring has positive effects on the attitudes and achievement of tutee and tutor.

Cultural pluralism (p. 114): the preservation of cultural differences among groups of people within one society. This view is in contrast to the melting-pot theory that says that ethnic cultures should melt into one.

Culture (p. 112): the way of life common to a group of people; includes knowledge deemed important, shared meanings, norms, values, attitudes, ideals, and view of the world.

Curriculum (p. 322): the school experiences, both planned and unplanned, that enhance (and sometimes impede) the education and growth of students.

D

Democratic classroom (p. 303): a classroom in which the teacher's leadership style encourages students to take more power and responsibility for their learning.

Departmentalization (p. 118): an organizational arrangement for schools in which students move from classroom to classroom for instruction in different subject areas.

Diversity (p. 112): differences among people in regard to gender, race, ethnicity, culture, and socioeconomic status.

E

Educare system (p. 478): A proposal that would combine education and day care to provide day-long, year-round schooling for children six months through twelve years of age.

Educational philosophy (p. 177): a set of ideas and beliefs about education that guide the professional behavior of educators.

English as a Second Language (ESL) (p. 139): specialized instruction in English for non-native speakers.

Epistemology (p. 183): a branch of philosophy concerned with the nature of knowledge and what it means to know something.

Essentialism (p. 191): formulated in part as a response to progressivism, this philosophical orientation holds that a core of common knowledge about the real world should be transmitted to students in a systematic, disciplined way.

Ethical dilemmas (p. 237): problem situations in which an ethical response is difficult to determine; that is, no single response can be called "right" or "wrong."

Ethics (p. 184): a branch of philosophy concerned with principles of conduct and determining what is good and evil, right and wrong, in human behavior.

Ethnic group (p. 115): individuals within a larger culture who share a racial or cultural identity and a set of beliefs, values, and attitudes and who consider themselves members of a distinct group or subculture.

Exceptional learners (p. 141): students whose growth and development deviate from the norm to the extent that their educational needs can be met more effectively through a modification of regular school programs.

Existentialism (p. 193): a philosophical orientation that emphasizes the individual's experiences and maintains that each individual must determine his or her own meaning of existence.

Explicit curriculum (p. 323): the behavior, attitudes, and knowledge that a school intends to teach students.

Expulsion (p. 246): a disciplinary action, used in extreme cases, which prohibits a student from returning to a particular school.

Extracurricular/cocurricular programs (p. 325): school-sponsored activities students may pursue outside of, or in addition to, academic study.

F

Field experiences (p. 62): opportunities for teachers-in-training to experience first-hand the world of the teacher, by observing, tutoring, and instructing small groups.

Focused observations (p. 63): classroom observations that focus on a particular aspect (or aspects) of teaching—for example, students' interests and ability levels, the teacher's approach to classroom management, or the teacher's questioning strategies.

Formal operations stage (p. 271): the stage of cognitive development (eleven to fifteen years of age) proposed by Jean Piaget in which cognitive abilities reach their highest level of development.

Formative evaluation (p. 309): an assessment, or diagnosis, of students' learning for the purpose of planning instruction.

Fringe benefits (p. 80): benefits (i.e., medical insurance, retirement, and tax-deferred investment opportunities) that are given to teachers in addition to base salary.

Full inclusion (p. 146): the policy and process of including exceptional learners in general education classrooms. According to the full-inclusion approach, included students need only benefit from such placement, and support services are *brought to* included students—they do not have to participate in pull-out programs.

Funding of education (p. 225): financial support of the school system at the local, provincial, or federal level.

Futurism (p. 374): the process of making forecasts about the future based on analyses of current social, economic, and technological trends.

G

Gender bias (p. 150): subtle bias or discrimination on the basis of gender; reduces the likelihood that the target of the bias will develop to the full extent of his or her capabilities.

Gender-fair curricula (p. 150): school curricula that are free of bias or discrimination on the basis of gender.

Gifted and talented (p. 147): exceptional learners who demonstrate high intelligence, high creativity, high achievement, or special talent(s).

H

Hidden curriculum (p. 118): the behaviors, attitudes, and knowledge the school culture unintentionally teaches students.

Higher-order questions (p. 301): questions that require the ability to engage in complex modes of thought (synthesis, analysis, and evaluation, for example).

Hypermedia (p. 390): an interactive instructional system consisting of a computer, CD-ROM drive, videodisc player, video monitor, and speakers. Hypermedia systems allow students to control and present sound, video images, text, and graphics in an almost limitless array of possibilities.

I

Individual education program (IEP) (p. 148): a plan for meeting an exceptional learner's educational needs, specifying goals, objectives, services, and procedures for evaluating progress.

Induction programs (p. 69): programs of support for beginning teachers, usually during their first year of teaching.

Information processing (p. 379): a branch of cognitive science concerned with how individuals use long- and short-term memory to acquire information and solve problems.

Inquiry-based curriculum (p. 335): a curriculum that teaches not only the content but also the thought processes of a discipline.

In-service workshops (p. 363): on-site professional development programs in which teachers meet to learn new techniques, develop curricular materials, share ideas, or solve problems.

Institution (p. 117): any organization a society establishes to maintain, and improve, its way of life.

Instructional Theory into Practice (p. 61): a systematic approach to developing lessons that contain seven essential elements: anticipatory set, objective and purpose, input, modeling, check for understanding, guided practice, and independent practice.

Integrated curriculum (p. 328): a school curriculum that draws from two or more subject areas and focuses on a theme or concept rather than on a single subject.

Intelligence (p. 262): the ability to learn; the cognitive capacity for thinking.

Interactive multimedia (p. 390): computer-supported media that allow the user to interact with a vast non-linear, multimedia database to combine textual, audio, video information.

Interactive teaching (p. 42): teaching characterized by face-to-face interactions between teachers and students in contrast to preactive teaching.

Internship programs (p. 69): programs of assistance and training for beginning teachers, usually for those who have not gone through a teacher education program.

J

Job analysis (p. 17): a procedure for determining the knowledge and skills needed for a job.

K

Knowledge base (p. 14): the body of knowledge that represents what teachers need to [know and be able to do].

L

Latchkey children (p. 259): children who, because of family circumstances, must spend part of each day unsupervised by a parent or guardian.

Learning (p. 378): changes in behavior the individual makes in response to environmental stimuli; the acquisition and organization of knowledge and skills.

Learning disability (LD) (p. 143): a limitation in one's ability to take in, organize, remember, and express information.

Learning style (p. 265): a set of cognitive, affective, and physiological behaviors through which an individual learns most effectively; determined by a combination of hereditary and environmental influences.

LEAST approach (p. 297): a sequence of steps teachers can follow to maintain discipline in the classroom.

Letter of application (p. 86): a letter written in application for a specific teaching vacancy in a school district.

Letter of inquiry (p. 86): a letter written to a school district inquiring about teaching vacancies.

Logic (p. 185): a branch of philosophy concerned with the processes of reasoning and the identification of rules that will enable thinkers to reach valid conclusions.

Lower-order questions (p. 301): questions that require students to recall specific information.

M

Magnet school (p. 120): a school offering a curriculum that focuses on a specific area such as the performing arts, mathematics, science, international studies, or technology. Magnet schools often draw students from a larger attendance area than regular schools.

Mainstreaming (p. 146): the policy and process of integrating disabled or otherwise exceptional learners into regular classrooms with nonexceptional students.

Measurement (p. 309): the gathering of data that indicate how much students have learned.

Mentor (p. 357): a wise, knowledgeable individual who provides guidance and encouragement to someone, a protégé.

Metaphysics (p. 181): a branch of philosophy concerned with the nature of reality.

Microcomputer (p. 387): a small, yet powerful computer with a wide variety of educational applications including computer-aided instruction, data analysis, and simulations.

Microcultural groups (p. 258): cultural subgroups within a larger (macro) culture.

Microteaching (p. 64): a brief, single-concept lesson taught by a teacher education student to a small group of students; usually designed to give the education student an opportunity to practice a specific teaching skill.

Minister of education (p. 223): a member of the provincial legislature appointed by the premier to be the central educational authority in the province.

Ministry of education (p. 223): the provincial agency responsible for the creation and implementation of educational policy.

Minority group (p. 134): a group of people who share certain characteristics, and is smaller in number than the majority of a population.

Model of teaching (p. 311): a coherent pattern of instructional strategies teachers may develop to obtain particular results in the classroom.

Modes of teaching (p. 31): different aspects of the teaching function—for example, teaching as a way of being, as a creative endeavor, as a live performance, and so on.

Moral reasoning (p. 271): the reasoning process people follow to decide what is right or wrong.

Multicultural (p. 110): a term used to describe a group whose members are from several different cultures; multiculturalism refers to diversity among students in classrooms in regard to their first language, religion, values, ethnicity, sex, and social class; reflections of concern with this diversity in curricula.

Multicultural education (p. 151): education that provides equal educational opportunities to all students—regardless of socioeconomic status, gender, or ethnic, racial, or cultural backgrounds—and is dedicated to reducing prejudice and celebrating the rich diversity of Canadian life.

Multiple intelligences (p. 264): a perspective on intellectual ability, proposed by Howard Gardner, suggesting that there are at least seven types of human intelligence.

N

Networking (p.387): the process of using computers to communicate—for example, exchanging information through electronic bulletin boards and electronic mail (e-mail).

No-lose method (p. 299): an approach to classroom management that begins with the teacher determining whether a classroom conflict is a teacher-owned problem, a student-owned problem, or a shared problem.

Null curriculum (p. 324): the intellectual processes and subject content that schools do not teach.

O

Open-space schools (p. 118): schools that have large instructional areas with movable walls and furniture that can be rearranged easily.

Opportunity to learn (OTL) (p. 294): the time during which a teacher provides students with challenging content and appropriate instructional strategies to learn that content.

P

Parent Advisory Council (PAC) (p. 217): a community group which gives parents the opportunity to influence and participate in educational policy.

Parent-Teacher Association (PTA) (p. 217): an organization made up of parents and teachers who share a concern for education.

Peer coaching (p. 381): an arrangement whereby teachers grow professionally by observing one another's teaching and providing constructive feedback.

Peer counseling (p. 381): an arrangement whereby students, monitored by a school counselor or teacher, counsel one another in such areas as low achievement, interpersonal problems, substance abuse, and career planning.

Peer tutoring (p. 292): an arrangement whereby students tutor other students in the same classroom or at the same grade level.

Perennialism (p. 186): a philosophical orientation that emphasizes the ideas contained in the Great Books and maintains that the true purpose of education is the discovery of the universal, or perennial, truths of life.

Permanent contract (p. 240): a secure form of employment granted to experienced teachers.

Personal-development view (p. 15): the belief that teachers become more effective by increasing their self-knowledge and developing themselves as persons.

Philosophy (p. 176): a field of study concerned with identifying basic truths about being, knowledge, and conduct.

Post degree programs (p. 60): professional education courses for which a bachelor's degree and other academic preparation are prerequisites.

Practicum (p. 65): a short field-based experience during which teacher education students spend time observing and assisting in classrooms.

Preactive teaching (p. 42): the stage of teaching when a teacher prepares to teach or reflects on previous teaching experiences in contrast with interactive teaching.

Preoperational stage (p. 271): the stage of cognitive development (two to seven years of age) proposed by Jean Piaget in which the individual begins to use language and symbols to think of objects and people outside of the immediate environment.

Probationary contract (p. 240): a temporary employment term whose length varies from province to province, granted to new teachers.

Problem-centered learning (p. 342): an approach to instruction in which students work in small groups on problems that have many or open-ended solutions.

Procedural fairness (p. 238): a principle which helps to protect the legal rights of teachers.

Profession (p. 350): an occupation that requires a high level of expertise, including advanced study in a specialized field, adherence to a code of ethics, and the ability to work without close supervision.

Professional code of ethics (p. 234): a set of values designed to guide teachers in their professional conduct and judgement; each provincial teachers' association has its own code of ethics.

Professional development school (PDS) (p. 364): a school that has formed a partnership with a college or university for the purpose of improving the school and contributing to the improvement of teacher preparation programs. Activites at a PDS may include collaborative research, team teaching, demonstration lessons by teacher education faculty, and various professional growth opportunities for teachers and teacher educators.

Professional empowerment (p. 12): a trend for teachers to have expanded opportunities to make decisions that affect their professional lives.

Professional portfolios (p. 22): a collection of various kinds of evidence (e.g., projects, written work, and video demonstrations of skills) documenting the achievement and performance of students.

Professionalization of teaching (p. 361): changes taking place in education that are enhancing the professional status of teachers; for example, longer and more rigorous preparation programs, higher salaries, and more opportunities to share in the governance of schools.

Progressivism (p. 188): a philosophical orientation based on the belief that life is evolving in a positive direction, that people may be trusted to act in their own best interests, and that education should focus on the needs and interests of students.

Psychosocial crisis (p. 271): a life crisis at one of eight different stages of growth and development. According to psychologist Erik Erikson, individuals must resolve each crisis to reach the next stage.

Psychosocial development (p. 271): the progression of an individual through various stages of psychological and social development.

R

Race (p. 135): a concept of human variation used to distinguish people on the basis of biological traits and characteristics.

Racism (p. 135): the prejudicial belief that one's ethnic or racial group is superior to others.

Realities of teaching (p. 35): actual conditions teachers face in the classroom; the demands as well as the rewards.

Reality therapy (p. 298): an approach to classroom management, developed by psychiatrist William Glasser, calling for teachers to create positive, caring relationships with students and requiring them to take responsibility for their behavior.

Reconstructionism (p. 196): a philosophical orientation that maintains that a better, more just society can be created by identifying, then correcting, social ills.

Reflection (p. 21): the process of thinking carefully and deliberately about the outcomes of one's teaching.

Reflection-in-action (p. 356): the process of engaging in serious, reflective thought about improving one's professional practicewhile one is engaged in that practice.

Reflective teaching (p. 60): an approach to teaching that encourages the teacher to use careful, deliberate reflection as the primary means of decision making.

Reflective teaching log (p. 68): a journal of classroom observations in which the teacher education student systematically analyzes specific episodes of teaching.

Regional unit (p. 224): an intermediate level of support and governance of schools, situated between the local and provincial levels.

Relevancy-based curriculum (p. 336): a curriculum that is relevant to students' needs, interests, and concerns with social issues.

Research-based competencies (p. 15): specific behaviors that educational research has identified as characteristic of effective teachers.

Restructuring (p. 17): reorganizing how schools are controlled at the local level so that teachers, principals, parents, and community members have greater authority.

Résumé (p. 86): a concise summary of an individual's professional experiences and education.

Ryerson, Edgerton (p. 162): an early proponent of public, nondenominational education.

S

School-based management (SBM) (p. 217): various approaches to school improvement in which teachers, principals, students, parents, and community members manage individual schools and share in the decision-making processes.

School board (p. 213): the primary governing body of a local school district.

School district (p. 212): a geographical region created by the provinces to divide responsibility for the operation of public schools.

School houses (p. 382): a method of organization in which teachers and students at a school are assigned to one of several houses within the school; sometimes referred to as the school-within-a-school concept.

School traditions (p. 118): the elements of a school's culture that reflect what the school wishes to be known for; for example, activities that emphasize academic excellence, accomplishments in the arts, or close school-community relations.

Self-assessment (p. 22): the process of measuring one's growth in regard to the knowledge, skills, and attitudes possessed by professional teachers.

Self-contained classroom (p. 117): an organizational structure for schools in which one teacher instructs a group of students (typically, twenty to thirty) in a single classroom.

Sexism (p. 149): the belief that one's sex is superior to the other; used to justify discrimination.

Sex-role socialization (p. 261): socially expected behavior patterns conveyed to individuals on the basis of gender.

Sex-role stereotyping (p. 262): beliefs that subtly encourage males and females to conform to certain behavioral norms regardless of abilities and interests.

Special education (p. 141): a teaching specialty for meeting the special educational needs of exceptional learners.

Staff teams (p. 381): an innovative teaching method whereby groups of teachers share in decision-making and classroom responsibilities.

Stages of development (p. 270): predictable stages through which individuals pass as they progress through life.

Stages of group development (p. 303): identifiable stages through which a group passes as its members learn to work together.

Stereotypes (p. 115): behavioral characteristics attributed to all members of a group; formulated on the basis of limited experiences with and information about the group coupled with an unwillingness to examine prejudices.

Student-centered curriculum (p. 328): curricula that are organized around students' needs and interests.

Student diversity (p. 8): differences among students in regard to gender, race, ethnicity, culture, and socioeconomic status.

Student variability (p. 8): differences among students in regard to their developmental needs, interests, abilities, and disabilities.

Students at risk (p. 122): students whose living conditions and backgrounds place them at risk for dropping out of school.

Students with disabilities (p. 267): students who need special education services because they possess one or more of the following disabilities: learning disabilities, speech or language impairments, mental retardation, serious emotional disturbance, hearing impairments, orthopedic impairments, visual impairments, or other health impairments.

Subject-centered curriculum (p. 328): a curriculum that emphasizes learning an academic discipline.

Summative evaluation (p. 309): an assessment of student learning made for the purpose of assigning grades at the end of a unit, semester, or year and deciding whether students are ready to proceed to the next phase of their education.

Superintendent (p. 215): the chief administrator of a school district.

Suspension (p. 246): a disciplinary action which prohibits a student from attending school for a certain amount of time.

T

Teacher centers (p. 363): centers where teachers provide other teachers with instructional materials and new methods and where teachers can exchange ideas.

Teacher effectiveness research (p. 45): educational research focused on identifying the significant differences between more and less effective teachers.

Teacher empowerment (p. 359): the trend to grant teachers greater power and more opportunities to make decisions that affect their professional lives.

Teacher supply and demand (p. 78): the number of school-age students compared to the number of available teachers; may also be projected based on estimated numbers of students and teachers.

Teachers' thought processes (p. 44): the thoughts that guide teachers' actions in classrooms. These thoughts typically consist of thoughts related to planning, theories and beliefs, and interactive thoughts and decisions.

Teaching certificate (p. 81): a license to teach issued by a state or, in a few cases, a large city.

Teaching functions (p. 58): instructional strategies that research has identified as enhancing students' learning of the basic skills.

Teaching simulations (p. 64): an activity in which teacher education students participate in role-plays designed to create situations comparable to those actually encountered by teachers.

Team teaching (p. 118): an arrangement whereby a team of teachers teaches a group of students equal in number to what the teachers would have in their self-contained classrooms.

Time on task (p. 293): the amount of time students are actively and directly engaged in learning tasks.

Tyler rationale (p. 326): a four-step model for curriculum development in which teachers identify purposes, select learning experiences, organize experiences, and evaluate.

V

Videodiscs (p. 389): twelve-inch plastic discs, each side of which holds about thirty minutes of motion video, or 54 000 frames of video; each frame can be frozen with a high degree of clarity.

Vocational education (p. 344): schooling that prepares students for particular jobs or provides them with the basic skills and career awareness needed to enter the world of work.

W

Whole-language movement (p. 339): the practice of teaching language skills (listening, reading, and writing) as part of students' everyday experiences rather than as isolated experiences.

Within-class ability grouping (p. 292): the practice of creating small, homogeneous groups of students within a single classroom for the purpose of instruction, usually in reading or mathematics, at the elementary level.

Y

Young Offenders Act, 1984 (p. 247): a set of principles which govern how minors who commit criminal offences should be handled.

Z

Zone of proximal development (p. 379): a term coined by Soviet psychologist L. S. Vygotsky to refer to the point at which students need assistance to continue learning.

Teacher's Resource Guide

STATEMENT OF BELIEFS

The Council of Ministers of Education, Canada (CMEC)

The CMEC comprises the Ministers of Education across Canada. Following their 64th meeting in Victoria, British Columbia on September 28, 1993, the CMEC issued a statement which included:

The ministers responsible for education hold the following beliefs in common:

We believe that education is a lifelong learning process. We also believe that the future of our society depends on informed and educated citizens who, while fulfilling their own goals of personal and professional development, contribute to the social, economic, and cultural development of the community and the country as a whole. Beyond our borders, Canadian education should reflect the priorities of Canadians while contributing to strengthening Canada's place internationally.

We share many common educational goals and we agree to ensure greater harmonization of the ways we set about achieving them. There is already in place a vast range of educational opportunities across Canada which should be fully accessible to individual learners. We jointly want to have the highest quality education based on shared and relevant goals, and to demonstrate accountability for achieving them.

Above all, we want all citizens to have a fair and equitable opportunity in whatever educational and training endeavours they may pursue.

More specifically, CMEC's actions will focus on the following four themes which we see as crucial in the coming years: quality of education, accountability, accessibility, and mobility.

After listing these four themes, the CMEC indicated that it will place priority on examining curriculum across the provinces to identify areas of commonality and possible joint initiatives. The Atlantic provinces have begun a regional approach to common core curriculum and the western provinces have given priority to expanding the work they have already completed in collaborating around curriculum initiatives.

The CMEC will also expand the current School Achievement Indicators Program adding science to reading, writing, and mathematics. In addition it will develop measurement tools to compare student completion rates, rates of successful transition to work, and satisfaction levels of students, educators, and the public.

Given the nature of education in Canada, this is the closest we can come to having a national statement of beliefs about education.

The Canadian School Boards Association

The Canadian School Boards Association believes the purpose of public education is to assist students to realize their full potential, contribute to society, and shape their individual and collective futures.

We believe every child has a right to a publicly-funded public elementary and secondary education. As a signatory of the United Nations Convention of the Rights of the Child, Canada has confirmed that right (Article 28).

We believe the nation has an interest in the education of children. Recognizing constitutional guarantees and responsibility of the provinces and territories for education, we believe there must be a national perspective in education.

We believe Canadian society as a whole, parents, local communities, educators, students, business, labour, and government must contribute towards the creation of a learning culture.

We believe that education encompasses all dimensions of a student's development.

We believe an educated populace is an essential foundation of our individual and collective economic and social well-being.

We believe governance by locally-elected school boards is the cornerstone of public education.

NATIONAL GOALS FOR ELEMENTARY/ SECONDARY EDUCATION IN CANADA

The Canadian School Boards Association

Intellectual Development

Students develop the knowledge, skills and attitudes to acquire, analyze and apply information necessary for lifelong learning.

Enabling Knowledge and Skills:
Competency in reading, computing, oral and written communication.
Knowledge and skills in the humanities, sciences, technology, mathematics, and the practical and fine arts.

Lifelong Learning:
Positive attitude towards learning throughout a lifetime.

Personal and Social Development

Students develop self-esteem, acceptance of responsibility for their own actions, and respect for the ideas and beliefs of others.

Values:
Ability to make moral and ethical decisions.

Social Justice:
Understanding and appreciation of fundamental human rights and of Canadian Charter of Rights and Freedoms.

Personal Development:
Development of a positive self-concept.
Sense of belonging to a community.
Openness to innovation, change and risk-taking.
Physical and mental well-being.
Ability to interact co-operatively with others.
Pride in one's heritage.

Citizenship:
Pride in Canada and in its multiculturalism.
Recognition of global interdependence.
Respect for law, property and the rights of others.

Career Development

Students develop an understanding of the link between ongoing education and economic and personal well-being. Students will be prepared to make the career and life decisions necessary to become productive Canadian citizens.

Awareness:
Knowledge, skills, attitudes and habits expected by the work world.
Awareness of choices with respect to a profession, trade or occupation.
Skills and strategies facilitating entry into the workforce.
Awareness and appreciation of entrepreneurship.

Change/Adaptability:
Confidence in making decisions.

RESOURCES IN EDUCATIONAL RESEARCH

Periodicals and Publications

Canada:
ABC Canada: Literacy at Work
Association of Canadian Educators of the Hearing Impaired Journal
Association for Canadian Studies Journal
Applying Research to the Classroom
Canadian Association for Health, Physical Education, Recreation, and Dance Journal
Canadian Association for Health, Physical Education, Recreation, and Dance Newsletter
Canadian Association of University Teachers Bulletin
Canadian Catholic School Trustees' Association Newsletter
Canadian Educational Association Newsletter
CM: A Reviewing Journal of Canadian Materials for Young People
Canadian Music Educators' Association Newsletter
Canadian Parents for French National News
Canadian School Boards Association Action Journal
Canadian Administrator
Canadian Children Journal
Canadian Home Economics Journal
Canadian and International Education Journal
Canadian Journal for Counselling
Canadian Journal of Education
Canadian Journal of Educational Communication
Canadian Journal of Higher Education

Canadian Journal of Native Education
Canadian Journal of University Continuing Education
Canadian Modern Language Review
Canadian Music Educator
Canadian Principal Journal
Canadian Review of Art Education
Canadian School Executive
Canadian Socials Studies Journal: The History and Social Science Teacher
Canadian Vocational Journal
Cognica: Canadian Guidance and Counselling Journal
Community (Canadian Association of Community Colleges)
Convergence (International Council for Adult Education)
Curriculum Inquiry
Dialogue (Council of Ministers of Education)
Education Canada
Education and Law Journal
Edulaw for Canadian Schools
English Quarterly (English and Language Arts Teachers)
Exceptionality Education Canada (Gifted Children)
Green Teacher
Guidance and Counselling
Health Promotion in Canada
Historical Studies in Education
Home and School
International Council for Adult Education News

Interchange: A Quarterly Review of Education
Journal of Educational Administration and Foundations
The Journal of Educational Thought
Learning (Canadian Association for Adult Education)
McGill Journal of Education
Media News (Association for Media and Technology in Education)
Mosaic Quarterly
Multiculturalism
Our Schools/Our Selves
PAIDEUSIS (Canadian Philosophy of Education Society)
Policy Exploration
Quill and Quire
School Libraries in Canada
Special Times: Special People
TESL Talk (Ontario Ministry of Citizenship)
Teach Magazine
University Affairs
UniWorld

The United States:

Academic Computing
Action in Teacher Education
Adolescence
American Biology Teacher
American Educational Research Journal
American Educator: The Professional Journal of the American Federation of Teachers
American Journal of Education
American School Board Journal
Arithmetic Teacher
Art Education
Bilingual Review
Black Scholar
Business Education Forum
Career Development for Exceptional Individuals
Career Development Quarterly
Child Abuse and Neglect: The International Journal
Child Development
Child Study Journal
Child Welfare
Childhood Education
Children Today
Children's Literature in Education
Classroom Computer Learning
Clearing House
Communication Education
Comparative Education
Computers and Education
Computers and the Humanities
Computers in the Schools
Computing Teacher
Contemporary Education
Curriculum and Teaching
Early Childhood Research Quarterly
Education and Computing
Education and Urban Society
Educational Forum

Educational Horizons
Educational Leadership
Educational Record
Educational Research
Educational Research Quarterly
Educational Researcher
Educational Review
Educational Technology
Educational Theory
Electronic Learning
Elementary School Journal
English Education
English Journal
English Language Teaching Journal (ELT Journal)
Equity and Choice
Equity and Excellence
Exceptional Children
Focus on Exceptional Children
Focus on Learning Problems in Mathematics
Forum for Reading
Geographical Education
Gifted Child Quarterly
Gifted Child Today
Gifted Education International
Harvard Educational Review
Health Education
Health Education Quarterly
High School Journal
History and Social Science Teacher
History Teacher
Home Economic Research Journal
Industrial Education
Instructor
International Journal of Early Childhood
International Journal of Educational Research
Journal for Research in Mathematics Education
Journal for Vocational Special Needs Education
Journal of Adolescence
Journal of Alcohol and Drug Education
Journal of American Indian Education
Journal of Black Studies
Journal of Classroom Interaction
Journal of Computer-Assisted Learning
Journal of Computer-Based Instruction
Journal of Computers in Mathematics and Science Teaching
Journal of Curriculum and Supervision
Journal of Curriculum Studies
Journal of Developmental Education
Journal of Drug Education
Journal of Early Intervention
Journal of Education
Journal of Educational Computing Research
Journal of Educational Research
Journal of Environmental Education
Journal of Home Economics
Journal of Humanistic Education and Development
Journal of Learning Disabilities
Journal of Negro Education

Journal of Physical Education, Recreation, and Dance
Journal of Reading
Journal of Reading Behavior
Journal of Research in Childhood Education
Journal of Research in Computing in Education
Journal of Research in Music Education
Journal of Research in Reading
Journal of Research in Science Teaching
Journal of Rural and Small Schools
Journal of Social Studies Research
Journal of Special Education
Journal of Teacher Education
Journal of Teaching in Physical Education
Journal of Youth and Adolescence
Kappa Delta Pi Record
Language Arts
Language, Speech, and Hearing Services in Schools
Learning
Learning Disabilities Focus
Learning Disabilities Research
Learning Disability Quarterly
Mathematics and Computer Education
Mathematics Teacher
Music Educators Journal
NABE: The Journal for the National Association for Bilingual Education
NASSP Bulletin
Negro Educational Review
New Directions for Child Development
New Directions for Teaching and Learning
Peabody Journal of Education
Phi Delta Kappan
Physical Educator
Physics Teacher
Preventing School Failure
Programmed Learning and Educational Technology
Psychology in the Schools
PTA Today
Reading Horizons
Reading Improvement
Reading Research and Instruction
Reading Research Quarterly
Reading Teacher
Remedial and Special Education
Research in Rural Education
Research in the Teaching of English
Review of Educational Research
Rural Educator
School Arts
School Science and Mathematics
Science and Children
Science Education
Science Teacher
Social Studies and the Young Learner
Social Studies Journal
Social Studies Professional
Sociology of Education
Studies in Art Education
Teacher Magazine
Teachers College Record

Teaching Exceptional Children
TESOL Quarterly
T.H.E. Journal (Technological Horizons in Education)
Theory and Research in Social Education
Theory into Practice

Topics in Early Childhood Special Education
Urban Education
Vocational Education Journal
Young Children
Youth and Society

Educational Resources Information Clearinghouses (ERIC)

Educational technology and library information science at all academic levels and with all populations, including the preparation of professionals. The media and devices of educational communication, as they pertain to teaching and learning (in both conventional and distance education settings). The operation and management of libraries and information services. All aspects of information management and information technology related to education.

ERIC Clearinghouse on Reading, English, and Communication (CS)

Indiana University
Smith Research Center, Suite 150
2806 East 10th Street
Bloomington, IN 47408-2696
Telephone: 812-855-6847
800: 800-769-4723
FAX: 812-855-4220
Internet: ericcs@ucs.indiana.edu

Reading and writing, English (as a first language), and communications skills (verbal and nonverbal), kindergarten through college. Includes family or intergenerational literacy. Research and instructional development in reading, writing, speaking, and listening. Identification, diagnosis, and remediation of reading problems. Speech communication (including forensics), mass communication (including journalism), interpersonal and small group interaction, oral interpretation, rhetorical and communication theory, and theater/drama. Preparation of instructional staff and related personnel in all the above areas.

ERIC Clearinghouse on Rural Education and Small Schools (RC)

Appalachia Educational Laboratory (AEL)
1031 Quarrier Street, P.O. Box 1348
Charleston, WV 26326-1848
Telephone: 304-347-0465; (800) 624-9120
FAX: 304-347-0487
Internet: u56d9@wvnvm.wvnet.edu

Curriculum and instructional programs and research/evaluation efforts that address the education of students in rural schools or districts, small schools wherever located, and schools of districts wherever located that serve American-Indian and Alaskan natives, Mexican Americans, and migrants, or that have programs related to outdoor education. Includes the cultural, ethnic, linguistic, economic, and social conditions that affect these educational institutions and groups. Preparation programs, including related services, that train education professionals to work in such contexts.

ERIC Clearinghouse on Science, Mathematics, and Environmental Education (SE)

Ohio State University
1929 Kenny Road
Columbus, OH 43210-1080
Telephone: 614-292-6717
FAX: 614-292-0263
Internet: haury.2@osu.edu

Science, mathematics, engineering/technology, and environmental education at all levels. The following topics when focused on any of the above broad scope areas: applications of learning theory; curriculum and instructional materials; teachers and teacher education; educational programs and projects; research and evaluative studies; applications of educational technology and media.

ERIC Clearinghouse for Social Studies/Social Science Education (SO)

Indiana University
Social Studies, Development Center
2805 East 10th Street, Suite 120
Bloomington, IN 47408-2698
Telephone: 812-855-3838
FAX: 812-855-0455
Internet: ericso@ucs.indiana.edu

All aspects of Social Studies and Social Science Education, including values education (and the social aspects of environmental education and sex education), international education, comparative education, and crosscultural studies in all subject areas (K–12). Ethnic heritage, gender equity, aging, and social bias/discrimination topics. Also covered are music, art, and architecture as related to the fine arts. Includes input from Adjunct ERIC Clearinghouses for U.S.–Japan Studies.

ERIC Clearinghouse on Teaching and Teacher Education (SP)

American Association of Colleges for Teacher Education (AACTE)
One Dupont Circle, N.W., Suite 810
Washington, DC 20036-1186
Telephone: 202-293-2450
FAX: 202-457-8095
Internet: jbeck@inet.ed.gov

School personnel at all levels. Teacher recruitment, selection, licensing, certification, training, preservice and inservice preparation, evaluation, retention, and refinement. The theory, philosophy, and practice of teaching. Organization, administration, finance, and legal issues relating to teacher education programs and institutions. All aspects of health, physical, recreation, and dance education.

ERIC Clearinghouse on Adult, Career, and Vocational Education (CE)
Ohio State University
Center on Education and Training for Employment
1900 Kenny Road
Columbus, OH 43210-1090
Telephone: 614-292-4353; (800) 848-4815
FAX: 614-292-1260
Internet: ericacve@magnue.ecs.ohio-state.edu

All levels of adult and continuing education from basic literacy training through professional skill upgrading. The focus is on factors contributing to the purposeful learning of adults in a variety of life situations usually related to adult roles (e.g., occupation, family, leisure time, citizenship, organization relationships, retirement, and so forth). Includes input from Adjunct ERIC Clearinghouse on Consumer Education.

ERIC Clearinghouse on Assessment and Evaluation (TM)
Catholic University of America
210 O'Boyle Hall
Washington, DC 20064-4035
Telephone: 202-319-5120
FAX: 202-342-5003
Internet: eric_ae@cua.edu

All aspects of tests and other measurement devices. The design and methodology of research, measurement, and evaluation. The evaluation of programs and projects. The application of tests, measurement, and evaluation devices/instrumentation in education projects and programs.

ERIC Clearinghouse for Community Colleges (JC)
University of California at Los Angeles (UCLA)
Math-Sciences Building, Room 8118
405 Hiligard Avenue
Los Angeles, CA 90024-1564
Telephone: 310-825-3931
FAX: 310-206-8095

Development, administration, and evaluation of two-year public and private community and junior colleges, technical institutes, and two-year branch university campuses. Two-year college students, faculty, staff, curricula, programs, support services, libraries, and community services. Linkages between two-year colleges and business/industrial/community organizations. Articulation of two-year colleges with secondary and four-year postsecondary institutions.

ERIC Clearinghouse on Counseling and Student Services (CG)
University of North Carolina at Greensboro
School of Education
Greensboro, NC 27412-5001
Telephone: 919-334-4114
FAX: 919-334-4116

Preparation, practice, and supervision of counselors at all educational levels and in all settings. Theoretical development of counseling and guidance, including the nature of relevant human characteristics. Use and results of personnel practices and procedures. Group process (counseling, therapy, dynamics) and case work.

ERIC Clearinghouse on Disabilities and Gifted Education (EC)
Council for Exceptional Children (CEC)
1920 Association Drive
Reston, VA 22091-1589
Telephone: 703-264-9474
FAX: 703-264-9494
Internet: ericec@gwuvm.gwu.edu

All aspects of the education and development of persons (of all ages) who have disabilities or who are gifted, including the delivery of all types of education-related services to these groups. Includes prevention, identification and assessment, intervention, and enrichment for these groups, in both regular and special education settings.

ERIC Clearinghouse on Educational Management (EA)
University of Oregon
1787 Agate Street
Eugene, OR 97403-5207
Telephone: 503-346-5043; 800-436-8641
FAX: 503-346-2334

All aspects of the governance, leadership, administration, and structure of public and private educational organizations at the elementary and secondary levels, including the provision of physical facilities for their operation.

ERIC Clearinghouse on Elementary and Early Childhood Education (PS)
University of Illinois
805 West Pennsylvania Avenue
Urbana, IL 61801-4897
Telephone: 217-333-1386
FAX: 217-333-3767
Internet: ericece@ux1.cso.uiuc.edu

All aspects of the physical, cognitive, social, emotional, educational, and cultural development of children, from birth through early adolescence. Among the topics covered are prenatal and infant development and care; parent education; home and school relationships; learning theory research and practice related to children's development;

preparation of early childhood teachers and caregivers; and educational programs and community service for children.

ERIC Clearinghouse on Higher Education (HE)
George Washington University
One Dupont Circle, N.W. Suite 630
Washington, DC 20036-1183
Telephone: 202-296-2607
FAX: 202-298-8379
Internet: eriche@inet.edu.gov

All aspects of the conditions, programs, and problems at colleges and universities providing higher education (i.e., four-year degrees and beyond). This includes governance and management; planning; finance; interinstitutional arrangements; business or industry programs leading to a degree; institutional research at the college/university level; federal programs; legal issue and legislation; professional education (e.g., medicine, law, etc.) and professional continuing education.

ERIC Clearinghouse on Information and Technology (IR)
Syracuse University
Center for Science and Technology, 4th Floor, Room 194
Syracuse, NY 13244-4100
Telephone: 315-443-3640
FAX: 315-443-5448
Internet: eric@ericir.syr.edu
AskERIC (Question service via Internet):
askeric@ericir.syr.ed

Educational Teaching Journals and Periodicals by Province

British Columbia
Abracadabra (Association of BC Drama Teachers)
BC Alternative Education Association Newsletter
BC Journal for Art Teachers
BC Association of Teachers of Modern Language Newsletter
BC Business Education Association Signature
BC English Teachers' Association Journal of Student Writing
BC Music Educator
BC Counsellor
Best of Teaching
Bookmark (BC Librarians' Association)
Catalyst (BC Science Teachers' Association)
Classroom Connection (BC Co-operative Learning Association)
Cue Journal (Computer Using Educators of BC)
Ecolacy (Environmental Educators)
First Nations Education Association Newsletter
Horizon (BC Social Studies Teachers)
Ideas Collection (BC Primary Teachers)
In Touch (BC Intermediate Teachers)
Journal of the Association of Educators of Gifted, Talented, and Creative Children of BC
Learning Assistant Teachers' Association Newsletter

Notes for ESL
Page (BC Teachers for Peace and Global Education)
Physical Education Provincial Specialist Association Newsletter
Prime Areas (BC Primary Teachers' Association)
Research Forum (BC Ministry of Education)
Rural Root Journal
Special Education Association Newsletter
Teacher (BCTF)
Thesa Newsletter (Teachers of Home Economics)
Update (BC English Teachers' Association)
Vector (Mathematics Teachers)
View (BC Technology Education Association)

Alberta
Agate (Gifted and Talented Education)
Alberta Counsellor
Alberta English
Alberta Journal of Educational Research
Alberta Modern Language Journal
Alberta Science Education Journal
ATA Magazine
ATA News
Computer Council of ATA Newsletter
Challenge (School Administrators)
Connections (Environmental Education)
delta-K (Mathematics Council)
Early Childhood Education
Fine (Fine Arts Council)
Journal of Home Economics Education
Multicultural Education Journal
One World (Social Studies Council)
Runner (Health and Physical Education)
Salt (Religious and Moral Education Council)
Spectrum (Alberta School Boards' Association)
Teacher-Librarian Today

Saskatchewan
AWASIS Journal/Newsletter (Indian and Native Education Council)
Accelerator Newsletter (Science Teachers' Society)
Art Education
Cadenza (Music Educators' Association)
Guidelines (Guidance and Counselling)
Hear Our Wings (Council for the Education of the Gifted)
In the Middle (Middle Years Association)
Insite (Industrial Education Association)
Intercom (Business Teachers' Association)
Lifeline (Health Educators' Association)
Medium (School Library Association)
On the Move (Physical Education Council)
Perspectives (Council of Social Sciences)
Prisma (Association of Teachers of German)
Query (Reading Council)
Saskatchewan Bulletin (Teachers' Federation)
Saskatchewan Educational Administrator
Saskatchewan Association for Computers in Education Bulletin

Saskatchewan Career/Work Education Bulletin
SDA Journal (Drama Association)
School Trustee
Skylark/Golden Taffy (Teachers of English and Language Arts)
SMTS News/Journal (Mathematics Teachers' Society)
TEMA (Teachers of Ukraine)
TRACE Newsletter (Teachers of Religion and Christian Ethics)
Venture Forth (Early Childhood Education Council)
VISTA (Home Economics Teachers' Association.

Manitoba
Classmate (Association of Teachers of English)
Colony Educators of Manitoba Newsletter
IMAGES (Association of Gifted Educators)
Impressions/Expressions (French Teachers' Association)
MAAE Bulletin (Association for Art Teachers)
Manitoba ALL Newsletter (Lifelong Learning)
Manitoba ACE Journal (Association of Computing Educators)
Manitoba CEC News (Council for Exceptional Children)
Manitoba ETA Journal (Elementary Teachers)
Manitoba Journal of Counselling
The Math Journal
Manitoba Music Educator
Manitoba OEEA Newsletter (Outdoor/Environmental Education)
Manitoba Science Teacher
Manitoba Social Science Teacher
Manitoba Spectra (Business Education)
Manitoba Teacher (Manitoba Teachers' Society)
MART Journal (Resource Teachers)
MAST Journal (Association of School Trustees)
MAST Newsletter
MHETA Journal (Home Economics Teachers' Association)
MPETA Journal (Physical Education Teachers' Association)
MSLA Journal (School Library Association)
Principal Issue
Reading Manitoba (Reading Council of Greater Winnipeg)
TEAM Journal (Technology Educators' Association)
TESL Manitoba (Teachers of English as a Second Language)
Today for Tomorrow (Early Childhood Education)
VITA Journal (Vocational Industrial Teachers' Association)

Ontario
Catholic Trustee
Crucible (Science Teachers' Association)
Education for a Global Perspective
Education Forum (Secondary Teachers)
Education Today (Public School Boards)
FWTAO Newsletter (Women Teachers)

Fast Reports (Public School Boards)
Indirections (Council of Teachers of English, Communications and Language Arts)
Monograph (Geographic and Environmental Education)
NEWS (Public School Teachers' Federation)
OTF/FEO Interaction (Ontario Teachers' Federation)
Ontario Mathematics Gazette
Orbit (Ontario Institute for Studies in Education)
OUTPUT (Educational Computing Organization)
Reporter (English Catholic Teachers' Association)
Reseau (French Teachers' Association)
Teachers in Charge (Ontario Teachers' Federation)
Trustee Times

Quebec
Geoscope (Quebec Association of Geography Teachers)
PACT Journal (Provincial Association of Catholic Teachers)
Quebec Home and School News

New Brunswick
Accents (Music Education Council)
Art Line
Business Education News
Canadian Quill (Council of Teachers of English)
Dialogue Immersion (Immersion Council)
Education New Brunswick (Department of Education)
Focus (Social Studies Council)
Functions (Mathematics Council)
Initiative (Junior High Technology Council)
Innovations (Home Economics Council)
NBTA News (New Brunswick Teachers' Association)
New Brunswick Counsellor
New Brunswick Educational Administrator
Output (Computer Services Council)
Pathways (Special Education Council)
Principals in Council (Principals' and Vice Principals' Council)
Rendezvous (French Second Language Council)
Resources (Library Council)
Tech Talk (Technical Vocation Council)
Solutions (Science Council)
Stopwatch (Health and Physical Education Council)
3r's (Elementary Council)

Nova Scotia
AVISO (Nova Scotia Teachers' Union)
NSSBA Newsletter (School Boards' Association)
The Teacher (Nova Scotia Teachers' Union)

Newfoundland
Atlantic Science Newsletter (Atlantic Provinces Council on Science)
The Morning Watch: Educational and Social Analysis
NTLA Bulletin (Newfoundland and Labrador Teachers' Association)

JOB SEARCH PLANNING AND DATA

Job Search—A Sequence of Planned Strategies

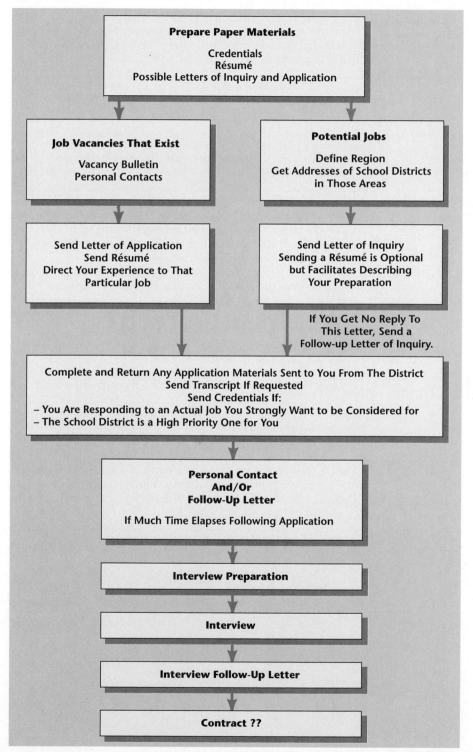

Source: Jan. E. Kilby, "Job Search—A Sequence of Planned Strategies," *The ASCUS Annual 1988: A Job Search Handbook for Educators* (Addison, Ill.: Associaiton for School, College and University Staffing), p. 16. Used with permission.

Job Search—A Timetable Checklist

Presented below is a job-search timetable checklist designed to help most graduating students seeking teaching positions make the best use of their time as they conduct a job search.

August/September (12 months prior to employment)	_____ _____	Attend any applicable orientations/workshops offered by your Faculty. Begin to define career goals by determining the types, sizes, and geographic locations of school systems in which you have an interest.
October (11 months prior to employment)	_____	Begin to identify references and ask them to prepare a letter of recommendation for your credential or placement file.
November (10 months prior to employment)	_____ _____	Begin developing a résumé and basic cover letter. Begin networking by contacting friends, faculty members, and so on to inform them of your career plans. If possible, give them a copy of your résumé.
December/January (8–9 months prior to employment)	_____ _____ _____ _____	Finalize your résumé and make arrangements for it to be reproduced. You may want to get some tips on résumé reproduction from your college placement office. Attend any career planning and placement workshops designed for education majors. Develop a list of school systems in which you have an interest. Contact school systems to request application materials.
February (7 months prior to employment)	_____ _____	Send completed application materials to school systems along with a résumé and cover letter. Inquire about school systems that will be recruiting at your university and about the procedures for interviewing with them.
March/April (5–6 months prior to employment)	_____ _____ _____	Research school systems with which you will be interviewing. Interview on campus and follow up with thank-you letters. Continue to follow up by phone with school systems of interest.
May/June (3–4 months prior to employment)	_____ _____ _____	Maintain communication with your network of contacts. Revise your résumé and cover letter if necessary. Interview off campus and follow up with thank-you letters.
July/August (1–2 months prior to employment)	_____ _____ _____	Continue to monitor job vacancy listings and apply when qualified and interested. Begin considering offers. Ask for more time to consider offers, if necessary. Select the best job offer. Inform individuals associated with your job search of your acceptance.

Source: 1991 ASCUS Annual: A Job Search Handbook for Educators (Evanston, Ill.: Association for School, College and University Staffing, Inc.), p. 5.

Fifteen Rules for Effectively Updating Your Résumé

Résumés have one purpose: to get an interview. The interview, not the résumé, leads to the job. Jobs come through people, not through paper. If you can get an interview any other way, skip the paperwork.

There is no right or wrong way to write a résumé although some ways are more effective and sophisticated than others. All rules are broken in this business, sometimes successfully. But each detail of the résumé-writing process should have your meticulous attention because people often are screened *out* on the basis of a poor letter and résumé. The following serve as guidelines and are based on books, articles, and the comments and preferences of hundreds of employers:

1. Résumés should be copied, preferably by laser printing. This is important because it will make your résumé stand out as professional looking. The *copy* of your résumé should always be accompanied by an *individually* typed cover letter.

2. Think of your résumé more as a piece of advertising than as a comprehensive data sheet. Use wide margins and plenty of spacing to make it easy to skim.

3. A listing of coursework does not belong on the résumé because it looks amateurish. If coursework is called for, send a transcript (or send a copy of your unofficial transcript).

4. Don't use a lot of dates or numbers that make the résumé hard to skim. Eliminate dates or place them at the end of a paragraph when describing experience. Don't use them for headlines.

5. Use action verbs. Avoid using forms of "to be." Use verbs such as *initiated, created, instructed, developed, supervised, managed, counseled, negotiated, maintained.*

6. Emphasize skills, especially those that transfer from one situation to another. The fact that you *coordinated* a fifth-grade field trip to Washington leads one to believe that you could coordinate other things as well.

7. Forget your best prose. Use short, choppy phrases. Short is sweet.

8. Use positive words. Don't apologize for lack of experience or for weaknesses. This is not the place to hang out your dirty laundry. Be positive, capitalize on strengths, and leave out the negative or neutral words.

9. Résumés should be one or two pages. Never more. Anything longer is an autobiography, not a résumé.

10. Expound on your relevant experiences and condense descriptions of jobs or experiences that are not directly related to the work you're seeking. This means that you slant your résumé to the type of job you are seeking. Hence, you will need more than one résumé if you are applying for different types of jobs.

11. Make every word count. Use the K.I.S.S. system of writing: *Keep It Short and Simple.*

12. Omit "professional objective" or "job objective" unless you know exactly what it is and are closed to all other possibilities. Your job objective doesn't add that much to the résumé, but it can serve to screen you out. The cover letter is the best place to detail your objectives.

13. List your telephone number, including area code. Employers usually call to set up an interview.

14. At the bottom of your résumé, write: "Credentials and references available on request." Have prospective employers request your credentials from you, not from your placement office. Don't list your references on your résumé.

15. Proofread your résumé. Then have a friend (or better, a professional proofreader) proofread your résumé. Even the pros have been known to send out résumés with humorous and embarrassing mistakes.

Source: Adapted from John William Zehring, "How to Get Another Teaching Job and What to Do If You Can't," *Learning* (February 1978): 48. Used by permission of the publisher.

Critical Information to Know about School Districts

In your interviews with K–12 school district administrators, it is very important that you know as much as possible about the school, district, and community in which you might be employed. Also, you should be prepared to ask about concerns and issues related to your employment that are of interest to you.

The following are topics about which job applicants typically have questions:

District

- Type of district (elementary, high school, or unit)
- History and development of the district
- Characteristics of the student population and community
- Size of the district (number of elementary, junior high/middle, and high schools)
- Central office administrators and their roles
- Grades included at each level of education

Curriculum

- Courses in the curriculum in your discipline and their content, sequence, prerequisites, and status as electives or required courses
- Typical schedule of courses in the curriculum (first and/or second semester courses)
- Textbook and supplementary materials, the recency of their adoption, and district adoption procedures
- Availability of AV materials and equipment for classroom use
- New and/or innovative curriculum developments in your discipline in recent years
- Curriculum developments currently being planned

Students

- Type and size of student body in which a position is available
- Typical class size
- Procedures for student placement
- Characteristics of entering and exiting students (i.e., number or percentage who are enrolled in vocational and college preparatory curricula and the number or percentage who enroll in college on graduation)

Instructional Assignment

- Reasons why the position is available (enrollment increase, retirement, resignation, etc.). Number and type of teaching preparations (i.e., self-contained classes or team-taught classes)
- Other instructional assignments
- Methods and frequency of teacher evaluation
- Availability of summer employment
- Assignments on department, school, or district committees

- Duties in the supervision/sponsorship of student activities
- Starting and ending dates of employment
- Contract length

Teaching Staff

- Number of administrators in the building and their responsibilities
- Size of the staff within departments and the building
- Number of new teachers hired each year
- Special interests and/or expertise of staff

Student Services

- Student clubs, organizations, and sports
- Counseling and guidance personnel and services
- Social worker, school nurse, librarian, and other support staff and their roles

Community

- Community support for education
- Involvement of parents and other community members in the school program
- Recreational and other facilities in the community
- Demographic information about community residents
- Cost of living and housing in the community

Salary and Fringe Benefits

- District salary schedule
- Pay for extracurricular responsibilities
- Reimbursement policies for graduate study
- District requirements for continuing professional education
- Vacation and sick leave, personal leave, and other leave policies
- Substitute teacher procedures
- Payroll schedule
- Medical insurance

Selection Procedures

- Number and type of interviews that job candidates can expect
- Individuals involved in the preliminary screening of candidates, interviews, and the final selection
- District requirements for residency of staff

Final Suggestions

- Be certain to read your employment contract carefully before signing it.

You might want to visit the district while classes are in session to visit the department and building in which you might be working. If at all possible, try to meet the department head and/or building principal by whom you would be supervised.

Source: Jan. E. Kilby, *The ASCUS Annual 1988: A Job Search Handbook for Educators* (Addison, Ill.: Associaiton for Schoo, College and University Staffing), p. 16. Used with permission.

Sample Interview Questions

Candidates Must Be Prepared to Ask Questions, Too

Many articles and books have been written about the art of interviewing, but few writers discuss the types of questions teacher candidates should ask their interviewers.

By asking pertinent and intelligent questions, a teacher tells the administrator or committee several things. First, the choice of questions lets the interviewer know whether or not the applicant understands fundamental issues related to teaching. Second, the questions also indicate whether or not the teacher is familiar with different issues related to nonteaching responsibilities.

Instructional Strategies

1. Which grades are responsible for what topics?
2. Who has the responsibility for a particular topic?
3. May I have a copy of the scope and sequence?
4. Tell me about supervision visits.
5. How does the administration work with teachers to improve instruction?
6. Are there school psychologists, counselors, or public agencies who help students and teachers?
7. What types of media resources are available?
8. How is the budget for this academic program developed?
9. What textbooks do you use in this subject area?
10. Describe the district's textbook adoption policies.

Staff/Students/Community

11. How would you describe the typical professional staff member in this district?
12. What professional skills do you expect of the person you hire?
13. Does the staff spend time together outside of normal school hours?
14. How does the staff feel about new teachers?
15. How active are teachers in working with community organizations?
16. Tell me about the students who attend this school.
17. How involved are parents in school activities?
18. What do parents expect of their teachers?

Extracurricular Responsibilities

19. What is the budget for this activity?
20. What does the community expect of activity sponsors?
21. Are there auxiliary groups involved in the activity?
22. Are there fund-raising requirements that are part of this activity?
23. May I have a copy of this year's activity calendar?
24. Are other faculty members also assigned to this activity?

Don't forget—the interview should go both ways. You need to ask questions not only to indicate your interest and knowledge, but also to determine if the position is one you want.

Source: C. Bruce Johnston, Michael A. Morehead, and Carter Burns, *1992 ASCUS Annual: The Job Search Handbook for Educators* (Evanston, Ill: Association for School, College and University Staffing, Inc.), p. 24. Used with permission.

Teacher Certification Categories by Provinces

Province/Territory	Certificates Available
Yukon	Professional (K-12) Basic Transitional (K-12) Cultural (K-12) Letter of Permission (K-12)
Northwest Territories	Professional (K-12) Standard (K-12) Vocational (Vocational Courses) Aboriginal Languages Specialist (K-12)
British Columbia	Professional (K-12) Standard (K-12) Basic (K-12) First Nations Language Teacher (K-12) Developmental Standard Term (K-12)
Alberta	Provisional (K-12) Professional (K-12)
Saskatchewan	Professional A & B (K-12) Vocational (K-12, limited subjects) Technical (K-12, limited subjects) Standard B (K-12, limited subjects) Probationary A & B (K-12) Letter of Eligibility (K-12)
Manitoba	Professional (K-12) Special Education (K-12) Vocational Industrial (K-12) Level 1 Administrator (K-12) Level 2 Principal (K-12)
Ontario	Ontario Teacher's Certificate (OTC) (Specified Levels) Temporary Letter of Standing (Specified Levels) Permanent Letter of Standing (Specified Courses)
Quebec	Teaching License (All Levels) Provisional Teaching Authorization (Secondary, Adult) Teaching Certificate (All Levels)
New Brunswick	Letter of Standing 4 (Industrial) Certificate 4, 5 & 6 (1-12) Letter of Standing for persons outside New Brunswick
Nova Scotia	Class 4, 5, 6, 7 & 8 (K-12)
Prince Edward Island	Certificate 4, 5, 5A, 5B (K-12)
Newfoundland	Certificate II, III, IV, V, VI, & VII (All Levels)

Directory of Provincial Certification Offices in Canada

Northwest Territories:
Office of the Registrar
Teacher Certification Northwest Territories
Department of Education, Culture and Employment
PO Box 1320
Yellowknife, N.W.T X1A 2L9

Yukon Territory:
Director of Personnel
Yukon Department of Education
PO Box 2703
Whitehorse, Yukon Y1A 2C6

British Columbia:
Registrar
British Columbia College of Teachers
405-1385 West 8th Avenue
Vancouver, British Columbia V6H 3V9

Alberta:
Teacher Certification and Development
Alberta Education
West Tower, Devonian Building
11160 Jasper Avenue
Edmonton, Alberta T5K 0L2

Saskatchewan:
Teacher Services
Saskatchewan Education Training and Employment
2220 College Avenue
Regina, Saskatchewan S4P 3V7

Manitoba:
Teacher Certification and Student Records
Manitoba Department of Education and Training
Box 700
Russell, Manitoba R0J 1W0

Ontario:
Registrar Services
Ontario Ministry of Education and Training
12th Floor, Mowat Block
Queen's Park
Toronto, Ontario M7A 1L2

Quebec:
> Director, Direction de la titularisation et de la
> classification du personnel enseignant
> Direction generale de la formation et des
> qualifications
> Ministere de l'Education
> 955 chemin Saint-Louis
> Quebec (Quebec) G1S 4S4

New Brunswick:
> Teacher Certification
> Human Resources
> New Brunswick Department of Education
> PO Box 6000
> Fredericton, New Brunswick E3B 5H1

Nova Scotia:
> Registrar, Teacher Certification
> Planning and Research Division Policy Branch
> Nova Scotia Department of Education
> PO Box 578
> Halifax, Nova Scotia B3J 2S9

Addresses of Departments of Education in Canada

British Columbia:
> Ministry of Education
> Parliament Buildings
> Victoria, British Columbia V8V 2M4
> (604) 387-4611 Local 391

Alberta:
> Alberta Education
> West Tower, Devonian Building
> 11160 Jasper Avenue
> Edmonton, Alberta
> (403) 297-6353

Saskatchewan
> Department of Education
> Parkview Place
> 2220 College Avenue
> Regina, Saskatchewan S4P 3V7
> (306) 525-6030

Manitoba:
> Department of Education
> Legislative Building
> Winnipeg, Manitoba R3C 0V8
> (204) 945-2211

Ontario:
> Ministry of Education
> Ministry of Colleges and Universities
> Mowat Block, 900 Bay Street
> Toronto, Ontario M7A 1L2
> (416) 965-6407

Quebec:
> Ministere de l'Education
> Edifice G
> 1035 rue de la Chevrotiere
> Ville de Quebec, Quebec G1R 5A5
> (418) 643-7095

Prince Edward Island:
> Office of the Registrar
> Administration and Finance Branch
> Prince Edward Island Department of Education
> Shaw Building, 95 Rochford Street
> Box 2000
> Charlottetown, Prince Edward Island C1A 7N8

Newfoundland and Labrador:
> Registrar, Teacher Certification
> Division of School Services and Professional
> Development
> Newfoundland and Labrador Department of
> Education
> Confederation Building, West Block
> PO Box 8700
> St. John's, Newfoundland A1B 4J6

New Brunswick:
> Department of Education
> PO Box 6000
> Fredericton, New Brunswick E3B 5H1
> (506) 453-3678

Nova Scotia:
> Department of Education
> PO Box 578
> Halifax, Nova Scotia B3J 2S9
> (902) 424-5605

Prince Edward Island
> Department of Education
> PO Box 2000
> Charlottetown, P.E.I. C1A 7N8

Newfoundland:
> Department of Education
> Government of Newfoundland and Labrador
> Confederation Building
> St. John's, Newfoundland A1C 5T7
> (709) 737-3027, (709) 737-2990

Northwest Territories:
> Department of Education
> Yellowknife, N.W.T. X1A 2C3
> (403) 873-2611

Yukon Territory:
> Department of Education
> Government of the Yukon Territory
> PO Box 2703
> Whitehorse, Yukon Y1A 2C3
> (403) 667-5811 (Inquiry Centre)

The Institutional Structure of Education in Canada

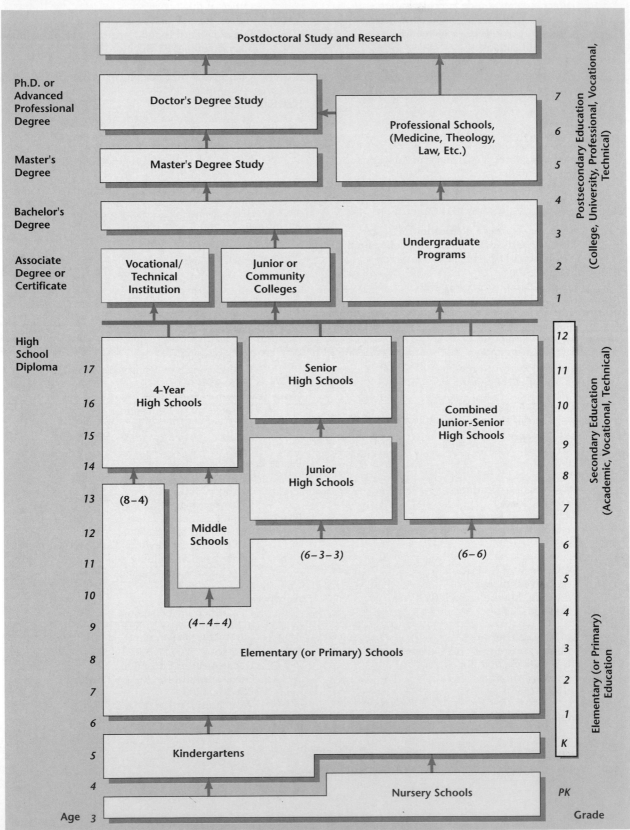

Organizational Structure of a Typical Provincial School System

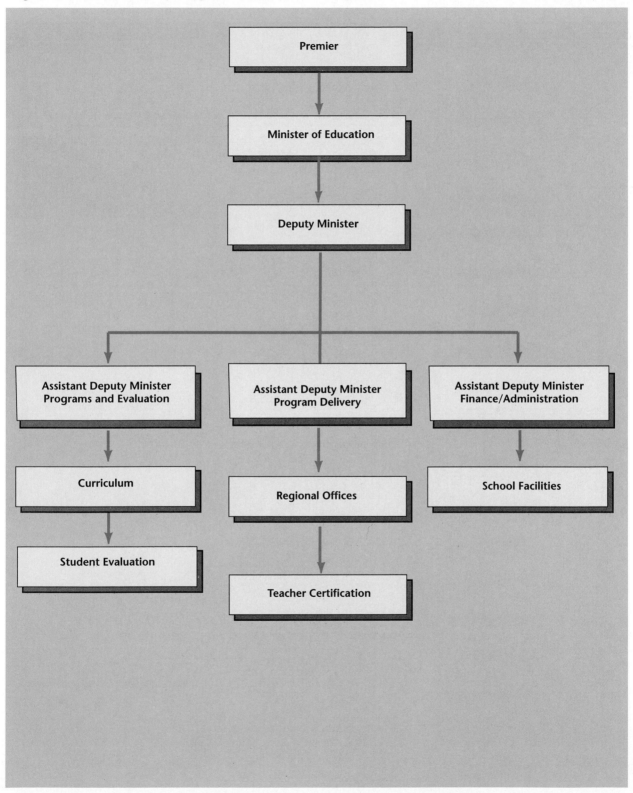

Organizational Chart for a Large School District

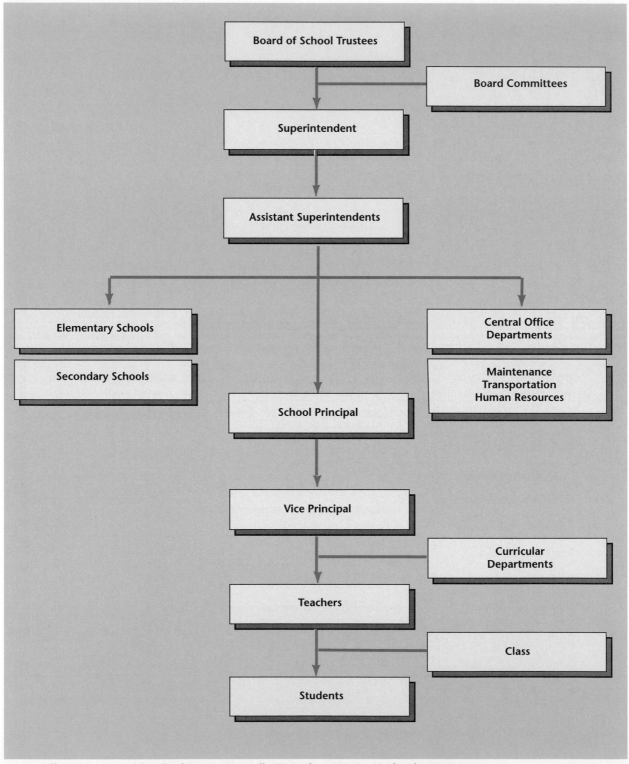

Source: Jefferson County Public School System, Louisville, Kentucky, 1990–91. Used with permission.

Typical Organizational Structure for a Medium-Sized School District (20,000 pupils)

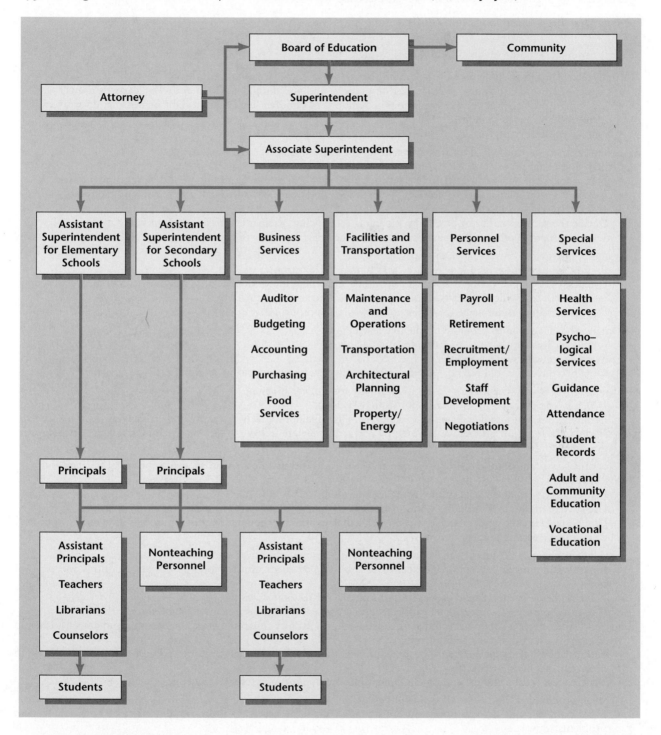

GENERAL INSTRUCTIONAL RESOURCES

Generic Teaching Knowledge and Skills

Teacher candidates should be able to do the following:

1. Analyze and interpret student abilities, cultural backgrounds, achievements, and needs:
   - Use school records, including standardized test scores, and anecdotal data, to identify the learner's needs
   - Recognize and interpret various exceptional conditions of children (e.g., limited sight or hearing, cognitive ability or outstanding gifted abilities)
   - Identify cultural backgrounds of students and interpret impact on learning

2. Design instruction that will meet learner needs through appropriate instructional materials, content, activities, format, and goals:
   - Plan a course of action for instruction over a school year, a semester, a grading period, a day, and a lesson
   - Develop lesson plans with objectives or expected outcomes, instructional sequences and activities, and an evaluation design
   - Decide the subject matter to be taught, including sequencing, pacing, emphases, activities, and evaluation
   - Select appropriate print, audiovisual, and computer materials according to established criteria and the needs of students

3. Conduct instruction to best facilitate learning:
   - Present subject matter and manage activities to maximize learning
   - Use a variety of instructional strategies including individual and small or large group instruction, peer teaching, independent study, field projects, computer-assisted instruction, lecture, etc.
   - Use instructional technology, including computers, as appropriate

4. Manage the classroom to promote productive learning:
   - Regulate classroom time to focus on learning activities
   - Manage student interaction with each other and the teacher
   - Organize the classroom physical setting to be an effective environment for learning activities

5. Manage student conduct to create a positive climate for student learning:
   - Develop, explain, and monitor rules for student conduct
   - Deal with distractions and competing tasks to maintain a smooth flow of attractive and challenging tasks for students
   - Maintain a focus on productive learning by correcting deviant behavior, varying teaching strategies, and praising desirable conduct

6. Promote classroom communication to evoke and express academic information as well as personal feelings and relationships:
   - Use and elicit Standard English in writing and speaking
   - Use correct mathematical symbols and processes
   - Use body language and other forms of nonverbal communication to express emotions as well as approval, disapproval, permission, etc.

7. Evaluate learning to determine the extent to which instructional objectives are achieved by students:
   - Relate evaluation to instructional objectives and be able to select and develop appropriate questions and types of tests
   - Elicit students' best efforts in preparation for and in taking examinations
   - Create an appropriate environment for test-taking that encourages conscientious and ethical behavior
   - Help students develop an acceptance of tests as an opportunity to demonstrate the accomplishment of goals and to identify areas that need strengthening
   - Summarize students' performance on units of instruction and report that performance honestly and accurately to both students and parents
   - Analyze test results and interpret achievement information meaningfully to students

8. Arrange for conferral and referral opportunities:
   - Refer parents/pupils to appropriate professional expertise as necessary following detection of apparent student problems
   - Conduct conferences as necessary with parents and special school personnel, such as the school nurse, psychologist, social worker, librarian/media specialist, and guidance counselor

Source: American Association of Colleges for Teacher Education, *Educating a Profession: Profile of a Beginning Teacher* (Washington, D.C.: American Association of Colleges for Teacher Education, 1983).

Selected Organizations that May Provide Resources for Including Exceptional Learners

Canadian Organizations

The Association for the Gifted—Canada
The University of Calgary
Department of Educational Psychology
2500 University Drive NW
Calgary AB T2N 1N4

Association of Visual Language Interpreters of Canada
House 144
11337-61 Avenue
Edmonton, AB T6H 1M3

Autism Society of Canada
Suite 2, 20 College Street
Toronto ON M5R 1B2

Canadian Cerebral Palsy Association
880 Wellington Street
Suite 612, City Centre
Ottawa ON K1R 6K7

Canadian Council for Exceptional Children
#750, 2 Robert Speck Parkway
Mississauga ON L4Z 1H8

Canadian Cystic Fibrosis Foundation
2221 Yonge Street
Suite 601
Toronto ON M4S 2B4

Canadian Diabetes Association
78 Bond Street
Toronto ON M5B 2J8

Canadian Down's Syndrome Society
Box 52027
Edmonton Trail RPO
Calgary AB T2E 8K9

Canadian Hard of Hearing Association
2435 Holly Lane
Suite 205
Ottawa On K1V 7P2

Canadian National Institute for the Blind
1929 Bayview Ave
Toronto ON M4G 3E8

Canadian Paraplegic Association
Suite 201
1500 Don Mills Road
Toronto ON M3B 3K4

Epilepsy Canada
PO Box 1560
Station C
Montreal PQ H2L 4K8

Learning Disabilities Association of Canada
323 Chapel Street
Ottawa ON K1N 7Z2

National Educational Association of Disabled Students
Carleton University
44th Floor, Unicentre
Ottawa ON K1S 5B6

Association of Early Childhood Educators
#211, 40 Orchard View Blvd
Toronto ON M4R 1B9

Selected American Resources

Behind Special Education
1991, Thomas Skrtic, Love Publishing Company, Denver, Colorado 80222.

Curriculum Considerations In Inclusive Schools 1992, William and Susan Stainback (Eds.), Brookes Publishing Company, P.O. Box 10624, Baltimore, Maryland 21285-0624.

Integrating General and Special Education
1993, John Goodlad and Thomas Lovitt (Eds.), Macmillan Publishing Company, 866 Third Avenue, New York, New York 10022.

Regular Lives
1988 video produced by Syracuse University. Available from the Council for Exceptional Children, 1920 Association Drive, Reston, Virginia 22091.

Report Card to the Nation on Inclusion in Education of Students with Mental Retardation
1992, The ARC, 500 E. Border Street, S-300, Arlington, Texas 76010.

Special Education at the Century's End: Evolution of Theory and Practice Since 1970
1992, Thomas Hehir and Thomas Latus (Eds.): Available from *Harvard Educational Review*, Gutman Library, Suite 349, 6 Appian Way, Cambridge, Massachusetts 02138.

Techniques for Including Students with Disabilities: A Step-by-Step Practical Guide for School Principals
1992, E. John Shinsky, Shinsky Seminars, Inc., 3101 North Cambridge Road, Lansing, Michigan 48911.

Winners All: A Call for Inclusive Schools

1992, National Association of State Boards of Education, 1012 Cameron Street, Alexandria, Virginia 22314.

Selected Canadian Resources for Achieving Gender Equity

Heather-jane Robertson
Literacy and Gender: Making Connections
Canadian Teachers' Federation
Ottawa
June 1991

Heather-jane Robertson
A Cappella: A Report on the Realities, Concerns, Expectations and Barriers Experienced by Adolescent Women in Canada
Canadian Teachers' Federation
Ottawa
1990

Janelle Holmes and Eliane Leslau Silverman
We're Here, Listen to Us! A Survey of Young Women in Canada
Canadian Advisory Council on the Status of Women
Ottawa
1992

Jennifer Smith
Encouraging Girls in Science: Facts, Theories, and Practical Suggestions
University of Lethbridge
1987

Literacy and Canada's Young Adults
Canadian Teachers' Federation
Ottawa
February 1988

Marlene Mackie
Constructing Women and Men: Gender Socialization
Holt, Rinehart and Winston
Toronto
1987

Maureen Baker
What will Tomorrow Bring?...A Study of the Aspirations of Adolescent Women
Canadian Advisory Council on the Status of Women
Ottawa
1985

Reporting Classroom Research
Ontario Education Research Council
Vol. 19:2
March/April 1990

Young Women in Nova Scotia: A Study of Attitudes, Behaviours and Aspirations
Nova Scotia Advisory Council on the Status of Women
Halifax
1990

Selected American Resources for Achieving Gender Equity

Beverly Hardcastle Stanford, "Gender Equity in the Classroom," in *Differences in Common: Anti-Bias Teaching in a Diverse Society*, eds. Deborah Byrnes and Gary Kiger (Washington, D.C., Association for Childhood Education International, 1992).

A-Gay-Yah: A Gender Equity Curriculum from Grades 6–12. A curriculum guide designed to increase gender equity and cultural awareness in middle and high school students through using Native-American history and culture. Developed by the American Indian Resource Center. Available from Women's Educational Equity Act Publishing Center, Education Development Center, Inc., 55 Chapel Street, Newton, MA 02160, (800) 225-3088.

Options for Girls: A Door to the Future. An anthology of readings that seek to encourage girls to pursue careers in mathematics and science. Foundation for Women's Resources, Pro-Ed, 8700 Shoal Creek Blvd., Austin, TX 78758.

Math & Science for Girls. A collection of symposium research results, classroom methods, position papers, and program descriptions focusing on teaching mathematics and science to girls. The National Coalition of Girls' Schools, 228 Main Street, Concord, MA 01742.

How Schools Shortchange Women: The A.A.U.W. Report. American Association of University Women Educational Foundation, 1111 16th Street, N.W., Washington, DC 20036-4873.

Teaching Mathematics Effectively and Equitably to Females. ERIC Clearinghouse on Urban Education, Institute for Urban and Minority Education, Box 40, Teachers College, Columbia University, New York, NY 10027. (Cite Report No. 17).

Teaching Tolerance is mailed twice a year at no charge to educators. It is published by the Southern Poverty Law Center, which founded Teaching Tolerance in 1991 to provide teachers with resources and ideas to help promote harmony in the classroom. The Law Center is a nonprofit legal and education foundation located at 400 Washington Ave., Montgomery, AL 36104.

Selected Resources for Multicultural Education.

Banks, James A., and Cherry A. McGee Banks (eds.), *Multicultural Education: Issues and Perspectives.* Boston: Allyn and Bacon, 1989. Issues and strategies for multicultural education in race, gender, social class, religion, and exceptionality.

Butler, Johnnella E., and John C. Walter (eds.), *Transforming the Curriculum: Ethnic Studies and Women Studies.* Albany: State University of New York Press, 1990.

Integrating content about ethnic groups and women into the mainstream curriculum, applicable to K–12.

Derman-Sparks, Louise, and the A.B.C. Task Force. *Anti-Bias Curriculum: Tools for Empowering Young Children.* Washington, D.C.: National Association for the Education of Young Children, 1989. Resources and activities for engendering positive intergroup attitudes.

Grant, Carl A., and Christine E. Sleeter. *Turning on Learning: Five Approaches for Multicultural Teaching Plans for Race, Class, and Disability.* Columbus, Ohio: Merrill/Macmillan, 1989.

King, Edith W. *Teaching Ethnic and Gender Awareness: Methods and Materials for the Elementary School*, 2d ed. Dubuque, IA: Kendall/Hunt Publishing Company, 1990. Rationale, activities, and teaching strategies for integrating ethnic and gender awareness into the elementary school curriculum.

Lee, Enid, *Letters to Marcia: A Teacher's Guide to Anti-Racist Education.* Toronto: Cross Cultural Communications Centre, 1985. Guide for reducing racism in the classroom and school.

Lynch, James. *Multicultural Education in a Global Society.* New York: Falmer Press, 1989.

Multicultural Leader. Quarterly newsletter published by the Educational Materials and Services Center, 144 Railroad Avenue, Suite 107, Edmonds, WA 98020. News on current theory, research, and teaching materials on race and ethnicity, gender, social class, and exceptionality.

Pedersen, Paul. *A Handbook for Developing Multicultural Awareness.* Alexandria, VA: American Association for Counseling and Development, 1988.

Sleeter, Christine E. (ed.), *Empowerment Through Multicultural Education.* Albany: State University of New York Press, 1991. Issues and problems of teaching in multicultural classrooms.

Sleeter, Christine E., and Carl A. Grant. *Making Choices for Multicultural Education: Five Approaches to Race, Class, and Gender.* Columbus, Ohio: Merrill/Macmillan, 1988. Multicultural teaching strategies.

Wasserman, Paul, and Alice E. Kennington. *Ethnic Information Sources of the United States*, 2d ed. Vols. 1 and 2. Detroit: Gale Research Company, 1983. Lists of organizations, agencies, foundations, institutions, and media that focus on ethnic groups in the United States.

SELECTED RESOURCES FOR TEACHING AT-RISK AND EXCEPTIONAL STUDENTS

Organizations from Canada

Addiction Intervention Association
2175 Sheppard Ave, Suite 110
Willowdale ON M2J 1W8

Against Drunk Driving
PO Box 397, Station A
Brampton ON L6V 2L3

Alliance for a Drug-Free Canada
PO Box 70007
Ottawa ON K2P 2M3

Council on Drug Abuse
698 Weston Road, Suite 17
Toronto ON M6N 3R3

Mothers Against Drinking Drivers
820A 12th Street
New Westminster BC V3M 4K3

Canadian AIDS Society
#400, 100 Sparks Street
Ottawa ON K1P 5B7

The Children's Wish Foundation of Canada
#8C, 1735 Bayly Street
Pickering ON L1W 3G7

Organizations from the United States

American Red Cross
431 18th Street NW
Washington, DC 20006
(202) 737-8300

Center for Early Adolescence
University of North Carolina at Chapel Hill
Carr Mill Town Center
Carboro, NC 27510
(919) 966-1148

Center for Successful Child Development
4848 South State Street
Chicago, IL 60609
(312) 373-8680

Child and Family Policy Center
100 Court Avenue, Suite 312
Des Moines, IA 50309
(515) 243-2000

Children's Defense Fund
25 E Street, NW
Washington, DC 20001
(202) 628-8787

The Family Resource Coalition
200 North Michigan Avenue
Suite 1520
Chicago, IL 60604
(312) 341-0900

Foundation for Child Development
345 E. 46th Street
Suite 700
New York, NY 10017
(212) 697-3150

Institute for Educational Leadership, et al.
1001 Connecticut Avenue, NW
Suite 310
Washington, DC 20036-5541
(202) 822-8405

National Coalition for an Urban Children's Agenda
c/o National Assoc. of State Boards of Education
Attn: Tom Schultz
1012 Cameron Street
Alexandria, VA 22314
(703) 684-4000

National Coalition of Hispanic Health and Human
Services Organizations
1501 16th Street NW
Washington, DC 20036
(202) 387-5000

National Collaboration for Youth
1319 F Street, NW
Suite 601
Washington, DC 20004
(202) 347-2080

National Community Education Association
3929 Old Lee Highway, Suite 91
Fairfax, VA 22314
(703) 359-8973

National Education Association
NEA Communications
1201 16th Street NW
Washington, DC 20036
(202) 833-4000

National Forum on the Future of Children and Their Families
National Research Council
2101 Constitution Avenue NW
Washington, DC 20418
(202) 334-3033

National Network of Runaway and Youth Services
1319 F Street, NW
Suite 401
Washington, DC 20004
(202) 783-7949

Networking Project for Disabled Women and Girls
YWCA of New York
610 Lexington Avenue
New York, NY 10022
(212) 755-4500

Outward Bound USA
Route 90, R2 Box 280
Garrison, NY 10524
(800) 243-8520

Parent Aide Support Service
Nebraska Dept. of Social Services
1050 N Street
Lincoln, NE 68508
(402) 471-7000

Parents as Teachers
9374 Olive Boulevard
St. Louis, MO 63132
(314) 432-4330

Teen Alternative Parents Program
Child Support Division
143 E. Market Street
Indianapolis, IN 46204
(317) 263-6100

Telephone Hotlines in Canada

Childfind Hotline
  Oakville   800-387-7962
  Calgary   800-561-1733

Missing Children's Society of Canada
  Calgary   800-661-6160

Suicide Hotline
  Samaritan Suicide Prevention Line
                800-667-8089

Canadian Association for Suicide Prevention
  Windsor   403-245-3900

Alcohol and Drug Concerns Canada
  Agincourt   416-293-3400

AIDS/STD Hotline
  Edmonton   800-772-2437

International Council of AIDS Service Organizations
  Ottawa   613-230-3580

Drug Abuse Hotline
                800-577-4742

Institute for the Prevention of Child Abuse
  Toronto   416-921-3151

Kids Help Foundation
  Toronto   800-268-3062

Kids Help Phone
  Toronto   800-668-6868

Video Productions

Canada

National Film Board
The National Film Board has expanded access to its productions by making many titles in its collection available to public libraries across Canada. Public library patrons can either borrow NFB videos free of charge or rent them according to local library policy. For information on public libraries that carry NFB videos, contact your nearest NFB office.

If you live outside the cities listed below, call the 800 numbers as follows:

Atlantic Canada	800-561-7104
Quebec	800-363-0328
Ontario	800-267-7710
Western and Northern Canada	800-661-9867

Alberta

NFB Video and Film Service
Canada Place
9700 Jasper Avenue, Suite 120
Edmonton AB T5J 4C3
403-495-3010

British Columbia

NFB Video and Film Service
1045 Howe Street, Suite 100
Vancouver BC V6Z 2B1
604-666-0716

Manitoba

NFB Video and Film Service
245 Main Street
Winnipeg MB R3C 1A7
204-983-4131

New Brunswick

NFB Video and Film Service
Terminal Plaza Building
1222 Main Street
Moncton NB E1C 1H6
506-851-6101

Newfoundland

NFB Video and Film Service
Sir Humphrey Gilbert Building
80 Water Street
St. John's Newfoundland A1C 1G4
709-772-5005

Northwest Territories

Government of the Northwest Territories
Department of Education
Media and Information Services
PO Box 1320
Yellowknife NWT X1A 2L9
403-873-7672

Nova Scotia

NFB Video and Film Service
Queen's Court
5475 Spring Garden Road, 2nd Floor
Halifax NS B3J 1G2
902-426-6001

Ontario

NFB Video and Film Service
Mercury Court
179 Rideau Street
Ottawa ON K1A 0M9
613-996-4861

Prince Edward Island

Government of Prince Edward Island
Department of Education
Media Centre
202 Richmond Street
Charlottetown PEI C1A 1K2
902-368-4641

Quebec

NFB Montreal
1564 St. Denis Street
Montreal PQ H2X 3K2
800-363-0328

Saskatchewan

NFB Video and Film Service
424-21st Street East
Saskatoon SK S7K 0C2
306-975-4245

Yukon

Government of Yukon
Department of Education
Libraries and Archives
PO Box 2703
Whitehorse Yukon Y1A 2C6
403-667-5240

The United States

The following six video productions are available from: Realizing America's Hope, South Carolina ETV, P.O. 1101, Columbia, SC 29211, (800) 277-0829.

"All Our Children with Bill Moyers," produced by Public Affairs Television, 90 minutes. Moyers and his colleagues examine the efforts of several programs and schools across the country that are achieving small victories in the lives of those young people who have known defeat.

"Investing in Our Youth," produced by South Carolina ETV, 30 minutes. Documentary edited from case studies produced for the legislators' teleconference, "Investing in Our Youth: A Nationwide Committee of the Whole."

"Investing in Our Youth: A Nationwide Committee of the Whole," produced by South Carolina ETV, 120 minutes. This teleconference aimed at state legislators demonstrated how collaborative strategies are proving to be highly cost-effective by cutting through bureaucratic red tape and serving clients more effectively.

"Making the American Dream Work for Our Children," produced by South Carolina ETV, 30 minutes. Documentary edited from the case studies produced for the guidance teleconference, "Making the American Dream Work for Our Children: A New Vision of School Guidance."

"Making the American Dream Work for Our Children: A New Vision of School Guidance," produced by South Carolina ETV, 60 minutes. This teleconference demonstrates how schools and businesses are being drawn into the school guidance process in order to better serve the nation's young people.

"Responding to 'All Our Children'—Bill Moyers Live from Longstreet Theatre," produced by South Carolina ETV, 60 minutes. Representatives from education, business, government, and the family engage in lively discussion with journalist Bill Moyers in response to the challenges facing the nation's youth described in the Moyers' documentary, "All Our Children with Bill Moyers."

"AIDS Prevention Program for Youth" A new program for high school students from the American Red Cross. Order from American Red Cross, AIDS Education Office, 431 18th Street NW, Washington, DC 20006. (202) 973-6000.

RESOURCES FOR EDUCATIONAL TECHNOLOGY

Associations and Organizations

Canada

The Alliance for Children and Television
    Toronto   416-515-0466

Association for Media and Technology in Education in Canada
    (No Phone Number Available)
    #1318, 3-1750 The Queensway
    Etobicoke ON M9C 5H5

Canadian Association for Distance Education
    Ottawa   613-230-3630

National SchoolNet Office
    Ottawa   800-268-6608

The United States

Association for Educational Communications and Technology
1025 Vermont Avenue, NW Suite 820
Washington, DC 20005
(202) 347-7834

Challenger Center for Space Science Education
1055 N. Fairfax Street, Suite 100
Alexandria, VA 22314
(703) 683-9740

Computer Equity Program of the Women's Action Alliance
370 Lexington Avenue, Suite 603
New York, NY 10017
(212) 532-8330

Computer Learning Foundation
2165 Park Boulevard
Palo Alto, CA 94306-0007

Institute for the Transfer of Technology to Education
1680 Duke Street
Alexandria, VA 22314
(703) 838-6722

International Society for Technology in Education
1787 Agate Street
Eugene, OR 97403-1923
(503) 346-4414

Public Broadcasting Service
1320 Braddock Place
Alexandria, VA 22314-1698
(703) 739-5038

Satellite Educational Resources Consortium
P.O. Box 50008
Columbia, SC 29250
(800) 476-5001

Selected Canadian Internet Service Providers

Acces Public LLC
CP 11 Station B
Quebec City, QC G1K 7A1
(418) 692-4711

ARnet
c/o Alberta Research Council
Box 8330
Edmonton, AB T6H 5X2
(403) 450-5189

INFOPUQ
Universite de Quebec
2875, boulevard Laurier
Sainte–Foy, QC G1V 2M3
(418) 657-4422

Internet Access Inc.
1916 Merivale Road, Suite 202
Nepean, ON K2G 1E8
(613) 225-5595

Lexicom Ltd.
#60 — 203 Lynnview Road S.E.
Calgary, AB T2C 2C6
(403) 279-0325

Maritime Internet Services
28–32 King Street
PO Box 6477, Partown Place
Saint John, NB E2L 4R9
(506) 652-3624

MINDLINK! Communications Corporation
#105 — 20381 62nd Avenue
Langley, BC V3A 5E6
(604) 534-5663

National Capital FreeNet
Carleton University
1125 Colonel By Drive
Ottawa, ON K1S 5B6
(613) 788-3947

Online Systems of Canada
383 Richmond Street, Suite 900
London, ON N6A 3C4
(416) 642-0731

WorldLinx Telecommunications
BCE Place
181 Bay Street, Suite 350
PO Box 851
Toronto, ON M5J 2T3
(800) 567-1811

World Tel Internet Canada
675 West Hastings Street, Suite 810
Vancouver, BC V6B 1N2
(604) 685-3877

Selected American Internet Service Providers

America Online
8619 Westwood Center Drive
Vienna, VA 22182
(800) 227-6364

CompuServe Inc.
Customer Service Ordering Department
500 Arlington Center Boulevard
Columbus, OH 43220
(800) 848-8199

GEnie
General Electric
401 N. Washington Street
Rockville, MD 20850
(800) 638-9636

GTE Education Services
5525 MacArthur Boulevard
Suite 320
Irving, TX 75038
(800) 659-3000

LinkNet Inc.
CEN
1400 E. Touhy Avenue, Suite 260
Des Plaines, IL 60018-3305
(708) 390-8700

Long Distance Learning Network
AT&T
5501 LBJ Freeway, Room 1015
Dallas, TX 75240
(800) 367-7225

NGS Kids Network
National Geographic Society
P.O. Box 98018
Washington DC 20090
(800) 368-2728

Other Services of Interest

IBM offers free posters for teachers of grades K–3, 4–8, and 9–12. They show students how to use computers to achieve their goals. Each one contains a lesson plan on the back. Contact: IBM Corp., P.O. Box 3900, Peoria, IL 61614; (800) IBM-7257.

Educational Photography
Through the Polaroid Education Program, teachers can receive a Polaroid camera and ideas on how to use it to enhance learning in the classroom. To get the camera and join the program, send ten proof-of-purchase seals from Polaroid 600 Plus film boxes. The program also provides inservice training for teachers around the country. Contact: Phillip Seymour, 95 Christopher Street, New York, NY 10014, (212) 741-0435.

Space Network
NASA Spacelink is an on-line information network that provides lesson plans and activities, NASA news, and historical information. Teachers can also post their own questions on a computer bulletin board. The service is free, although there may be phone costs. To log onto the network directly via modem, dial (205) 895-0028. To get a brochure or more information, contact: NASA Education Affairs, Code XE, NASA Headquarters, Washington, DC 20546; (202) 453-8388.

Special Education
The Council for Exceptional Children's Center for Special Education Technology offers free tech use guides, which summarize important ways technology can be used in special education, and resource inventories, which list state and national technology resources. Teachers with questions about special education technology or wanting to request materials can call (800) 873-8255 between 8:30 A.M. and 4:30 P.M. (EST). The organization also provides access to a bulletin board called TECH LINE, on SpecialNet, an international special education computer network. Contact: CSET, 1920 Association Drive, Reston, VA 22091; (800) 873-8255.

Whole Language
Using Whole Language Software is a free quarterly newsletter and catalog for K–8 teachers. The newsletter gives specific advice for using commercial software with a whole-language approach. Contact: Willy Billy's Workshop, P.O. Box 6104, Cleveland, OH 44101; (800) 628-4623.

Source: Mary Koepke and Sharon K. Williams, "Resources," *Teacher Magazine* (January 1991): 54, 56–57.

Sources of Interactive Multimedia Materials

ABC News Interactive
7 West 66th Street, 4th Floor
New York, NY 10023

Agency for Instructional Technology
Box A
Bloomington, IN 47402-0120

AIMS Media
9710 DeSoto Avenue
Chatsworth, CA 91311

In Canada:
Britannica Learning Materials
Britannica Place, Box 2249
Cambridge, Ontario N3C 3N4

David C. Cook Publishing Co.
850 N. Grove Avenue
Elgin, IL 60120

In Canada:
Educational Services Canada
211 Watline Avenue, Suite 210
Mississauga, Ontario L4C 1P3

IBM Corp.
Multimedia & Education Division
4111 Northside Parkway
Atlanta, GA 30327

Intellimation
P.O. Box 1530
Santa Barbara CA 93116-1530

Laser Learning Technologies
3114 37th Place, South
Seattle, WA 98114

MECC
6160 Summit Drive North
Minneapolis, MN 55430

National Geographic Society
Educational Services
Washington, DC 20090-8019

Optical Data Corp.
30 Technology Drive
Warren, NJ 07059

Quantum Leap Technologies
1399 SE 9th Avenue
Hialeah, FL 33010-5999

Synapse Technologies
3400 Wilshire Boulevard, Bungalow H
Los Angeles, CA 90010

Texas Learning Technology Group
7703 North Lamar Boulevard
Austin, TX 78752

The Discovery Channel
Interactive Multimedia Division
7700 Wisconsin Road, Suite 900
Bethesda, MD 20814-3522

Turner Educational Services Inc.
1 CNN Center
Box 105336
Atlanta, GA 30348-5366

Videodiscovery, Inc.
1515 Dexter Avenue N., #400
Seattle, WA 98109

The Voyager Company
1351 Pacific Coast Highway
Santa Monica, CA 90401

Ztek Co.
P.O. Box 1055
Louisville, KY 40201-1055

Software Evaluation Criteria

1. *Educational content and value:* Is the content accurate? Clearly presented? Appropriate for the intended audience? Free of stereotypes? Important? Does the program seem to achieve its objectives? Is it easily integrated with classwork?

2. *Mode of instruction:* What is the program intended to teach: concepts, principles, skills, visualization, and/or problem solving? Is the appropriate form of instruction or are the appropriate classroom aids (such as simulation, tutorial, drill and practice, visualization materials, problem-solving materials) being used?

3. *Technical features:* Did you have any technical problems with the program? Is the layout visually attractive? Are graphics, color, and sound used effectively to enhance instruction? Could you modify the program?

4. *Ease of use:* Are the instructions clear? Can students operate the program easily? Control the pace? Review the instructions? End the program? How is inappropriate input handled?

5. *Motivation:* Does the program hold students' interest? Do students want to use it again? Does the program vary when repeated?

6. *Feedback:* Is the feedback positive and constructive? Appropriate for the grade level? Immediate? Varied? Does it provide help or an explanation?

7. *Record keeping:* Are students' records stored on disk for later retrieval? What information is stored? For how many students? Is the record-keeping system easy to use? Is it reasonably secure?

8. *Documentation:* Are the written instructions clear? Well organized? Comprehensive? Are the objectives, prerequisites, and intended audience specified?

9. *Summary and recommendations:* What are the program's strengths? What are its weaknesses? Does it take advantage of the computer's capabilities? Does it involve the learner in the learning process? How does it compare with others with similar objectives? Would you buy and use it?

Source: Janice L. Flake, C. Edwin McClintock, and Sandra Turner, *Fundamentals of Computer Education* (Belmont, Calif.: Wadsworth, 1990), pp. 286–288.

Name Index

A
Aburdene, Patricia, 374, 376
Adler, Mortimer, 186, 187
Alvin, Duane, 325
Anyon, Jean, 120-21, 132
Arbeau, Ron, 93
Austin, Nancy, 29

B
Bagley, William C., 191
Bandura, Albert, 41
Banks, James a., 135, 152, 153
Barth, John, 5
Barth, Roland, 29
Beard, Charles, 342
Bennett, Linda, 66
Bennett, William J., 336
Bettelheim, Bruno, 331
Binet, Alfred, 262
Blakey, Lillian, 169
Bloom, Kathryn, 344
Borich, Gary D., 284
Borrowman, M.L., 60
Boyer, Ernest, 384
Brameld, Theodore, 196, 198
Brophy, Jere, 293, 301, 302
Broudy, Harry, 184
Brown, Dan, 220
Brown, Joanne, 52
Bruner, Jerome, 335
Brushett, Ray, 165
Bullough, Robert, 59
Burnaby, Robert, 276

C
Caldwell, Bettye, 384
Canter, Lee, 297
Carew, Jean, 55
Castle, Margaret, 142
Champlain, Samuel de, 159
Clark, Christopher, 307
Coleman, James S., 137
Coleman, Laurence, 269
Combs, Arthur, 14, 40
Copperman, Paul, 191
Counts, George S., 122
Cruickshank, Donald, 60-61
Currie, Audrey, 384
Cutter, Milo, 382

D
David, Morgan, 325
Day, 141
Denton, David, 31
Dewey, John, 39, 40, 176, 188-89
Dillman, Don, 168
Dreikurs, Rudolph, 259, 298

E
Eisner, Elliot, 322, 324
Erikson, Erik, 271-72, 274, 278-79
Ernst, Gisela, 140, 142
Etzioni, Amitai, 351

F
Fernandez, Joseph A., 219
Fisher, Charles, 293
Fliegler, Louis, 268
Friesen, John W., 191
Frostad, Lauren C., 142
Frymier, Jack, 119
Fuchs, Estelle, 286

G
Gallagher, 141
Galloway, Charles, 287
Galton, M., 314
Gardner, Howard, 264
Gilligan, Carol, 273
Ginott, Haim, 29
Glasser, William, 298
Good, Tom, 293, 301, 302
Goodlad, John, 61, 119, 326, 350
Gordon, Thomas, 299
Grant, Gerald, 117
Guderyan, Ellen, 53-54
Guerriero, Maureen, 144

H
Hallahan, Daniel P., 146
Hayden, Torey, 34
Heck, Shirley, 33
Hewlett, Sylvia Ann, 260
Holt, John, 34
Howsam, Robert B., 352
Hunter, Madeline, 61
Hutchins, Robert Maynard, 186-87

I
Imber, Michael, 232

J
Jackson, Philip, 36, 38, 39, 42, 327
Janz, Edwin, 296
Jay, Susan, 144
Jersild, Arthur, 15, 55
Johnson, David, 291
Johnson, Roger, 291
Joyce, Bruce, 311, 313
Juel, Martin O., 63

K
Kauffman, James M., 146
Kellagan, Thomas, 337
Kirk, 141
Koerner, James D., 191
Kohl, Herbert, 34
Kohlberg, Lawrence, 272-73
Kounin, Jacob, 295
Krogh, Suzanne, 328

L
Lanier, Judith, 60
Lengesfeld, Ryan, 111
Levin, Benjamin, 208
Lewin, Kurt, 58
Lieberman, Ann, 32, 55, 348
Lightfoot, Sara Lawrence, 12, 35, 55
Little, Judith, 60
Lortie, Dan, 9, 352

M
MacDonald, Carolyn, 218
McGrath, Tom, 197
MacLeod, Ray, 366
McMurray, Foster, 174
Madaus, George, 337
Mann, Horace, 158
Mappin, Mike, 111
Marland, Sidney, 268
Marshall, Sybil, 33
Matte, Marcel, 296
Meister, Carla, 58
Miller, Lynne, 32, 55
Montagu, Ashley, 135
Moyers, Bill, 12

Subject Index